Fixed Charge Coverage =

$$\frac{\text{Recurring Earnings, Excluding Inte\ldots} \text{Expense, Equity Earnings, and M\ldots} + \text{Interest Portion of R\ldots}}{\text{Interest Expense, Including \ldots} \text{Interest + Interest Portion \ldots}}$$

$$\text{Debt Ratio} = \frac{\text{Total Liabilities}}{\text{Total Assets}}$$

$$\text{Debt/Equity Ratio} = \frac{\text{Total Liabilities}}{\text{Shareholders' Equity}}$$

$$\text{Debt to Tangible Net Worth} = \frac{\text{Total Liabilities}}{\text{Shareholders' Equity} - \text{Intangible Assets}}$$

$$\text{Operating Cash Flow/Total Debt} = \frac{\text{Operating Cash Flow}}{\text{Total Debt}}$$

Profitability

$$\text{Net Profit Margin} = \frac{\text{Net Income before Minority Share of Earnings and Nonrecurring Items}}{\text{Net Sales}}$$

$$\text{Total Asset Turnover} = \frac{\text{Net Sales}}{\text{Average Total Assets}}$$

$$\text{Return on Assets} = \frac{\text{Net Income before Minority Share of Earnings and Nonrecurring Items}}{\text{Average Total Assets}}$$

$$\text{DuPont Return on Assets} = \text{Net Profit Margin} \times \text{Total Asset Turnover}$$

$$\text{Operating Income Margin} = \frac{\text{Operating Income}}{\text{Net Sales}}$$

$$\text{Operating Asset Turnover} = \frac{\text{Net Sales}}{\text{Average Operating Assets}}$$

$$\text{Return on Operating Assets} = \frac{\text{Operating Income}}{\text{Average Operating Assets}}$$

$$\begin{array}{l}\text{DuPont Return} \\ \text{on Operating Assets}\end{array} = \begin{array}{c}\text{Operating} \\ \text{Income} \\ \text{Margin}\end{array} \times \begin{array}{c}\text{Operating} \\ \text{Asset} \\ \text{Turnover}\end{array}$$

$$\text{Sales to Fixed Assets} = \frac{\text{Net Sales}}{\text{Average Net Fixed Assets}}$$

7TH **EDITION**

FINANCIAL STATEMENT ANALYSIS

USING FINANCIAL ACCOUNTING INFORMATION

CHARLES H. GIBSON
THE UNIVERSITY OF TOLEDO

SOUTH-WESTERN College Publishing

An International Thomson Publishing Company

Accounting Team Director: Richard Lindgren
Senior Acquisitions Editor: David L. Shaut
Marketing Manager: Matthew Filimonov
Senior Developmental Editor: Ken Martin
Production Editors: Jason Fisher/Mark Sears
Production House: CompuText Productions, Inc.
Internal Design: The Book Company
Cover Design: Matulionis Design
Cover Photo: Amos Chan/Direct Stock

Copyright © 1998
by South-Western College Publishing
Cincinnati, Ohio

I(T)P

International Thomson Publishing
South-Western is an ITP Company. The ITP trademark is used under license.

Material from the Uniform CPA Examination Questions and Unofficial Answers (copyright © 1953,
1969, 1971, 1972, 1974, 1976, 1978, 1981, by the American Institute of Certified Public Accountants,
Inc.) is adapted with permission.

Material from the Certified Management Accountant Examination, Copyright © 1973, 1975, 1976,
1977, 1978, 1979, 1980, 1984, 1988, by the Institute of Certified Management Accountants, is reprinted
and/or adapted with permission.

Materials identified as CFA Examination I, June 1988 and June 1987, are reproduced with permission
from The Association of Investment Management and Research and The Institute of Chartered
Financial Analysts.

Material copyrighted by the Financial Accounting Standards Board, 401 Merritt 7, P.O. Box 5116,
Norwalk, Connecticut 06856-5116, U.S.A., is reprinted with permission. Copies of the complete
documents are available from the FASB.

Library of Congress Cataloging-in-Publication Data

Gibson, Charles H.
    Financial statement analysis : using financial accounting
information / Charles H. Gibson. -- 7th ed.
        p.   cm.
    Includes bibliographical references and index.
    ISBN 0-538-86689-6 (hc : alk. paper)
    1. Financial statements. I. Title.
HF5681.B2G49   1997
657' .3--dc21   97-12998
                                                             CIP

1 2 3 4 5 6 7 C5 3 2 1 0 9 8 7

Printed in the United States of America

Preface

Tell me, I'll forget.
Show me, I may remember.
Involve me, I'll understand.

This old proverb describes the approach of the 7th edition—involving students in actual financial statements and their analysis and interpretation. Its premise is that students are better prepared to understand and analyze real financial reports when learning is not based on oversimplified financial statements.

ACTUAL COMPANIES

The text explains financial reporting differences among industries, including manufacturing, retailing, and service firms, and regulated and nonregulated industries. Statements of actual companies, such as Delta Air Lines (page 129), Lands' End (page 149), and Intel Corporation (page 373) are used in illustrations, problems, and cases. The actual financial statements highlight current financial reporting problems, including leases, pensions, options, postretirement benefits, financial instrument disclosures, deferred taxes, and the harmonization of international accounting standards. The text includes a new section on using the Internet in financial analysis (pages 221-223).

EXTENSIVE USE OF ONE FIRM

An important feature of this text is that one firm, Cooper Tire & Rubber Company, is used extensively as an illustration. By using Cooper's 1995 financial statements and industry data, readers become familiar with a typical competitive market and a meaningful example for viewing financial statement analysis as a whole. (See Chapters 6 and 12 and pages 126, 273, 386, 482, and 572.) In addition, in an appendix at the end of the text, another actual company—Worthington Industries—is used as the basis for a comprehensive case.

FLEXIBLE ORGANIZATION

This book provides the flexibility necessary to meet the needs of accounting and finance courses varying in content and length. Sufficient text, problem materials, and cases are presented to allow the instructor latitude in the depth of coverage. Accounting principles are the basis for all discussion so that students may understand the methods used as well as the implications for analysis.

Chapter 1 develops the basic principles of accounting on which financial reports are based. A review of the evolution of GAAP and the traditional assumptions of the accounting model helps the reader understand the statements and thus analyze them better.

Chapter 2 describes the forms of business entities and introduces financial statements. This chapter also reviews the sequence of accounting procedures completed during each accounting period. This chapter includes other financial reporting topics that contribute to the understanding of financial reporting, such as the auditor's report, management's responsibility for financial statements, and the SEC's integrated disclosure system.

Chapter 3 presents an in-depth review of the balance sheet and introduces consolidated statements and problems in balance sheet presentation. This chapter gives special emphasis to inventories and tangible assets.

Chapter 4 presents an in-depth review of the income statement, including special income statement items. Other topics included are the reconciliation of retained earnings and dividends and stock splits.

Chapter 5 is an introduction to analysis and comparative statistics. Techniques include ratio analysis, common-size analysis, examination of relative size among firms, comparison of results with other types of data, study of differences of components of financial statements among industries, and review of descriptive material.

Chapter 6 introduces Cooper Tire & Rubber Company and information about the tire industry. Information from Cooper's financial statements is used in illustrations of ratios in subsequent chapters. Chapter 12 summarizes the analysis of Cooper.

Chapter 7 covers short-term liquidity. This chapter includes suggested procedures for analyzing short-term assets and the short-term debt-paying ability of an entity. This chapter includes a detailed discussion of four very important assets: cash, marketable securities, accounts receivable, and inventory.

Chapter 8 covers long-term debt-paying ability. Topics reviewed in this chapter include: financial instruments with off-balance-sheet risk, financial instruments with concentrations of credit risk, and disclosures about fair value of financial instruments.

Chapter 9 covers the analysis of profitability, which is of vital concern to stockholders, creditors, and management.

Chapter 10, although not intended as a comprehensive guide to investment analysis, introduces analysis useful to the investor.

Chapter 11 reviews the statement of cash flows, including ratios that relate to this statement. A brief historical presentation conveys a perspective on the development of the statement of cash flows.

Chapter 13 covers an expanded utility of financial ratios. This includes the perception of financial ratios, the degree of conservatism and quality of earnings, forecasting financial failure, analytical review procedures, management's use of analysis, use of LIFO reserves, and graphing financial information.

Chapter 14 reviews the impact of changing prices on financial statements.

Chapter 15 covers problems in analyzing six specialized industries: banks, electric utilities, oil and gas, transportation, insurance, and real estate. The chapter notes the differences in statements and suggests changes or additions to their analysis.

Chapter 16 covers personal financial statements and financial reporting for governments and other not-for-profit institutions.

Worthington Industries, another actual company, is used as the basis for a comprehensive case at the end of the text.

An extensive glossary defines terms frequently found in annual reports. The text also includes a bibliography of references that can be used in exploring further the topics in the text.

SUPPLEMENTARY MATERIALS

For the student:

A Study Guide includes objective problems that aid in reviewing chapter material. The types of problems provided are: (1) fill-ins, (2) multiple choice, (3) true/false, (4) matching, (5) classification, (6) effect of selected transactions, and (7) problems.

For the instructor:

1. A Solutions Manual includes a suggested solution for each question, problem, and case.
2. A Test Bank includes problems, multiple-choice, true/false, and other objective material for each chapter. The Test Bank is available in both printed and microcomputer versions.

ACKNOWLEDGMENTS

I am grateful to many people for their help and encouragement during the writing of this book. Comments received from colleagues and students who used the first six editions resulted in many changes. I especially want to thank Susan Mangiero of Sacred Heart University for her valuable comments, and Jim Emig of Villanova University for verifying the Solutions Manual, Test Bank, and Study Guide. I also want to extend my appreciation to Cooper Tire & Rubber Company for permission to use its statements as illustrations. I am grateful to the numerous other firms and organizations that granted permission to reproduce their materials. Special thanks go to the American Institute of Certified Public Accountants, the Institute of Chartered Financial Analysts, the Institute of Certified Management Accountants, and the Financial Accounting Standards Board.

Charles H. Gibson

ACTUAL COMPANIES

Real-world business examples were used extensively in the text, illustrations, problems, and cases. Organizations and companies include the following:

AMP
Aetna Life & Casualty
Amerada Hess Corporation
American Accounting Association
American Airlines
American Institute of Certified Public
    Accountants (AICPA)
American Maise-Products Company
Amgen
Arbor Drugs, Inc.
Ashland Coal, Inc.
Bassett Furniture Industries
Best Buy Co., Inc.
Bristol-Myers Squibb Company
Chesapeake Utilities Corporation
Chevron Corporation
Chrysler Corporation
Cooper Tire & Rubber Company
Crown Cork & Seal Company, Inc.
Dana Corporation
Delta Air Lines
Dibrell Brothers, Inc.
Eastman Kodak Company
Electronic Data Systems Corporation
Financial Accounting Standards Board
    (FASB)
Flowers Industries, Inc.
Fluor
Foote, Cone & Belding Communica-
    tions, Inc.
Ford Motor Company
Freeport-McMoran Inc.
General Dynamics
General Motors Corporation
Georgia Power Company
HFS Incorporated
Harsco Corporation
Hewlett-Packard Company

Honeywell, Inc.
Houston Industries Incorporated
Huntington Bancshares
Institute of Management Accountants,
    Inc.
Intel
The Interpublic Group of Companies
JC Penney
JLG Industries
Johanson Company
LTV Corporation
Lands' End, Inc.
La-Z-Boy Chair Company
Lucas County, Ohio
Lufkin Industries, Inc.
McDonnell Douglas Corporation
Micron Technology, Inc.
Mid Am, Inc.
The Money Store Inc.
Mosinee Paper Corporation
Motorola
Nacco Industries
New England Electric System
Nordson Corporation
Norfolk Southern
Novell
Orange and Rockland Utilities, Inc.
Osmonics
Overseas Shipholding Group, Inc.
Potash Corporation
Procter & Gamble Company
Public Service Company of Colorado
Quanex
Reeves Industries, Inc.
The Roose Company
Seaway Food Town, Inc.
Securities and Exchange Commission
    (SEC)

Snap On, Inc.
The Southern Company
Southern Indiana Gas and Electric
  Company
Southern New England
  Telecommunications Corpora-
  tion
Spectrum Control, Inc.
Sylvania Savings Bank
Telephone and Data Systems, Inc.
City of Toledo
Tribune Company
Tyco International Ltd. Company
Union Carbide
Union Texas Petroleum Holdings
United Airlines Corporation

United Realty Trust
United States Surgical Corporation
United Technologies
Utilicorp United
Vivra
W. T. Grant
Warford Corporation
Warner-Lambert
Wausau Paper Mills Company
Wisconsin Energy Corporation
Worthington Industries
York
Zapata
Zurn

About the Author

Charles Gibson is a certified public accountant who practiced with a big six accounting firm for four years and has had more than twenty-five years of teaching experience. His teaching experience encompasses a variety of accounting courses, including financial, managerial, tax, cost, and financial analysis.

Professor Gibson teaches seminars on financial analysis to financial executives, bank commercial loan officers, lawyers, and others. He has also taught financial reporting seminars for CPAs and review courses for both CPAs and CMAs.

Dr. Gibson has written more than sixty articles in such journals as the *Journal of Accountancy, Accounting Horizons, Journal of Commercial Bank Lending, CPA Journal, Ohio CPA, Management Accounting, Risk Management, Taxation for Accountants, Advanced Management Journal, Taxation for Lawyers, California Management Review,* and *Journal of Small Business Management.* He is a co-author of the Financial Executives Research Foundation Study entitled "Discounting in Financial Accounting and Reporting."

Dr. Gibson has co-authored *Cases in Financial Reporting*, published by PWS-KENT Publishing Company. He has also co-authored two continuing education courses consisting of books and cassette tapes, published by the American Institute of Certified Public Accountants. These courses are entitled "Funds Flow Evaluation" and "Profitability and the Quality of Earnings."

Professor Gibson is a member of the American Accounting Association, American Institute of Certified Public Accountants, Institute of Management Accountants, Ohio Society of Certified Public Accountants, Institute of Internal Auditors, and Financial Executives Institute. He has been particularly active in the American Accounting Association and the Ohio Society of Certified Public Accountants.

Dr. Gibson received the 1989 Outstanding Ohio Accounting Educator Award jointly presented by The Ohio Society of Certified Public Accountants and the Ohio Regional American Accounting Association. In 1993, he received the College of Business Research Award at The University of Toledo. In 1996, Dr. Gibson was honored as an "Accomplished Graduate" of the College of Business at Bowling Green State University.

Dedication

This book is dedicated to my wife Patricia and daughters Anne Elizabeth and Laura.

Contents

4 INCOME STATEMENT 157

14 IMPACT OF CHANGING PRICES ON FINANCIAL STATEMENTS   603

15 STATEMENT ANALYSIS FOR SPECIAL INDUSTRIES: BANKS, UTILITIES, OIL AND GAS, TRANSPORTATION, INSURANCE, REAL ESTATE COMPANIES   625

1   Fundamental Concepts and Introduction to Financial Reporting

USERS OF FINANCIAL STATEMENTS INCLUDE a company's managers, stockholders, bondholders, security analysts, suppliers, lending institutions, employees, labor unions, regulatory authorities, and the general public. They use the financial reports to make decisions. For example, potential investors use the financial reports as an aid in deciding whether or not to buy the stock. Suppliers use the financial reports to decide whether or not to sell merchandise to a company on credit. Labor unions use the financial reports to help determine their demands when they negotiate for employees. Management could use the financial reports to determine the company's profitability.

Demand for financial reports exists because users believe that the reports help them in decision making. In addition to the financial reports, users often consult competing information sources, such as new wage contracts and economy-oriented releases.

This textbook concentrates on using financial accounting information properly. Users must have a basic understanding of generally accepted accounting principles and traditional assumptions of the accounting model in order to recognize the limits of financial reports.

The ideas that underlie financial reports have developed over several hundred years. This development continues today to meet the needs of a changing society. A review of the evolution of generally accepted accounting principles and the traditional assumptions of the accounting model should help the reader understand the financial reports and thus analyze them better.

DEVELOPMENT OF GENERALLY ACCEPTED ACCOUNTING PRINCIPLES (GAAP)

Generally accepted accounting principles (GAAP) are accounting principles that have substantial authoritative support. The accountant must be familiar with acceptable reference sources in order to decide whether any particular accounting principle has substantial authoritative support.

The formal process of developing accounting principles that exist today in the United States began with the Securities Acts of 1933 and 1934. The Securities Act of 1933 was designed to protect investors from abuses in financial reporting that developed during the 1920s. This act was intended to regulate the initial offering and sale of securities in interstate commerce.

In general, the Securities Exchange Act of 1934 was intended to regulate securities trading on the national exchanges, and it was under this authority that the **Securities and Exchange Commission (SEC)** was created. In effect, the SEC has the authority to determine GAAP and to regulate the accounting profession. The SEC has elected to leave much of the determination of GAAP and the regulation of the accounting profession to the private sector. At times, the SEC will issue its own standards.

Currently the SEC issues Financial Reporting Releases (FRRs) that pertain to financial reporting requirements. FRRs are part of GAAP and are used to give the SEC's official position on matters relating to financial statements. Thus, the formal process that exists today is a blend of the private and public sectors.

A number of parties in the private sector have played a role in the development of GAAP. The American Institute of Certified Public Accountants (AICPA) and the Financial Accounting Standards Board (FASB) have had the most influence.

American Institute of Certified Public Accountants (AICPA)

The **AICPA** is a professional accounting organization whose members are certified public accountants (CPAs). During the 1930s, the AICPA had a special committee working with the New York Stock Exchange on matters of common interest. An outgrowth of this special committee was the establishment in 1939 of two standing committees, the **Committee on Accounting Procedures** and the **Committee on Accounting Terminology**. These committees were active from 1939 to 1959 and issued 51 Accounting Research Bulletins. These committees took a problem-by-problem approach, because they tended to review an issue only when there was a problem related to that issue. This method became known as the brushfire approach. They were only partially successful in developing a well-structured body of accounting principles.

In 1959, the AICPA replaced the two committees with the **Accounting Principles Board (APB)** and the **Accounting Research Division**. The Accounting Research Division provided research to aid the APB in making decisions regarding accounting principles. Basic postulates would be developed that would aid in the development of accounting principles, and the entire process was intended to be based on research prior to an APB decision. However, the APB and the Accounting Research Division were not successful in formulating broad principles.

The combination of the APB and the Accounting Research Division lasted from 1959 to 1973. During this time, the Accounting Research Division issued 14 Accounting Research Studies. The APB issued 31 Opinions (APBO) and 4 Statements (APBS). The Opinions represented official positions of the Board, whereas the Statements represented the views of the Board but not the official opinions. APBOs are part of GAAP.

Various sources, including the public, generated pressure to find another way of developing GAAP. In 1972, a special study group of the AICPA recommended another approach—the establishment of the **Financial Accounting Standards Board (FASB)**. The AICPA adopted these recommendations in 1973.

Financial Accounting Standards Board (FASB)

The Financial Accounting Standards Board, independent of the AICPA, is governed by the **Financial Accounting Foundation (FAF)**. The FAF consists of eight public members and eight private industry members. The public members consist of five at-large members and three state and local government members. The FAF appoints the seven members of the FASB and appoints the **Financial Accounting Standards Advisory Council (FASAC)**. The FASAC is responsible for advising the FASB.

The FASB issues four types of pronouncements:

1. **Statements of Financial Accounting Standards (SFAS).** These Statements establish GAAP for specific accounting issues.

2. **Interpretations.** These pronouncements provide clarifications to previously issued standards, including SFASs, APB Opinions, and Accounting Research Bulletins. The interpretations have the same authority and require the same majority votes for passage as standards (a supermajority of five or more of the seven members). Interpretations are part of GAAP.

3. **Technical bulletins.** These bulletins provide timely guidance on financial accounting and reporting problems. They may be used when the effect will not cause a major change in accounting practice for a number of companies and when they do not conflict with any broad fundamental accounting principle. Technical bulletins are part of GAAP.

4. **Statements of Financial Accounting Concepts (SFAC).** These Statements provide a theoretical foundation upon which to base GAAP. They are the output of the FASB's Conceptual Framework project, but they are not part of GAAP.

Operating Procedure for Statements of Financial Accounting Standards (SFAS)

The process of considering a SFAS begins when the Board elects to add a topic to its technical agenda. The Board receives suggestions and advice on topics from many sources, including the Financial Accounting Standards Advisory Council, the SEC, the AICPA, and industry organizations.

For its technical agenda, the Board considers only "broken" items. In other words, the Board must be convinced that a major issue needs to be addressed in a new area or an old issue needs to be reexamined.

The Board must rely on staff members for the day-to-day work on projects. A project is assigned a staff project manager, and informal discussions frequently take place among Board members, the staff project manager, and staff. In this way, Board members gain an understanding of the accounting issues and the economic relationships that underlie those issues.

On projects with a broad impact, a **Discussion Memorandum** (DM) or an **Invitation to Comment** is issued. A Discussion Memorandum presents all known facts and points of view on a topic. An Invitation to Comment sets forth the Board's tentative conclusions on some issues related to the topic or represents the views of others.

The Discussion Memorandum or Invitation to Comment is distributed as a basis for public comment. There is usually a 60-day period for written comments, followed by a public hearing. A transcript of the public hearing and the written comments become part of the public record. Then the Board begins deliberations on an **Exposure Draft** (ED) of a proposed Statement of Financial Accounting Standards. When completed, the Exposure Draft is issued for public comment. The Board may call for written comments only, or it may announce another public hearing. After considering the written comments and the public hearing comments, the Board resumes deliberations in one or more public Board meetings. The final Statement must receive affirmative votes from five of the seven members of the Board. The Rules of Procedure require dissenting Board members to set forth their reasons in the Statement. Developing a Statement on a major project generally takes at least two years, sometimes much longer. Some people believe that the time should be shortened to permit faster decision making.

The FASB standard-setting process includes aspects of accounting theory and political aspects. Many organizations, companies, and individuals have input into the process. Some input is directed toward achieving a standard less than desirable in terms of a strict accounting perspective. Often the end result is a standard that is not the best representation of economic reality.

FASB Conceptual Framework

The Conceptual Framework for Accounting and Reporting was on the agenda of the FASB from its inception in 1973. The Framework is intended to set forth a system of interrelated objectives and underlying concepts that will serve as the basis for evaluating existing standards of financial accounting and reporting.

Under this project, the FASB has established a series of pronouncements, **Statements of Financial Accounting Concepts** (SFACs), intended to provide the Board with a common foundation and the basic reasons for considering the merits of various alternative accounting principles. SFACs *do not* establish GAAP; rather, the FASB eventually intends to evaluate current principles in terms of the concepts established.

To date, the Framework project has six Concept Statements. There may be additional Concepts Statements in the future, and Concept Statements are expected to undergo periodic reviews with a view toward improvement. The six Concepts Statements include:

1. *Statement of Financial Accounting Concepts No. 1,* "Objectives of Financial Reporting by Business Enterprises."

2. *Statement of Financial Accounting Concepts No. 2,* "Qualitative Characteristics of Accounting Information."

3. *Statement of Financial Accounting Concepts No. 3,* "Elements of Financial Statements of Business Enterprises."

4. *Statement of Financial Accounting Concepts No. 4,* "Objectives of Financial Reporting by Nonbusiness Organizations."

5. *Statement of Financial Accounting Concepts No. 5,* "Recognition and Measurement in Financial Statements of Business Enterprises."

6. *Statement of Financial Accounting Concepts No. 6,* "Elements of Financial Statements" (a replacement of No. 3).

Concepts Statement No. 1 deals with identifying the objectives of financial reporting for business entities and establishes the focus for subsequent concept projects for business entities. Concepts Statement No. 1 pertains to general-purpose external financial reporting and is not restricted to financial statements. Listed below is a summary of the highlights of Concepts Statement No. 1.[1]

1. Financial reporting is intended to provide information useful in making business and economic decisions.

2. The information should be comprehensible to those having a reasonable understanding of business and economic activities.

These individuals should be willing to study the information with reasonable diligence.

3. Financial reporting should be helpful to users in assessing the amounts, timing, and uncertainty of future cash flows.

4. The primary focus is information about earnings and its components.

5. Information should be provided about the economic resources of an enterprise and the claims against those resources.

Issued in May 1980, "Qualitative Characteristics of Accounting Information" (SFAC No. 2) examines the characteristics that make accounting information useful for investment, credit, and similar decisions. Those characteristics of information that make it a desirable commodity can be viewed as a hierarchy of qualities, with *understandability* and *usefulness for decision making* of most importance. See Exhibit 1-1.

Relevance and **reliability,** the two primary qualities, make accounting information useful for decision making. SFAC No. 2 indicates that, to be relevant, the information needs to have *predictive* and feedback value and must be *timely.* The SFAC also indicates that, to be reliable, the information must be *verifiable*, subject to representational faithfulness, and *neutral.* **Comparability**, which includes consistency, interacts with relevance and reliability to contribute to the usefulness of information.

The hierarchy includes *two constraints.* To be useful and worth providing, the information should have *benefits that exceed its cost.* In addition, all of the qualities of information shown are *subject to a materiality threshold.*

SFAC No. 6, "Elements of Financial Statements," which replaced SFAC No. 3 in 1985, defines ten interrelated elements directly related to measuring performance and financial status of an enterprise. The ten *elements* are defined as follows:[2]

1. **Assets.**   Assets are probable future economic benefits obtained or controlled by a particular entity as a result of past transactions or events.

2. **Liabilities.**   Liabilities are probable future sacrifices of economic benefits arising from present obligations of a particular entity to transfer assets or provide services to other entities in the future as a result of past transactions or events.

3. **Equity.**   Equity is the residual interest in the assets of an entity that remains after deducting its liabilities:

$$\text{Equity} = \text{Assets} - \text{Liabilities}$$

4. **Investments by owners.**   Investments by owners are increases in equity of a particular business enterprise resulting from

EXHIBIT 1-1   **A Hierarchy of Accounting Qualities**

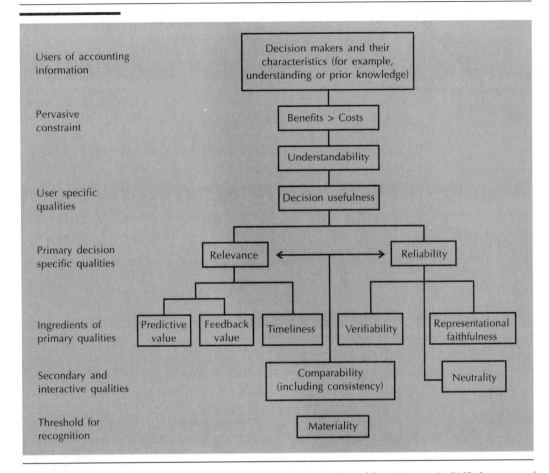

Source: "Qualitative Characteristics of Accounting Information." Adapted from Figure 1 in FASB *Statement of Financial Accounting Concepts No. 2* (Stamford, CT: Financial Accounting Standards Board, 1980).

transfers to the enterprise from other entities of something of value to obtain or increase ownership interests (or equity) in it. Assets, most commonly received as investments by owners, may also include services or satisfaction or conversion of liabilities of the enterprise.

5. **Distribution to owners.**   Distribution to owners is a decrease in equity of a particular business enterprise resulting from transferring assets, rendering services, or incurring liabilities by the enterprise to owners. Distributions to owners decrease ownership interest (or equity) in an enterprise.

6. **Comprehensive income.** Comprehensive income is the change in equity (net assets) of a business enterprise during a period from transactions and other events and circumstances from nonowner sources. It includes all changes in equity during a period except those resulting from investments by owners and distributions to owners. (This concept has not been directly incorporated in an FASB standard.)

7. **Revenues.** Revenues are inflows or other enhancements of assets of an entity or settlements of its liabilities (or a combination of both) from delivering or producing goods, rendering services, or other activities that constitute the entity's ongoing major or central operations.

8. **Expenses.** Expenses are outflows or other consumption or using up of assets or incurrences of liabilities (or a combination of both) from delivering or producing goods, rendering services, or carrying out other activities that constitute the entity's ongoing major or central operations.

9. **Gains.** Gains are increases in equity (net assets) from peripheral or incidental transactions of an entity and from all other transactions and other events and circumstances affecting the entity during a period except those that result from revenues or investments by owners.

10. **Losses.** Losses are decreases in equity (net assets) from peripheral or incidental transactions of an entity and from all other transactions and other events and circumstances affecting the entity during a period except those that result from expenses or distributions to owners.

"Objectives of Financial Reporting by Nonbusiness Organizations" (SFAC No. 4) was completed in December 1980. Organizations that fall within the focus of this statement include churches, foundations, and human service organizations. Performance indicators for nonbusiness organizations include formal budgets and donor restrictions. These types of indicators are not ordinarily related to competition in markets.

Issued in December 1984, "Recognition and Measurement in Financial Statements of Business Enterprises" (SFAC No. 5) indicates that an item, to be recognized, should meet four criteria, subject to the cost-benefit constraint and materiality threshold:[3]

1. **Definition.** The item fits one of the definitions of the elements.
2. **Measurability.** The item has a relevant attribute measurable with sufficient reliability.
3. **Relevance.** The information related to the item is relevant.
4. **Reliability.** The information related to the item is reliable.

SFAC No. 5 identifies *five* different *measurement attributes* currently used in practice:[4]

1. **Historical cost (historical proceeds).** Property, plant, and equipment and most inventories are reported at their historical cost: the amount of cash, or its equivalent, paid to acquire an asset, commonly adjusted after acquisition for amortization or other allocations. Liabilities that involve obligations to provide goods or services to customers are generally reported at historical proceeds: the amount of cash, or its equivalent, received when the obligation was incurred and may be adjusted after acquisition for amortization or other allocations.

2. **Current cost.** Some inventories are reported at their current (replacement) cost: the amount of cash, or its equivalent, that would have to be paid if the same or an equivalent asset were acquired currently.

3. **Current market value.** Some investments in marketable securities are reported at their current market value: the amount of cash, or its equivalent, that could be obtained by selling an asset in an orderly liquidation. Current market value is also generally used for assets expected to be sold at prices lower than previous carrying amounts. Some liabilities that involve marketable commodities and securities are reported at current market value. These liabilities include the obligations of writers of options or sellers of common shares who do not own the underlying commodities or securities.

4. **Net realizable (settlement) value.** Short-term receivables and some inventories are reported at their net realizable value: the nondiscounted amount of cash, or its equivalent, into which an asset is expected to be converted in due course of business, less direct costs, if any, necessary to make that conversion. Liabilities that involve known or estimated amounts of money payable at unknown future dates, such as trade payables or warranty obligations, are generally reported at their net settlement value: the nondiscounted amounts of cash, or its equivalent, expected to be paid to liquidate an obligation in the due course of business, including direct costs, if any, necessary to make that payment.

5. **Present (or discounted) value of future cash flows.** Long-term receivables are reported at their present value (discounted at the implicit or historical rate): the present or discounted value of future cash inflows into which an asset is expected to be converted in due course of business less present values of cash outflows necessary to obtain those inflows. Long-term

payables are similarly reported at their present value (discounted at the implicit or historical rate): the present or discounted value of future cash outflows expected to be required to satisfy the liability in the due course of business.

SFAC No. 5 probably accomplished little, because a firm, consistent position on recognition and measurement could not be agreed upon. SFAC No. 5 states: "Rather than attempt to select a single attribute and force changes in practice so that all classes of assets and liabilities use that attribute, this concept statement suggests that use of different attributes will continue."[5]

The FASB Conceptual Framework for Accounting and Reporting project represents the most extensive effort undertaken to provide a conceptual framework for financial accounting. Potentially, the project can have a significant influence on financial accounting.

ADDITIONAL INPUT—AMERICAN INSTITUTE OF CERTIFIED PUBLIC ACCOUNTANTS (AICPA)

As indicated earlier, the AICPA played the primary role in the private sector in establishing GAAP prior to 1973. However, the AICPA continues to play a substantial part, primarily through its Accounting Standards Division. The Accounting Standards Executive Committee (AcSEC) serves as the official voice of the AICPA in matters relating to financial accounting and reporting standards.

The Accounting Standards Division publishes numerous documents considered as sources of GAAP. These include Industry Audit Guides, Industry Accounting Guides, and Statements of Position (SOP).

Industry Audit Guides and Industry Accounting Guides are designed to assist auditors in examining and reporting on financial statements of companies in specialized industries, such as insurance. SOPs are issued to influence the development of accounting standards. Some SOPs are revisions or clarifications to recommendations on accounting standards contained in Industry Audit Guides and Industry Accounting Guides.

Industry Audit Guides, Industry Accounting Guides, and SOPs are considered a lower level of authority than FASB Statements of Financial Accounting Standards (SFASs), FASB Interpretations, APB Opinions, and Accounting Research Bulletins. However, since the Industry Audit Guides, Industry Accounting Guides, and SOPs deal with material not covered in the primary sources, they, in effect, become the guide to standards for the areas they cover. They are part of GAAP.

EMERGING ISSUES TASK FORCE (EITF)

The FASB established the Emerging Issues Task Force (EITF) in July 1984 to help identify emerging issues affecting reporting and problems in implementing authoritative pronouncements. The Task Force has 15 members—senior technical partners of major national CPA firms and representatives of major associations of preparers of financial statements. The FASB's Director of Research and Technical Activities serves as Task Force chairperson. The SEC's Chief Accountant and the chairperson of the AICPA's Accounting Standards Executive Committee participate in Task Force meetings as observers.

The SEC's Chief Accountant has stated that any accounting that conflicts with the position of a consensus of the Task Force would be challenged. Agreement of the Task Force is recognized as a consensus if no more than two members disagree with a position.

Task Force meetings are held about once every six weeks. Issues come to the Task Force from a variety of sources, including the EITF members, the SEC, and other federal agencies. The FASB also brings issues to the EITF in response to issues submitted by auditors and preparers of financial statements.

The EITF statements have become a very important source of GAAP. The Task Force has the capability to review a number of issues within a relatively short period of time, in contrast to the lengthy deliberations that go into an SFAS.

EITF statements are considered to be less authoritative than the sources previously discussed in this chapter. However, since EITF addresses issues not covered by the other sources, its statements become important guidelines to standards for the areas they cover.

TRADITIONAL ASSUMPTIONS OF THE ACCOUNTING MODEL

The FASB's Conceptual Framework was influenced by several underlying assumptions. Some of these assumptions were addressed in the Conceptual Framework, and others are implicit in the Framework. These assumptions, along with the Conceptual Framework, are considered when a GAAP is established. Accountants, when confronted with a situation lacking an explicit standard, should resolve the situation by considering the Conceptual Framework and the traditional assumptions of the accounting model.

In all cases, accountants are required to make a "fair representation." Even when there is an explicit GAAP, following the GAAP is not appropriate unless the end result is a "fair representation."

Business Entity

The concept of separate **entity** means that the business or entity for which the financial statements are prepared is separate and distinct from the owners of the entity. In other words, the entity is viewed as an economic unit that stands on its own.

For example, an individual may own a grocery store, a farm, and numerous personal assets. To determine the economic success of the grocery store, we would view it separately from the other resources owned by the individual. The grocery store would be treated as a separate entity.

A corporation such as the Ford Motor Company has many owners (stockholders). The entity concept enables us to account for the Ford Motor Company entity separately from the transactions of the owners of the Ford Motor Company.

Going Concern or Continuity

The **going-concern assumption,** that the entity in question will remain in business for an indefinite period of time, provides perspective on the future of the entity. The going-concern assumption deliberately disregards the possibility that the entity will go bankrupt or be liquidated. If a particular entity is in fact threatened with bankruptcy or liquidation, then the going-concern assumption should be dropped. In such a case, the reader of the financial statements is interested in the liquidation values, not the values that can be used when making the assumption that the business will continue indefinitely. If the going-concern assumption has not been used for a particular set of financial statements, because of the threat of liquidation or bankruptcy, the financial statements must clearly disclose that the statements were prepared with the view that the entity will be liquidated or that it is a failing concern. In this case, conventional financial statement analysis would not apply.

Many of our present financial statement figures would be misleading if it were not for the going-concern assumption. For instance, under the going-concern assumption, the value of prepaid insurance is computed by spreading the cost of the insurance over the period of the policy. If the entity were liquidated, then only the cancellation value of the policy would be meaningful. Inventories are basically carried at their accumulated cost. If the entity were liquidated, then the amount realized from the sale of the inventory, in a manner other than through the usual channels, usually would be substantially less than the cost. Therefore, to carry the inventory at cost would fail to recognize the loss that is represented by the difference between the liquidation value and the cost.

The going-concern assumption also influences liabilities. If the entity were liquidating, some liabilities would have to be stated at amounts in excess of those stated on the conventional statement. Also, the amounts provided for warranties and guarantees would not be realistic if the entity were liquidating.

The going-concern assumption also influences the classification of assets and liabilities. Without the going-concern assumption, all assets and liabilities would be current, with the expectation that the assets would be liquidated and the liabilities paid in the near future.

The audit opinion for a particular firm may indicate that the auditors have reservations as to the going-concern status of the firm. This puts the reader on guard that the statements are misleading if the firm does not continue as a going concern. For example, the 1994 annual report of Brown Disc Products Company indicated a concern over the company's ability to continue as a going concern.

The Brown Disc Products Company's annual report included these comments in Note 1 and the auditor's report.

Note 1 (in Part)

BASIS OF PRESENTATION—The accompanying financial statements have been prepared on a going-concern basis, which contemplates the realization of assets and the liquidation of liabilities in the normal course of business. However, Brown Disc has sustained substantial operating losses in recent years. In addition, total liabilities exceed total assets as of June 30, 1994. These factors, among others, adversely affect the ability of Brown Disc to continue as a going concern. The financial statements do not include any adjustments relating to the recoverability and classification of recorded asset amounts or the amount and classification of liabilities that might be necessary should Brown Disc be unable to continue as a going concern.

Auditor's Report (in Part)

The accompanying financial statements have been prepared assuming that the Company will continue as a going concern. As discussed in Note 1 to the financial statements, the Company emerged from bankruptcy proceedings on May 5, 1993. The Company had a net capital deficiency as of June 30, 1994, and losses have continued subsequent to emerging from bankruptcy. These factors, among others, raise substantial doubt about its ability to continue as a going concern. Management's plans concerning these matters are also described in Note 1. The financial statements do not include any adjustments that might arise from the outcome of this uncertainty.

Time Period

The only accurate way to account for the success or failure of an entity is to accumulate all transactions from the opening of business until the business eventually liquidates. Many years ago, this time period for reporting was acceptable, because it would be feasible to account for and divide up what remained at the completion of the venture. Today, the typical business has a relatively long duration, so it is not feasible to wait until the business liquidates before accounting for its success or failure.

This presents a problem: Accounting for the success or failure of the business in midstream involves inaccuracies. Many transactions and commitments are incomplete at any particular time between the opening and the closing of business. An attempt is made to eliminate the inaccuracies when statements are prepared for a period of time short of an entity's life span, but the inaccuracies cannot be eliminated completely. For example, the entity typically carries accounts receivable at the amount expected to be collected. Only when the receivables are collected can the entity account for them accurately. Until receivables are collected, there exists the possibility that collection cannot be made. The entity will have outstanding obligations at any time, and these obligations cannot be accurately accounted for until they are met. An example would be a warranty on products sold. An entity may also have a considerable investment in the production of inventories. Usually, until the inventory is sold in the normal course of business, the entity cannot accurately account for the investment in inventory.

With the time period assumption, we accept some inaccuracies of accounting for the entity short of its complete life span. We assume that the entity can be accounted for with reasonable accuracy for a particular period of time. In other words, the decision is made to accept some inaccuracy, because of incomplete information about the future, in exchange for more timely reporting.

Some businesses select an accounting period, known as a **natural business year**, that ends when operations are at a low ebb in order to facilitate a better measurement of income and financial position. Other businesses use the **calendar year** and thus end the accounting period on December 31. Some select a 12-month accounting period, known as a **fiscal year**, which closes at the end of a month other than December. The accounting period may be shorter than a year, such as a month. The shorter the period of time, the more inaccuracies we typically expect in the reporting.

Monetary Unit

Accountants need some standard of measure to bring financial transactions together in a meaningful way. Without some standard of measure, accountants would be forced to report in such terms as 5 cars, 1 factory, and 100 acres. This type of reporting would not be very meaningful.

There are a number of standards of measure, such as a yard, a gallon, and money. Of the possible standards of measure, accountants have concluded that money is the best for the purpose of measuring financial transactions.

Different countries call their monetary units by different names: Germany uses the **mark**, France uses the **franc**, and Japan uses the **yen**. Different countries also attach different values to their money—1 mark is not equal to 1 yen. Thus, financial transactions may be measured in terms of money in each country, but the statements from various countries cannot be compared directly or added together until they are converted to a common monetary unit, such as the U.S. dollar.

In various countries, the stability of the monetary unit has been a problem. The loss in value of money is called **inflation**. In some countries, inflation has been more than 300% per year. In countries where inflation has been significant, financial statements are adjusted by an inflation factor that restores the significance of money as a measuring unit. However, a completely acceptable restoration of money as a measuring unit cannot be made in such cases because of the problems involved in determining an accurate index. To indicate one such problem, consider the price of a car in 1988 and in 1998. The price of the car in 1998 would be higher, but the explanation would not be simply that the general price level has increased. Part of the reason for the price increase would be that the type and quality of the equipment have changed between 1988 and 1998. Thus, an index that relates the 1998 price to the 1988 price is a mixture of inflation, technological advancement, and quality changes.

The rate of inflation in the United States prior to the 1970s was relatively low. Therefore, it was thought that an adjustment of money as a measuring unit was not appropriate, because the added expense and inaccuracies of adjusting for inflation were greater than the benefits. During the 1970s, however, the United States experienced double-digit inflation. This made it increasingly desirable to implement some formal recognition of inflation.

In September 1979, the FASB issued *Statement of Financial Accounting Standards No. 33*, "Financial Reporting and Changing Prices," which required that certain large, publicly held companies disclose certain supplementary information concerning the impact of changing prices in their annual reports for fiscal years ending on or after December 25, 1979. This disclosure later became optional in 1986, when the FASB issued SFAS No. 89.

Historical Cost

SFAC No. 5 identified five different measurement attributes currently used in practice: historical cost, current cost, current market value, net realizable value, and present value. Usually, historical cost is used in practice because it is objective and determinable. A deviation from historical cost is accepted when it becomes apparent that the historical cost cannot be recovered. This deviation is justified by the conservatism concept. A deviation from historical cost is also found in practice where specific standards call for another measurement attribute such as current market value, net realizable value, or present value.

Conservatism

The accountant is often faced with a choice of different measurements of a situation, with each measurement having reasonable support. According to the concept of **conservatism**, the accountant must select the measurement with the least favorable effect on net income and financial position in the current period.

To apply the concept of conservatism to any given situation, there must be alternative measurements, each of which must have reasonable support. The accountant cannot use the conservatism concept to justify arbitrarily low figures. For example, writing inventory down to an arbitrarily low figure in order to recognize any possible loss from selling the inventory constitutes inaccurate accounting and cannot be justified under the concept of conservatism. An acceptable use of conservatism would be to value inventory at the lower of historical cost or market value.

The conservatism concept is used in many other situations, such as writing down or writing off obsolete inventory prior to sale, recognizing a loss on a long-term construction contract when it can be reasonably anticipated, and taking a conservative approach in determining the application of overhead to inventory. In estimating the lives of fixed assets, a conservative view is taken. Conservatism requires that the estimate of warranty expense reflects the least favorable effect on net income and the financial position of the current period.

Realization

Accountants face a problem of when to recognize revenue. All parts of an entity contribute to revenue, including the janitor, the receiving department, and the production employees. The problem becomes how to determine objectively the contribution of each of the segments toward revenue. Since this is not practical, accountants must determine *when* it is practical to recognize revenue. Revenue recognition *guidance* is in SFAC No. 5, "Recognition and Measurement in Financial Statements of Business Enterprises"; SFAC No. 6, "Elements of Financial Statements of Business Enterprises"; and APB Statement No. 4, "Basic Concepts and Accounting Principles Underlying Financial Statements of Business Enterprises." Also, SFAS No. 48, "Revenue Recognition When Right of Return Exists," provides specific conditions for recognizing revenue when there is a right of return.

In practice, revenue recognition has been the subject of much debate. This has resulted in fairly wide interpretations. The issue of revenue recognition has represented the basis of many SEC enforcement actions. In general, the point of recognition of revenue should be the point in time when revenue can be reasonably and objectively determined.

Point of Sale   Revenue is usually recognized at the point of sale. At this time, the earning process is virtually complete, and the exchange value can be determined. It is essential that there be some uniformity between firms regarding when revenue is recognized, so as to make financial statements meaningful and comparable.

There are times when the use of the point-of-sale approach does not give a fair result. An example would be the sale of land on credit to a buyer who does not have a reasonable ability to pay. If revenue were recognized at the point of sale, there would be a reasonable chance that sales had been overstated because of the material risk of default. In such cases, there are other acceptable methods of recognizing revenue that should be considered, such as the following:

1.   End of production
2.   Receipt of cash
3.   Revenue recognized during production
4.   Cost recovery

End of Production   The recognition of revenue at the completion of the production process is acceptable when the price of the item is known and there is a ready market. The mining of gold or silver is an example, and the harvesting of some farm products would also fit these criteria. If corn is harvested in the fall and held over the winter in order to obtain a higher price in the spring, the realization of revenue from the growing of corn should be recognized in the fall, at the point of harvest. The gain or loss from the holding of the corn represents a separate consideration from the growing of the corn.

Receipt of Cash   The receipt of cash is another basis for revenue recognition. This method should be used when collection is not capable of reasonable estimation at the time of sale. The land sales business, where the purchaser makes only a nominal down payment, is one type of business where the collection of the full amount is especially doubtful. Experience has shown that many purchasers default on the contract.

During Production   Some long-term construction projects recognize revenue as the construction progresses. This exception tends to give a fairer picture of the results for a given period of time. For example, in the building of a utility plant, which may take several years, recognizing revenue as work progresses gives a fairer picture of the results than does having the entire revenue recognized in the period when the plant is completed.

Cost Recovery   The cost recovery approach is acceptable for highly speculative transactions. For example, an entity may invest in a venture search for gold, the outcome of which is completely unpredictable. In this case, the first revenue can be handled as a return of the investment. If more is received than has been invested, the excess would be considered revenue.

In addition to the methods of recognizing revenue described in this chapter, there are many other methods that are usually industry specific. Being aware of the method(s) used by a specific firm can be important to your understanding of the financial reports.

Matching

The revenue realization concept involves when to recognize revenue. Accountants need a related concept that addresses when to recognize the costs associated with the recognized revenue: the **matching concept**. The basic intent is to determine the revenue first and then match the appropriate costs against this revenue.

Some costs, such as the cost of inventory, can be easily matched with revenue. When we sell the inventory and recognize the revenue, the cost of the inventory can be matched against the revenue. Other costs have no direct connection with revenue, so some systematic policy must be adopted in order to allocate these costs reasonably against revenues. Examples are research and development costs and public relations costs. Both research and development costs and public relations costs are charged off in the period incurred. This is inconsistent with the matching concept because the cost would benefit beyond the current period, but it is in accordance with the concept of conservatism.

Consistency

The **consistency concept** requires the entity to give the same treatment to comparable transactions from period to period. This adds to the usefulness of the reports, since the reports from one period are comparable to the reports from another period. It also facilitates the detection of trends.

Many accounting methods could be used for any single item, such as inventory. If inventory were determined in one period on the FIFO basis (first-in, first-out) and in the next period on the LIFO basis (last-in, first-out), the resulting inventory and profits would not be comparable from period to period.

Entities sometimes need to change particular accounting methods in order to adapt to changing environments. If the entity can justify the use of an alternative accounting method, the change can be made. The entity must be ready to defend the change—a responsibility that should not be taken lightly in view of the liability for misleading financial statements. Sometimes the change will be based on a new accounting pronouncement. When an entity makes a change in accounting methods, the justification for the change must be disclosed, along with an explanation of the effect on the statements.

Full Disclosure

The accounting reports must disclose all facts that may influence the judgment of an informed reader. If the entity uses an accounting method that represents a departure from the official position of the FASB, disclosure of the departure must be made, along with the justification for it.

Several methods of disclosure exist, such as parenthetical explanations, supporting schedules, cross-references, and footnotes. Often, the additional disclosures must be made by a footnote in order to explain the situation properly. For example, details of a pension plan, long-term leases, and provisions of a bond issue are often disclosed in footnotes.

The financial statements are expected to summarize significant financial information. If all the financial information is presented in detail, it could be misleading. Excessive disclosure could violate the concept of full disclosure. Therefore, a reasonable summarization of financial information is required.

Because of the complexity of many businesses and the increased expectations of the public, full disclosure has become one of the most difficult concepts for the accountant to apply. Lawsuits frequently charge accountants with failure to make proper disclosure. Since disclosure is often a judgment decision, it is not surprising that others (especially those who have suffered losses) would disagree with the adequacy of the disclosure.

Materiality

The accountant must consider many concepts and principles when determining how to handle a particular item. The proper use of the various concepts and principles may be costly and time-consuming. The **materiality concept** involves the relative size and importance of an item to a firm. A material item to one entity may not be material to another. For example, an item that costs $100 might be expensed by General Motors, but the same item might be carried as an asset by a small entity.

It is essential that material items be properly handled on the financial statements. Immaterial items are not subject to the concepts and principles that bind the accountant. They may be handled in the most economical and expedient manner possible. However, the accountant faces a judgment situation when determining materiality. It is better to err in favor of an item being material than the other way around.

A basic question when determining whether an item is material is: "Would this item influence an informed reader of the financial statements?" In answering this question, the accountant should consider the statements as a whole.

Industry Practices

Some industry practices lead to accounting reports that do not conform to the general theory that underlies accounting. Some of these practices are the result of government regulation. For example, some differences can be found in highly regulated industries, such as insurance, railroad, and utilities.

In the utility industry, an allowance for funds used during the construction period of a new plant is treated as part of the cost of the plant. The offsetting amount is reflected as other income. This amount is based on the utility's hypothetical cost of funds, including funds from debt and stock. This type of accounting is found only in the utility industry.

In some industries, it is very difficult to determine the cost of the inventory. Examples include the meat-packing industry, the flower industry, and farming. In these areas, it may be necessary to determine the inventory value by working backward from the anticipated selling price and subtracting the estimated cost to complete and dispose of the inventory. The inventory would thus be valued at a net realizable value, which would depart from the cost concept and the usual interpretation of the revenue realization concept. If inventory is valued at net realizable value, then the profit has already been recognized and is part of the inventory amount.

The accounting profession is making an effort to reduce or eliminate specific industry practices. However, industry practices that depart from typical accounting procedures will probably never be eliminated completely. Some industries have legitimate peculiarities that call for accounting procedures other than the customary ones.

Transaction Approach

The accountant records only events that affect the financial position of the entity and, at the same time, can be reasonably determined in monetary terms. For example, if the entity purchases merchandise on account (on credit), the financial position of the entity changes. This change can be determined in monetary terms as the inventory asset is obtained and the liability, accounts payable, is incurred.

Many important events that influence the prospects for the entity are not recorded and, therefore, are not reflected in the financial statements because they fall outside the transaction approach. The death of a top executive could have a material influence on future prospects, especially for a small company. One of the company's major suppliers could go bankrupt at a time when the entity does not have an alternative source. The entity may have experienced a long strike by its employees or have a history of labor problems. A major competitor may go out of business. All these events may be significant to the entity. They are not recorded because they are not transactions. When projecting the future prospects of an entity, it is necessary to go beyond current financial reports.

Present Value Considerations

Some assets and most liabilities represent current purchasing power or legal obligations to pay out a fixed number of dollars. These assets and liabilities, known as monetary items, include cash, accounts receivable, accounts payable, and notes payable. The timing of the cash receipt for a monetary asset and the cash payment to extinguish a liability is important to the worth of the asset and the amount of the liability. The characteristic that money to be received or paid out in the future is not worth as much as money available today is referred to as the time value of money or the present value.

Accountants usually must reflect the time value of money on monetary assets and liabilities when a material difference occurs between the monetary amount involved in the transaction and the present value of the item. For example, if a company sells an item for $1,000 and in return receives a three-year, non-interest-bearing note, the note and the sales price would need to be adjusted downward to reflect the present value of the money. The entity would use its going rate of interest to determine the amount of the adjustment. If the entity had accepted a one-year, non-interest-bearing note, no adjustment to the $1,000 amount would be made. The difference between the stated monetary amount and the projected present value would be considered immaterial, since the note would be relatively short term. This illustrates that the time value of money consideration is not applied to relatively short-term assets or liabilities.

Accountants take into consideration the time value of money when preparing the financial statements for such areas as long-term leases, pensions, and other long-term situations where the future payments or receipts are not indicative of the present value of the asset or the obligation. However, the way accountants consider the time value of money is not always consistent. For example, an interest rate at the time of the original transaction is used for leases, whereas an annual consideration of the interest rate is used for pensions.

Cash Basis

The **cash basis** recognizes revenue when cash is received and recognizes expenses when cash is paid. The cash basis usually does *not* provide reasonable information about the earning capability of the entity in the short run. Therefore, the cash basis is usually *not* acceptable.

Accrual Basis

The **accrual basis** of accounting recognizes revenue when realized (realization concept) and expenses when incurred (matching concept). If the difference between the accrual basis and the cash basis is not material, the entity may use the cash basis as an alternative to the accrual basis for income determination. Usually, the difference between the accrual basis and the cash basis is material.

A modified cash basis is sometimes used by professional practices and service organizations. The modified cash basis adjusts for such items as buildings and equipment.

The accrual basis requires numerous adjustments at the end of the accounting period. For instance, if insurance has been paid for in advance, the accountant must determine the amounts that belong in prepaid insurance and insurance expense. If employees have not been paid all of their wages, the unpaid wages must be determined and recorded as an expense and as a liability. If revenue has been collected in advance, such as rent received in advance, this revenue relates to future periods and must, therefore, be deferred to those periods. At the end of the accounting period, the unearned rent would be considered a liability.

The use of the accrual basis complicates the accounting process, but the end result is more representative of an entity's financial condition than the cash basis. Without the accrual basis, accountants would not usually be able to make the time period assumption—that the entity can be accounted for with reasonable accuracy for a particular period of time.

The following illustration indicates why the accrual basis is generally regarded as a better measure of a firm's performance than the cash basis.

Assumptions:

1. Sold merchandise (inventory) for $25,000 on credit this year. The merchandise cost $12,500 when purchased in the prior year.
2. Purchased merchandise this year in the amount of $30,000 on credit.
3. Paid suppliers of merchandise $18,000 this year.
4. Collected $15,000 from sales.

	Accrual Basis		**Cash Basis**	
Sales	$ 25,000	Receipts	$ 15,000
Cost of sales (expenses)	(12,500)	Expenditures	(18,000)
Income	$ 12,500	Loss	$ (3,000)

The accrual basis indicates a profitable business, whereas the cash basis indicates a loss. The cash basis does not reasonably indicate when the revenue was earned or when to recognize the cost that relates to the earned revenue. The cash basis does indicate when the receipts and payments (disbursements) occurred. The points in time when cash is received and paid do not usually constitute a good gauge of profitability. However, knowing the points in time is important; the flow of cash will be presented in a separate financial statement (statement of cash flows).

In practice the accrual basis is modified. Immaterial items are frequently handled on a cash basis, and some specific standards have allowed the cash basis.

SUMMARY

This chapter has reviewed the development of generally accepted accounting principles (GAAP) and the traditional assumptions of the accounting model. The user needs a broad understanding of GAAP and the traditional assumptions to reasonably understand financial reports. The financial reports can be no better than the accounting principles and the assumptions of the accounting model that are the basis for preparation.

QUESTIONS

Q 1-1. Discuss the role of each of the following in the formulation of accounting principles:

a. American Institute of Certified Public Accountants
b. Financial Accounting Standards Board
c. Securities and Exchange Commission

Q 1-2. How does the concept of consistency aid in the analysis of financial statements? What type of accounting disclosure is required if this concept is not applied?

Q 1-3. The president of your firm, Lesky and Lesky, has little background in accounting. Today he walked into your office and said, "A year ago we bought a piece of land for $100,000. This year inflation has driven prices up by 6%, and an appraiser just told us we could easily resell the land for $115,000. Yet our balance sheet still shows it at $100,000. It should be valued at $115,000. That's what it's worth. Or, at a minimum, at $106,000." Respond to this statement with specific reference to accounting principles applicable in this situation.

Q 1-4.   Identify the accounting principle(s) applicable to each of the following situations:

    a.   Tim Roberts owns a bar and a rental apartment and operates a consulting service. He has separate financial statements for each.

    b.   An advance collection for magazine subscriptions is reported as a liability titled Unearned Subscriptions.

    c.   Purchases for office or store equipment for less than $25 are entered in Miscellaneous Expense.

    d.   A company uses the lower of cost or market for valuation of its inventory.

    e.   Although inflation of 6% occurred during the year, no adjustment for this was made on the books.

    f.   Partially completed television sets are carried at the sum of the cost incurred to date.

    g.   Land purchased 15 years ago for $40,500 is now worth $346,000. It is still carried on the books at $40,500.

    h.   Zero Corporation is being sued for $1,000,000 for breach of contract. Its lawyers believe that the damages will be minimal. Zero reports the possible loss in a footnote.

Q 1-5.   A corporation like General Motors has many owners (stockholders). Which concept enables the accountant to account for transactions of General Motors, separate and distinct from the personal transactions of the owners of General Motors?

Q 1-6.   Zebra Company has incurred substantial financial losses in recent years. Because of its financial condition, the ability of the company to keep operating is in question. Management prepares a set of financial statements that conform to generally accepted accounting principles. Comment on the use of GAAP under these conditions.

Q 1-7.   Because of assumptions and estimates that go into the preparation of financial statements, the statements are inaccurate and are, therefore, not a very meaningful tool to determine the profits or losses of an entity or the financial position of an entity. Comment.

Q 1-8.   The only accurate way to account for the success or failure of an entity is to accumulate all transactions from the opening of business until the business eventually liquidates. Comment on whether this is true. Discuss the necessity of having completely accurate statements.

Q 1-9.   Describe the following terms, which indicate the period of time included in the financial statements:

    a.   Natural business year

    b.   Calendar year

    c.   Fiscal year

Q 1-10.   Which standard of measure is the best for measuring financial transactions?

Q 1-11.   Countries have had problems with the stability of their money. Briefly describe the problem caused for financial statements when money does not hold a stable value.

Q 1-12.   In some countries where inflation has been material, an effort has been made to retain the significance of money as a measuring unit by adjusting the financial statements by an inflation factor. Can an accurate adjustment for inflation be made to the statements? Can a reasonable adjustment to the statements be made? Discuss.

Q 1-13.   An arbitrary write-off of inventory can be justified under the conservatism concept. Is this statement true or false? Discuss.

Q 1-14.   Inventory that has a market value below the historical cost should be written down in order to recognize a loss. Comment.

Q 1-15.   There are other acceptable methods of recognizing revenue when the point of sale is not acceptable. List and discuss the other methods reviewed in this chapter, and indicate when they can be used.

Q 1-16.   The matching concept involves the determination of when to recognize the costs associated with the revenue that is being recognized. For some costs, such as administrative costs, the matching concept is difficult to apply. Comment on when it is difficult to apply the matching concept. What do accountants often do under these circumstances?

Q 1-17.   The consistency concept requires the entity to give the same treatment to comparable transactions from period to period. Under what circumstances can an entity change its accounting methods, provided it makes full disclosure?

Q 1-18.   Discuss why the concept of full disclosure is difficult to apply.

Q 1-19.   No estimates or subjectivity is allowed in the preparation of financial statements. Discuss.

Q 1-20.   It is proper to handle immaterial items in the most economical, expedient manner possible. In other words, generally accepted accounting principles do not apply. Comment, including a concept that justifies your answer.

Q 1-21.   The same generally accepted accounting principles apply to all companies. Comment.

Q 1-22.   Many important events that influence the prospect for the entity are not recorded in the financial records. Comment and give an example.

Q 1-23.   If a company has a long-term lease and the lease payments are $20,000 a year for the next ten years, then the amount of the liability that appears on the financial statements would be $200,000. Comment.

Q 1-24.   An entity may choose between the use of the accrual basis of accounting and the cash basis. Comment.

Q 1-25.   Generally accepted accounting principles have substantial authoritative support. Indicate the problem with determining substantial authoritative support.

Q 1-26.   Would an accountant record the personal assets and liabilities of the owners in the accounts of the business? Explain.

Q 1-27.   At which point is revenue from sales on account commonly recognized?

Q 1-28.   Elliott Company constructed a building at a cost of $50,000. A local contractor had submitted a bid to construct it for $60,000.

    a. At what amount should the building be recorded?

    b. Should revenue be recorded for the savings between the cost of $50,000 and the bid of $60,000?

Q 1-29.   Dexter Company charges to expense all equipment that costs $25 or less. What concept supports this policy?

Q 1-30.   Which U.S. government body has the legal power to determine generally accepted accounting principles?

Q 1-31.   What is the basic problem with the monetary assumption when there has been significant inflation?

Q 1-32.   Explain the matching principle. How is the matching principle related to the realization concept?

Q 1-33.   Briefly explain the term *generally accepted accounting principles*.

Q 1-34.   Briefly describe the operating procedure for Statements of Financial Accounting Standards.

Q 1-35.   What is the FASB Conceptual Framework for Accounting and Reporting intended to provide?

Q 1-36.   Briefly describe the following:

    a. Committee on Accounting Procedures

    b. Committee on Accounting Terminology

    c. Accounting Principles Board

    d. Financial Accounting Standards Board

Q 1-37.   Describe the role of Statements of Financial Accounting Concepts (SFACs) in the development of generally accepted accounting principles.

Q 1-38.   The objectives of general-purpose external financial reporting are primarily to serve the needs of management. Comment.

Q 1-39.   Financial accounting is designed to measure directly the value of a business enterprise. Comment.

Q 1-40.   According to Concepts Statement No. 2, relevance and reliability are the two primary qualities that make accounting information useful for decision making. Comment on what is meant by relevance and reliability.

Q 1-41.   SFAC No. 5 indicates that, to be recognized, an item should meet four criteria, subject to the cost-benefit constraint and materiality threshold. List these criteria.

Q 1-42.   SFAC No. 5 identifies five different measurement attributes currently used in practice. List these measurement attributes.

Q 1-43.   Briefly explain the difference between an accrual basis income statement and a cash basis income statement.

Q 1-44.   The cash basis does not reasonably indicate when the revenue was earned and when the cost should be recognized. Comment.

Q 1-45.   It is not important to know when cash is received and when payment is made. Comment.

PROBLEMS

P 1-1. FASB Statement of Concepts No. 2 indicates several qualitative characteristics of useful accounting information. Below is a list of some of these qualities, as well as a list of statements and phrases describing the qualities.

a. Benefits > costs
b. Decision usefulness
c. Relevance
d. Reliability
e. Predictive value, feedback value, timeliness

f. Verifiability, neutrality, representational faithfulness
g. Comparability
h. Materiality
i. Relevance, reliability

___ 1. Without usefulness, there would be no benefits from information to set against its cost.

___ 2. Pervasive constraint imposed upon financial accounting information.

___ 3. Constraint that guides the threshold for recognition.

___ 4. A quality requiring that the information be timely and that it also have predictive value, or feedback value, or both.

___ 5. A quality requiring that the information have representational faithfulness and that it be verifiable and neutral.

___ 6. These are the two primary qualities that make accounting information useful for decision making.

___ 7. These are the ingredients needed to ensure that the information is relevant.

___ 8. These are the ingredients needed to ensure that the information is reliable.

___ 9. Includes consistency and interacts with relevance and reliability to contribute to the usefulness of information.

Required Place the appropriate letter identifying each quality on the line in front of the statement or phrase describing the quality.

P 1-2. Certain underlying considerations have had an important impact on the development of generally accepted accounting principles. Below is a list of these underlying considerations, as well as a list of statements describing them.

a. Going concern or continuity
b. Monetary unit
c. Conservatism
d. Matching
e. Full disclosure
f. Materiality
g. Transaction approach
h. Accrual basis

i. Industry practices
j. Verifiability
k. Consistency
l. Realization
m. Historical cost
n. Time period
o. Business entity

____ 1. The business for which the financial statements are prepared is separate and distinct from the owners.

____ 2. The assumption is made that the entity will remain in business for an indefinite period of time.

____ 3. Accountants need some standard of measure to bring financial transactions together in a meaningful way.

____ 4. Revenue should be recognized when the earning process is virtually complete and the exchange value can be objectively determined.

____ 5. This concept deals with when to recognize the costs that are associated with the recognized revenue.

____ 6. Accounting reports must disclose all facts that may influence the judgment of an informed reader.

____ 7. This concept involves the relative size and importance of an item to a firm.

____ 8. The accountant is required to adhere as closely as possible to verifiable data.

____ 9. Some companies use accounting reports that do not conform to the general theory that underlies accounting.

____ 10. The accountant records only events that affect the financial position of the entity and, at the same time, can be reasonably determined in monetary terms.

____ 11. Revenue must be recognized when it is realized (realization concept), and expenses are recognized when incurred (matching concept).

____ 12. The entity must give the same treatment to comparable transactions from period to period.

____ 13. The measurement with the least favorable effect on net income and financial position in the current period must be selected.

____ 14. Of the various values that could be used, this value has been selected because it is objective and determinable.

____ 15. With this assumption, inaccuracies of accounting for the entity short of its complete life span are accepted.

Required   Place the appropriate letter identifying each quality on the line in front of the statement describing the quality.

P 1-3.

Required   Answer the following multiple-choice questions:

a. Which of the following is a characteristic of information provided by external financial reports?
1. The information is exact and not subject to change.
2. The information is frequently the result of reasonable estimates.
3. The information pertains to the economy as a whole.
4. The information is provided at the least possible cost.
5. None of the above.

b. Which of the following is not an objective of financial reporting?
1. Financial reporting should provide information that is useful to present and potential investors and creditors and other users in making rational investment, credit, and similar decisions.
2. Financial reporting should provide information to help present and potential investors and creditors and other users in assessing the amounts, timing, and uncertainty of prospective cash receipts from dividends or interest and the proceeds from the sale, redemption, or maturity of securities or loans.
3. Financial reporting should provide information about the economic resources of an enterprise, the claims against those resources, and the effects of transactions, events, and circumstances that change the resources and claims against those resources.
4. Financial accounting is designed to measure directly the value of a business enterprise.
5. None of the above.

c. According to FASB Statement of Concepts No. 2, which of the following is an ingredient of the quality of relevance?
1. Verifiability
2. Representational faithfulness
3. Neutrality
4. Timeliness
5. None of the above

d. The primary current source of generally accepted accounting principles for nongovernment operations is the
1. New York Stock Exchange
2. Financial Accounting Standards Board
3. Securities and Exchange Commission
4. American Institute of Certified Public Accountants
5. None of the above

e. What is the underlying concept that supports the immediate recognition of a loss?
1. Matching
2. Consistency
3. Judgment
4. Conservatism
5. Going concern

    f.   Which statement is not true?
1. The Securities and Exchange Commission is a source of some generally accepted accounting principles.
2. The American Institute of Certified Public Accountants is a source of some generally accepted accounting principles.
3. The Internal Revenue Service is a source of some generally accepted accounting principles.
4. The Financial Accounting Standards Board is a source of some generally accepted accounting principles.
5. Numbers 1, 2, and 4 are sources of generally accepted accounting principles.

    g.   Which pronouncements are not issued by the Financial Accounting Standards Board?
1. Statements of Financial Accounting Standards
2. Statements of Financial Accounting Concepts
3. Technical bulletins
4. Interpretations
5. Opinions

P 1-4.

Required   Answer the following multiple-choice questions:

    a.   Which of the following does the Financial Accounting Standards Board not issue?
1. Statements of Position (SOPs)
2. Statements of Financial Accounting Standards (SFASs)
3. Interpretations
4. Technical bulletins
5. Statements of Financial Accounting Concepts (SFACs)

    b.   According to SFAC No. 6, assets can be defined by which of the following?
1. Probable future sacrifices of economic benefits arising from present obligations of a particular entity to transfer assets or provide services to other entities in the future as a result of past transactions or events.
2. Probable future economic benefits obtained or controlled by a particular entity as a result of past transactions or events.
3. Residual interest on the assets of an entity that remains after deducting its liabilities.
4. Increases in equity of a particular business enterprise resulting from transfers to the enterprise from other entities of something of value to obtain or increase ownership interests (or equity) in it.
5. Decrease in equity of a particular business enterprise resulting from transferring assets, rendering services, or incurring liabilities by the enterprise.

c. According to SFAC No. 6, expenses can be defined by which of the following?

1. Inflows or other enhancements of assets of an entity or settlements of its liabilities (or a combination of both) from delivering or producing goods, rendering services, or other activities that constitute the entity's ongoing major or central operations.
2. Outflows or other consumption or using up of assets or incurrences of liabilities (or a combination of both) from delivering or producing goods, rendering services, or carrying out other activities that constitute the entity's ongoing major or central operations.
3. Increases in equity (net assets) from peripheral or incidental transactions of an entity and from all other transactions and other events and circumstances affecting the entity during a period, except those that result from revenues or investments.
4. Decreases in equity (net assets) from peripheral or incidental transactions of an entity and from all other transactions and other events and circumstances affecting the entity during a period, except those that result from expenses or distributions to owners.
5. Probable future economic benefits obtained or controlled by a particular entity as a result of past transactions or events.

d. SFAC No. 5 indicates that an item, to be recognized, should meet four criteria, subject to the cost-benefit constraint and the materiality threshold. Which of the following is not one of the four criteria?

1. The item fits one of the definitions of the elements.
2. The item has a relevant attribute measurable with sufficient reliability.
3. The information related to the item is relevant.
4. The information related to the item is reliable.
5. The item has comparability, including consistency.

e. SFAC No. 5 identifies five different measurement attributes currently used in practice. Which of the following is not one of the measurement attributes currently used in practice?

1. Historical cost
2. Future cost
3. Current market value
4. Net realizable value
5. Present, or discounted, value of future cash flows

f. Which of the following indicates how revenue is usually recognized?

1. Point of sale
2. End of production
3. Receipt of cash
4. During production
5. Cost recovery

g. *Statement of Financial Accounting Concepts No. 1,* "Objectives of Financial Reporting by Business Enterprises," includes all of the following objectives, except for one. Which objective does it not include?
1. Financial accounting is designed to measure directly the value of a business enterprise.
2. Investors, creditors, and others may use reported earnings and information about the elements of financial statements in various ways to assess the prospects for cash flows.
3. The primary focus of financial reporting is information about earnings and its components.
4. Financial reporting should provide information that is useful to present and potential investors and creditors and other users in making rational investment, credit, and similar decisions.
5. The objectives are those of general-purpose external financial reporting by business enterprises.

P 1-5.   The following data relate to Jones Company for the year ended December 31, 1998:

Sales on credit	$80,000
Cost of inventory sold on credit	65,000
Collections from customers	60,000
Purchase of inventory on credit	50,000
Payment for purchases	55,000
Cash collections for common stock	30,000
Dividends paid	10,000
Payment to sales clerk	10,000

Required   a. Determine income on an accrual basis.
           b. Determine income on a cash basis.

Cases

CASE 1-1   Standards Overload?*

Even though accounting records go back hundreds of years, there was little effort to develop accounting standards until the 1900s. The first major effort to develop accounting standards in the United States came in 1939 when the American Institute of Certified Public Accountants formed the Committee on Accounting Procedures.

As the number of standards increased, an issue called "standards overload" emerged. Essentially the charge of "standards overload" is that there are too many accounting standards and that the standards are too complicated. Many individuals charging that standards overload is a problem maintain that more professional judgment should be allowed in financial accounting. Some individuals take a position that selected standards should not apply to nonpublic companies. Others take a position that "little" companies should be exempt from selected standards. There has been some selective exclusion from standards in the past. Examples of selective exclusion are the following:

1. *Statement of Financial Accounting Standards No. 21,* "Suspension of the Reporting of Earnings per Share and Segment Information by Nonpublic Enterprises."

    "Although the presentation of earnings per share and segment information is not required in the financial statements of nonpublic enterprises, any such information that is presented in the financial statements of nonpublic enterprises shall be consistent with the requirements of APB Opinion No. 15 and FASB Statement No. 14."

2. *Statement of Financial Accounting Standards No. 33,* "Financial Reporting and Changing Prices."

    This statement required supplemental reporting on the effects of price changes. Only large public companies were required to present this information on a supplementary basis.

---

*Note: The standards referenced in this case should not be considered current standards. The financial reporting issues referenced in this case are discussed in subsequent chapters using current requirements.

Required   a.   Financial statements should aid the user of the statements in making decisions. In your opinion, would the user of the statements be aided if there were a distinction between financial reporting standards for public vs. nonpublic companies? Between little and big companies?

b.   In your opinion, would CPAs favor a distinction between financial reporting standards for public vs. nonpublic companies? Discuss.

c.   In your opinion, would small business owner-managers favor a distinction between financial reporting standards for small and large companies? Discuss.

d.   In your opinion, would CPAs in a small CPA firm view standards overload as a bigger problem than CPAs in a large CPA firm? Discuss.

e.   Comment on standards overload, considering *Statement of Financial Accounting Concepts No. 1,* "Objectives of Financial Reporting by Business Enterprises." Particularly consider the following objective:

> Financial reporting should provide information useful to present and potential investors and creditors and other users in making rational investment, credit, and similar decisions. The information should be comprehensible to those having a reasonable understanding of business and economic activities and willing to study the information with reasonable diligence.

CASE 1-2   Standard Setting: "A Political Aspect"

This case consists of a letter from Dennis R. Beresford, chairperson of the Financial Accounting Standards Board, to Senator Joseph I. Lieberman. The specific issue was proposed legislation relating to the accounting for employee stock options.

Permission to reprint the following letter was obtained from the Financial Accounting Standards Board.

August 3, 1993

Senator Joseph I. Lieberman
United States Senate
Hart Senate Office Building
Room 316
Washington, DC 20510

Dear Senator Lieberman:

Members of the Financial Accounting Standards Board (the FASB or the Board) and its staff routinely consult with members of Congress, their staffs, and other government officials on matters involving financial accounting. For example, FASB members and staff met with Senator Levin both before and after the introduction of his proposed legislation, Senate Bill 259, which also addresses accounting for employee stock options.

The attachment to this letter discusses the accounting issues (we have not addressed the tax issues) raised in your proposed legislation, Senate Bill 1175, and issues raised in remarks introduced in the *Congressional Record*. My comments in this letter address an issue that is more important than any particular legislation or any particular accounting issue: why we have a defined process for setting financial reporting standards and why it is harmful to the public interest to distort accounting reports in an attempt to attain other worthwhile goals.

Financial Reporting

Markets are enormously efficient information processors—when they have the information and that information faithfully portrays economic events. Financial statements are one of the basic tools for communicating that information. The U.S. capital market system is well-developed and efficient because of users' confidence that the financial information they receive is reliable. Common accounting standards for the preparation of financial reports contribute to their credibility. The mission of the FASB, an organization designed to be independent of all other business and professional organizations, is to establish and improve financial accounting and reporting standards in the United States.

Investors, creditors, regulators, and other users of financial reports make business and economic decisions based on information in financial statements. Credibility is critical whether the user is an individual contemplating a stock investment, a bank making lending decisions, or a regulatory agency reviewing solvency. Users count on financial reports that are evenhanded, neutral, and unbiased.

An efficiently functioning economy requires credible financial information as a basis for decisions about allocation of resources. If financial statements are to be useful, they must report economic activity without coloring the message to influence behavior in a particular direction. They must not intentionally favor one party over another. Financial statements must provide a neutral scorecard of the effects of transactions.

Economic Consequences of Accounting Standards

The Board often hears that we should take a broader view, that we must consider the economic consequences of a new accounting standard. The FASB should not act, critics maintain, if a new accounting standard would have undesirable economic consequences. We have been told that the effects of accounting standards could cause lasting damage to American companies and their employees. Some have suggested, for example, that recording the liability for retiree health care or the costs for stock-based compensation will place U.S. companies at a competitive disadvantage. These critics suggest that because of accounting standards, companies may reduce benefits or move operations overseas to areas where workers do not demand the same benefits. These assertions are usually combined with statements about desirable goals, like providing retiree health care or creating employee incentives.

There is a common element in those assertions. The goals are desirable, but the means require that the Board abandon neutrality and establish reporting standards that conceal the financial impact of certain transactions from those who use financial statements. Costs of transactions exist whether or not the FASB mandates their recognition in financial statements. For example, not requiring the recognition of the cost of stock options or ignoring the liabilities for retiree health benefits does not alter the economics of the transactions. It only withholds information from investors, creditors, policy makers, and others who need to make informed decisions and, eventually, impairs the credibility of financial reports.

One need only look to the collapse of the thrift industry to demonstrate the consequences of abandoning neutrality. During the 1970s and 1980s, regulatory accounting principles (RAP) were altered to obscure problems in troubled institutions. Preserving the industry was considered a "greater good." Many observers believe that the effect was to delay action and hide the true dimensions of the problem. The public interest is best served by neutral accounting standards that inform policy rather than promote it. Stated simply, truth in accounting is always good policy.

Neutrality does not mean that accounting should not influence human behavior. We expect that changes in financial reporting will have economic consequences, just as economic consequences are inherent in existing financial reporting practices. Changes in behavior naturally flow from more complete and representationally faithful financial statements. The fundamental question, however, is whether those who measure and report on economic events should somehow screen the information before reporting it to achieve some objective. In FASB Concepts Statement No. 2, "Qualitative Characteristics of Accounting Information" (paragraph 102), the Board observed:

> Indeed, most people are repelled by the notion that some "big brother," whether government or private, would tamper with scales or speedometers surreptitiously to induce people to lose weight or obey speed limits or would slant the scoring of athletic events or examinations to enhance or decrease someone's chances of winning or graduating. There is no more reason to abandon neutrality in accounting measurement.

The Board continues to hold that view. The Board does not set out to achieve particular economic results through accounting pronouncements. We could not if we tried. Beyond that, it is seldom clear which result we should seek because our constituents often have opposing viewpoints. Governments, and the policy goals they adopt, frequently change.

Standard Setting in the Private Sector

While the SEC and congressional committees maintain active oversight of the FASB to ensure that the public interest is served, throughout its history the SEC has relied on the Board and its predecessors in the private sector to establish and improve financial accounting and reporting standards. In fulfilling the Board's mission of improving financial reporting, accounting standards are established through a system of due process and open deliberation. On all of our major projects, this involves open Board meetings, proposals published for comment, "field testing" of proposals, public hearings, and redeliberation of the issues in light of comments.

Our due process has allowed us to deal with complex and highly controversial accounting issues, ranging from pensions and retiree health care to abandonment of nuclear power plants. This open, orderly process for standard setting precludes placing any particular special interest above the interests of the many who rely on financial information. The Board believes that the public interest is best served by developing neutral accounting standards that result in accounting for similar transactions similarly and different transactions differently. The resulting financial statements provide as complete and faithful a picture of an entity as possible.

Corporations, accounting firms, users of financial statements, and most other interested parties have long supported the process of establishing accounting standards in the private sector without intervention by Congress or other branches of government. Despite numerous individual issues on which the FASB and many of its constituents have disagreed, that support has continued. The resulting system of accounting standards and financial reporting, while not perfect, is the best in the world.

Conclusion

We understand that there are a number of people who believe that their particular short-term interests are more important than an effectively functioning financial reporting system. We sincerely hope, however, that you and others in the Congress will review the reasons that have led generations of lawmakers and regulators to conclude that neutral financial reporting is critical to the functioning of our economic system and that the best way to achieve that end is to allow the existing private sector process to proceed. We respectfully submit that the public interest will be best served by that course. As former SEC Chairman Richard Breeden said in testimony to the Senate Banking Committee in 1990:

> The purpose of accounting standards is to assure that financial information is presented in a way that enables decision-makers to make informed judgments. To the extent that accounting standards are subverted to achieve objectives unrelated to a fair and accurate presentation, they fail in their purpose.

The attachment to this letter discusses your proposed legislation. It also describes some aspects of our project on stock compensation and the steps in our due process procedures that remain before the project will be completed. In your remarks in the *Congressional Record*, you said that you will address future issues, including an examination of the current treatment of employee stock options, over the next weeks and months. We would be pleased to meet with you or your staff to discuss these topics and the details of our project. I will phone your appointments person in the next two weeks to see if it is convenient for you to meet with me.

Sincerely,

Dennis R. Beresford

Dennis R. Beresford

Enclosure

cc: The Honorable Connie Mack
     The Honorable Dianne Feinstein
     The Honorable Barbara Boxer
     The Honorable Carl S. Levin
     The Honorable Christopher J. Dodd
     The Honorable Arthur J. Levitt

Required

a. "Financial statements must provide a neutral scorecard of the effects of transactions." Comment.
b. "Costs of transactions exist whether or not the FASB mandates their recognition in financial statements." Comment.
c. In the United States, standard setting is in the private sector. Comment.
d. Few, if any, accounting standards are without some economic impact. Comment.

CASE 1-3   Standard Setting: "By the Way of the United States Congress"

In the summer of 1993, the Senate and the House introduced identical bills to amend the Internal Revenue Code of 1986. Section 4 of these bills addressed stock option compensation and financial reporting.

SEC. 4   STOCK OPTION COMPENSATION.

Section 14 of the Securities Exchange Act of 1934 (15 U.S.C. 78n) is amended by adding at the end the following new subsection:

"(h) STOCK OPTION COMPENSATION—The Commission shall not require or permit an issuer to recognize any expense or other charge in financial statements furnished to its security holders resulting from, or attributable to, either the grant, vesting, or exercise of any option or other right to acquire any equity security of such issuer (even if the right to exercise such option or right is subject to any conditions, contingencies or other criteria including, without limitation, the continued performance of services, achievement of performance objectives, or the occurrence of any event) which is granted to its directors, officers, employees, or other persons in connection with the performance of services, where the exercise price of such option or right is not less than the fair market value of the underlying security at the time such option or right is granted."

Required
a. The United States Congress is well qualified to debate and set generally accepted accounting principles. Comment.
b. Speculate on why these bills were directed to amend the Securities Exchange Act of 1934.

CASE 1-4   Recognizing Revenue and Related Costs— Consider These Situations (Part I)

A. American Maize-Products Company

American Maize-Products Company reported net sales of $603,988,000 in 1994. The following was disclosed relating to by-product revenues: "Certain by-products are produced from the Company's corn processing operations. Revenues from by-products are included in net sales and aggregated $73,482, $71,903, and $78,454, in 1994, 1993, and 1992, respectively."

Required
a. How material are by-product sales for American Maize-Products?
b. What revenue recognition method should be used by American Maize-Products Company for by-products?

B. Electronic Data Systems Corporation

Electronic Data Systems Corporation included the following related to revenue recognition in its 1994 annual report:

Revenue Recognition

The Company provides services under level-of-effort and fixed-price contracts, with the length of the Company's contracts ranging up to ten years. For level-of-effort types of contracts, revenue is earned based on the agreed-upon billing amounts as services are provided to the customer. For certain fixed-price contracts, revenue is recognized on the percentage-of-completion method. Revenue earned is based on the percentage that incurred costs to date bear to total estimated costs after giving effect to the most recent estimates of total cost.

Level-of-Effort Contracts

Required   a. Comment on the apparent degree of estimating in determining the revenue recognition for level-of-effort contracts.

b. For these contracts, does the effort occur in the period of revenue recognition?

Fixed-Price Contracts

Required   a. Comment on the apparent degree of estimating in determining the revenue recognition for fixed-price contracts.

b. For these contracts, does the effort occur in the period of revenue recognition?

C. General Motors Corporation

General Motors Corporation included the following in its 1994 annual report:

Revenue Recognition (in Part)

Sales are generally recorded by the Corporation when products are shipped to independent dealers. Provisions for normal dealer sales incentives, returns and allowances, and GM Card rebates are made at the time of vehicle sale. Costs related to special sales incentive programs are recognized as reductions to sales when determinable.

Required   a. Sales are generally recorded by the Corporation when products are shipped to independent dealers. Apparently when does the title pass to the independent dealers? Does this method resemble point of sale?

b. Provisions for normal dealer sales incentives, returns and allowances, and GM Card rebates are made at the time of vehicle sale. Speculate on the time lag between recognizing sales and the reduction for these items. Would this time lag represent a problem when matching these related costs to revenue? Comment.

c. Costs related to special sales incentive programs are recognized as reductions to sales when determinable. Comment on any matching problem that this may represent.

CASE 1-5 Recognizing Revenue and Related Costs— Consider These Situations (Part II)

A. Wisconsin Energy Corporation

Wisconsin Energy Corporation reported the following in its 1994 annual report: "Revenues: Utility revenues are recognized on the accrual basis and include estimated amounts for service rendered but not billed."

Required
   a. Briefly describe the accrual basis.
   b. Give your opinion of the difficulty of estimating amounts of service rendered but not billed.
   c. Give your opinion of a matching problem (cost) for estimated amounts for service rendered but not billed.

B. Houston Industries Incorporated

Houston Industries Incorporated included the following related to revenue recognition in its 1994 annual report:

"Revenues—H L & P records electricity sales under the full accrual method, whereby unbilled electricity sales are estimated and recorded each month in order to better match revenues with expenses. Prior to January 1, 1992, electric revenues were recognized as bills were rendered (see Note 6).

Cable television revenues are recognized as the services are provided to subscribers, and advertising revenues are recorded when earned."

Note 6—Change in Accounting Method for Revenues

During the fourth quarter of 1992, H L & P adopted a change in accounting method for revenues from a cycle billing to a full accrual method, effective January 1, 1992. Unbilled revenues represent the estimated amount customers will be charged for service received, but not yet billed, as of the end of each month. The accrual of unbilled revenues results in a better matching of revenues and expenses. The cumulative effect of this accounting change, less income taxes of $48.5 million, amounted to $94.2 million, and was included in 1992 income.

Required
   a. H L & P records electricity sales under the full accrual method, whereby unbilled electricity sales are estimated and recorded each month in order to better match revenues with expenses. Prior to January 1, 1992, electric revenues were recognized as bills were rendered. Would this change in revenue recognition be an improvement in financial reporting? Speculate on the reasons for the change.

b. Cable television revenues are recognized as the services are provided to subscribers. Speculate on the difficulty of determining when services are provided to subscribers.

c. Advertising revenues are recorded when earned. Would this represent an application of the accrual or cash basis of recognizing revenue?

C. Osmonics

In February 1993, Autotrol, prior to acquisition by Osmonics, discovered that a former employee of its French subsidiary had been embezzling funds for several years. The funds were embezzled through the issuing of fraudulent checks by the former employee and the falsifying of value added tax (VAT) returns and diverting the funds received from the French government.

Autotrol's investigation of the embezzlement revealed that approximately $4,750,000 was embezzled from 1988 to 1992. Of this total, $2,342,000 related to 1992. The prior years' financial statements reflected embezzlement losses in the year the embezzlement initially occurred. The Company had net recoveries of $562,000 in 1993 from insurance and reductions in VAT payable.

Required
a. How much embezzlement losses were recorded in 1988 to 1991?
b. In what year were the recoveries recorded?
c. Comment on the embezzlement losses and recoveries in terms of revenue recognition and recording of embezzlement losses.

CASE 1-6   Cash Basis—Accrual Basis?

1994 Annual Report—Dibrell Brothers Inc.

Note F—Employee Benefits (in Part)
Postretirement Health and Life Insurance Benefits

Effective July 1, 1992, the Company adopted Statement of Financial Accounting Standards, No. 106, "Employer's Accounting for Postretirement Benefits Other Than Pensions," for its U.S. operations. Employees retiring from the Company on or after attaining age 55 who have rendered at least ten years of service to the Company are eligible for postretirement health care coverage. The benefits are subject to deductibles, co-payment provisions, and other limitations. The Company reserves the right to change or terminate these benefits at any time.

SFAS 106 requires that the cost of postretirement benefits to the Company be recognized over the service lives of the employees, rather than on the cash basis. Employees of the Company are currently eligible to receive specified company-paid health care and life insurance benefits during retirement.

Required
    a. Prior to July 1, 1992, what was the basis used to account for postretirement health care coverage?

    b. Effective July 1, 1992, what was the basis used to account for postretirement health care coverage?

    c. Why was the change made for reporting postretirement health care coverage?

    d. Assume that this company used the accrual basis of accounting. Speculate on why such a company could report a potentially significant item on a cash basis.

CASE 1-7   Going Concern?

1994 Annual Report—Fountain Powerboard Industries Inc.

Note 12—Financial Condition (in Part)

. . . The Company's financial statements have been prepared on the basis that it is a going concern, which contemplates the realization of assets and the satisfaction of liabilities in the normal course of business. The financial statements do not include any adjustments relating to recoverability and classification of assets, or the amounts and classification of liabilities that might be necessary in the event the company cannot continue in existence.

The Company reported a net loss of $2,993,344 for Fiscal 1994 and its current liabilities exceeded its current assets by $9,340,951. The Company's continual existence is dependent upon its ability to achieve profitable operations. The Company's Fiscal 1995 operating plan includes a substantial increase in sales and a restructuring of its operations to reduce its operating costs.

If management cannot achieve the Fiscal 1995 operating plan because of sales shortfalls or greater than anticipated costs and expenses, then the Company may not be able to meet its obligations on a timely basis, its operations may be significantly restricted, and it may not be able to continue on in business as a going concern . . .

Required
    a. What is the going-concern assumption?

    b. Has Fountain Powerboard Industries Inc. prepared financial statements using the going-concern assumption? What appears to be the potential problem with using the going-concern assumption in this case?

    c. What is the significance of the disclosure that this company may not be able to continue as a going concern?

CASE 1-8   Economics and Accounting: The Uncongenial Twins*

"Economics and accountancy are two disciplines which draw their raw material from much the same mines. From these raw materials, however, they seem to fashion remarkably different products. They both study the operations of firms; they both are concerned with such concepts as income, expenditure, profits, capital, value, and prices. In spite of an apparently common subject-matter, however, they often seem to inhabit totally different worlds, between which there is remarkably little communication."

"It is not surprising that the economist regards much accounting procedure as in the nature of ritual. To call these procedures ritualistic is in no way to deny or decry their validity. Ritual is always the proper response when a man has to give an answer to a question, the answer to which he cannot really know. Ritual under these circumstances has two functions. It is comforting (and in the face of the great uncertainties of the future, comfort is not to be despised), and it is also an answer sufficient for action. It is the sufficient answer rather than the right answer which the accountant really seeks. Under these circumstances, however, it is important that we should know what the accountant's answer means, which means that we should know what procedure he has employed. The wise businessman will not believe his accountant although he takes what his accountant tells him as important evidence. The quality of that evidence, however, depends in considerable degree on the simplicity of the procedures and the awareness which we have of them. What the accountant tells us may not be true, but, if we know what he has done, we have a fair idea of what it means. For this reason, I am somewhat suspicious of many current efforts to reform accounting in the direction of making it more 'accurate'."

"If accounts are bound to be untruths anyhow, as I have argued, there is much to be said for the simple untruth as against a complicated untruth, for if the untruth is simple, it seems to me that we have a fair chance of knowing what kind of an untruth it is. A known untruth is much better than a lie, and provided that the accounting rituals are well known and understood, accounting may be untrue but it is not lies; it does not deceive because we know that it does not tell the truth, and we are able to make our own adjustment in each individual case, using the results of the accountant as evidence rather than as definitive information."

---

*Note: This case consists of quotes from the article "Economics and Accounting: The Uncongenial Twins," Kenneth E. Boulding. Professor Boulding was a professor of economics. *Source*: From *Studies in Accounting Theory*, edited by W. T. Baxter and Sidney Davidson (Homewood, IL: R. D. Irwin, 1962), pp. 44-55.

Required   a.   Assume that accounting procedures are in the form of ritual. Does this imply that the accountant's product does not serve a useful function? Discuss.

b.   Does it appear that Kenneth Boulding would support complicated procedures and a complicated end product for the accountant? Discuss.

c.   Accounting reports must be accurate in order to serve a useful function. Discuss.

Endnotes

1   *Statement of Financial Accounting Concepts No. 1,* "Objectives of Financial Reporting by Business Enterprises" (Stamford, CT: Financial Accounting Standards Board, 1978).

2   *Statement of Financial Accounting Concepts No. 6,* "Elements of Financial Statements" (Stamford, CT: Financial Accounting Standards Board, 1985).

3   *Statement of Financial Accounting Concepts No. 5,* "Recognition and Measurement of Financial Statements of Business Enterprises" (Stamford, CT: Financial Accounting Standards Board, 1984), paragraph 63.

4   *Statement of Financial Accounting Concepts No. 5,* paragraph 67.

5   *Statement of Financial Accounting Concepts No. 5,* pp. 24-25.

2   Introduction to Financial Statements and Other Financial Reporting Topics

THIS CHAPTER INTRODUCES FINANCIAL STATEMENTS. Subsequent chapters present a detailed review of the principal financial statements. Chapter 3 covers the balance sheet, Chapter 4 covers the income statement, and Chapter 11 covers the statement of cash flows.

This chapter also reviews the forms of business entities, and the sequence of accounting procedures (called the accounting cycle). Other financial reporting topics included in this chapter that contribute to the understanding of financial reporting are: human resources and social accounting, the auditor's report, management's responsibility for financial statements, the SEC's integrated disclosure system, the summary annual report, ethics, and international accounting standards.

FORMS OF BUSINESS ENTITIES

A business entity may be a sole proprietorship, a partnership, or a corporation. A **sole proprietorship**, a business owned by one person, is not a legal entity separate from its owner. Although the owner is responsible for the debts of the sole proprietorship, the accountant treats the business as a separate accounting entity.

A **partnership** is a business owned by two or more individuals. Each owner, called a *partner*, is personally responsible for the debts of the partnership. The accountant treats the partners and the business as separate accounting entities.

In the United States, a **business corporation** is a legal entity incorporated in a particular state. Ownership is evidenced by shares of stock. A corporation is considered to be separate and distinct from the stockholders. The stockholders risk only their investment; they are not responsible for the debts of the corporation.

In the United States, most businesses operate as proprietorships, but corporations perform the bulk of business activity. Since the bulk of business activity is carried on in corporations and because much of financial accounting is concerned with reporting to the public, this text focuses on the corporate form of business.

Accounting for corporations, sole proprietorships, and partnerships is the same, except for the owners' equity section of the balance sheet. The owners' equity section for a sole proprietorship consists of the owner's capital account, while the owners' equity section for a partnership has a capital account for each partner. The more complicated owners' equity section for a corporation will be described in detail in this book.

THE FINANCIAL STATEMENTS

The principal financial statements of a corporation are the balance sheet, income statement, and statement of cash flows. Footnotes (notes) accompany these financial statements. To evaluate the financial condition, the profitability, and cash flows of an entity, the user needs to understand the statements and related notes.

Exhibit 2-1 illustrates the interrelationship of the balance sheet, income statement, retained earnings, and statement of cash flows. The most basic statement is the balance sheet. The other statements explain the changes between two balance sheet dates.

Balance Sheet (Statement of Financial Position)

A **balance sheet** shows the financial condition of an accounting entity as of a particular date. The balance sheet consists of three major sections: assets, the resources of the firm; liabilities, the debts of the firm; and owners' equity, the owners' interest in the firm.

At any point in time, the total assets amount must equal the total amount of the contributions of the creditors and owners. This is expressed in the accounting equation:

$$\textbf{Assets = Liabilities + Owners' Equity}$$

In simplistic form, the owners' equity of a corporation appears as follows:

Owners' Equity	
Common stock	$200,000
Retained earnings	50,000
	$250,000

This indicates that stockholders contributed (invested) $200,000, and prior earnings less prior dividends have been retained in the entity in the net amount of $50,000.

EXHIBIT 2-1   ABC COMPANY—The Interrelationship of Financial Statements

Balance Sheet December 31, 1997		Statement of Cash Flows For the Year Ended December 31, 1998		Balance Sheet December 31, 1998	
Assets		**Cash flows from operating activities:**		**Assets**	
Cash	$25,000	Net income	$20,000	Cash	$ 40,000
Receivables	20,000	+ Decrease in		Receivables	20,000
Inventory	30,000	inventory	10,000	Inventory	20,000
Land	10,000	− Decrease in		Land	20,000
Other assets	10,000	accounts payable	(5,000)	Other assets	10,000
Total assets	$95,000	Net cash flow from		Total assets	$110,000
		operating activities	25,000		
Liabilities		**Cash flow from investing activities:**		**Liabilities**	
Accounts payable	$25,000	− Increase in land	(10,000)	Accounts payable	$ 20,000
Wages payable	5,000	Net cash flow from		Wages payable	5,000
Total liabilities	30,000	investing activities	(10,000)	Total liabilities	25,000
		Cash flow from financing activities:			
Stockholders' equity		+ Capital stock	10,000	**Stockholders' equity**	
Capital stock	40,000	− Dividends	(10,000)	Capital stock	50,000
Retained earnings	25,000	Net cash flow from		Retained earnings	35,000
Total stockholders' equity	65,000	financing activities	—0—	Total stockholders' equity	85,000
Total liabilities and stockholders' equity	$95,000	Net increase in cash	15,000	Total liabilities and stockholders' equity	$110,000
		Cash at beginning of year	25,000		
		Cash at end of year	$40,000		

Income Statement For the Year Ended December 31, 1998	
Revenues	$ 120,000
− Expenses	(100,000)
Net income	$ 20,000

Statement of Retained Earnings For the Year Ended December 31, 1998	
Beginning balance	$25,000
+ Net income	20,000
− Dividends	(10,000)
Ending balance	$35,000

Income Statement (Statement of Earnings)

The **income statement** summarizes revenues and expenses and gains and losses, ending with net income. It summarizes the results of operations for a particular period of time. Net income is included in retained earnings in the owners' equity section of the balance sheet. (This is necessary for the balance sheet to balance.)

Statement of Owners' Equity (Reconciliation of Owners' Equity Accounts)

Firms are required to present reconciliations of the beginning and ending balances of their owners' equity accounts. This is often accomplished by presenting a "statement of owners' equity." Retained earnings is one of the accounts in owners' equity.

Retained earnings links the balance sheet to the income statement. Retained earnings is increased by net income and decreased by net losses and dividends paid to stockholders. There are some other possible increases or decreases to retained earnings besides income (losses) and dividends. For the purposes of this chapter, retained earnings will be described as prior earnings less prior dividends.

Firms sometimes present the reconciliation of retained earnings within a "statement of owners' equity." Some firms present the reconciliation of retained earnings at the bottom of the income statement (combined income statement and retained earnings). In this case the other owners' equity accounts may be reconciled in a statement that excludes retained earnings. (Alternative presentations of the reconciliation of retained earnings are illustrated in Chapter 4, along with a more detailed review of retained earnings.)

Statement of Cash Flows (Statement of Inflows and Outflows of Cash)

The **statement of cash flows** details the inflows and outflows of cash during a specified period of time—the same period that is used for the income statement. The statement of cash flows consists of three sections: cash flows from operating activities, cash flows from investing activities, and cash flows from financing activities.

Footnotes (Notes)

The footnotes to the financial statements are used to present additional information about items included in the financial statements and to present additional financial information. Footnotes are an integral part of financial statements. A detailed review of footnotes is essential to understanding the financial statements.

Certain information must be presented in footnotes. APB Opinion No. 22 requires that accounting policies be disclosed as the first note or be disclosed in a separate summary of significant accounting policies (preceding the first note). Accounting policies include such items as the method of inventory valuation and depreciation policies. (Inventory valuation and depreciation policies are described in a subsequent chapter.) Other information specifically requiring footnote disclosure is the existence of contingent liabilities and some subsequent events.

Contingent liabilities are dependent upon the occurrence or nonoccurrence of one or more future events to confirm the liability. The settlement of litigation or the ruling of a tax court would be examples of the confirmation of a contingent liability. Signing as guarantor on a loan creates another type of contingent liability.

SFAS No. 5 recommends that an estimated loss from a contingent liability be charged to income, and that it be established as a liability only if the loss is considered probable and the amount is reasonably determinable. A contingent liability that is recorded is also frequently described in a footnote. A loss contingency that is reasonably possible, but not probable, must be disclosed even if the loss is not reasonably estimable. (This loss contingency is not charged to income or established as a liability.) A loss contingency that is less than reasonably possible does not need to be disclosed, but disclosure may be desirable if there is an unusually large potential loss. Exhibit 2-2 illustrates a contingent liability footnote.

EXHIBIT 2-2 YORK
Contingent Liabilities

Note 13. Contingent Liabilities

It is the opinion of the Company's management and its general counsel that various claims and litigation in which the Company is currently involved have been adequately provided for or are covered by insurance and, therefore, the resolution of such matters will not materially affect the Company's financial position or future earnings.

At December 31, 1995, $27.4 million in standby letters of credit and $23.9 million of performance guarantees issued for the account of the Company were outstanding. These items are expected to expire and be replaced with similar items in the normal course of the Company's business.

Subsequent events occur after the balance sheet date, but before the statements are issued. Two varieties of subsequent events occur. The first type consists of events related to conditions that existed at the balance sheet date, affect the estimates in the statements, and require adjustment of the statements before issuance. For example, if additional information is obtained indicating that a major customer's account receivable is not collectible, an adjustment would be made. The second type consists of events that provide evidence about conditions that did not exist at the balance sheet date and do not require adjustment of the statements. If failure to disclose these events would be misleading, disclosure should take the form of footnotes or supplementary schedules. Examples of the second type of such events include the sale of securities, the settlement of litigation, a casualty loss, or the purchase of a subsidiary. Other examples of subsequent events might be debt incurred, reduced, or refinanced; business combinations pending or effected; discontinued operations; litigation; employee benefit plans; and capital stock issued or purchased. Exhibit 2-3 describes a subsequent event for Quanex, whose year-end was October 31, 1995.

THE ACCOUNTING CYCLE

The sequence of accounting procedures completed during each accounting period is called the **accounting cycle**. A broad summary of the steps of the accounting cycle include:

1. Recording transactions
2. Recording adjusting entries
3. Preparing the financial statements

EXHIBIT 2-3   QUANEX
Subsequent Events

16. Subsequent Event

On December 29, 1995, the Company acquired all of its outstanding 10.77% Senior Notes for a purchase price equal to 107.5% of the principal amount plus accrued interest. The acquisition and related expenses will result in a one-time, after-tax extraordinary charge of approximately $2.5 million in the first quarter of 1996.

Recording Transactions

A **transaction** is an event that causes a change in a company's assets, liabilities, or owners' equity, thus changing the company's financial position. Transactions may be external or internal to the company. External transactions involve outside parties, while internal transactions are confined within the company. For example, sales is an external transaction, while the use of equipment is internal.

Transactions must be recorded in a **journal** (book of original entry). All transactions could be recorded in the general journal. However, companies use a number of special journals to record most transactions. The special journals are designed to improve record keeping efficiency that could not be obtained by using only the general journal. The general journal is then used only to record transactions for which the company does not have a special journal. A transaction recorded in a journal is referred to as a **journal entry**.

All transactions are recorded in a journal (journal entry) and are later posted from the journals to a **general ledger** (group of accounts for a company). After posting, the general ledger accounts contain the same information as in the journals, but the information has been summarized by account.

Accounts store the monetary information from the recording of transactions. Examples of accounts include Cash, Land, and Buildings. An accounting system can be computerized or manual. A manual system using T-accounts is usually used for textbook explanations because a T-account is a logical format.

T-accounts have a left (debit) side and a right (credit) side. An example T-account follows:

Cash

Debit	Credit
10,000	

A double-entry system has been devised to handle the recording of transactions. In a double-entry system, each transaction is recorded with the total dollar amount of the debits equal to the total dollar amount of the credits. The scheme of the double-entry system revolves around the **accounting equation**:

Assets = Liabilities + Owners' Equity

With the double-entry system, *debit* merely means the left side of an account, while *credit* means the right side. Each transaction recorded must have an equal number of dollars on the left side as it does on the right side. Several accounts could be involved in a single transaction, but the debits and credits must still be equal.

The debit and credit approach is a technique that has gained acceptance over a long period of time. This book will not make you competent in the use of the double-entry (debit and credit) technique. This book will enhance your understanding of the end result of the accounting process and enable you to use the financial accounting information in a meaningful way.

Asset, liability, and owners' equity accounts are referred to as **permanent accounts** because the balances in these accounts carry forward to the next accounting period. Balances in revenue, expense, gain, loss, and dividend accounts, described as **temporary accounts**, are closed to retained earnings and not carried into the next period.

Exhibit 2-4 illustrates the double-entry system. Notice that the permanent accounts are represented by the accounting equation: **assets = liabilities + owners' equity**. The temporary accounts are represented by revenue, expense, and dividends (gains and losses would be treated like revenue and expense, respectively). The balance sheet will not balance until the temporary accounts are closed to retained earnings.

Recording Adjusting Entries

Earlier a distinction was made between the accrual basis of accounting and the cash basis. It was indicated that the accrual basis requires that revenue be recognized when realized (realization concept) and expenses recognized when incurred (matching concept). The point of cash receipt for revenue and cash disbursement for expenses is not important under the accrual basis when determining income. Usually a company must use the accrual basis to achieve a reasonable result for the balance sheet and the income statement.

The accrual basis needs numerous adjustments to account balances at the end of the accounting period. For example, $1,000 paid for insurance on October 1 for a one-year period (October 1-September 30) could have been recorded as a debit to Insurance Expense ($1,000) and a credit to Cash ($1,000). If this company prepares financial statements on December 31, it would be necessary to adjust Insurance Expense because not all of the insurance expense should be recognized in the three-month period October 1-December 31. The adjustment would debit Prepaid Insurance, an asset account, for $750 and credit Insurance Expense for $750. Thus, insurance expense would be presented on the income statement for this period as $250, and an asset, prepaid insurance, would be presented on the balance sheet at $750.

Adjusting entries are recorded in the general journal and then posted to the general ledger. Once the accounts are adjusted to the accrual basis, the financial statements can be prepared.

EXHIBIT 2-4 **Double-Entry System**
(Illustrating Relationship Between Permanent and Temporary Accounts)

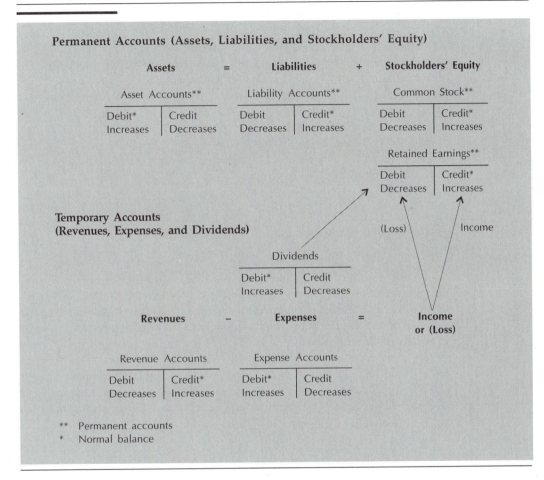

Preparing the Financial Statements

The accountant uses the accounts after the adjustments have been made to prepare the financial statements. These statements represent the output of the accounting system. Two of the principal financial statements, the income statement and the balance sheet, can be prepared directly from the adjusted accounts. Preparation of the statement of cash flows requires further analysis of the accounts.

HUMAN RESOURCES AND SOCIAL ACCOUNTING

American business has become acutely aware of the influence of social pressures and of the value of its employees. This has been reflected by two developments in the accounting area—human resources accounting and social accounting. **Human resources accounting** attempts to account for the services of employees, while **social accounting** attempts to account for the benefits to the social environment within which the firm operates. Although reporting of these areas is still in the development stage, many firms have begun to include such information in their annual reports. Such information may enhance the analyst's subjective opinion regarding the company. Exhibit 2-5 presents one firm's attempt to show its concern for the social environment.

AUDITOR'S REPORT

An auditor (certified public accountant) conducts an independent examination of the accounting information presented by the business and issues a report thereon. An **auditor's report** is the formal statement of the auditor's opinion of the financial statements after conducting an audit. Audit opinions are classified as follows:

1. **Unqualified opinion.** This opinion states that the financial statements present fairly, in all material respects, the financial position, results of operations, and cash flows of the entity, in conformity with generally accepted accounting principles.

2. **Qualified opinion.** A qualified opinion states that, except for the effects of the matter(s) to which the qualification relates, the financial statements present fairly, in all material respects, the financial position, results of operations, and cash flows of the entity, in conformity with generally accepted accounting principles.

3. **Adverse opinion.** This opinion states that the financial statements do *not* present fairly the financial position, results of operations, and cash flows of the entity, in conformity with generally accepted accounting principles.

4. **Disclaimer of opinion.** A disclaimer of opinion states that the auditor does not express an opinion on the financial statements. A disclaimer of opinion is rendered when the auditor has not performed an audit sufficient in scope to form an opinion.

EXHIBIT 2-5 JC PENNEY
Social Environment

Community relations. During 1995, the Company's charitable contributions totaled $27 million nationwide, most of which was contributed to community charitable organizations by JC Penney stores and other units. Priority was given to programs that address our target issues of pre-kindergarten through twelfth-grade education; encouraging and promoting volunteerism; and supporting the United Way. In addition to financial support for education, JC Penney hosted its first Education Expo, a one-day conference for Home Office associates on parenting and education issues, and broadcast the first in a series of broadcasts titled the "JC Penney Leadership Institute of School Improvement" to 160 stores nationwide.

Major commitments in our support of volunteerism included the expansion of our Golden Rule Award Program to 220 markets. These awards publicly honor community volunteers and support their work with contributions. The James Cash Penney Awards for Community Service provide similar recognition to JC Penney associates for outstanding volunteer activities. The two programs contributed approximately $1.8 million to local charitable organizations. The 1995 United Way campaign raised a Company record of over $16 million in JC Penney associate and unit pledges for nearly 1,000 United Way Organizations.

The Company has a number of programs that support wellness and physical fitness for women and children. JC Penney continued as the national presenting sponsor of the Susan G. Komen Breast Cancer Foundation Race for the Cure, and JC Penney associates supported local races in 57 cities as volunteers, runners, or walkers. Raising more than $620,000 for the prevention and cure of birth defects, associates actively supported the March of Dimes Walk America in 101 markets. More than 46,000 children were photographed and fingerprinted at JC Penney stores nationwide during a two-day child health and safety event, with proceeds of over $225,000 benefiting St. Jude's Children's Research Hospital. Now in its 19th year, the JC Penney Golf Classic has raised $8.4 million for Suncoast Charities of Florida since its inception. Additionally, the JC Penney/LPGA Skins Tournament raised over $350,000 for Easter Seals of North Texas in 1995.

The fourth JC Penney Juanita Kreps Award Honoring the Spirit of the American Woman was awarded to Sally Ride, the first American woman to fly into space. She was recognized for her contributions as a former NASA astronaut, a university professor of astrophysics, and as the director of the California Space Institute. In 32 U.S. cities, JC Penney actively supported women's conferences and expos, bringing together exhibits, information, fun, and entertainment focusing on fashion, home decorating, health and fitness, finance, travel, and food. Included in these conference programs is the Spirit of the American Woman Award given to an outstanding local woman for her contribution to her community, her involvement with her family, or her achievements in her career. During 1995, the Company participated in over 30 special events and conferences through our Multicultural Affairs Department, including our Seventh Annual Hispanic Designers Model Search. Since 1993, the Company has served as the retail sponsor of the Essence Awards and, in 1995, served as a major sponsor of the first Bravo Awards in cooperation with the Nation Council of La Raza.

The typical unqualified (or clean) opinion has three paragraphs. The first paragraph indicates *the financial statements that have been audited* and states that these *statements are the responsibility of the company's management.* This paragraph indicates that the auditors have the responsibility to express an opinion on these statements based on the audit or to disclaim an opinion.

The second paragraph indicates that the audit has been conducted *in accordance with generally accepted auditing standards.* Auditing standards define the required level of audit quality. These standards are classified as to "general standards," "fieldwork standards," and "reporting standards." The paragraph goes on to state that these standards require the auditor to plan and perform the audit to obtain reasonable assurance that the financial statements are free of material misstatement. The second paragraph also includes a brief description of what is included in an audit.

The third paragraph gives an opinion on the statements—that they are in conformity with GAAP. In certain circumstances, an unqualified opinion on the financial statements may require that the auditor add an explanatory paragraph after the opinion paragraph. In this paragraph, the auditor may express agreement with a departure from a designated principle, describe a material uncertainty, describe a change in accounting principle, or express doubt as to the ability of the entity to continue as a going concern. An explanatory paragraph may also be added to emphasize a matter. Exhibit 2-6 illustrates a typical unqualified report.

When examining financial statements, review the independent auditor's report. It can be important to your analysis. From the point of view of analysis, financial statements accompanied by an unqualified opinion without an explanatory paragraph or explanatory language carry the highest degree of reliability. This type of report indicates that the financial statements do not contain a material departure from GAAP and that the audit was not limited as to scope.

When an unqualified opinion contains an explanatory paragraph or explanatory language, try to decide how seriously to regard the departure from a straight unqualified opinion. For example, an explanatory paragraph because of a change in accounting principle would not usually be regarded as serious, although it would be important to your analysis. An explanatory paragraph because of a material uncertainty would often be regarded as a serious matter.

You are likely to regard a qualified opinion or an adverse opinion as casting serious doubts on the reliability of the financial statements. In each case, you must read the auditor's report carefully to form your opinion.

A disclaimer of opinion indicates that you should not look to the auditor's report as an indication of the reliability of the statements. When rendering this type of report, the auditor has not performed an audit sufficient in scope to form an opinion, or the auditor is not independent.

EXHIBIT 2-6   JLG INDUSTRIES
Report—Unqualified Opinion (Report of Independent Auditors)

JLG INDUSTRIES, INC.
MCCONNELLSBURG, PENNSYLVANIA
**To The Board of Directors and
Shareholders:**

We have audited the accompanying consolidated balance sheets of JLG Industries, Inc. as of July 31, 1995 and 1994, and the related consolidated statements of income, shareholders' equity, and cash flows for each of the three years in the period ended July 31, 1995. These financial statements are the responsibility of the Company's management. Our responsibility is to express an opinion on these financial statements based on our audits.

We conducted our audits in accordance with generally accepted auditing standards. Those standards require that we plan and perform the audit to obtain reasonable assurance about whether the financial statements are free of material misstatement. An audit includes examining, on a test basis, evidence supporting the amounts and disclosures in the financial statements. An audit also includes assessing the accounting principles used and significant estimates made by management, as well as evaluating the overall financial statement presentation. We believe that our audits provide a reasonable basis for our opinion.

In our opinion, the financial statements referred to above present fairly, in all material respects, the consolidated financial position of JLG Industries, Inc. at July 31, 1995 and 1994, and the consolidated results of its operations and its cash flows for each of the three years in the period ended July 31, 1995, in conformity with generally accepted accounting principles.

Ernst & Young LLP

ERNST & YOUNG LLP

Baltimore, Maryland
September 7, 1995

In some cases, outside accountants are associated with financial statements when they have performed less than an audit. The accountant's report then indicates that the financial statements have been reviewed or compiled.

A **review** consists principally of inquiries made to company personnel and analytical procedures applied to financial data. It has substantially less scope than an examination in accordance with generally accepted auditing standards, the objective of which is the expression of an opinion regarding the financial statements taken as a whole. Accordingly, the accountant does not express an opinion. The accountant's report will indicate that the accountants are not aware of any material modifications that should be made to the financial statements in order for them to be in conformity with GAAP; or the report will indicate departures from GAAP. A departure from GAAP may result from using one or more accounting principles without reasonable justification, the omission of necessary footnote disclosures, or the omission of the statement of cash flows.

In general, the reliance that can be placed on financial statements accompanied by an accountant's review report is substantially less than those accompanied by an audit report. Remember that the accountant's report does not express an opinion on reviewed financial statements.

When the outside accountant presents only financial information as provided by management, he or she is said to have **compiled** the financial statements. The compilation report states that the accountant has not audited or reviewed the financial statements. Therefore, the accountant does not express an opinion or any other form of assurance about them. If an accountant performs a compilation and becomes aware of deficiencies in the statements, then the accountant's report characterizes the deficiencies as follows:

— Omission of substantially all disclosures
— Omission of statement of cash flows
— Accounting principles not generally accepted

Sometimes financial statements are presented without an accompanying accountant's report. This means that the statements have not been audited, reviewed, or compiled. Such statements are solely the representation of management.

Management's Responsibility for Financial Statements

The responsibility for the preparation and for the integrity of financial statements rests with management. The auditor is responsible for conducting an independent examination of the statements. To make financial statement users aware of management's responsibility, companies have presented management statements to shareholders as part of the annual report. Exhibit 2-7 shows an example.

The SEC's Integrated Disclosure System

In general, the SEC has the authority to prescribe external financial reporting requirements for companies with securities sold to the general public. Under this jurisdiction, the SEC requires that certain financial

EXHIBIT 2-7   MOSINEE PAPER CORPORATION & SUBSIDIARIES
Management's Responsibility for Financial Reporting

The management of Mosinee Paper Corporation is responsible for the integrity and objectivity of the consolidated financial statements. Such financial statements were prepared in conformity with generally accepted accounting principles. Some of the amounts included in these financial statements are estimates based upon management's best judgment of current conditions and circumstances. Management is also responsible for preparing other financial information included in this annual report.

The company's management depends on the company's system of internal accounting controls to assure itself of the reliability of the financial statements. The internal control system is designed to provide reasonable assurance, at appropriate cost, that assets are safeguarded and transactions are executed in accordance with management's authorizations and recorded properly to permit the preparation of financial statements in accordance with generally accepted accounting principles. Periodic reviews of internal controls are made by management and the internal audit function and corrective action is taken if needed.

The Audit Committee of the Board of Directors, consisting of outside directors, provides oversight of financial reporting. The company's internal audit function and independent public accountants meet with the Audit Committee to discuss financial reporting and internal control issues and have full and free access to the Audit Committee.

The consolidated financial statements have been audited by the company's independent auditors and their report is presented on the following page. The independent auditors are approved each year at the annual shareholders' meeting based on a recommendation by the Audit Committee and the Board of Directors.

Daniel R. Olvey

Daniel R. Olvey
President
Chief Executive Officer

Gary P. Peterson

Gary P. Peterson
Senior Vice President Finance
Secretary and Treasurer

statement information be included in the annual report to shareholders. This annual report, along with certain supplementary information, must then be included, or incorporated by reference, in the annual filing to the SEC, known as the **10-K report** or **Form 10-K**. The Form 10-K is due three months following the end of the company's fiscal year. The annual report and the Form 10-K include audited financial statements.

The SEC promotes an integrated disclosure system between the annual report and the Form 10-K. The goals are to improve the quality of disclosure, lighten the disclosure load, standardize information requirements, and achieve uniformity of annual reports and Form 10-K filings.

In addition to the company's primary financial statements, the Form 10-K must include the following:

1. Information on the market for holders of common stock and related securities, including high and low sales price, frequency and amount of dividends, and number of shares.

2. Five-year summary of selected financial data, including net sales or operating revenues, income from continuing operations, total assets, long-term obligations, redeemable preferred stock, and cash dividends per share. (Some companies elect to present data for more than five years and/or expand the disclosure.) Trend analysis is emphasized.

3. Management's discussion and analysis (MDA) of financial condition and results of operations. Specifically required is discussion of liquidity, capital resources, and results of operations.

4. Two years of audited balance sheets and three years of audited income statements and statements of cash flow.

5. Disclosure of the domestic and foreign components of pretax income, unless foreign components are considered to be immaterial.

SEC requirements force management to focus on the financial statements as a whole, rather than on just the income statement and operations. Where trend information is relevant, discussion should center on the five-year summary. Emphasis should be on favorable or unfavorable trends and on identification of significant events or uncertainties. This discussion should provide the analyst with a reasonable summary of the position of the firm. Chapter 12 presents specific management discussion for Cooper Tire & Rubber Company.

Exhibit 2-8 presents a summary of the major parts of the Form 10-K. In practice, much of the required information in the Form 10-K is *incorporated by reference*. Incorporated by reference means that the information is presented outside the Form 10-K, and a reference in the Form 10-K indicates where the information can be found. Usually the financial statements are incorporated into the Form 10-K by referencing the annual report.

A review of a company's Form 10-K can reveal information that is not available in the annual report. Exhibit 2-9 contains Item 2, Properties, from the 1995 Form 10-K of Cooper Tire & Rubber Company. Notice that this

EXHIBIT 2-8 **General Summary of Form 10-K**

PART I

Item 1.   Business.
Item 2.   Properties.
Item 3.   Legal Proceedings.
Item 4.   Submission of Matters to a Vote of Security Holders.

PART II

Item 5.   Market for Registrant's Common Equity and Related Stockholder Matters.
Item 6.   Selected Financial Data.
Item 7.   Management's Discussion and Analysis of Financial Condition and Results of Operations.
Item 8.   Financial Statements and Supplementary Data.
Item 9.   Changes in and Disagreements with Accountants on Accounting and Financial Disclosure.

PART III

Item 10. Directors and Executive Officers of Registrant.
Item 11. Executive Compensation.
Item 12. Security Ownership of Certain Beneficial Owners and Management.
Item 13. Certain Relationships and Related Transactions.
Item 14. Exhibits, Financial Statement Schedules, and Reports on Form 8-K.

section on properties includes a detailed listing of properties and indicates if the property is leased or owned.

The SEC requires that a quarterly report (Form 10-Q), containing financial statements and a management discussion and analysis, be submitted within 45 days following the end of the quarter. (The Form 10-Q is not required for the fourth quarter of the fiscal year.) Most companies also issue a quarterly report to stockholders. The Form 10-Q and quarterly reports are unaudited.

In addition to the Form 10-K and Form 10-Q, a Form 8-K must be submitted to the SEC to report special events. Special events required to be reported are changes in principal stockholders, changes in auditors, acquisitions and divestitures, bankruptcy, and resignation of directors. The Form 8-K is due 15 days following the event.

The Forms 10-K, 10-Q, and 8-K filings are available to the public. Typically a company provides these reports to stockholders upon request only.

EXHIBIT 2-9   **COOPER TIRE & RUBBER COMPANY**
1995 Form 10-K—Item 2 Properties

Item 2.   Properties.

The Company owns its headquarters facility which is adjacent to its Findlay, Ohio, tire manufacturing plant.   Properties are located in various sections of the United States for use in the ordinary course of business. Such properties consist of the following:

Location	Use	Title
3300 Sylvester Rd., Albany, GA 31703	Tire plant and regional distribution center	Leased
725 West Eleventh St., Auburn, IN 46706	Engineered products plant	Owned
1175 North Main St., Bowling Green, OH 43402	Engineered products plant	Owned
400 Van Camp Rd., Bowling Green, OH 43402	Engineered products plant	Owned
2205 Dr. Martin Luther King Blvd., Clarksdale, MS 38614	Inner tube plant	Owned
166 Cooper Dr., El Dorado, AR 71730	Engineered products plant	Owned
701 Lima Ave., Findlay, OH 45840	Tire plant	Owned
2025 Production Dr., Findlay, OH 45840	Metal fabrication and assembly plant	Owned
3571 Owingsville Rd., Mt. Sterling, KY 40353	Engineered products plant (under construction)	Owned
3500 E. Washington Rd., Texarkana, AR 71854	Tire plant and regional distribution center	Owned
1689 South Green St., Tupelo, MS 38802	Tire plant and regional distribution center	Owned/ Leased
6340 Artesia Blvd., Buena Park, CA 90620	Regional distribution center	Owned
1300 Lunt Ave., Elk Grove Village, IL 60007	Regional distribution center	Owned
4200-D Industry Dr., Fife, WA 98424	Regional distribution center	Leased
Lake Cascades Pkwy., Findlay, OH 45840	Regional distribution center	Owned
1026 North Century Ave., Kansas City, MO 64120	Regional distribution center	Leased
3601 Dryden Rd., Moraine, OH 45439	Regional distribution center	Owned
Terminal Rd. & Industrial Dr., New Brunswick, NJ 08901	Regional distribution center	Owned

The Company also owns a manufacturing facility located in Mexico which produces inner tubes and engineered rubber parts. The Company believes its properties have been adequately maintained and generally are in good condition.

Cooper's tire plants are operating at rated capacity levels. The Tupelo, Mississippi, and Albany, Georgia, plants operate on a 24-hour day, seven-day production schedule. The other plants are operating 24 hours per day, five days per week.

The Company's capacity to manufacture a full range of radial passenger, light truck, and medium truck tires using the most advanced technology continues to be incrementally expanded. The Mt. Sterling, Kentucky, plant, currently under construction, is planned to commence production of engineered rubber products during the second quarter of 1996.

Additional information concerning the Company's facilities appears on pages 29 and 32 of this Annual Report on Form 10-K. Information related to leased properties appears on page 23.

Proxy

The **proxy**, the solicitation sent to stockholders for the election of directors and for the approval of other corporation actions, represents the shareholder authorization regarding the casting of that shareholder's vote. The proxy contains notice of the annual meeting, beneficial ownership (name, address, and share ownership data of shareholders holding more than 5% of outstanding shares), board of directors, standing committees, compensation of directors, compensation of executive officers, employee benefit plans, certain transactions with officers and directors, relationship with independent accountants, and other business.

The proxy rules provided under the 1934 Securities Exchange Act are applicable to all securities registered under Section 12 of the Act. The SEC gains its influence over the annual report through provisions of the Act that cover proxy statements.

The SEC's proxy rules of particular interest to investors involve executive compensation disclosure, performance graph, and retirement plans for executive officers. These rules are designed to improve shareholders' understanding of the compensation paid to senior executives and directors, the criteria used in reaching compensation decisions, and the relationship between compensation and corporate performance.

Among other matters, the executive compensation rules call for four highly formatted disclosure tables and the disclosure of the compensation committee's basis for compensation decisions.

The four tables disclosing executive compensation are:

— A summary executive compensation table covering compensation for the company's chief executive officer and its four other most highly compensated executives for the last three years.

— Two tables detailing options and stock appreciation rights.

— A long-term incentive plan award table.

The performance graph is a line graph comparing the cumulative total shareholder return with performance indicators of the overall stock market and either the published industry index or the registrant-determined peer comparison. This performance graph must be presented for a five-year period.

The pension plan table for executive officers discloses the estimated annual benefits payable upon retirement for any defined benefit or actuarial plan under which benefits are determined primarily by final compensation (or average final compensation) and years of service. Immediately following the table, additional disclosure is required. This disclosure includes items such as the relationship of the covered compensation to the compensation reported in the summary compensation table and the estimated credited years of service for each of the named executive officers.

SUMMARY ANNUAL REPORT

A reporting option available to public companies is to issue a summary annual report. The concept of a summary annual report was approved by the Securities and Exchange Commission in January 1987.

A **summary annual report**, a condensed report, omits much of the financial information typically included in an annual report. A typical full annual report has more financial pages than nonfinancial pages. A summary annual report generally has more nonfinancial pages.[1] When a company issues a summary annual report, the proxy materials it sends to shareholders must include a set of fully audited statements and other required financial disclosures.

A summary annual report is *not* adequate for reasonable analysis. For companies that issue a summary annual report, request a copy of their proxy and the Form 10-K. Even for companies that issue a full annual report, it is also good to obtain a copy of the proxy materials and the Form 10-K. Some companies issue a joint annual report and Form 10-K, while other companies issue a joint annual report and proxy.

ETHICS

"Ethics and morals are synonymous. While *ethics* is derived from Greek, *morals* is derived from Latin. They are interchangeable terms referring to ideals of character and conduct. These ideals, in the form of codes of conduct, furnish criteria for distinguishing between right and wrong."[2] Ethics has been a subject of investigation for hundreds of years. Individuals in financial positions must be able to recognize ethical issues and resolve them in an appropriate manner.

Ethics affect all individuals—from the financial clerk to the high-level financial executive. Individuals make daily decisions based on their individual values. Some companies and professional organizations have formulated a code of ethics as a statement of aspirations and a standard of integrity beyond that required by law (which can be viewed as the minimum standard of ethics).

Ten essential values can be considered central to relations between people.[3]

1. Caring
2. Honesty
3. Accountability
4. Promise keeping

5.   Pursuit of excellence

6.   Loyalty

7.   Fairness

8.   Integrity

9.   Respect for others

10.   Responsible citizenship

Ethics can be a particular problem with financial reports. Accepted accounting principles leave ample room for arriving at different results in the short run. Highly subjective estimates can substantially influence earnings. What provision should be made for warranty costs? What should be the loan loss reserve? What should be the allowance for doubtful accounts?

The American Accounting Association initiated a project in 1988 on professionalism and ethics. One of the goals of this project was to provide students with a framework for evaluating their courses of action when encountering ethical dilemmas. The American Accounting Association developed a decision model for focusing on ethical issues.[4]

1.   Determine the facts—what, who, where, when, how.

2.   Define the ethical issues (includes identifying the identifiable parties affected by the decision made or action taken).

3.   Identify major principles, rules, and values.

4.   Specify the alternatives.

5.   Compare norms, principles, and values with alternatives to see if a clear decision can be reached.

6.   Assess the consequences.

7.   Make your decision.

Example 1: Questionable Ethics in Savings and Loans   In connection with the savings and loan (S & L) scandal, it was revealed that several auditors of thrift institutions borrowed substantial amounts from the S & L that their firm was auditing. It was charged that some of the loans involved special consideration.[5] In one case, dozens of partners of a major accounting firm borrowed money for commercial real estate loans, and some of the partners defaulted on their loans when the real estate market collapsed.[6] It was not clear whether these particular loans violated professional ethics standards. The AICPA subsequently changed its ethics standards to ban all such loans.

In another case, an accounting firm paid $1.5 million to settle charges by the California State Board of Accountancy that the accounting firm was grossly negligent in its 1987 audit of Lincoln Savings & Loan. The accounting board charged that the firm had agreed to the improper recognition of approximately $62 million in profits.[7]

Example 2: Questionable Ethics in the Motion Picture Industry
Hollywood's accounting practices have often been labeled "mysterious."[8]
A case in point is Art Buchwald's lawsuit against Paramount Pictures for breach of contract regarding the film *Coming to America*. Paramount took an option on Buchwald's story "King for a Day" in 1983 and promised Buchwald 1.5% of the net profits of the film. Buchwald's attorney, Pierce O'Donnell, accused Paramount Studios of "fatal subtraction" in determining the amount of profit. Although the film grossed $350 million worldwide, Paramount claimed an $18 million net loss. As a result of the studio's accounting practices, Buchwald was to get 1.5% of nothing.[9] Buchwald was eventually awarded $150,000 in a 1992 court decision.[10]

Many Hollywood celebrities, in addition to Art Buchwald, have sued over Hollywood style accounting. These include Winston Groom over the movie rights to *Forrest Gump,* Jane Fonda over a larger share of profits relating to *On Golden Pond*, and James Garner over his share of profits from *The Rockford Files* (a television program). Some of the best creative work in Hollywood is in accounting.

HARMONIZATION OF INTERNATIONAL ACCOUNTING STANDARDS

The impetus for changes in accounting practice has come from the needs of the business community and governments. With the expansion of international business and global capital markets, the business community and governments have shown an increased interest in the harmonization of international accounting standards.

Suggested problems caused by lack of harmonization of international accounting standards include:

1. A need for employment of key personnel in multinational companies to bridge the "gap" in accounting requirements between countries.

2. Difficulties in reconciling local standards for access to other capital markets.

3. Difficulties in accessing capital markets for companies from less developed countries.[11]

4. Negative effect on the international trade of accounting practice and services.[12]

International interest in harmonization of international accounting standards has been especially strong since the early 1970s. In 1973, nine countries, including the United States, formed the International Accounting Standards Committee (IASC). IASC includes approximately 100 member nations and well over 100 professional accounting bodies. The IASC is the only private sector body involved in setting international accounting standards.

The IASC's objectives include:

1. Developing international accounting standards and disclosure to meet the needs of international capital markets and the international business community.

2. Developing accounting standards to meet the needs of developing and newly industrialized countries.

3. Working toward increased comparability between national and international accounting standards.[13]

The IASC does not have authority to enforce its standards, but these standards have been adopted in whole or in part by many countries. Some see the lack of enforcement authority as a positive factor because it enables the passing of standards that would not have had the necessary votes if they could be enforced. This allows standards to be more ideal than they would otherwise be if they were enforceable.

IASC follows a due-process procedure similar to that of the FASB. This includes exposure drafts and a comment period. All proposed standards and guidelines are exposed for comment for about six months.[14]

The United Nations (UN) has shown a substantial interest in harmonization of international accounting standards. The UN appointed a group to study harmonization of international accounting standards in 1973. This has evolved into an ad hoc working group. Members of the working group represent governments and not the private sector. The working group does not issue standards but rather facilitates their development. The UN's concern is with how multinational corporations affect the developing countries.[15]

Many other organizations, in addition to the IASC and the UN, have played a role in the harmonization of international accounting standards. Some of these organizations include the Financial Accounting Standards Board (FASB), the European Economic Community (EEC), the Organization for Economic Corporation and Development (OECD), and the International Federation of Accountants (IFAC).

Domestic accounting standards have developed to meet the needs of domestic environments. A few of the factors that influence accounting standards locally are:

1. A litigious environment in the United States that has led to a demand for more detailed standards in many cases.

2. High rates of inflation in some countries that have resulted in periodic revaluation of fixed assets and other price-level adjustments or disclosures.

3. More emphasis on financial reporting/income tax conformity in certain countries (for example, Japan and Germany) that no doubt greatly influences domestic financial reporting.

4. Reliance on open markets as the principal means of intermediating capital flows that has increased the demand for information to be included in financial reports in the United States and some other developed countries.[16]

The following have been observed to have an impact on a country's financial accounting operation:

1. Who the investors and creditors—the information users—are (individuals, banks, the government).

2. How many investors and creditors there are.

3. How close the relationship is between businesses and the investor/creditor group.

4. How developed the stock exchanges and bond markets are.

5. The extent of use of international financial markets.[17]

With this backdrop of fragmentation, it will be difficult in the short run, if not impossible, to bring national standards into agreement with a meaningful body of international standards. But many see benefits to harmonization of international accounting standards and feel that accounting must move in that direction. In the short run, ways exist to cope with incomparable standards. One possible interim solution involves dual standards. International companies would prepare two sets of financial statements. One would be prepared under domestic GAAP, while the other would be prepared under international GAAP. This would likely put pressure on domestic GAAP to move towards international GAAP.

In the United States, a conflict exists between the SEC and the securities exchanges, such as the New York Stock Exchange (NYSE). In general, the SEC requires foreign registrants to conform to U.S. GAAP, either directly or by reconciliation. This approach achieves a degree of comparability in the U.S. capital market, but it does not achieve comparability for investors who want to invest in several national capital markets. This approach poses a problem for U.S. securities exchanges, because the U.S. standards are perceived to be the most stringent. This puts exchanges such as the NYSE at a competitive disadvantage with foreign exchanges that have lower standards. The development of international standards would alleviate this problem.

In the United States, the FASB did not show a critical interest in harmonization of international accounting standards until the early 1990s. The FASB now actively participates in the harmonization of international accounting standards. This includes cooperating with the IASC and the UN.

SUMMARY

This chapter includes an introduction to the basic financial statements. Subsequent chapters will cover these statements in detail.

An understanding of the sequence of accounting procedures completed during each accounting period, called the accounting cycle, will help in understanding the end result—financial statements.

This chapter describes the forms of business entities, which are sole proprietorship, partnership, and corporation.

Human resources accounting attempts to account for the services of employees, while social accounting attempts to account for the benefits to the social environment.

Management is responsible for financial statements. These statements are examined by auditors who express an opinion regarding the statements' conformity to GAAP in the auditor's report. The auditor's report often points out key factors that can affect financial statement analysis. The SEC has begun a program to integrate the Form 10-K requirements with those of the annual report.

A reporting option available to public companies, a summary annual report (a condensed annual report), omits much of the financial information included in a typical annual report.

Individuals in financial positions must be able to recognize ethical issues and resolve them appropriately.

With the expansion of international business and global capital markets, the business community and governments have shown an increased interest in the harmonization of international accounting standards.

QUESTIONS

Q 2-1.   Name the type of opinion indicated by each of the following situations:

a. There is a material uncertainty.

b. There was a change in accounting principle.

c. There is no material scope limitation or material departure from GAAP.

d. The financial statements do not present fairly the financial position, results of operations, or cash flows of the entity in conformity with GAAP.

e. Except for the effects of the matter(s) to which the qualification relates, the financial statements present fairly, in all material respects, the financial position, results of operations, and cash flows of the entity, in conformity with GAAP.

Q 2-2.   What are the roles of management and the auditor in the preparation and integrity of the financial statements?

Q 2-3.   What is the purpose of the SEC's integrated disclosure system for financial reporting?

Q 2-4.   Why do some unqualified opinions have explanatory paragraphs?

Q 2-5.   Describe an auditor's review of financial statements.

Q 2-6.   Will the accountant express an opinion on reviewed financial statements? Describe the accountant's report for reviewed financial statements.

Q 2-7.   What type of opinion is expressed on a compilation?

Q 2-8.   Are all financial statements presented with some kind of an accountant's report? Explain.

Q 2-9.   What are the principal financial statements of a corporation? Briefly describe the purpose of each statement.

Q 2-10.   Why are footnotes to statements necessary?

Q 2-11.   What are contingent liabilities? Are lawsuits against the firm contingent liabilities?

Q 2-12.   Which of the following events, occurring subsequent to the balance sheet date, would require a footnote?

    a.   Major fire in one of the firm's plants
    b.   Increase in competitor's advertising
    c.   Purchase of another company
    d.   Introduction of new management techniques
    e.   Death of the corporate treasurer

Q 2-13.   Why are the firm's employees not valued as assets on the balance sheet?

Q 2-14.   Briefly describe a summary annual report.

Q 2-15.   If a company issues a summary annual report, where can the more extensive financial information be found?

Q 2-16.   Comment on the typical number of financial pages in a summary annual report as compared to a full annual report.

Q 2-17.   What are the major sections of a statement of cash flows?

Q 2-18.   Which major financial statements explain the difference between two balance sheet dates?

Q 2-19.   What are the three major categories on a balance sheet?

Q 2-20.   Can cash dividends be paid from retained earnings? Comment.

Q 2-21.   Why review footnotes to financial statements?

Q 2-22.   Where do we find a description of a firm's accounting policies?

Q 2-23.   Describe the relationship between the terms *ethics* and *morals*.

Q 2-24.   What is the relationship between *ethics* and *law*?

Q 2-25.   Identify the basic accounting equation.

Q 2-26.   What is the relationship between the accounting equation and the double-entry system of recording transactions?

Q 2-27.   Define the following:

    a. Permanent accounts

    b. Temporary accounts

Q 2-28.   A typical accrual recognition for salaries is as follows:

Salaries Expense	$1,000 (increase)
Salaries Payable	1,000 (increase)

    Explain how the matching concept applies in this situation.

Q 2-29.   Why are adjusting entries necessary?

Q 2-30.   Why are not all transactions recorded in the general journal?

Q 2-31.   The NYSE has trouble competing with many foreign exchanges in the listing of foreign stocks. Discuss.

Q 2-32.   Identify the usual forms of a business entity and describe the ownership characteristic of each.

Q 2-33.   Describe a proxy statement.

PROBLEMS

P 2-1.   The Mike Szabo Company engaged in the following transactions during the month of December:

    December   2   Made credit sales of $4,000 (accepted accounts receivable).

                 6   Made cash sales of $2,500.

              10   Paid office salaries of $500.

              14   Sold land that originally cost $2,200 for $3,000 cash.

              17   Paid $6,000 for equipment.

              21   Billed clients $900 for services (accepted accounts receivable).

              24   Collected $1,200 on an account receivable.

              28   Paid an account payable of $700.

Required   Record the transactions, using T-accounts.

P 2-2.

Required   Answer the following multiple-choice questions:

    a. The balance sheet equation can be defined as which of the following?

        1.   Assets + Owners' Equity = Liabilities

        2.   Assets + Liabilities = Owners' Equity

        3.   Assets = Liabilities − Owners' Equity

        4.   Assets − Liabilities = Owners' Equity

        5.   None of the above

b. If assets are $40,000 and owners' equity is $10,000, how much are liabilities?
  1. $30,000
  2. $50,000
  3. $20,000
  4. $60,000
  5. $10,000

c. If assets are $100,000 and liabilities are $40,000, how much is owners' equity?
  1. $40,000
  2. $50,000
  3. $60,000
  4. $30,000
  5. $140,000

d. Which is a permanent account?
  1. Revenue
  2. Advertising Expense
  3. Accounts Receivable
  4. Dividends
  5. Insurance Expense

e. Which is a temporary account?
  1. Cash
  2. Accounts Receivable
  3. Insurance Expense
  4. Accounts Payable
  5. Notes Payable

f. In terms of debits and credits, which accounts have the same normal balances?
  1. Dividends, retained earnings, liabilities
  2. Capital stock, liabilities, expenses
  3. Revenues, capital stock, expenses
  4. Expenses, assets, dividends
  5. Dividends, assets, liabilities

P 2-3.

Required   Answer the following multiple-choice questions:

a. Audit opinions cannot be classified as which of the following?
  1. All-purpose
  2. Disclaimer of opinion
  3. Adverse opinion
  4. Qualified opinion
  5. Unqualified opinion

b. From the point of view of analysis, which classification of an audit opinion indicates that the financial statements carry the highest degree of reliability?

       1.   Unqualified opinion
       2.   All-purpose
       3.   Disclaimer of opinion
       4.   Qualified opinion
       5.   Adverse opinion

c. Which one of the following statements is false?

    1.   The reliance that can be placed on financial statements that have been reviewed is substantially less than for those that have been audited.
    2.   An accountant's report described as a compilation presents only financial information as provided by management.
    3.   A disclaimer of opinion indicates that you should not look to the auditor's report as an indication of the reliability of the statements.
    4.   A review has substantially less scope than an examination in accordance with generally accepted auditing standards.
    5.   The typical unqualified opinion has one paragraph.

d. If an accountant performs a compilation and becomes aware of deficiencies in the statements, the accountant's report characterizes the deficiencies by all but one of the following:

    1.   Omission of substantially all disclosures
    2.   Omission of statement of cash flows
    3.   Accounting principles not generally accepted
    4.   All of the above
    5.   None of the above

e. In addition to the company's primary financial statements, the Form 10-K and shareholder annual reports must include all but one of the following:

    1.   Information on the market for holders of common stock and related securities, including high and low sales price, frequency and amount of dividends, and number of shares.
    2.   Five-year summary of selected financial data.
    3.   Management's discussion and analysis of financial condition and results of operations.
    4.   Two years of audited balance sheets, three years of audited statements of income, and two years of statements of cash flows.
    5.   Disclosure of the domestic and foreign components of pretax income.

f. Which of these is not a suggested problem caused by lack of harmonization of international accounting standards?

    1.   Positive effect on the international trade of accounting practice and services.
    2.   A need for employment of key personnel in multinational companies to bridge the "gap" in accounting requirements between countries.
    3.   Difficulties in reconciling local standards for access to other capital markets.
    4.   Difficulties in accessing capital markets for companies from less developed countries.
    5.   Negative effect on the international trade of accounting practice and services.

g. Which of these organizations has not played a role in the harmonization of international accounting standards?
1. United Nations (UN)
2. Internal Revenue Service (IRS)
3. International Accounting Standards Committee (IASC)
4. Financial Accounting Standards Board (FASB)
5. European Economic Community (EEC)

h. The Form 10-K is submitted to the
1. American Institute of Certified Public Accountants
2. Securities and Exchange Commission
3. Internal Revenue Service
4. American Accounting Association
5. Emerging Issues Task Force

P 2-4. The following are selected accounts of the Laura Gibson Company on December 31:

	Permanent (P) or Temporary (T)	Normal Balance (Dr.) or (Cr.)
Cash		
Accounts Receivable		
Equipment		
Accounts Payable		
Common Stock		
Sales		
Purchases		
Rent Expense		
Utility Expense		
Selling Expense		

Required   In the space provided:

1. Indicate if the account is a permanent (P) or temporary (T) account.

2. Indicate the normal balance in terms of debit (Dr.) or credit (Cr.).

P 2-5. An auditor's report is the formal presentation of all the effort that goes into an audit. Below is a list of the classifications of audit opinions that can be found in an auditor's report as well as a list of phrases describing the opinions.

Classifications of Audit Opinions

a. Unqualified opinion
b. Qualified opinion
c. Adverse opinion
d. Disclaimer of opinion

Phrases

___ 1. This opinion states that the financial statements do not present fairly the financial position, results of operations, or cash flows of the entity, in conformity with generally accepted accounting principles.

___ 2. This type of report is rendered when the auditor has not performed an audit sufficient in scope to form an opinion.

___ 3. This opinion states that, except for the effects of the matters to which the qualification relates, the financial statements present fairly, in all material respects, the financial position, results of operations, and cash flows of the entity, in conformity with generally accepted accounting principles.

___ 4. This opinion states that the financial statements present fairly, in all material respects, the financial position, results of operations, and cash flows of the entity, in conformity with generally accepted accounting principles.

Required   Place the appropriate letter identifying each type of opinion on the line in front of the statement or phrase describing the type of opinion.

P 2-6.   A company prepares financial statements in order to summarize financial information. Below is a list of financial statements and a list of descriptions.

Financial Statements
a. Balance sheet
b. Income statement
c. Statement of cash flows

Descriptions

___ 1. Details the sources and uses of cash during a specified period of time.

___ 2. Summary of revenues and expenses and gains and losses for a specific period of time.

___ 3. Shows the financial condition of an accounting entity as of a specific date.

Required   Match each financial statement with its description.

Cases

CASE 2-1   The CEO Retires*

Dan Murphy awoke at 5:45 a.m., just like he did every workday morning. No matter that he went to sleep only four hours ago. The Orange Bowl game had gone late into the evening, and the New Year's Day party was so good, no one wanted to leave. At least Dan could awake easily this morning. Some of his guests had lost a little control celebrating the first day of the new year, and Dan was not a person who ever lost control.

The drive to the office was easier than most days. Perhaps there were a great many parties last night. All the better as it gave Dan time to think. The dawn of a new year; his last year. Dan would turn 65 next December, and the company had a mandatory retirement policy. A good idea he thought; to get new blood in the organization. At least that's what he thought on the climb up. From just another college graduate within the corporate staff, all the way to the Chief Executive Officer's suite. It certainly is a magnificent view from the top.

To be CEO of his own company. Well not really, as it was the stockholders' company, but he had been CEO for the past eight years. Now he too must turn the reins over. "Must," now that's the operative word. He knew it was the best thing for the company. Turnover kept middle management aggressive, but he also knew that he wouldn't leave if he had a choice. So Dan resolved to make his last year the company's best year ever.

It was that thought which kept his attention, yet the focus of consideration and related motivations supporting such a strategy changed as he continued to strategize. At first, Dan thought that it would be a fine way to give something back to a company that had given him so much. His 43 years with the company had given him challenges which filled his life with meaning and satisfaction, provided him with a good living, and made him a man respected and listened to in the business community. But the thought that the company was also forcing him to give all that up made his thoughts turn more inward.

Prepared by Professor William H. Coyle, Babson College.

*Note: From "Ethics in the Accounting Curriculum: Cases & Readings," American Accounting Association, included with permission.

Of course, the company had done many things for him, but what of all the sacrifices he had made? His whole heart and soul were tied to the company. In fact, one could hardly think of Dan Murphy without thinking of the company, in much the same way as prominent corporate leaders and their firms are intrinsically linked. But the company would still be here this time next year, and what of him? Yes, he would leave the company strong, because by leaving it strong, it would strengthen his reputation as a great leader. His legacy would carry and sustain him over the years. But would it? One must also live in a manner consistent with such esteem.

Being the CEO of a major company also has its creature comforts. Dan was accustomed to a certain style of living. How much will that suffer after the salary, bonuses, and stock options are no more?

Arriving at the office by 7:30 a.m., he left a note for his secretary that he was not to be disturbed until 9 a.m. He pulled out the compensation file and examined the incentive clauses in his own contract. The contract was created by the compensation committee of the Board of Directors. All of the committee members were outsiders; that is, not a part of the company's management. This lends the appearance of independence, but most were CEOs of their own companies, and Dan knew that, by and large, CEOs take care of their own. His suspicions were confirmed. If the company's financial results were the best ever this year, then so too would be his own personal compensation.

Yet what if there were uncontrollable problems? The general economy appeared fairly stable. However, another oil shock, some more bank failures, or a list of other disasters could turn things into a downward spiral quickly. Economies are easily influenced and consumer and corporate psychology can play a large part in determining outcomes. But even in apparently uncontrollable circumstances, Dan knew he could protect himself and the financial fortunes of his company during the short-term, which after all, was the only thing that mattered.

Upon further review of his compensation contract, Dan saw that a large portion of his bonus and stock options was a function of operating income levels, earnings per share, and return on assets. So the trick was to maximize those items. If he did, the company would appear vibrant and posed for future growth at the time of his forced retirement, he reminded himself. Furthermore, his total compensation in the last year of his employment would reach record proportions. Additionally, since his pension is based on the average of his last three years' compensation, Dan will continue to reap the benefits of this year's results for hopefully a long time to come. And who says CEOs don't think long-term?

Two remaining issues needed to be addressed. Those were (1) how to ensure a record-breaking year and (2) how to overcome any objections raised in attaining those results? Actually, the former was a relatively simple goal to achieve. Since accounting allows so many alternatives in the way financial events are measured, Dan could just select a package of alternatives which would maximize the company's earnings and return on assets. Some alternatives may result in changing an accounting method, but since the new auditing standards were issued, his company could still receive an unqualified opinion from his auditors, with only a passing reference to any accounting changes in the auditor's opinion and its effects disclosed in the footnotes. As long as the alternative was allowed by generally accepted accounting principles, and the justification for the change was reasonable, the auditors should not object. If there were objections, Dan could always threaten to change auditors. But still the best avenue to pursue would be a change in accounting estimates, since those changes did not even need to be explicitly disclosed.

So Dan began to mull over what changes in estimates or methods he could employ in order to maximize his firm's financial appearance. In the area of accounting estimates, Dan could lower the rate of estimated default on his accounts receivable, thus lowering bad debt expense. The estimated useful lives of his plant and equipment could be extended, thus lowering depreciation expense. In arguing that quality improvements have been implemented in the manufacturing process, the warranty expense on the products sold could also be lowered. In examining pension expense, he noted that the assumed rate of return on pension assets was at a modest 6.5%, so if that rate could be increased, the corresponding pension expense could be reduced.

Other possibilities occurred to Murphy. Perhaps items normally expensed, such as repairs, could be capitalized. Those repairs that could not be capitalized could simply be deferred. The company could also defer short-term expenses for the training of staff. Since research and development costs must now be fully expensed as incurred, a reduction in those expenditures would increase net income. Return on assets would be increased by not acquiring any new fixed assets. Production levels for inventory could be increased, thus spreading fixed costs over a greater number of units and reducing the total average cost per unit. Therefore, gross profit per unit will increase. Inventory levels would be a little bloated, but that should be easily handled by Dan's successor.

The prior examples are subtle changes that could be made. As a last resort, a change in accounting methods could be employed. This would require explicit footnote disclosure and a comment in the auditor's report, but if it came to that, it would still be tolerable. Examples of such changes would be to switch from accelerated to straight-line depreciation or to change from LIFO to FIFO.

How to make changes to the financial results of the company appeared easier than he first thought. Now back to the other potential problem of "getting away with it." At first thought, Dan considered the degree of resistance by the other members of top management. Mike Harrington, Dan's chief financial officer, would have to review any accounting changes that he suggested. Since Dan had brought Mike up the organization with him, Dan didn't foresee any strong resistance from Mike. As for the others, Dan believed he had two things going for him. One was their ambition. Dan knew that they all coveted his job, and a clear successor to Dan had yet to be chosen. Dan would only make a recommendation to the promotion committee of the Board of Directors, but everyone knew his recommendation carried a great deal of weight. Therefore, resistance to any accounting changes by any individual would surely end his or her hope to succeed him as CEO. Secondly, although not as lucrative as Dan's, their bonus package is tied to the exact same accounting numbers. So any actions taken by Dan to increase his compensation will also increase theirs.

Dan was actually beginning to enjoy this situation, even considering it one of his final challenges. Dan realized that any changes he implemented would have the tendency to reverse themselves over time. That would undoubtedly hurt the company's performance down the road, but all of his potential successors were in their mid-to-late 50s, so there would be plenty of time for them to turn things around in the years ahead. Besides, any near-term reversals would merely enhance his reputation as an excellent corporate leader, as problems would arise *after* his departure.

At that moment, his secretary called to inform him that Mike Harrington wanted to see him. Mike was just the man Dan wanted to see.

What are the ethical issues?

What should Mike do?

Required
a. Determine the facts—what, who, where, when, how.
b. Define the ethical issues.
c. Identify major principles, rules, and values.
d. Specify the alternatives.
e. Compare norms, principles, and values with alternatives to see if a clear decision can be reached.
f. Assess the consequences.
g. Make your decision.

CASE 2-2 The Dangerous Morality of Managing Earnings*

The Majority of Managers Surveyed Say It's Not Wrong to Manage Earnings

Occasionally, the morals and ethics executives use to manage their businesses are examined and discussed. Unfortunately, the morals that guide the timing of nonoperating events and choices of accounting policies largely have been ignored.

---

*Note: Prepared by William J. Bruns, Jr., Professor of Business Administration, Harvard University Graduate School of Business Administration, and Kenneth A. Merchant, Professor of Accounting, University of Southern California.

Reprinted from *Management Accounting*, August 1990. Copyright by National Association of Accountants, Montvale, NJ.

The ethical framework used by managers in reporting short-term earnings probably has received less attention than its operating counterpart because accountants prepare financial disclosures consistent with laws and generally accepted accounting principles (GAAP). Those disclosures are reviewed by objective auditors.

Managers determine the short-term reported earnings of their companies by:

— Managing, providing leadership, and directing the use of resources in operations.
— Selecting the timing of some nonoperating events, such as the sale of excess assets or the placement of gains or losses into a particular reporting period.
— Choosing the accounting methods that are used to measure short-term earnings.

Casual observers of the financial reporting process may assume that time, laws, regulation, and professional standards have restricted accounting practices to those which are moral, ethical, fair, and precise. But most managers and their accountants know otherwise—that managing short-term earnings can be part of a manager's job.

To understand the morals of short-term earnings management, we surveyed general managers and finance, control, and audit managers. The results are frightening.

We found striking disagreements among managers in all groups. Furthermore, the liberal definitions revealed in many responses of what is moral or ethical should raise profound questions about the quality of financial information that is used for decision-making purposes by parties both inside and outside a company. It seems many managers are convinced that if a practice is not explicitly prohibited or is only a slight deviation from rules, it is an ethical practice regardless of who might be affected either by the practice or the information that flows from it. This means that anyone who uses information on short-term earnings is vulnerable to misinterpretation, manipulation, or deliberate deception.

The Morals of Managing Earnings

To find a "revealed" consensus concerning the morality of engaging in earnings-management activities, we prepared a questionnaire describing 13 earnings-management situations we had observed either directly or indirectly. The actions described in the incidents were all legal (although some were in violation of GAAP), but each could be construed as involving short-term earnings management.

A total of 649 managers completed our questionnaire. Table 1 classifies respondents by job function. Table 2 summarizes the views on the acceptability of various earnings-management practices.

A major finding of the survey was a striking lack of agreement. None of the respondent groups viewed any of the 13 practices unanimously as an

TABLE 1 **Survey Respondents**

	Total Sample
General Managers	119
Finance, Control, & Audit Managers	262
Others or Position Not Known	268
	649

TABLE 2 **Managing Short-Term Earnings**

	Proportion of Managers Who Judge the Practice		
	Ethical	*Questionable, or a Minor Infraction*	*Unethical, or a Serious Infraction*
1. Managing short-term earnings by changing or manipulating operating decisions or procedures:			
When the result is to reduce earnings	79%	19%	2%
When the result is to increase earnings	57%	31%	12%
2. Managing short-term earnings by changing or manipulating accounting methods:			
When the change to earnings is small	5%	45%	50%
When the change to earnings is large	3%	21%	76%
3. Managing short-term earnings by deferring discretionary expenditures into the next accounting period:			
To meet an interim quarterly budget target	47%	41%	12%
To meet an annual budget target	41%	35%	24%
4. Increasing short-term earnings to meet a budget target:			
By selling excess assets and realizing a profit	80%	16%	4%
By ordering overtime work at year-end to ship as much as possible	74%	21%	5%
By offering customers special credit terms to accept delivery without obligation to pay until the following year	43%	44%	15%

Percentages are calculated from *Harvard Business Review* readers' sample.

ethical or unethical practice. The dispersion of judgments about many of the incidents was great. For example, here is one hypothetical earnings-management practice described in the questionnaire:

> In September, a general manager realized that his division would need a strong performance in the last quarter of the year in order to reach its budget targets. He decided to implement a sales program offering liberal payment terms to pull some sales that would normally occur next year into the current year. Customers accepting delivery in the fourth quarter would not have to pay the invoice for 120 days.

The survey respondents' judgments of the acceptability of this practice were distributed as follows:

Ethical	279
Questionable	288
Unethical	82
Total	**649**

Perhaps you are not surprised by these data. The ethical basis of an early shipment/liberal payment program may not be something you have considered, but, with the prevalence of such diverse views, how can any user of a short-term earnings report know the quality of the information?

Although the judgments about all earnings-management practices varied considerably, there are some other generalizations that can be made from the findings summarized in Table 2.

— On average, the respondents viewed management of short-term earnings by *accounting* methods as significantly less acceptable than accomplishing the same ends by changing or manipulating *operating decisions or procedures*.

— The direction of the effect on earnings matters. *Increasing* earnings is judged less acceptable than *reducing* earnings.

— Materiality matters. Short-term earnings management is judged less acceptable if the earnings effect is *large* rather than *small*.

— The time period of the effect may affect ethical judgments. Managing short-term earnings at the end of an interim *quarterly* reporting period is viewed as somewhat more acceptable than engaging in the same activity at the end of an *annual* reporting period.

— The method of managing earnings has an effect. Increasing profits by offering *extended credit terms* is seen as less acceptable than accomplishing the same end by *selling excess assets or using overtime* to increase shipments.

Managers Interviewed

Were the survey results simply hypothetical, or did managers recognize they can manage earnings and choose to do so? To find the answers, we talked to a large number of the respondents. What they told us was rarely reassuring.

On accounting manipulations, a profit center controller reported:

"Accounting is grey. Very little is absolute . . . You can save your company by doing things with sales and expenses, and, if it's legal, then you are justified in doing it."

A divisional general manager spoke to us about squeezing reserves to generate additional reported profit:

"If we get a call asking for additional profit, and that's not inconceivable, I would look at our reserves. Our reserves tend to be realistic, but we may have a product claim that could range from $50,000 to $500,000. Who knows what the right amount for something like that is? We would review our reserves, and if we felt some were on the high side, we would not be uncomfortable reducing them."

We also heard about operating manipulations. One corporate group controller noted:

"[To boost sales] we have paid overtime and shipped on Saturday, the last day of the fiscal quarter. If we totally left responsibility for the shipping function to the divisions, it could even slip over to 12:30 a.m. Sunday. There are people who would do that and not know it's wrong."

Managers often recognize that such actions "move" earnings from one period to another. For example, a division controller told us:

"Last year we called our customers and asked if they would take early delivery. We generated an extra $300,000 in sales at the last minute. We were scratching for everything. We made our plans, but we cleaned out our backlog and started in the hole this year. We missed our first quarter sales plan. We will catch up by the end of the second quarter."

And a group vice president said:

"I recently was involved in a situation where the manager wanted to delay the production costs for the advertising that would appear in the fall [so that he could meet his quarterly budget]."

Thus, in practice, it appears that a large majority of managers use at least some methods to manage short-term earnings. Although legal, these methods do not seem to be consistent with a strict ethical framework. While the managers' actions have the desired effect on reported earnings, the managers know there are no real positive economic benefits, and the actions might actually be quite costly in the long run. These actions are at best questionable because they involve deceptions that are not disclosed. Most managers who manage earnings, however, do not believe they are doing anything wrong.

We see two major problems. The most important is the generally high tolerance for operating manipulations. The other is the dispersion in managers' views about which practices are moral and ethical.

The Dangerous Allure

The essence of a moral or ethical approach to management is achieving a balance between individual interests and obligations to those who have a stake in what happens in the corporation (or what happens to a division or group within the corporation). These stakeholders include not only people who work in the firm, but customers, suppliers, creditors, shareholders, and investors as well.

Managers who take unproductive actions to boost short-term earnings may be acting totally within the laws and rules. Also they may be acting in the best interest of the corporation. But, if they fail to consider the adverse effects of their actions on other stakeholders, we may conclude that they are acting unethically.

The managers we interviewed explained that they rated accounting manipulations harshly because in such cases the "truth" has somehow been denied or misstated. The recipients of the earnings reports do not know what earnings would have been if no manipulation had taken place. Even if the accounting methods used are consistent with GAAP, they reason, the actions are not ethical because the interests of major stakeholder groups—including the recipients of the earnings reports—have been ignored.

The managers judge the operating manipulations more favorably because the earnings numbers are indicative of what actually took place. The operating manipulations have changed reality, and "truth" is fairly reported.

We see flaws in that reasoning. One is that the truth has not necessarily been disclosed completely. When sales and profits are borrowed from the future, for example, it is a rare company that discloses the borrowed nature of some of the profits reported.

A second flaw in the reasoning about the acceptability of operating manipulations is that it ignores a few or all of the effects of some types of operating manipulations on the full range of stakeholders. Many managers consider operating manipulations as a kind of "victimless crime."

But victims do exist. Consider, for example, the relatively common operating manipulation of early shipments. As one manager told us:

"Would I ship extra product if I was faced with a sales shortfall? You have to be careful there; you're playing with fire. I would let whatever happened fall to the bottom line. I've been in companies that did whatever they could to make the sales number, such as shipping lower quality product. That's way too short-term. You have to draw the line there. You must maintain the level of quality and customer service. You'll end up paying for bad shipments eventually. You'll have returns, repairs, adjustments, ill will that will cause you to lose the account . . . [In addition] it's tough to go to your employees one day and say ship everything you can and then turn around the next day and say that the quality standards must be maintained."

Another reported:

"We've had to go to [one of our biggest customers] and say we need an order. That kills us in the negotiations. Our last sale was at a price just over our cost of materials."

These comments point out that customers—and sometimes even the corporation—may be victims.

Without a full analysis of the costs of operating manipulations, the dangers of such manipulations to the corporation are easily underestimated. Mistakes will be made because the quality of information is misjudged. The short term will be emphasized at the expense of the long term. If managers consistently manage short-term earnings, the messages sent to other employees create a corporate culture that lacks mutual trust, integrity, and loyalty.

A Lack of Moral Agreement

We also are troubled by the managers' inability to agree on the types of earnings-management activities that are acceptable. This lack of agreement exists even within corporations.

What this suggests is that many managers are doing their analyses in different ways. The danger is obfuscation of the reality behind the financial reports. Because managers are using different standards, individuals who try to use the information reported may be unable to assess accurately the quality of that information.

If differences in opinions exist, it is likely that financial reporting practices will sink to their lowest and most manipulative level. As a result, managers with strict definitions of what is moral and ethical will find it difficult to compete with managers who are not playing by the same rules. Ethical managers either will loosen their moral standards or fail to be promoted into positions of greater power.

Actions for Concerned Managers

We believe most corporations would benefit if they established clearer accounting and operating standards for all employees to follow. The standard-setting process should involve managers in discussions of the practices related to short-term earnings measurements.

Until these standards are in place, different managers will use widely varying criteria in assessing the acceptability of various earnings-management practices. These variations will have an adverse effect on the quality of the firm's financial information. Companies can use a questionnaire similar to the one in our study to encourage discussion and to communicate corporate standards and the reason for them.

Standards also enable internal and external auditors and management to judge whether or not the desired quality of earnings is being maintained. In most companies, auditors can depend on good standards to identify and judge the acceptability of the operating manipulations.

Ultimately, the line management chain-of-command, not auditors or financial staff, bears the primary responsibility for controlling operating manipulations. Often managers must rely on their prior experience and good judgment to distinguish between a decision that will have positive long-term benefits and one that has a positive short-term effect but a deleterious long-term effect.

Finally, it is important to manage the corporate culture. A culture that promotes openness and cooperative problem-solving among managers is likely to result in less short-term earnings management than one that is more competitive and where annual, and even quarterly, performance shortfalls are punished. A corporate culture that is more concerned with managing for excellence rather than for reporting short-term profits will be less likely to support the widespread use of immoral earnings-management practices.

Required   a. Time, laws, regulation, and professional standards have restricted accounting practices to those that are moral, ethical, fair, and precise. Comment.

b. Most managers surveyed had a conservative, strict interpretation of what is moral or ethical in financial reporting. Comment.

c. The managers surveyed exhibited a surprising agreement as to what constitutes an ethical or unethical practice. Comment.

d. List the five generalizations from the findings in this study relating to managing earnings.

e. Comment on management's ability to manage earnings in the long run by influencing financial accounting.

CASE 2-3   Frequent-Flier Awards—Tick-Tick, Tick-Tick, Tick-Tick

In the early 1980s, airlines introduced frequent-flier awards to develop passenger loyalty to a single airline. Free tickets and possibly other awards were made available to passengers when they accumulated a certain number of miles or flights on a particular air carrier. These programs were potentially good for the passenger and the airline as long as the awards were not too generous and the airlines could minimize revenue displacement from a paying passenger.

These programs were introduced by American Airlines in 1981. Originally there were no restrictions. Anyone with the necessary miles could take any flight that had an available seat. In the late 1980s, most airlines changed their no-restriction programs to programs with restrictions and blackout days. Airlines typically compensated passengers for these changes by cutting mileage requirements. The airlines also added partners in frequent-flier programs, such as car rental companies and hotels. These partners handed out frequent-flier miles compensating the airlines in some manner for the miles distributed. Airlines also added triple-mileage deals.

A consequence of these expanding frequent-flier programs was a surge in the number of passengers flying free and a surge in unused miles. To get a handle on the cost and the unused miles, airlines increased the frequent-flier miles needed for a flight and placed time limits on the award miles. Thus —tick-tick, tick-tick, tick-tick.

The increased frequent-flier miles needed for a flight and the time limits prompted lawsuits. Many of these lawsuits were filed in state courts. One of the suits filed in the District Court in Chicago in 1989 made its way to the United States Supreme Court. In 1995 the Supreme Court ruled that federal airline deregulation law would not bar the breach-of-contract claim in the state court. In June of 1995 a District Court in Dallas ruled in favor of the airline in a case involving an increase in miles needed to earn a trip. Airlines interpret this decision as upholding their right to make changes to their frequent-flier programs.

Required   a. In your opinion, are the outstanding (unused) miles a liability to the airline? (Substantiate your answer.)

           b. Comment on the potential problems involved in estimating the dollar amount of any potential liability.

           c. 1. What is a contingent liability?

                  2. In your opinion, are unused miles a contingent liability to the air carrier?

                  3. Recommend the recognition (if any) for unused miles.

CASE 2-4   International Accounting—Harmonization in Practice

Dennis R. Beresford, Chairman, Financial Accounting Standards Board, included these comments in the June, 1995, Financial Accounting Series of the Financial Accounting Foundation. This case represents a quote from page 2, Notes from the Chairman. (Permission to reprint obtained from the Financial Accounting Standards Board.)

Notes from the Chairman (in Part)

Last month Jim Leisenring and I attended what is now becoming more or less an annual meeting of accounting standards setters from more than a dozen countries. The first of those meetings, initiated by the FASB, was held in 1991 in Brussels, and similar get-togethers have followed in our offices, London, and now Amsterdam. This year's meeting was held in conjunction with a regular meeting of the International Accounting Standards Committee and the centenary celebrations of NIVRA, the professional accounting body in the Netherlands.

Earlier, this group had devoted its attention mainly to conceptual issues and general communications about what the various countries were working on at the time. For example, the first gathering concentrated on the objectives of external financial reporting and whether individual countries had explicit or implicit conceptual frameworks. In London, most of the time was spent on how future events are considered in accounting recognition and measurement decisions. That discussion was facilitated by a paper prepared by the FASB and our counterparts from Australia, Canada, the United Kingdom, and the IASC. The paper later was jointly published as the Special Report, "Future Events—A Conceptual Study of Their Significance for Recognition and Measurement."

In Amsterdam, we spent most of the time on two specific technical issues that are hot topics here as well as in the rest of the world: accounting for environmental liabilities and derivative financial instruments. Papers were presented by Canada, Denmark,

England, and the European Commission, which covered the current
state-of-the-art regarding disclosure of and accounting for environmental costs. As in the U.S., the key issues are deciding when an
obligation has been incurred, under what circumstances can any resulting debit be considered an asset (e.g., costs incurred to "improve"
a productive facility), and when an amount is measurable with sufficient reliability.

Required   a.   Comment on the trend in harmonization of international accounting as
represented by the comments included in this case.

b.   Can we expect harmonization of international accounting to be accomplished in the foreseeable future? Comment.

Endnotes

1   Charles H. Gibson and Nicholas Schroeder, "How 21 Companies Handled Their Summary Annual Reports," *Financial Executive* (November/December 1989), pp. 45-46.

2   Mary E. Guy, *Ethical Decision Making in Everyday Work Situations* (New York, NY: Quarum Books, 1990), p. 5.

3   Guy, p. 14.

4   William W. May, ed., *Ethics in the Accounting Curriculum: Cases & Readings* (Sarasota, FL: American Accounting Association, 1990), pp. 1-2.

5   "Regulators Investigate Peat on Its Auditing of S & L," *New York Times* (May 23, 1991), p. D-1.

6   "S.E.C. Inquiry Is Reported on Loans to Accountants," *New York Times* (February 7, 1991), p. D-1.

7   "Ernst & Young Settles Negligence Charge," *Business Insurance* (May 6, 1991), p. 2.

8   Ronald Grover, "Curtains for Tinseltown Accounting?" *Business Week* (January 14, 1991), p. 35.

9   Shahram Victory, "Pierce O'Donnell Pans 'Fatal Subtraction,'" *American Lawyer* (March 1991), p. 43.

10 "Buchwald Wins Just $150,000 in Film Lawsuit," *The Wall Street Journal* (March 17, 1992), p. B-1.

11 Dennis E. Peavey and Stuart K. Webster, "Is GAAP the Gap to International Markets?" *Management Accounting* (August 1990), pp. 31-32.

12 John Hagarty, "Why We Can't Let GATT Die," *Journal of Accountancy* (April 1991), p. 74.

13 Peavey and Webster, p. 34.

14 Anthony B. Creamer, "Auditing Beyond U.S. Shores: What the U.S. CPA Should Know," *Journal of Accountancy* (November 1987), p. 92.

15 Gerhard G. Mueller, Helen Gernan, and Gary Meek, *Accounting: An International Perspective*, 2d ed. (Homewood, IL: Richard D. Irwin, Inc., 1991), pp. 45-46.

16 Dennis Beresford, "Internationalization of Accounting Standards," *Accounting Horizons* (March 1990), p. 10.

17 Mueller, Gernan, and Meek, pp. 11-12.

3 ___ Balance Sheet

THE BASIC FINANCIAL STATEMENTS ARE THE balance sheet, income statement, and statement of cash flows. Since these statements may be titled "consolidated," a brief description of consolidated statements is in order before reviewing the balance sheet. Also, a brief description of how a business combination can impact the basic statements is in order.

CONSOLIDATED STATEMENTS

Financial statements of legally separate entities may be issued to show financial position, income, and cash flow as they would appear if the companies were a single entity (consolidated). Such statements reflect an economic, rather than a legal, concept of the entity. For consolidated statements, all transactions between the entities being consolidated—intercompany transactions—must be eliminated.

One corporation can own stock in another corporation in an amount sufficient to hold substantial voting rights in that corporation. The corporation owning the stock is the *parent corporation*. The corporation whose stock is owned is the *subsidiary corporation*. The financial statements of the parent and the subsidiary are consolidated for all majority-owned subsidiaries unless control is temporary or does not rest with the majority owner. These are termed **consolidated financial statements**. An *unconsolidated* subsidiary is accounted for as an investment on the parent's balance sheet.

When a subsidiary is less than 100% owned and its statements are consolidated, minority shareholders must be recognized in the consolidated financial statements by showing the minority interest in net assets on the balance sheet and the minority share of earnings on the income statement. Minority-related accounts are discussed in detail later in this chapter and in the next chapter.

Consolidation of financial statements has been a practice in the United States for years; however, this has not been the case for many other nations. In some countries like Japan, parent-only financial statements are the norm. In other countries like Germany, consolidation only includes domestic subsidiaries.

The International Accounting Standards Committee passed IAS 27, which requires that all controlled subsidiaries be consolidated. Although IASC standards cannot be enforced, IAS 27 will likely increase the acceptance of consolidation.

ACCOUNTING FOR BUSINESS COMBINATIONS

The combination of business entities by merger or acquisition is very frequent. There are many possible reasons for this external business expansion, including achieving economies of scale and savings of time in entering a new market.

There are two methods of accounting for a business combination—the **pooling of interests method** and the **purchase method**. The accounting for a merger or acquisition is under APB Opinion No. 16. APB Opinion No. 16 presents 12 specific criteria to judge a combination. If the 12 criteria are met, then the acquisition *must* be accounted for as a pooling of interests. The criteria leave some room for judgment in determining if the pooling method should be used.

A pooling of interests involves an exchange of voting common stock. (Common stock is reviewed under owners' equity later in this chapter.) With the pooling method, the recorded assets and liabilities of the firms involved are carried forward to the combined entity at their previous recorded amounts. Income of the combined firm includes income of the constituents for the entire period. The prior years are restated to show the combined firms as merged (pooled).

Since the pooling method results in the acquired assets and liabilities being carried forward at the amount that they were previously recorded, this results in a net understatement of assets, liabilities, and owners' equity in relation to the acquisition values. This will lead to a subsequent overstatement of income because of the reduced expenses subsequently recognized. With the pooling method, the resulting retained earnings in owners' equity represents the prior retained earnings of both companies.

The purchase method views the business combination as the acquisition of one entity by another. The firm doing the acquiring records the identifiable assets and liabilities at fair value at the date of acquisition. The difference between the fair value of the identifiable assets and liabilities and the amount paid is recorded as goodwill. Since goodwill must be amortized to expense over its useful life, but not longer than 40 years, this can result in substantial subsequent expense.

With a purchase, the acquiring firm picks up the income of the acquired firm from the date of acquisition. Retained earnings of the acquired firm do not continue.

BASIC ELEMENTS OF THE BALANCE SHEET

A **balance sheet** shows the financial condition of an accounting entity as of a particular date. The balance sheet consists of assets, the resources of the firm; liabilities, the debts of the firm; and stockholders' equity, the owners' interest in the firm.

The assets are derived from two sources, creditors and owners. At any point in time, the assets must equal the contribution of the creditors and owners. The accounting equation expresses this relationship:

Assets = Liabilities + Owners' Equity

On the balance sheet, the assets equal the liabilities plus the owners' equity. This may be presented side by side (account form) or with the assets at the top and the liabilities and owners' equity at the bottom (report form). Exhibit 3-1, pages 96 and 97, presents a typical account form format, and Exhibit 3-2, page 98, presents a typical report form format.

Balance sheet formats differ across nations. For example, nations influenced by British financial reporting report the least liquid assets first and cash last.

Assets

Assets are probable future economic benefits obtained or controlled by an entity as a result of past transactions or events.[1] Assets may be *physical,* such as land, buildings, inventory of supplies, material, or finished products. Assets may also be *intangible,* such as patents and trademarks.

Assets are normally divided into two major categories: current and noncurrent (long-term). **Current assets** are assets (1) in the form of cash, (2) that will normally be realized in cash, or (3) that conserve the use of cash during the operating cycle of a firm or for one year, whichever is longer. The *operating cycle* covers the time between the acquisition of inventory and the realization of cash from selling the inventory. Noncurrent or **long-term assets** take longer than a year or an operating cycle to be converted to cash or to conserve cash. Some industries, such as banking (financial institutions), insurance, and real estate, do not divide assets (or liabilities) into current and noncurrent.

When a significant subsidiary is consolidated from an industry that does not use the concept of current and noncurrent, then the consolidated statements will not use the concept of current and noncurrent. These companies often present supplementary statements, handling the subsidiary as an investment (nonconsolidated).

For example, the Dana Corporation is primarily in the business of manufacturing and marketing vehicular and industrial components.

EXHIBIT 3-1 **FLOWERS INDUSTRIES, INC.**
Consolidated Balance Sheets (Statement of Financial Position)
Account Form

(In thousands, except share data)	July 1, 1995	July 2, 1994
Assets		
Current assets:		
Cash and temporary investments (Note 1)	$ 31,836	$ 19,758
Accounts receivable (Note 1)	93,134	81,161
Inventories (Notes 1 and 2)	53,634	59,714
Prepaid expenses	3,675	3,525
Deferred income taxes (Note 9)	6,755	11,273
	189,034	175,431
Property, plant, and equipment (Notes 1 and 4):		
Land	21,439	15,475
Buildings	153,947	142,116
Machinery and equipment	371,869	332,804
Furniture, fixtures, and transportation equipment	22,264	34,858
Construction in progress	60,865	38,849
	630,384	564,102
Less: Accumulated depreciation	(255,919)	(243,846)
	374,465	320,256
Other assets and deferred charges:		
Notes receivable from distributors (Notes 1 and 3)	55,699	37,746
Other long-term assets	27,442	16,631
	83,141	54,377
Cost in-excess of net tangible assets	10,337	10,442
Less: Accumulated amortization (Note 1)	(1,056)	(824)
	9,281	9,618
	$ 655,921	$ 559,682

Dana has a significant financial subsidiary, Dana Credit Corporation (DCC). Dana consolidates this subsidiary and presents the balance sheet without the concept of current and noncurrent. Dana presents the balance sheet and income statement of DCC in Footnote 22, Significant Subsidiary.

Current Assets Current assets are listed on the balance sheet in order of **liquidity** (the ability to be converted to cash). Current assets typically include cash, marketable securities, short-term receivables, inventories, and prepaids. In some cases, assets other than these may be classified as current. If so, management is indicating that it expects the asset to be converted into

EXHIBIT 3-1 (concluded)

Liabilities and Stockholders' Equity		
Current liabilities:		
Long-term debt (Note 4)	$ 6,243	$ 7,659
Obligations under capital leases	1,677	1,299
Accounts payable	66,159	58,916
Accrued taxes other than income taxes	4,599	4,398
Income taxes (Note 9)	3,321	833
Accrued compensation, interest, and other liabilities		
(Note 6)	64,655	47,239
	146,654	120,344
Long-term notes payable (Note 4)	99,251	77,422
Obligations under capital leases	3,798	3,900
Industrial revenue bonds (Note 4)	17,895	11,564
Deferred income taxes (Note 9)	39,538	36,296
Deferred income (Note 1)	44,804	28,925
Other long-term liabilities (Note 4)		5,500
Commitments and contingencies (Note 5)		
Common stockholders' equity (Note 7):		
Common stock—$.625 par value, authorized		
100,000,000 shares, issued 39,393,817		
and 38,342,075 shares, respectively	24,621	23,964
Capital in excess of par value	67,617	51,038
Retained earnings	236,645	225,601
Less: Common stock in treasury, 985,337		
and 840,301 shares, respectively	(17,763)	(15,200)
Restricted Stock Award and Executive		
Incentive Award (Note 7)	(7,139)	(9,672)
	509,267	439,338
	$ 655,921	$ 559,682

cash during the operating cycle or within a year, whichever is longer. An example is land held for immediate disposal. Exhibit 3-3, page 99, includes the items that the 1995 edition of *Accounting Trends & Techniques* reported as being disclosed as other current assets. The definition of current assets excludes restricted cash, investments for purposes of control, long-term receivables, the cash surrender value of life insurance, land and other natural resources, depreciable assets, and long-term prepayments.

Cash **Cash,** the most liquid asset, includes negotiable checks and unrestricted balances in checking accounts, as well as cash on hand. Savings accounts are classified as cash even though the bank may not release the money for a specific period of time. Exhibit 3-4, page 100, illustrates the presentation of cash.

EXHIBIT 3-2   HARSCO CORPORATION
Consolidated Balance Sheets (Statement of Financial Position)
Report Form

	December 31	
(In thousands, except share amounts)	1995	1994
Assets		
Current assets:		
Cash and cash equivalents	$ 76,669	$ 43,550
Notes and accounts receivables, less allowance		
for uncollectible accounts ($8,256 and $7,285)	272,858	350,578
Inventories	123,285	121,199
Other current assets	60,954	21,432
Total current assets	533,766	536,759
Property, plant, and equipment, net	459,809	434,968
Cost in excess of net assets of business acquired, less		
accumulated amortization ($34,464 and $25,912)	205,801	213,480
Investments	21,007	43,711
Investments in unconsolidated entities	45,604	32,312
Other assets	44,675	53,419
	$1,310,662	$1,314,649
Liabilities		
Current liabilities:		
Short-term borrowing	$ 5,704	$ 14,236
Current maturities of long-term debt	103,043	11,502
Accounts payable	112,736	92,166
Accrued compensation	41,304	37,837
Income taxes	17,671	10,971
Dividends payable	9,520	9,317
Other current liabilities	98,534	106,392
Total current liabilities	388,512	282,421
Long-term debt	179,926	340,246
Deferred income taxes	36,061	29,217
Insurance liabilities	37,298	44,560
Other liabilities	42,874	36,983
	684,671	733,427
COMMITMENTS AND CONTINGENCIES		
Shareholders' equity		
Preferred stock, Series A junior participating		
cumulative preferred stock	—	—
Common stock, par value $1.25; issued 32,537,880		
and 32,343,553 shares, respectively	40,672	40,429
Additional paid-in capital	101,183	94,070
Cumulative translation adjustments	(19,852)	(16,020)
Cumulative pension liability adjustments	(413)	(99)
Retained earnings	713,774	653,996
	835,364	772,376
Treasury stock, at cost (7,486,331 and 7,161,303		
shares, respectively)	(209,373)	(191,154)
	625,991	581,222
	$1,310,662	$1,314,649

EXHIBIT 3-3   **Other Current Asset Items**

	Number of Companies			
Nature of Asset	*1994*	*1993*	*1992*	*1991*
Deferred income taxes	363	317	247	192
Property held for sale	36	36	28	35
Unbilled costs	28	20	23	24
Advances or deposits	9	10	6	10
Other—identified	29	33	29	35

Source: Accounting Trends & Techniques, copyright © 1995 by American Institute of Certified Public Accountants, Inc., p. 182.   Reprinted with permission.

Marketable Securities   **Marketable securities** (also labeled short-term investments) are characterized by their marketability at a readily determinable market price.   A firm holds marketable securities to earn a return on near-cash resources.   Management must intend to convert these assets to cash during the current period for them to be classified as marketable securities.

The carrying basis of debt and equity marketable securities is fair value. Refer to Exhibit 3-4 for a presentation of marketable securities.

Accounts Receivable   **Accounts receivable** are monies due on accounts from customers that arise from sales or services rendered.   Accounts receivable are shown net of allowances to reflect their realizable value.   This amount is expected to be collected.   The most typical allowances are for bad debts (uncollectible accounts).   Other allowances may account for expected sales discounts, which are given for prompt payment or for sales returns. These types of allowances recognize expenses in the period of sale, at which time the allowance is established.   In future periods, when the losses occur, they are charged to the allowance.   Exhibit 3-4 presents the accounts receivable of Norfolk Southern (less allowances).   At year-end 1995, the firm expects to realize $703,500,000.   The gross receivables can be reconciled as follows:

Receivables, net	$703,500,000
Plus: Allowances	19,100,000
Receivables, gross	$722,600,000

Other receivables may also be included in current assets.   These receivables may result from tax refund claims, contracts, investees, finance installment notes or accounts, employees, and the sale of assets.[2]

EXHIBIT 3-4   NORFOLK SOUTHERN
Illustration of Cash, Marketable Securities, and Accounts Receivable

	As of December 31	
	1995	1994
	($ in millions)	
Assets		
Current assets:		
Cash and cash equivalents	$ 67.7	$ 57.0
Short-term investments	261.3	249.7
Accounts receivable net of allowance		
for doubtful accounts of $19.1 million		
and $21.9 million, respectively	703.5	726.6
Materials and supplies	61.7	61.9
Deferred income taxes (Note 3)	144.7	137.0
Other current assets	103.9	105.3
Total current assets	1,342.8	1,337.5
Investments (Note 4)	231.7	172.8
Properties less accumulated depreciation (Note 5)	9,258.8	8,987.1
Other assets	71.5	90.4
Total assets	$10,904.8	$10,587.8

Inventories   **Inventories** are the balance of goods on hand. In a manufacturing firm, they include raw materials, work in process, and finished goods, which are carried at the lower of cost or market.

Raw Materials   These are goods purchased for direct use in manufacturing a product, and they become part of the product. For example, in the manufacture of shirts, the fabric and buttons would be raw materials.

Work in Process   Work in process represents goods started but not ready for sale. Work in process includes the cost of materials, labor costs for workers directly involved in the manufacture, and factory overhead. Factory overhead includes such cost items as rent, indirect wages, and maintenance.

Finished Goods   Finished goods are inventory ready for sale. These inventory costs also include the cost of materials, labor costs for workers directly involved in the manufacture, and a portion of factory overhead.

Supplies   These are items used indirectly in the production of goods or services. They could include register tapes, pencils, or sewing machine needles for the shirt factory.

Since retailing and wholesaling firms do not engage in the manufacture of a product but only in the sale, their only inventory item is merchandise. These firms do not have raw materials or work in process inventory.

Inventory Cost   The costing of inventory is a difficult problem. For example, a firm buys two units of raw materials. The first unit costs $5; the second, $7. If, at the end of the year, the firm has used only one of them, what is the cost (expense) of the unit used? What is the cost assigned to the unit in inventory? Various costing methods exist; four methods are explained briefly in the paragraphs that follow.

FIFO   **FIFO, "First-in, first-out,"** assumes that those units first purchased are the first sold. By necessity, this would be the flow pattern for a product such as bananas. In the above example, the cost of sales would be $5; inventory, $7. FIFO can be selected as the cost flow assumption even if this assumption does not agree with the actual physical flow.

LIFO   **LIFO, "Last-in, first-out,"** assumes that those units last purchased are the first sold. This would apply to the sale of bulk nails, where new shipments are poured on top of old ones and subsequently sold first. In our example, the cost of goods sold would be $7; the inventory, $5. Again, this method can be selected as the cost flow assumption even if this assumption does not agree with the actual physical flow.

In a period of rising prices, LIFO results in the most realistic figure for cost of goods sold, in terms of current cost. LIFO also has the advantage of providing the largest tax break during such periods. FIFO results in the most realistic current value for inventory, but results in higher taxes.

The inventory costing method can have a material effect not only on the inventory account on the balance sheet, but also on cost of goods sold and reported income. The inventory costing method can be particularly important during times of significant inflation. During times of inflation, LIFO can result in materially lower income and lower inventory balance than would FIFO.

Under LIFO, a reduction in inventory matches old costs against current year's revenue. These old costs are often substantially less than the current costs to replace the inventory. Thus, income is increased as revenue is matched with old costs. The effect of matching old costs against current revenue is referred to as the *LIFO layers effect.*

A footnote in the 1995 annual report of General Motors described a reduction in LIFO inventory. This footnote reads in part as follows:

As a result of decreases in U.S. inventories, certain inventory quantities carried at lower LIFO costs prevailing in prior years, as compared with current purchases, were liquidated in 1993. This inventory adjustment improved pretax operating results by approximately $134.4 million in 1993, primarily from the sale of AGT.

LIFO accounting was started in the United States. It is now accepted in some other countries.

Average   **Averaging methods** lump the costs to determine a midpoint. In the example, the average is $6. The cost of goods sold would be $6; inventory would also be $6. An average method falls between LIFO and FIFO.

Specific Identification   The **specific identification method** identifies the items in inventory as coming from specific purchases. Assume that the item in inventory was the second item, costing $7. The inventory cost would be $7, and the cost of sales would be $5.

Exhibit 3-5 presents the inventory of General Motors. This includes the footnotes that relate to inventories. Notice that more than one costing method is used.

Lower-of-Cost-or-Market Rule   We have reviewed the inventory cost-based measurements of FIFO, LIFO, average, and specific identification. These cost-based measurements are all considered to be historical cost approaches. The accounting profession decided that "a departure from the cost basis of inventory pricing is required when the utility of the goods is no longer as great as its cost."[3] Utility of the goods has been measured through market values. When market value of inventory falls below cost, it is necessary to write the inventory down to the lower market value. This is known as the **lower-of-cost-or-market (LCM) rule**. Market is defined in terms of current replacement cost, either by purchase or manufacture.

Following the LCM rule, inventories can be written down below cost but never up above cost. The LCM rule provides for the recognition of the loss in utility during the period in which the loss occurs. The LCM rule is consistent with both the matching and the conservatism assumptions.

The LCM rule is used by countries other than the United States. As indicated, market is defined in the United States in terms of current replacement cost. Market in other countries may be defined differently, such as "net realizable value."

Prepaids   A **prepaid** is an expenditure made in advance of the use of the service or goods. It represents future benefits that have resulted from past transactions. For example, if insurance is paid in advance for three years, at the end of the first year, two years' worth of the outlay will be prepaid. The entity retains the right to be covered by insurance for two more years.

EXHIBIT 3-5   **GENERAL MOTORS**
Inventory

Consolidated Balance Sheet (in Part)

Assets

	December 31	
(Dollars in millions)	**1995**	**1994**
Inventories (less allowances) (Note 5)	$11,529.5	$10,127.8

Note 5. Inventories
Major Classes of Inventories

	December 31	
(Dollars in millions)	**1995**	**1994**
Productive material, work in process, and supplies	$ 6,570.4	$ 5,478.3
Finished product, service parts, etc.	4,959.1	4,649.5
Total	$11,529.5	$10,127.8
Memo: Increase in LIFO inventories if valued at FIFO	$ 2,424.4	$ 2,535.9

Inventories are stated generally at cost, which is not in excess of market. The cost of substantially all U.S. inventories other than the inventories of Saturn Corporation (Saturn) and Hughes is determined by the last-in, first-out (LIFO) method. The cost of non-U.S. Saturn and Hughes inventories is determined generally by the first-in, first-out (FIFO) or average cost methods.

As a result of decreases in U.S. inventories, certain inventory quantities carried at lower LIFO costs prevailing in prior years, as compared with current purchases, were liquidated in 1993. This inventory adjustment improved pretax operating results by approximately $134.4 million in 1993, primarily from the sale of AGT.

Typical prepaids include advertising, taxes, insurance, promotion costs, and early payments on long-term contracts. Prepaids are often not disclosed separately but are part of "other." In Exhibit 3-1, the prepaid account is disclosed separately. In Exhibit 3-2, prepaids are part of "other."

Long-Term Assets   Long-term assets are usually divided into four categories: tangible assets, investments, intangible assets, and other.

Tangible Assets   These are the physical facilities used in the operations of the business. The tangible assets of land, buildings, machinery, and construction in progress will now be reviewed. Accumulated depreciation related to buildings and machinery will also be reviewed.

Land   Land is shown at acquisition cost and is not depreciated because land does not get used up. Land containing resources that will be used up, however, such as mineral deposits and timberlands, is subject to depletion. Depletion expense attempts to measure the wearing away of these resources. It is similar to depreciation except that depreciation deals with a tangible fixed asset and depletion deals with a natural resource.

Buildings   Structures are presented at cost plus the cost of permanent improvements. Buildings are depreciated (expensed) over their estimated useful life.

Machinery   Machinery is listed at historical cost, including delivery and installation, plus any material improvements that extend its life or increase the quantity or quality of service. Machinery is depreciated (expensed) over its estimated useful life.

Construction in Progress   Construction in progress represents cost incurred for projects under construction. These costs will be transferred to the proper tangible asset account upon completion of construction. The firm cannot use these assets while they are under construction. Some analysis is directed at how efficiently the company is using operating assets. This analysis can be distorted by construction in progress, since construction in progress is classified as part of tangible assets. To avoid this distortion, classify construction in progress under long-term assets, other.

Accumulated Depreciation   Depreciation is the process of allocating the cost of buildings and machinery over the periods benefited. The depreciation expense taken each period is accumulated in a separate account (Accumulated Depreciation). Accumulated depreciation, a contra asset, is subtracted from the cost of plant and equipment. The net amount is the **book value** of the asset. It does not represent the current market value of the asset.

There are a number of depreciation methods that a firm can use. Often a firm depreciates an asset under one method for financial statements and another for income tax returns. A firm often wants to depreciate slowly for the financial statements because this results in the highest immediate income and highest asset balance. The same firm would want to depreciate faster for income tax returns because this results in the lowest immediate income and thus lower income taxes. Over the life of an asset, the total depreciation will be the same regardless of the depreciation method selected.

Three factors are usually considered when computing depreciation: (1) the asset cost, (2) length of the life of the asset, and (3) its salvage value when retired from service. The length of the asset's life and the salvage value must be estimated at the time that the asset is placed in service. These estimates may be later changed, if warranted.

Exhibit 3-6 indicates the depreciation methods used for financial reporting purposes by the firms surveyed for the 1995 edition of *Accounting*

EXHIBIT 3-6 Depreciation Methods, 1991-1994

	Number of Companies			
	1994	*1993*	*1992*	*1991*
Straight-line	573	570	564	558
Declining-balance	27	26	26	28
Sum-of-the-years'-digits	9	9	12	8
Accelerated method—not specified	49	56	62	70
Units-of-production	49	46	47	50
Other	11	9	5	7

Source: Accounting Trends & Techniques, copyright © 1995 by American Institute of Certified Public Accountants, Inc., p. 386. Reprinted with permission.

Trends & Techniques. The most popular methods were straight-line, accelerated methods, and units-of-production. Many firms use more than one depreciation method.

The following assumptions will be made to illustrate depreciation methods:

1. Cost of asset—$10,000

2. Estimated life of asset—5 years

3. Estimated salvage (or residual) value—$2,000

4. Estimated total hours of use—16,000

Straight-Line Method   The **straight-line method** recognizes depreciation in equal amounts over the estimated life of the asset. Compute depreciation using the straight-line method as follows:

$$\frac{\textbf{Cost – Salvage value}}{\textbf{Estimated life}} = \textbf{Annual depreciation}$$

For the asset used for illustration, the annual depreciation would be computed as follows:

$$\frac{\textbf{\$10,000 – \$2,000}}{\textbf{5 years}} = \textbf{\$1,600}$$

The $1,600 depreciation amount would be recognized each year of the five-year life of the asset. Do not depreciate the salvage value.

Declining-Balance Method   The **declining-balance method**, an accelerated method, applies double the straight-line rate to the declining book value
(cost minus accumulated depreciation) to achieve a declining depreciation
charge over the estimated life of the asset. Compute depreciation using the
declining balance method as follows:

$$\frac{1}{\text{Estimated life of asset}} \times 2 \times \begin{matrix}\text{Book amount} \\ \text{at beginning of} \\ \text{the year}\end{matrix} = \text{Annual depreciation}$$

For the asset used for illustration, the first year's depreciation would
be computed as follows:

$$\frac{1}{5} \times 2 \times (\$10,000 - 0) = \$4,000$$

The declining-balance method results in the following depreciation
amounts for each of the five years of the asset's life.

Year	Cost	Accumulated Depreciation at Beginning of Year	Book Amount at Beginning of Year	Depreciation for Year	Book Amount at End of Year
1	$10,000	—	$10,000	$4,000	$6,000
2	10,000	$4,000	6,000	2,400	3,600
3	10,000	6,400	3,600	1,440	2,160
4	10,000	7,840	2,160	160	2,000
5	10,000	8,000	2,000	—	2,000

Estimated salvage value is not considered in the formula, but the asset
should not be depreciated below the estimated salvage value. For the sample
asset, the formula produced a depreciation amount of $864 in the fourth
year. Only $160 depreciation can be used in the fourth year because the $160
amount brings the book amount of the asset down to the salvage value.
Once the book amount is equal to the salvage value, no additional depreciation may be taken.

Sum-of-the-Years'-Digits Method   The **sum-of-the-years'-digits
method** is an accelerated depreciation method. Thus, the depreciation
expense declines steadily over the estimated life of the asset. This method
takes a fraction each year times the cost less salvage value. The numerator
of the fraction changes each year. It is the remaining number of years of
the asset's life. The denominator of the fraction remains constant; it is the
sum of the digits representing the years of the asset's life. Compute depreciation using the sum-of-the-years'-digits method as follows:

Remaining number of years
of life

$$\frac{\text{Remaining number of years of life}}{\text{Sum of the digits representing the years of life}} \quad \text{x} \quad (\text{Cost} - \text{Salvage}) \quad = \quad \text{Annual depreciation}$$

For the asset used for illustration, the first year's depreciation would be computed as follows:

$$\frac{5}{(5 + 4 + 3 + 2 + 1) \text{ or } 15} \quad \text{x} \quad (\$10,000 - \$2,000) \quad = \quad \$2,666.67$$

The sum-of-the-years'-digits method results in the following depreciation amounts for each year of the five years of the asset's life.

Year	Cost Less Salvage Value	Fraction	Depreciation for Year	Accumulated Depreciation at End of Year	Book Amount at End of Year
1	$8,000	5/15	$2,666.67	$2,666.67	$7,333.33
2	8,000	4/15	2,133.33	4,800.00	5,200.00
3	8,000	3/15	1,600.00	6,400.00	3,600.00
4	8,000	2/15	1,066.67	7,466.67	2,533.33
5	8,000	1/15	533.33	8,000.00	2,000.00

Unit-of-Production Method   The **unit-of-production method** relates depreciation to the output capacity of the asset, estimated for the life of the asset. The capacity is stated in terms most appropriate for the asset, such as units of production, hours of use, or miles. Hours of use will be used for the asset in our example. For the life of the asset, it is estimated that there will be 16,000 hours of use. The estimated output capacity is divided into the cost of the asset less the salvage value to determine the depreciation per unit of output. For the example asset, the depreciation per hour of use would be $.50 [(cost of asset, $10,000 – salvage, $2,000) divided by 16,000 hours].

The depreciation for each year is then determined by multiplying the depreciation per unit of output by the output for that year. Assuming that the output was 2,000 hours during the first year, the depreciation for that year would be $1,000 ($.50 x 2,000). Further depreciation cannot be taken when the accumulated depreciation equals the cost of the asset less the salvage value. For the example asset, this will be when accumulated depreciation equals $8,000.

In Exhibit 3-7, Dana Corporation presents these assets as property, plant, and equipment, net. This is a typical presentation—not disclosing the detail

EXHIBIT 3-7   DANA CORPORATION
Properties and Depreciation

Balance Sheet (in Part)

(In millions)	December 31 1994	1995
Assets (in Part)		
Property, plant, and equipment, net	$1,347.2	$1,649.5

Note 1 (in Part)

Properties and Depreciation

Property, plant, and equipment is valued at historical cost. Depreciation is computed over the estimated useful lives of property, plant, and equipment using primarily the straight-line method for financial reporting purposes and primarily accelerated depreciation methods for federal income tax purposes.

contents. Dana uses primarily the straight-line method of depreciation for financial reporting purposes and primarily accelerated depreciation methods for federal income tax purposes.

Leases   Leases are classified as *operating* leases or *capital* leases. If the lease is in substance an ownership arrangement, it is a capital lease; otherwise, the lease is an operating lease. According to FASB Statement No. 13, equipment leased under a capital lease is classified as a long-term asset. It is shown net of amortization (depreciation) and listed with plant, property, and equipment. (The discounted value of the obligation, a liability, will be part current and part long term.) Chapter 8 covers the topic of leases in more length.

Investments   Long-term investments, usually stocks and bonds of other companies, are often held to maintain a business relationship or to exercise control. Long-term investments are different from marketable securities, where the intent is to hold for short-term profits and to achieve liquidity. (Financial reports often refer to marketable securities as investments.)

SFAS No. 115 directs that debt securities under investments are to be classified as held-to-maturity securities or available-for-sale securities. *Held-to-maturity securities* are securities that the firm has the intent and ability to hold to maturity. Debt securities classified as held-to-maturity securities are carried at amortized cost. Debt securities classified as available-for-sale securities are carried at fair value.

SFAS No. 115 directs that equity securities under investments are to be carried at fair value. An exception for fair value is used for common stock where there is significant influence. For these common stock investments, the investment is carried under the equity method. Under the equity method, the cost is adjusted for the proportionate share of the rise (fall) in retained profits of the subsidiary (investee). For example, a parent company owns 40% of a subsidiary company, purchased at a cost of $400,000. When the subsidiary company earns $100,000, the parent company increases the investment account by 40% of $100,000, or $40,000. When the subsidiary company declares dividends of $20,000, the parent company decreases the investment account by 40% of $20,000, or $8,000. This decrease occurs because the investment account changes in direct proportion to the retained earnings of the subsidiary (investee).

Investments can also include tangible assets not currently used in operations, such as an idle plant, as well as monies set aside in special funds, such as sinking funds or pensions. The investments of Zurn are illustrated in Exhibit 3-8, page 110.

Intangibles   **Intangibles** are nonphysical assets, such as patents and copyrights. Intangibles are recorded at historical cost and amortized over their useful lives or their legal lives, whichever is shorter. Current GAAP requires amortization for intangibles over a period of time that cannot exceed 40 years (APB Opinion No. 17). Intangibles purchased prior to 1970 (the passage of APB Opinion No. 17) do not have to be amortized. Also, research and development costs must be expensed as incurred (FASB Statement No. 2). This requirement is not common in many other countries. The following are examples of intangibles that are recorded in the United States:

Goodwill   **Goodwill** arises from the acquisition of a business for a sum greater than the physical asset value, usually because the business has unusual earning power. It may result from good customer relations, a well-respected owner, and so on.

Goodwill can be a substantial asset. Therefore, the amortization period selected can have a material influence on earnings. In the United States the maximum amortization period is **40 years**.

The global treatment of goodwill varies significantly. In some countries, goodwill is not recorded because it is charged to owners' equity. In this case there is no influence to reported income. In some countries, goodwill is expensed in the year acquired. In many countries that record goodwill, the maximum amortization period is much less than it is in the United States.

Patents   **Patents**, exclusive legal rights granted to an inventor for a period of 20 years, are valued at their acquisition cost, not their future benefits.

Trademarks   Distinctive names or symbols are termed **trademarks**. Rights are granted to the holder for 10 years and may be renewed every 10 years thereafter.

EXHIBIT 3-8 ZURN
Investments

Consolidated Financial Position (in Part)

(Thousands)	March 31 1995	1994
Assets		
Current assets:		
Cash and equivalents	$ 6,360	$ 4,137
Marketable securities	48,478	61,296
Accounts receivable	115,373	132,328
Inventories and contracts in progress	84,264	86,379
Income taxes	38,751	41,880
Other assets	5,153	5,642
Total current assets	298,379	331,662
Property, plant, and equipment	56,162	57,003
Investments (Note)	35,447	35,958
Other assets	24,708	23,270
	$414,696	$447,893

Note
Investments

(Thousands)	March 31 1995	1994
Irrevocable trust securities for nonqualified pension, deferred compensation, and other employee plans	$15,350	$15,611
Notes receivable	8,426	8,180
Sales-type leases	3,726	3,786
Business ventures	7,659	7,843
Other	286	538
	$35,447	$35,958

Organizational Costs The legal costs incurred when a business is organized are carried as an asset and are usually written off over a period of five years or longer.

Franchises These are the legal right to operate under a particular corporate name, providing trade-name products or services.

Exhibit 3-9 displays the Lands' End presentation of intangibles. It consists primarily of goodwill, less accumulated amortization.

EXHIBIT 3-9 LANDS' END, INC.
Intangibles

Consolidated Balance Sheets (in Part)

(In thousands)	February 1, 1996	January 27, 1995
Assets		
Total current assets (detail excluded)	$ 222,089	$ 198,168
Property, plant, and equipment, net (detail excluded)	98,985	96,991
Intangibles	2,423	2,453
Total assets	$ 323,497	$ 297,612

Note to Consolidated Financial Statements
Note 1. Summary of significant accounting policies (in part)

Intangibles

Intangible assets consist primarily of goodwill which is being amortized over 40 years on a straight-line basis. Other intangibles are amortized up to a period of 5 years. Total accumulated amortization of these intangibles was $0.4 million and $.03 million at February 2, 1996, and January 27, 1995, respectively.

Other Assets Firms will occasionally have assets that do not fit into one of the previously discussed classifications. These assets, termed "other," might include noncurrent receivables and noncurrent prepaids. Exhibit 3-10, page 112, summarizes types of other assets from a financial statement compilation in *Accounting Trends & Techniques*.

Liabilities

Liabilities are probable future sacrifices of economic benefits arising from present obligations of a particular entity to transfer assets or provide services to other entities in the future as a result of past transactions or events.[4] Liabilities are usually classified as either *current* or *long-term* liabilities.

Current Liabilities Current liabilities are obligations whose liquidation is reasonably expected to require the use of existing current assets or the creation of other current liabilities within a year or an operating cycle, whichever is longer. They include the following items.

Payables These include short-term obligations created by the acquisition of goods and services, such as accounts payable (for materials or goods bought for use or resale), wages payable, and taxes payable. Payables may also be in the form of a written promissory note, notes payable.

EXHIBIT 3-10   Other Noncurrent Assets

	Number of Companies			
	1994	*1993*	*1992*	*1991*
Deferred income taxes	167	169	95	34
Prepaid pension costs	95	83	81	87
Property held for sale	55	63	73	60
Debt issue costs	47	46	34	45
Software	41	37	29	35
Segregated cash or securities	38	23	33	33
Assets of nonhomogeneous operations	25	30	29	26
Cash surrender value of life insurance	24	18	18	18
Assets leased to others	23	14	19	25
Start-up costs	20	19	17	15
Other identified noncurrent assets	50	42	50	48

Source: Accounting Trends & Techniques, copyright © 1995 by American Institute of Certified Public Accountants, Inc., p. 220. Reprinted with permission.

Unearned Income   Payments collected in advance of the performance of service are termed *unearned.* They include rent income and subscription income. Rather than cash, a future service or good is due the customer.

Exhibit 3-11 shows the current liabilities of Wausau Paper Mills Company.

Other Current Liabilities   There are many other current obligations requiring payment during the year. Exhibit 3-12 displays other current liabilities reported by *Accounting Trends & Techniques* in 1995.

Long-Term Liabilities   Long-term liabilities are those due in a period exceeding one year or one operating cycle, whichever is longer. Long-term liabilities are generally of two types: financing arrangements of assets and operational obligations.

Liabilities Relating to Financing Agreements   The long-term liabilities that are financing arrangements of assets usually require systematic payment of principal and interest. They include notes payable, bonds payable, and credit agreements.

Notes Payable   Promissory notes due in periods greater than one year or one operating cycle, whichever is longer, are classified as long term. If secured by a claim against real property, they are called *mortgage notes.*

Bonds Payable   A **bond** is a debt security normally issued with $1,000 par per bond and requiring semiannual interest payments based on the coupon rate.

EXHIBIT 3-11 **WAUSAU PAPER MILLS COMPANY**
Current Liabilities

Consolidated Balance Sheets (in Part)

	As of August 31	
(All dollar amounts in thousands)	**1995**	**1994**
Current liabilities:		
Current maturities of long-term debt	$ 6,425	$ 462
Accounts payable	24,426	25,325
Accrued salaries and wages	7,480	8,960
Accrued and other liabilities	13,161	11,117
Accrued income taxes	1,259	192
Total current liabilities	$ 52,751	$46,056

EXHIBIT 3-12 **Other Current Liabilities**

	Number of Companies			
	1994	*1993*	*1992*	*1991*
Taxes other than federal income taxes	139	132	138	149
Estimated costs related to discontinued operations	130	142	114	91
Interest	124	121	137	139
Dividends payable	78	82	88	84
Insurance	78	75	79	83
Customer advances, deposits	55	58	49	54
Warranties	54	54	51	48
Deferred revenue	54	47	48	53
Deferred taxes	53	42	33	34
Environmental costs	53	39	27	23
Advertising	39	44	40	33
Billings on uncompleted contracts	31	31	28	25
Due to affiliated companies	22	24	14	19
Other—described	115	101	100	104

Source: Accounting Trends & Techniques, copyright © 1995 by American Institute of Certified Public Accountants, Inc., p. 243. Reprinted with permission.

Bonds are not necessarily sold at par. They are sold at a premium if the stated rate of interest exceeds the market rate and at a discount if the stated rate of interest is less than the market rate. If sold for more than par, a premium on bonds payable arises and increases bonds payable to obtain the current carrying value. Similarly, if sold at less than par, a discount on bonds payable arises and decreases bonds payable on the balance sheet. Each of these accounts, discount or premium, will be gradually written off (amortized) to interest expense over the life of the bond. At the maturity date, the carrying value of bonds payable will be equal to the par value. Amortization of bond discount increases interest expense; amortization of bond premium reduces it. APB Opinion No. 21 establishes the accounting and reporting requirements for discounts and premiums.

Bonds that are convertible into common stock at the option of the bondholder (creditor) are exchanged for a specified number of common shares, and the bondholder becomes a common stockholder. Often, convertible bonds are issued when the common stock price is low, in management's opinion, and the firm eventually wants to increase its common equity. By issuing a convertible bond, the firm may get more for the specified number of common shares than could be obtained by issuing the common shares. The conversion feature allows the firm to issue the bond at a more favorable interest rate than would be the case with a bond lacking the conversion feature. Also, the tax deductible interest paid on the convertible bond reduces the firm's cost for these funds. If common stock had been issued, the dividend on the common stock would not be tax deductible. Thus, a firm may find that issuing a convertible bond can be an attractive means of raising common equity funds in the long run. However, if the firm's stock price stays depressed after issuing a convertible bond, then the firm will have the convertible bond liability until the bond comes due. Convertible bonds of Freeport-McMoran are displayed in Exhibit 3-13.

Credit Agreements   Many firms arrange loan commitments from banks or insurance companies for future loans. Often, the firm does not intend to obtain these loans but has arranged the credit agreement just in case a need exists for additional funds. Such credit agreements do not represent a liability unless the firm actually requests the funds. From the point of view of analysis, the existence of a substantial credit agreement is a positive condition in that it could relieve pressure on the firm if there is a problem in meeting existing liabilities.

In return for giving a credit agreement, the bank or insurance company obtains a fee. This commitment fee is usually a percentage of the unused portion of the commitment. Also, banks often require the firm to keep a specified sum in its bank account, referred to as a **compensating balance**. Exhibit 3-14 shows a credit agreement.

EXHIBIT 3-13   FREEPORT-McMORAN INC.
Convertible Bonds

Balance Sheets (in Part)

	December 31	
	1995	1994
	(In thousands)	
Liabilities (in Part)		
Long-term debt, less current portion (Note 4)	$359,501	$ 1,122,070

Note 4. Long-Term Debt

	December 31	
	1995	1994
	(In thousands)	
Notes payable:		
FTX credit agreement, average rate 7.1% in 1995 and 5.4% in 1994	$196,400	$ 370,000
Other	13,440	13,951
Publicly traded notes and debentures:		
Zero coupon convertible subordinated debentures	—	270,196
6.55% convertible subordinated notes	—	318,237
FRP 8 3/4% senior subordinated notes due 2004	150,000	150,000
	359,840	1,122,384
Less current portion, included in accounts payable	339	314
	$359,501	$ 1,122,070

EXHIBIT 3-14   COOPER TIRE & RUBBER COMPANY
Credit Agreements

1995 Annual Report
Note
Long-Term Debt (in Part) (Dollar amounts in thousands)

The Company has an agreement with four banks authorizing borrowings up to $120,000 with interest at varying rates. The proceeds may be used for general corporate purposes. The agreement provides that on March 1, 1999, the Company may convert any outstanding borrowings into a four-year term loan. A commitment fee is payable quarterly and is based on the daily unused portion of the $120,000. The credit facility supports the issuance of commercial paper. There were no borrowings under the agreement at December 31, 1995.

Liabilities Relating to Operational Obligations   Long-term liabilities relating to operational obligations include obligations arising from the operation of a business, mostly of a service nature such as pension obligations, postretirement benefit obligations other than pension plans, deferred taxes, and service warranties. Chapter 8 covers at length pensions and postretirement benefit obligations other than pension plans.

Deferred Taxes   Deferred taxes are caused by using different accounting methods for tax and reporting purposes. For example, a firm may use accelerated depreciation for tax purposes and straight-line depreciation for reporting purposes. This causes tax expense for reporting purposes to be higher than taxes payable according to the tax return. The difference is deferred tax. Any situation where revenue or expense is recognized in the financial statements in a different time period than for the tax return will create a deferred tax situation (asset or liability). For example, in the later years of the life of a fixed asset, straight-line depreciation will give higher depreciation and, therefore, lower net income than an accelerated method. Then tax expense for reporting purposes will be lower than taxes payable, and the deferred tax will be reduced (paid). Since firms often buy more and higher priced assets, however, the increase in deferred taxes may exceed the decrease. In this case a partial or a total reversal will not occur. The taxes may be deferred for a very long time, perhaps permanently. Chapter 8 covers deferred taxes in more detail.

Warranty Obligations   Warranty obligations are estimated obligations arising out of product warranties. Product warranties require the seller to correct any deficiencies in quantity, quality, or performance of the product or service for a specific period of time after the sale. Warranty obligations are estimated in order to recognize the obligation at the balance sheet date and to charge the expense to the period of the sale.

Exhibit 3-15 shows warranty obligations of the Ford Motor Company. Notice that these obligations are disclosed in both current liabilities and noncurrent liabilities as "dealer and customer allowances and claims."

Minority Interest   Minority interest reflects the ownership of minority shareholders in the equity of consolidated subsidiaries less than wholly owned. Minority interest does not represent a liability or stockholders' equity in the firm being analyzed. Consider the following simple example. Parent P owns 90% of the common stock of Subsidiary S.

	Parent P Balance Sheet December 31, 1996	Subsidiary S Balance Sheet December 31, 1996
	(In millions)	
Current assets	$100	$10
Investment in Subsidiary S	18	–
Other long-term assets	382	40
	$500	$50
Current liabilities	$100	$10
Long-term liabilities	200	20
Stockholders' equity	200	20
	$500	$50

EXHIBIT 3-15 FORD MOTOR COMPANY
Warranty Obligations

Note 7. Liabilities—Automotive

Current Liabilities
Included in accrued liabilities at December 31 were the following in millions.

	1995	1994
Dealer and customer allowances and claims	$ 7,824	$ 7,115
Employee benefit plans	2,225	2,130
Salaries, wages, and employer taxes	843	598
Postretirement benefits other than pensions	782	688
Other	1,718	1,412
Total accrued liabilities	$13,392	$11,943

Noncurrent Liabilities
Included in other liabilities at December 31 were the following in millions.

	1995	1994
Postretirement benefits other than pensions	$14,533	$14,025
Dealer and customer allowances and claims	5,514	6,044
Employee benefit plans	2,657	2,232
Unfunded pension obligation	627	362
Minority interest in net assets of subsidiaries	121	118
Other	2,225	2,139
Total other liabilities	$25,677	$24,920

In consolidation, the assets and liabilities of the subsidiary are added to those of the parent, with the elimination of the investment in Subsidiary S. Parent P owns 90% of the subsidiary's net assets of $20 ($50 – $30), and the minority shareholders own 10%.

This will be shown on the consolidated balance sheet:

PARENT P AND SUBSIDIARY
Consolidated Balance Sheet
December 31, 1996

	(In millions)
Current assets	$110
Long-term assets	422
	$532
Current liabilities	$110
Long-term liabilities	220
Minority interest	2
Stockholders' equity	200
	$532

Because of the nature of minority interest, it is usually presented after liabilities and before stockholders' equity. Some firms include minority interest in liabilities; others present it in stockholders' equity. Since minority interest is seldom material, consider it a liability to simplify the analysis. In a firm where the minority interest is material, the analysis can be performed twice—once with minority interest as a liability and then as a stockholders' equity item.

Including minority interest as a long-term liability is also conservative when analyzing a firm. The primary analysis should be conservative. Refer to Exhibit 3-16 for an illustration of minority interest.

Other Noncurrent Liabilities Many other noncurrent liabilities may be disclosed. It would not be practical to discuss all of the possibilities. An example would be deferred profit on sales.

Redeemable Preferred Stock Redeemable preferred stock is subject to mandatory redemption requirements or has a redemption feature outside the control of the issuer. If this feature is coupled with such characteristics as no vote or fixed return, often preferred stock and bond characteristics, then this type of preferred stock is more like debt than equity. For this reason, in 1979 the SEC issued Accounting Series Release No. 268, which requires that the three categories of stock—redeemable preferred stock, non-redeemable preferred stock, and common stock—not be totaled in the

EXHIBIT 3-16 FREEPORT-McMORAN INC.
Minority Interest

	December 31	
	1995	**1994**
	(In thousands)	
Liabilities and Stockholders' Equity		
Accounts payable and accrued liabilities	$ 180,766	$ 191,553
Long-term debt, less current portion	359,501	1,122,070
Accrued postretirement benefits and pension costs	170,542	158,707
Reclamation and mine shutdown reserves	128,981	112,777
Other liabilities and deferred credits	92,722	77,034
Minority interest	196,021	217,768
Stockholders' equity:		
Convertible exchangeable preferred stock, par value $1, at liquidation value, authorized 50,000,000 shares	50,084	250,000
Common stock, par value $0.01 and $1 per share, respectively, authorized 100,000,000 shares and 300,000,000 shares, respectively	337	166,365
Capital in excess of par value of common stock	522,694	—
Retained earnings (deficit)	92,746	(221,925)
Cumulative foreign currency translation adjustment	—	(2,555)
Common stock held in treasury— 6,016,800 and 4,863,200 shares, respectively, at cost	(473,924)	(422,352)
	191,937	(230,467)
Total liabilities and stockholders' equity	$ 1,320,470	$1,649,442

balance sheet. Further, the owners' equity section should not include redeemable preferred stock. Redeemable preferred stock is illustrated in Exhibit 3-17, page 120. Because redeemable preferred stock is more like debt than equity, consider it as part of total liabilities for purposes of financial statement analysis.

Owners' Equity

Ownership equity is the residual ownership interest in the assets of an entity that remains after deducting its liabilities.[5] Usually divided into two basic categories, paid-in capital and retained earnings, other accounts may appear in owners' equity that are usually presented separately from paid-in capital and retained earnings. Other accounts include foreign currency translation adjustments, unrealized decline in market value of investments, equity-oriented deferred compensation, and employee stock ownership plans (ESOPs).

EXHIBIT 3-17 TELEPHONE AND DATA SYSTEMS, INC.
Redeemable Preferred Stock

	December 31	
	1995	1994
Liabilities and Stockholders' Equity	(Dollars in thousands)	
Current Liabilities:		
Current portion of long-term debt and preferred shares	$ 49,233	$ 37,447
Notes payable	184,320	98,608
Accounts payable	122,886	112,967
Due to FCC-PCS licenses	—	42,897
Advance billings and customer deposits	27,706	20,898
Accrued interest	11,573	10,054
Accrued taxes	2,525	3,894
Other	29,481	19,419
	427,724	346,184
Deferred Liabilities and Credits:		
Net deferred income tax liability	103,206	80,274
Postretirement benefits obligation other than pensions	12,146	14,379
Other	22,943	24,423
	138,295	119,076
Long-Term Debt, excluding current portion	858,857	536,509
Redeemable Preferred Shares, excluding current portion	1,587	13,209
Minority Interest, in subsidiaries	328,544	272,292
Nonredeemable Preferred Stock	29,710	29,819
Common Stockholders' Equity:		
Common shares, par value $1 per share; authorized 100,000,000 shares; issued and outstanding 51,137,426 and 47,937,570 shares, respectively	51,137	47,938
Series A common shares, par value $1 per share; authorized 25,000,000 shares; issued and outstanding 6,893,101 and 6,886,684 shares, respectively	6,893	6,887
Common shares issuable, 31,431 and 41,908 shares, respectively	1,496	1,995
Capital in excess of par value	1,417,513	1,288,453
Retained earnings	207,326	127,765
	1,684,365	1,473,038
	$3,469,082	$2,790,127

Corporations do not use a standard title for owners' equity. Exhibit 3-18 shows the titles for owners' equity used by the companies surveyed by *Accounting Trends & Techniques*.

Paid-in Capital   The first type of paid-in capital account is capital stock. Two basic types of capital stock are preferred and common.

Both preferred stock and common stock may be issued as par-value stock. (Some states call this *stated value stock*.) The articles of incorporation establish the par value, a designated dollar amount per share. Most states stipulate that the par value of issued stock times the number of shares outstanding constitutes the **legal capital**. Most states also designate that, if original-issue stock is sold below par value, the buyer is contingently liable for the difference between the par value and the lower amount paid. This does not usually pose a problem because the par value has no direct relationship to market value, the selling price of the stock. To avoid selling a stock below par, the par value is usually set very low in relation to the intended selling price. For example, the intended selling price may be $25.00, and the par value may be $1.00.

Some states allow the issuance of no-par stock (either common or preferred). Some of these states require that the entire proceeds received from the sale of the no-par stock be designated as legal capital.

Additional paid-in capital arises from the excess of amounts paid for stock over the par or stated value of the common and preferred stock. Also included here are amounts over cost from the sale of treasury stock (discussed later in this chapter), capital arising from the donation of assets to the firm, and transfer from retained earnings through stock dividends when the market price of the stock exceeds par.

EXHIBIT 3-18   **Titles of Owners' Equity**

	1994	1993	1992	1991
Shareholders' Equity	255	257	254	251
Stockholders' Equity	249	249	239	241
Shareowners' Equity	24	20	20	19
Common Stockholders' Equity	13	12	15	14
Shareholders' Investment	9	15	14	9
Stockholders' Investment	9	10	10	15
Common Shareholders' Equity	8	7	11	14
Other or not titled	33	30	37	37
Total companies	600	600	600	600

Common Stock   Common stock shares in all the stockholders' rights and represents ownership that has voting and liquidation rights. Common stockholders elect the board of directors and vote on major corporate decisions. In the event of liquidation, the liquidation rights of common stockholders give them claims to company assets after all creditors' and preferred stockholders' rights have been fulfilled.

Preferred Stock   Preferred stock seldom has voting rights. When preferred stock has voting rights, it is usually because of missed dividends. For example, the preferred stockholders may receive voting rights if their dividends have been missed two consecutive times. Some other preferred stock characteristics include the following:

— Preference as to dividends
— Accumulation of dividends
— Participation in excess of stated dividend rate
— Convertibility into common stock
— Callability by the corporation
— Redemption at future maturity date (see the previous discussion of redeemable preferred stock)
— Preference in liquidation

Preference as to Dividends   When preferred stock has a preference as to dividends, the current year's preferred dividend must be paid before a dividend can be paid to common stockholders. For par-value (or stated value) stock, the dividend rate is usually stated as a percentage of par. For example, if the dividend rate were 9% and the par were $100 per share, then the dividend per share would be $9. For no-par stock, if the dividend rate is stated as $7, then each share should receive $7 if a dividend is paid. A preference as to dividends does not guarantee that a preferred dividend will be paid in a given year. The Board of Directors must declare a dividend before a dividend is paid. The lack of a fixed commitment to pay dividends and the lack of a due date on the principal are the primary reasons that many firms elect to issue preferred stock instead of bonds. Preferred stock usually represents an expensive source of funds, compared to bonds. The preferred stock dividends are not tax deductible, while interest on bonds is deductible.

Accumulation of Dividends   If the Board of Directors does not declare dividends in a particular year, a holder of noncumulative preferred stock will never be paid that dividend. To make the preferred stock more attractive to investors, a corporation typically issues cumulative preferred stock. If a corporation fails to declare the usual dividend on the cumulative preferred stock, the amount of passed dividends becomes **dividends in arrears**. Common stockholders cannot be paid any dividends until the preferred dividends in arrears and the current preferred dividends are paid.

To illustrate dividends in arrears, assume a corporation has outstanding 10,000 shares of 8%, $100 par cumulative preferred stock. If dividends are not declared in 1995 and 1996, but are declared in 1997, the preferred stockholders would be entitled to dividends in arrears of $160,000 and current dividends in 1997 of $80,000 before any dividends could be paid to common shareholders.

Participation in Excess of Stated Dividend Rate   When preferred stock is participating, preferred stockholders may receive an extra dividend beyond the stated dividend rate. The terms of the participation depend on the terms included with the stock certificate. For example, the terms may state that any dividend to common stockholders over $10 per share will also be given to preferred stockholders.

To illustrate participating preferred stock, assume that a corporation has 8%, $100 par preferred stock. The terms of the participation are that any dividend paid on common shares over $10 per share will also be paid to preferred stockholders. For the current year, a dividend of $12 per share is declared on the common stock. Therefore, a dividend of $10 must be paid per share of preferred stock for the current year: (8% x $100) + $2.00 = $10.00.

Convertibility into Common Stock   Convertible preferred stock contains a provision that allows the preferred stockholders, at their option, to convert the share of preferred stock at a specific exchange ratio into another security of the corporation. The other security is almost always common stock. The conversion feature is very attractive to investors. For example, the terms may be that each share of preferred stock can be converted to four shares of common stock.

Convertible preferred stock is similar to a convertible bond, except that there are no fixed payout commitments with the convertible preferred stock. The preferred dividend need not be declared, and the preferred stock does not have a due date. The major reason for issuing convertible preferred stock is similar to that for issuing convertible bonds: If the current common stock price is low, in the opinion of management, and the firm eventually wants to increase its common equity, then the firm can raise more money for a given number of common shares by first issuing convertible preferred stock.

A firm usually prefers to issue convertible bonds rather than convertible preferred stock if its capital structure can carry more debt without taking on too much risk. The interest on the convertible bond is tax deductible while the dividend on the preferred stock is not.

Callability by the Corporation   Callable preferred stock may be retired (recalled) by the corporation at its option. The call price is part of the original stock contract. When the preferred stock is also cumulative, the call terms normally require payment of dividends in arrears before the call is executed.

The call provision favors the company because the company decides when to call. Investors do not like call provisions. Therefore, to make a security that has a call provision marketable, the call provision can normally not be exercised for a given number of years. For example, callable preferred stock issued in 1998 may have a provision that the call option cannot be exercised prior to 2008.

Preference in Liquidation   Should the corporation liquidate, the preferred stockholders normally have priority over common stockholders for settlement of claims. However, the claims of preferred stockholders are secondary to the claims of creditors, including bondholders.

Preference in liquidation for preferred stock over common stock is not usually considered to be an important provision. This is because often, in liquidation, funds are not sufficient to pay claims of preferred stock. Even creditors may receive only a few cents on the dollar in satisfaction of their claims.

Disclosures   Preferred stock may carry various combinations of provisions. The provisions of each preferred stock issue should be disclosed either parenthetically in the owners' equity section of the balance sheet or in a footnote. A company may have various preferred stock issues, each with different provisions.

Preferred stock is illustrated in Exhibit 3-19. This particular preferred stock is convertible preferred stock.

Donated Capital   Donated capital may be included in the paid-in capital. Capital is donated to the company by stockholders, creditors, or other parties (such as a city). For example, a city may offer land to a company as an inducement to locate a factory there to increase the level of employment. The firm records the donated land at the appraised amount and records an equal amount as donated capital in stockholders' equity.

Another example would be a company that needs to increase its available cash. A plan is devised, calling for existing common stockholders to donate a percentage of their stock to the company. When the stock is sold, the proceeds are added to the cash account, and the donated capital in owners' equity is increased. Exhibit 3-20, page 126, illustrates the presentation of donated capital by Lands' End, Inc.

Retained Earnings   **Retained earnings** are the undistributed earnings of the corporation—that is, the net income for all past periods minus the dividends (both cash and stock) that have been declared. Retained earnings are legally available as a basis for dividends unless they have been restricted. A firm may elect, or be required by law or contract, to restrict dividends. For example, bond indenture agreements frequently contain dividend restrictions to require the firm to conserve cash for debt coverage. A restriction of retained earnings accomplished through an appropriation makes the amount unavailable for dividends. A restriction of retained earnings will be disclosed. The disclosure is usually in a footnote. (Caution should be exercised not to confuse retained earnings or appropriated retained earnings with cash or any other asset. There is no cash or any other asset in retained earnings.)

EXHIBIT 3-19   FREEPORT-McMORAN INC.
Preferred Stock

	December 31	
	1995	1994
	(In thousands)	
Stockholders' equity:		
Convertible exchangeable preferred stock, par value $1, at liquidation value, authorized 50,000,000 shares	$ 50,084	$ 250,000
Common stock, par value $0.01 and $1 per share, respectively, authorized 100,000,000 shares and 300,000,000 shares, respectively	337	166,365
Capital in excess of par value of common stock	522,694	—
Retained earnings (deficit)	92,746	(221,925)
Cumulative foreign currency translation adjustment	—	(2,555)
Common stock held in treasury—6,016,800 and 4,863,200 shares, respectively, at cost	(473,924)	(422,352)
	191,937	(230,467)
Total liabilities and stockholders' equity	$ 1,320,470	$ 1,649,442

Notes to Financial Statements (in Part)

7. Stockholders' Equity

Preferred Stock. In April 1995, FTX exchanged 1.9 million FTX common shares for 4 million shares of its $4.375 convertible exchangeable preferred stock ($4.375 preferred stock) in accordance with an exchange offer whereby FTX temporarily increased the FTX shares issuable upon conversion. As a result of the exchange offer, FTX recorded a noncash charge of $33.5 million to preferred dividends. As of December 31, 1995, 1 million shares of $4.375 preferred stock remained outstanding and are convertible into FTX common stock at a conversion price of $27.36 per share or the equivalent of 1.8 shares of FTX common stock for each share of $4.375 preferred stock. Beginning March 1997, FTX may redeem this preferred stock for cash at $52.1875 per share (declining ratably to $50 per share in March 2002) plus accrued and unpaid dividends.

Exhibit 3-21, page 126, illustrates the presentation of retained earnings. This illustration includes restrictive covenants (appropriation).

Quasi-Reorganization

A **quasi-reorganization** is an accounting procedure equivalent to an accounting fresh start. A company with a deficit balance in retained earnings "starts over" with a zero balance rather than a deficit. A

EXHIBIT 3-20   LANDS' END, INC.
Donated Capital

(In thousands)	February 2, 1996	January 27, 1995
Shareholders' investment:		
Common stock, 40,221 shares issued	$ 402	$ 402
Donated capital	8,400	8,400
Additional paid-in capital	26,165	25,817
Deferred compensation	(1,193)	(1,421)
Currency translation adjustments	360	284
Retained earnings	260,109	229,554
Treasury stock, 6,561 and 5,395 shares at cost, respectively	(93,051)	(73,908)
Total shareholders' investment	201,192	189,128
Total liabilities and shareholders' investment	$ 323,497	$ 297,612

EXHIBIT 3-21   COOPER TIRE & RUBBER COMPANY
Retained Earnings—(Restricted/Appropriation)

(In thousands)	December 31	
	1995	1994
Stockholders' equity:		
Preferred stock, $1 par value; 5,000,000 shares authorized; none issued		
Common stock, $1 par value; 300,000,000 shares authorized; 83,661,972 shares outstanding (83,634,072 in 1994)	$ 83,662	$ 83,634
Capital in excess of par value	1,931	1,656
Retained earnings	672,373	582,137
Minimum pension liability	(9,167)	(5,350)
Total stockholders' equity	748,799	662,077
	$ 1,143,701	$ 1,039,731

Significant Accounting Policies (in Part)

Long-Term Debt (in Part)

The most restrictive covenants under the loan agreements require the maintenance of $65,000 in working capital and restrict the payment of dividends. The amount of retained earnings not restricted was $540,703 at December 31, 1995.

quasi-reorganization involves the reclassification of a deficit in retained earnings. It removes the deficit and an equal amount from paid-in capital. A quasi-reorganization may also include a restatement of the carrying values of assets and liabilities to reflect current values.

When a quasi-reorganization is performed, the retained earnings should be dated as of the readjustment date and disclosed in the financial statements for a period of five to ten years. Exhibit 3-22 illustrates a quasi-reorganization of ZAPATA.

EXHIBIT 3-22 **ZAPATA**
Quasi-Reorganization

	September 30	
(In thousands)	1994	1993
Stockholders' equity:		
$6.00 cumulative preferred stock (no par), outstanding: 22,498 shares (1994) and 44,943 shares (1993)	$ 2,255	$ 4,500
$2.00 noncumulative convertible preference stock ($1.00 par), outstanding: 2,627 shares (1994) and 2,637 shares (1993)	3	3
Common stock ($.025 par), outstanding: 31,716,991 shares (1994) and 28,940,592 shares (1993)	7,930	36,176
Capital in excess of par value	138,293	92,906
Reinvested earnings, from October 1, 1990 (deficit balance prior to quasi-reorganization at September 30, 1990: $296,850,000)	1,785	12,679
Investment in equity securities— unrealized gain, net of taxes	4,276	—
Total stockholders' equity	$ 154,542	$ 146,264

Notes (in Part)

Quasi-Reorganization

In connection with the comprehensive restructuring accomplished in 1991, the Company implemented, for accounting purposes, a "quasi-reorganization," an elective accounting procedure that permits a company which has emerged from previous financial difficulty to restate its accounts and establish a fresh start in an accounting sense. After implementation of the accounting quasi-reorganization, the Company's assets and liabilities were revalued and its deficit in reinvested earnings was charged to capital in excess of par value. The Company effected the accounting quasi-reorganization as of October 1, 1990.

Foreign Currency Translation

The expansion of international business and extensive currency realignments have created special accounting problems. The biggest difficulty has been related to translating foreign financial statements into the financial statements of a U.S. enterprise by consolidation, combination, or the equity method of accounting. Through 1981, following SFAS No. 8, financial statements were translated, and the resulting unrealized exchange gains or losses were included in determining net income. This mandate caused income statement amounts to fluctuate widely. These fluctuations and public sentiment about the impact of changes on earnings caused the FASB to rethink this matter.

After considerable deliberation and research effort, the FASB passed SFAS No. 52 in late 1981. It calls for postponing the recognition of *unrealized* exchange gains and losses until the foreign operation is substantially liquidated. This postponement will be accomplished by creating a stockholders' equity account to carry unrealized exchange gains and losses. This method eliminates the wide fluctuations in earnings from translation adjustments for most firms. For subsidiaries operating in highly inflationary economies, translation adjustments are charged to net earnings. Also, *actual* foreign currency exchange gains (losses) are included in net income. Exhibit 3-23 illustrates the presentation of translation adjustments in stockholders' equity.

Unrealized Holding Gains and Losses

Under SFAS No. 115, *debt and equity* securities classified as available-for-sale securities are carried at *fair value*. Unrealized holding gains and losses are included as a separate component of stockholders' equity until realized. Thus, the unrealized holding gains and losses are not included in income. Note that this accounting only applies to securities available for sale. Trading securities are reported at their fair values on the balance sheet date, and unrealized holding gains and losses are included in income of the current period. Debt securities held to maturity are reported at their amortized cost on the balance sheet date.

Exhibit 3-24 discloses an unrealized gain for Delta Air Lines. For some firms, this account is substantial. It represents a balance sheet recognition that has not been recognized in earnings.

Equity-Oriented Deferred Compensation

Equity-oriented deferred compensation arrangements encompass a wide variety of plans. The deferred compensation element of an equity-based deferred compensation arrangement is the amount of compensation cost

EXHIBIT 3-23 **FLUOR**
Foreign Currency Translation

(In thousands)	October 31	
	1995	1994
Shareholders' equity:		
Capital stock:		
Preferred—authorized 20,000,000 shares without par value, none issued		
Common—authorized 150,000,000 shares of $.625 par value; issued and outstanding in 1995—83,164,866 shares and in 1994—82,507,568 shares	$ 51,978	$ 51,567
Additional capital	538,503	498,804
Retained earnings (since October 31, 1987)	866,305	684,249
Unamortized executive stock plan expense	(26,865)	(14,472)
Cumulative translation adjustment	893	308
Total shareholders' equity	$1,430,814	$1,220,456

EXHIBIT 3-24 **DELTA AIR LINES**
Unrealized Gain (Loss)

(In millions, except share data)	June 30	
	1995	1994
Shareholders' equity:		
Series C convertible preferred stock, $1.00 par value, $50,000 liquidation preference; issued and outstanding 23,000 shares at June 30, 1995 and 1994	—	—
Common stock, $3.00 par value; authorized 150,000,000 shares; issued 54,537,103 shares at June 30, 1995, and 54,469,491 shares at June 30, 1994	$ 164	$ 163
Additional paid-in capital	2,016	2,013
Accumulated deficit	(184)	(490)
Net unrealized gain on marketable securities	83	53
Less: Treasury stock at cost, 3,721,093 shares at June 30, 1995, and 4,016,219 shares at June 30, 1994	(252)	(272)
Total shareholders' equity	$ 1,827	$ 1,467

deferred and amortized (expensed) to future periods as the services are provided.

APB Opinion No. 25 directs that if stock is issued in a plan before some or all of the services are performed, the unearned compensation should be shown as a separate contra (reduction) item to owners' equity. This unearned compensation amount should be accounted for as an expense of future period(s) as services are performed. Thus, the unearned compensation amount is removed from owners' equity (amortized) and is recognized as an expense in future periods.

When a plan involves the potential issuance of only stock, then the unearned compensation is shown as a reduction in owners' equity, and the offsetting amount is also in the owners' equity section. If the plan involves cash or a subsequent election of either cash or stock, the unearned compensation appears as a reduction in owners' equity, and the offsetting amount appears as a liability.

Exhibit 3-25 illustrates an equity-oriented deferred compensation plan for AMP. It is apparently a stock-only plan. The deferred compensation will be amortized to expense over subsequent periods.

Employee Stock Ownership Plans (ESOPs)

An **ESOP** is a qualified stock-bonus, or combination stock-bonus and money-purchase pension plan, designed to invest primarily in the

EXHIBIT 3-25 **AMP**
Equity-Oriented Deferred Compensation

	December 31	
(Dollars in thousands)	1995	1994
Shareholders' equity:		
Common stock, without par value— authorized 700,000,000 shares, issued 232,491,889 shares	$ 79,580	$ 70,135
Other capital	83,454	80,105
Deferred compensation	(2,489)	(4,568)
Cumulative translation adjustments	156,837	129,612
Net unrealized investment gains	19,423	21,585
Retained earnings	2,667,755	2,442,317
Treasury stock, at cost	(236,532)	(243,431)
Total shareholders' equity	$ 2,768,028	$ 2,495,755

employer's securities. A qualified plan must satisfy certain requirements of the Internal Revenue Code. An ESOP must be a permanent trusteed plan for the exclusive benefit of the employees.

The trust that is part of the plan is exempt from tax on its income, and the employer/sponsor gets a current deduction for contributions to the plan. The plan participants become eligible for favorable taxation of distributions from the plan.

An ESOP may borrow the funds necessary to purchase the employer stock. These funds may be borrowed from the company, its shareholders, or a third party such as a bank. The company can guarantee the loan to the ESOP. Financial leverage—the ability of the ESOP to borrow in order to buy employer securities—is an important aspect.

The Internal Revenue Code favors borrowing for an ESOP. Commercial lending institutions, insurance companies, and mutual funds are permitted an exclusion from income for 50% of the interest received on loans used to finance an ESOP's acquisition of company stock. Thus, these institutions are willing to charge a reduced rate of interest for the loan.

From a company's perspective, there are advantages and disadvantages to an ESOP. One advantage is that an ESOP serves as a source of funds for expansion at a reasonable rate. Other possible advantages follow:

1. A means to buy the stock from a major shareholder or possibly an unwanted shareholder.

2. Help financing a leveraged buyout.

3. Reduction of potential of an unfriendly takeover.

4. Help in creating a market for the company's stock.

Some firms do not find an ESOP attractive, because it can result in a significant amount of voting stock in the hands of their employees. Existing stockholders may not find an ESOP desirable because it will probably dilute their proportional ownership.

The employer contribution to an ESOP reduces cash, and an unearned compensation item decreases stockholders' equity. The unearned compensation is amortized on the income statement in subsequent periods. When an ESOP borrows funds and the firm (in either an informal or formal guarantee) commits to future contributions to the ESOP to meet the debt-service requirements, then the firm records this commitment as a liability and as a deferred compensation deduction within stockholders' equity. As the debt is liquidated, the liability and deferred compensation are reduced.

Exhibit 3-26 shows the reporting of the ESOP of the Southern New England Telecommunications Corporation.

Treasury Stock

A firm creates **treasury stock** when it repurchases its own stock and does not retire it. Since treasury stock lowers the stock outstanding, it is

EXHIBIT 3-26   **SOUTHERN NEW ENGLAND TELECOMMUNICATIONS CORPORATION**
Employee Stock Ownership Plan (ESOP)

(In thousands)	October 29, 1995	October 30, 1994
Shareholders' equity:		
Preferred shares, no par value; 10,000,000 shares authorized; none issued		
Common shares, no par value; 80,000,000 shares authorized; 24,506,000 shares issued	$ 12,253	$ 12,253
Capital in excess of stated value	60,142	57,590
Cumulative translation adjustments	10,944	10,977
Retained earnings	341,223	300,223
Common shares in treasury, at cost	(192,099)	(166,098)
Deferred stock-based compensation	(1,133)	(2,521)
Total shareholders' equity	$ 231,330	$ 212,424

Note 12 (in Part)

Employee Stock Ownership Plan—The Company sponsors a leveraged Employee Stock Ownership Plan (ESOP) covering all domestic employees. Company contributions are discretionary and funded annually by a combination of cash and shares of the Company's common stock. Suspense shares are committed to be released as the ESOP's debt is repaid. Allocations to the participants' accounts are made on December 31 on the basis of their compensation for the year. Each participant vests in his account at a rate of 20 percent per year from date of employment. Distribution of a participant's account occurs at retirement, death, or termination of employment.

ESOP compensation expense was $2,411,000 in 1995 ($1,642,000 in 1994, and $1,681,000 in 1993). Contributions to the plan were $1,795,000, $1,567,000, and $2,068,000 in 1995, 1994, and 1993, respectively. The number of ESOP shares outstanding is as follows:

	1995	1994
Allocated shares	426,424	384,231
Committed-to-be-released shares	2,324	7,411
Suspense shares	13,721	47,335
Total ESOP shares	442,469	438,977

subtracted from owners' equity. Treasury stock is, in essence, a reduction in paid-in capital.

A firm may record treasury stock in two ways. One records the treasury stock at par or stated value, referred to as the par value method of recording treasury stock. This method removes the paid-in capital in excess of par (or stated value) from the original issue. The treasury stock appears as a reduction of paid-in capital.

The other method, referred to as the *cost method*, records treasury stock at the cost of the stock (presented as a reduction of owners' equity). Most firms record treasury stock at cost.

Exhibit 3-27 illustrates the presentation of treasury stock for Warner-Lambert. Note that a firm cannot record gains or losses from dealing in its own stock. Any apparent gains or losses related to treasury stock must impact owners' equity, such as a reduction in retained earnings.

Owners' Equity in Unincorporated Firms

Owners' equity in an unincorporated firm is termed *capital*. The amount invested by the owner plus the retained earnings may be shown as one sum, since no restriction applies on the removal (drawing or withdrawal) of profits. A sole proprietorship form of business has only one

EXHIBIT 3-27 **WARNER-LAMBERT**
Treasury Stock

	December 31	
	1995	1994
	(Dollars in millions)	
Shareholders' equity:		
Preferred stock—none issued	—	—
Common stock—160,330,268 shares issued	$ 160.3	$ 160.3
Capital in excess of par value	217.5	152.2
Retained earnings	3,042.9	2,654.5
Cumulative translation adjustments	(216.3)	(181.0)
Treasury stock, at cost:		
1995—24,731,378 shares; 1994—25,734,568 shares	(958.3)	(969.6)
Total shareholders' equity	$2,246.1	$1,816.4

owner (one capital account). A partnership form of business has more than one owner (capital account for each owner). Chapter 2 reviewed these forms of business.

PROBLEMS IN BALANCE SHEET PRESENTATION

Numerous problems inherent in balance sheet presentation may cause difficulty in analysis. First, most assets are valued at cost, so one cannot determine the market value or replacement cost of many assets and should not assume that their balance sheet amount approximates current valuation.

Second, varying methods are used for asset valuation. For example, inventories may be valued differently from firm to firm and, within a firm, from product to product. A simple illustration may help. In a period, a firm buys two units of goods for resale, the first at $10 and the second at $12. The goods are placed on the shelf and are indistinguishable. After sales for the period, one unit remains. Different methods of inventory valuation allow a cost of $10, $12, or the average of $11 to be used. This lack of uniformity causes problems in comparison. Similar problems exist with long-term asset valuation and the related depreciation alternatives. Methods to alleviate these problems will be discussed in relationship to the ratios where these asset valuations are used.

A third and different type of problem exists in that not all items of value to the firm are included as assets. For example, such characteristics as good employees, outstanding management, and a well-chosen location do not appear on the balance sheet. In the same vein, liabilities related to contingencies also may not appear on the balance sheet. Chapters 7 and 8 present many of the problems of the balance sheet.

These problems do not make statement analysis impossible. They merely require that qualitative judgment be applied to quantitative ratio and trend analyses in order to assess the impact of these problem areas.

SUMMARY

The balance sheet shows the financial condition of an accounting entity as of a particular date. It is the most basic financial statement, and it is read by various users as part of their decision-making process.

QUESTIONS

Q 3-1.   Name and describe the three major categories of balance sheet accounts.

Q 3-2.   Are the following balance sheet items (A) assets, (L) liabilities, or (E) stockholders' equity?

a. Cash dividends payable	k. Retained earnings
b. Mortgage notes payable	l. Donated capital
c. Investments in stock	m. Accounts receivable
d. Cash	n. Taxes payable
e. Land	o. Accounts payable
f. Inventory	p. Organizational costs
g. Unearned rent	q. Prepaid expenses
h. Marketable securities	r. Goodwill
i. Patents	s. Tools
j. Capital stock	t. Buildings

Q 3-3.   Classify the following as (CA) current asset, (IV) investments, (IA) intangible asset, or (TA) tangible asset:

a. Land	g. Tools
b. Cash	h. Prepaids
c. Copyrights	i. Buildings
d. Marketable securities	j. Accounts receivable
e. Goodwill	k. Long-term investment in stock
f. Inventories	l. Machinery

Q 3-4.   Current assets are listed in specific order, starting with cash. What is the objective of this order of listing?

Q 3-5.   Differentiate between marketable securities and long-term investments. What is the purpose of owning each?

Q 3-6.   Differentiate between accounts receivable and accounts payable.

Q 3-7.   What types of inventory will a retailing firm have? A manufacturing firm?

Q 3-8.   Why does LIFO result in a very unrealistic ending inventory figure in a period of rising prices?

Q 3-9.   What is depreciation? Which tangible assets are depreciated and which are not? Why?

Q 3-10.   For reporting purposes, management prefers higher profits; for tax purposes, lower taxable income is desired. To meet these goals, firms often use different methods of depreciation for tax and reporting purposes. Which depreciation method is best for reporting and which for tax purposes? Why?

Q 3-11.   A rental agency collects rent in advance. Why is the rent collected treated as a liability?

Q 3-12.   A bond carries a stated rate of interest of 6% and par of $1,000. It matures in 20 years. It is sold at 83 (83% of $1,000, or $830).

a. Under normal conditions, why would the bond sell at less than par?
b. How would the discount be disclosed on the statements?

Q 3-13.   To be conservative, how should minority interest on the balance sheet be handled for primary analysis?

Q 3-14.   Firms value many assets at historical cost. Why does this accounting principle cause difficulties in financial statement analysis?

Q 3-15.   Explain how the issuance of a convertible bond can be a very attractive means of raising common equity funds.

Q 3-16.   Classify each of the following as a (CA) current asset, (NA) noncurrent asset, (CL) current liability, (NL) noncurrent liability, or (E) equity account. Choose the best or most frequently used classification.

a. Supplies   k. Wages payable
b. Notes receivable   l. Mortgage bonds payable
c. Unearned subscription   m. Unearned interest
   revenue   n. Marketable securities
d. Accounts payable   o. Paid-in capital from
e. Retained earnings   sale of treasury stock
f. Accounts receivable   p. Land
g. Preferred stock   q. Inventories
h. Plant   r. Taxes accrued
i. Prepaid rent   s. Cash
j. Capital

Q 3-17.   Explain these preferred stock characteristics:

a. Accumulation of dividends
b. Participation in excess of stated dividend rate
c. Convertibility into common stock
d. Callability by the corporation
e. Preference in liquidation

Q 3-18.   Describe the account "unrealized exchange gains or losses."

Q 3-19.   What is treasury stock? Why is it deducted from stockholders' equity?

Q 3-20.   A firm, with no opening inventory, buys ten units at $6 each during the period. In which accounts might the $60 appear on the financial statements?

Q 3-21.   Consolidated statements may be issued to show financial position as it would appear if two or more companies were one entity. What is the objective of these statements?

Q 3-22.   How is an unconsolidated subsidiary presented on a balance sheet?

Q 3-23.   When would minority interest be presented on a balance sheet?

Q 3-24.   What is the basic guideline for consolidation?

Q 3-25. DeLand Company owns 100% of Little Florida, Inc. Will DeLand Company show a minority interest on its balance sheet? Would the answer change if it owned only 60%? Will there ever be a case in which the subsidiary, Little Florida, is not consolidated?

Q 3-26. Describe the item "unrealized decline in market value of noncurrent equity investments."

Q 3-27. What is redeemable preferred stock? Why should it be included with debt for purposes of financial statement analysis?

Q 3-28. Describe donated capital.

Q 3-29. Assume that a city donated land to a company. What accounts would be affected by this donation, and what would be the value?

Q 3-30. Describe quasi-reorganization.

Q 3-31. Assume that an equity-oriented deferred compensation plan involves cash or a subsequent election of either cash or stock. Describe the presentation of this plan on the balance sheet.

Q 3-32. Describe employee stock ownership plans (ESOPs).

Q 3-33. Why are commercial lending institutions, insurance companies, and mutual funds willing to grant loans to an employee stock ownership plan at favorable rates?

Q 3-34. What are some possible disadvantages of an employee stock ownership plan?

Q 3-35. How does a company recognize, in an informal or formal way, that it has guaranteed commitments to future contributions to an ESOP to meet debt-service requirements?

Q 3-36. Describe depreciation, amortization, and depletion. How do they differ?

Q 3-37. What are the three factors usually considered when computing depreciation?

Q 3-38. An accelerated system of depreciation is often used for income tax purposes but not for financial reporting. Why?

Q 3-39. Which depreciation method will result in the most depreciation over the life of an asset?

Q 3-40. Should depreciation be recognized on a building in a year in which the cost of replacing the building rises? Explain.

Q 3-41. The cost of inventory at the close of the calendar year of the first year of operation is $40,000, using LIFO inventory, resulting in a profit before tax of $100,000. If the FIFO inventory would have been $50,000, what would the reported profit before tax have been? If the average cost method would have resulted in an inventory of $45,000, what would the reported profit before tax have been? Should the inventory costing method be disclosed? Why?

Q 3-42. Describe the two methods of accounting for a business combination.

PROBLEMS

P 3-1.   The following are the inventory records of Herrick House:

	Units	Cost	Total
January 1	10	$ 8	$ 80
Purchases:			
April 18	32	9	288
November 3	41	10	410
December 10	4	11	44

Ending inventory consists of 6 units. These units are from the November purchase.

Required   Calculate ending inventory and cost of sales using: (a) FIFO, (b) LIFO, (c) average, and (d) specific identification.

P 3-2.   The following information was obtained from the accounts of Airlines International dated December 31, 1997. It is presented in scrambled order.

Accounts payable	$ 77,916
Accounts receivable	67,551
Accrued expenses	23,952
Accumulated depreciation	220,541
Allowance for doubtful accounts	248
Capital in excess of par	72,913
Cash	28,837
Common stock (par $.50, authorized 20,000 shares, issued 14,304 shares)	7,152
Current installments of long-term debt	36,875
Deferred income tax liability (long term)	42,070
Inventory	16,643
Investments and special funds	11,901
Long-term debt, less current portion	393,808
Marketable securities	10,042
Other assets	727
Prepaid expenses	3,963
Property, plant, and equipment at cost	809,980
Retained earnings	67,361
Unearned transportation revenue (airline tickets expiring within one year)	6,808

Required   Prepare a classified balance sheet in report form.

P 3-3. The following information was obtained from the accounts of Lukes, Inc. as of December 31, 1997. It is presented in scrambled order.

Common stock, no par value, 10,000 shares authorized, 5,724 shares issued	$ 3,180
Retained earnings	129,950
Deferred income tax liability (long term)	24,000
Long-term debt	99,870
Accounts payable	35,000
Buildings	75,000
Machinery and equipment	300,000
Land	11,000
Accumulated depreciation	200,000
Cash	3,000
Receivables, less allowance of $3,000	58,000
Accrued income taxes	3,000
Inventories	54,000
Other accrued expenses	8,000
Current portion of long-term debt	7,000
Prepaid expenses	2,000
Other assets (long term)	7,000

Required Prepare a classified balance sheet in report form. For assets, use the classifications of current assets, plant and equipment, and other assets. For liabilities, use the classifications of current liabilities and long-term liabilities.

P 3-4. The following information was obtained from the accounts of Alleg, Inc. as of December 31, 1997. It is presented in scrambled order.

Common stock, authorized 21,000 shares at $1 par value, issued 10,000 shares	$ 10,000
Additional paid-in capital	38,000
Cash	13,000
Marketable securities	17,000
Accounts receivable	26,000
Accounts payable	15,000
Current maturities of long-term debt	11,000
Mortgages payable	80,000
Bonds payable	70,000
Inventories	30,000
Land and buildings	57,000
Machinery and equipment	125,000
Goodwill	8,000
Patents	10,000
Other assets	50,000
Deferred income taxes (long-term liability)	18,000
Retained earnings	33,000
Accumulated depreciation	61,000

Required   Prepare a classified balance sheet in report form. For assets, use the classifications of current assets, plant and equipment, intangibles, and other assets. For liabilities, use the classifications of current liabilities and long-term liabilities.

P 3-5.   Presented below is the balance sheet of Ingram Industries.

INGRAM INDUSTRIES
Balance Sheet
June 30, 1997

Assets
Current assets:
  Cash (including $13,000 in
    sinking fund for bonds
    payable) $ 70,000
  Marketable securities   23,400
  Investment in subsidiary company   23,000
  Accounts receivable   21,000
  Inventories (lower-of-cost-
    or-market)   117,000 $ 254,400

Plant assets:
  Land and buildings $ 160,000
  Less: Accumulated depreciation   100,000   60,000

Investments:
  Treasury stock   4,000
Deferred charges:
  Discount on bonds payable $ 6,000
  Prepaid expenses   2,000   8,000
                                                                          $ 326,400

Liabilities and Stockholders' Equity
Liabilities:
  Notes payable to bank $ 60,000
  Accounts payable   18,000
  Bonds payable   61,000
      Total liabilities $ 139,000
Stockholders' equity:
  Preferred and common (each $10 par, 5,000
    shares preferred and 6,000 shares common) $ 110,000
  Capital in excess of par   61,000
  Retained earnings,
    beginning of year $ 11,400
  Net income   15,000
  Less: Dividends   10,000   16,400   187,400

Total liabilities and
  stockholders' equity $ 326,400

Required   Indicate your criticisms of the balance sheet and briefly explain the proper treatment of any item criticized.

P 3-6.   Presented below is the balance sheet of Rubber Industries.

RUBBER INDUSTRIES
Balance Sheet
For the Year Ended December 31, 1997

Assets

Current assets:	
Cash	$ 50,000
Marketable equity securities (market $15,000 at lower-of-cost-or-market)	19,000
Accounts receivable, net	60,000
Inventories (lower-of-cost-or-market)	30,000
Treasury stock	20,000
Total current assets	179,000
Plant assets:	
Land and buildings, net	160,000
Investments:	
Short-term U.S. notes	20,000
Other assets:	
Supplies	4,000
Total assets	$363,000

Liabilities and Stockholders' Equity

Liabilities:	
Bonds payable	$120,000
Accounts payable	40,000
Wages payable	10,000
Premium on bonds payable	3,000
Total liabilities	173,000
Stockholders' equity:	
Common stock ($20 par, 20,000 shares authorized, 6,000 shares outstanding)	120,000
Retained earnings	30,000
Minority interest	20,000
Redeemable preferred stock	20,000
Total liabilities and stockholders' equity	$363,000

Required   Indicate your criticisms of the balance sheet and briefly explain the proper treatment of any item criticized.

P 3-7.   The balance sheet of McDonald Company is presented for your review.

McDONALD COMPANY
December 31, 1997

Assets
    Current assets:

Cash (including $10,000 restricted for payment of note)	$ 40,000	
Marketable equity securities	20,000	
Accounts receivable, less allowance for doubtful accounts of $12,000	70,000	
Inventory (lower-of-cost-or-market)	60,000	
Total current assets		$ 190,000
Plant assets:		
Land	40,000	
Buildings, net	100,000	
Equipment	$ 80,000	
Less: Accumulated depreciation	20,000	60,000
Patent	20,000	
Organizational costs	15,000	
		235,000
Other assets:		
Prepaid insurance		5,000
Total assets		$ 430,000

Liabilities and Stockholders' Equity

Current liabilities:		
Accounts payable	$ 60,000	
Wages payable	10,000	
Notes payable, due July 1, 2000	20,000	
Bonds payable, due December 2010	100,000	
Total current liabilities		$ 190,000
Dividends payable		4,000
Deferred tax liability, long term		30,000
Stockholders' equity:		
Common stock ($10 par, 10,000 shares authorized, 5,000 shares outstanding)	50,000	
Retained earnings	156,000	
Total stockholders' equity		206,000
Total liabilities and stockholders' equity		$ 430,000

Required   Indicate your criticisms of the balance sheet and briefly explain the proper treatment of any item criticized.

P 3-8.   You have just started as a staff auditor for a small CPA firm. During the course of the audit, you discover the following items related to a single client firm:
    a. During the year, the firm declared and paid $10,000 in dividends.
    b. Your client has been named defendant in a legal suit involving a material

account. You have received from the client's counsel a statement indicating little likelihood of loss.

c. Because of cost control actions and general employee dissatisfaction, it is likely that the client will suffer a costly strike in the near future.

d. During the year, the firm changed its inventory method from average to LIFO.

e. Twenty days after closing, the client suffered a major fire in one of its plants.

f. The cash account includes a substantial amount set aside for payment of pension obligations.

g. Marketable securities include a large quantity of shares of stock purchased for control purposes.

h. Land is listed on the balance sheet at its market value of $1,000,000. It cost $670,000 to purchase 12 years ago.

i. During the year, the government of Uganda expropriated a plant located in that country. There was substantial loss.

Required   How would each of these items be reflected in the year-end balance sheet, including footnotes?

P 3-9.   Corvallis Corporation owns 80% of the stock of Little Harrisburg, Inc. At December 31, 1997, Little Harrisburg had the following summarized balance sheet:

LITTLE HARRISBURG, INC.
Balance Sheet
December 31, 1997

Current assets	$100,000	Current liabilities	$ 50,000
Property, plant, and		Long-term debt	150,000
equipment (net)	400,000	Capital stock	50,000
		Retained earnings	250,000
	$500,000		$500,000

The earnings of Little Harrisburg, Inc. for 1997 were $50,000 after tax.

Required   a. What would be the amount of minority interest on the balance sheet of Corvallis Corporation? How should the balance sheet minority interest be classified for financial statement analysis purposes?

b. What would be the minority share of earnings on the income statement of Corvallis Corporation?

P 3-10.   The Aggarwal Company has had 10,000 shares of 10%, $100 par-value preferred stock and 80,000 shares of $5 stated-value common stock outstanding for the last three years. During that period, dividends paid totaled $0, $200,000, and $220,000 for each year, respectively.

Required   Compute the amount of dividends that must have been paid to preferred
                 stockholders and common stockholders in each of the three years, given the
                 following four independent assumptions:

a.   Preferred stock is nonparticipating and cumulative.
b.   Preferred stock participates up to 12% of its par value and is cumulative.
c.   Preferred stock is fully participating and cumulative.
d.   Preferred stock is nonparticipating and noncumulative.

P 3-11.   The Rosewell Company has had 5,000 shares of 9%, $100 par-value preferred
                 stock and 10,000 shares of $10 par-value common stock outstanding for the
                 last two years. During the most recent year, dividends paid totaled $65,000;
                 in the prior year, dividends paid totaled $40,000.

Required   Compute the amount of dividends that must have been paid to preferred
                 stockholders and common stockholders in each year, given the following
                 independent assumptions:

a.   Preferred stock is fully participating and cumulative.
b.   Preferred stock is nonparticipating and noncumulative.
c.   Preferred stock participates up to 10% of its par value and is cumulative.
d.   Preferred stock is nonparticipating and cumulative.

P 3-12.   An item of equipment acquired on January 1 at a cost of $100,000 has an
                 estimated life of ten years.

Required   Assuming that the equipment will have a salvage value of $10,000, determine
                 the depreciation for each of the first three years by the:

a.   Straight-line method
b.   Declining-balance method
c.   Sum-of-the-years'-digits method

P 3-13.   An item of equipment acquired on January 1 at a cost of $60,000 has an esti-
                 mated use of 25,000 hours. During the first three years, the equipment was
                 used 5,000, 6,000, and 4,000 hours, respectively. The estimated salvage value
                 of the equipment is $10,000.

Required   Determine the depreciation for each of the three years, using the unit-of-
                 production method.

P 3-14.   An item of equipment acquired on January 1 at a cost of $50,000 has an
                 estimated life of five years and an estimated salvage of $10,000.

Required   a. From a management perspective, from among the straight-line method,
                 declining-balance method, and the sum-of-the-years'-digits method of
                 depreciation, which method should be chosen for the financial state-
                 ments if income is to be at a maximum the first year? Which method
                 should be chosen for the income tax returns, assuming that the tax rate
                 stays the same each year? Explain and show computations.
              b. Is it permissible to use different depreciation methods in financial state-
                 ments than those used in tax returns?

Cases

CASE 3-1   Balance Sheet Review

The December 31, 1995 and 1994 consolidated balance sheets of Lufkin Industries, Inc. follow.

(Thousands of dollars)	December 31 1995	December 31 1994
Assets		
Current assets:		
Cash	$ 277	$ 207
Temporary investments	33,040	36,716
Receivables, net	36,204	28,262
Inventories	24,737	21,919
Deferred income tax assets	3,853	4,522
Total current assets	98,111	91,626
Property, plant, and equipment:		
Land and improvements	8,784	8,801
Buildings	52,555	52,076
Machinery and equipment	172,437	167,387
Total property, plant, and equipment	233,776	228,264
Less: Accumulated depreciation	(172,953)	(167,558)
Total property, plant, and equipment, net	60,823	60,706
Prepaid pension costs	20,936	17,784
Other assets	6,426	6,658
Total	$ 186,296	$ 176,774

(continued)

Liabilities and Shareholders' Equity

Current liabilities:

Accounts payable	$ 11,430	$ 10,661
Accrued liabilities:		
Payrolls and benefits	5,084	4,574
Accrued warranty expenses	2,032	2,265
Taxes payable	2,849	2,158
Commissions and other	1,774	1,137
Total current liabilities	23,169	20,795
Deferred income tax liabilities	8,500	6,172
Postretirement benefits liability	12,035	11,843
Shareholders' equity:		
Common stock, par $1 per share; 20,000 shares authorized; 6,792,381 shares issued	6,792	6,792
Capital in excess of par	15,367	15,372
Retained earnings	121,692	116,845
Treasury stock, 16,108 shares, at cost	(311)	—
Cumulative translation adjustment	(948)	(1,045)
Total shareholders' equity	142,592	137,964
Total	$186,296	$176,774

(1) Summary of Major Accounting Policies (Partial)

Principles of Consolidation   The consolidated financial statements include the accounts of Lufkin Industries, Inc. and Subsidiaries (the Company) after elimination of all significant intercompany accounts and transactions.

Use of Estimates   The preparation of the financial statements in conformity with generally accepted accounting principles requires the use of certain estimates by management in determining the Company's assets, liabilities, revenue, and expenses.

Translation of Foreign Currencies   Assets and liabilities of foreign operations are translated into U.S. dollars at the exchange rate in effect at the end of each accounting period, and income statement accounts are translated at the average exchange rates prevailing during the period.

Temporary Investments   The Company's temporary investments consisting of highly liquid government and corporate debt securities have been classified as trading securities which are carried at market value.   All realized and unrealized gains and losses are recognized currently in investment income.

Receivables   The following is a summary of the Company's receivable balances:

(Thousands of dollars)	1995	1994
Accounts receivable	$ 34,645	$ 25,024
Notes receivable	2,159	3,838
	36,804	28,862
Allowance for doubtful accounts	(600)	(600)
Net receivables	$ 36,204	$ 28,262

Inventories   The Company reports its inventories by using the last-in, first-out (LIFO) and the first-in, first-out (FIFO) methods less reserves necessary to report inventories at the lower of cost or estimated market. Inventory costs include material, labor, and factory overhead.

Property, Plant, and Equipment   The Company records investments in these assets at cost. Improvements are capitalized, while repair and maintenance costs are charged to operations as incurred. Gains or losses realized on the sale or retirement of these assets are reflected in income. Depreciation for financial reporting purposes is provided by a straight-line method based upon the estimated useful lives of the assets. Accelerated depreciation methods are used for tax purposes. Expenditures for maintenance and repairs were $10,902,000 in 1995, $8,924,000 in 1994, and $8,240,000 in 1993.

Other   Certain prior year amounts have been reclassified to conform with the current year presentation.

Required

a. The statement is entitled "Consolidated Balance Sheet." What does it mean to have a consolidated balance sheet?

b. Does it appear that the subsidiaries are wholly owned? Explain.

c. 1. What are the gross receivables at December 31, 1995?
    2. What is the estimated amount that will be collected on receivables outstanding at December 31, 1995?
    3. What is the amount of the allowance for doubtful accounts at December 31, 1995?

d. 1. What is the net property, plant, and equipment at December 31, 1995? What does this figure represent?
    2. What is the gross property, plant, and equipment at December 31, 1995?
    3. What depreciation method is used for financial reporting purposes?
    4. What depreciation method is used for tax purposes?
    5. Does it appear that property, plant, and equipment is relatively old? Explain.

e. What is the total amount of current assets at December 31, 1995?

f.   What is the total shareholders' equity at December 31, 1995?

g.   Describe the account "accrued warranty expenses."

h.   1.   Describe treasury stock.

      2.   How many shares of treasury stock are held at December 31, 1995?

i.   1.   How many common stock shares have been issued at December 31, 1995?

      2.   How many common stock shares are outstanding at December 31, 1995?

j.   In general, describe deferred taxes.

k.   1.   What is the total amount of assets at December 31, 1995?

      2.   What is the total amount of liabilities at December 31, 1995?

      3.   What is the total amount of shareholders' equity at December 31, 1995?

      4.   Demonstrate that the balance sheet balances at December 31, 1995.

CASE 3-2   Insight on Liabilities and Shareholders' Equity

The December 31, 1995 and 1994 consolidated statement of financial position of Eastman Kodak Company included the liabilities and shareowners' equity shown at the top of the next page.

Required   a.   The statement is entitled "Consolidated Statement of Financial Position." What does it mean to have a consolidated balance sheet?

b.   Does it appear that the subsidiaries are wholly owned? Explain.

c.   Describe "payables."

d.   Describe deferred income tax credits.

e.   Describe long-term borrowings.

f.   Describe retained earnings.

g.   Describe accumulated translation adjustments.

h.   Describe treasury stock.

i.   1.   How many shares of common stock have been issued as of December 31, 1995?

      2.   How many shares of treasury stock are held at December 31, 1995?

      3.   How many shares of common stock are outstanding at December 31, 1995?

j.   1.   What are the total liabilities at December 31, 1995?

      2.   What is the total shareowners' equity at December 31, 1995?

      3.   What is the total asset amount at December 31, 1995?

Eastman Kodak Company
Liabilities and Shareowners' Equity

(In millions)	At December 31	
	1995	1994
Liabilities and Shareowners' Equity		
Current liabilities:		
Payables	$ 3,327	$ 3,398
Short-term borrowings	586	371
Taxes—income and other	567	1,701
Dividends payable	137	136
Deferred income tax credits	26	129
Total current liabilities	4,643	5,735
Other liabilities:		
Long-term borrowings	665	660
Postemployment liabilities	3,247	3,671
Other long-term liabilities	704	790
Deferred income tax credits	97	95
Total liabilities	9,356	10,951
Shareowners' equity:		
Common stock, par value $2.50 per share, 950,000,000 shares authorized; issued 389,574,619 in 1995 and 386,343,903 in 1994	974	966
Additional capital paid in or transferred from retained earnings	803	515
Retained earnings	5,184	4,485
Accumulated translation adjustment	93	8
	7,054	5,974
Treasury stock, at cost, 43,685,196 shares in 1995 and 46,587,211 shares in 1994	1,933	1,957
Total shareowners' equity	5,121	4,017
Total Liabilities and Shareowners' Equity	$14,477	$14,968

CASE 3-3   Insight on Shareholders' Investment

The 1995 annual report of Lands' End, Inc. included the shareholders' investment as shown at the top of the next page.

Consolidated Balance Sheets (in Part) (In thousands)	January 27, 1995	January 28, 1994
Shareholder's investment:		
Common stock, 40,221 and 20,110 shares issued	$ 402	$ 201
Donated capital	8,400	8,400
Paid-in capital	25,817	24,888
Deferred compensation	(1,421)	(2,001)
Currency translation adjustments	284	246
Retained earnings	229,554	193,460
Treasury stock, 5,395 and 2,154 shares at cost	(73,908)	(47,909)
Total shareholders' investment	$189,128	$177,285

Required   a.   Describe shareholders' investment.
b.   Describe the account deferred compensation.
c.   Describe the account donated capital.
d.   Describe the account currency translation adjustments.
e.   Describe the account retained earnings.
f.   Describe the account treasury stock.
g.   How many shares of common stock are outstanding at January 27, 1995?

CASE 3-4   Insight on Assets

The October 31, 1995 and 1994 consolidated balance sheets of Hewlett-Packard Company included the following assets:

(In millions, except par value and number of shares)	October 31 1995	October 31 1994
Assets		
Current assets:		
Cash and cash equivalents	$ 1,973	$ 1,357
Short-term investments	643	1,121
Accounts and notes receivable	6,735	5,028
Inventories:		
Finished goods	3,368	2,466
Purchased parts and fabricated assemblies	2,645	1,807
Other current assets	875	730
Total current assets	16,239	12,509
Property, plant, and equipment:		
Land	485	508
Buildings and leasehold improvements	3,810	3,472
Machinery and equipment	4,452	3,958
	8,747	7,938
Accumulated depreciation	(4,036)	(3,610)
	4,711	4,328
Long-term investments and other assets	3,477	2,730
Total assets	$24,427	$19,567

Required a. The statement is entitled "Consolidated Balance Sheets." What does it mean to have consolidated balance sheets?

b. What is the estimated amount that will be collected from accounts and notes receivable at October 31, 1995?

c. What is the gross amount of property, plant, and equipment at October 31, 1995?

d. What is the net amount of property, plant, and equipment at October 31, 1995?

e. Describe the account accumulated depreciation.

f. What would be the accumulated depreciation related to land at October 31, 1995?

g. What is the amount of total assets at October 31, 1995?

CASE 3-5   Selective Review of Balance Sheet

The consolidated balance sheets and selected footnotes from the 1995 annual report of AMP follow:

Consolidated Balance Sheet	December 31	
(Dollars in thousands)	**1995**	**1994**
Assets		
Current assets:		
Cash and cash equivalents	$ 212,538	$ 244,568
Securities available for sale	58,197	156,708
Receivables	1,011,460	908,390
Inventories	762,803	641,953
Deferred income taxes	137,043	135,498
Other current assets	95,867	87,183
Total current assets	2,277,908	2,174,300
Property, plant, and equipment	4,352,026	3,713,660
Less: Accumulated depreciation	2,413,760	2,138,978
Property, plant, and equipment, net	1,938,266	1,574,682
Investments and other assets	288,565	343,564
Total assets	$4,504,739	$4,092,546

(continued)

Liabilities and Shareholders' Equity

Current liabilities:

Short-term debt	$ 318,169	$ 182,338
Payables, trade and other	460,892	403,947
Accrued payrolls and employee benefits	168,667	156,322
Accrued income taxes	196,417	247,997
Other accrued liabilities	121,948	116,318
Total current liabilities	1,266,093	1,106,922
Long-term debt	212,485	278,843
Deferred income taxes	45,768	34,249
Other liabilities	212,365	176,777
Total liabilities	1,736,711	1,596,791

Shareholders' equity:

Common stock, without par value—authorized 700,000,000 shares, issued 232,491,889 shares	79,580	70,135
Other capital	83,454	80,105
Deferred compensation	(2,489)	(4,568)
Cumulative translation adjustments	156,837	129,612
Net unrealized investment gains	19,423	21,585
Retained earnings	2,667,755	2,442,317
Treasury stock, at cost	(236,532)	(243,431)
Total shareholders' equity	2,768,028	2,495,755
Total liabilities and shareholders' equity	$ 4,504,739	$ 4,092,546

Notes to Consolidated Financial Statements (in Part)

1. Summary of Accounting Principles (in Part)

Principles of Consolidation The consolidated financial statements include the accounts of the Company and its wholly owned subsidiaries. Investments representing ownership of 20% to 50% in affiliates and corporate joint ventures are accounted for using the equity method.

Inventories Inventories, consisting of material, labor, and overhead, are stated at the lower of first-in, first-out (FIFO) cost or market.

Property, Plant, and Equipment and Depreciation Property, plant, and equipment is stated at cost, adjusted to current exchange rates where applicable. Depreciation is computed by applying principally the straight-line method to individual items. Depreciation rate ranges are substantially as follows:

Buildings	5%
Leasehold improvements	Life of lease
Machinery and equipment	7 1/2% to 33 1/3%
Machines and tools with customers	20% to 33 1/3%

Where different depreciation methods or lives are used for tax purposes, deferred income taxes are recorded.

3. Property, Plant, and Equipment

At December 31, property, plant, and equipment were comprised of the following:

(Dollars in thousands)	1995	1994
Land	$ 81,656	$ 66,135
Buildings and leasehold improvement	898,362	747,996
Machinery and equipment	3,003,591	2,546,700
Machines and tools with customers	368,508	352,829
	$ 4,352,117	$ 3,713,660

6. Inventories

At December 31, inventories were comprised of the following:

(Dollars in thousands)	1995	1994
Finished goods and work in process	$411,504	$373,094
Purchased and manufactured parts	263,926	199,493
Raw materials	87,373	69,366
	$762,803	$641,953

Required

a. The statement is entitled "Consolidated Balance Sheet." What does it mean to have a consolidated balance sheet?

b. Does it appear that the subsidiaries are wholly owned? Explain.

c. What is the dollar amount of stockholders' equity at December 31, 1995?

d. Would the dollar amount of stockholders' equity at December 31, 1995 equal the market value of the common stock at December 31, 1995? Explain.

e. Describe the retained earnings account. Is there cash in the retained earnings account?

f. Describe the treasury stock account. Why is this account deducted from shareholders' equity?

g. Describe the cumulative translation adjustments.

h. What inventory costing method is used? What comprised the major proportion of inventories at December 31, 1995?

i. What is the gross amount of property, plant, and equipment at December 31, 1995?

j. For the property, plant, and equipment on hand at December 31, 1995, what has been the depreciation recognized?

k. 1. What depreciation method is used?
    2. Will straight-line depreciation result in a relative slow recognition
        of depreciation expense? Comment.
l. 1. What is the amount for total assets at December 31, 1995?
    2. What is the amount for total liabilities at December 31, 1995?
    3. What is the amount for shareholders' equity at December 31, 1995?

CASE 3-6 Our Principal Asset Is Our People

Foote, Cone & Belding Communications, Inc. included the following in
its 1992 financial report.

BUSINESS PROFILE

FCB is a global marketing communications company that provides advertising, direct marketing, sales promotion, and other specialized services to
clients worldwide. The Company's activities are conducted through an
organization of 180 offices in 46 countries on six continents, including the
combined Publicis-FCB group in Europe.

In 1992, the Company ranked as one of the largest marketing communications companies in the world. On a combined basis, FCB and Publicis had
revenues of $884 million and billings of more than $6.1 billion.

PERSONNEL

Our principal asset is our people. Our success depends in large part on
our ability to attract and retain personnel who are competent in the various
aspects of our business. As of December 31, 1992, FCB employed 3,631 persons
in its majority-owned offices: 2,411 were employed in the domestic offices and
1,220 were employed in the international offices. Of the 3,631 total employees,
1,100 were engaged in the creation and production of advertising, 1,176 in
account management, 505 in media and research activities, and 850 in administrative and clerical functions.

We believe that it is important for the success of FCB that our people own
a significant portion of FCB's outstanding Common Stock. Our employees
owned approximately 20% of the outstanding Common Stock of the Company
at December 31, 1992, either directly or through various employee benefit
plans.

Required   a. Foote, Cone & Belding states that "Our principal asset is our people."
                 Currently, generally accepted principles do not recognize people as an
                 asset. Speculate on why people are not considered to be an asset.
             b. Speculate on what concept of an asset that Foote, Cone & Belding is
                 considering when they state "Our principal asset is our people."

CASE 3-7 Brands Are Dead?

The September 1, 1993 issue of *Financial World* estimated that the brand value of Intel was $178 billion. *Financial World* arrived at this estimate using a valuation method developed by London-based Intrbrand Group.

Required
a. Define an asset.
b. In your opinion, do brands represent a valuable asset? Comment.
c. Under generally accepted accounting principles, should an internally generated brand value be recognized as an asset? Comment.
d. If the brand was purchased, should it be recognized as an asset? Comment.

CASE 3-8 Advertising—Asset?

The Big Car Company did substantial advertising in late December. The company's year-end date was December 31. The president of the firm was concerned that this advertising campaign would reduce profits.

Required
a. Define an asset.
b. Would the advertising represent an asset? Comment.

Endnotes

1 *Statement of Financial Accounting Concepts No. 6*, "Elements of Financial Statements" (Stamford, CT: Financial Accounting Standards Board, 1985), paragraph 25.

2 *Accounting Trends & Techniques* (Jersey City, NJ), p. 165. Copyright © 1995 by the American Institute of Certified Public Accountants, Inc.

3 Accounting Research Bulletin No. 43 (New York: AICPA, 1953), Ch. 4, paragraph 8.

4 *Statement of Financial Accounting Concepts No. 6*, paragraph 35.

5 *Statement of Financial Accounting Concepts No. 6*, paragraph 212.

4   Income Statement

THE INCOME STATEMENT IS OFTEN CONSIDERED to be the most important financial statement. Frequently used titles for this statement include Statement of Income, Statement of Earnings, and Statement of Operations. This chapter covers the income statement in detail.

BASIC ELEMENTS OF THE INCOME STATEMENT

An income statement summarizes revenues and expenses and gains and losses, and ends with the net income for a specific period.

A simplified multiple-step income statement might look as follows:

	Net Sales	$ XXX
–	*Cost of Goods Sold (cost of sales)*	XXX
	Gross Profit	XXX
–	*Operating Expenses (selling and administrative)*	XXX
	Operating Income	XXX
+(–)	*Other Income or Expense*	XXX
	Income Before Income Taxes	XXX
–	*Income Taxes*	XXX
	Net Income	$ XXX
	Earnings per Share	$X.XX

A multiple-step income statement usually presents separately the gross profit, operating income, income before income taxes, and net income. Many firms use a single-step income statement, which totals revenues and gains (sales, other income, etc.) and then deducts total expenses and losses (cost of goods sold, operating expenses, other expenses, etc.). A simplified single-step income statement might look as follows:

Revenue:	
Net Sales	$ XXX
Other Income	XXX
Total Revenue	XXX
Expenses:	
Cost of Goods Sold (cost of sales)	XXX
Operating Expenses (selling and administrative)	XXX
Other Expense	XXX
Income Tax Expense	XXX
Total Expenses	XXX
Net Income	$ XXX
Earnings per Share	$X.XX

A single-step income statement lists all revenues and gains (usually in order of amount), then lists all expenses and losses (usually in order of amount). Total expense and loss items deducted from total revenue and gain items determine the net income. Most firms that present a single-step income statement modify it in some way, such as presenting federal income tax expense as a separate item.

Exhibits 4-1 and 4-2 illustrate the different types of income statements. In Exhibit 4-1, The Money Store Inc. uses a single-step income statement, while in Exhibit 4-2, page 160, La-Z-Boy Chair Company uses a multiple-step format. Exhibit 4-3, page 161, contains a comprehensive multiple-step income statement illustration.

To permit comparison, the formats of income statements must be similar. The multiple-step format should be used because it provides intermediate profit figures useful in financial statement analysis. You may need to construct the multiple-step format from the single-step.

Net Sales (Revenues)

Sales represent revenue from goods or services sold to customers. The firm earns revenue from the sale of its principal products. Sales are usually shown net of any discounts, returns, and allowances.

Cost of Goods Sold or Cost of Sales

This shows the cost of goods sold to produce revenue. For a retailing firm, the cost of goods sold equals beginning inventory plus purchases minus ending inventory. In a manufacturing firm, the cost of goods manufactured replaces purchases since the goods are produced rather than purchased. A service firm will not have cost of goods sold or cost of sales, but it will often have cost of services.

EXHIBIT 4-1 **THE MONEY STORE INC. AND SUBSIDIARIES**
Consolidated Statements of Income
Single-Step Income Statement

	Years Ended December 31		
(Dollars in thousands)	**1995**	**1994**	**1993**
Revenues:			
Gain on sale of receivables	$ 353,995	$ 259,913	$ 159,576
Finance income, fees earned and other	156,563	70,557	60,233
	510,558	330,470	219,809
Expenses:			
Salaries and employee benefits	119,423	85,596	53,844
Other operating expenses	123,394	96,188	53,462
Provision for credit losses	90,723	52,600	42,746
Interest	93,985	43,059	29,184
	427,525	277,443	179,236
Income before income taxes	83,033	53,027	40,573
Income taxes	34,318	21,706	18,802
Net income	$ 48,715	$ 31,321	$ 21,771
Net income per share	$ 0.95	$ 0.62	$ 0.48
Weighted average number of shares outstanding	51,023,609	50,804,963	45,347,486

Other Operating Revenue

Depending on the operations of the business, there may be other operating revenue, such as lease revenue and royalties.

Operating Expenses

Operating expenses consist of two types: selling and administrative. **Selling expenses**, resulting from the company's effort to create sales, include advertising, sales commissions, sales supplies used, and so on. **Administrative expenses** relate to the general administration of the company's operation. They include office salaries, insurance, telephone, bad debt expense, and other costs difficult to allocate.

Other Income and Expense

These categories are secondary activities of the firm, not directly related to the operations. For example, if a manufacturing firm has a

EXHIBIT 4-2   **LA-Z-BOY CHAIR COMPANY**
Consolidated Statements of Income
Multiple-Step Income Statement

Year Ended	(Dollar amounts in thousands, except per share data)		
	April 29, 1995 (52 weeks)	April 30, 1994 (53 weeks)	April 24, 1993 (52 weeks)
Sales	$ 850,271	$ 804,898	$ 684,122
Cost of sales	629,222	593,890	506,435
Gross profit	221,049	211,008	177,687
Selling, general, and administrative expenses	158,551	151,756	131,894
Operating profit	62,498	59,252	45,793
Interest expense	(3,334)	(2,822)	(3,260)
Interest income	1,628	1,076	1,474
Other income	1,229	649	1,292
Income before income tax expense	62,021	58,155	45,299
Income tax expense:			
Federal—current	22,716	19,719	16,726
—deferred	(1,205)	(445)	(1,965)
State —current	4,177	4,283	3,254
—deferred	31	(119)	—
Total tax expense	25,719	23,438	18,015
Net income before accounting change	36,302	34,717	27,284
Accounting change	—	3,352	—
Net income	$ 36,302	$ 38,069	$ 27,284
Weighted average shares	18,044	18,268	18,172
Net income per share before accounting change	$ 2.01	$ 1.90	$ 1.50
Accounting change	—	0.18	—
Net income per share	$ 2.01	$ 2.08	$ 1.50

warehouse rented, this lease income would be other income. Dividend and interest income and gains and losses from the sale of assets are also included here. Interest expense is categorized as other expense.

SPECIAL INCOME STATEMENT ITEMS

To comprehend and analyze profits, you need to understand income statement items that require special disclosure. Exhibit 4-3 contains items

EXHIBIT 4-3　**Illustration of Special Items**

G AND F COMPANY
Income Statement (Multiple-Step Format)
For the Year Ended December 31, 1995

Net sales		$ XXX
Cost of products sold		XXX
Gross profit		XXX
Other operating revenue		XXX
Operating expenses:		
Selling expenses	$ XXX	
General expenses	XXX	(XXX)
Operating income		XXX
Other income (includes interest income)		XXX
Other expenses (includes interest expense)		(XXX)
[A] Unusual or infrequent item disclosed separately [loss]		(XXX)
[B] Equity in earnings of nonconsolidated subsidiaries [loss]		XXX
Income before taxes		XXX
Income taxes related to operations		XXX
Net income from operations		XXX
[C] Discontinued operations:		
Income [loss] from operations of discontinued segment		
(less applicable income taxes of $XXX)	$(XXX)	
Income [loss] on disposal of division X (less applicable		
income taxes of $XXX)	(XXX)	(XXX)
[D] Extraordinary gain [loss] (less applicable income taxes of $XXX)		(XXX)
[E] Cumulative effect of change in accounting principle [loss]		
(less applicable income taxes of $XXX)		XXX
Net income before minority interest		XXX
[F] Minority share of earnings (income) loss		(XXX)
Net income		$ XXX
Earnings per share		$X.XX

that require special disclosure. These items are lettered to identify them for discussion. Note that some of these items are presented before tax and some are presented net of tax.

(A) Unusual or Infrequent Item Disclosed Separately

Certain income statement items are either unusual or occur infrequently. They might include such items as a gain on sale of securities, write-downs of receivables, or write-downs of inventory. These items are shown with normal, recurring revenues and expenses, and gains and losses. If material, they will be disclosed separately, before tax. Unusual or infrequent items are typically left in primary analysis because they relate to operations.

In supplementary analysis, unusual or infrequent items should be removed net after tax. Usually an estimate of the tax effect will be necessary. A reasonable estimate of the tax effect can be made by using the effective income tax rate, usually disclosed in a footnote, or by dividing income taxes by income before taxes.

Refer to Exhibit 4-4, which illustrates an unusual or infrequent item disclosed separately for Lufkin Industries in 1994. Since Lufkin had a loss in 1994, we compare income tax benefits to the loss to estimate the tax rate of 33% ($592,000/$1,799,000). (Income tax benefits relates to receiving a refund on prior taxes because of the 1994 loss.)

EXHIBIT 4-4 LUFKIN INDUSTRIES, INC. AND SUBSIDIARIES
Consolidated Statement of Earnings
Unusual or Infrequent Item (Special Inventory Provisions)

For the Year Ended December 31 (In thousands except per-share data)	1995	1994	1993
Sales	$ 248,909	$ 217,273	$ 202,225
Costs and expenses:			
Cost of sales	216,733	189,999	176,099
Selling, general, and administrative expenses	22,171	20,725	24,737
→ Special inventory provisions	—	11,224	—
Other income, net	(481)	(1,610)	(347)
Total costs and expenses	238,423	220,338	200,489
Operating income (loss)	10,486	(3,065)	1,736
Investment income	3,118	1,266	2,558
Earnings (loss) before income taxes	13,604	(1,799)	4,294
Income taxes (benefits)	4,686	(592)	1,745
Net earnings (loss)	$ 8,918	$ (1,207)	$ 2,549
Net earnings (loss) per share	$ 1.31	$ (.18)	$ .38

The Lufkin Industries, Inc. unusual item for 1994 would be removed as follows:

Special inventory provisions, before tax	$11,224,000
Less estimated tax effect (33% x $11,224,000)	3,703,920
Special inventory provision, net of tax	$ 7,520,080

Net earnings (loss) would be increased by $7,520,080, resulting in an adjusted net earnings (loss) of $6,313,080 ($1,207,000 loss + $7,520,080 gain).

(B) Equity in Earnings of Nonconsolidated Subsidiaries

When a firm accounts for its investments in stocks using the equity method (the investment is not consolidated), the investor reports equity earnings (losses). **Equity earnings** (losses) are the investor's proportionate share of the investee's earnings (losses). If the investor owns 20% of the stock of the investee, for example, and the investee reports income of $100,000, then the investor reports $20,000 on its income statement. In this book, the term *equity earnings* will be used unless equity losses are specifically intended.

To the extent that equity earnings are not accompanied by cash dividends, the investor reports earnings greater than the cash flow from the investment. If an investor company reports material equity earnings, its net income could be much greater than its ability to pay dividends or cover maturing liabilities.

For purposes of analysis, the equity in the net income of non-consolidated subsidiaries raises practical problems. For example, the equity earnings represent earnings of other companies, not earnings from the operations of the business. Thus, equity earnings can distort the reported results of a business' operations. For each ratio influenced by equity earnings, this book suggests a recommended approach described when the ratio is introduced.

Refer to Exhibit 4-5, which illustrates equity in earnings of non-consolidated subsidiaries for Chevron. Leaving these accounts in the statements presents a problem for profitability analysis because most of the profitability measures relate income figures to other figures (usually balance sheet figures). Because these earnings are from nonconsolidated subsidiaries, an inconsistency can result between the numerator and the denominator when computing a ratio.

Some ratios are distorted more than others by equity earnings. (Chapter 5 presents a detailed discussion of ratios.) For example, the ratio that relates income to sales can be distorted because of equity earnings. The numerator of the ratio includes the earnings of the operating company and the equity earnings of nonconsolidated subsidiaries. The denominator (sales)

EXHIBIT 4-5   CHEVRON CORPORATION
Consolidated Statements of Income
Equity in Earnings of Nonconsolidated Subsidiaries

(Millions of dollars, except per-share amounts)	Year Ended December 31		
	1995	1994	1993
REVENUES			
Sales and other operating revenues*	$36,310	$35,130	$36,191
Equity in net income of affiliated companies	553	440	440
Other income	219	284	451
TOTAL REVENUES	37,082	35,854	37,082
COSTS AND OTHER DEDUCTIONS			
Purchased crude oil and products	18,033	16,990	18,007
Operating expenses	5,974	6,383	7,104
Exploration expenses	372	379	360
Selling, general, and administrative expenses	1,384	963	1,530
Depreciation, depletion, and amortization	3,381	2,431	2,452
Taxes other than income*	5,748	5,559	4,886
Interest and debt expense	401	346	317
TOTAL COSTS AND OTHER DEDUCTIONS	35,293	33,051	34,656
INCOME BEFORE INCOME TAX EXPENSE	1,789	2,803	2,426
INCOME TAX EXPENSE	859	1,110	1,161
NET INCOME PER SHARE OF COMMON STOCK	$1.43	$2.60	$1.94
WEIGHTED AVERAGE NUMBER OF SHARES OUTSTANDING	652,083,804	651,672,238	650,957,752
*Includes consumer excise taxes	$4,988	$4,790	$4,068

includes only the sales of the operating company. The sales of the unconsolidated subsidiaries will not appear on the investor's income statement
because the subsidiary was not consolidated. This causes the ratio to be
distorted.

Equity in earnings of nonconsolidated subsidiaries (equity earnings) will
be presented before tax. Any tax will be related to the dividend
received, and it will typically be immaterial. When removing equity earnings for analysis, do not attempt a tax computation.

Income Taxes Related to Operations

Federal, state, and local income taxes, based on reported accounting
profit, are shown here. Income tax expense includes taxes paid and taxes

deferred. Income taxes reported here will not include taxes on items presented net of tax.

(C) Discontinued Operations

A common type of unusual item is the disposal of a business or product line. APB Opinion No. 30 established disclosure requirements to provide the information necessary to assess the impact of discontinued operations on the business enterprise. If the disposal meets the criteria of APB Opinion No. 30, a separate income statement category for the gain or loss from disposal of a segment of the business must be provided. In addition, the results of operations of the segment that has been or will be disposed of are reported in conjunction with the gain or loss on disposal. These effects appear as a separate category after continuing operations.

Discontinued operations pose a problem for profitability analysis. Ideally, income from continuing operations would be the better figure to use to project future income. Several practical problems associated with the removal of a gain or loss from the discontinued operations occur in the primary profitability analysis. These problems revolve around two points: (1) an inadequate disclosure of data related to the discontinued operations, in order to remove the balance sheet amounts associated with the discontinued operations; and (2) the lack of past profit and loss data associated with the discontinued operations.

Exhibit 4-6, page 166-167, illustrates the presentation of discontinued operations in net income. The best analysis would remove the income statement item that relates to the discontinued operations.

The income statement items that relate to a discontinued operation are always presented net of applicable income taxes. Therefore, the items as presented on the income statement can be removed for primary analysis without further adjustment for income taxes. Supplementary analysis considers discontinued operations in order to avoid completely disregarding these items.

Ideally, the balance sheet accounts that relate to the discontinued operations should be removed for primary analysis. Consider these items on a supplemental basis because they will not contribute to future operating revenue. However, inadequate disclosure often makes it impossible to remove these items from your analysis.

The balance sheet items related to discontinued operations are frequently disposed of when the business or product line has been disposed of prior to the year-end balance sheet date. In this case, the balance sheet accounts related to discontinued operations do not present a problem for the current year.

EXHIBIT 4-6 BRISTOL-MYERS SQUIBB COMPANY
Consolidated Statements of Earnings
Discontinued Operations

	Year Ended December 31		
(In millions, except per-share data)	1995	1994	1993
Revenues			
Sales	$ 8,799	$ 7,853	$ 7,211
Service and rentals	6,804	6,229	5,954
Finance income	1,008	1,006	1,064
Total Revenues	16,611	15,088	14,229
Costs and Expenses			
Cost of sales	4,962	4,653	4,098
Cost of service and rentals	3,437	3,016	2,986
Equipment financing interest	509	502	537
Research and development expenses	951	895	883
Selling, administrative, and general expenses	4,770	4,394	4,477
Special charges, net	—	—	1,373
Other, net	135	114	155
Total Costs and Expenses	14,764	13,574	14,509
Income (Loss) Before Income Taxes, Equity Income, and Minorities' Interests	1,847	1,514	(280)
Income Taxes (Benefits)	615	595	(78)
Equity in Net Income of Unconsolidated Affiliates	132	88	87
Minorities' Interests in Earnings of Subsidiaries	190	213	78
Income (Loss) from Continuing Operations	1,174	794	(193)
Discontinued Operations	(1,646)	—	67
Net Income (Loss)	$ (472)	$ 794	$ (126)
Primary Earnings (Loss) per Share			
Continuing Operations	$ 10.20	$ 6.73	$ (2.50)
Discontinued Operations	(14.89)	—	.66
Primary Earnings per Share	$ (4.69)	$ 6.73	$ (1.84)
Fully Diluted Earnings (Loss) per Share			
Continuing Operations	$ 9.63	$ 6.44	$ (2.50)
Discontinued Operations	(14.89)	—	.66
Fully Diluted Earnings per Share	$ (5.26)	$ 6.44	$ (1.84)

Note 1—Summary of Significant Accounting Policies (in Part)

Discontinued Operations. In January 1993, the Company announced its intent to sell or otherwise disengage from its Insurance and Other Financial Services businesses, which is consistent with the strategy that began in 1990. A formal plan for

EXHIBIT 4-6   **(concluded)**

the disposal of Other Financial Services was adopted in 1993, at which time the Other Financial Services businesses were accounted for as discontinued operations. The Insurance business, which now consists of Talegen Holdings, Inc. (Talegen), The Resolution Group, Inc. (TRG), Ridge Reinsurance Limited, and headquarters costs and interest expense associated with the insurance activities of Xerox Financial, Inc., remained a continuing operation of the Company at that time.

During 1995, two of the seven operating groups of Talegen were sold. In January 1996, the Company announced separate agreements to sell all of the remaining insurance units of Talegen and TRG to investor groups led by Kohlberg Kravis Roberts & Co. and existing management. The sales are subject to customary closing conditions, including buyer financing and regulatory approvals. As a result, the Insurance businesses have been accounted for as a discontinued operation, and all prior periods have been restated. See Note 9 on Page 60 for additional information.

The announced sale agreements, on closing, effectively complete the Company's strategy to exit financial services.

(D) Extraordinary Items

APB Opinion No. 30 established criteria for extraordinary items; that is, material events and transactions distinguished by their unusual nature and by the infrequency of their occurrence. Examples include a major casualty (such as a fire), prohibition under a newly enacted law, or an expropriation. These items, net of their tax effects, must be shown separately. Other pronouncements have specified items that must be considered extraordinary, including material tax loss carryovers and gains and losses from extinguishment of debt. The effect of an extraordinary item on earnings per share must also be shown separately. Exhibit 4-7, page 168, presents an extraordinary gain on extinguishment of debt.

In analysis of income for purposes of determining a trend, extraordinary items should be eliminated since the extraordinary item is not expected to recur. In supplementary analysis, these extraordinary items should be considered, as this approach avoids completely disregarding these items.

Extraordinary items are always presented net of applicable income taxes. Therefore, the items as presented on the income statement are removed without further adjustment for income taxes.

EXHIBIT 4-7 SPECTRUM CONTROL INC.
Consolidated Statements of Income
Extraordinary Gain (Loss)

Year Ended November 30	(Dollars in thousands except per-share data)		
	1995	1994	1993
Net sales	$49,297	$43,659	$41,336
Cost of products sold	33,236	30,629	26,271
Selling, general, and administrative expense	11,016	9,734	9,916
	44,252	40,363	36,187
Income from operations	5,045	3,296	5,149
Other income (expense)			
Interest expense	(908)	(1,003)	(1,157)
Other income and expense, net (Note 9)	(42)	364	226
	(950)	(639)	(931)
Income from continuing operations before provision for income taxes	4,095	2,657	4,218
Provision for income taxes (Note 10)	1,111	602	320
Income from continuing operations	2,984	2,055	3,898
Discontinued operations (Note 3):			
Loss from hybrid integrated circuit operations	—	—	(483)
Loss on disposal of hybrid integrated circuit operations, including operating losses of $653 during phase-out period	—	—	(2,433)
	—	—	(2,916)
Income before extraordinary item and cumulative effect of a change in accounting principle	2,984	2,055	982
Extraordinary item (Note 8):			
Gain on extinguishment of debt, net of applicable income taxes of $446	—	—	4,012
Income before cumulative effect of a change in accounting principle	2,984	2,055	4,994
Cumulative effect on prior years of changing the method of accounting for income taxes (Note 2)	—	1,845	—
Net income	$ 2,984	$ 3,900	$ 4,994
Earnings (loss) per common share:			
Continuing operations	$ 0.28	$ 0.19	$ 0.38
Discontinued operations	—	—	(0.28)
Extraordinary item	—	—	0.39
Accounting change	—	0.18	—
Net income	$ 0.28	$ 0.37	$ 0.49

(E) Cumulative Effect of Change in Accounting Principle

Some changes in accounting principles do not require retroactive adjustments to reflect the adoption of a new accounting principle. The new principle is used for the current year, while the prior years continue to be presented based on the prior accounting principle. This makes comparability a problem. The comparability problem is compounded by the additional reporting guideline that directs that the income effect of the change on prior years be reported net of tax as a cumulative effect of a change in accounting principle on the income statement in the year of change. The cumulative effect is shown separately on the income statement in the year of change. It is usually shown just above net income.

When there is a cumulative effect of a change in accounting principle, the reporting standards require that income before extraordinary items and net income, computed on a pro forma basis (as if the new principle had been in effect), should be shown on the face of the income statements for all periods as if the newly adopted accounting principle had been applied during all periods affected. The pro forma presentation is an additional presentation at the bottom of the income statement. In practice this pro forma material is often not presented or only partially presented.

The accounting standard of not changing the statements retroactively is the general case when an accounting principle changes. APB Opinion No. 20, the basis of this reporting standard, provides for only a few exceptions. For most exceptions, the prior statements are retroactively changed using the new accounting principle. In the case when the cumulative effect cannot be determined, the firm should include a footnote explaining the change in accounting principle and the fact that the cumulative effect is not determinable.

The most common situation in which the cumulative effect is not determinable has been a switch to LIFO inventory. The base-year inventory is the opening inventory in the year that LIFO is adopted. There is no restatement of prior years or cumulative effect treatment. Thus, when a firm switches to LIFO, a major problem develops in profitability analysis. The year of change and subsequent years are in LIFO, while years prior to the change are reported using the previous inventory method. Be aware that these years are not comparable with the years using LIFO.

The accounting standard of not changing the statements retroactively when there has been a change in accounting principle is not always followed in practice. APB opinions subsequent to No. 20 and later SFASs frequently directed that the new principles included in the respective pronouncement be handled retroactively by changing prior years' statements.

The accounting standard of not changing the statements retroactively when there has been a change in accounting principle presents major problems for analysis. It is not good theory because it places on the income statement, in the year of change, a potentially material income or loss amount that has nothing to do with operations of that year. Comparability with prior years (consistency) is also a problem.

Statement of Financial Accounting Concepts No. 5 (December 1985) recommends that the cumulative effects of changes in accounting principles not be included in earnings in the year of change in principle. To date, this recommendation has not been the subject of a FASB statement.

No ideal way exists to handle the analysis problem when a change in accounting principle is not handled retroactively. The cumulative effect of a change in accounting principle should be removed from the income statement for primary analysis. This still leaves the comparability problem that the income in the year of change, and subsequent years, is based on the new principle; while the years prior to the change are based on the prior principle. If, in your opinion, the income effect is so extreme that comparability is materially distorted, then do not use years prior to the change in comparability analysis. Also note the pro forma presentation, if provided, at the bottom of the income statement. The pro forma numbers will be comparable, but limited. Exhibit 4-8 illustrates a cumulative effect of a change in accounting principle. Exhibit 4-8 does not include a pro forma presentation.

(F) Minority Share of Earnings

If a firm consolidates subsidiaries not wholly owned, the total revenues and expenses of the subsidiaries are included with those of the parent. However, to determine the income that would accrue to the parent, it is necessary to deduct the portion of income that would belong to the minority owners. This is labeled "minority share of earnings" or "minority interest in net income." Note that this item sometimes appears before and sometimes after the tax provision on the income statement. When presented before the tax provision, it is usually presented gross of tax. When presented after the tax provision, it is presented net of tax. In this book, assume net-of-tax treatment. Exhibit 4-9, page 172, illustrates a minority share of earnings.

Some ratios can be distorted because of a minority share of earnings. For each ratio influenced by a minority share of earnings, this book suggests a recommended approach described later.

EARNINGS PER SHARE

In general, **earnings per share** is earnings divided by the number of shares of outstanding common stock. Chapter 10 presents earnings per share in detail, and explains its computation. Meanwhile, use the formula of net income divided by outstanding shares of common stock.

EXHIBIT 4-8 BASSETT FURNITURE INDUSTRIES, INCORPORATED AND SUBSIDIARIES
Consolidated Statements of Income
Cumulative Effect of Change in Accounting Principle

	Year Ended November 30		
	1995	**1994**	**1993**
Net sales	$ 490,816,681	$ 510,560,858	$ 503,770,060
Costs and expenses:			
Cost of sales	407,749,396	419,393,531	413,055,371
Selling, general, and administrative	65,938,061	66,044,399	63,472,078
	473,687,457	485,437,930	476,527,449
INCOME FROM OPERATIONS	17,129,224	25,122,928	27,242,611
Other income, net	12,999,562	9,657,476	9,270,219
Income before income taxes and cumulative effect of a change in accounting principle	30,128,786	34,780,404	36,512,830
Income taxes:			
Federal	6,455,000	8,521,000	9,223,000
State	879,000	1,361,000	1,077,000
Deferred	(108,000)	(78,000)	344,000
	7,226,000	9,804,000	10,644,000
Income before cumulative effect of a change in accounting principle	22,902,786	24,976,404	25,868,830
Cumulative effect of a change in accounting principle	—	(510,200)	—
NET INCOME	$ 22,902,786	$ 24,466,204	$ 25,868,830
EARNINGS PER SHARE			
Income before cumulative effect of a change in accounting principle	$ 1.63	$ 1.75	$ 1.79
Cumulative effect of a change in accounting principle	—	(.04)	—
NET INCOME PER SHARE	$ 1.63	$ 1.71	$ 1.79

RETAINED EARNINGS

Retained earnings are the undistributed earnings of the corporation. A reconciliation of retained earnings summarizes the changes in retained earnings. It shows the retained earnings at the beginning of the year, the net income for the year as an addition, the dividends as a subtraction, and

EXHIBIT 4-9 UNITED TECHNOLOGIES
Consolidated Statements of Operations
Minority Share of Earnings

| | Year Ended December 31 | | |
(In thousands, except per share)	1995	1994	1993
Revenues			
Net sales	$ 1,495,466	$ 1,357,715	$ 1,422,308
Equity in income of unconsolidated entities	57,031	64,120	2,415
Gain on sale of investments	—	5,966	17,555
Other revenues	1,520	37,980	2,018
Total revenues	1,554,017	1,465,781	1,444,296
Costs and expenses			
Cost of sales	1,147,467	1,060,695	1,107,187
Selling, general, and administrative expenses	198,706	199,837	180,375
Research and development expenses	4,876	5,463	5,167
Facilities discontinuance and reorganization costs	22,809	17,143	2,419
Other	(5,018)	6,158	(493)
Total costs and expenses	1,368,840	1,289,296	1,294,655
Income before interest, taxes, minority interest, and cumulative effect of accounting change	185,177	176,485	149,641
Interest income	7,472	6,403	7,586
Interest expense	(28,921)	(34,048)	(19,974)
Income before taxes, minority interest, and cumulative effect of accounting change	163,728	148,840	137,253
Provision for income taxes	63,854	59,536	56,335
Income before minority interest and cumulative effect of accounting change	99,874	89,304	80,918
Minority interest in net income	2,497	2,751	102
Income before cumulative effect of accounting change	97,377	86,553	80,816
Cumulative effect of accounting change	—	—	6,802
Net income	$ 97,377	$ 86,553	$ 87,618
Earnings per common share			
Income before cumulative effect of accounting change	$ 3.86	$ 3.45	$ 3.23
Cumulative effect of accounting change	—	—	0.27
Net income per common share	$ 3.86	$ 3.45	$ 3.50
Average shares of common stock outstanding	25,246	25,115	25,036

concludes with end-of-year retained earnings. It also includes, if appropriate, prior period adjustments (net of tax) and some adjustments for changes in accounting principles (net of tax). These restate beginning retained earnings. Other possible changes to retained earnings are beyond the scope of this book.

Sometimes a portion of retained earnings may be unavailable for dividends because it has been appropriated (restricted). Appropriated retained earnings remain part of retained earnings. The appropriation of retained earnings may or may not have significance.

Appropriations that result from legal requirements (usually state law) and appropriations that result from contractual agreements are potentially significant. They may leave unappropriated retained earnings inadequate to pay dividends. (Note: A corporation will not be able to pay a cash dividend even with an adequate unrestricted balance in retained earnings unless it has adequate cash.)

Most appropriations result from management decisions. These are usually not significant, because management can choose to remove the appropriation.

The reason for an appropriation will be disclosed either in the reconciliation of retained earnings or in a footnote. From this disclosure, try to arrive at an opinion as to the significance, if any. For example, Cooper Tire & Rubber Company had retained earnings of $672,373,000 at December 31, 1995. A footnote indicates restricted retained earnings because of loan agreements. The amount of retained earnings not restricted was $540,703,000 at December 31, 1995. This is likely not significant because the dividends paid were only $22,584,000 in 1995.

The reconciliation of retained earnings usually appears as part of a statement of owners' equity. Sometimes it is combined with the income statement. Exhibit 4-10, page 174, gives an example of a reconciliation of retained earnings being presented with an owners' equity statement. Exhibit 4-11, page 175, illustrates a combined income statement and reconciliation of retained earnings. This clearly shows the connection between the income statement and retained earnings on the balance sheet.

DIVIDENDS AND STOCK SPLITS

Dividends return profits to the owners of a corporation. A cash dividend declared by the board of directors reduces retained earnings by the amount of the dividends declared and creates the current liability, dividends payable. The date of payment occurs after the date of declaration. The dividend payment eliminates the liability, dividends payable, and reduces cash. Note that the date of the declaration of dividends, not the date of the dividend payment, affects retained earnings and creates the liability.

EXHIBIT 4-10   THE MONEY STORE INC. AND SUBSIDIARIES
Consolidated Statements of Shareholders' Equity

(Dollars in thousands)	Common Stock		Retained	
	Shares	Amount	Earnings	Total
Balance, December 31, 1992	45,168,750	$38,888	$ 87,267	$126,155
Proceeds from exercise of stock options	11,250	32	—	32
Issuance of common stock	5,625,000	19,043	—	19,043
Dividends	—	—	(1,688)	(1,688)
Net income	—	—	21,771	21,771
Balance, December 31, 1993	50,805,000	57,963	107,350	165,313
Purchase of fractional shares	(37)	—	—	—
Dividends	—	—	(2,371)	(2,371)
Net income	—	—	31,321	31,321
Balance, December 31, 1994	50,804,963	57,963	136,300	194,263
Proceeds from exercise of stock options	534,933	1,640	—	1,640
Dividends	—	—	(3,492)	(3,492)
Net income	—	—	48,715	48,715
Balance, December 31, 1995	51,339,896	$59,603	$181,523	$241,126

The board of directors may elect to declare and issue another type of dividend, termed a *stock dividend*. The firm issues a percentage of outstanding stock as new shares to existing shareholders. If the board declares a 10% stock dividend, for example, an owner holding 1,000 shares would receive an additional 100 shares of new stock. The accounting for a stock dividend, assuming a relatively small distribution (less than 25% of the existing stock), requires removing the fair market value of the stock at the date of declaration from retained earnings and transferring it to paid-in capital. With a material stock dividend, the amount removed from retained earnings and transferred to paid-in capital is determined by multiplying the par value of the stock by the number of additional shares. Note that the overall effect of a stock dividend leaves total stockholders' equity and each owner's share of stockholders' equity unchanged. However, the total number of outstanding shares increases.

A stock dividend should reduce the market value of individual shares by the percentage of the stock dividend. Total market value considering all outstanding shares should not change in theory. In practice, the market value change may not be the same percentage as the stock dividend.

A more drastic device to change the market value of individual shares is by declaring a stock split. A 2-for-1 split should reduce the market value per share to one half the amount prior to the split. The market value per

EXHIBIT 4-11 OVERSEAS SHIPHOLDING GROUP, INC.
Consolidated Statements of Operations and Retained Earnings

	Year Ended December 31		
(In thousands, except per-share amounts)	1995	1994	1993
Shipping Revenues:			
Revenues from voyages—Note B	$ 407,834	$ 358,537	$ 376,885
Income attributable to bulk shipping joint			
ventures—Note E	6,083	5,599	5,695
	413,917	364,136	382,580
Shipping Expenses:			
Vessel and voyage—Note H	272,778	243,684	252,153
Depreciation of vessels and amortization of			
capital leases	66,134	59,992	58,734
Agency fees—Note H	34,105	30,302	30,225
General and administrative	10,515	9,825	8,826
	383,532	343,803	349,938
Income from Vessel Operations	30,385	20,333	32,642
Equity in Results of Celebrity Cruise			
Lines Inc.—Note D	(1,208)	797	6,841
Other Income (Net)—Note K	23,371	25,908	30,674
	52,548	47,038	70,157
Interest Expense	66,440	56,988	43,311
Income/(Loss) Before Federal Income Taxes	(13,892)	(9,950)	26,846
Provision/(Credit) for Federal Income Taxes—Note J	(5,260)	(3,750)	8,900
Net Income/(Loss)	(8,632)	(6,200)	17,946
Retained Earnings at Beginning of Year	737,583	764,987	766,647
	728,951	758,787	784,593
Cash Dividends Declared and Paid	21,731	21,204	19,606
Retained Earnings at End of Year	$ 707,220	$ 737,583	$ 764,987
Per Share Amounts—Note N:			
Net income/(Loss)	$ (0.24)	$ (0.17)	$ 0.55
Cash dividends declared and paid	$ 0.60	$ 0.60	$ 0.60

share in practice may not change exactly in proportion to the split. The market value will result from the supply and demand for the stock.

Lowering the market value is sometimes desirable for stocks selling at high prices (as perceived by management). Stocks with high prices are less readily traded. A stock dividend or stock split can influence the demand for the stock.

A stock split merely increases the number of shares of stock. It does not usually change retained earnings or paid-in capital. For example, if a firm had 1,000 shares of common stock, a 2-for-1 stock split would result in 2,000 shares.

For a stock split, the par or stated value of the stock is changed in proportion to the stock split, and no change is made to retained earnings, additional paid-in capital, or capital stock. For example, a firm with $10 par common stock that declares a 2-for-1 stock split would reduce the par value to $5.

Since the number of shares changes under both a stock dividend and stock split, any ratio based on the number of shares must be restated for a meaningful comparison. For example, if a firm had earnings per share of $4.00 in 1996, a 2-for-1 stock split in 1997 would require restatement of the earnings per share to $2.00 in 1996 because of the increase in the shares. Restatement will be made for all prior financial statements presented with the current financial statements, including a five- or ten-year summary.

SUMMARY

The income statement summarizes the profit for a specific period of time. To understand and analyze profitability, the reader must be familiar with the components of income, as well as income statement items that require special disclosure. This chapter presented special income statement items, such as unusual or infrequent items disclosed separately, equity in earnings of nonconsolidated subsidiaries, discontinued operations, extraordinary items, changes in accounting principle, and minority shares of earnings. This chapter also reviewed the reconciliation of retained earnings, as well as dividends and stock splits.

QUESTIONS

Q 4-1.   What are extraordinary items? How are they shown on the income statement? Why are they shown in that manner?

Q 4-2.   Which of the following would be classified as extraordinary?

a. Selling expense
b. Interest expense
c. Gain on the sale of marketable securities
d. Loss from flood
e. Income tax expense
f. Loss from prohibition of red dye
g. Loss from the write-down of inventory

Q 4-3.   Give three examples of unusual or infrequent items that are disclosed separately. Why are they shown separately? Are they presented before or after tax? Why or why not?

Q 4-4.   Why is the equity in earnings of nonconsolidated subsidiaries sometimes a problem in profitability analysis? Discuss with respect to income versus cash flow.

Q 4-5.   A health food distributor selling wholesale dairy products and vitamins decides to discontinue the division that sells vitamins. How should this discontinuance be classified on the income statement?

Q 4-6.   Why are unusual or infrequent items disclosed before tax?

Q 4-7.   In 1996, Jensen Company decided to change its depreciation method from units-of-production to straight-line. The cumulative effect of the change to the new method, prior to 1996, was to increase depreciation by $30,000 before tax. How would the change be presented in the financial statements?

Q 4-8.   How does the declaration of a cash dividend affect the financial statements? How does the payment of a cash dividend affect the financial statements?

Q 4-9.   What is the difference in the impact on financial statements of a stock dividend versus a stock split?

Q 4-10.   Why is minority share of earnings deducted before arriving at net income?

Q 4-11.   Explain the relationship between the income statement and the reconciliation of retained earnings.

Q 4-12.   List the three types of appropriated retained earnings accounts. Which of these types is most likely not a detriment to the payment of a dividend? Explain.

Q 4-13.   A balance sheet represents a specific date, such as "December 31," while an income statement covers a period of time, such as "For the Year Ended December 31, 1997." Why does this difference exist?

Q 4-14.   Describe the following items:

a. Minority interest
b. Equity in earnings of nonconsolidated subsidiaries
c. Minority share of earnings

Q 4-15.   An income statement is a summary of revenues and expenses and gains and losses, ending with net income for a specific period of time. Indicate the two traditional formats for presenting the income statement. Which of these formats is preferable for analysis? Why?

Q 4-16.   Melcher Company reported earnings per share in 1996 and 1995 of $2.00 and $1.60, respectively. In 1997 there was a 2-for-1 stock split, and the earnings per share for 1997 were reported to be $1.40. Give a three-year presentation of earnings per share (1995-1997).

PROBLEMS

P 4-1.   The following information for Decher Automotives covers the year ended 1997:

Administrative expenses	$ 62,000
Dividend income	10,000
Income taxes	100,000
Interest expense	20,000
Merchandise inventory, 1/1	650,000
Merchandise inventory, 12/31	440,000
Flood loss (net of tax)	30,000
Purchases	460,000
Sales	1,000,000
Selling expenses	43,000

Required   a.   Prepare a multiple-step income statement.
              b.   Assuming that 100,000 shares of common stock are outstanding, calculate the earnings per share before extraordinary items and the net earnings per share.
              c.   Prepare a single-step income statement.

P 4-2.   The following information for Lesky Corporation covers the year ended December 31, 1997:

LESKY CORPORATION
Income Statement
For the Year Ended December 31, 1997

Revenue:		
Revenues from sales		$ 362,000
Rental income		1,000
Interest		2,400
Total revenue		365,400
Expenses:		
Cost of products sold	$242,000	
Selling expenses	47,000	
Administrative and general expenses	11,400	
Interest expense	2,200	
Federal and state income taxes	20,300	
Total expenses		322,900
Net income		$ 42,500

Required   Change this statement to a multiple-step format, as illustrated in this chapter.

P 4-3.   The accounts of Consolidated Can contain the following amounts at December 31, 1997:

Cost of products sold	$410,000
Dividends	3,000
Extraordinary gain (net of tax)	1,000
Income taxes	9,300
Interest expense	8,700
Other income	1,600
Retained earnings, 1/1	270,000
Sales	480,000
Selling and administrative expense	42,000

Required   Prepare a multiple-step income statement combined with a reconciliation of retained earnings for the year ended December 31, 1997.

P 4-4.   The following items are from Taperline Corporation on December 31, 1997. Assume a flat 40% corporate tax rate on all items, including the casualty loss.

Sales	$670,000
Rental income	3,600
Gain on the sale of fixed assets	3,000
General and administrative expenses	110,000
Selling expenses	97,000
Interest expense	1,900
Depreciation for the period	10,000
Extraordinary item (casualty loss—pretax)	30,000
Cost of sales	300,000
Common stock (30,000 shares outstanding)	150,000

Required   a. Prepare a single-step income statement for the year ended December 31, 1997. Include earnings per share for earnings before extraordinary items and net income.

b. Prepare a multiple-step income statement. Include earnings per share for earnings before extraordinary items and net income.

P 4-5.   The income statement of Rawl Company for the year ended December 31, 1997 shows:

Net sales	$ 360,000
Cost of sales	190,000
Gross profit	170,000
Selling, general, and administrative expense	80,000
Income before unusual write-offs	90,000
Provision for unusual write-offs	50,000
Earnings from operations before income taxes	40,000
Income taxes	20,000
Net earnings from operations before extraordinary charge	20,000
Extraordinary charge, net of tax of $10,000	(50,000)
Net earnings (loss)	$ (30,000)

Required   Compute the net earnings remaining after removing unusual write-offs and the extraordinary charge. Remove these items net of tax. Estimate the tax rate for unusual write-offs based on the taxes on operating income.

P 4-6.   At the end of 1997, vandals destroyed your financial records. Fortunately, the controller had kept certain statistical data related to the income statement, as follows:

  a. Cost of goods sold was $2,000,000.
  b. Administrative expenses were 20% of the cost of sales but only 10% of sales.
  c. Selling expenses were 150% of administrative expenses.
  d. Bonds payable were $1,000,000, with an average interest rate of 11%.
  e. The tax rate was 48%.
  f. 50,000 shares of common stock were outstanding for the entire year.

Required   From the information given, reconstruct a multiple-step income statement for the year. Include earnings per share.

P 4-7.   The following information applies to Bowling Green Metals Corporation for the year ended December 31, 1997.

Total revenues from regular operations	$832,000
Total expenses from regular operations	776,000
Extraordinary gain, net of applicable income taxes	30,000
Dividends paid	20,000
Number of shares of common stock	
outstanding during the year	10,000

Required   Compute earnings per share before extraordinary items and net earnings. Show how this might be presented in the financial statements.

P 4-8.   You were recently hired as the assistant treasurer for Victor, Inc. Yesterday the treasurer was injured in a bicycle accident and is now hospitalized, unconscious. Your boss, Mr. Fernandes, just informed you that the financial statements are due today. Searching through the treasurer's desk, you find the following notes:

  a. Income from continuing operations, based on computations done so far, is $400,000. No taxes are accounted for yet. The tax rate is 30%.
  b. Dividends declared and paid were $20,000. During the year, 100,000 shares of stock were outstanding.
  c. The corporation experienced an uninsured loss from a freak hail storm of $20,000 pretax. Such a storm is considered to be unusual and infrequent.
  d. The company decided to change its inventory pricing method from average cost to the FIFO method. The effect of this change is to increase prior years'

income by $30,000 pretax. The FIFO method has been used for 1997. (Hint: This adjustment should be placed just prior to net income.)

e. In 1997, the company settled a lawsuit against it for $10,000 pretax. The settlement was not previously accrued and is due for payment in February 1998.

f. In 1997, the firm sold a portion of its long-term securities at a gain of $30,000 pretax.

g. The corporation disposed of its consumer products division in August 1997, at a loss of $90,000 pretax. The loss from operations through August was $60,000 pretax.

Required   Prepare an income statement for 1997, in good form, starting with income from continuing operations. Compute earnings per share for income from continuing operations, discontinued operations, extraordinary loss, cumulative effect of a change in accounting principle, and net income.

P 4-9.   List the statement on which each of the following items may appear. Choose from (A) income statement, (B) balance sheet, or (C) neither.

a. Net income
b. Cost of goods sold
c. Gross profit
d. Retained earnings
e. Paid-in capital in excess of par
f. Sales
g. Supplies expense
h. Investment in G. Company
i. Dividends
j. Inventory
k. Common stock

l. Interest payable
m. Loss from flood
n. Land
o. Taxes payable
p. Interest income
q. Gain on sale of property
r. Dividend income
s. Depreciation expense
t. Accounts receivable
u. Accumulated depreciation
v. Sales commissions

P 4-10.   List where each of the following items may appear. Choose from (A) income statement, (B) balance sheet, or (C) reconciliation of retained earnings.

a. Dividends paid
b. Notes payable
c. Minority share of earnings
d. Accrued payroll
e. Loss on disposal of equipment
f. Minority interest in consolidated subsidiary
g. Adjustments of prior periods
h. Redeemable preferred stock
i. Treasury stock
j. Extraordinary loss

k. Unrealized exchange gains and losses
l. Equity in net income of affiliates
m. Goodwill
n. Unrealized decline in market value of equity investment
o. Cumulative effect of change in accounting principle
p. Common stock
q. Cost of goods sold
r. Supplies
s. Land

P 4-11.   The income statement of Tawls Company for the year ended December 31, 1997 shows:

Revenue from sales		$ 980,000
Cost of products sold		510,000
Gross profit		470,000
Operating expenses:		
Selling expenses	$110,000	
General expenses	140,000	250,000
Operating income		220,000
Equity on earnings of nonconsolidated subsidiary		60,000
Operating income before income taxes		280,000
Taxes related to operations		100,000
Net income from operations		180,000
Extraordinary loss from flood		
(less applicable taxes of $50,000)		(120,000)
Minority share of earnings		(40,000)
Net income		$ 20,000

Required   a.   Compute the net earnings remaining after removing nonrecurring items.
b.   Determine the earnings from the nonconsolidated subsidiary.
c.   For the subsidiary that was not consolidated, what amount of income would have been included if this subsidiary had been consolidated?
d.   What earnings relate to minority shareholders of a subsidiary that was consolidated?
e.   Determine the total tax amount.

P 4-12.   The income statement of Jones Company for the year ended December 31, 1997 shows:

Revenue from sales		$ 790,000
Cost of products sold		410,000
Gross profit		380,000
Operating expenses:		
Selling expenses	$ 40,000	
General expenses	80,000	120,000
Operating income		260,000
Equity in earnings of non-		
consolidated subsidiaries (loss)		(20,000)
Operating income before income taxes		240,000
Taxes related to operations		(94,000)
Net income from operations		146,000

(continued)

Net income from operations (brought forward)		$146,000
Discontinued operations:		
Loss from operations of discontinued		
segment (less applicable income		
tax credit of $30,000)	$(70,000)	
Loss on disposal of segment		
(less applicable income tax		
credit of $50,000)	(100,000)	(170,000)
Income before cumulative effect		
of change in accounting		
principle		(24,000)
Cumulative effect of change in accounting		
principle (less applicable income taxes of		
$25,000)		50,000
Net income		$ 26,000

Required

a. Compute the net earnings remaining after removing nonrecurring items.
b. Determine the earnings (loss) from the nonconsolidated subsidiary.
c. Determine the total tax amount.

P 4-13.   Uranium Mining Company, founded in 1970 to mine and market uranium, purchased a mine in 1971 for $900 million. It estimated that the uranium had a market value of $150 per ounce. By 1997, the market value had increased to $300 per ounce. Records for 1997 indicate the following:

Production	200,000 ounces
Sales	230,000 ounces
Deliveries	190,000 ounces
Cash collection	210,000 ounces
Costs of production including depletion*	$50,000,000
Selling expense	$2,000,000
Administrative expenses	$1,250,000
Tax rate	50%

*Production cost per ounce has remained constant over the last few years, and the company has maintained the same production level.

Required

a. Compute the income for 1997, using each of the following bases:
   1.   Receipt of cash
   2.   Point of sale
   3.   End of production
   4.   Based on delivery
b. Comment on when each of the methods should be used. Which method should be used by Uranium Mining Company?

P 4-14.   Each of the following statements represents a decision made by the accountant of Growth Industries:

a. A tornado destroyed $200,000 in uninsured inventory. This loss is included in the cost of goods sold.

b. Land was purchased ten years ago for $50,000. The accountant adjusts the land account to $100,000, which is the estimated current value.

c. The cost of machinery and equipment is charged to a fixed asset account. The machinery and equipment will be expensed over the period of use.

d. The value of equipment increased this year, so no depreciation of equipment was recorded this year.

e. During the year, inventory that cost $5,000 was stolen by employees. This loss has been included in the cost of goods sold for the financial statements. The total amount of the cost of goods sold was $1,000,000.

f. The president of the company, who owns the business, used company funds to buy a car for personal use. The car was recorded on the company's books.

Required   State whether you agree or disagree with each decision.

Cases

CASE 4-1 Single-Step/Multiple-Step Income Statement

Motorola presented these statements of consolidated earnings for the years ended December 31.

Statements of Consolidated Earnings	Years Ended December 31		
(In millions, except per-share amounts)	1995	1994	1993
Net sales	$ 27,037	$ 22,245	$ 16,963
Cost and expenses:			
Manufacturing and other costs of sales	17,545	13,760	10,351
Selling, general, and administrative expenses	4,642	4,381	3,776
Depreciation expenses	1,919	1,525	1,170
Interest expense, net	149	142	141
Total costs and expenses	24,255	19,808	15,438
Earnings before income taxes	2,782	2,437	1,525
Income taxes provided on earnings	1,001	877	503
Net earnings	$ 1,781	$ 1,560	$ 1,022
Fully diluted net earnings per common and common equivalent share[1,2]	$ 2.93	$ 2.65	$ 1.78
Fully diluted average common and common equivalent shares outstanding[1,2]	609.8	592.7	583.7

1. Primary earnings per common and common equivalent share were the same as fully diluted for all years shown, except in 1994 when they were one cent higher than fully diluted. Average primary common and common equivalent shares outstanding for 1995, 1994, and 1993 were 609.7, 591.7, and 582.6, respectively (which includes the dilutive effects of the convertible zero coupon notes and the outstanding stock options).

2. Includes adjustments for the 1994 two-for-one stock split effected in the form of a 100 percent stock dividend.

Required   a. Does it appear that there is 100% ownership in all consolidated sub-sidiaries? Discuss.
b. If a subsidiary were not consolidated but rather accounted for using the equity method, would this change net income? Explain.
c. Present a multiple-step income statement. (Do not present earnings per share.)

CASE 4-2   Identify Nonrecurrent Items

Tyco International Ltd. Company presented these consolidated statements of income for 1995, 1994, and 1993.

Consolidated Statements of Income

(In thousands, except per-share data)	Years Ended June 30		
	1995	1994	1993
Sales	$ 4,534,651	$ 4,076,383	$ 3,919,357
Costs and Expenses:			
Cost of sales	3,313,301	3,003,194	2,909,947
Nonrecurring inventory charge	—	—	22,485
Selling, general, and administrative	735,917	682,568	682,520
Merger and transaction related costs	37,170	—	—
Restructuring and severance charges	—	—	39,325
Interest	63,385	62,431	85,785
	4,149,773	3,748,193	3,740,062
Income before income taxes, extraordinary item, and cumulative effect of accounting changes	384,878	328,190	179,295
Income taxes	168,285	138,999	84,837
Income before extraordinary item and cumulative effect of accounting changes	216,593	189,191	94,458
Extraordinary item, net of taxes	(2,600)	—	(2,816)
Income before cumulative effect of accounting changes	213,993	189,191	91,642
Cumulative effect of accounting changes	—	—	(71,040)
Net Income	$ 213,993	$ 189,191	$ 20,602
Income per Share:			
Before extraordinary item and cumulative effect of accounting changes	$ 2.87	$ 2.56	$ 1.30
Extraordinary item	(.03)	—	(.04)
Cumulative effect of accounting changes	—	—	(.98)
Net Income	$ 2.83	$ 2.56	$ .28
Common equivalent shares	75,509	73,770	72,316

Required   a. Identify nonrecurring items.

          b. Determine the net income (loss) for each year with the nonrecurring items excluded.

          c. Determine the amount to remove from the statements of operations if these items are removed:

              1. Merger and transaction-related costs.

              2. Restructuring and severance charges.

CASE 4-3   Review of Income

General Dynamics presented these consolidated statements of income for 1995, 1994, and 1993:

Consolidated Statements of Earnings

	Years Ended December 31		
(Dollars in millions, except per-share amounts)	**1995**	**1994**	**1993**
Net Sales	$ 3,067	$ 3,058	$ 3,187
Operating Costs and Expenses	2,752	2,737	2,878
Operating Earnings	315	321	309
Interest, net	55	22	36
Other income, net	5	—	68
Earnings from Continuing Operations Before Income Taxes	375	343	413
Provision for income taxes	128	120	143
Earnings from Continuing Operations	247	223	270
Discontinued Operations, Net of Income Taxes:			
Earnings (loss) from operations	55	—	(30)
Gain on disposal	19	15	645
	74	15	615
Net Earnings	$ 321	$ 238	$ 885
Net Earnings per Share:			
Continuing operations	$ 3.92	$ 3.53	$ 4.34
Discontinued operations:			
Earnings (loss) from operations	.88	—	(.48)
Gain on disposal	.30	.24	10.37
	$ 5.10	$ 3.77	$ 14.23

Required   a. Identify nonrecurring items.

          b. Determine the net income (loss) for each year with the nonrecurring items excluded.

          c. What does it mean that the statement is titled "Consolidated Statement of Earnings"?

          d. Does it appear that there are minority interests in the subsidiaries?

CASE 4-4   Examination of Income Statement

Vivra presented this consolidated statement of earnings for the years ended November 30, 1995, 1994, and 1993.

Consolidated Statement of Earnings

	Years Ended November 30		
In thousands, except per-share amounts	1995	1994	1993
Revenues:			
Operating revenues	$350,490	$284,649	$ 216,760
Other income	5,157	1,870	1,221
Total Revenues	355,647	286,519	217,981
Costs and Expenses:			
Operating	238,730	188,529	148,046
General and administrative	43,531	37,495	20,722
Depreciation	10,767	9,552	7,196
Interest	360	523	912
Total Costs and Expenses	293,388	236,099	176,876
Earnings from continuing operations, before minority interest and income taxes	62,259	50,420	41,105
Minority interest	(95)	(10)	—
Earnings from continuing operations, before income taxes	62,164	50,410	41,105
Income taxes (Note 6)	24,224	20,668	17,263
Net earnings from continuing operations	37,940	29,742	23,842
Earnings from discontinued operations, less applicable taxes (Note 3)	—	—	554
Gain on sale of discontinued operations, less applicable taxes (Note 3)	—	697	—
Net Earnings	$ 37,940	$ 30,439	$ 24,396
Earnings per Share (Primary and Fully Diluted):			
Net earnings from continuing operations	$ 1.08	$ .96	$ .79
Earnings from discontinued operations	—	—	.02
Gain on sale of discontinued operations	—	.02	—
Net earnings	$ 1.08	$ .99[1]	$ .81
Average Number of Common Shares:			
Primary	35,068	30,834	30,075
Fully diluted	35,068	30,834	30,110

1. As a result of rounding, year-to-date earnings per share was $.99 rather than $.98.

Required a. 1. What does it mean that the statement is titled "Consolidated Statement of Earnings"?

2. Identify minority interest.
3. Describe what it means to have minority interest.

b. Identify nonrecurring items.
c. Identify net earnings with the nonrecurring items removed.

CASE 4-5 The Big Order

On October 15, 1990, United Airlines (UAL Corporation) placed the largest widebody aircraft order in commercial aviation history—60 Boeing 747-400s and 68 Boeing 777s—with an estimated value of $22 billion. With this order, United became the launch customer for the B777. This order was equally split between firm orders and options.

Required

a. Comment on when United Airlines should record the purchase of these planes.
b. Comment on when Boeing should record the revenue from selling these planes.
c. Speculate on how firm the commitment was on the part of United Airlines to accept delivery of these planes.
d. 1. Speculate on the disclosure for this order in the 1990 financial statements and footnotes of United Airlines.
   2. Speculate on the disclosure for this order in the 1990 annual report of United Airlines (exclude the financial statements and footnotes).
e. 1. Speculate on the disclosure for this order in the 1990 financial statements and footnotes of The Boeing Company.
   2. Speculate on the disclosure for this order in the 1990 annual report of The Boeing Company (exclude the financial statements and footnotes).

5   Basics of Analysis

THE ANALYSIS OF FINANCIAL DATA EMPLOYS various techniques to emphasize the comparative and relative importance of the data presented and to evaluate the position of the firm. These techniques include ratio analysis, common-size analysis, study of differences in components of financial statements among industries, review of descriptive material, and comparisons of results with other types of data. The information derived from these types of analyses should be blended to determine the overall financial position. No one type of analysis supports overall findings or serves all types of users. This chapter provides an introduction to different analyses and uses of financial information.

Financial statement analysis is a judgmental process. One of the primary objectives is identification of major changes (turning points) in trends, amounts, and relationships and investigation of the reasons underlying those changes. Often, a turning point may signal an early warning of a significant shift in the future success or failure of the business. The judgment process can be improved by experience and by the use of analytical tools.

RATIO ANALYSIS

Financial ratios are usually expressed as a percent or as times per period. The ratios listed below will be discussed fully in future chapters.

1. Liquidity ratios measure a firm's ability to meet its current obligations. They may include ratios that measure the efficiency of the use of current assets (Chapter 7).

2. Borrowing capacity (leverage) ratios measure the degree of protection of suppliers of long-term funds (Chapter 8).

3. Profitability ratios measure the earning ability of a firm. Discussion will include measures of the use of assets in general (Chapter 9).

191

4. Investors are interested in a special group of ratios, in addition to liquidity, debt, and profitability ratios (Chapter 10).

5. Cash flow ratios can indicate liquidity, borrowing capacity, or profitability (Chapter 11).

A ratio can be computed from any pair of numbers. Given the large quantity of variables included in financial statements, a very long list of meaningful ratios can be derived. A standard list of ratios or standard computation of them does not exist. Each author and source on financial analysis uses a different list. This text presents frequently utilized and discussed ratios.

Comparison of income statement and balance sheet numbers, in the form of ratios, can create difficulties due to the timing of the financial statements. Specifically, the income statement covers the entire fiscal period; whereas, the balance sheet applies to a single point in time, the end of the period. Ideally, then, to compare an income statement figure such as sales to a balance sheet figure such as receivables, we need to know the average receivables for the year that the sales figure covers. However, these data are not available to the external analyst. In some cases, the analyst uses an average of the beginning and ending balance sheet figures. This approach smooths out changes from beginning to end, but it does not eliminate problems due to seasonal and cyclical changes. It also does not reflect changes that occur unevenly throughout the year.

Be aware that computing averages from two similar balance sheet dates can be misleading. It is possible that a representative average cannot be computed from externally published statements.

A ratio will usually represent a fairly accurate trend, even when the ratio is distorted. If the ratio is distorted, then it does not represent a good absolute number.

Applying the U.S. techniques of ratio analysis to statements prepared in other countries can be misleading. The ratio analysis must be understood in terms of the accounting principles used and the business practices and culture of the country.

COMMON-SIZE ANALYSIS (VERTICAL AND HORIZONTAL)

Common-size analysis expresses comparisons in percentages. For example, if cash is $40,000 and total assets is $1,000,000, then cash represents 4% of total assets. The use of percentages is usually preferable to the use of absolute amounts. An illustration will make this clear. If Firm A earns $10,000 and Firm B earns $1,000, which is more profitable? Firm

A is probably your response. However, the total owners' equity of A is $1,000,000, and B's is $10,000. The return on owners' equity is as follows:

	Firm A	Firm B
$\dfrac{\text{Earnings}}{\text{Owners' Equity}}$	$\dfrac{\$10,000}{\$1,000,000} = 1\%$	$\dfrac{\$1,000}{\$10,000} = 10\%$

The use of common-size analysis makes comparisons of firms of different sizes much more meaningful. Care must be exercised in the use of common-size analysis with small absolute amounts because a small change in amount can result in a very substantial percentage change. For instance, if profits last year amounted to $100 and increased this year to $500, this would be an increase of only $400 in profits, but it would represent a substantial percentage increase.

Vertical analysis compares each amount with a base amount selected from the same year. For example, if advertising expenses were $1,000 in 1997 and sales were $100,000, the advertising would have been 1% of sales.

Horizontal analysis compares each amount with a base amount for a selected base year. For example, if sales were $400,000 in 1996 and $600,000 in 1997, then sales increased to 150% of the 1996 level in 1997, an increase of 50%.

Exhibit 5-1, page 194, illustrates common-size analysis (vertical and horizontal).

FINANCIAL STATEMENT VARIATIONS BY TYPE OF INDUSTRY

The components of financial statements, especially the balance sheet and the income statement, will vary by type of industry. Exhibits 5-2, 5-3, and 5-4 illustrate, respectively, a merchandising firm (Arbor Drugs, Inc.), a service firm (The Interpublic Group of Companies), and a manufacturing firm (Union Carbide Corporation).

Merchandising (retail-wholesale) firms sell products purchased from other firms. A principal asset is inventory, which consists of finished goods. For some merchandising firms, a large amount of sales may be for cash. In such cases, the receivables balance will be relatively low. Other merchandising firms have a large amount of sales charged but also accept credit cards such as VISA, so they also have a relatively low balance in receivables. Other firms extend credit and carry the accounts receivable and thus have a relatively large receivables balance. Because of the competitive nature of the industry, profit ratios on the income statement are often quite low, with the cost of sales and operating expenses constituting a large portion of expenses. Refer to Exhibit 5-2, pages 195-196, Arbor Drugs.

A service firm generates its revenue from the service provided. Because service cannot typically be stored, inventory is low or nonexistent.

EXHIBIT 5-1 MELCHER COMPANY
Income Statement
Illustration of Common-Size Analysis (Vertical and Horizontal)

(Absolute dollars)	For the Years Ended December 31		
	1997	1996	1995
Revenue from sales	$100,000	$95,000	$91,000
Cost of products sold	65,000	60,800	56,420
Gross profit	35,000	34,200	34,580
Operating expenses:			
Selling expenses	14,000	11,400	10,000
General expenses	16,000	15,200	13,650
Total operating expenses	30,000	26,600	23,650
Operating income before income taxes	5,000	7,600	10,930
Taxes related to operations	1,500	2,280	3,279
Net income	$ 3,500	$ 5,320	$ 7,651
Vertical Common Size			
Revenue from sales	100.0%	100.0%	100.0%
Cost of goods sold	65.0	64.0	62.0
Gross profit	35.0	36.0	38.0
Operating expenses:			
Selling expenses	14.0	12.0	11.0
General expenses	16.0	16.0	15.0
Total operating expenses	30.0	28.0	26.0
Operating income before income taxes	5.0	8.0	12.0
Taxes related to operations	1.5	2.4	3.6
Net income	3.5%	5.6%	8.4%
Horizontal Common Size			
Revenue from sales	109.9%	104.4%	100.0%
Cost of goods sold	115.2	107.8	100.0
Gross profit	101.2	98.9	100.0
Operating expenses:			
Selling expenses	140.0	114.0	100.0
General expenses	117.2	111.4	100.0
Total operating expenses	126.8	112.5	100.0
Operating income before income taxes	45.7	69.5	100.0
Taxes related to operations	45.7	69.5	100.0
Net income	45.7%	69.5%	100.0%

Handwritten annotations: "inc statement ITEM REVENUE"; "IS ITEM YR. X / IS ITEM BASE YR."; "1995 Base yr"; "EARLIST YEAR"; "3500/7651 5320/7651 7651/7651"

EXHIBIT 5-2   ARBOR DRUGS, INC. AND SUBSIDIARIES
Financial Statements—Merchandising Firm

Consolidated Balance Sheets
Arbor Drugs, Inc. and Subsidiaries

	July 31	
(Dollars in thousands)	1995	1994
Assets		
Current assets:		
Cash and cash equivalents	$ 39,798	$ 36,420
Short-term investments	170	1,264
Accounts receivable	14,020	12,782
Inventory	89,553	83,398
Prepaid expenses	4,904	6,733
Total current assets	148,445	140,597
Property and equipment:		
Land and land improvements	14,591	10,477
Buildings	17,433	14,824
Furniture, fixtures, and equipment	58,369	51,563
Leasehold improvements	35,695	34,156
Less: Accumulated depreciation	(49,705)	(40,451)
	76,383	70,569
Intangible assets	21,766	22,494
Total assets	$ 246,594	$ 233,660
Liabilities		
Current liabilities:		
Notes payable, current portion	$ 1,529	$ 1,483
Accounts payable	50,341	52,918
Liability for third-party settlement and related expenses	—	5,000
Accrued rent and other	7,712	7,080
Accrued compensation and benefits	5,144	4,765
Income tax payable	2,333	1,197
Total current liabilities	67,059	72,443
Notes payable, net of current portion	22,260	23,679
Deferred income tax	5,938	6,991
Minority interest in subsidiaries	621	583
	28,819	31,253
Shareholders' Equity		
Preferred stock: $.01 par value; 2,000,000 shares authorized; none issued	—	—
Common stock: $.01 par value; 40,000,000 shares authorized; 24,765,602 and 24,510,290 issued and outstanding, respectively	248	163
Additional paid-in capital	48,902	46,621
Retained earnings	101,566	83,180
	150,716	129,964
Total liabilities & shareholders' equity	$ 246,594	$ 233,660

(continued)

EXHIBIT 5-2   (concluded)

Consolidated Statement of Income Arbor Drugs, Inc. and Subsidiaries Fiscal Years Ended July 31	1995	1994	1993
(Dollars in thousands, except per-share data)			
Net sales	$ 707,150	$ 618,562	$ 534,966
Costs and expenses:			
Cost of sales	(521,707)	(454,207)	(390,896)
Selling, general, and administrative	(149,829)	(132,759)	(117,337)
Provision for third-party settlement and related expenses	—	(7,000)	(16,000)
Income from operations	35,614	24,596	10,733
Interest expense	(2,035)	(1,667)	(1,738)
Interest income	1,359	995	961
Income before income tax	34,938	23,924	9,956
Provision for income tax	11,871	9,846	3,047
Net income	$ 23,067	$ 14,078	$ 6,909
Weighted average number of common shares outstanding (in thousands)	24,646	24,427	24,326
Earnings per common share	$0.94	$0.58	$0.28
Cash dividend per common share	$0.190	$0.153	$0.123

In people-intensive services, such as advertising, investment in property and equipment is also low compared with that of manufacturing firms. Refer to Exhibit 5-3, pages 197-199, The Interpublic Group of Companies.

A manufacturing firm will usually have large inventories composed of raw materials, work in process, and finished goods, as well as a material investment in property, plant, and equipment. Notes and accounts receivable may also be material, depending on the terms of sale. The cost of sales often represents the major expense. Refer to Exhibit 5-4, Union Carbide, pages 200-201.

REVIEW OF DESCRIPTIVE INFORMATION

The descriptive information found in an annual report, in trade periodicals, and in industry reviews helps us understand the financial position of a firm. Descriptive material might discuss the role of research and development in producing future sales, present data on capital expansion and the goals related thereto, discuss aspects of employee relations such as minority hiring or union negotiations, or help explain the dividend policy of the firm.

EXHIBIT 5-3 **THE INTERPUBLIC GROUP OF COMPANIES**
Financial Statements—Service Firm

CONSOLIDATED BALANCE SHEET

	December 31	
(Dollars in thousands except per share data)	**1995**	**1994**
ASSETS		
Current Assets:		
Cash and cash equivalents (includes certificates of deposit:		
1995—$114,182; 1994—$151,341)	$ 418,448	$ 413,709
Marketable securities, at cost which approximates market	38,926	27,893
Receivables (net of allowance for doubtful accounts:		
1995—$21,941; 1994—$22,656)	2,320,248	2,072,764
Expenditures billable to clients	108,165	104,787
Prepaid expenses and other current assets	88,611	56,154
Total current assets	2,974,398	2,675,307
Other Assets:		
Investment in unconsolidated affiliates	119,473	63,824
Deferred taxes on income	103,497	84,788
Other investments and miscellaneous assets	144,963	120,242
Total other assets	367,933	268,854
Fixed Assets, at cost:		
Land and buildings	76,813	73,370
Furniture and equipment	360,653	320,164
	437,466	393,534
Less: Accumulated depreciation	240,274	212,755
	197,192	180,779
Unamortized leasehold improvements	82,075	67,348
Total fixed assets	279,267	248,127
Intangible Assets (net of accumulated amortization:		
1995—$157,673; 1994—$130,045)	638,168	601,130
Total Assets	$4,259,766	$3,793,418

(continued)

EXHIBIT 5-3   (continued)

CONSOLIDATED BALANCE SHEET—CONCLUDED

December 31	1995	1994
LIABILITIES AND STOCKHOLDERS' EQUITY		
Current Liabilities:		
Payable to banks	$ 162,524	$ 128,529
Accounts payable	2,291,208	2,090,406
Accrued expenses	256,408	292,436
Accrued income taxes	116,557	83,802
Total current liabilities	2,826,697	2,595,173
Noncurrent Liabilities:		
Long-term debt	170,262	131,276
Convertible subordinated debentures	113,235	110,527
Deferred compensation and reserve for termination allowances	235,325	215,893
Accrued postretirement benefits	46,461	45,751
Other noncurrent liabilities	102,909	32,886
Minority interests in consolidated subsidiaries	15,171	12,485
Total noncurrent liabilities	683,363	548,818
Stockholders' Equity:		
Preferred Stock, no par value		
shares authorized: 20,000,000		
shares issued: none	—	—
Common Stock, $.10 par value		
shares authorized: 150,000,000		
shares issued:		
1995—89,630,568;		
1994—87,705,760	8,963	8,771
Additional paid-in capital	446,931	383,678
Retained earnings	704,946	619,627
Adjustment for minimum pension liability	(9,088)	(6,422)
Cumulative translation adjustment	(93,436)	(97,587)
	1,058,316	908,067
Less:		
Treasury stock, at cost:		
1995—10,002,567 shares;		
1994—10,001,680 shares	(268,946)	(222,698)
Unamortized expense of restricted stock grants	(39,664)	(35,942)
Total stockholders' equity	749,706	649,427
Commitments and Contingencies (See Note 15)		
Total Liabilities and Stockholders' Equity	$ 4,259,766	$ 3,793,418

EXHIBIT 5-3 (concluded)

CONSOLIDATED STATEMENT OF INCOME

Year Ended December 31	1995	1994	1993
(Dollars in thousands except per share data)			
Income:			
Commissions and fees	$2,093,832	$1,916,376	$1,739,778
Other income	85,907	67,879	54,078
Gross income	2,179,739	1,984,255	1,793,856
Costs and Expenses:			
Salaries and related expenses	1,149,964	1,040,579	917,185
Office and general expenses	699,423	661,238	618,466
Interest expense	38,020	32,924	26,445
Write-down of goodwill and other related assets	38,177	—	—
Restructuring charges	—	48,715	—
Total costs and expenses	1,925,584	1,783,456	1,562,096
Income before provision for income taxes and effect of accounting changes	254,155	200,799	231,760
Provision for Income Taxes:			
United States—federal	40,900	26,816	29,277
—state and local	12,366	9,862	14,289
Foreign	69,477	49,655	56,253
Total provision for income taxes	122,743	86,333	99,819
Income of consolidated companies	131,412	114,466	131,941
Income applicable to minority interests	(7,686)	(3,262)	(7,606)
Equity in net income of unconsolidated affiliates	6,086	4,043	944
Income before effect of accounting changes	129,812	115,247	125,279
Effect of Accounting Changes:			
Postemployment benefits	—	(21,780)	—
Income taxes	—	—	(512)
Net Income	$ 129,812	$ 93,467	$ 124,767

COMPARISONS

Absolute figures or ratios appear meaningless unless compared to other figures or ratios. If you were asked if ten dollars is a lot of money, the frame of reference would determine the answer. To a small child, still in awe of a quarter, ten dollars is a lot. To a millionaire, a ten-dollar bill is nothing. Similarly, having 60% of total assets composed of buildings and equipment would be normal for some firms but disastrous for others. One must have a guide to determine the meaning of the ratios and other measures. Several types of comparisons offer insight.

EXHIBIT 5-4 UNION CARBIDE CORPORATION AND SUBSIDIARIES
Financial Statements—Manufacturing Firm

Consolidated Balance Sheet
Union Carbide Corporation and Subsidiaries

(Millions of dollars at December 31)	1995	1994
Assets		
Cash and cash equivalents	$ 449	$ 109
Notes and accounts receivable	996	898
Inventories	544	390
Other current assets	207	217
Total Current Assets	2,196	1,614
Property, plant, and equipment	6,357	5,889
Less: Accumulated depreciation	3,549	3,347
Net Fixed Assets	2,808	2,542
Companies carried at equity	739	418
Other investments and advances	84	88
Total Investments and Advances	823	506
Other assets	429	366
Total Assets	$ 6,256	$ 5,028
Liabilities and Stockholders' Equity		
Accounts payable	$ 316	$ 326
Short-term debt and current portion of long-term debt	38	47
Accrued income and other taxes	259	179
Other accrued liabilities	725	733
Total Current Liabilities	1,338	1,285
Long-term debt	1,285	899
Postretirement benefit obligation	480	488
Other long-term obligations	834	537
Deferred credits	201	242
Minority stockholders' equity in consolidated subsidiaries	24	24
Convertible preferred stock—ESOP	146	148
Unearned employee compensation—ESOP	(97)	(104)
Total Liabilities	4,211	3,519
UCC stockholders' equity:		
Common stock		
Authorized—500,000,000 shares		
Issued—154,609,669 shares	155	155
Additional paid-in capital	343	369
Translation and other equity adjustments	(15)	(59)
Retained earnings	2,145	1,333
	2,628	1,798
Less: Treasury stock, at cost—19,501,701 shares (10,197,367 in 1994)	583	289
Total UCC Stockholders' Equity	2,045	1,509
Total Liabilities and Stockholders' Equity	$ 6,256	$ 5,028

EXHIBIT 5-4 (concluded)

Consolidated Statement of Income
Union Carbide Corporation and Subsidiaries

(Millions of dollars except per-share figures) Year Ended December 31	1995	1994	1993
Net Sales	$ 5,888	$ 4,865	$ 4,640
Cost of sales, exclusive of depreciation and amortization	(4,100)	(3,673)	(3,589)
Research and development	(144)	(136)	(139)
Selling, administration, and other expenses	(387)	(290)	(340)
Depreciation and amortization	(306)	(274)	(276)
Interest expense	(89)	(80)	(70)
Partnership income	152	98	67
Other income (expense)—net	245	(39)	(66)
Income Before Provision for Income Taxes	1,259	471	227
Provision for income taxes	380	137	78
Income of Consolidated Companies	879	334	149
Income from corporate investments carried at equity	46	55	16
Net Income Before Cumulative Effect of Change in Accounting Principle	925	389	165
Cumulative effect of change in accounting principle	—	—	(97)
Net Income	925	389	68
Preferred stock dividends, net of income taxes	10	10	10
Net Income—Common Stockholders	$ 915	$ 379	$ 58
Earnings per Common Share			
Primary—Net income before cumulative effect of change in accounting principle	$ 6.44	$ 2.44	$ 1.00
—Cumulative effect of change in accounting principle	—	—	(0.64)
—Net income—common stockholders	$ 6.44	$ 2.44	$ 0.36
Fully diluted	$ 5.83	$ 2.27	—
Cash Dividends Declared per Common Share	$ 0.75	$ 0.75	$ 0.75

Trend Analysis

Trend analysis studies the financial history of a firm for comparison. By looking at the trend of a particular ratio, one sees whether that ratio is falling, rising, or remaining relatively constant. This helps detect problems or observe good management.

Standard Industrial Classification Manual (SIC)

The Standard Industrial Classification, a statistical classification of business by industry, is used in compiling federal economic statistics. The

National Technical Information Service publishes the classification manual. The manual is the responsibility of the Office of Management and Budget, which is under the executive office of the President.

Use of the SIC promotes comparability of various facets of the U.S. economy and defines industries in accordance with the composition and structure of the economy. An organization's SIC consists of a two-digit major group number, a three-digit industry group number, and a four-digit industry number. These numbers describe the business' identifiable level of industrial detail.

Determining a company's SIC is a good starting point in researching a company, industry, or product. Many library sources use the SIC number as a method of classification.

Industry Averages and Comparison with Competitors

The analysis of an entity's financial statements is more meaningful if the results are compared with industry averages and with results of competitors. Several financial services provide composite data on various industries.

The analyst faces a problem when the industries reported do not clearly include the company being examined because the company is diversified into many industrial areas. Since many companies do not clearly fit into any one industry, it is often necessary to use an industry that best fits the firm. The financial services have a similar problem in selecting an industry in which to place a company. Thus, a financial service uses its best judgment as to which industry the firm best fits.

This section briefly describes some financial services. For a more extensive explanation, consult the service's literature. Each service explains how it computes its ratios and the data it provides.

The Department of Commerce Financial Report (Exhibit 5-5) is a publication of the federal government for manufacturing, mining, and trade corporations. Published by the Economic Surveys Division of the Bureau of the Census, it includes income statement data and balance sheet data in total industry dollars. It also includes an industry-wide common-size vertical income statement (Income Statement in Ratio Format) and an industry-wide common-size vertical balance sheet (Selected Balance Sheet Ratios). This source also includes selected operating and balance sheet ratios.

This report, updated quarterly, probably offers the most current source. It typically becomes available within six or seven months after the end of the quarter. It is a unique source of industry data in total dollars and would enable a company to compare its dollars (such as sales) with the industry dollars (sales).

Robert Morris Associates Annual Statement Studies (Exhibit 5-6) is published by Robert Morris Associates, the association of lending and credit risk professionals. Submitted by institutional members of Robert Morris Associates, the data cover 450 different industries in manufacturing, wholesaling, retailing, service, agriculture, and construction.

Annual Statement Studies groups the data by industry, using the SIC code. It provides common-size balance sheets, income statements, and 16 selected ratios.

The data are sorted by assets and sales and are particularly useful because the financial position and operations of small firms are often quite different from those of larger firms. The Robert Morris presentation also includes a five-year comparison of historical data that presents all firms under a particular SIC.

In each category, the ratios are computed for the median and the upper and lower quartiles. For example:

Number of firms (9)
Ratio—Return on total assets
Results for the nine firms (in order, from highest to lowest):
      12%, 11%, 10.5%, 10%, 9.8%, 9.7%, 9.6%, 7.0%, 6.5%
The middle result is the median: 9.8%
The result halfway between the top result and the median is the
      upper quartile: 10.5%
The result halfway between the bottom result and the median
      is the lower quartile: 9.6%

For ratios in which a low value is desirable, the results are presented from low values to high: For example, 2% (upper quartile), 5% (median), and 8% (lower quartile).

Because of the combination of common-size statements, selected ratios, and comparative historical data, *Robert Morris Associates Annual Statement Studies* is one of the most extensively used sources of industry data. Commercial loan officers in banks frequently use this source.

Notice the section called "Interpretation of Statement Studies Figures," which indicates that statement studies should be "regarded only as general guidelines and not as absolute industry norms." It then proceeds to list reasons why the data may not be fully representative of a given industry. This word of caution is useful in keeping the user from concluding that the data represent an absolute norm for a given industry.

Standard & Poor's Industry Surveys contains a five-year summary on several firms within an industry group. Some of the data include:

1. Operating revenues
2. Net income
3. Return on revenues (%)
4. Return on assets (%)

5.   Return on equity (%)

6.   Current ratio

7.   Debt/capital ratio (%)

8.   Debt as a percent of net working capital

9.   Price-earnings ratio (high-low)

10.   Dividend payout ratio (%)

11.   Yield (high %-low %)

12.   Earnings per share

13.   Book value per share

14.   Share price (high-low)

Industry Surveys also includes composite industry data. Industry surveys are of particular interest to investors.

The Almanac of Business and Industrial Financial Ratios by Leo Troy is a compilation of corporate tax return data published by Prentice Hall. It includes a broad range of industries and presents 50 statistics for 11 size categories of firms. Some of the industries include manufacturing, construction, transportation, retail trade, banking, and wholesale trade. Each Almanac industry is cross-referenced to an SIC number.

Industry Norms and Key Business Ratios, desktop edition published by Dun & Bradstreet, includes over 800 different lines of business as defined by the U.S. Standard Industrial Classification (SIC) code numbers. It includes one-year data consisting of a condensed balance sheet and income statement in dollars and common size. It also includes working capital and ratios.

There are 14 ratios presented for the upper quartile, median, and lower quartile. The 14 ratios are:

Solvency
>   Quick Ratio
>   Current Liabilities to Net Worth (%)
>   Current Liabilities to Inventory (%)
>   Total Liabilities to Net Worth (%)
>   Fixed Assets to Net Worth (%)

Efficiency
>   Collection Period (days)
>   Sales to Inventory (times per period)
>   Assets to Sales (%)
>   Sales to Net Working Capital (times per period)

Profitability
>   Return on Sales (%)
>   Return on Assets (%)
>   Return on Net Working Capital (%)

Dun & Bradstreet advises users that the industry norms and key business ratios are to be used as yardsticks and not as absolutes. *Industry Norms and Key Business Ratios* is also published in an expanded set in the following five segments:

1. Agriculture/Mining/Construction/Transportation/Communication/Utilities
2. Manufacturing
3. Wholesaling
4. Retailing
5. Finance/Real Estate/Services

All five segments are available in three different formats, for a total of 15 books. The three formats follow:

1. Industry Norms for last three years
2. Industry Norms one-year edition
3. Key Business Ratios one-year edition

Value Line Investment Service contains profitability and investment data for 1,700 individual firms and for industries in general. *Value Line* places companies in 1 of 96 industries. This service rates each stock's timeliness and safety. It is very popular with investors.

The data included in *Value Line* for a company are largely for a relatively long period of time (five to ten years). Some of the data provided for each company are as follows:

1. Revenues per share
2. Cash flow per share
3. Earnings per share
4. Dividends declared per share
5. Capital spending per share
6. Book value per share
7. Common shares outstanding
8. Average annual P/E ratio
9. Relative P/E ratio
10. Average annual dividend yield
11. Revenues
12. Net profit
13. Income tax rate
14. AFUDC % to net profit

15.   Long-term debt ratio
16.   Common equity ratio
17.   Total capital
18.   Net plant
19.   Percent earned total capital
20.   Percent earned net worth
21.   Percent earned common equity
22.   Percent retained to common equity
23.   Percent all dividends to net profit

Tax Financial Statement Benchmarks, published by John Wiley & Sons, provides industry benchmarks from IRS tax return data representing approximately 4 million corporations in the United States. The data are aggregated into 235 industries and industry groups, identified by both SIC and IRS Principal Business Activity (PBA) codes. The corporations in each industry are categorized by asset size into 13 size-classes. Income statement, balance sheet, and operating data are presented in percentage form. There are also profitability, liquidity, leverage, and other financial ratios.

As indicated previously, comparison has become more difficult in recent years as more firms become conglomerates and diversify into many product lines. To counteract this problem, the Securities and Exchange Commission (SEC) has implemented line-of-business reporting requirements for companies that must submit their reports to the SEC. These reports are made available to the public. SFAS No. 14 also addresses line-of-business reporting requirements. Such reporting requirements ease the analysis problem created by conglomerates but cannot eliminate it because the entity must decide how to allocate administrative and joint costs.

If industry figures are unavailable or if comparison with a competitor is desired, another firm's statements may be analyzed. Remember, however, that the other firm is not necessarily good or bad, nor does it represent a norm or standard for its industry.

Alternative accounting methods are acceptable in many situations. Since identical companies may use different valuation or expense methods, read statements and footnotes carefully to determine if the statements are reasonably comparable.

Ideally, the use of all types of comparison would be best. Using trend analysis, industry averages, and comparisons with a major competitor will give support to findings and will provide a concrete basis for problem solving.

In analyzing ratios, the analyst will sometimes encounter negative profit figures. *Analysis of ratios that have negative numerators or denominators is meaningless, and the negative sign of the ratio should simply be noted.*

Caution in Using Industry Averages

Financial analysis requires judgment decisions on the part of the analyst. Users of financial statements must be careful not to place complete confidence in ratios or comparisons.

Remember that ratios are simply fractions with a numerator (top) and a denominator (bottom). There are as many for financial analysis as there are pairs of figures. There is no set group, nor is a particular ratio always computed using the same figures. Even the industry ratio formulas vary from source to source. Adequate detailed disclosure of how the industry ratios are computed is often lacking. Major problems can result from analyzing a firm according to the recommendations of a book and then making comparisons to industry ratios that may have been computed differently.

The use of different accounting methods causes a problem. Since identical firms may use different valuation or revenue recognition methods, read statements and footnotes carefully to determine the degree of comparability between statements. For example, if one firm uses FIFO and another uses LIFO inventory, their inventory and cost of sales figures will be so different that comparisons of ratios that utilize these figures will be meaningless in an absolute sense. Trend analysis for each firm, however, will usually be meaningful. Industry averages group firms that use different accounting principles.

Different year-ends can also produce different results. Consider the difference in the inventory of two toy stores if one ends November 30 and the other ends December 31. The ratios of firms with differing year-ends are all grouped together in industry averages.

Firms with differing financial policies might be included in the same industry average. Possibly capital-intensive firms are grouped with labor-intensive companies. Firms with large amounts of debt may be included in the same average as firms that prefer to avoid the risk of debt.

Some industry averages come from small samples that may not be representative of the industry. An extreme statement, such as one containing a large loss, can also distort industry data.

Ratios may have alternative forms of computation. In comparing one year to the next, one firm to another, or a company to its industry, meaningful analysis requires that the ratios be computed using the same formula. For example, Robert Morris computes income ratios before tax; Dun & Bradstreet profit figures are after tax. The analyst should compute the enterprise ratios on the same basis as is used for industry comparisons, but this is often not possible.

Finally, ratios are not absolute norms. They are general guidelines to be combined with other methods in formulating an evaluation of the financial condition of a firm. Despite the problems with using ratios, they can be very informative if reasonably used.

EXHIBIT 5-5   DEPARTMENT OF COMMERCE QUARTERLY FINANCIAL REPORT

TABLE 1.0—INCOME STATEMENT
FOR CORPORATIONS INCLUDED IN ALL MANUFACTURING
AND ALL NONDURABLE MANUFACTURING INDUSTRIES

Item	All Manufacturing[1][2]				
	4Q 1994	1Q 1995	2Q 1995	3Q 1995	4Q 1995
	(million dollars)				
Net sales, receipts, and operating revenues	$854,917	$843,285	$888,572	$877,996	$908,753
Less: Depreciation, depletion, and amortization of property, plant, and equipment	(32,159)	(31,669)	(32,270)	(32,274)	(34,033)
Less: All other operating costs and expenses, including cost of goods sold and selling, general, and administrative expenses	(762,813)	(746,768)	(781,118)	(775,928)	(814,246)
Income (or loss) from operations	59,945	64,847	75,184	69,794	60,474
Net nonoperating income (expense)	4,491	8,557	4,336	1,009	(5,548)
Income (or loss) before income taxes	64,436	73,405	79,520	70,803	54,926
Less: Provision for current and deferred domestic income taxes	17,140	20,862	22,156	20,109	14,218
Income (or loss) after income taxes	47,295	52,543	57,365	50,694	40,708
Cash dividends charged to retained earnings in current quarter	18,988	18,298	20,658	20,946	20,977
Net income retained in business	28,307	34,245	36,707	29,748	19,730
Retained earnings at beginning of quarter	718,751	737,628	768,748	808,583	824,540
Other direct credits (or charges) to retained earnings (net), including stock and other noncash dividends, etc.	(4,574)	3,072	5,280	(9,694)	(8,492)
Retained earnings at end of quarter	$742,484	$774,945	$810,735	$828,637	$835,778
INCOME STATEMENT IN RATIO FORMAT	(percent of net sales)				
Net sales, receipts, and operating revenues	100.0	100.0	100.0	100.0	100.0
Less: Depreciation, depletion, and amortization of property, plant, and equipment	(3.8)	(3.8)	(3.6)	(3.7)	(3.7)
Less: All other operating costs and expenses	(89.2)	(88.6)	(87.9)	(88.4)	(89.6)

Income (or loss) from operations	7.0	7.7	8.5	7.9	6.7
Net nonoperating income (expenses)	0.5	1.0	0.5	0.1	(0.6)
Income (or loss) before income taxes	7.5	8.7	8.9	8.1	6.0
Less: Provision for current and deferred domestic income taxes	2.0	2.5	2.5	2.3	1.6
Income (or loss) after income taxes	5.5	6.2	6.5	5.8	4.5
OPERATING RATIOS (see explanatory notes) *(percent)*					
Annual rate of profit on stockholders' equity at end of period:					
Before income taxes	22.35	24.57	25.77	22.61	17.22
After income taxes	16.41	17.59	18.59	16.19	12.76
Annual rate of profit on total assets:					
Before income taxes	8.37	9.36	9.91	8.69	6.63
After income taxes	6.14	6.70	7.15	6.23	4.91
BALANCE SHEET RATIOS (based on succeeding table)					
Total current assets to total current liabilities	1.39	1.40	1.42	1.41	1.41
Total cash, U.S. Government and other securities to total current liabilities	0.21	0.19	0.21	0.20	0.21
Total stockholders' equity to total debt	1.41	1.42	1.42	1.44	1.46

[1] Beginning in the fourth quarter of 1995, the threshold for sampling on less than a 1:1 ratio was raised from $50 million to $250 million in assets. To provide comparability, data for the fourth quarter of 1994 and the first three quarters of 1995 have been restated to reflect this change.
[2] Prior quarters' data are revised to reflect additional information and/or corrections submitted by respondents subsequent to last quarter's publication.

(continued)

EXHIBIT 5-5 (continued)

TABLE 1.1—BALANCE SHEET
FOR CORPORATIONS INCLUDED IN ALL MANUFACTURING AND ALL NONDURABLE MANUFACTURING INDUSTRIES

Item	All Manufacturing[1] [2] (million dollars)				
	4Q 1994	1Q 1995	2Q 1995	3Q 1995	4Q 1995
ASSETS					
Cash and demand deposits in the United States	$ 56,423	$ 52,785	$ 53,922	$ 56,945	$ 62,999
Time deposits in the United States, including negotiable certificates of deposit	26,151	22,268	24,629	25,102	25,607
Total cash on hand and in U.S. banks	82,573	75,053	78,552	82,047	88,606
Other short-term financial investments, including marketable and government securities, commercial paper, etc.	80,099	75,284	85,374	76,434	80,708
Total cash, U.S. Government and other securities	162,673	150,337	163,925	158,480	169,314
Trade accounts and trade notes receivable (less allowances for doubtful receivables)	403,383	411,133	420,441	437,236	432,181
Inventories	390,284	408,348	414,718	419,516	419,593
All other current assets	124,486	130,103	133,100	131,894	133,852
Total current assets	1,080,826	1,099,921	1,132,184	1,147,126	1,154,940
Depreciable and amortizable fixed assets, including construction in progress	1,805,293	1,823,244	1,854,589	1,883,647	1,915,159
Land and mineral rights	119,766	118,741	118,936	118,265	116,674
Less: Accumulated depreciation, depletion, and amortization	(950,776)	(964,342)	(980,471)	(996,496)	(1,007,113)
Net property, plant, and equipment	974,283	977,644	993,053	1,005,417	1,024,720
All other noncurrent assets, including investment in nonconsolidated entities, long-term investments, intangibles, etc.	1,025,122	1,058,538	1,084,504	1,104,762	1,133,627
Total Assets	$3,080,231	$3,136,103	$3,209,741	$3,257,305	$3,313,287
LIABILITIES AND STOCKHOLDERS' EQUITY					
Short-term debt, original maturity of 1 year or less:					
a. Loans from banks	$ 51,634	$ 57,897	$ 59,449	$ 58,455	$ 55,924
b. Other short-term debt, including commercial paper	66,674	71,730	80,073	81,990	68,241

Trade accounts and trade notes payable	248,556	247,246	249,181	259,000	271,618
Income taxes accrued, prior and current years, net of payments	28,351	34,809	28,726	29,750	28,553
Installments, due in 1 year or less, on long-term debt:					
a. Loans from banks	20,397	20,367	22,114	21,628	21,864
b. Other long-term debt	30,083	28,298	32,617	32,378	34,074
All other current liabilities, including excise and sales taxes, and accrued expenses	329,532	324,312	323,618	328,743	341,011
Total current liabilities	775,227	784,659	795,777	811,944	821,284
Long-term debt (due in more than 1 year):					
a. Loans from banks	188,685	197,626	202,092	202,119	206,007
b. Other long-term debt	463,025	465,082	472,043	473,555	485,247
All other noncurrent liabilities, including deferred income taxes, capitalized leases, and minority stockholders' interest in consolidated domestic corporations	500,295	493,880	505,555	517,069	525,127
Total liabilities	1,927,233	1,941,247	1,975,467	2,004,687	2,037,666
Capital stock and other capital (less treasury stock)	410,514	419,910	423,539	423,980	439,844
Retained earnings	742,484	774,945	810,735	828,637	835,778
Stockholders' equity	1,152,998	1,194,855	1,234,274	1,252,618	1,275,622
Total Liabilities and Stockholders' Equity	$3,080,231	$3,136,103	$3,209,741	$3,257,305	$3,313,287
NET WORKING CAPITAL					
Excess of total current assets over total current liabilities	$ 305,599	$ 315,262	$ 336,407	$ 335,183	$ 333,656

SELECTED BALANCE SHEET RATIOS

(percent of total assets)

Total cash, U.S. Government and other securities	5.3	4.8	5.1	4.9	5.1
Trade accounts and trade notes receivable	13.1	13.1	13.1	13.4	13.0
Inventories	12.7	13.0	12.9	12.9	12.7
Total current assets	35.1	35.1	35.3	35.2	34.9
Net property, plant, and equipment	31.6	31.2	30.9	30.9	30.9
Short-term debt including installments on long-term debt	5.6	5.6	6.1	6.0	5.5
Total current liabilities	25.2	25.0	24.8	24.9	24.8
Long-term debt	21.1	21.1	21.0	20.7	20.8
Total liabilities	62.6	61.9	61.5	61.5	61.5
Stockholders' equity	37.4	38.1	38.5	38.5	38.5

[1] Beginning in the fourth quarter of 1995, the threshold for sampling on less than a 1:1 ratio was raised from $50 million to $250 million in assets. To provide comparability, data for the fourth quarter of 1994 and the first three quarters of 1995 have been restated to reflect this change.

[2] Prior quarters' data are revised to reflect additional information and/or corrections submitted by respondents subsequent to last quarter's publication.

EXHIBIT 5-6 ROBERT MORRIS ASSOCIATES ANNUAL STATEMENT STUDIES

MANUFACTURERS—DRUGS & MEDICINES. SIC# 2833 (34-36)

	Comparative Historical Data					Current Data Sorted by Sales					
							30 (4/1-9/30/95)		110 (10/1/95-3/31/96)		
	4/1/91-3/31/92	4/1/92-3/31/93	4/1/93-3/31/94	4/1/94-3/31/95	4/1/95-3/31/96	0-1MM	1-3MM	3-5MM	5-10MM	10-25MM	25MM & OVER
	ALL	ALL	ALL	ALL	ALL						
# Postretirement Benefits	3	16	12	16	22	1	1	1	5	5	9
Type of Statement											
Unqualified	64	78	66	79	61	2		4	11	14	30
Reviewed	26	16	17	9	13	1		1	5	4	2
Compiled	12	11	21	17	12	1	5	2	3	1	
Tax Returns			1	1	4	2	1	1			
Other	22	30	35	49	50	3	5	6	8	5	23
NUMBER OF STATEMENTS	124	135	140	155	140	9	11	14	27	24	55
	%	%	%	%	%	%	%	%	%	%	%
ASSETS											
Cash & Equivalents	13.6	13.5	13.8	13.8	10.8		10.1	12.3	7.5	11.6	11.3
Trade Receivables—(net)	21.0	23.1	20.3	22.6	22.7		23.1	23.0	23.5	23.1	22.0
Inventory	23.6	24.0	22.2	24.1	24.9		28.2	30.3	22.5	26.3	24.1
All Other Current	1.5	1.9	2.6	1.9	1.6		1.1	.9	2.7	.8	2.0
Total Current	59.8	62.6	58.9	62.4	60.0		62.5	66.6	56.1	61.8	59.3
Fixed Assets (net)	28.2	26.6	28.4	26.3	27.0		32.0	24.9	29.2	27.0	25.6
Intangibles (net)	5.0	4.7	5.1	4.7	4.4		.2	.7	4.7	2.6	6.3
All Other Non-Current	7.1	6.2	7.6	6.7	8.6		5.3	7.9	10.0	8.5	8.8
Total	100.0	100.0	100.0	100.0	100.0		100.0	100.0	100.0	100.0	100.0
LIABILITIES											
Notes Payable–Short Term	6.4	5.1	5.7	5.7	8.0		6.6	10.6	4.6	5.3	8.6
Cur. Mat.–L/T/D	3.4	2.6	2.8	2.6	2.9		2.5	3.7	3.4	3.7	2.4
Trade Payables	12.0	14.2	11.6	12.6	13.0		12.4	14.9	11.1	14.9	12.8
Income Taxes Payable	.5	.8	.7	.8	1.1		.0	.7	.7	1.4	.9
All Other Current	9.5	9.4	8.9	8.4	8.9		7.5	7.6	10.3	7.3	9.2
Total Current	31.7	32.1	29.7	30.1	33.9		29.0	37.4	30.1	32.5	34.0
Long Term Debt	13.0	14.1	12.6	13.0	14.6		16.9	11.7	15.9	15.1	13.6
Deferred Taxes	1.1	.8	.8	.8	.7		.3	.0	.6	.5	1.1
All Other Non-Current	1.6	2.5	4.5	4.5	5.0		7.5	15.1	3.2	6.2	1.6
Net Worth	52.6	50.5	52.4	51.6	45.8		46.3	35.7	50.2	45.8	49.8
Total Liabilities & Net Worth	100.0	100.0	100.0	100.0	100.0		100.0	100.0	100.0	100.0	100.0
INCOME DATA											
Net Sales	100.0	100.0	100.0	100.0	100.0		100.0	100.0	100.0	100.0	100.0
Gross Profit	42.9	43.3	43.9	44.7	42.6		42.5	36.0	47.4	42.8	41.6
Operating Expenses	36.0	35.4	37.5	37.7	35.9		42.3	34.2	40.2	35.2	32.6
Operating Profit	6.8	7.9	6.4	7.0	6.7		.2	1.8	7.2	7.6	9.0
All Other Expenses (net)	2.0	1.2	.9	1.1	1.2		1.8	.9	.6	.6	1.5
Profit Before Taxes	4.9	6.8	5.5	5.9	5.5		-1.6	.9	6.6	7.0	7.5

Values shown for each ratio are Upper Quartile / Median / Lower Quartile. Day-count figures precede the ratio for turnover items. Figures in parentheses indicate number of statements used.

RATIOS	3673718M / 3283608M	3577511M / 3064841M	4657531M / 3594841M	5760718M / 5015516M	5109650M / 4067220M	4913M / 3105M	20822M / 16263M	58927M / 36203M	184820M / 160577M	382211M / 255545M	4457957M / 3595527M
Current	3.3 / 2.1 / 1.4	3.6 / 2.1 / 1.3	3.7 / 2.2 / 1.4	3.6 / 2.1 / 1.4	2.9 / 1.9 / 1.3	3.3 / 2.2 / 1.9	3.0 / 2.0 / 1.4	3.0 / 1.9 / 1.1	3.0 / 1.9 / 1.1	2.8 / 2.2 / 1.3	2.9 / 1.8 / 1.3
Quick	2.0 / 1.1 / .6	2.1 / 1.1 / .7	2.1 / 1.1 / .8	2.0 / 1.1 / .6	1.7 / 1.0 / .6	2.1 / 1.2 / .7	1.6 / 1.1 / .8	1.8 / 1.0 / .5	1.8 / 1.0 / .5	1.9 / 1.0 / .7	2.0 / 1.0 / .5
Sales/Receivables	35 10.3 / 47 7.7 / 68 5.4	36 10.1 / 47 7.7 / 62 5.9	39 9.4 / 50 7.6 / 64 5.9	37 9.3 / 50 7.3 / 64 5.7	37 9.9 / 50 7.3 / 64 5.7	32 11.3 / 47 7.8 / 56 6.5	41 14.8 / 52 9.7 / 65 6.7	34 9.0 / 46 7.0 / 53 5.6	34 9.0 / 46 7.0 / 53 5.6	34 10.7 / 46 8.0 / 53 6.9	42 8.6 / 56 6.5 / 73 5.0
Cost of Sales/Inventory	59 6.2 / 96 3.8 / 166 2.2	56 6.5 / 104 3.5 / 166 2.2	57 6.4 / 99 3.9 / 159 2.3	62 5.9 / 111 3.3 / 166 2.2	57 6.4 / 99 3.7 / 159 2.3	68 5.4 / 76 4.8 / 135 2.7	51 9.2 / 85 4.5 / 166 2.4	53 7.2 / 89 4.3 / 130 2.2	51 7.2 / 85 4.3 / 166 2.2	53 6.9 / 89 4.1 / 130 2.8	83 4.4 / 122 3.0 / 166 2.2
Cost of Sales/Payables	28 13.0 / 43 8.4 / 69 5.3	31 11.9 / 43 8.5 / 69 5.3	29 12.6 / 51 7.3 / 74 5.4	24 12.7 / 47 7.2 / 69 4.9	24 15.2 / 47 7.8 / 69 5.3	22 16.6 / 32 11.3 / 65 5.6	23 25.0 / 48 13.0 / 76 6.4	25 15.8 / 46 7.6 / 73 4.8	25 15.8 / 46 7.6 / 73 4.8	25 14.6 / 46 7.9 / 73 5.0	31 11.9 / 54 6.7 / 72 5.1
Sales/Working Capital	3.0 / 6.0 / 11.8	2.9 / 5.7 / 14.2	3.0 / 5.1 / 11.9	2.7 / 5.1 / 11.1	4.1 / 7.1 / 15.7	4.7 / 5.2 / 8.7	2.8 / 7.6 / 15.2	4.5 / 7.9 / 35.9	4.5 / 7.9 / 35.9	4.5 / 7.8 / 15.4	3.4 / 5.6 / 16.0
EBIT/Interest	(113) 11.1 / 4.4 / 1.8	(120) 17.1 / 6.5 / 1.8	(130) 29.1 / 7.1 / 2.3	(127) 23.0 / 5.2 / 2.2	14.8 / 5.4 / 1.5	(10) 2.7 / 1.0 / -.7	(12) 16.0 / 5.9 / .8	(26) 12.9 / 6.7 / 1.9	(22) 12.9 / 6.7 / 1.9	(50) 21.8 / 10.5 / 2.4	14.8 / 5.1 / 1.8
Net Profit + Depr., Depr., Amort./Cur. Mat. L/T/D	(69) 6.9 / 3.2 / 1.0	(68) 14.1 / 6.5 / 2.2	(77) 10.1 / 3.8 / 1.2	(50) 15.3 / 3.1 / 1.2	10.2 / 3.8 / 1.3		(12) 5.6 / 3.4 / 2.1			(24)	10.2 / 3.0 / .6
Fixed/Worth	.3 / .6 / 1.1	.3 / .5 / 1.0	.3 / .6 / .9	.3 / .6 / 1.1	.3 / .7 / 1.4	.2 / .6 / 2.9	.2 / .5 / 1.7	.4 / .7 / 1.2	.5 / .6 / 1.2	.4 / .6 / 1.2	.3 / .7 / 1.2
Debt/Worth	.4 / .9 / 1.9	.4 / .9 / 2.5	.4 / 1.0 / 2.7	.4 / .9 / 2.5	.5 / 1.5 / 3.1	.4 / 1.0 / 5.2	.6 / 2.0 / 4.4	.5 / 1.1 / 2.5	.6 / 1.6 / 2.5	.6 / 1.6 / 2.5	.4 / 1.4 / 3.1
% Profit Before Taxes/Tangible Net Worth	(118) 35.4 / 21.7 / 4.8	(129) 42.3 / 24.4 / 6.4	(147) 53.1 / 24.5 / 7.3	(134) 41.8 / 19.7 / 4.0	49.7 / 25.5 / 4.8	5.2 / 3.3 / -11.6	33.0 / 24.1 / 5.4	52.5 / 19.8 / 2.6	57.2 / 29.8 / 17.8	(53) 57.2 / 29.8 / 17.8	45.0 / 28.6 / 8.7
% Profit Before Taxes/Total Assets	16.6 / 9.4 / 1.8	18.5 / 10.3 / 2.5	22.7 / 9.9 / 2.7	17.4 / 8.4 / 1.4	18.8 / 8.7 / 2.3	2.7 / 2.3 / -5.1	13.7 / 9.2 / .8	21.1 / 8.2 / 1.9	29.4 / 11.0 / 6.3	29.4 / 11.0 / 6.3	17.7 / 10.4 / 4.1
Sales/Net Fixed Assets	12.9 / 5.6 / 3.4	16.6 / 6.1 / 3.5	13.2 / 6.9 / 3.5	9.6 / 4.8 / 2.8	15.2 / 6.0 / 3.3	32.2 / 5.1 / 2.6	28.3 / 8.6 / 3.9	19.1 / 10.1 / 2.5	17.8 / 9.5 / 3.4	17.8 / 9.5 / 3.4	10.8 / 5.0 / 3.5
Sales/Total Assets	2.2 / 1.5 / 1.0	2.4 / 1.5 / 1.1	2.5 / 1.5 / 1.2	2.0 / 1.3 / .9	2.4 / 1.6 / 1.0	2.6 / 2.1 / 1.3	3.0 / 2.0 / 1.3	2.9 / 1.8 / .8	2.4 / 2.0 / 1.3	2.4 / 2.1 / 1.2	1.8 / 1.4 / 1.0
% Depr., Depr., Amort./Sales	(107) 1.9 / 3.1 / 5.5	(121) 1.8 / 2.8 / 4.4	(138) 1.4 / 2.7 / 4.1	(115) 1.9 / 2.9 / 4.6	1.3 / 2.6 / 4.2		(12) 2.2 / 2.8	1.2 / 2.2 / 6.1	(23) .5 / 2.2 / 2.8	(21) 1.1 / 1.7 / 3.5	(45) 1.7 / 3.1 / 4.0
% Officers', Directors', Owners' Comp/Sales	(32) 2.8 / 6.7 / 10.4	(28) 2.8 / 6.6 / 14.4	(24) 2.5 / 6.5 / 10.4	(31) 2.5 / 4.8 / 9.2	1.9 / 7.0 / 9.5						
Net Sales ($)	3673718M	3577511M	4657531M	5760718M	5109650M	4913M	20822M	58927M	184820M	382211M	4457957M
Total Assets ($)	3283608M	3064841M	3594841M	5015516M	4067220M	3105M	16263M	36203M	160577M	255545M	3595527M

M = $ thousands   MM = $ millions

See Pages 1 through 21 for Explanation of Ratios and Data

(continued)

EXHIBIT 5-6 **(continued)**

MANUFACTURERS—DRUGS & MEDICINES. SIC# 2833 (34-36)

		Current Data Sorted by Assets				
	1	2	6	8	3	2
		30 (4/1-9/30/95)		110 (10/1/95-3/31/96)		
	0-500M	500M-2MM	2-10MM	10-50MM	50-100MM	100-250MM
# Postretirement Benefits						
Type of Statement						
Unqualified	1	2	17	25	10	6
Reviewed		3	8	2		
Compiled	2	8	2			
Tax Returns	2	1	1			
Other	2	10	14	14	5	5
NUMBER OF STATEMENTS	7	24	42	41	15	11
ASSETS	%	%	%	%	%	%
Cash & Equivalents		8.8	9.6	10.7	10.5	16.3
Trade Receivables—(net)		25.8	25.1	19.3	21.2	18.9
Inventory		30.6	26.8	22.6	23.6	17.0
All Other Current		.8	2.2	2.1	.6	1.3
Total Current		66.1	63.7	54.7	56.0	53.5
Fixed Assets (net)		25.6	26.5	31.4	23.9	24.2
Intangibles (net)		2.4	1.8	6.1	10.0	6.3
All Other Non-Current		5.9	8.0	7.8	10.2	15.9
Total		100.0	100.0	100.0	100.0	100.0
LIABILITIES						
Notes Payable–Short Term		7.7	6.8	9.1	4.3	7.4
Cur. Mat.–L/T/D		2.7	3.9	3.3	1.6	.3
Trade Payables		14.4	14.1	12.5	10.8	9.0
Income Taxes Payable		.1	.9	1.1	.4	2.1
All Other Current		11.1	7.5	9.1	6.7	12.7
Total Current		36.1	33.2	35.0	23.8	31.4
Long Term Debt		17.9	15.5	16.2	15.9	4.7
Deferred Taxes		.3	.3	1.0	.9	1.9
All Other Non-Current		10.4	5.8	2.4	3.3	.9
Net Worth		35.2	45.2	45.5	56.1	61.0
Total Liabilities & Net Worth		100.0	100.0	100.0	100.0	100.0
INCOME DATA						
Net Sales		100.0	100.0	100.0	100.0	100.0
Gross Profit		34.9	44.0	44.4	40.6	50.5
Operating Expenses		32.1	38.1	34.8	34.0	40.5
Operating Profit		2.8	5.9	9.5	6.6	10.0
All Other Expenses (net)		1.5	1.3	1.2	1.1	.6
Profit Before Taxes		1.3	4.7	8.3	5.4	9.4

RATIOS											
			2.3		3.4		2.4		3.3		3.8
Current			2.0		2.2		1.4		2.5		2.3
			1.5		1.3		1.1		1.7		1.0
			1.2		1.9		1.7		2.3		2.9
Quick			1.0		1.0		.8		1.3		1.0
			.7		.7		.4		.9		.5
		23	15.8	37	10.0	42	8.6	43	8.5	54	6.7
Sales/Receivables		47	7.8	46	7.9	52	7.0	59	6.2	72	5.1
		59	6.2	54	6.8	68	5.4	76	4.8	81	4.5
		47	7.7	54	6.7	85	4.3	89	4.1	87	4.2
Cost of Sales/Inventory		73	5.0	91	4.0	118	3.1	107	3.4	152	2.4
		122	3.0	152	2.4	159	2.3	183	2.0	183	2.0
		20	18.3	22	16.7	36	10.2	28	13.1	41	9.0
Cost of Sales/Payables		31	11.9	40	9.1	58	6.3	49	7.4	64	5.7
		49	7.5	66	5.5	76	4.8	70	5.2	135	2.7
			5.0		4.0		4.6		3.0		2.1
Sales/Working Capital			8.1		6.7		7.9		3.9		5.2
			15.3		15.5		24.4		5.7		100.9
			12.1		16.8		13.8		13.4		152.4
EBIT/Interest		(23)	2.7	(37)	6.7	(40)	5.1	(12)	4.2	(10)	13.6
			1.4		1.5		2.1		1.6		-5.3
					6.8		12.1				
Net Profit + Depr., Dep., Amort./Cur. Mat. L/T/D				(14)	3.4	(21)	3.8				
					1.8		1.1				
			.2		.3		.6		.3		.3
Fixed/Worth			.7		.6		1.0		.6		.4
			3.2		1.4		1.6		.9		.7
			.6		.5		.8		.3		.2
Debt/Worth			1.8		1.5		1.6		.9		.5
			6.3		3.3		3.0		1.6		1.5
			55.3		51.5		44.7		47.5		38.0
% Profit Before Taxes/Tangible Net Worth		(21)	17.4	(41)	26.3	(40)	27.6	(14)	32.7		23.3
			3.8		3.5		11.6		4.8		-5.2
			17.6		21.1		17.8		16.7		19.5
% Profit Before Taxes/Total Assets			5.2		8.8		9.5		12.6		12.3
			1.6		1.8		4.3		2.4		-4.5
			32.2		16.3		9.7		10.8		4.8
Sales/Net Fixed Assets			10.3		10.3		4.3		5.2		4.0
			3.1		3.9		2.3		3.5		3.7
			3.5		2.5		1.8		1.7		1.4
Sales/Total Assets			2.5		2.1		1.3		1.2		1.0
			1.5		1.2		.9		.9		.8
			.7		1.1		1.9		1.3		
% Depr., Dep., Amort./Sales		(19)	2.6	(37)	1.5	(36)	3.7	(11)	2.9		
			6.8		2.7		6.7		4.1		
			5.6		2.7						
% Officers', Directors', Owners' Comp/Sales		(10)	7.5	(12)	5.1						
			9.5		9.8						
Net Sales ($)	6046M		79044M		432743M		1408078M		1338432M		1845307M
Total Assets ($)	1733M		27614M		218208M		1050013M		1047656M		1721996M

M = $ thousands MM = $ millions

See Pages 1 through 21 for Explanation of Ratios and Data

(continued)

EXHIBIT 5-6   (continued)

Interpretation of Statement Studies Figures

RMA recommends that *Statement Studies* data be regarded only as general guidelines and not as absolute industry norms. There are several reasons why the data may not be fully representative of a given industry.

(1)   The financial statements used in the *Statement Studies* are not selected by any random or statistically reliable method. RMA member banks voluntarily submit the raw data they have available each year with no limitation on company size.

(2)   Many companies have varied product lines; however, the *Statement Studies* categorize them by their primary product Standard Industrial Classification (SIC) number only.

(3)   Some of our industry samples are rather small in relation to the total number of firms in a given industry. A relatively small sample can increase the chances that some of our composites do not fully represent an industry.

(4)   There is the chance that an extreme statement can be present in a sample, causing a disproportionate influence on the industry composite. This is particularly true in a relatively small sample.

(5)   Companies within the same industry may differ in their method of operations which in turn can directly influence their financial statements. Since they are included in our sample, too, these statements can significantly affect our composite calculations.

(6)   Other considerations that can result in variations among different companies engaged in the same general line of business are different labor markets; geographical location; different accounting methods; quality of products handled; sources and methods of financing; and terms of sale.

For these reasons, RMA does not recommend the Statement Studies figures be considered as absolute norms for a given industry. Rather the figures should be used only as general guidelines and in addition to the other methods of financial analysis. RMA makes no claim as to the representativeness of the figures printed in this book.

Robert Morris Associates
One Liberty Place
Philadelphia, PA 19103

©1996 by Robert Morris Associates

Reprinted with permission, copyright Robert Morris Associates, 1996.

RELATIVE SIZE OF FIRM

Comparisons of firms of different sizes may be more difficult than comparison of firms of equal size. For example, larger firms often have access to wider and more sophisticated capital markets, can buy in large quantities, and service wider markets. Ratios and common-size analysis help to eliminate some of the problems related to the use of absolute numbers.

Be aware of the different sizes of firms under comparison. These differences can be seen by looking at relative sales, assets, or profit sizes. Investment services such as *Value Line*, a securities analysis and rating service, often make available another meaningful figure—percent of market.

OTHER LIBRARY SOURCES

The typical business library has many sources of information relating to a particular company, industry, and product. Some of these sources are described here to aid you in your search for information about a company, its industry, and its products.

Standard & Poor's Reports

The *Standard & Poor's Reports* cover companies on the New York Stock Exchange, American Stock Exchange, over-the-counter companies, and regional exchanges. Arranged alphabetically by stock exchange, they contain a brief narrative analysis of companies regularly traded and provide key financial data. Company information is updated four times per year on a rotating basis.

Standard & Poor's Register of Corporations, Directors, and Executives

This annual source is arranged in three volumes. Volume 1 contains an alphabetical list of approximately 55,000 corporations, including such data as ZIP Codes, telephone numbers, and functions of officers, directors, and other principals.

Volume 2 contains an alphabetical list of individuals serving as officers, directors, trustees, partners, and so on. It provides such data as principal business affiliations, business address, and residence address.

Volume 3 contains seven sections:

— *Section 1*—Explains the constructions and use of the SIC code numbers and lists these numbers by major groups and by alphabetical and numerical division of major groups.

— *Section 2*—Lists corporations under the four-digit standard industrial classification codes, which are arranged in numerical order.

— *Section 3*—Lists companies geographically by states and by major cities.

— *Section 4*—Lists and cross-references subsidiaries, divisions, and affiliates in alphabetical sequence and links them to their ultimate parent company listed in Volume 1.

— *Section 5*—Lists the deaths of which publishers have been notified in the past year.

— *Section 6*—Lists individuals whose names appear in the Register for the first time.

— *Section 7*—Lists the companies appearing in the Register for the first time.

Standard & Poor's Analyst's Handbook

This source contains selected income account and balance sheet items and related ratios as applied to the Standard & Poor's industry group stock price indexes. The progress of a given company may possibly be compared with a composite of its industry groups. Brief monthly updates for selected industries supplement the annual editions of the handbook.

Standard & Poor's Corporation Records

This source provides background information and detailed financial statistics on U.S. corporations, with extensive coverage for some corporations. Historical information is arranged in a multivalue section separate from the "Daily News" section. The contents and the index are updated throughout the year.

America's Corporate Families:™
The Billion Dollar Directory®

The directory listings include 9,000 parent companies that have $500,000 or more of net worth, at least one subsidiary, and at least two principal business locations. Corporate family listings are alphabetical, geographical, and by product (SIC) classification. This annual directory provides a cross-reference index of divisions, subsidiaries, and ultimate parent companies, as well as such data as lines of business and telephone numbers of parent and subsidiary companies.

Million Dollar Directory®

This directory provides information on more than 160,000 U.S. companies with a net worth of over $500,000. Company listings are shown alphabetically, geographically, and by SIC classification. Data include lines of business, accounting firm, legal counsel, stock ticker symbol, and names of officers.

Directory of Corporate Affiliations

This directory gives an in-depth view of companies and their divisions, subsidiaries, and affiliates. It contains an alphabetical index, geographical index, and SIC classifications. The parent company listing consists of address, telephone number, ticker symbol, stock exchange(s), approximate sales, number of employees, type of business, and top corporate officers.

Thomas Register of American Manufacturers and Thomas Register

This is a comprehensive "yellow pages" of products and services, as follows:

— *Red section*—Products and services listed alphabetically.
— *Yellow section*—Company profiles with addresses, ZIP Codes, telephone numbers, branch officials, asset ratings, and company officials.
— *Blue section*—Catalogs of companies; cross-referenced to the red volumes.

Moody's Investors' Services

Moody's Industrial Manual examines corporations with detailed summary coverage of the history, principal products and services, and detailed financial tables. They are color-coded and arranged in major industry/service groups: Bank and finance, Industrial, OTC industrial, OTC unlisted, International, Municipal government, Public utility, and Transportation.

Also available from Moody's are the following:

— *Moody's Bond Record*
— *Moody's Bond Survey*
— *Moody's Dividend Record*
— *Moody's Handbook of Common Stock*

Securities Owner's Stock Guide

This monthly guide, published by Standard & Poor's, covers over 5,300 common and preferred stocks. It contains trading activity, price range, dividends, and so on for companies traded on the New York Stock Exchange (NYSE), American Stock Exchange (AMEX), over the counter (OTC), and regional exchanges. The information is displayed with numerous abbreviations and footnotes, in order to fit concisely into one single line, for each publicly traded security.

Wall Street Transcript

The *Wall Street Transcript* newspaper provides access to corporate management presentations to financial analysts and brokerage house assessment reports of corporations and industries. Each issue contains a cumulative index for the current quarter. Each issue also has a reference to the cumulative index for a relatively long period of time, such as for the prior year.

The Wall Street Journal Index

This index provides abstracts and comprehensive indexing of all articles in the 3-Star Eastern Edition of *The Wall Street Journal.* Some of the items included are feature articles, editorials, news items, and earnings reports.

The Official Index to the Financial Times

This index is compiled from the final London editions of *The Financial Times* and *The Weekend Financial Times.* It can be used to locate reports and articles in these publications.

Predicasts F & S Index

This family of indexes, previously known as the Funk & Scott Index of Corporations and Industries, includes:

— *Predicasts F & S Index—United States*
— *Predicasts F & S Index—Europe*
— *Predicasts F & S Index—International*

This comprehensive family of indexes to articles on corporations and industries issued monthly covers 1965 to the present. Each listing includes business periodicals, newspapers, government documents, and investment services reports. The material is arranged by company and industry by SIC code.

Reference Book of Corporate Managements

The four volumes contain profile information on over 200,000 principal corporate officers in over 12,000 companies. The information includes the year of birth, education, military service, present business position, and previous positions. Names and titles of other officers, as well as names of directors who are not officers, are also provided.

Compact Disclosure

This database of textual and financial information on approximately 14,000 public companies can be accessed by a menu-driven screen. The information is taken from annual and periodic reports filed by each company with the Securities and Exchange Commission. A full printout for a company is approximately 14 pages. It includes the major financial statements (annual and quarterly), many financial ratios for the prior three years, institutional holdings, ownership by insiders, president's letter, and financial footnotes.

A company can be accessed by keying its name or ticker symbol. In addition, the system can be searched by type of business (SIC), by geographic area (state, city, ZIP Code, or telephone area code), stock price financial ratios, and much more.

USING THE INTERNET

The **Internet** is a global collection of computer networks linked together and available for your use. Information passes easily among these networks because all connected networks use a common communication protocol. The Internet includes local, regional, national, and international backbone networks. The Internet is often referred to as the "Information Highway."

There are many reasons for using the Internet. Some of these reasons include: (1) retrieving information, (2) finding information, (3) sending and receiving electronic mail, (4) conducting research, and (5) accessing information databases.

The Internet is a valuable tool to use when performing financial analysis. In this section, using the Internet for financial analysis will be introduced.

Company's Internet Home Page

The majority of publicly held companies in the United States have established a home page on the Internet. The contents of these home pages vary. A few companies only provide advertisements and product information. In these cases a phone number may be given to order more information. Other companies provide limited financial information, such as total revenues, net income, and earnings per share. These companies may also provide advertisements and a phone number for more information. The majority of companies provide comprehensive financial information and possibly advertisements. The comprehensive financial information may include the annual report, 10-K, and quarterly report. It may also include the current stock price and the history of the stock price.

Networth (networth.galt.com) lists home pages of approximately 2,000 public companies. One of these companies is Ford Motor Co., whose Internet address is http://www.Ford.com.

Accounting-Oriented Home Pages

There are a number of accounting-oriented home pages. These home pages can be very useful when performing analysis. Many of these home pages are known as *directory sites*. A directory site contains hyperlinks in which highlighted text or graphics can be used to go to another related site.

Several excellent accounting-oriented home pages follow:

1. SEC Edgar Database

   Address: http://sec.gov/edgarhp.htm

   The Securities and Exchange Commission provides a home page that includes its Edgar Database. This site allows users to download publicly available electronic filings submitted to the SEC from 1994 to the present. By citing the company name, you can select from a menu of recent filings. This will include the 10-K report and the 10-Q.

2. Rutgers Accounting Web

   Address: http://www.rutgers.edu/Accounting/raw.htm

   This site provides links to many other accounting sites. RAW provides rapid access to many accounting sites without separately targeting each site. These include Edgar, the International Accounting Network, and many other accounting resources. Accounting organizations include the American Accounting Association, American Institute of Certified Public Accountants, and Institute of Management Accountants.

3. Accounting Resources on Internet

   Address: http://www.rutgers.edu/Accounting/raw/internet/internet.htm

   This site provides links to many other related sites. Some of these related sites include financial markets, government agencies, SEC corporate filings, Financial Accounting Standards Board, and accounting journals.

4. ANet—The Accounting Network—Southern Cross University

   Address: http://anet.scu.edu.au/anet

   This site has accounting mailing lists and a list of accounting organizations and journals. It is part of the International Accounting Network.

5. Summa Project—Chartered Accountants of England

   Address: http://www.ex.ac.uk/~BjSpaul/1CAEW/1CAEW.html

   This site is the home page for the Institute of Chartered Accountants in England and Wales. It is linked to the Summa Project, an international accounting project.

6. Yancey's Home Page

   Address: http://zeta.is.tcu.edu/~yancey

   Yancey's home page provides links to accounting related sites, such as articles, accounting sites, and finance sites. It consists of sites that Will Yancey thinks are helpful to an accountant.

7. WWW Virtual Library—Finance

   Address: http://www.cob.ohio-state.edu/dept/fin/overview.htm

   Contains substantial financial information.

8. Financial markets—stock exchanges
   a. Exchange: American Stock Exchange
      Address: http://www.amex.com
   b. Exchange: Chicago Mercantile Exchange
      Address: http://www.cme.com
   c. Exchange: NASDAQ Stock Market
      Address: http://www.nasdaq.com
   d. Exchange: New York Stock Exchange
      Address: http//www.nyse.com

The contents of these sites vary and are expanding. Each provides information relating to the stock exchange.

THE USERS OF FINANCIAL STATEMENTS

The financial statements are prepared for a group of diversified users. Users of financial data have their own objectives in analysis.

Management, an obvious user of financial data, must analyze the data from the viewpoints of both investors and creditors. Management must be concerned about the current position of the entity to meet its obligations, as well as the future earning prospects of the firm.

Management is interested in the financial structure of the entity in order to determine a proper mix of short-term debt, long-term debt, and equity from owners. Also of interest is the asset structure of the entity: the combination of cash, inventory, receivables, investments, and fixed assets.

Management must guide the entity toward sound short-term and long-term financial policies and also earn a profit. For example, liquidity and profitability are competitive since the most highly liquid assets (cash and marketable securities) are usually the least profitable. It does the entity little good to be guided toward a maximum profitability goal if resources are not available to meet current obligations. The entity would soon find itself in bankruptcy as creditors cut off lines of credit and demand payment. Similarly, management must utilize resources properly to obtain a reasonable return.

The investing public, another category of users, is interested in specific types of analysis. Investors are concerned with the financial position of the entity and its ability to earn future profits. The investor uses an analysis of past trends and the current position of the entity to project the future prospects of the entity.

Credit grantors are interested in the financial statements of the entity. Pure credit grantors obtain a limited return from extending credit: a fixed rate of interest (as in the case of banks) or the profit on the merchandise or services provided (as in the case of suppliers). Since these rewards are limited and the possibility exists that the principal will not be repaid, credit grantors tend to be conservative in extending credit.

The same principle applies to suppliers that extend credit. If merchandise with a 20% markup is sold on credit, it takes five successful sales of the same amount to make up for one sale not collected. In addition, the creditor considers the cost of the funds when extending credit. Extending credit really amounts to financing the entity.

A difference exists between the objectives of short-time grantors of credit and those of long-term grantors. The short-term creditor can look primarily to current resources that appear on the financial statements in order to determine if credit should be extended. Long-term creditors must usually look to the future prospects of earnings in order to be repaid. For example, if bonds are issued that are to be repaid in 30 years, the current resources of the entity will not be an indication of its ability to meet this obligation. The repayment for this obligation will come from future earnings. Thus, the objectives of financial analysis by credit grantors will vary, based on such factors as the term of the credit and the purpose. Profitability of the entity may not be a major consideration, as long as the resources for repayment can be projected.

The financial structure of the entity is of interest to creditors because the amount of equity capital in relation to debt indicates the risk that the owners bear in relation to the creditors. The equity capital provides creditors with a cushion against loss. When this equity cushion is small, creditors are bearing the risk of the entity.

Many other parties are interested in analyzing financial statements. Unions that represent employees are interested in the ability of the entity to grant wage increases and fringe benefits, such as pension plans. The government also has an interest in analyzing financial statements for tax purposes and to ensure compliance with antitrust laws.

SUMMARY

Financial analysis consists of the quantitative and qualitative aspects of measuring the relative financial position among firms and among industries. Analysis can be done in different ways, depending on the type of firm or industry and the specific needs of the user. Financial statements will vary by size of firm and among industries. These basics of analysis will be extensively illustrated. Chapter 6 presents an actual set of financial statements for Cooper Tire & Rubber Company. Financial analysis is applied to the firm in Chapters 7 through 12.

QUESTIONS

Q 5-1.   What is a ratio? How do ratios help to alleviate the problems of size differences among firms?

Q 5-2.   What does each of the following categories of ratios attempt to measure? (a) liquidity; (b) long-term borrowing capacity; (c) profitability. Name a group of users who might be interested in each category.

Q 5-3.   Brown Company earned 5.5% on sales in 1997. What further information would be needed to evaluate this result?

Q 5-4.   Differentiate between absolute and percentage changes. Which is generally a better measure of change, and why?

Q 5-5.   Differentiate between horizontal and vertical analyses. Using sales as a component for each type, give an example that explains the difference.

Q 5-6.   What is trend analysis? Can it be used for ratios? For absolute figures?

Q 5-7.   Suppose you are comparing two firms within an industry. One is large and the other is small. Will relative or absolute numbers be of more value in each case? What kinds of statistics can help evaluate relative size?

Q 5-8.   Are managers the only users of financial reports? Discuss.

Q 5-9.   Briefly describe how each of these groups might use financial reports: managers, investors, and creditors.

Q 5-10.   Refer to Exhibits 5-2, 5-3, and 5-4 to answer the following questions:

   a.   For each of the firms illustrated, what is the single largest asset category? Does this seem typical of this type of firm?

b.   Which of the three firms has the largest amount in current assets in relation to the amount in current liabilities? Does this seem logical? Explain.

Q 5-11.   Differentiate between the types of inventory typically held by a retailing and a manufacturing firm.

Q 5-12.   Sometimes manufacturing firms have only raw materials and finished goods listed on their balance sheets. This is true of Avon Products, a manufacturer of cosmetics, and it might be true of food canners also. Explain the absence of work in process.

Q 5-13.   Using the sample industry ratios from *Robert Morris Associates Annual Statement Studies* (Exhibit 5-6), answer the following:

a.   Describe the common-size statements included in Exhibit 5-6.
b.   Describe some possible uses of these common-size statements by a firm in the same industry.
c.   Speculate on why the current data are broken down by size of firm.
d.   Current data sorted by assets indicates that the sales/total assets ratio has three numbers. Explain these three numbers.
e.   For the following ratios in Exhibit 5-6, indicate if the ratio is expressed in percent, times per period, or days.
        1.   Current
        2.   Fixed/worth
        3.   Sales/receivables
        4.   Sales/total assets

Q 5-14.   You want profile information on the president of a company. Which reference book should be consulted?

Q 5-15.   Answer the following concerning *The Almanac of Business and Industrial Financial Ratios*:

a.   This service presents statistics for how many size categories of firms?
b.   Indicate the industries covered by this service.

Q 5-16.   Using *Department of Commerce Quarterly Financial Report* (Exhibit 5-5) and the discussion of it in the text, answer the following:

a.   Could we determine the percentage of total income after income taxes that a particular firm had in relation to the total industry? Explain.
b.   Could we determine the percentage of total assets that a particular firm had in relation to the total industry? Explain.
c.   What statements are presented in common-size format? Are they in vertical or horizontal format?
d.   For the fourth quarter of 1995, a firm in the same industry as illustrated in Exhibit 5-5 has a 5.0% annual rate of profit on total assets after taxes. How does this compare with the industry?

Q 5-17.   What is the SIC? How can it aid in the search of a company, industry, or product?

Q 5-18.   You want to know if there have been any reported deaths of officers of a company you are researching. What library source will aid you in your search?

Q 5-19.   You want to compare the progress of a given company with a composite of that company's industry group for selected income statement and balance sheet items. Which library source will aid you?

Q 5-20.   You are considering buying the stock of a large publicly traded company. You need an opinion of timeliness of the industry and the company. Which publication could you use?

Q 5-21.   You want to know the trading activity (volume of its stock sold) for a company. Which service provides this information?

Q 5-22.   You need to research articles on a company that you are analyzing. Which source will aid you?

Q 5-23.   You read in your local newspaper that an executive of a company that you are interested in is giving a presentation to financial analysts in New York. How could you learn the content of the presentation without getting in touch with the company?

Q 5-24.   You would like to determine the principal business affiliations of the president of a company you are analyzing. Which reference service may have this information?

Q 5-25.   Indicate some sources that contain an appraisal of the outlook for particular industries.

Q 5-26.   You want to determine if there is a fairly recent brokerage house assessment report on a company that you are analyzing. Which reference may aid you?

PROBLEMS

P 5-1.   The Arbor Drugs, Inc. balance sheet from its 1995 annual report is presented in Exhibit 5-2.

Required   a.   Using the balance sheet, prepare a vertical common- size analysis for 1995 and 1994. Use total assets as a base.
   b.   Using the balance sheet, prepare a horizontal common-size analysis for 1995 and 1994. Use 1994 as the base.
   c.   Comment on significant trends that appear in (a) and (b).

P 5-2.   The Arbor Drugs, Inc. income statement from its 1995 annual report is presented in Exhibit 5-2.

Required   a.   Using the income statement, prepare a vertical common-size analysis for 1995, 1994, and 1993. Use net sales as a base.
   b.   Using the income statement, prepare a horizontal common-size analysis for 1995, 1994, and 1993. Use 1993 as the base.
   c.   Comment on significant trends that appear in (a) and (b).

P 5-3.   The Interpublic Group of Companies balance sheet from its 1995 annual report is presented in Exhibit 5-3.

Required a. Using the balance sheet, prepare a vertical common- size analysis for 1995, and 1994. Use total assets as a base.

b. Using the balance sheet, prepare a horizontal common-size analysis for 1995 and 1994. Use 1994 as the base.

c. Comment on significant trends that appear in (a) and (b).

P 5-4. The Interpublic Group of Companies income statement from its 1995 annual report is presented in Exhibit 5-3.

Required a. Using the income statement, prepare a vertical common-size analysis for 1995, 1994, and 1993. Use gross income as the base.

b. Using the income statement, prepare a horizontal common-size analysis for 1995, 1994, and 1993. Use 1993 as the base.

c. Comment on significant trends that appear in (a) and (b).

6 An Illustration of Statement Analysis: Part I—Cooper Tire & Rubber Company

USERS MUST BE ABLE TO APPLY and understand financial statement analysis. They must study ratio and trend analysis for meaning. This analysis is the difficult aspect of interpreting financial statements. Chapters 6 through 12 will illustrate the technique of calculating ratios for financial statement analysis.

This chapter presents the statements of an actual firm, Cooper Tire & Rubber Company (Cooper) and information pertaining to Cooper and the tire industry. It also indicates some sources of extensive data relating to the tire industry. Illustrative financial statements are often oversimplified and, therefore, of limited value in learning to analyze actual statements received by users. Thus, although the statements of Cooper may seem difficult because of their comprehensiveness, they provide a typical and meaningful real-world example for financial statement analysis.

COOPER TIRE & RUBBER COMPANY OPERATIONS

The original company from which Cooper evolved started in 1914. On March 26, 1930, the company incorporated as Master Tire & Rubber Company and changed its name to Cooper Tire & Rubber Company on July 20, 1946.

Fortune magazine's list of America's 1,000 largest publicly held firms ranked Cooper number 701 in sales for 1995. Cooper is ranked fourth among 14 generally recognized producers of new tires. The Company's shipments of automobile and truck tires in 1995 represented approximately 12% of all domestic, original equipment, and replacement tire sales.

Products and Sales

Cooper Tire & Rubber Company primarily converts natural and synthetic rubbers into a variety of carbon black reinforced rubber products. The Company manufactures and markets automobile and truck tires, inner tubes, vibration control products, hose and hose assemblies, automotive sealing products, and specialty seating components.

The Company sells tire products nationally and internationally in the replacement tire market, primarily through independent dealers and distributors. This channel of marketing accounted for 68% of Cooper's replacement passenger tire sales in the United States during 1995. During 1994 and 1993, this share approximated 68% and 67%, respectively.

Cooper also supplies original equipment manufacturers with a wide range of rubber products. Cooper manufactures rubber parts for automobile companies and produces tires for mobile home and travel trailer manufacturers.

Current market data indicate an increasing demand for replacement tires and engineered rubber products. Essentially, no economical or practical substitutes for tires or certain rubber automotive parts exist.

During recent years, Cooper has exported to many countries. These include Canada and countries in Latin America, Western Europe, the Middle East, Asia, Africa, and Oceania. Net sales from international operations accounted for approximately 8%, 7%, and 5% of Cooper's sales in 1995, 1994, and 1993, respectively. During 1995, Cooper's ten largest customers accounted for approximately 55% of total sales. Sales to one major customer represented 14%, 13%, and 14% of net sales in 1995, 1994, and 1993, respectively.

Raw Materials

The primary raw materials used by the Company include synthetic and natural rubbers, polyester and nylon fabrics, steel tire cord, and carbon black, which the Company acquires from multiple sources. The Company generally bases contractual relationships with its raw material suppliers on purchase order arrangements.

Research, Development, and Product Improvement

Cooper generally directs its research activities toward product development, improvements in quality, and operating efficiency. Raw material suppliers perform a significant portion of basic research for the rubber industry.

1995 FINANCIAL STATEMENTS FOR COOPER TIRE & RUBBER COMPANY

The 1995 annual report of Cooper included the following sections:

1. *Financial Highlights.* A summary of selected items that would be used in analysis, especially if you are not doing your own analysis. (Not included in this chapter.)

2. *To the Stockholders.* Management comments to stockholders. (Not included in this chapter.)

3. *Operations Review.* (Some of this information has been included in this chapter under "Operations.")

4. *Product Overview.* (Not included in this chapter.)

5. *Financial Review.* The financial review includes the following:

   a. Management's responsibility for financial reporting (included in this chapter).
   b. Management's analysis (included in this chapter).
   c. Notes to financial statements (typically presented with the financial statements; included in this chapter).

6. *Financial Statements* (included in this chapter). The financial statements are the following:

   a. Consolidated Balance Sheets.
   b. Consolidated Statements of Income.
   c. Consolidated Statements of Stockholders' Equity.
   d. Consolidated Statements of Cash Flows.

7. *Report of Independent Auditors* (included in this chapter).

8. *Eleven-Year Summary of Operations and Financial Data* (included in Chapter 12).

9. *Selected Quarterly Data* (included in this chapter).

10. *Directory* (not included in this chapter).

THE TIRE INDUSTRY

For the tire industry, sources of extensive industry data include:

1. *Modern Tire Dealer.*   Published 14 times a year by Bill Communications, Rubber/Automotive Division, 633 Third Ave., New York, NY 10017.

2. *Tire Industry Quarterly.*   Published by Merrill Lynch, Pierce, Fenner & Smith, Inc., One Liberty Plaza, 165 Broadway, New York, NY 10080.

3. *Standard & Poor's Industry Surveys, Autos-Auto Parts*, includes *Rubber Fabricating.*   Published by Standard & Poor's, Equity Research Department, 25 Broadway, New York, NY 10004.

4. *Rubber & Plastics News.*   Published by Crain Communications, Inc., Executive Offices, 1725 Merriman Road, Suite 300, Akron, OH 44313.

FINANCIAL REVIEW
Including MANAGEMENT'S ANALYSIS and NOTES TO FINANCIAL STATEMENTS

MANAGEMENT'S RESPONSIBILITY FOR FINANCIAL REPORTING

The management of Cooper Tire & Rubber Company is responsible for the integrity, objectivity, and accuracy of the financial statements of the Company. The statements have been prepared by the Company in accordance with generally accepted accounting principles and, where appropriate, are based on management's best estimates and judgment. The financial information presented in this report is consistent with the statements.

The accounting systems established and maintained by the Company are supported by adequate internal controls augmented by written policies, internal audits, and the training of qualified personnel.

The accompanying financial statements have been audited by Ernst & Young LLP, independent auditors, whose report appears herein.

The Audit Committee of the Board of Directors is composed solely of directors who are not officers or employees of the Company. The committee meets regularly with management, the Company's internal auditors, and its independent auditors to discuss their evaluations of internal accounting controls, the audit scopes, and the quality of financial reporting. The independent auditors and the internal auditors have free access to the committee, without management's presence, to discuss the results of their respective audits.

Financial Condition

The financial position of the Company continues to be excellent. Strong operating cash flows provided funds for investment in capacity expansion and technological advances and contributed to growing financial strength.

Working capital amounted to $272 million at year-end 1995 compared to $303 million one year earlier. A current ratio of 2.7 indicates a strong liquidity position, although down slightly from the excellent year-end 1994 current ratio of 3.0.

Accounts receivable increased to $257 million versus $221 million at year-end 1994, reflecting strong fourth quarter sales and a delay of customer payments. However, collection experience has been excellent. Adequate allowances have been made for possible collection losses.

Total inventories at $138 million were up from $116 million at year-end 1994. Finished goods inventories were $88 million, or 28 percent higher than one year ago. This increase resulted from restoration of inventory from the low levels at December, 1994 and the building of inventory to provide for new customers coming on stream in 1996. Raw materials and supplies inventories were slightly lower compared to one year ago. Work-in-process inventories were $3 million higher compared with

FINANCIAL REVIEW

(Dollar amounts in thousands; per-share amounts in dollars)

the prior year reflecting current production levels.

Prepaid expenses and deferred income taxes at December 31, 1995 include $11 million in deferred tax assets which are considered fully realizable within one year.

In 1995 additions to property, plant, and equipment were $195 million compared with $78 million in 1994. This increase reflects modernization and expansion projects begun in 1994 as well as similar projects during 1995. The Company invested significant amounts for property, plant, and equipment in recent years primarily for expansions and improving manufacturing technology. The Company's capital expenditure commitments approximated $73 million and $32 million at December 31, 1995 and 1994, respectively. Continuation of high levels of capital expenditures is anticipated. Funding for these expenditures will be available from operating cash flows with additional funding available, if needed, under a credit agreement and a shelf registration. Depreciation and amortization were $63 million in 1995, a 13 percent increase from $56 million in 1994, resulting from the significant capital expenditures in recent years.

Current liabilities of $158 million were $6 million higher than the $152 million at year-end 1994 reflecting increases in income taxes.

Long-term debt decreased $5 million from year-end 1994 to $29 million due to scheduled debt payments. Long-term debt, as a percent of total capitalization, decreased to 3.7 percent at December 31, 1995 form 4.8 percent one year earlier.

The Company has a shelf registration statement with the Securities and Exchange Commission covering the proposed sale of debt securities in an aggregate amount of up to $200 million. The net proceeds received by the Company from any sale of the debt securities would be available for general corporate purposes.

The Company currently provides certain health care and life insurance benefits for its active and retired employees. If the Company does not terminate such benefits, or modify coverage or eligibility requirements, substantially all of the Company's United States employees may become eligible for these benefits upon retirement. The Company uses the accrual method of accounting for such benefits. These benefit costs are funded as claims are incurred. The Company adjusted certain demographic and actuarial assumptions used to derive the liabilities for pensions and postretirement benefits other than pensions at December 31, 1995. These adjustments included a decrease in the discount rate for pensions from 8 percent to 7.5 percent and a decrease in the assumed rate of increase in compensation from 6 percent to 5.5 percent. The discount rate for postretirement benefits other than pensions was decreased from 8.5 percent at December 31, 1994 to 8 percent at December 31, 1995.

Noncurrent deferred income taxes increased to $37 million at December 31, 1995 from $30 million one year earlier, primarily reflecting the excess of tax depreciation over book depreciation.

The Company has been named in environmental matters asserting potential joint and several liability for past and future cleanup, state and Federal claims, site remediation, and attorney fees. The Company has determined that it has no material liability for these matters. In addition, the Company is a defendant in unrelated product liability actions in Federal and state courts throughout the United States in which plaintiffs assert monetary damages. While the outcome of litigation cannot be predicted with certainty, in the opinion of counsel for the Company the pending claims and lawsuits against the Company have not had and should not have

FINANCIAL REVIEW

(Dollar amounts in thousands; per-share amounts in dollars)

a material adverse effect on its financial condition or results of operations.

Stockholders' equity increased $86 million during the year reaching $749 million at year-end. Earnings retentions for 1995 (net income less dividends paid) added $90 million to stockholders' equity but was offset by a $4 million minimum pension liability adjustment. Stockholders' equity per share was $8.95 at year-end 1995, an increase of 13 percent over $7.92 per share at year-end 1994.

Results of Operations

Customer demand was strong for the Company's tires in spite of a decreased industry market, and was excellent for the Company's engineered rubber products as new and larger contracts with our automotive customers were achieved. Capacity utilization was maintained at high levels. Sales increased over 6 percent in 1995 to a record of nearly $1.5 billion. This followed an 18 percent increase in sales in 1994 which resulted primarily from growth in customer demand.

Sales margins were lower in 1995 than in 1994, and were higher in 1994 than in 1993. Raw material cost increases and intense pricing pressure in the replacement tire industry, which restricted recovery of the increased costs, contributed to the reduction in 1995. During 1994 higher operating rates, more favorable product mix, and higher finished goods pricing more than offset raw material cost increases.

The costs of certain raw materials increased significantly during 1994 and more so in 1995, and are expected to continue at high levels during the first half of 1996. In addition, some of these materials are likely to be in short supply if the high levels of global demand experienced in 1994 recur in 1996. Sales margins during 1996 may be affected by these situations. The effects of inflation on sales and operations were not material during 1995 and 1994.

Other income was higher in 1995 compared with 1994, and higher in 1994 compared to 1993. These changes were related to the investments of cash reserves and interest earned thereon.

Increases in 1995 and 1994 selling, general, and administrative expenses were normal considering sales activity levels. As a percent of net sales, these expenses were unchanged.

Effective income tax rates were lower in 1995 than in 1994 due to a reduction in the effective state and local income tax rate. The increased rate in 1994 over 1993 was due primarily to changes in tax credits.

Significant Accounting Policies

The Company employs accounting policies that are based on generally accepted accounting principles. The preparation of financial statements in conformity with these principles requires management to make estimates and assumptions that affect reported amounts of (1) revenues and expenses during the reporting period, and (2) assets and liabilities, as well as disclosure of contingent assets and liabilities, at the date of the financial statements. Actual results could differ from those estimates.

The following summary of significant accounting policies is presented for assistance in the elevation and interpretation of the financial statements and supplementary data. Certain amounts for prior years have been reclassified to conform to 1995 presentations.

Consolidation—The consolidated financial statements include the accounts of the Company and its subsidiaries, all of which are wholly owned. All material intercompany accounts and transactions have been eliminated.

FINANCIAL REVIEW

(Dollar amounts in thousands; per-share amounts in dollars)

Cash and short-term investments—The Company considers all highly liquid investments with an original maturity of three months or less to be short-term investments (cash equivalents). The carrying amount reported in the balance sheets for cash and short-term investments approximates fair value.

Inventories—Substantially all inventories are valued at cost, using the last-in, first-out (LIFO) cost method, which is not in excess of market.

Property, plant, and equipment—Assets are recorded at cost and depreciated or amortized using the straight-line method over their expected useful lives. For income tax purposes accelerated depreciation methods and shorter lives are used.

Stock options—The Company accounts for employee stock options in accordance with Accounting Principles Board Opinion No. 25, "Accounting for Stock Issued to Employees."

Revenue recognition—Revenues are recognized when goods are shipped to customers in accordance with their purchase orders.

Warranties—Estimated costs for product warranties are charged to income at the time of sale.

Research and development—Costs are charged to expense as incurred and amounted to approximately $16,800, $14,700, and $15,100 in 1995, 1994, and 1993, respectively.

Business

The Company, a specialist in the rubber industry, manufactures and markets automobile and truck tires, inner tubes, vibration control products, hoses and hose assemblies, and automotive sealing systems. Product shipments to original equipment vehicle manufacturers historically have approximated 15 to 20 percent of net sales.

The Company manufactures products for the transportation industry. Shipments to customers outside of the United States approximated eight, seven, and five percent of net sales in 1995, 1994, and 1993, respectively. Sales to one major customer approximated 14, 13, and 14 percent of net sales in 1995, 1994, and 1993, respectively.

Inventories

Under the LIFO method, inventories have been reduced by approximately $76,309 and $64,653 at December 31, 1995 and 1994, respectively, from current cost which would be reported under the first-in, first-out method.

Long-Term Debt

The Company has an agreement with four banks authorizing borrowings up to $120,000 with interest at varying rates. The proceeds may be used for general corporate purposes. The agreement provides that on March 1, 1999 the Company may convert any outstanding borrowings into a four-year term loan. A commitment fee is payable quarterly and is based on the daily unused portion of the $120,000. The credit facility supports the issuance of commercial paper. There were no borrowings under the agreement at December 31, 1995.

The 9% Senior Notes, due October 1, 2001, provide for semiannual interest payments on April 1 and October 1 and annual principal prepayments of $4,545 on October 1 through the year 2000. Based on the borrowing rates available to the Company for instruments with similar term and maturity at December 31, 1995 and 1994, the fair value of the senior notes, including the current portion, was $29,733 and $32,536, respectively.

FINANCIAL REVIEW

(Dollar amounts in thousands; per-share amounts in dollars)

Other long-term debt at December 31 comprises the following:

	1995	1994
Capitalized lease obligations	$5,133	$5,137
$8^7/_8$% mortgage note, payable $47 monthly including interest	714	1,204
	$5,847	$6,341

The mortgage note is secured by real and personal property with a carrying value of $7,662 at December 31, 1995.

The most restrictive covenants under the loan agreements require the maintenance of $65,000 in working capital and restrict the payment of dividends. The amount of retained earnings not restricted was $540,703 at December 31, 1995.

Interest paid on debt during 1995, 1994, and 1993 was $3,515, $3,911, and $4,723, respectively. The amount of interest capitalized was $2,694, $1,170, and $2,297 during 1995, 1994, and 1993, respectively.

The required principal payments for long-term debt during the next five years are as follows: 1996—$5,035; 1997—$5,081; 1998—$4,723; 1999—$4,545; 2000—$4,545. See the note on lease commitments for information on capitalized lease obligations.

The Company has a Registration Statement with the Securities and Exchange Commission covering the proposed sale of its debt securities in an aggregate amount of up to $200,000. The Company may sell the securities to or through underwriters, and may also sell the securities directly to other purchasers or through agents or dealers. The net proceeds received by the Company from any sale of the debt securities would be available for general corporate purposes.

Accrued Liabilities

Accrued liabilities at December 31 were as follows:

	1995	1994
Payroll	$29,422	$32,403
Other	34,254	31,024
	$63,676	$63,427

Preferred Stock

At December 31, 1995, 5,000,000 shares of preferred stock were authorized but unissued. The rights of the preferred stock will be determined upon issuance by the Board of Directors.

Preferred Stock Purchase Right

Each stockholder is entitled to the right to purchase 1/100th of a newly issued share of Series A preferred stock of the Company at an exercise price of $16.88. The rights will be exercisable only if a person or group acquires beneficial ownership of 20 percent or more of the Company's outstanding common stock, or commences a tender or exchange offer which upon consummation would result in such person or group beneficially owning 30 percent or more of the Company's outstanding common stock.

If any person becomes the beneficial owner of 25 percent or more of the Company's outstanding common stock, or if a holder of 20 percent or more of the Company's common stock engages in certain self-dealing transactions or a merger transaction in which the Company is the surviving corporation and its common stock remains outstanding, then each right not owned by such person or certain related parties will entitle its holder to purchase a number of shares of the Company's Series A preferred stock having a market value equal to

FINANCIAL REVIEW

(Dollar amounts in thousands; per-share amounts in dollars)

twice the then current exercise price of the right. In addition, if the Company is involved in a merger or other business combination transaction with another person after which the Company's common stock does not remain outstanding, or if the Company sells 50 percent or more of its assets or earning power to another person, each right will entitle its holder to purchase a number of shares of common stock of such other person having a market value equal to twice the then current exercise price of the right.

The Company will generally be entitled to redeem the rights at one cent per right, or as adjusted to reflect stock splits or similar transactions, at any time until the tenth day following public announcement that a person or group has acquired 20 percent or more of the Company's common stock.

Common Stock

There were 7,717,468 common shares reserved for the exercise of stock options and contributions to the Company's Thrift and Profit Sharing and Pre-Tax Savings plans at December 31, 1995.

Stock Options

The Company's 1981 and 1986 incentive stock option plans provide for granting options to key employees to purchase common shares at prices not less than market at the date of grant. These plans were amended in 1988 to allow the granting of nonqualified stock options. Nonqualified stock options are not intended to qualify for the tax treatment applicable to incentive stock options under provisions of the Internal Revenue Code.

Options under these plans may have terms of up to ten years becoming exercisable in whole or in consecutive installments, cumulative or otherwise. The plans also permit the granting

of stock appreciation rights with the options. Stock appreciation rights enable an optionee to surrender exercisable options and receive common stock and/or cash measured by the difference between the option price and the market value of the common stock on the date of surrender.

The options granted under these plans which were outstanding at December 31, 1995 have a term of 10 years and become exercisable 50 percent after the first year and 100 percent after the second year.

The Company's 1991 nonqualified stock option plan provides for granting options to directors, who are not current or former employees of the Company, to purchase common shares at prices not less than market at the date of grant. Options granted under this plan have a term of ten years and are exercisable in full beginning one year after the date of grant.

Summarized information for the plans follows:

	Number of Shares	Price Range per Share
Outstanding at December 31, 1993	454,769	$5.09–$34.69
Granted under 1986 plan	75,000	24.50
Granted under 1991 plan	2,910	26.44
Exercised	(52,304)	5.09–15.19
Cancelled	(5,143)	12.16–34.69
Outstanding at December 31, 1994	475,232	$5.09–$34.69
Granted under 1986 plan	103,800	24.13
Granted under 1991 plan	3,153	24.25
Exercised	(27,900)	5.09–25.00
Cancelled	(13,110)	24.13–25.00
Outstanding at December 31, 1995	541,175	$5.09–$34.69

FINANCIAL REVIEW

(Dollar amounts in thousands; per-share amounts in dollars)

At December 31, 1995, under the 1981 plan, options were exercisable on 22,424 shares and no shares were available for future grants. At December 31, 1994, options were exercisable on 24,024 shares and no shares were available for future grants.

Under the 1986 plan, at December 31, 1995, options were exercisable on 367,012 shares and 1,146,300 shares were available for future grants. At December 31, 1994, options were exercisable on 326,022 shares and 1,236,990 shares were available for future grants.

At December 31, 1995, under the 1991 plan, 8,386 options were exercisable and 88,225 shares were available for future grants. At December 31, 1994, 5,476 options were exercisable and 91,378 shares were available for future grants.

Earnings per Share

Net income per share is based upon the weighted average number of shares outstanding which were 83,645,864 in 1995, 83,623,234 in 1994, and 83,549,566 in 1993. The effect of common stock equivalents is not significant for any period presented.

Pensions

The Company has defined benefit plans covering substantially all employees. The salary plan provides pension benefits based on an employee's years of service and average earnings for the five highest calendar years during the ten years immediately preceding retirement. The hourly plans provide benefits of stated amounts for each year of service. The Company's general funding policy is to contribute amounts deductible for federal income tax purposes.

Pension expense for 1995, 1994, and 1993 included the following components:

	1995	1994	1993
Service cost— benefits earned during period	$ 9,833	$ 9,769	$ 7,641
Interest cost on projected benefit obligation	20,374	17,485	16,327
Actual return on assets	(54,268)	1,565	(12,875)
Net amortization and deferral	38,966	(17,201)	(879)
Net periodic pension cost	$14,905	$11,618	$ 10,214

The actuarial present value of benefit obligations in 1995 reflects changes in certain actuarial assumptions including demographics and decreases in the discount rate and the rate of increase in future compensation levels. The expected long-term rate of return on the plans' assets was ten percent in 1995, 1994, and 1993. The assumptions used to determine the status of the Company's plans at December 31 were as follows:

	1995	1994
Increase in future compensation levels	5.5%	6.0%
Discount rate	7.5	8.0

The information presented above includes an unfunded, nonqualified supplemental executive retirement plan covering certain employees whose participation in the qualified plan is limited by provisions of the Internal Revenue Code.

FINANCIAL REVIEW

(Dollar amounts in thousands; per-share amounts in dollars)

The Company sponsors several defined contribution plans for its employees. Substantially all employees are eligible to participate upon attaining minimum continuous service requirements. Participation is voluntary and participants' contributions are based on their compensation. The Company matches certain plan participants' contributions up to various limits. Company contributions are based on the lesser of (a) participants' contributions up to a specified percent of each participant's compensation, less any forfeitures, or (b) an amount equal to fifteen percent of the Company's pretax earnings in excess of ten percent of stock-

holders' equity at the beginning of the year. Expense for these plans was $8,277, $7,485, and $6,027 for 1995, 1994, and 1993, respectively.

Postretirement Benefits Other than Pensions

The Company currently provides certain health care and life insurance benefits for its active and retired employees. If the Company does not terminate such benefits, or modify coverage or eligibility requirements, substantially all of the Company's United States employees may become eligible for these benefits

The plans' assets consists of cash, cash equivalents, and marketable securities. The funded status of the Company's plans at December 31, 1995 and 1994 was as follows:

| | December 31, 1995 | | December 31, 1994 | |
| | Plans for Which | | Plans for Which | |
	Assets Exceed Accumulated Benefits	Accumulated Benefits Exceed Assets	Assets Exceed Accumulated Benefits	Accumulated Benefits Exceed Assets
Actuarial present value of benefit obligations:				
Vested benefit obligation	$ 131,996	$ 108,028	$ 106,291	$ 86,629
Accumulated benefit obligation	$ 135,171	$ 111,320	$ 108,824	$ 88,350
Projected benefit obligation	$ 203,446	$ 112,845	$ 159,326	$ 90,310
Plans' assets at fair value	187,831	82,144	148,488	63,059
Projected benefit obligation in excess of plan assets	(15,615)	(30,701)	(10,838)	(27,251)
Unrecognized transition amount	5,175	2,723	5,814	3,172
Unrecognized prior service cost	—	8,014	173	10,498
Unrecognized net loss	33,093	15,895	26,344	9,707
Adjustment for minimum liability	—	(26,117)	—	(22,673)
Pension asset (liability) recognized in the Balance Sheet	$ 22,653	$ (30,186)	$ 21,493	$ (26,547)

FINANCIAL REVIEW

(Dollar amounts in thousands; per-share amounts in dollars)

upon retirement if they meet certain age and service requirements. The Company has reserved the right to modify or terminate such benefits at any time. In recent years benefit changes have been implemented throughout the Company.

The Company continues to fund these benefit costs as claims are incurred. Post-retirement benefits expense for 1995, 1994, and 1993 included the following components:

	1995	1994	1993
Service cost	$ 2,607	$ 3,022	$ 2,226
Interest cost	9,810	10,803	9,805
Amortization	(333)	261	—
	$12,084	$14,086	$12,031

The status of the Company's plans at December 31, 1995 and 1994 was as follows:

	1995	1994
Accumulated postretirement benefit obligation (APBO):		
Retirees	$ 71,077	$ 61,280
Fully eligible active plan participants	25,131	22,525
Other active plan participants	37,314	31,881
	133,522	115,686
Deferred gain	6,041	17,561
Postretirement benefits liability	$139,563	$133,247

These amounts are included in the accompanying balance sheet captions:

	1995	1994
Accrued liabilities	$ 6,600	$ 5,900
Postretirement benefits other than pensions	132,963	127,347
	$139,563	$133,247

The discount rate used in determining the APBO was 8.0 percent and 8.5 percent for 1995 and 1994, respectively. The increase in the APBO is due primarily to the decrease in the assumption for the discount rate. At December 31, 1995, the assumed average annual rate of increase in the cost of health care benefits (health care cost trend rate) was 9.5 percent for 1996 declining by 1/2 percent per year through 2004 when the ultimate rate of 5.5 percent is attained. This trend rate assumption has a significant effect on the amounts reported above. A one percent increase in the health care cost trend rate would increase the APBO by $6,216 and the net periodic expense by $483 for the year.

The Company has a Voluntary Employees' Beneficiary Trust and Welfare Benefits Plan (VEBA) to fund health benefits for eligible active and retired employees. The pre-funded amount was $11,000 in 1995 and $9,900 in 1994.

Income Taxes

The provision for income taxes consists of the following:

	1995	1994	1993
Current:			
Federal	$51,141	$60,819	$44,531
State and local	6,753	9,798	6,983
	57,894	70,617	51,514
Deferred:			
Federal	8,062	7,677	8,849
State and local	1,294	1,306	1,677
	9,356	8,983	10,526
	$67,250	$79,600	$62,040

The effective income tax rate differs from the statutory Federal tax rate as follows:

FINANCIAL REVIEW

(Dollar amounts in thousands; per-share amounts in dollars)

	1995	1994	1993
Statutory Federal tax rate	35.0%	35.0%	35.0%
State and local income taxes, net of Federal income tax benefit	2.9	3.5	3.4
Other	(0.6)	(0.3)	(0.6)
Effective income tax rate	37.3%	38.2%	37.8%

Payments for income taxes in 1995, 1994, and 1993 were $53,110, $70,634 and $54,712, respectively.

Deferred income taxes reflect the net tax effects of temporary differences between the carrying amount of assets and liabilities for financial reporting purposes and the amounts used for income tax purposes. Significant components of the Company's deferred tax liabilities and assets as of December 31, 1995 and 1994 are as follows:

	1995	1994
Deferred tax liabilities:		
Tax depreciation over book depreciation	$75,238	$65,638
Other	23,945	20,852
Total deferred tax liabilities	99,183	86,490
Deferred tax assets:		
Postretirement benefits other than pensions	48,163	46,119
Other	25,025	21,326
Total deferred tax assets	73,188	67,445
Net deferred tax liabilities	$25,995	$19,045

These amounts are included in the accompanying balance sheet captions:

	1995	1994
Prepaid expenses and deferred income taxes	$ 10,661	$ 10,692
Deferred income taxes	36,656	29,737
Net deferred tax liabilities	$ 25,995	$ 19,045

Lease Commitments

The Company rents certain manufacturing facilities and equipment under long-term leases expiring at various dates. The leases generally contain renewal or purchase options and provide that the Company shall pay for insurance, property taxes, and maintenance.

Included in property, plant, and equipment are the following capitalized lease amounts at December 31, 1995 and 1994:

	1995	1994
Land and land improvements	$ 378	$ 378
Buildings	9,788	9,788
Machinery and equipment	13,339	13,640
	23,505	23,806
Less accumulated amortization	20,410	20,444
	$ 3,095	$ 3,362

Rental expense for operating leases was $6,696 for 1995, $6,235 for 1994, and $5,362 for 1993.

Future minimum payments for all noncancelable leases at December 31, 1995 are summarized below:

	Capital Leases	Operating Leases
1996	$ 298	$ 2,444
1997	298	1,428
1998	298	1,074
1999	298	676
2000	298	254
2001 and later	11,156	94
	12,646	$ 5,970
Less amount representing interest	7,513	
Present value of minimum lease payments	$ 5,133	

CONSOLIDATED BALANCE SHEETS   December 31

(Dollar amounts in thousands; per-share amounts in dollars)

Assets	1995	1994
Current assets:		
Cash, including short-term investments of $14,000 in 1995 and $83,000 in 1994	$ 23,187	$ 103,285
Accounts receivable, less allowances of $3,600	257,049	221,237
Inventories:		
Finished goods	88,470	69,098
Work in process	13,154	10,341
Raw materials and supplies	36,340	37,084
	137,964	116,523
Prepaid expenses and deferred income taxes	12,384	13,666
Total current assets	430,584	454,711
Property, plant, and equipment:		
Land and land improvements	23,038	20,228
Buildings	228,877	190,129
Machinery and equipment	765,192	631,711
Molds, cores, and rings	50,626	38,546
	1,067,733	880,614
Less accumulated depreciation and amortization	388,857	331,013
Net property, plant, and equipment	678,876	549,601
Other assets	34,241	35,419
	$ 1,143,701	$ 1,039,731

CONSOLIDATED BALANCE SHEETS   December 31

(Dollar amounts in thousands; per-share amounts in dollars)

Liabilities and Stockholders' Equity	1995	1994
Current liabilities:		
Accounts payable	$ 78,823	$ 77,020
Accrued liabilities	63,676	63,427
Income taxes	10,834	6,049
Current portion of debt	5,035	5,112
Total current liabilities	158,368	151,608
Long-term debt:		
9% senior notes payable, due 2001	22,727	27,273
Other	5,847	6,341
Total long-term debt	28,574	33,614
Postretirement benefits other than pensions	132,963	127,347
Other long-term liabilities	38,341	35,348
Deferred income taxes	36,656	29,737
Commitments	—	—
Stockholders' equity:		
Preferred stock, $1 par value; 5,000,000 shares authorized; none issued	—	—
Common stock, $1 par value; 300,000,000 shares authorized; 83,661,972 shares outstanding (83,634,072 in 1994)	83,662	83,634
Capital in excess of par value	1,931	1,656
Retained earnings	672,373	582,137
Minimum pension liability	(9,167)	(5,350)
Total stockholders' equity	748,799	662,077
	$ 1,143,701	$ 1,039,731

CONSOLIDATED STATEMENTS OF INCOME   Years Ended December 31

(Dollar amounts in thousands; per-share amounts in dollars)

	1995	1994	1993
Revenues:			
Net sales	$ 1,493,622	$ 1,403,243	$ 1,193,648
Other income	3,836	2,282	588
	1,497,458	1,405,525	1,194,236
Costs and expenses:			
Cost of products sold	1,242,895	1,125,978	965,353
Selling, general, and administrative	73,796	68,748	62,282
Interest	697	2,680	2,351
	1,317,388	1,197,406	1,029,986
Income before income taxes	180,070	208,119	164,250
Provision for income taxes	67,250	79,600	62,040
Net income	$ 112,820	$ 128,519	$ 102,210
Net income per share	$ 1.35	$ 1.54	$ 1.22

CONSOLIDATED STATEMENTS OF STOCKHOLDERS' EQUITY

(Dollar amounts in thousands; per-share amounts in dollars)

	Common Stock $1 Par Value	Capital In Excess of Par Value	Retained Earnings	Minimum Pension Liability	Total
Balance at December 31, 1992	$ 83,511	$ 611	$387,352	$ —	$ 471,474
Net income			102,210		102,210
Exercise of stock options	71	604			675
Cash dividends—$.20 per share			(16,710)		(16,710)
Minimum pension liability adjustment, net of income taxes				(7,463)	(7,463)
Balance at December 31, 1993	83,582	1,215	472,852	(7,463)	550,186
Net income			128,519		128,519
Exercise of stock options	52	441			493
Cash dividends—$.23 per share			(19,234)		(19,234)
Minimum pension liability adjustment, net of income taxes				2,113	2,113
Balance at December 31, 1994	83,634	1,656	582,137	(5,350)	662,077
Net income			112,820		112,820
Exercise of stock options	28	275			303
Cash dividends—$.27 per share			(22,584)		(22,584)
Minimum pension liability adjustment, net of income taxes				(3,817)	(3,817)
Balance at December 31, 1995	$ 83,662	$ 1,931	$672,373	$ (9,167)	$ 748,799

CONSOLIDATED STATEMENTS OF CASH FLOWS

Years Ended December 31

(Dollar amounts in thousands; per-share amounts in dollars)

	1995	1994	1993
Operating activities:			
Net income	$ 112,820	$ 128,519	$ 102,210
Adjustments to reconcile net income to net cash provided by operating activities:			
Depreciation and amortization	63,313	55,603	46,352
Deferred income taxes	9,356	8,983	10,526
Changes in operating assets and liabilities:			
Accounts receivable	(35,812)	(39,034)	(980)
Inventories and prepaid expenses	(20,159)	(6,174)	(45,623)
Accounts payable and accrued liabilities	2,052	24,698	(12,800)
Postretirement benefits other than pensions	6,315	8,170	8,400
Other	3,051	(828)	1,979
Net cash provided by operating activities	140,936	179,937	110,064
Investing activities:			
Property, plant, and equipment	(194,894)	(78,449)	(117,249)
Other	1,258	88	3,226
Net cash used in investing activities	(193,636)	(78,361)	(114,023)
Financing activities:			
Payment on debt	(5,117)	(18,349)	(33,318)
Issuance of debt	—	13,000	24,000
Issuance of common stock	303	493	675
Payment of dividends	(22,584)	(19,234)	(16,710)
Net cash used in financing activities	(27,398)	(24,090)	(25,353)
Changes in cash and short-term investments	(80,098)	77,486	(29,312)
Cash and short-term investments at beginning of year	103,285	25,799	55,111
Cash and short-term investments at end of year	$ 23,187	$ 103,285	$ 25,799

REPORT OF
INDEPENDENT AUDITORS

The Board of Directors
Cooper Tire & Rubber Company

    We have audited the accompanying consolidated balance sheets of Cooper Tire & Rubber Company as of December 31, 1995 and 1994 and the related consolidated statements of income, stockholders' equity, and cash flows for each of the three years in the period ended December 31, 1995. These financial statements are the responsibility of the Company's management. Our responsibility is to express an opinion on these financial statements based on our audits.

    We conducted our audits in accordance with generally accepted auditing standards. Those standards require that we plan and perform the audit to obtain reasonable assurance about whether the financial statements are free of material misstatement. An audit includes examining, on a test basis, evidence supporting the amounts and disclosures in the financial statements. An audit also includes assessing the accounting principles used and significant estimates made by management, as well as evaluating the overall financial statement presentation. We believe that our audits provide a reasonable basis for our opinion.

    In our opinion, the financial statements referred to above present fairly, in all material respects, the consolidated financial position of Cooper Tire & Rubber Company at December 31, 1995 and 1994 and the consolidated results of its operations and its cash flows for each of the three years in the period ended December 31, 1995, in conformity with generally accepted accounting principles.

Ernst & Young LLP

Toledo, Ohio
February 13, 1996

SELECTED QUARTERLY DATA   (Unaudited)

(Dollar amounts in thousands; per-share amounts in dollars)

1995	Net Sales	Gross Margin	Net Income	Net Income per Share	Dividend per Share	Stock Price High	Stock Price Low
Fourth	$381,899	$70,224	$33,894	$.41	$.075	$25³/₄	$22¹/₄
Third	375,004	61,505	27,048	.32	.075	27³/₈	23⁵/₈
Second	371,366	57,576	24,661	.29	.060	29¹/₈	22⁷/₈
First	365,353	61,422	27,217	.33	.060	29⁵/₈	23³/₈
1994							
Fourth	$361,316	$77,999	$39,100	$.47	$.060	$25³/₈	$21⁵/₈
Third	383,456	76,087	35,454	.42	.060	26¹/₈	22³/₄
Second	329,339	61,691	27,459	.33	.055	28	22¹/₂
First	329,132	61,488	26,506	.32	.055	29¹/₂	23¹/₂

QUESTIONS

Q 6-1.   Cooper—Significant Accounting Policies—Research and Development. "Costs are charged to expense as incurred and amounted to approximately $16,800,000, $14,700,000, and $15,100,000 in 1995, 1994, and 1993, respectively.

a.   Would this policy be considered conservative? Comment.
b.   Is the policy of expensing research and development a policy chosen by management?
c.   Rationalize how research and development expenditures could be viewed as a hidden asset.

Q 6-2.   Cooper—Significant Accounting Policies—Inventory Valuation. "Substantially all inventories are valued at cost, using the last-in, first-out (LIFO) cost method, which is not in excess of market."

a.   Would this policy usually be considered conservative? Comment.
b.   Would the use of LIFO usually result in a reasonable matching of current cost against revenue?
c.   What would be the balance of inventory at December 31, 1995 if Cooper had costed its 1995 inventory using FIFO?

Q 6-3.   Cooper—Significant Accounting Policies—Property, Plant, and Equipment. "Assets are recorded at cost and depreciated or amortized using the straight-line method over their expected useful lives. For income tax purposes accelerated depreciation methods and shorter lives are used."

a.   Would this policy usually be considered conservative? Comment.
b.   Would this policy result in depreciation being recognized on a slower basis for the financial statements or for the tax return? Comment.
c.   Speculate on why management may want to select a different policy for the financial statements than for the tax return.
d.   How much did tax depreciation exceed book (financial) depreciation in 1995 and 1994?

Q 6-4.   Cooper—Significant Accounting Policies—Warranties. "Estimated costs for product warranties are charged to income at the time of sale."

a.   Does this result in warranty expense being recognized in the same period that warranty costs are incurred? Explain.
b.   Explain this policy in terms of the matching concept.

Q 6-5.   Comment on any potential minority interest to be disclosed on the statement of income or on the balance sheet for Cooper.

Q 6-6.   Comment on the concentration of sales by Cooper to an individual customer.

Q 6-7.   Does Cooper have any retained earnings restricted at December 31, 1995? If so, indicate the amount and the purpose of the restriction.

Q 6-8.   Comment on the materiality of export sales in 1995, 1994, and 1993.

Q 6-9.   Using the Consolidated Statement of Stockholders' Equity for Cooper, comment on cash dividends in relation to net income for the three-year period ended December 31, 1995.

Q 6-10.　　Comment on the method of revenue recognition.

Q 6-11.　　Comment on "Management's Responsibility for Financial Reporting." How is this responsibility recognized by Cooper on its annual report?

PROBLEMS

P 6-1.　　Use the Cooper Tire & Rubber Company income statement from the 1995 annual report.

Required　　a.　Prepare a vertical common-size analysis for 1995, 1994, and 1993. Use net sales as the base.

b.　Prepare a horizontal common-size analysis for 1995, 1994, and 1993. Use 1993 as the base year.

c.　Comment on significant trends that appear in the common-size statements prepared in (a) and (b).

P 6-2.　　Use the Cooper Tire & Rubber Company balance sheet from the 1995 annual report.

Required　　a.　Prepare a vertical common-size analysis for 1995 and 1994. Use total assets as the base.

b.　Prepare a horizontal common-size analysis for 1995 and 1994. Use 1994 as the base year.

c.　Comment on significant trends that appear in the common-size statements prepared in (a) and (b).

Cases

CASE 6-1　Comprehensive Review of Statements

Use the financial statements of Cooper Tire & Rubber Company presented in this chapter.

Required　a.　The statements are entitled "Consolidated." What does it mean to have consolidated financial statements?

b.　Does it appear that the subsidiaries are wholly owned? Explain, using the financial statements and the notes.

c.　1.　What are the gross receivables at December 31, 1995?
　　2.　What is the estimated amount that will be collected on receivables outstanding at December 31, 1995?

d.　1.　What is the gross amount in property, plant, and equipment at December 31, 1995? What does this figure represent?
　　2.　What is the net amount in property, plant, and equipment at December 31, 1995? What does this figure represent?

e.　1.　What is the dominant inventory method being used by Cooper?
　　2.　At December 31, 1995, what was the total inventory under LIFO?
　　3.　At December 31, 1995, what was the total inventory under FIFO?

f.　Describe the purpose of the liability account, "Postretirement benefits other than pensions."

g.　1.　What is the total balance in retained earnings at December 31, 1995?
　　2.　How much of this balance is not restricted?

h.　What were the cash dividends per share in 1995?

i.　What type of audit report was received for 1995?

7   Liquidity of Short-Term Assets; Related Debt-Paying Ability

AN ENTITY'S ABILITY TO MAINTAIN ITS short-term debt-paying ability is important to all users of financial statements. If the entity cannot maintain a short-term debt-paying ability, it will not be able to maintain a long-term debt-paying ability, nor will it be able to satisfy its stockholders. Even a very profitable entity will find itself bankrupt if it fails to meet its obligations to short-term creditors. The ability to pay current obligations when due is also related to the cash-generating ability of the firm. This will be discussed in Chapter 11.

When analyzing the short-term debt-paying ability of the firm, we find a close relationship between the current assets and the current liabilities. Generally, the current liabilities will be paid with cash generated from the current assets. As previously indicated, the profitability of the firm does not determine the short-term debt-paying ability. In other words, using accrual accounting, the entity may report very high profits but may not have the ability to pay its current bills, because it lacks available funds. If the entity reports a loss, it may still be able to pay short-term obligations.

This chapter suggests procedures for analyzing short-term assets and the short-term debt-paying ability of an entity. The procedures require an understanding of current assets, current liabilities, and the notes to financial statements.

This chapter also includes a detailed discussion of four very important assets—cash, marketable securities, accounts receivable, and inventory. Accounts receivable and inventory, two critical assets, often substantially influence the liquidity and profitability of a firm.

CURRENT ASSETS, CURRENT LIABILITIES, AND THE OPERATING CYCLE

Current assets (1) are in the form of cash, (2) will be realized in cash, or (3) conserve the use of cash *within the operating cycle of a business or one year, whichever is longer.*[1]

The five categories of assets usually found in current assets, listed in their order of liquidity, include cash, marketable securities, receivables, inventories, and prepayments. Other assets may also be classified in current assets, such as assets held for sale. This chapter will examine in detail each type current asset.

The **operating cycle** for a company is the time period between the acquisition of goods and the final cash realization resulting from sales and subsequent collections. For example, a food store purchases inventory and then sells the inventory for cash. The relatively short time that the inventory remains an asset of the food store represents a very short operating cycle. In another example, a car manufacturer purchases materials and then uses labor and overhead to convert these materials into a finished car. A dealer buys the car on credit and then pays the manufacturer. Compared to the food store, the car manufacturer has a much longer operating cycle, but it is still less than a year. Only a few businesses have an operating cycle longer than a year. For instance, if a business is involved in selling resort property, the average time period that the property is held before sale, plus the average collection period, is typically longer than a year.

Cash

Cash is a medium of exchange that a bank will accept for deposit and a creditor will accept for payment. To be classified as a current asset, cash must be free from any restrictions that would prevent its deposit or use to pay creditors classified as current. If restricted for specific short-term creditors, many firms still classify this cash under current assets, but they disclose the restrictions. Cash restricted for short-term creditors should be eliminated along with the related amount of short-term debt when determining the short-term debt-paying ability. Cash should be available to pay general short-term creditors to be considered as part of the firm's short-term debt-paying ability.

It has become common for banks to require a portion of any loan to remain on deposit in the bank for the duration of the loan period. These deposits, termed **compensating balances**, reduce the amount of cash available to the borrower to meet obligations, and they increase the borrower's effective interest rate.

Compensating balances against short-term borrowings are separately stated in the current asset section or footnoted. Compensating balances for long-term borrowings are separately stated as noncurrent assets under either investments or other assets.

The cash account on the balance sheet is usually entitled *cash, cash and equivalents,* or *cash and certificates of deposit.* The cash classification typically includes currency and unrestricted funds on deposit with a bank.

There are two major problems encountered when analyzing a current asset: determining a fair valuation for the asset and determining the liquidity of the asset. These problems apply to the cash asset only when it has been restricted. Thus, it is usually a simple matter to decide on the amount of cash to use when determining the short-term debt-paying ability of an entity.

Marketable Securities

The business entity has varying cash needs throughout the year. Because an inferred cost arises from keeping money available, management does not want to keep all of the entity's cash needs in the form of cash throughout the year. The available alternative turns some of the cash into productive use through short-term investments (marketable securities), which can be converted into cash as the need arises.

To qualify as a **marketable security**, the investment must be readily marketable, and it must be the intent of management to convert the investment to cash within the current operating cycle or one year, whichever is longer. The key element of this test is **managerial intent**.

It is to management's advantage to show investments under marketable securities, instead of long-term investments, because this classification improves the liquidity appearance of the firm. When the same securities are carried as marketable securities year after year, they are likely held for a business purpose. For example, the other company may be a major supplier or customer of the firm being analyzed. The firm would not want to sell these securities to pay short-term creditors. Therefore, to be conservative, it is better to reclassify them as investments for analysis purposes.

Investments classified as marketable securities should be temporary. Examples of marketable securities include treasury bills, short-term notes of corporations, government bonds, corporate bonds, preferred stock, and common stock. Investments in preferred stock and common stock are referred to as *marketable equity securities.*

Debt and equity securities are to be carried at fair value. An exception is that debt securities can be carried at amortized cost if classified as held-to-maturity securities, but these debt securities would be classified under investments (not classified under current assets).[2]

A security's liquidity must be determined in order for it to be classified as a marketable security. The analyst must assume that securities classified as marketable securities are readily marketable.

Exhibit 7-1, page 256, presents the marketable securities on the 1995 annual report of Chrysler Corporation. It discloses the detail of the marketable securities account. Many companies do not disclose this detail.

EXHIBIT 7-1   **CHRYSLER CORPORATION**
Marketable Securities (Short-Term Investments)

	December 31	
	1995	1994
	(In millions of dollars)	
Assets:		
Cash and equivalents (Note 1)	$5,543	$5,145
Marketable securities (Note 1)	2,582	3,226

Notes to Consolidated Financial Statements

Note 1 (in Part)

At December 31, 1995 and 1994, Chrysler had investments in securities (including cash equivalents) with an aggregate carrying value of $7.3 billion and $7.9 billion, respectively, accounted for in accordance with SFAS No. 115. These securities consisted primarily of commercial paper, federal government agency securities, and corporate debt. At December 31, 1995, securities categorized as available-for-sale and held-to-maturity totaled $6.6 billion and $677 million, respectively. At December 31, 1994, securities categorized as available-for-sale and held-to-maturity totaled $5.5 billion and $2.4 billion, respectively. Substantially all such securities have maturities within one year.

Receivables

An entity usually has a number of claims to future inflows of cash. These claims are usually classified as **accounts receivable** and **notes receivable** on the financial statements. The primary claim that most entities have comes from the selling of merchandise or services on account to customers, referred to as *trade receivables,* with the customer promising to pay within a limited period of time, such as 30 days. Other claims may be from sources such as loans to employees or a federal tax refund.

Claims from customers, usually in the form of accounts receivable, neither bear interest nor involve claims against specific resources of the customer. In some cases, however, the customer signs a note instead of being granted the privilege of having an open account. Usually, the interest-bearing note will be for a longer period of time than an account receivable. In some cases, a customer who does not pay an account receivable when due signs a *note receivable* in place of the account receivable.

The common characteristic of receivables is that the company expects to receive cash some time in the future. This causes two valuation problems. First, a period of time must pass before the receivable can be collected, so the entity incurs costs for the use of these funds. Second, collection may not be made.

The valuation problem from waiting to collect is *ignored in the valuation of receivables and of notes classified as current assets* because of the short waiting period and the immaterial difference in value. The waiting period problem is not ignored if the receivable or note is long-term and classified as an investment. The stipulated rate of interest is presumed to be fair, except when:

1.   No interest is stated.
2.   The stated rate of interest is clearly unreasonable.
3.   The face value of the note is materially different from the cash sales price of the property, goods, or services, or the market value of the note at the date of the transaction.[3]

Under the condition that the face amount of the note does not represent the fair value of the consideration exchanged, *the note is recorded as a present value amount on the date of the original transaction.* The note is recorded at less than (or more than) the face amount, taking into consideration the time value of money. The difference between the recorded amount and the face amount is subsequently amortized as interest income (note receivable) or as interest expense (note payable).

The second problem in valuing receivables or notes is that collection may not be made. Usually, an allowance provides for estimated uncollectible accounts. Estimated losses must be accrued against income and the impairment of the asset must be recognized (or liability recorded) under the following conditions:

1.   Information available prior to the issuance of the financial statements indicates that it is probable that an asset has been impaired, or a liability has been incurred at the date of the financial statements.
2.   The amount of the loss can be reasonably estimated.[4]

Both of these conditions are normally met with respect to the uncollectibility of receivables, and the amount subject to being uncollectible is usually material. Thus, in most cases, the company must estimate bad debt expense and indicate the impairment of the receivable. The expense is placed on the income statement, and the impairment of the receivable is disclosed by the use of an account, **Allowance for Doubtful Accounts**, which is subtracted from the gross receivable account. Later, a specific customer's account, identified as being uncollectible, is charged against Allowance for Doubtful Accounts and the gross receivable account on the balance sheet. (This does *not* mean that the firm will stop efforts to collect.)

It is difficult for the firm to estimate the collectibility of any individual receivable, but when it considers all of the receivables in setting up the allowance, the total estimate should be reasonably accurate. The problem of collection applies to each type of receivable, including notes. The company normally provides for only one allowance account as a matter of convenience, but it considers possible collection problems with all types of receivables and notes when determining the allowance account.

The impairment of receivables may come from causes other than uncollectibility, such as cash discounts allowed, sales returns, and allowances given. Usually, the company considers all of the causes that impair receivables in Allowance for Doubtful Accounts, rather than setting up a separate allowance account for each cause.

Cooper Tire & Rubber Company presented its receivable account for December 31, 1995 and 1994 as follows:

	1995	1994
Accounts receivable, less allowance of $3,600,000 in 1995 and $3,600,000 in 1994	$257,049,000	$221,237,000

This indicates that net receivables were $257,049,000 at December 31, 1995 and $221,237,000 at December 31, 1994 after subtracting allowances for doubtful accounts of $3,600,000.

The use of the Allowance for Doubtful Accounts approach results in the bad debt expense being charged to the period of sale, thus matching this expense with its related revenue. It also results in the recognition of the impairment of the asset. The later charge-off of a specified account receivable does not influence the income statement or net receivables on the balance sheet. The charge-off reduces Accounts Receivable and Allowance for Doubtful Accounts.

When both conditions specified are not met, or the receivables are immaterial, the entity recognizes bad debt expense using the direct write-off method. With this method, bad debt expense is recognized when a specific customer's account is identified as being uncollectible. At this time, the bad debt expense is recognized on the income statement, and gross accounts receivable is decreased on the balance sheet. This method recognizes the bad debt expense in the same period for both the income statement and the tax return.

The direct write-off method frequently results in the bad debt expense being recognized in the year subsequent to the sale, and thus does not result in a proper matching of expense with revenue. This method reports gross receivables, which does not recognize the impairment of the asset from uncollectibility.

When a company has receivables that are due beyond one year (or accounting cycle) from the balance sheet date, and when it is the industry practice to include these receivables in current assets, they are included in current assets even though they do not technically meet the guidelines to qualify as a current asset. The company should disclose the fact that these receivables do not meet the technical guidelines for current assets. Exhibit 7-2 indicates the disclosure made by Snap On, Inc. in its 1994 annual report.

When a company has receivables classified as current, but due later than one year from the balance sheet date, the analyst should make special note of this when making comparisons with competitors. If competitors do not have the same type of receivables, the receivables may not be comparable. For example, a retail company that has substantial installment receivables, with many of them over a year from their due date, is not comparable to a retail company that does not have installment receivables. Installment receivables are considered to be of lower quality than other receivables because of the length of time needed to collect the installment receivables. More importantly, the company with installment receivables should have high standards when granting credit and should closely monitor its receivables.

Customer concentration can be an important consideration in the quality of receivables. When a large portion of receivables is from a few customers, the firm can be highly dependent on those customers. This information is usually not available in the annual report but will be available in the Form 10-K. Cooper's Form 10-K disclosed that "during 1995 Cooper's ten largest customers accounted for approximately 55 percent of total sales. Sales to one major customer were approximately 14, 13, and 14 percent of net sales in 1995, 1994, and 1993, respectively." Thus a moderately high concentration of Cooper's sales involves ten customers.

The liquidity of the trade receivables for a company can be examined by making *two computations*. *One computation* determines the number of days' sales in receivables at the end of the accounting period, and the *second computation* determines the accounts receivable turnover. The turnover

EXHIBIT 7-2 **SNAP ON, INC.**
Receivable Due Beyond One Year

December 31, 1994 Annual Report

Note 1 Summary of Accounting Policies (in Part)

D. ACCOUNTS RECEIVABLE: Accounts receivable includes installment receivable amounts which are due subsequent to one year from balance sheet dates. These amounts were approximately $28.2 million and $27.9 million at the end of 1994 and 1993.

figure can be computed to show the number of times per year receivables turn over or to show how many days on the average it takes to collect the receivables.

Days' Sales in Receivables The number of days' sales in receivables relates the amount of the accounts receivable to the average daily sales on account. For this computation, the accounts receivable amount should include trade notes receivable. Other receivables not related to sales on account should not be included in this computation. Compute the days' sales in receivables as follows:

$$\text{Days' Sales in Receivables} = \frac{\text{Gross Receivables}}{\text{Net Sales} / 365}$$

This formula divides the number of days in a year into net sales on account, and then divides the resulting figure into gross receivables. Exhibit 7-3 presents the computation for Cooper at the end of 1995 and 1994. The increase in days' sales in receivables from 58.48 days at the end of 1994 to 63.70 days at the end of 1995 appears to indicate a slight deterioration in the control of receivables. It could also indicate an increase in sales on account late in 1995.

An internal analyst compares days' sales in receivables with the company's credit terms as an indication of how efficiently the company manages its receivables. For example, if the credit term is 30 days, days' sales in receivables should not be materially over 30 days. If days' sales in receivables are materially more than the credit terms, the company has a collection problem. An effort should be made to keep the days' sales in receivables close to the credit terms.

EXHIBIT 7-3 **COOPER TIRE & RUBBER COMPANY**
Days' Sales in Receivables
December 31, 1995 and 1994

	1995	1994
	(Dollar amounts in thousands)	
Receivables, less allowance for doubtful accounts of $3,600 in 1995 and $3,600 in 1994	$ 257,049	$ 221,237
Gross receivables (net plus allowance) [A]	260,649	224,837
Net sales	1,493,622	1,403,243
Average daily sales on account (net sales on account divided by 365) [B]	4,092	3,845
Days' sales in receivables [A÷B]	63.70 days	58.48 days

Consider the effect on the quality of receivables from a change in the *credit terms*. Shortening the credit terms indicates that there will be less risk in the collection of future receivables, and a lengthening of the credit terms indicates a greater risk. Credit term information is readily available for internal analysis and may be available in footnotes.

Right of return privileges can also be important to the quality of receivables. Liberal right of return privileges can be a negative factor in the quality of receivables and on sales that have already been recorded. Pay particular attention to any change in the right of return privileges. Right of return privileges can readily be determined for internal analysis, and this information should be available in a footnote if considered to be material.

The net sales figure includes collectible and uncollectible accounts. The uncollectible accounts *would not exist* if there were an accurate way, prior to sale, of determining which credit customers would not pay. Firms make an effort to determine credit standing when they approve a customer for credit, but this process does not eliminate uncollectible accounts. Since the net sales figure includes both collectible and uncollectible accounts (gross sales), the comparable receivables figure should include gross receivables, rather than the net receivables figure that remains after the allowance for doubtful accounts is deducted.

The days' sales in receivables gives an indication of the length of time that the receivables have been outstanding at the end of the year. *The indication can be misleading if sales are seasonal and/or the company uses a natural business year*. If the company uses a natural business year for its accounting period, the days' sales in receivables will tend to be understated, because the actual sales per day at the end of the year will be low when compared to the average sales per day for the year. The understatement of days' sales in receivables can also be explained by the fact that gross receivables will tend to be below average at that time of year.

The following is an example of how days' sales in receivables will tend to be understated when a company uses a natural business year:

Average sales per day for the entire year	$ 2,000
Sales per day at the end of the natural business year	1,000
Gross receivables at the end of the year	100,000

Days' sales in receivables based on the formula:

$$\frac{\$100,000}{\$2,000} = 50 \text{ Days}$$

Days' sales in receivables based on sales per day at the end of the natural business year:

$$\frac{\$100,000}{\$1,000} = 100 \text{ Days}$$

The liquidity of a company that uses a natural business year tends to be overstated. However, the only positive way to know if a company uses a natural business year is through research. The information may not be readily available.

It is unlikely that a company that has a seasonal business will close the accounting year during peak activity. At the peak of the business cycle, company personnel are busy and receivables are likely to be at their highest levels. If a company closed during peak activity, the days' sales in receivables would tend to be overstated and the liquidity understated.

The length of time that the receivables have been outstanding gives an indication of their collectibility. The days' sales in receivables should be compared for several years. A comparison should also be made between the days' sales in receivables for a particular company and comparable figures for other firms in the industry and industry averages. This type of comparison can be made when doing either internal or external analysis.

Assuming that the days' sales in receivables computation is *not* distorted because of a seasonal business and/or the company's use of a natural business year, consider the following reasons to explain why the days' sales in receivables appears to be abnormally high:

1. Sales volume expands materially late in the year.
2. Receivables are uncollectible and should have been written off.
3. The company seasonally dates invoices. (An example would be a toy manufacturer that ships in August with the receivable due at the end of December.)
4. A large portion of receivables are on the installment basis.

Assuming that the distortion is *not* from a seasonal situation or the company's use of a natural business year, the following should be considered as possible reasons why the days' sales in receivables appears to be abnormally low:

1. Sales volume decreases materially late in the year.
2. A material amount of sales are on a cash basis.
3. The company has a factoring arrangement in which a material amount of the receivables are sold. (With a factoring arrangement, the receivables are sold to an outside party.)

When doing external analysis, many of the reasons why the days' sales in receivables is abnormally high or low cannot be determined without access to internal information.

Accounts Receivable Turnover Another computation, accounts receivable turnover, indicates the liquidity of the receivables. Compute the accounts receivable turnover measured in times per year as follows:

$$\text{Accounts Receivable Turnover} = \frac{\text{Net Sales}}{\text{Average Gross Receivables}}$$

Exhibit 7-4 presents the computation for Cooper at the end of 1995 and 1994. The turnover of receivables slightly decreased between 1994 and 1995 from 6.84 times per year to 6.15 times per year.

Computing the average gross receivables based on beginning-of-year and end-of-year receivables can be misleading, if the business has seasonal fluctuations or if the company uses a natural business year. To avoid problems of seasonal fluctuations or of comparing a company that uses a natural business year with one that uses a calendar year, the monthly balances (or even weekly balances) of accounts receivable should be used in the computation. This is feasible when performing internal analysis, but not when performing external analysis. In the latter case, quarterly figures can be used to help eliminate these problems. If these problems cannot be eliminated, companies not on the same basis should not be compared. The company with the natural business year tends to overstate its accounts receivable turnover, thus overstating its liquidity.

EXHIBIT 7-4 **COOPER TIRE & RUBBER COMPANY**
Accounts Receivable Turnover
For the Years Ended December 31, 1995 and 1994

	1995	1994
	(Dollars in thousands)	
Net sales [A]	$1,493,622	$1,403,243
End-of-year receivables, less allowance for doubtful accounts	257,049	221,237
Beginning-of-year receivables, less allowance for doubtful accounts	221,237	182,203
Allowance for doubtful accounts:		
End of 1995 $3,600		
End of 1994 $3,600		
End of 1993 $3,100		
Ending gross receivables (net plus allowance)	260,649	224,837
Beginning gross receivables (net plus allowance)	224,837	185,303
Average gross receivables [B]	242,743	205,070
Accounts receivable turnover [A÷B]	6.15 times per year	6.84 times per year

Accounts Receivable Turnover in Days   The accounts receivable turnover can be expressed in terms of days instead of times per year. Turnover in number of days also gives a comparison with the number of days' sales in the ending receivables. The accounts receivable turnover in days also results in an answer directly related to the firm's credit terms. Compute the accounts receivable turnover in days as follows:

$$\text{Accounts Receivable Turnover in Days} = \frac{\text{Average Gross Receivables}}{\text{Net Sales} / 365}$$

This formula is the same as that for determining number of days' sales in receivables, except that the accounts receivable turnover in days is computed using the average gross receivables. Exhibit 7-5 presents the computation for Cooper at the end of 1995 and 1994. Accounts receivable turnover in days increased from 53.34 days in 1994 to 59.32 days in 1995.

The accounts receivable turnover in times per year and days can both be computed by alternative formulas, using Cooper's 1995 figures, as follows:

1. Accounts Receivable Turnover in Times per Year

$$\frac{365}{\text{Accounts Receivable Turnover in Days}} = \frac{365}{59.32 \text{ Days}} = 6.15 \text{ Times per Year}$$

2. Accounts Receivable Turnover in Days

$$\frac{365}{\text{Accounts Receivable Turnover in Times per Year}} = \frac{365}{6.15 \text{ Times per Year}} = 59.35 \text{ Days}$$

EXHIBIT 7-5   **COOPER TIRE & RUBBER COMPANY**
Accounts Receivable Turnover in Days
For the Years Ended December 31, 1995 and 1994

	1995	1994
	(Dollars in thousands)	
Net sales	$1,493,622	$1,403,243
Average gross receivables [A]	242,743	205,070
Sales per day (net sales divided by 365) [B]	4,092	3,845
Accounts receivable turnover in days [A÷B]	59.32 days	53.34 days

The answers obtained for both accounts receivable turnover in number of times per year and accounts receivable turnover in days, using the alternative formulas, may differ slightly from the answers obtained with the previous formulas. The difference is due to rounding.

Credit Sales Versus Cash Sales   A difficulty in computing receivables' liquidity is the problem of credit sales versus cash sales. Net sales includes both credit sales and cash sales. To have a realistic indication of the liquidity of receivables, only the credit sales should be included in the computations. If cash sales are included, the liquidity will be overstated.

The internal analyst determines the credit sales figure and eliminates the problem of credit sales versus cash sales. The external analyst should be aware of this problem, and not be misled by the liquidity figures. The distinction between cash sales and credit sales is not usually a major problem for the external analyst because certain types of businesses tend to sell only on cash terms, and others sell only on credit terms. For instance, a manufacturer usually sells only on credit terms. Some businesses, such as a retail department store, have a mixture of credit sales and cash sales.

In cases of mixed sales, the proportion of credit and cash sales tends to stay rather constant. Therefore, the liquidity figures are comparable (but overstated), enabling the reader to compare figures from period to period as well as figures of similar companies.

Inventories

Inventory is often the most significant asset in determining the short-term debt-paying ability of an entity. Often the inventory account is more than half of the total current assets. Because of the significance of inventories, a special effort should be made to analyze properly this important area.

To be classified as **inventory**, the asset should be for sale in the ordinary course of business, or used or consumed in the production of goods. A trading concern purchases merchandise in a form to sell to customers. Inventories of a trading concern, whether wholesale or retail, usually appear in one inventory account (Merchandise Inventory). A manufacturing concern produces goods to be sold. Inventories of a manufacturing concern are normally classified in three distinct inventory accounts: inventory available to use in production (Raw Materials Inventory), inventory in production (Work in Process Inventory), and inventory completed (Finished Goods Inventory). Usually, the determination of the inventory figures is much more difficult in a manufacturing concern than in a trading concern. The manufacturing concern deals with materials, labor, and overhead when determining the inventory figures, while the trading concern only deals with purchased merchandise. The overhead portion of the work in process inventory and the finished goods inventory is often a problem when determining a manufacturer's inventory. The overhead consists of all the costs of the factory other than direct materials and direct labor. From an analysis viewpoint, however, many of the problems of determining the proper inventory are solved before the entity publishes financial statements.

Inventory is particularly sensitive to changes in business activity, so management must keep inventory in balance with business activity. Failure to do so leads to excessive costs (such as storage cost), production disruptions, and employee layoffs. For example, it is difficult for automobile manufacturers to balance inventories with business activities. When sales decline rapidly, the industry has difficulty adjusting production and the resulting inventory to match the decline. Manufacturers have to use customer incentives, such as price rebates, to get the large inventory buildup back to a manageable level. When business activity increases, inventory shortages can lead to overtime costs. The increase in activity can also lead to cash shortages because of the length of time necessary to acquire inventory, sell the merchandise, and collect receivables.

Determining valuation and liquidity is a fairly complicated problem when analyzing inventories. The basic approach to the valuation of inventory uses cost. The cost figure is often difficult to determine, especially when dealing with manufacturing inventory. Because of the concept of conservatism, the cost figure may not be acceptable if it cannot be recovered. Therefore, if the market figure is below cost, the inventory is reduced to market. Inventory is stated at lower of cost or market on the financial statements.

Inventory Cost   The most critical problem that most entities face is determining which cost to use, since the cost prices have usually varied over time. If it were practical to determine the specific cost of an item, this would be a good cost figure to use in theory. It would also substantially reduce inventory valuation problems. In practice, because of the different types of inventory items and the constant flow of these items, it is not practical to determine the specific costs. Exceptions to this are large items and/or expensive items. For example, it would be practical to determine the specific cost of a new car in the dealer's showroom or the specific cost of an expensive diamond in a jewelry store.

Because the cost of specific items is not usually practical to determine and because other things are considered (such as the income result), companies typically use a cost flow assumption. The most common cost flow assumptions are first-in, first-out (FIFO), last-in, first-out (LIFO), or some average computation. These assumptions can produce substantially different results, because of changing prices.

The **FIFO method** assumes that the first inventory acquired is the first sold. This means that the cost of goods sold account consists of beginning inventory and the earliest items purchased. The latest items purchased remain in inventory. These latest costs are fairly representative of the current costs to replace the inventory. If the inventory flows slowly (low turnover), or if there has been substantial inflation, even FIFO may not produce an inventory figure for the balance sheet representative of the replacement cost. Part of the inventory cost of a manufacturing concern consists of overhead, some of which may represent costs from several years prior, such as depreciation on the plant and equipment. Often the costs transferred to Cost of Goods Sold under FIFO are low in relation to current costs, so current costs are not matched against current revenue. During a time of inflation the resulting profit is overstated. To the extent that inventory does not represent replacement cost, an understatement of the inventory cost occurs.

The **LIFO method** assumes that the costs of the latest items bought or produced are matched against current sales. This assumption materially improves the matching of current costs against current revenue, so the resulting profit figure is usually fairly realistic. The first items (and oldest costs) in inventory can materially distort the reported inventory figure in comparison with its replacement cost. A firm that has been on LIFO for many years may have some inventory costs that go back 20 years or more. Because of inflation, the resulting inventory figure will not reflect current replacement costs.

An average cost computation for inventories results in an inventory amount and a cost of goods sold amount somewhere between FIFO and LIFO. During times of inflation, the resulting inventory is more than LIFO and less than FIFO. The resulting cost of goods sold is less than LIFO and more than FIFO.

Exhibit 7-6, page 268, summarizes the inventory methods used by the 600 companies surveyed for *Accounting Trends & Techniques*. The table covers the years 1994, 1993, 1992, and 1991. (Notice that the number of the companies in the table do not add up to 600, because many companies use more than one method.) Exhibit 7-6 indicates that the most popular inventory methods are FIFO and LIFO. It is perceived that LIFO requires more cost to administer than FIFO. LIFO is not as popular during times of relatively low inflation. During times of relatively high inflation, LIFO becomes more popular because LIFO matches the latest costs against revenue. LIFO results in tax benefits because of the matching of recent higher costs against revenue.

Exhibit 7-6 includes a summary of companies that use LIFO for all inventories, 50% or more of inventories, less than 50% of inventories, and not determinable. This summary indicates that only a small percentage of companies that use LIFO use it for all of their inventories.

Inventory quantities and costs may be accounted for using either the **perpetual** or **periodic** system. Using the perpetual system, the company maintains a continuous record of physical quantities in its inventory. When the perpetual system includes costs (versus quantities only), then the company updates its inventory and cost of goods sold continually as purchases and sales take place. (The inventory needs to be verified by a physical count at least once a year.)

EXHIBIT 7-6   **Inventory Cost Determination**

	Number of Companies			
	1994	**1993**	**1992**	**1991**
Methods:				
First-in, first-out (FIFO)	417	417	415	421
Last-in, first-out (LIFO)	351	350	358	361
Average cost	192	189	193	200
Other	42	42	45	50
Use of LIFO:				
All inventories	17	17	23	23
50% or more of inventories	186	191	189	186
Less than 50% of inventories	98	92	91	95
Not determinable	50	50	55	57
Companies using LIFO	351	350	358	361

Source: Accounting Trends & Techniques, copyright © 1995 by American Institute of Certified Public Accountants, Inc., p. 177. Reprinted with permission.

Using the periodic system, physical counts are taken periodically, which should be at least once a year. The cost of the ending inventory is determined by attaching costs to the physical quantities on hand based on the cost flow assumption used. The cost of goods sold is calculated by subtracting the ending inventory from the cost of goods available for sale.

For the following illustration, the periodic system is used with the inventory count at the end of the year. The same answer would result for FIFO and specific identification under either the perpetual or periodic system. A different answer would result for LIFO and average cost, depending on whether a perpetual or periodic system is used.

To illustrate the major costing methods for determining which costs apply to the units remaining in inventory at the end of the year and which costs are allocated to cost of goods sold, consider the following:

Date	Description	Number of Units	Cost per Unit	Total Cost
January 1	Beginning inventory	200	$6	$ 1,200
March 1	Purchase	1,200	7	8,400
July 1	Purchase	300	9	2,700
October 1	Purchase	400	11	4,400
		2,100		$16,700

A physical inventory on December 31 indicates 800 units on hand. There were 2,100 units available during the year, and 800 remained at the end of the year; therefore, 1,300 units were sold.

Four cost assumptions will be used to illustrate the determination of the ending inventory costs and the related cost of goods sold: *first-in, first-out (FIFO), last-in, first-out (LIFO), average cost,* and *specific identification.*

First-In, First-Out Method (FIFO)   The cost of ending inventory is found by attaching cost to the physical quantities on hand, based on the FIFO cost flow assumption. The costs of goods sold is calculated by subtracting the ending inventory cost from the cost of goods available for sale.

				Inventory Cost	Cost of Goods Sold
October 1	Purchase	400 @ $11		$4,400	
July 1	Purchase	300 @ 9		2,700	
March 1	Purchase	100 @ 7		700	
Ending inventory		800		$7,800	
Cost of goods sold ($16,700 − $7,800) =					$8,900

Last-In, First-Out Method (LIFO)   The cost of the ending inventory is found by attaching costs to the physical quantities on hand, based on the LIFO cost flow assumption. The cost of goods sold is calculated by subtracting the ending inventory cost from the cost of goods available for sale.

				Inventory Cost	Cost of Goods Sold
January 1	Beginning inventory	200 @ $6		$1,200	
March 1	Purchase	600 @ 7		4,200	
Ending inventory		800		$5,400	
Cost of goods sold ($16,700 − $5,400) =					$11,300

Average Cost   There are several ways to compute the average cost. The weighted average divides the total units into the total cost to determine the average cost per unit. The average cost per unit is multiplied by the inventory quantity to determine inventory cost. The cost of goods sold is calculated by subtracting the ending inventory cost from the cost of goods available for sale.

			Inventory Cost	Cost of Goods Sold
$\dfrac{\text{Total cost} \quad \$16,700}{\text{Total units} \quad 2,100} = \$7.95$				
Ending inventory (800 × $7.95)			$6,360	
Cost of goods sold ($16,700 − $6,360) =				$10,340

Specific Identification   With the specific identification method, the items in inventory are identified as coming from specific purchases. The example assumes that the 800 items in inventory can be identified with the March 1 purchase. The cost of goods sold is calculated by subtracting the ending inventory cost from the cost of goods available for sale.

	Inventory Cost	Cost of Goods Sold
Ending inventory (800 x $7.00)	$5,600	
Cost of goods sold ($16,700 – $5,600) =		$11,100

The difference in results on inventory cost and cost of goods sold from using different inventory methods may be material or immaterial. The major impact on the results usually comes from the rate of inflation. In general, the higher the inflation rate, the greater the differences between the inventory methods.

Because the inventory amounts can be substantially different under the various inventory flow assumptions, the analyst should be cautious when comparing the liquidity of firms that have different inventory flow assumptions. Caution is particularly necessary when one of the firms is using the LIFO inventory method, because LIFO may prove meaningless with regard to the firm's short-term debt-paying ability. If two firms that have different inventory flow assumptions need to be compared, this problem should be kept in mind to avoid being misled by the indicated short-term debt-paying ability.

Since the resulting inventory amount will not be equal to the cost of replacing the inventory, regardless of the cost method, another problem needs to be considered when determining the short-term debt-paying ability of the firm: The inventory must be sold for more than cost in order to realize a profit. To the extent that the inventory is sold for more than cost, the short-term debt-paying ability has been understated. However, the extent of the understatement is materially reduced by several factors. One, the firm will incur substantial selling and administrative costs in addition to the inventory cost, thereby reducing the understatement of liquidity to the resulting net profit. Two, the replacement cost of the inventory usually exceeds the reported inventory cost, even if FIFO is used. Therefore, more funds will be required to replace the inventory sold. This will reduce the future short-term debt-paying ability of the firm. Also, since accountants support the conservatism concept, they would rather have a slight understatement of the short-term debt-paying ability of the firm than an overstatement.

The impact on the entity of the different inventory methods must be understood. Since the extremes in inventory costing are LIFO and FIFO, these methods have been summarized. This summary assumes that the entity faces a period of inflation. The conclusions arrived at in this summary would be reversed if the entity faces a deflationary period.

A summary of a LIFO-FIFO comparison follows:

1. LIFO generally results in a lower profit than does FIFO, and this difference can be substantial.

2. Generally, reported profit under LIFO is closer to reality than profit reported under FIFO because the cost of goods sold is closer to replacement cost under LIFO. This is the case under both inflationary and deflationary conditions.

3. FIFO reports a higher inventory ending balance (closer to replacement cost). However, this figure falls short of true replacement cost.

4. LIFO results in a lower profit figure than does FIFO, the result of a higher cost of goods sold.

5. The cash flow under LIFO is greater than the cash flow under FIFO because of the difference in tax liability between the two methods, an important reason why a company selects LIFO.

6. Some companies use a periodic inventory system, which updates the inventory in the general ledger once a year. Purchases made late in the year become part of the cost of goods sold under LIFO. If prices have increased during the period, the cost of goods sold will increase and profits will decrease. It is important that accountants inform management that profits will be lower if substantial purchases of inventory are made near the end of the year, and a periodic inventory system is used.

7. A company using LIFO could face a severe tax problem and a severe cash problem if sales reduce or eliminate the amount of inventory normally carried. The reduction in inventory would result in older costs being matched against current sales. This distorts profits on the high side. Because of the high reported profit, income taxes would increase. When the firm has to replenish the inventory, it has to use additional cash. These problems can be reduced by planning and close supervision of production and purchases. A method called dollar-value LIFO is now frequently used by companies that use LIFO. This method can essentially eliminate the problem addressed in item 7. The dollar-value LIFO method uses price indexes related to the inventory instead of units and unit costs. With dollar-value LIFO, inventory each period is determined for pools of inventory dollars. (See an intermediate accounting book for a detailed explanation of dollar-value LIFO.)

8. LIFO would probably not be used for inventory that has a high turnover rate, because there would be an immaterial difference in the results between LIFO and FIFO.

A firm using LIFO must disclose a LIFO reserve account, usually in a footnote. Usually the amount disclosed must be added to inventory to approximate the inventory at FIFO. An inventory at FIFO is usually a reasonable approximation of the current replacement cost of the inventory.

The Cooper footnote reads, "Under the LIFO method, inventories have been reduced by approximately $76,309,000 and $64,653,000 at December 31, 1995 and 1994, respectively, from current cost which would have been reported under the first-in, first-out method." The approximate current costs of the Cooper inventory for December 31, 1995 and 1994 follow:

	1995	1994
Balance sheet inventories	$137,964,000	$116,523,000
Additional amount in footnote (LIFO reserve)	76,309,000	64,653,000
Approximate current costs	$214,273,000	$181,176,000

In a later chapter, we will examine the possibility of using the adjusted inventory amount to improve the analysis of inventory and of the liquidity of the firm in general.

Liquidity of Inventory   The analysis of the liquidity of the inventories can be approached in a manner similar to that taken to analyze the liquidity of accounts receivable. One computation determines the *number of days' sales in inventory* at the end of the accounting period, another computation determines the *inventory turnover in times per year,* and a third determines the *inventory turnover in days.*

Days' Sales in Inventory   The number of days' sales in inventory ratio relates the amount of the ending inventory to the average daily cost of goods sold. All of the inventory accounts should be included in the computation. The computation gives an indication of the length of time that it will take to use up the inventory through sales. This can be misleading if sales are seasonal or if the company uses a natural business year.

If the company uses a natural business year for its accounting period, the number of days' sales in inventory will tend to be understated, because the average daily cost of goods sold will be at a low point at this time of year. If the days' sales in inventory is understated, the liquidity of the inventory is overstated. The same caution should be observed here as was suggested for determining the liquidity of receivables, when one company uses a natural business year and the other uses a calendar year.

If the company closes its year during peak activity, the number of days' sales in inventory would tend to be overstated and the liquidity would be understated. As indicated with receivables, no good business reason exists for closing the year when activities are at a peak, so this situation should rarely occur.

Compute the number of days' sales in inventory as follows:

$$\text{Days' Sales in Inventory} \quad = \quad \frac{\textbf{Ending Inventory}}{\textbf{Cost of Goods Sold} / \textbf{365}}$$

The formula divides the number of days in a year into the cost of goods sold, and then divides the resulting figure into the ending inventory. Exhibit 7-7 presents the number of days' sales in inventory for Cooper for December 31, 1995 and December 31, 1994. The number of days' sales in inventory has increased from 37.77 days at the end of 1994 to 40.52 days at the end of 1995.

If sales are approximately constant, then the lower the number of days' sales in inventory, the better the inventory control. An inventory buildup can be burdensome if business volume decreases. However, it can be good if business volume expands, since the increased inventory would be available for customers. Because Cooper has expanding sales, an inventory buildup may be in order.

The days' sales in inventory estimates the number of days that it will take to sell the current inventory. For several reasons, this estimate may not be very accurate. The cost of goods sold figure is based on last year's sales, divided by the number of days in a year. Sales next year may not be at the same pace as last year. Also, the ending inventory figure may not be representative of the quantity of inventory actually on hand, especially if using LIFO. This possibly is the case with Cooper because of the large LIFO reserve in relation to the reported inventory.

A seasonal situation, with inventory unusually low or high at the end of the year, would also result in an unrealistic days' sales in inventory computation. Also, a natural business year with low inventory at the end of the year would result in an unrealistic days' sales in inventory. Therefore,

EXHIBIT 7-7 **COOPER TIRE & RUBBER COMPANY**
Days' Sales in Inventory
December 31, 1995 and 1994

	1995	1994
	(Dollars in thousands)	
Inventories, end of year [A]	$ 137,964	$ 116,523
Cost of goods sold	1,242,895	1,125,978
Average daily cost of goods sold (cost of goods sold divided by 365) [B]	3,405	3,085
Number of days' sales in inventory [A÷B]	40.52 days	37.77 days

the resulting answer should be taken as a rough estimate, but it helps when comparing periods or similar companies.

The number of days' sales in inventory could become too low, resulting in lost sales. A good knowledge of the industry and the company is required to determine if the number of days' sales in inventory is too low.

In some cases, not only will the cost of goods sold not be reported separately, but the figure reported will not be a close approximation of the cost of goods sold. This, of course, presents a problem for the external analyst. In such cases, use net sales in place of the cost of goods sold. The result will not be a realistic number of days' sales in inventory, but it can be useful in comparing periods within one firm and in comparing one firm with another. Using net sales produces a much lower number of days' sales in inventory, which materially overstates the liquidity of the ending inventory. Therefore, only the trend determined from comparing one period with another and one firm with other firms should be taken seriously (not actual absolute figures). When you suspect that the days' sales in inventory computation does not result in a reasonable answer, consider using this ratio only to indicate a trend.

If the dollar figures for inventory and/or the cost of goods sold are not reasonable, the ratios calculated with these figures may be distorted. These distortions can be eliminated to some extent by using quantities rather than dollars in the computation. The use of quantities in the computation may work very well for single products or groups of similar products. It does not work very well for a large diversified inventory because of possible changes in the mix of the inventory. Also, using quantities rather than dollars will not be feasible when using externally published statements.

An example of the use of quantities, instead of dollars, follows:

Ending inventory	50 units
Cost of goods sold	500 units

$$\text{Days' sales in inventory} = \frac{50}{500\ /\ 365} = 36.50 \text{ Days}$$

Inventory Turnover   Inventory turnover indicates the liquidity of the inventory. This computation is similar to the receivables turnover computation.

The inventory turnover formula follows:

$$\textbf{Inventory Turnover} = \frac{\textbf{Cost of Goods Sold}}{\textbf{Average Inventory}}$$

Exhibit 7-8 presents the inventory turnover using the 1995 and 1994 figures for Cooper. For Cooper, the inventory turnover was down slightly in 1995.

Computing the average inventory based on the beginning-of-year and end-of-year inventories can be misleading if the company has seasonal fluctuations or if the company uses a natural business year. The solution to the problem is similar to that used when computing the receivables turnover—that is, use the monthly balances of inventory. Monthly estimates of inventory are available for internal analysis, but not for external analysis. Quarterly figures may be available for external analysis. If adequate information is not available, avoid comparing a company on a natural business year with a company on a calendar year. The company with the natural business year tends to overstate inventory turnover and therefore the liquidity of its inventory.

Over time, the difference between the inventory turnover for a firm that uses LIFO and one that uses a method that results in a higher inventory figure can become very material. The LIFO firm will have a much lower inventory and therefore a much higher turnover. Also, it may not be reasonable to compare firms in different industries.

When you suspect that the inventory turnover computation does not result in a reasonable answer because of inventory and/or cost of goods sold dollar figures not being reasonable, perform the computation using quantities rather than dollars. As with the days' sales in inventory, this alternative is feasible only when performing internal analysis. (It may not be feasible even for internal analysis because of product line changes.)

EXHIBIT 7-8 **COOPER TIRE & RUBBER COMPANY**
Merchandise Inventory Turnover
December 31, 1995 and 1994

	1995	1994
	(Dollar amounts in thousands)	
Cost of goods sold [A]	$1,242,895	$1,125,978
Inventories:		
Beginning of year	116,523	111,111
End of year	137,964	116,523
Total	254,487	227,634
Average inventory [B]	127,244	113,817
Merchandise inventory turnover [A÷B]	9.77 times per year	9.89 times per year

Inventory Turnover in Days The inventory turnover figure can be expressed in number of days instead of times per year. This is comparable to the computation that expressed accounts receivable turnover in days. Compute the inventory turnover in days as follows:

$$\text{Inventory Turnover in Days} = \frac{\text{Average Inventory}}{\text{Cost of Goods Sold} / 365}$$

This is the same formula for determining the days' sales in inventory, except that it uses the average inventory. Exhibit 7-9 uses the 1995 and 1994 Cooper data to compute the inventory turnover in days. There was a slight increase in inventory turnover in days for Cooper in 1995.

The inventory turnover in days can be used to compute the inventory turnover per year, as follows:

$$\frac{365}{\text{Inventory Turnover in Days}} = \text{Inventory Turnover per Year}$$

Using the 1995 Cooper data, the inventory turnover is as follows:

$$\frac{365}{\text{Inventory Turnover in Days}} = \frac{365}{37.37} = 9.77 \text{ Times per Year}$$

Operating Cycle The operating cycle represents the period of time elapsing between the acquisition of goods and the final cash realization resulting from sales and subsequent collections. An approximation of the

EXHIBIT 7-9 COOPER TIRE & RUBBER COMPANY
Inventory Turnover in Days
December 31, 1995 and 1994

	1995	1994
	(Dollar amounts in thousands)	
Cost of goods sold	$1,242,895	$1,125,978
Average inventory [A]	127,244	113,817
Sales of inventory per day (cost of goods sold divided by 365) [B]	3,405	3,085
Inventory turnover in days [A÷B]	37.37 days	36.90 days

operating cycle can be determined from the receivables liquidity figures and the inventory liquidity figures. Compute the operating cycle as follows:

$$\text{Operating Cycle} = \frac{\text{Accounts Receivable}}{\text{Turnover in Days}} + \frac{\text{Inventory Turnover}}{\text{in Days}}$$

Exhibit 7-10 uses the 1995 and 1994 Cooper data to compute the operating cycle.

The estimate of the operating cycle is not realistic if the accounts receivable turnover in days and the inventory turnover in days are not realistic. Remember that the accounts receivable turnover in days and the inventory turnover in days are understated, and thus the liquidity overstated, if the company uses a natural business year and computed the averages based on beginning-of-year and end-of-year data. It should also be remembered that the inventory turnover in days is understated, and the liquidity of the inventory overstated, if the company uses LIFO inventory. Also note that accounts receivable turnover in days is understated, and liquidity of receivables overstated, if the sales figures used included cash and credit sales.

The operating cycle should be helpful when comparing a firm from period to period and when comparing a firm with similar companies. This would be the case, even if understated or overstated, as long as the figures in the computation are comparable.

Related to the operating cycle figure is a computation that indicates how long it will take to realize cash from the ending inventory. This computation consists of combining the number of days' sales in ending receivables and the number of days' sales in ending inventory. The 1995 Cooper data produced a days' sales in ending receivables of 63.70 days and a days' sales in ending inventory of 40.52 days, for a total of 104.22 days. In this case, there is a moderate increase, considering the year-end numbers. Therefore, the receivables and inventory at the end of the year are higher than the receivables and inventory carried during the year. This indicates less liquidity at the end of the year than during the year.

EXHIBIT 7-10 **COOPER TIRE & RUBBER COMPANY**
Operating Cycle
For the Years Ended December 31, 1995 and 1994

	1995	1994
Accounts receivable turnover in days [A]	59.32	53.34
Inventory turnover in days [B]	37.37	36.90
Operating cycle [A+B]	96.69 days	90.24 days

Prepayments

Prepayments consist of unexpired costs for which payment has been made. These current assets are expected to be consumed within the operating cycle or one year, whichever is longer. Prepayments normally represent an immaterial portion of the current assets. Therefore, they have little influence on the short-term debt-paying ability of the firm.

Since prepayments have been paid for and will not generate cash in the future, they differ from other current assets. Prepayments relate to the short-term debt-paying ability of the entity because they conserve the use of cash.

Because of the nature of prepayments, the problems of valuation and liquidity are handled in a simple manner. Valuation is taken as the cost that has been paid. Since a prepayment is a current asset that has been paid for in a relatively short period before the balance sheet date, the cost paid fairly represents the cash used for the prepayment. Except in rare circumstances, a prepayment will not result in a receipt of cash; therefore, no liquidity computation is needed. An example of a circumstance where cash is received would be an insurance policy canceled early. No liquidity computation is possible, even in this case.

Other Current Assets

Current assets other than cash, marketable securities, receivables, inventories, and prepayments are usually listed under Other Current Assets. These other current assets may be very material in any one year and, unless they are recurring, may distort the firm's liquidity.

These assets will, in management's opinion, be realized in cash or conserve the use of cash within the operating cycle of the business or one year, whichever is longer. Examples of other current assets include property held for sale and advances or deposits, often explained in a footnote.

Current Liabilities

Current liabilities are "obligations whose liquidation is reasonably expected to require the use of existing resources properly classifiable as current assets or the creation of other current liabilities."[5] Thus, the definition of current liabilities correlates with the definition of current assets.

Typical items found in current liabilities include accounts payable, notes payable, accrued wages, accrued taxes, collections received in advance, and current portions of long-term liabilities. The 1995 Cooper annual report listed current liabilities as follows:

Current liabilities:	
Accounts payable	$ 78,823,000
Accrued liabilities	63,676,000
Income taxes	10,834,000
Current portion of long-term debt	5,035,000
Total current liabilities	$158,368,000

For a current liability, liquidity is not a problem, and the valuation problem is immaterial and is disregarded. Theoretically, the valuation of a current liability should be the present value of the required future outlay of money. Since the difference between the present value and the amount that will be paid in the future is immaterial, the current liability is carried at its face value.

CURRENT ASSETS COMPARED WITH CURRENT LIABILITIES

A comparison of current assets with current liabilities gives an indication of the short-term debt-paying ability of the entity. Several comparisons can be made to determine this ability:

1. Working capital
2. Current ratio
3. Acid-test ratio
4. Cash ratio

Working Capital

The working capital of a business is an indication of the short-run solvency of the business. Compute working capital as follows:

NET
Working Capital = Current Assets – Current Liabilities

Exhibit 7-11, page 280, presents the working capital for Cooper at the end of 1995 and 1994. Cooper had $272,216,000 in working capital in 1995 and $303,103,000 in working capital in 1994. These figures tend to be understated, because some of the current assets, such as inventory, may be understated, based on the book figures.

The inventory as reported may be much less than its replacement cost. The difference between the reported inventory amount and the replacement

EXHIBIT 7-11   COOPER TIRE & RUBBER COMPANY
Working Capital
December 31, 1995 and 1994

	1995	1994
	(Dollar amounts in thousands)	
Current assets [A]	$430,584	$454,711
Current liabilities [B]	158,368	151,608
Working capital [A–B]	$272,216	$303,103

amount is normally material when the firm is using LIFO inventory. The difference may also be material when using one of the other cost methods.

The current working capital amount should be compared with past amounts to determine if working capital is reasonable. Because the relative size of a firm may be expanding or contracting, comparing working capital of one firm with that of another firm is usually meaningless because of their size differences. If the working capital appears to be out of line, find the reasons by analyzing the individual current asset and current liability accounts.

Current Ratio

Another indicator, the current ratio, determines short-term debt-paying ability and is computed as follows:

$$\text{Current Ratio} = \frac{\text{Current Assets}}{\text{Current Liabilities}}$$

Exhibit 7-12 presents the current ratio for Cooper at the end of 1995 and 1994. For Cooper, the current ratio was 2.72 at the end of 1995 and 3.00 at the end of 1994.

For many years, the guideline for the minimum current ratio has been 2.00. Until the mid-1960s, the typical firm successfully maintained a current ratio of 2.00 or better. Since that time, the current ratio of many firms has declined to a point below the 2.00 guideline. Currently, many firms are not successful in staying above a current ratio of 2.00. This indicates a decline in the liquidity of many firms.

A comparison with industry averages should be made to determine the typical current ratio for similar firms. In some industries, a current ratio

EXHIBIT 7-12   **COOPER TIRE & RUBBER COMPANY**
Current Ratio
December 31, 1995 and 1994

	1995	1994
	(Dollar amounts in thousands)	
Current assets [A]	$430,584	$454,711
Current liabilities [B]	158,368	151,608
Current ratio [A÷B]	2.72	3.00

substantially below 2.00 is adequate, while other industries require a much larger ratio. In general, the shorter the operating cycle, the lower the current ratio. The longer the operating cycle, the higher the current ratio.

A comparison of the firm's current ratio with prior periods, and a comparison with industry averages, will help to determine if the ratio is high or low. These comparisons do not indicate why it is high or low. Possible reasons can be found from an analysis of the individual current asset and current liability accounts. Often, the major reasons for the current ratio being out of line will be found in a detailed analysis of accounts receivable and inventory.

The current ratio is considered to be more indicative of the short-term debt-paying ability than the working capital. Working capital only determines the absolute difference between the current assets and current liabilities. The current ratio shows the relationship between the size of the current assets and the size of the current liabilities, making it feasible to compare the current ratio, for instance, between Motorola and Intel. A comparison of the working capital of these two firms would be meaningless because Motorola is a larger firm than Intel.

LIFO inventory can cause major problems with the current ratio because of the understatement of inventory. The result is an understated current ratio. Extreme caution should be exercised when comparing a firm that uses LIFO and a firm that uses some other costing method.

Before computing the current ratio, the analyst should compute the accounts receivable turnover and the merchandise inventory turnover. These computations enable the analyst to formulate an opinion as to whether liquidity problems exist with receivables and/or inventory. An opinion as to the quality of receivables and inventory should influence the analyst's opinion of the current ratio. If liquidity problems exist with receivables and/or inventory, the current ratio needs to be much higher.

Acid-Test Ratio (Quick Ratio)

The current ratio evaluates an enterprise's overall liquidity position, considering current assets and current liabilities. At times, it is desirable to access a more immediate position than that indicated by the current ratio. The acid-test (or quick) ratio relates the most liquid assets to current liabilities.

Inventory is removed from current assets when computing the acid-test ratio. Some of the reasons for removing inventory are that inventory may be slow-moving or possibly obsolete, and parts of the inventory may have been pledged to specific creditors. For example, a winery's inventory requires considerable time for aging and, therefore, a considerable time before sale. To include the wine inventory in the acid-test computation would overstate the liquidity. A valuation problem with inventory also exists, because it is stated at a cost figure that may be materially different from a fair current valuation.

Compute the acid-test ratio as follows:

$$\text{Acid-Test Ratio} = \frac{\text{Current Assets} - \text{Inventory}}{\text{Current Liabilities}}$$

Exhibit 7-13 presents the acid-test ratio for Cooper at the end of 1995 and 1994. For Cooper, the acid-test ratio was 1.85 at the end of 1995 and 2.23 at the end of 1994.

It may also be desirable to exclude some other items from current assets that may not represent current cash flow, such as prepaid and miscellaneous items. Compute the more conservative acid-test ratio as follows:

$$\text{Acid-Test Ratio} = \frac{\text{Cash Equivalents} + \text{Marketable Securities} + \text{Net Receivables}}{\text{Current Liabilities}}$$

Usually a very immaterial difference occurs between the acid-test ratios computed under the first method and this second method. Frequently, the only difference is the inclusion of prepayments in the first computation.

Exhibit 7-14 presents the conservative acid-test ratio for Cooper at the end of 1995 and 1994. This approach resulted in an acid-test ratio of 1.77 at the end of 1995 and 2.14 at the end of 1994.

For Cooper, the difference in the results between the two alternative computations is immaterial. From this point on in this text, the more conservative computations will be used for the acid-test ratio. When a company

EXHIBIT 7-13   **COOPER TIRE & RUBBER COMPANY**
Acid-Test Ratio
December 31, 1995 and 1994

	1995	1994
	(Dollar amounts in thousands)	
Current assets	$430,584	$454,711
Less ending inventory	137,964	116,523
Remaining current assets [A]	292,620	338,188
Current liabilities [B]	158,368	151,608
Acid-test ratio [A÷B]	1.85	2.23

needs to view liquidity with only inventory removed, the alternative computation should be used.

The usual guideline for the acid-test ratio is 1.00. A comparison should be made with the firm's past acid-test ratios and with major competitors and the industry averages. Some industries find that a ratio less than 1.00 is adequate, while others need a ratio greater than 1.00. For example, a grocery store may sell only for cash and not have receivables. This type of business can have an acid-test ratio substantially below the 1.00 guideline and still have adequate liquidity.

Before computing the acid-test ratio, compute the accounts receivable turnover. An opinion as to the quality of receivables should help the analyst form an opinion of the acid-test ratio.

There has been a major decline in the liquidity of companies in the United States, as measured by the current ratio and the acid-test ratio.

EXHIBIT 7-14   **COOPER TIRE & RUBBER COMPANY**
Acid-Test Ratio (Conservative Approach)
December 31, 1995 and 1994

	1995	1994
	(Dollar amounts in thousands)	
Cash, including short-term investments	$ 23,187	$103,285
Net receivables	257,049	221,237
Total quick assets [A]	280,236	324,522
Current liabilities [B]	158,368	151,608
Acid-test ratio [A÷B]	1.77	2.14

Exhibit 7-15 shows the dramatically reduced liquidity of U.S. companies. Reduced liquidity leads to more bankruptcies and greater risk for creditors and investors.

Cash Ratio

Sometimes an analyst needs to view the liquidity of a firm from an extremely conservative point of view. For example, the company may have pledged its receivables and its inventory, or the analyst suspects severe

EXHIBIT 7-15   **Trends in Current Ratio and Acid-Test Ratio**
All U.S. Manufacturing Companies, 1947-1995*

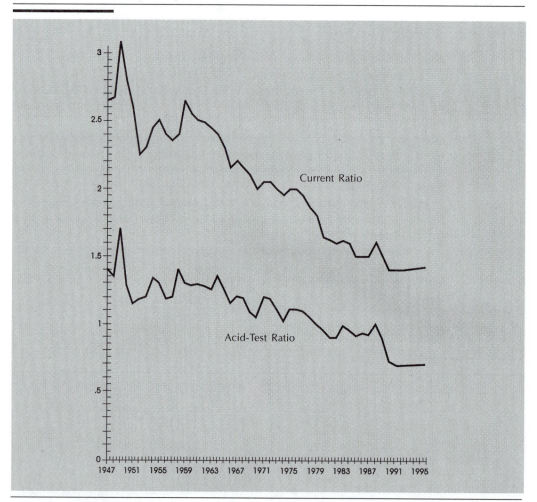

* 1980-1995 extended by author.
Source: Financial Accounting Standards Board, "FASB Discussion Memorandum—Reporting Funds Flows, Liquidity, and Financial Flexibility," 1980, p. 7.

liquidity problems with inventory and receivables. The best indicator of the company's short-run liquidity may be the cash ratio. Compute the cash ratio as follows:

$$\text{Cash Ratio} = \frac{\textbf{Cash Equivalents + Marketable Securities}}{\textbf{Current Liabilities}}$$

The analyst seldom gives the cash ratio much weight when evaluating the liquidity of a firm because it is not realistic to expect a firm to have enough cash equivalents and marketable securities to cover current liabilities. If the firm must depend on cash equivalents and marketable securities for its liquidity, its solvency may be impaired.

Analysts should consider the cash ratio of companies that have naturally slow-moving inventories and receivables and companies that are highly speculative. For instance, a land development company in Florida may sell lots paid for over a number of years on the installment basis; or the success of a new company may be in doubt, such as the Bricklin car company started in Canada during the early 1970s.

The cash ratio indicates the immediate liquidity of the firm. A high cash ratio indicates that the firm is not using its cash to its best advantage; cash should be put to work in the operations of the company. Detailed knowledge of the firm is required, however, before drawing a definite conclusion. Management may have plans for the cash, such as a building expansion program. A cash ratio that is too low could indicate an immediate problem with paying bills.

Exhibit 7-16 presents this ratio for Cooper at the end of 1995 and 1994. For Cooper, the cash ratio was .15 at the end of 1995 and .68 at the end of 1994. Cooper's cash ratio decreased materially at the end of 1995 in relation to the end of 1994. The cash ratio at the end of 1994 was over four times the cash ratio at the end 1995.

EXHIBIT 7-16   COOPER TIRE & RUBBER COMPANY
Cash Ratio
December 31, 1995 and 1994

	1995	1994
	(Dollar amounts in thousands)	
Cash, including short-term investments [A]	$ 23,187	$103,285
Current liabilities [B]	158,368	151,608
Cash ratio [A÷B]	0.15	0.68

OTHER LIQUIDITY CONSIDERATIONS

Another ratio that may be useful to the analyst is the sales to working capital ratio. In addition, there may be liquidity considerations that are not on the face of the statements. This ratio and other liquidity considerations are discussed in this section.

Sales to Working Capital (Working Capital Turnover)

Relating sales to working capital gives an indication of the turnover in working capital per year. The analyst needs to compare this ratio with the past, with competitors, and with industry averages in order to form an opinion as to the adequacy of the working capital turnover. Like many ratios, no rules of thumb exist as to what it should be. Since this ratio relates a balance sheet number (working capital) to an income statement number (sales), a problem exists if the balance sheet number is not representative of the year. To avoid this problem, use the average monthly working capital figure when available. Compute the working capital turnover as follows:

$$\text{Sales to Working Capital} \ = \ \frac{\text{Sales}}{\text{Average Working Capital}}$$

A low working capital turnover ratio tentatively indicates an unprofitable use of working capital. In other words, sales are not adequate in relation to the available working capital. A high ratio tentatively indicates that the firm is undercapitalized (overtrading). An undercapitalized firm is particularly susceptible to liquidity problems when a major adverse change in business conditions occurs.

Exhibit 7-17 presents this ratio for Cooper at the end of 1995 and 1994. The sales to working capital ratio decreased slightly from 1994 to 1995. (Working capital in 1995 was higher in relation to sales than it was in 1994.) This tentatively indicates a slightly less profitable use of working capital in 1995 in relation to 1994.

Liquidity Considerations Not on the Face of the Statements

A firm may have a better liquidity position than indicated by the face of the financial statements. The following paragraphs present several examples:

EXHIBIT 7-17   COOPER TIRE & RUBBER COMPANY
Sales to Working Capital
For the Years Ended December 31, 1995 and 1994

	1995	1994
	(Dollar amounts in thousands)	
Net sales [A]	$1,493,622	$1,403,243
Working capital at beginning of year	303,103	204,857
Working capital at end of year	272,216	303,103
Average working capital [B]	287,660	253,980
Sales to working capital [A÷B]	5.19 times per year	5.53 times per year

1. Unused bank credit lines would be a positive addition to liquidity. They are frequently disclosed in footnotes. Cooper includes this statement in its long-term debt footnote: "The Company has a credit agreement with four banks authorizing borrowings up to $120,000,000 with interest at varying rates. The proceeds may be used for general corporate purposes. The agreement provides that on March 1, 1999 the Company may convert any outstanding borrowings into a four-year term loan. A commitment fee is payable quarterly and is based on the daily unused portion of the $120,000,000. The credit facility supports the issuance of commercial paper. There were no borrowings under the agreement at December 31, 1995."

2. A firm may have some long-term assets that could be converted to cash quickly. This would add to the firm's liquidity. Extreme caution is advised if there is any reliance on long-term assets for liquidity. For one thing, the long-term assets are usually needed in operations. Second, even excess long-term assets may not be easily converted into cash in a short period of time. An exception might be investments, depending on the nature of the investments.

3. A firm may be in a very good long-term debt position and therefore have the capability to issue debt or stock. Thus, the firm could relieve a severe liquidity problem in a reasonable amount of time.

A firm may not be in as good a position of liquidity as indicated by the ratios, as the following examples show:

1. A firm may have notes discounted on which the other party has full recourse against the firm. Discounted notes should be disclosed in a footnote. (A company that discounts a customer note receivable is in essence selling the note to the bank with recourse.)

2.   A firm may have major contingent liabilities that have not been recorded, such as a disputed tax claim. Unrecorded contingencies that are material are disclosed in a footnote.

3.   A firm may have guaranteed a bank note for another company. This would be disclosed in a footnote.

An example of additional potential liabilities not disclosed on the face of the statements appeared in the following footnote of Intel in its 1995 annual report.

Contingencies (in Part)

Intel has been named to the California and U.S. Superfund lists for three of its sites and has completed, along with two other companies, a Remedial Investigation/Feasibility study with the U.S. Environmental Protection Agency (EPA) to evaluate the groundwater in areas adjacent to one of its former sites. The EPA has issued a Record of Decision with respect to a groundwater cleanup plan at that site, including expected costs to complete. Under the California and U.S. Superfund statutes, liability for cleanup of this site and the adjacent area is joint and several. The Company, however, has reached agreement with those same two companies which significantly limits the Company's liabilities under the proposed cleanup plan. Also, the Company has completed extensive studies at its other sites and is engaged in cleanup at several of these sites. In the opinion of management, including internal counsel, the potential losses to the Company in excess of amounts already accrued arising out of these matters will not have a material adverse effect on the Company's financial position or overall trends in results of operations, even if joint and several liability were to be assessed.

The Company is party to various other legal proceedings. In the opinion of management, including internal counsel, these proceedings will not have a material adverse effect on the financial position or overall trends in results of operations of the Company.

The estimate of the potential impact on the Company's financial position or overall results of operations for the above legal proceedings could change in the future.

SUMMARY

The ratios related to the liquidity of short-term assets and the short-term debt-paying ability follow:

$$\text{Days' Sales in Receivables} = \frac{\text{Gross Receivables}}{\text{Net Sales} / 365}$$

$$\text{Accounts Receivable Turnover} = \frac{\text{Net Sales}}{\text{Average Gross Receivables}}$$

$$\text{Accounts Receivable Turnover in Days} = \frac{\text{Average Gross Receivables}}{\text{Net Sales} / 365}$$

$$\text{Days' Sales in Inventory} = \frac{\text{Ending Inventory}}{\text{Cost of Goods Sold} / 365}$$

$$\text{Inventory Turnover} = \frac{\text{Cost of Goods Sold}}{\text{Average Inventory}}$$

$$\text{Inventory Turnover in Days} = \frac{\text{Average Inventory}}{\text{Cost of Goods Sold} / 365}$$

$$\text{Operating Cycle} = \text{Accounts Receivable Turnover in Days} + \text{Inventory Turnover in Days}$$

$$\text{Working Capital} = \text{Current Assets} - \text{Current Liabilities}$$

$$\text{Current Ratio} = \frac{\text{Current Assets}}{\text{Current Liabilities}}$$

$$\text{Acid-Test Ratio} = \frac{\text{Cash Equivalents} + \text{Marketable Securities} + \text{Net Receivables}}{\text{Current Liabilities}}$$

$$\text{Cash Ratio} = \frac{\text{Cash Equivalents} + \text{Marketable Securities}}{\text{Current Liabilities}}$$

$$\text{Sales to Working Capital} = \frac{\text{Sales}}{\text{Average Working Capital}}$$

QUESTIONS

Q 7-1. It is proposed at a stockholders' meeting that the firm slow its rate of payments on accounts payable in order to make more funds available for operations. It is contended that this procedure will enable the firm to expand inventory, which will in turn enable the firm to generate more sales. Comment on this proposal.

Q 7-2. Jones Wholesale Company has been one of the fastest growing wholesale firms in the United States for the last five years in terms of sales and profits. The firm has maintained a current ratio above the average for the wholesale industry. Mr. Jones has asked you to explain possible reasons why the firm is having difficulty meeting its payroll and its accounts payable. What would you tell Mr. Jones?

Q 7-3. What is the reason for separating current assets from the rest of the assets found on the balance sheet?

Q 7-4. Define the operating cycle.

Q 7-5. Define current assets.

Q 7-6. List the major categories of items usually found in current assets.

Q 7-7. Rachit Company has cash that has been frozen in a bank in Cuba. Should this cash be classified as a current asset? Discuss.

Q 7-8. A. B. Smith Company has guaranteed a $1,000,000 bank note for Alender Company. How would this influence the liquidity ratios of A. B. Smith Company? How should this situation be considered?

Q 7-9. Arrow Company has invested funds in a supplier to help ensure a steady supply of needed materials. Would this investment be classified as a marketable security (current asset)?

Q 7-10. List the two computations that are used to determine the liquidity of receivables.

Q 7-11. List the two computations that are used to determine the liquidity of inventory.

Q 7-12. Would a company that uses a natural business year tend to overstate or understate the liquidity of its receivables? Explain.

Q 7-13. T. Melcher Company uses the calendar year. Sales are at a peak during the holiday season, and T. Melcher Company extends 30-day credit terms to customers. Comment on the expected liquidity of its receivables, based on the days' sales in receivables and the accounts receivable turnover.

Q 7-14. A company that uses a natural business year, or ends its year when business is at a peak, will tend to distort the liquidity of its receivables when end-of-year and beginning-of-year receivables are used in the computation. Explain how a company that uses a natural business year or ends its year when business is at a peak can eliminate the distortion in its liquidity computations.

Q 7-15. If a company has substantial cash sales and credit sales, is there any meaning to the receivable liquidity computations that are based on gross sales?

Q 7-16. Describe the difference in inventories between a firm that is a trading concern and a firm that is a manufacturing concern.

Q 7-17.   During times of inflation, which of the inventory costing methods listed below would give the most realistic valuation in inventory? Which method would give the least realistic valuation of inventory? Explain.

   a.   LIFO
   b.   Average
   c.   FIFO

Q 7-18.   The number of days' sales in inventory relates the amount of the ending inventory to the average daily cost of goods sold. Explain why this computation may be misleading under the following conditions:

   a.   The company uses a natural business year for its accounting period.
   b.   The company closes the year when activities are at a peak.
   c.   The company uses LIFO inventory, and inflation has been a problem for a number of years.

Q 7-19.   The days' sales in inventory is an estimate of the number of days that it will take to sell the current inventory.

   a.   What is the ideal number of days' sales in inventory?
   b.   In general, does a company want many days' sales in inventory?
   c.   Can days' sales in inventory be too low?

Q 7-20.   Some firms do not report the cost of goods sold separately on their income statements. In such a case, how should you proceed to compute days' sales in inventory? Will this procedure produce a realistic days' sales in inventory?

Q 7-21.   One of the computations used to determine the liquidity of inventory determines the inventory turnover. In this computation, usually the average inventory is determined by using the beginning-of-the-year and the end-of-the-year inventory figures, but this computation can be misleading if the company has seasonal fluctuations or uses a natural business year. Suggest how to eliminate these distortions.

Q 7-22.   Explain the influence of the use of LIFO inventory on the inventory turnover.

Q 7-23.   Define working capital.

Q 7-24.   Define current liabilities.

Q 7-25.   Several comparisons can be made to determine the short-term debt-paying ability of an entity. Some of these are:

   a.   Working capital   c.   Acid-test ratio
   b.   Current ratio   d.   Cash ratio

      1.   Define each of these terms.
      2.   If the book figures are based on cost, will the results of the preceding computations tend to be understated or overstated? Explain.
      3.   What figures should be used in order to avoid the problem referred to in (2)?

Q 7-26.   Discuss how to use working capital in analysis.

Q 7-27.   Both current assets and current liabilities are used in the computation of working capital and the current ratio, yet the current ratio is considered to be more indicative of the short-term debt-paying ability. Explain.

Q 7-28.   In determining the short-term liquidity of a firm, the current ratio is usually considered to be a better guide than the acid-test ratio, and the acid-test ratio is considered to be a better guide than the cash ratio. Discuss when the acid-test ratio would be preferred over the current ratio and when the cash ratio would be preferred over the acid-test ratio.

Q 7-29.   Discuss some benefits that may accrue to a firm from reducing its operating cycle. Suggest some ways that may be used to reduce a company's operating cycle.

Q 7-30.   Discuss why some firms have longer natural operating cycles than other firms.

Q 7-31.   Would a firm with a relatively long operating cycle tend to charge a higher markup on its inventory cost than a firm with a short operating cycle? Discuss.

Q 7-32.   Is the profitability of the entity considered to be of major importance in determining the short-term debt-paying ability? Discuss.

Q 7-33.   Does the allowance method for bad debts or the direct write-off method result in the fairest presentation of receivables on the balance sheet and the fairest matching of expenses against revenue?

Q 7-34.   When a firm faces an inflationary condition and the LIFO inventory method is based on a periodic basis, purchases late in the year can have a substantial influence on profits. Comment.

Q 7-35.   Why could a current asset such as "net assets of business held for sale" distort a firm's liquidity, in terms of working capital or the current ratio?

Q 7-36.   Before computing the current ratio, the accounts receivable turnover and the inventory turnover should be computed. Why?

Q 7-37.   Before computing the acid-test ratio, compute the accounts receivable turnover. Comment.

Q 7-38.   Which inventory costing method results in the highest balance sheet amount for inventory? (Assume inflationary conditions.)

Q 7-39.   Indicate the single most important factor that motivates a company to select LIFO.

Q 7-40.   A relatively low sales to working capital ratio is a tentative indication of an efficient use of working capital. Comment. A relatively high sales to working capital ratio is a tentative indication that the firm is undercapitalized. Comment.

Q 7-41.   List three situations in which the liquidity position of the firm may be better than that indicated by the liquidity ratios.

Q 7-42.   List three situations in which the liquidity position of the firm may not be as good as that indicated by the liquidity ratios.

Q 7-43.   Indicate the objective of the sales to working capital ratio.

PROBLEMS

P 7-1.   In this problem, compute the acid-test ratio as follows:

$$\frac{\text{Current Assets} - \text{Inventory}}{\text{Current Liabilities}}$$

Required   Determine the cost of sales of a firm with the financial data given below:

Current ratio	2.5
Quick ratio or acid-test ratio	2.0
Current liabilities	$400,000
Inventory turnover	3 times

P 7-2.   The Hawk Company wants to determine the liquidity of its receivables. It has supplied you with the following data regarding selected accounts for December 31, 1995 and 1994.

	1995	1994
Net sales	$1,180,178	$2,200,000
Receivables, less allowance		
for losses and discounts:		
Beginning of year (allowance		
for losses and discounts,		
1995—$12,300; 1994—$7,180)	240,360	230,180
End of year (allowance for		
losses and discounts,		
1995—$11,180; 1994—$12,300)	220,385	240,360

Required   a. Compute the number of days' sales in receivables at December 31, 1995 and 1994.
          b. Compute the accounts receivable turnover for 1995 and 1994. (Use year-end gross receivables.)
          c. Comment on the liquidity of the Hawk Company receivables.

P 7-3.   Mr. Williams, the owner of Williams Produce, wants to maintain control over accounts receivable. He understands that days' sales in receivables and accounts receivable turnover will give a good indication of how well receivables are being managed. Williams Produce does 60% of its business during June, July, and August. Mr. Williams provided the pertinent data. *(See table at top of page 294.)*

Required   a. Compute the days' sales in receivables for July 31, 1995 and December 31, 1995, based on the accompanying data.
          b. Compute the accounts receivable turnover for the period ended July 31, 1995, and December 31, 1995. (Use year-end gross receivables.)
          c. Comment on the results from (a) and (b).

	For Year Ended December 31, 1995	For Year Ended July 31, 1995
Net sales	$800,000	$790,000
Receivables, less allowance for doubtful accounts:		
Beginning of period (allowance January 1, $3,000; August 1, $4,000)	50,000	89,000
End of period (allowance December 31, $3,500; July 31, $4,100)	55,400	90,150

P 7-4. L. Solomon Company would like to compare its days' sales in receivables with that of a competitor, L. Konrath Company. Both companies have had similar sales results in the past, but L. Konrath Company has had better profit results. L. Solomon Company suspects that one reason for the better profit results is that L. Konrath Company did a better job of managing receivables. L. Solomon Company uses a calendar year that ends on December 31, while L. Konrath Company uses a fiscal year that ends on July 31. Information related to sales and receivables of the two companies follows:

	For Year Ended December 31, 19XX
L. Solomon Company	
Net sales	$1,800,000
Receivables, less allowance for doubtful accounts of $8,000	110,000

	For Year Ended July 31, 19XX
L. Konrath Company	
Net sales	$1,850,000
Receivables, less allowance for doubtful accounts of $4,000	60,000

Required a. Compute the days' sales in receivables for both companies. (Use year-end gross receivables.)
b. Comment on the results.

P 7-5a. The P. Gibson Company has computed its accounts receivable turnover in days to be 36.

Required Compute the accounts receivable turnover per year.

P 7-5b. The P. Gibson Company has computed its accounts receivable turnover per year to be 12.

Required Compute the accounts receivable turnover in days.

P 7-5c.   The P. Gibson Company has gross receivables at the end of the year of $280,000 and net sales for the year of $2,158,000.

Required   Compute the days' sales in receivables at the end of the year.

P 7-5d.   The P. Gibson Company has net sales of $3,500,000 and average gross receivables of $324,000.

Required   Compute the accounts receivable turnover.

P 7-6.   The J. Shaffer Company has an ending inventory of $360,500 and a cost of goods sold for the year of $2,100,000. It has used LIFO inventory for a number of years because of persistent inflation.

Required   a. Compute the days' sales in inventory.
     b. Is the J. Shaffer Company days' sales in inventory as computed realistic in comparison with the actual days' sales in inventory?
     c. Would the days' sales in inventory computed for the J. Shaffer Company be a helpful guide?

P 7-7.   The J. Szabo Company had an average inventory of $280,000 and a cost of goods sold of $1,250,000.

Required   Compute the following:
     a. The inventory turnover in days
     b. The inventory turnover

P 7-8.   The following inventory and sales data for this year for G. Rabbit Company are:

	End of Year	Beginning of Year
Net sales	$3,150,000	
Gross receivables	180,000	$160,000
Inventory	480,000	390,000
Cost of goods sold	2,250,000	

Required   Using the above data from the G. Rabbit Company, compute:
     a. The accounts receivable turnover in days
     b. The inventory turnover in days
     c. The operating cycle

P 7-9.   The Anna Banana Company would like to estimate how long it will take to realize cash from its ending inventory. For this purpose, the following data are submitted:

Accounts receivable, less allowance for doubtful accounts of $30,000	$ 560,000
Ending inventory	680,000
Net sales	4,350,000
Cost of goods sold	3,600,000

Required   Estimate how long it will take to realize cash from the ending inventory.

P 7-10.   The Laura Badora Company has been using LIFO inventory. The Company is required to disclose the replacement cost of its inventory and the replacement cost of its cost of goods sold on its annual statements. Selected data for the year 1996 are as follows:

Ending accounts receivable, less allowance for doubtful accounts of $25,000	$ 480,000
Ending inventory, LIFO (estimated replacement cost $900,000)	570,000
Net sales	3,650,000
Cost of goods sold (estimated replacement cost $3,150,000)	2,850,000

Required   a. Compute the days' sales in receivables.
b. Compute the days' sales in inventory, using the cost figure.
c. Compute the days' sales in inventory, using the replacement cost for the inventory and the cost of goods sold.
d. Should replacement cost of inventory and cost of goods sold be used, when possible, when computing days' sales in inventory? Discuss.

P 7-11.   A partial balance sheet and income statement for the King Corporation follows:

KING CORPORATION
Partial Balance Sheet
December 31, 1996

Assets
Current assets:

Cash	$ 33,493
Marketable securities	215,147
Trade receivables, less allowance of $6,000	255,000
Inventories, LIFO	523,000
Prepaid expenses	26,180
Total current assets	$ 1,052,820

Liabilities
Current liabilities:

Trade accounts payable	$ 103,689
Notes payable (primarily to banks) and commercial paper	210,381
Accrued expenses and other liabilities	120,602
Income taxes payable	3,120
Current maturities of long-term debt	22,050
Total current liabilities	$ 459,842

KING CORPORATION
Partial Income Statement
For the Year Ended December 31, 1996

Net sales	$ 3,050,600
Miscellaneous income	45,060
	3,095,660
Cost and expenses:	
Cost of sales	2,185,100
Selling, general, and administrative expenses	350,265
Interest expense	45,600
Income taxes	300,000
	2,880,965
Net income	$ 214,695

Note: The trade receivables at December 31, 1995 were $280,000, net of an allowance of $8,000, for a gross receivables figure of $288,000. The inventory at December 31, 1995 was $565,000.

Required   Compute the following:

a. Working capital
b. Current ratio
c. Acid-test ratio
d. Cash ratio
e. Days' sales in receivables

f. Accounts receivable turnover in days
g. Days' sales in inventory
h. Inventory turnover in days
i. Operating cycle

P 7-12.   Individual transactions often have a significant impact on ratios. This problem will consider the direction of such an impact.

	Total Current Assets	Total Current Liabilities	Net Working Capital	Current Ratio
a. Cash is acquired through issuance of additional common stock.	_____	_____	_____	_____
b. Merchandise is sold for cash. (Assume a profit.)	_____	_____	_____	_____
c. A fixed asset is sold for more than book value.	_____	_____	_____	_____
d. Payment is made to trade creditors for previous purchases.	_____	_____	_____	_____
e. A cash dividend is declared and paid.	_____	_____	_____	_____
f. A stock dividend is declared and paid.	_____	_____	_____	_____

g. Cash is obtained through
    long-term bank loans.   _____ _____ _____ _____

h. A profitable firm increases
    its fixed assets deprecia-
    tion allowance account.   _____ _____ _____ _____

i. Current operating
    expenses are paid.   _____ _____ _____ _____

j. Ten-year notes are
    issued to pay off
    accounts payable.   _____ _____ _____ _____

k. Accounts receivable
    are collected.   _____ _____ _____ _____

l. Equipment is purchased
    with short-term notes.   _____ _____ _____ _____

m. Merchandise is
    purchased on credit.   _____ _____ _____ _____

n. The estimated taxes
    payable are increased.   _____ _____ _____ _____

o. Marketable securities
    are sold below cost.   _____ _____ _____ _____

Required   Indicate the effects of the transactions listed above on each of the following:
total current assets, total current liabilities, net working capital, and current
ratio. Use + to indicate an increase, – to indicate a decrease, and 0 to indicate
no effect. Assume an initial current ratio of more than 1 to 1.

P 7-13.   Current assets and current liabilities data for companies D and E are summarized as follows:

	Company D	Company E
Current assets	$400,000	$900,000
Current liabilities	200,000	700,000
Working capital	$200,000	$200,000

Required   Evaluate the relative solvency of companies D and E.

P 7-14.   Current assets and current liabilities for companies R and T are summarized
as follows:

	Company R	Company T
Current assets	$400,000	$800,000
Current liabilities	200,000	400,000
Working capital	$200,000	$400,000

Required   Evaluate the relative solvency of companies R and T.

P 7-15.   The accompanying financial data were taken from the annual financial statements of Smith Corporation.

	1994	1995	1996
Current assets	$ 450,000	$ 400,000	$ 500,000
Current liabilities	390,000	300,000	340,000
Sales	1,450,000	1,500,000	1,400,000
Cost of goods sold	1,180,000	1,020,000	1,120,000
Inventory	280,000	200,000	250,000
Accounts receivable	120,000	110,000	105,000

Required   a. Based on these data, calculate the following for 1995 and 1996:

1.	Working capital	4.	Accounts receivable turnover
2.	Current ratio	5.	Merchandise inventory turnover
3.	Acid-test ratio	6.	Inventory turnover in days

b. Evaluate the results of your computations in regard to the short-term liquidity of the firm.

P 7-16.   Anne Elizabeth Corporation is engaged in the business of making toys. A high percentage of its products are sold to consumers during November and December. Therefore, retailers need to have the toys in stock prior to November. The corporation produces on a relatively stable basis during the year in order to retain its skilled employees and to minimize its investment in plant and equipment. The seasonal nature of its business requires a substantial capacity to store inventory.

The gross receivables balance at April 30, 1995 was $75,000, and the inventory balance was $350,000 on this date. Sales for the year ended April 30, 1996 totaled $4,000,000 and the cost of goods sold totaled $1,800,000.

Anne Elizabeth Corporation uses a natural business year that ends on April 30. Inventory and accounts receivable data are given in the following table for the year ended April 30, 1996.

	Month-End Balance	
Month	Gross Receivables	Inventory
May, 1995	$ 60,000	$525,000
June, 1995	40,000	650,000
July, 1995	50,000	775,000
August, 1995	60,000	900,000
September, 1995	200,000	975,000
October, 1995	800,000	700,000
November, 1995	1,500,000	400,000
December, 1995	1,800,000	25,000
January, 1996	1,000,000	100,000
February, 1996	600,000	150,000
March, 1996	200,000	275,000
April, 1996	50,000	400,000

Required   a. Using averages based on the year-end figures, compute the following:
1.   Accounts receivable turnover in days
2.   Accounts receivable turnover per year
3.   Inventory turnover in days
4.   Inventory turnover per year

b. Using averages based on the monthly figures, compute the following:
1.   Accounts receivable turnover in days
2.   Accounts receivable turnover per year
3.   Inventory turnover in days
4.   Inventory turnover per year

c. Comment on the difference between the ratios computed in (a) and (b).

d. Compute the days' sales in receivables.

e. Compute the days' sales in inventory.

f. How realistic are the days' sales in receivables and the days' sales in inventory that were computed in (d) and (e)?

P 7-17.   The following data relate to inventory for the year ended December 31, 1995.

Date	Description	Number of Units	Cost per Unit	Total Cost
January 1	Beginning inventory	400	$5.00	$ 2,000
March 1	Purchase	1,000	6.00	6,000
August 1	Purchase	200	7.00	1,400
November 1	Purchase	200	7.50	1,500
		1,800		$10,900

A physical inventory on December 31, 1995 indicates that 400 units are on hand and that they came from the March 1 purchase.

Required   Compute the cost of goods sold for the year ended December 31, 1995 and the ending inventory under the following cost assumptions.

a. First-in, first-out (FIFO)

b. Last-in, first-out (LIFO)

c. Average cost (weighted average)

d. Specific identification

P 7-18.   The data in the following table relate to inventory for the year ended December 31, 1996. A physical inventory on December 31, 1996 indicates that 600 units are on hand, and that they came from the July 1 purchase.

Date	Description	Number of Units	Cost per Unit	Total Cost
January 1	Beginning inventory	1,000	$4.00	$ 4,000
February 20	Purchase	800	4.50	3,600
April 1	Purchase	900	4.75	4,275
July 1	Purchase	700	5.00	3,500
October 22	Purchase	500	4.90	2,450
December 10	Purchase	500	5.00	2,500
		4,400		$20,325

Required   Compute the cost of goods sold for the year ended December 31, 1996 and the ending inventory under the following cost assumptions:
a.   First-in, first-out (FIFO)
b.   Last-in, first-out (LIFO)
c.   Average cost (weighted average)
d.   Specific identification

P 7-19.   J.A. Appliance Company has supplied you with the following data regarding working capital and sales for the years 1996, 1995, and 1994.

	1996	1995	1994
Working capital	$270,000	$260,000	$240,000
Sales	$650,000	$600,000	$500,000
Industry average for the ratio sales to working capital	4.10 times	4.05 times	4.00 times

Required   a.   Compute the sales to working capital ratio for each year.
b.   Comment on the sales to working capital ratio for J. A. Appliance in relation to the industry average and what this may indicate.

P 7-20.   Depoole Company manufactures industrial products and employs a calendar year for financial reporting purposes. Items (a) through (e) present several of Depoole's transactions during 1996. The total of cash equivalents, marketable securities, and net receivables exceeded total current liabilities both before and after each transaction described. Depoole has positive profits in 1996 and a credit balance throughout 1996 in its retained earnings account.

Required   Answer the following multiple-choice questions:
a.   Payment of a trade account payable of $64,500 would:
   1.   Increase the current ratio, but the acid-test ratio would not be affected.
   2.   Increase the acid-test ratio, but the current ratio would not be affected.
   3.   Increase both the current and acid-test ratios.
   4.   Decrease both the current and acid-test ratios.
   5.   Have no effect on the current and acid-test ratios.

b. The purchase of raw materials for $85,000 on open account would:
1. Increase the current ratio
2. Decrease the current ratio
3. Increase net working capital
4. Decrease net working capital
5. Increase both the current ratio and net working capital

c. The collection of a current accounts receivable of $29,000 would:
1. Increase the current ratio
2. Decrease the current ratio
3. Increase the acid-test ratio
4. Decrease the acid-test ratio
5. Not affect the current or acid-test ratios

d. Obsolete inventory of $125,000 was written off during 1996. This would:
1. Decrease the acid-test ratio
2. Increase the acid-test ratio
3. Increase net working capital
4. Decrease the current ratio
5. Decrease both the current and acid-test ratios

e. The early liquidation of a long-term note with cash would:
1. Affect the current ratio to a greater degree than the acid-test ratio.
2. Affect the acid-test ratio to a greater degree than the current ratio.
3. Affect the current and acid-test ratios to the same degree.
4. Affect the current ratio, but not the acid-test ratio.
5. Affect the acid-test ratio, but not the current ratio.

CMA Adapted

P 7-21. The following data apply to items (a) and (b). Mr. Sparks, the owner of School Supplies, Inc. wants to maintain control over accounts receivable. He understands that accounts receivable turnover will give a good indication of how well receivables are being managed. School Supplies, Inc. does 70% of its business during June, July, and August. The terms of sale are 2/10, net/60.

Net sales for the year ended December 31, 1996 and receivables balances are given below.

Net sales	$1,500,000
Receivables, less allowance for doubtful accounts of $8,000 at January 1, 1996	72,000
Receivables, less allowance for doubtful accounts of $10,000 at December 31, 1996	60,000

Required   Answer the following multiple-choice questions:

    a.   The average accounts receivable turnover calculated from the data above is:
        1.   20.0 times per year
        2.   25.0 times per year
        3.   22.7 times per year
        4.   18.75 times per year
        5.   20.8 times per year

    b.   The average accounts receivable turnover computed for School Supplies, Inc. in item (a) above is:
        1.   Representative for the entire year
        2.   Overstated
        3.   Understated

                                                             CMA Adapted

P 7-22.   Information from Greg Company's balance sheet follows:

Current assets:	
Cash	$ 2,100,000
Marketable securities	7,200,000
Accounts receivable	50,500,000
Inventories	65,000,000
Prepaid expenses	1,000,000
Total current assets	$125,800,000
Current liabilities:	
Notes payable	$ 1,400,000
Accounts payable	18,000,000
Accrued expenses	11,000,000
Income taxes payable	600,000
Payments due within one year on	
long-term debt	3,000,000
Total current liabilities	$ 34,000,000

Required   Answer the following multiple-choice questions:

    a.   What is the conservative acid-test ratio for Greg Company?
        1.   1.60   3.   1.90
        2.   1.76   4.   2.20

    b.   What is the effect of the collection of accounts receivable on the current ratio and net working capital, respectively?

	Current Ratio	Net Working Capital
1.	No effect	No effect
2.	Increase	Increase
3.	Increase	No effect
4.	No effect	Increase

P 7-23.   Items (a) through (d) are based on the following information:

SHARKEY CORPORATION
Selected Financial Data

	As of December 31	
	1996	**1995**
Cash	$ 8,000	$ 60,000
Marketable securities	32,000	8,000
Accounts receivable	40,000	110,000
Inventory	80,000	140,000
Net property, plant, and equipment	240,000	280,000
Accounts payable	60,000	100,000
Short-term notes payable	30,000	50,000
Cash sales	1,500,000	1,400,000
Credit sales	600,000	900,000
Cost of goods sold	1,260,000	1,403,000

Required   Answer the following multiple-choice questions:

a. Sharkey's conservative acid-test ratio as of December 31, 1996 is:
    1. 0.63
    2. 0.70
    3. 0.89
    4. 0.99

b. Sharkey's receivable turnover for 1996 is:
    1. 8 times
    2. 6 times
    3. 12 times
    4. 14 times

c. Sharkey's inventory turnover for 1996 is:
    1. 11.45 times
    2. 10.50 times
    3. 9.85 times
    4. 8.45 times

d. Sharkey's current ratio at December 31, 1996 is:
    1. 1.40
    2. 2.60
    3. 1.90
    4. 1.78

e. If current assets exceed current liabilities, payments to creditors made on
    the last day of the year will:
    1. Decrease the current ratio
    2. Increase the current ratio
    3. Decrease working capital
    4. Increase working capital

P 7-24.

Required   Answer the following multiple-choice questions:

a. A company's current ratio is 2.2 to 1 and quick (acid-test) ratio is 1.0 to 1 at the beginning of the year. At the end of the year, the company has a current ratio of 2.5 to 1 and a quick ratio of .8 to 1. Which of the following could help explain the divergence in the ratios from the beginning to the end of the year?
1. An increase in inventory levels during the current year.
2. An increase in credit sales in relationship to cash sales.
3. An increase in the use of trade payables during the current year.
4. An increase in the collection rate of accounts receivable.
5. The sale of marketable securities at a price below cost.

b. If, just prior to a period of rising prices, a company changed its inventory measurement method from FIFO to LIFO, the effect in the next period would be:
1. Increase in both the current ratio and inventory turnover.
2. Decrease in both the current ratio and inventory turnover.
3. Increase in the current ratio and decrease in inventory turnover.
4. Decrease in the current ratio and increase in inventory turnover.
5. The current ratio and inventory turnover would not change.

c. Selected year-end data for the Bayer Company are as follows:

Current liabilities	$600,000
Acid-test ratio	2.5
Current ratio	3.0
Cost of sales	$500,000

Bayer Company's inventory turnover based on this year-end data is:
1. 1.20
2. 2.40
3. 1.67
4. Some amount other than those given above
5. Not determinable from the data given

d. If a firm has a high current ratio but a low acid-test ratio, one can conclude that:
1. The firm has a large outstanding accounts receivable balance.
2. The firm has a large investment in inventory.
3. The firm has a large amount of current liabilities.
4. The cash ratio is extremely high.
5. The two ratios must be recalculated because both conditions cannot occur simultaneously.

e. Investment instruments used to invest temporarily idle cash balances should have the following characteristics:
1. High expected return, low marketability, and a short term to maturity.
2. High expected return, readily marketable, and no maturity date.
3. Low default risk, low marketability, and a short term to maturity.
4. Low default risk, readily marketable, and a long term to maturity.
5. Low default risk, readily marketable, and a short term to maturity.

f. The primary objective in the management of accounts receivable is:
1. To achieve a combination of sales volume, bad debt experience, and receivables turnover that maximizes the profits of the corporation.
2. To realize no bad debts because of the opportunity cost involved.
3. To provide the treasurer of the corporation with sufficient cash to pay the company's bills on time.
4. To coordinate the activities of manufacturing, marketing, and financing so that the corporation can maximize its profits.
5. To allow the most liberal credit acceptance policy because increased sales mean increased profits.

g. A firm requires short-term funds to cover payroll expenses. These funds can come from:
1. Trade credit
2. Collections of receivables
3. Bank loans
4. Delayed payments of accounts payable
5. All of the above

CMA Adapted

P 7-25.   Text-of-the-Quarter, Inc. (TQI) is a new retailer of accounting texts. Sales are made via contracts that provide for TQI to send the customer an accounting text each quarter for 12 quarters. The selling price of each text is $15, with payment due within 30 days of delivery. Sales can be accurately estimated because of the contracts.

The number of contracts TQI sold in its first four quarters of existence, along with the number of texts purchased by TQI, were as follows:

Quarter	Contracts Sold	Texts Purchased	Texts Remaining from Each Quarter's Purchases at End of First Year
First	10,000	50,000	0
Second	20,000	40,000	0
Third	30,000	50,000	10,000
Fourth	40,000	120,000	50,000

All deliveries start in the quarter of contract sale, and all deliveries are up-to-date. Texts were purchased from the publisher at an average cost of $9 for the first quarter, $10 for the second and third quarters, and $11 for the fourth quarter. Selling and administrative costs for the year were $270,000. TQI's tax rate is 40%.

Required   Using generally accepted accounting principles for revenue and expense recognition and inventory accounting, prepare an income statement in such a way as to minimize the company's taxes.

CFA Adapted

P 7-26.   Consecutive five-year balance sheets and income statements of the Anne Gibson Corporation follow:

ANNE GIBSON CORPORATION
Balance Sheet
December 31, 1993 through December 31, 1997

Dollars in thousands	1997	1996	1995	1994	1993
Assets					
Current assets:					
Cash	$ 47,200	$ 46,000	$ 45,000	$ 44,000	$ 43,000
Marketable securities	2,000	2,500	3,000	3,000	3,000
Accounts receivable,					
less allowance of					
$1,000, December 31, 1997					
$ 900, December 31, 1996					
$ 900, December 31, 1995					
$ 800, December 31, 1994					
$1,200, December 31, 1993	131,000	128,000	127,000	126,000	125,000
Inventories	122,000	124,000	126,000	127,000	125,000
Prepaid expenses	3,000	2,500	2,000	1,000	1,000
Total current assets	305,200	303,000	303,000	301,000	297,000
Property, plant, and					
equipment, net	240,000	239,000	238,000	237,500	234,000
Other assets	10,000	8,000	7,000	6,500	7,000
Total assets	$555,200	$550,000	$548,000	$545,000	$538,000
Liabilities and Stockholders' Equity					
Current liabilities:					
Accounts payable	$ 72,000	$ 73,000	$ 75,000	$ 76,000	$ 78,500
Accrued compensation	26,000	25,000	25,500	26,000	26,000
Income taxes	11,500	12,000	13,000	12,500	11,000
Total current liabilities	109,500	110,000	113,500	114,500	115,500
Long-term debt	68,000	60,000	58,000	60,000	62,000
Deferred income taxes	25,000	24,000	23,000	22,000	21,000
Stockholders' equity	352,700	356,000	353,500	348,500	339,500
Total liabilities and					
stockholders' equity	$555,200	$550,000	$548,000	$545,000	$538,000

ANNE GIBSON CORPORATION
Statement of Earnings
For Years Ended December 31, 1993-1997

In thousands, except per share	1997	1996	1995	1994	1993
Net sales	$880,000	$910,000	$840,000	$825,000	$820,000
Cost of goods sold	740,000	760,000	704,000	695,000	692,000
Gross profit	140,000	150,000	136,000	130,000	128,000
Selling and administrative expense	53,000	52,000	50,000	49,800	49,000
Interest expense	6,700	5,900	5,800	5,900	6,000
Earnings from continuing operations before income taxes	80,300	92,100	80,200	74,300	73,000
Income taxes	26,000	27,500	28,000	23,000	22,500
Net earnings	$ 54,300	$ 64,600	$ 52,200	$ 51,300	$ 50,500
Earnings per share	$1.40	$1.65	$1.38	$1.36	$1.33

Required a. Using year-end balance sheet figures, compute the following for the maximum number of years based on the available data.
   1. Days' sales in receivables
   2. Accounts receivable turnover
   3. Accounts receivable turnover in days
   4. Days' sales in inventory
   5. Inventory turnover
   6. Inventory turnover in days
   7. Operating cycle
   8. Working capital
   9. Current ratio
   10. Acid-test ratio (conservative)
   11. Cash ratio
   12. Sales to working capital

   b. Using average balance sheet figures, as suggested in the chapter, compute the following for the maximum number of years, based on the available data.
   1. Days' sales in receivables
   2. Accounts receivable turnover
   3. Accounts receivable turnover in days
   4. Days' sales in inventory
   5. Inventory turnover
   6. Inventory turnover in days
   7. Operating cycle
   8. Working capital
   9. Current ratio
   10. Acid-test ratio (conservative)
   11. Cash ratio
   12. Sales to working capital

   c. Comment on trends indicated in short-term liquidity.

Cases

CASE 7-1   LIFO-FIFO

The current assets and current liabilities section of the NACCO Industries balance sheet is presented for 1995 and 1994, along with selected footnotes.

| | December 31 | |
	1995	1994
	(In thousands)	
Assets		
Current assets:		
Cash and cash equivalents	$ 30,924	$ 19,541
Accounts receivable, net	284,235	236,215
Inventories	388,819	298,987
Prepaid expenses and other	18,027	31,893
Total current assets	$722,005	$586,636
Liabilities		
Current liabilities:		
Accounts payable	$250,662	$226,892
Revolving credit agreements	95,736	30,760
Current maturities of long-term obligations	19,864	63,509
Income taxes	4,672	18,662
Accrued payroll	29,827	28,018
Other current liabilities	122,961	113,597
Total current liabilities	$523,722	$481,438

Note 2—Accounting Policies (in Part)

Inventories: Inventories are stated at the lower-of-cost-or-market. Cost is determined under the last-in, first-out (LIFO) method for manufacturing inventories in the United States and under the first-in, first-out (FIFO) method with respect to all other inventories.

Note 5—Inventories

Inventories are summarized as follows:

	December 31	
	1995	1994
	(In millions)	
Manufacturing inventories:		
Finished goods and service parts—		
NACCO Materials Handling Group	$ 117.4	$ 82.3
Hamilton Beach; Proctor-Silex	43.3	32.8
	160.7	115.1
Raw materials and work in process—		
NACCO Materials Handling Group	182.0	137.9
Hamilton Beach; Proctor-Silex	15.7	15.9
	197.7	153.8
LIFO reserve—		
NACCO Materials Handling Group	(13.3)	(11.4)
Hamilton Beach; Proctor-Silex	(.3)	(.1)
	(13.6)	(11.5)
Total manufacturing inventories	344.8	257.4
North American Coal—		
Coal	10.6	8.4
Mining supplies	19.1	18.8
Retail inventories—Kitchen Collection	14.3	14.4
	$ 388.8	$ 299.0

The cost of manufacturing inventories has been determined by the LIFO method for 66 percent and 69 percent of such inventories at December 31, 1995 and 1994, respectively.

Required   a.   What is the working capital at the end of 1995?

b.   What is the LIFO reserve account?

c.   If the LIFO reserve account was added to the inventory at LIFO, what would be the resulting inventory number at the end of 1995? Which inventory amount do you consider to be more realistic?

d.   Does the use of LIFO or FIFO produce higher, lower, or the same income during (1) price increases, (2) price decreases, and (3) constant prices? (Assume no decrease or increase in inventory quantity.)

e.   Does the use of LIFO or FIFO produce higher, lower, or the same amount of cash flow during (1) price increases, (2) price decreases, and (3) constant costs? Answer the question for both pretax cash flows and after-tax cash flows. (Assume no decrease or increase in inventory quantity.)

f.   Assume that the company purchased inventory on the last day of the year, beginning inventory equaled ending inventory, and inventory records for the item purchased were maintained periodically on the LIFO basis. Would that purchase be included on the income statement or the balance sheet at year-end?

CASE 7-2 Rising Prices, a Time to Switch Off LIFO?

The following information was taken directly from an annual report of a firm that wishes to remain anonymous (the dates have been changed).

Financial Summary

Effects of LIFO Accounting

For a number of years, the corporation has used the last-in, first-out (LIFO) method of accounting for its steel inventories. In periods of extended inflation, coupled with uncertain supplies of raw materials from foreign sources, and rapid increases and fluctuations in prices of raw materials such as nickel and chrome nickel scrap, earnings can be affected unrealistically for any given year.

Because of these factors, the corporation will apply to the Internal Revenue Service for permission to discontinue using the LIFO method of accounting for valuing those inventories for which this method has been used. If such application is granted, the LIFO reserve at December 31, 1996, of $12,300,000 would be eliminated, which would require a provision for income taxes of approximately $6,150,000. The corporation will also seek permission to pay the increased taxes over a ten-year period. If the corporation had not used the LIFO method of accounting during 1995, net earnings for the year would have been increased by approximately $1,500,000.

The 1996 annual report also disclosed the following:

	1996	1995
1. Sales and revenues	$536,467,782	$487,886,449
2. Earnings per common share	$3.44	$3.58

Required a. The corporation indicates that earnings can be affected unrealistically by rapid increases and fluctuations in prices when using LIFO. Comment.

b. How much taxes will need to be paid on past earnings from the switch from LIFO? How will the switch from LIFO influence taxes in the future?

c. How will a switch from LIFO affect 1996 profits?

d. How will a switch from LIFO affect future profits?

e. How will a switch from LIFO affect 1996 cash flow?

f. How will a switch from LIFO affect future cash flow?

g. Speculate on the real reason that the corporation wishes to switch from LIFO.

CASE 7-3   The Other Side of LIFO

What happens when a company using LIFO sells a greater quantity of goods than it purchases? In the following article,[*] Allen I. Schiff, Ph.D., Associate Professor of Accounting at Fordham University, New York City, discusses the implications of this phenomenon, which is known as LIFO liquidation.

Discussion of the LIFO cost basis for inventory valuation usually focuses on the superiority of this method and its widespread adoption. The conventional rationale for LIFO is its consistency with the matching principle during a period of rising prices. Historically, the most significant adoption of LIFO by U.S. corporations occurred during the period from 1973 to 1974, which was characterized by rapidly rising prices and sharp increases in interest rates. However, the motivation for the widespread use of LIFO didn't derive from the desire to achieve better matching of cost and revenue but, rather, from the reduced reported income that led to tax savings and increased cash flow.

Recently, another facet of LIFO has appeared in the annual reports of some companies. Known as LIFO liquidation, this process occurs during a reporting period when a company sells (withdraws) goods in a greater quantity than the quantity purchased (entered). As a result, inventories are reduced to a point at which cost layers of prior years are related to current inflated sales prices.

Relatively little attention has been given to the implications of LIFO inventory liquidations. Accounting texts discuss LIFO liquidations in a superficial fashion—and for good reason, it wasn't a phenomenon frequently encountered in the past. Indeed, until recently the only significant attempted LIFO liquidation related to the steel industry during the Korean War period. During this period, the demand for steel was strong, prices were high, and a steelworker's strike contributed to decreasing inventory levels. Congress was petitioned to modify the tax result from a matching of "old" costs against their then-current high-selling prices. Congress refused and steel inventories weren't liquidated despite market demand.

The Incentives for LIFO Liquidation

The economic environment at this writing is quite different. Possible factors causing LIFO liquidations at present are:

— Decreased expected demand associated with a recessionary economy.

— High interest rates resulting in high inventory carrying costs. These high rates also present alternative economic opportu-

---

[*] Copyright © 1983 by the AICPA, Inc. Opinions expressed in the *Journal of Accountancy* are those of the editors and contributors. Publication in the *Journal of Accountancy* does not constitute endorsement by the AICPA or its committees.

nities for funds invested in inventories if there is a belief that the inflation rate will decrease in relation to interest rates.

— A sluggish economy that could lead management to minimize losses or improve reported profit.

To get a notion about the extent, if any, to which companies that recorded a LIFO liquidation increased net income, the financial reports of 17 LIFO companies for the years 1980 and 1981 were randomly selected. Nine of these companies reported an increase in pretax income (or a reduction of loss) of at least 10 percent for either 1980, 1981 or both as a direct result of LIFO liquidation. What these preliminary results suggest is that there are other aspects of LIFO which require more extensive study. The original justification for LIFO was its superiority in reflecting results consistent with the matching principle. The liquidation of LIFO layers in recent years has had the opposite effect, it mismatches current revenues and historical costs, which results in the inclusion of inventory holding gains in reported income.

Conclusion

Thus, we have come full circle. FIFO valuation methods, originally criticized for poor matching when compared to LIFO, may actually be superior in the sense that, compared to companies experiencing LIFO liquidations, FIFO companies match costs and revenues relatively well. Furthermore, it may be argued that the sole motivation attributed to companies for switching to LIFO—to improve cash flows—may need broadening. Since the timing of the decision to liquidate LIFO inventories is entirely up to management, it would appear that such liquidations may give rise to income smoothing; it must be stressed that the smoothing may enhance the image conveyed by financial statements, but it has a negative impact on cash flow to the extent that taxes are paid (or loss carryforwards reduced) on the incremental profit associated with the sale of the liquidated inventories.

More extensive research is, of course, needed to fully document the incidence of LIFO inventory liquidation during the last two years. Even my limited examination of reports suggests the need to emphasize the "other side of LIFO."

Required a. Briefly describe why an inventory method that uses historical costs (such as LIFO) can distort profits.

    b. Indicate probable reasons why the steel industry did not sell its available inventory during the steel strike.

    c. For the firms that were using LIFO, explain the anticipated effect on the following variables because of reducing inventories during 1980 and 1981.

      1. Profits
      2. Taxes paid
      3. Cash flow

    d. In your opinion, what effect did the reduction in inventories during 1980 and 1981, for the LIFO firms, have on the quality of earnings?

    e. Explain why many firms voluntarily reduced their inventories during 1980 and 1981.

CASE 7-4   Booming Retail

The Grand retail firm reported the following financial data for the past several years:

	Year				
	5	4	3	2	1
	(amounts in 000s)				
Sales	$1,254,131	$1,210,918	$1,096,152	$979,458	$920,797
Net accounts receivable	419,731	368,267	312,776	272,450	230,427

The Grand retail firm had a decentralized credit operation allowing each store to administer its credit operation. Many stores provided installment plans allowing the customer up to 36 months to pay. Gross profits on install-ment sales were reflected in the financial statements in the period when the sales were made.

Required

a. Using Year 1 as the base, prepare horizontal common-size analysis for sales and net accounts receivable.

b. Compute the accounts receivable turnover for Years 2-5. (Use net accounts receivable.)

c. Would financial control of accounts receivable be more important with installment sales than with sales on 30-day credit? Comment.

d. Comment on what is apparently happening at The Grand retail firm.

Endnotes

1   *Accounting Research Bulletins No. 43,* "Restatement and Revision of Accounting Research Bulletins," 1953, Chapter 3, Section A, paragraph 4.

2   *Statement of Financial Accounting Standards No. 115,* "Accounting for Certain Investments in Debt and Equity Securities" (Norwalk, CT: Financial Accounting Standards Board, 1993).

3   *Opinions of the Accounting Principles Board No. 21,* "Interest on Receivables and Payables" (New York, NY: American Institute of Certified Public Accountants, 1971), paragraph 11.

4   *Statement of Financial Accounting Standards No. 5,* "Accounting for Contingencies" (Stamford, CT: Financial Accounting Standards Board, 1975), paragraph 8.

5   Committee on Accounting Procedure, American Institute of Certified Public Accountants, "Accounting Research and Terminology Bulletins" (New York, NY: American Institute of Certified Public Accountants, 1961), p. 21.

8   Long-Term Debt-Paying Ability

THIS CHAPTER COVERS TWO APPROACHES TO viewing a firm's long-term debt-paying ability. One approach views the firm's ability to carry the debt as indicated by the income statement, and the other considers the firm's ability to carry debt as indicated by the balance sheet.

In the long run, a relationship exists between the reported income resulting from the use of accrual accounting and the ability of the firm to meet its long-term obligations. Although the reported income does not agree with the cash available in the short run, the revenue and expense items eventually do result in cash movements. Because of the close relationship between the reported income and the ability of the firm to meet its long-run obligations, the entity's profitability is an important factor when determining long-term debt-paying ability.

In addition to the profitability of the firm, the amount of debt in relation to the size of the firm should be analyzed. This analysis indicates the amount of funds provided by outsiders in relation to those provided by owners of the firm. If a high proportion of the resources has been provided by outsiders, the risks of the business have been substantially shifted to the outsiders. A large proportion of debt in the capital structure increases the risk of not meeting the principal or interest obligation because the company may not generate adequate funds to meet these obligations.

INCOME STATEMENT CONSIDERATION WHEN DETERMINING LONG-TERM DEBT-PAYING ABILITY

The firm's ability to carry debt, as indicated by the income statement, can be viewed by considering the times interest earned and the fixed charge coverage. These ratios are now reviewed.

Times Interest Earned

The **times interest earned ratio** indicates a firm's long-term debt-paying ability from the income statement view. If the times interest earned is adequate, little danger exists that the firm will not be able to meet its interest obligation. If the firm has good coverage of the interest obligation, it should also be able to refinance the principal when it comes due. In effect, the funds will probably never be required to pay off the principal if the company has a good record of covering the interest expense. A relatively high, stable coverage of interest over the years indicates a good record. A low, fluctuating coverage from year to year indicates a poor record.

Companies that maintain a good record can finance a relatively high proportion of debt in relation to stockholders' equity and, at the same time, obtain funds at favorable rates. Utility companies have traditionally been examples of companies that have a high debt structure, in relation to stockholders' equity. They accomplished this because of their relatively high, stable coverage of interest over the years. This stability evolved in an industry with a regulated profit and a relatively stable demand. During the 1970s, 1980s, and 1990s, utilities experienced a severe strain on their profits, as rate increases did not keep pace with inflation. In addition, the demand was not as predictable as in prior years. The strain on profits and the uncertainty of demand influenced investors to demand higher interest rates from utilities than had been previously required in relation to other companies.

A company issues debt obligations to obtain funds at an interest rate less than the earnings from these funds. This is called **trading on the equity** or **leverage**. With a high interest rate, the added risk exists that the company will not be able to earn more on the funds than the interest cost on them.

Compute times interest earned as follows:

$$\text{Times Interest Earned} = \frac{\substack{\textbf{Recurring Earnings, Excluding Interest} \\ \textbf{Expense, Tax Expense, Equity Earnings,} \\ \textbf{and Minority Earnings}}}{\substack{\textbf{Interest Expense, Including Capitalized} \\ \textbf{Interest}}}$$

The income statement contains several figures that might be used in this analysis. In general, the primary analysis of the firm's ability to carry the debt as indicated by the income statement should include only income expected to occur in subsequent periods. Thus, the following nonrecurring items should be excluded:

1. Discontinued operations
2. Extraordinary items
3. Cumulative effect of a change in accounting principle

In addition to these nonrecurring items, additional items that should be excluded for the times interest earned computation include:

1. **Interest expense.** This is added back to net income because the interest coverage would be understated by one if interest expense were deducted before computing times interest earned.

2. **Income tax expense.** Income taxes are computed after deducting interest expense, so they do not affect the safety of the interest payments.

3. **Equity earnings (losses) of nonconsolidated subsidiaries.** These are excluded because they are not available to cover interest payments, except to the extent that they are accompanied by cash dividends.

4. **Minority income (loss).** This adjustment at the bottom of the income statement should be excluded; use income before minority interest. Minority income (loss) results from consolidating a firm in which a company has control but less than 100% ownership. All of the interest expense of the firm consolidated is included in the consolidated income statement. Therefore, all of the income of the firm consolidated should be considered in the coverage.

Capitalization of interest results in interest being added to a fixed asset instead of expensed. The interest capitalized should be included with the total interest expense in the denominator of the times interest earned ratio because it is part of the interest payment. The capitalized interest must be added to the interest expense disclosed on the income statement or in footnotes.

An example of capitalized interest would be interest during the current year on a bond issued to build a factory. As long as the factory is under construction, this interest would be added to the asset account, Construction in Process, on the balance sheet. This interest does not appear on the income statement, but it is as much of a commitment as the interest expense deducted on the income statement.

When the factory is completed, the annual interest on the bond issued to build the factory will be expensed. When expensed, interest appears on the income statement.

Capitalized interest is usually disclosed in a footnote. Some firms describe the capitalized interest on the face of the income statement. Cooper Tire & Rubber Company disclosed in the footnotes that the amount of interest capitalized was $2,694,000, $1,170,000, and $2,297,000 during 1995, 1994, and 1993, respectively.

Exhibit 8-1, page 320, shows times interest earned for Cooper for the years 1995 and 1994. Note that the ratio is very, very high. To evaluate the adequacy of coverage, the times interest earned ratio should be computed for a period of three to five years and compared to competitors and the industry average. Computing interest earned for three to five years provides insight on the stability of the interest coverage. Because the firm needs to cover interest in the bad years as well as the good years, the lowest times interest earned in the period is used as the primary indication of the interest coverage. A cyclical firm may have a very high times interest earned ratio in highly profitable years, but interest may not be covered in low profit years.

EXHIBIT 8-1   COOPER TIRE & RUBBER COMPANY
Times Interest Earned
For the Years Ended December 31, 1995 and 1994

	(Dollar amounts in thousands)	
	1995	1994
Income before income taxes	$180,070	$208,119
Plus: Interest expense	697	2,680
Earnings before interest and tax [A]	$180,767	$210,799
Interest expense	$ 697	$ 2,680
Capitalized interest	2,694	1,170
Total interest paid [B]	$ 3,391	$ 3,850
Times interest earned [A÷B]	53.31 times per year	54.75 times per year

Interest coverage on long-term debt is sometimes computed separately from the normal times interest earned. For this purpose only, use the interest on long-term debt, thus focusing on the long-term interest coverage. Since times interest earned indicates long-term debt-paying ability, this revised computation helps focus on the long-term position. For external analysis, it is usually not practical to compute times interest coverage on long-term debt because of the lack of data. However, this computation can be made for internal analysis.

In the long run, a firm must have the funds to meet all of its expenses. In the short run, a firm can often meet its interest obligations even when the times interest earned is less than 1.00. Some of the expenses, such as depreciation expense, amortization expense, and depletion expense, do not require funds in the short run. The airline industry has had several bad periods when the times interest earned was less than 1.00, but it was able to maintain the interest payments.

To get a better indication of a firm's ability to cover interest payments in the short run, the noncash expenses such as depreciation, depletion, and amortization can be added back to the numerator of the times interest earned ratio. The resulting ratio, which is less conservative, gives a type of cash basis times interest earned useful for evaluating the firm in the short run.

Exhibit 8-2 shows that Cooper's short-run times interest earned ratio is substantially higher than its long-run ratio.

Fixed Charge Coverage

The **fixed charge coverage ratio**, an extension of the times interest earned ratio, also indicates a firm's long-term debt-paying ability from the income

EXHIBIT 8-2 COOPER TIRE & RUBBER COMPANY
Times Interest Earned (Short-Run Perspective)
For the Years Ended December 31, 1995 and 1994

	(Dollar amounts in thousands)	
	1995	**1994**
Income before income taxes	$180,070	$208,119
Plus: Interest expense	697	2,680
Depreciation and amortization	63,313	55,603
Earnings adjusted [A]	$244,080	$266,402
Interest expense	$ 697	$ 2,680
Capitalized interest	2,694	1,170
Total interest paid [B]	$ 3,391	$ 3,850
Times interest earned (short-run perspective) [A÷B]	71.98 times per year	69.20 times per year

statement view. The fixed charge coverage ratio indicates a firm's ability to cover fixed charges. It is computed as follows:

$$\text{Fixed Charge Coverage} = \frac{\begin{array}{c}\textbf{Recurring Earnings, Excluding Interest}\\ \textbf{Expense, Tax Expense, Equity Earnings,}\\ \textbf{and Minority Earnings}\\ \textbf{+ Interest Portion of Rentals}\end{array}}{\begin{array}{c}\textbf{Interest Expense, Including Capitalized}\\ \textbf{Interest + Interest Portion of Rentals}\end{array}}$$

A difference of opinion occurs in practice as to what should be included in the fixed charges. When assets are leased, the lessee classifies leases as either capital leases or operating leases. The lessee treats a capital lease as an acquisition and includes the leased asset in fixed assets and the related obligation in liabilities. Part of the lease payment is considered to be interest expense. Therefore, the interest expense on the income statement includes interest related to capital leases.

A portion of operating lease payments is an item frequently included in addition to interest expense. Operating leases are not on the balance sheet, but they are reflected on the income statement in the rent expense. An operating lease for a relatively long term is a type of long-term financing, so part of the lease payment is really interest. When a portion of operating lease payments is included in fixed charges, it is an effort to recognize the true total interest that the firm pays.

SEC reporting may require a more conservative computation than the times interest earned ratio in order to determine the firm's long-term debt-paying ability. The SEC refers to its ratio as the **ratio of earnings to fixed charges**. The major difference between the times interest earned computation and the ratio of earnings to fixed charges is that the latter computation includes a portion of the operating leases.

Usually, one-third of the operating leases' rental charges is included in the fixed charges because this is an approximation of the proportion of lease payments that is interest. The SEC does not accept the one-third approximation automatically, but requires a more specific estimate of the interest portion based on the terms of the lease. Individuals interested in a company's ratio of earnings to fixed charges can find this ratio on the face of the income statement included with the SEC registration statement (Form S-7) when debt securities are registered.

The same adjusted earnings figure is used in the fixed charge coverage ratio as is used for the times interest earned ratio, except that the interest portion of operating leases (rentals) is added to the adjusted earnings for the fixed charge coverage ratio. The interest portion of operating leases is added to the adjusted earnings because it was previously deducted on the income statement as rental charges.

Cooper's 1995 annual report disclosed its rent expense attributable to all operating leases as $6,696,000 and $6,235,000, respectively, for 1995 and 1994. Using one-third as the approximation of the rent expense, which would be interest expense if financed, the interest expense would be increased by $2,232,000 in 1995 and by $2,078,333 in 1994.

Exhibit 8-3 shows the fixed charge coverage for Cooper for 1995 and 1994, with the interest portion of rentals considered. This figure, more conservative than the times interest earned, is still very good for Cooper.

Among the other items sometimes considered as fixed charges are depreciation, depletion and amortization, debt principal payments, and pension payments. Substantial preferred dividends may also be included, or a separate ratio may be computed to consider preferred dividends. The more items considered as fixed charges, the more conservative the ratio. The trend is usually similar to that found for the times interest earned ratio.

BALANCE SHEET CONSIDERATION WHEN DETERMINING LONG-TERM DEBT-PAYING ABILITY

The firm's ability to carry debt, as indicated by the balance sheet, can be viewed by considering the debt ratio and the debt/equity ratio. These ratios are now reviewed.

EXHIBIT 8-3 **COOPER TIRE & RUBBER COMPANY**
Fixed Charge Coverage
For the Years Ended December 31, 1995 and 1994

	(Dollar amounts in thousands)	
	1995	**1994**
Income before income taxes	$180,070	$208,119
Plus: Interest expense	697	2,680
Interest portion of rentals	2,232	2,078
Earnings adjusted [A]	$182,999	$212,877
Interest expense	$ 697	$ 2,680
Capitalized interest	2,694	1,170
Interest portion of rental	2,232	2,078
Adjusted interest [B]	$ 5,623	$ 5,928
Fixed charge coverage [A÷B]	32.54 times per year	35.91 times per year

Debt Ratio

The **debt ratio** indicates the firm's long-term debt-paying ability. It is computed as follows:

$$\text{Debt Ratio} = \frac{\textbf{Total Liabilities}}{\textbf{Total Assets}}$$

Total liabilities includes short-term liabilities, reserves, deferred tax liabilities, minority shareholders' interests, redeemable preferred stock, and any other noncurrent liability. It does not include shareholders' equity (convertible preferred stock, preferred stock, common stock, capital in excess of stated value, foreign currency equity accounts, unrealized holding gains and losses, retained earnings, treasury stock, or any other shareholders' equity account).

The debt ratio indicates the percentage of assets financed by creditors, and it helps to determine how well creditors are protected in case of insolvency. If creditors are not well protected, the company is not in a position to issue additional long-term debt. From the perspective of long-term debt-paying ability, the lower this ratio, the better the company's position.

Exhibit 8-4 shows the debt ratio for Cooper for December 31, 1995, and December 31, 1994. The exhibit indicates that substantially less than

EXHIBIT 8-4 **COOPER TIRE & RUBBER COMPANY**
Debt Ratio
December 31, 1995 and 1994

	(Dollar amounts in thousands)	
	1995	1994
Total liabilities compiled:		
Current liabilities	$ 158,368	$ 151,608
Long-term debt	28,574	33,614
Postretirement benefits other than pensions	132,963	127,347
Other long-term liabilities	38,341	35,348
Deferred federal income taxes	36,656	29,737
Total liabilities [A]	$ 394,902	$ 377,654
Total assets [B]	$1,143,701	$1,039,731
Debt ratio [A÷B]	34.53%	36.32%

one-half of the Cooper assets were financed by outsiders in both 1995 and 1994. This debt ratio is a conservative computation because all of the liabilities and near liabilities have been included. At the same time, the assets are understated because no adjustments have been made for assets that have a fair market value greater than book value.

The debt ratio should be compared with industry averages. Industries that have stable earnings can handle more debt than industries that have cyclical earnings. This comparison can be misleading if one firm has substantial hidden assets that other firms do not (such as substantial land carried at historical cost).

In practice, substantial disagreement occurs on the details of the formula to compute the debt ratio. Some of the disagreement revolves around whether short-term liabilities should be included. Some firms exclude short-term liabilities because they are not long-term sources of funds and are, therefore, not a valid indication of the firm's long-term debt position. Other firms include short-term liabilities because these liabilities become part of the total source of outside funds in the long run. For example, individual accounts payable are relatively short term, but accounts payable in total becomes a rather permanent part of the entire sources of funds. This book takes a conservative position that includes the short-term liabilities in the debt ratio.

Another issue involves whether certain other items should be included in liabilities. Under current GAAP, some liabilities clearly represent a commitment to pay out funds in the future, whereas other items may never result in a future payment. Items that present particular problems as to a future payment of funds include reserves, deferred taxes, minority shareholders' interests, and redeemable preferred stock. Each of these items will be reviewed in the sections that follow.

Reserves The reserve accounts classified under liabilities (some short-term and some long-term) result from an expense charge to the income statement and an equal increase in the reserve account on the balance sheet. These reserve accounts do not represent definite commitments to pay out funds in the future, but they are estimates of funds that will be paid out.

Reserve accounts are used infrequently in U.S. financial reporting. It is thought that they provide too much discretion in determining the amount of the reserve and the related impact on reported income. When the reserve account is increased, income is reduced. When the reserve account is decreased, income is increased. Reserve accounts are popular in some other countries such as Germany. This book takes a conservative position that includes the reserves in liabilities in the debt ratio.

An example of a reserve appeared in the 1995 United Technologies annual report. Footnote 15 reads in part:

> The Corporation extends performance and operating cost guarantees, which are beyond its normal warranty and service policies, for extended periods on some of its products, particularly commercial aircraft engines. Liability under such guarantees is contingent upon future product performance and durability. The Corporation has accrued its estimated liabilities that may result under these guarantees.

This book takes a conservative position that includes the reserves in liabilities in the debt ratio.

Deferred Taxes (Interperiod Tax Allocation) In the United States, a firm may recognize certain income and expense items in one period for the financial statements and in another period for the federal tax return. This can result in financial statement income in any one period that is substantially different from tax return income. For many other countries this is not the case. For example, there are few timing differences in Germany, and there are no timing differences in Japan. For these countries, deferred taxes are not a substantial issue or are not an issue. In the United States, taxes payable based on the tax return can be substantially different from income tax expense based on financial statement income. Current GAAP directs that the tax expense for the financial statements be based on the tax-related items on the financial statements. Taxes payable are based on the actual current taxes payable, determined by the tax return. (The Internal Revenue Code specifies the procedures for determining taxable income.)

The tax expense for the financial statements often does not agree with the taxes payable. The difference between tax expense and taxes payable is recorded as deferred income taxes. The concept that results in deferred income taxes is called **interperiod tax allocation**.

As an illustration of deferred taxes, consider the following facts related to machinery purchased for $100,000:

Three-year write-off for tax purposes:
1st year	$ 25,000
2d year	38,000
3d year	37,000
	$ 100,000

Five-year write-off for financial statements:
1st year	$ 20,000
2d year	20,000
3d year	20,000
4th year	20,000
5th year	20,000
	$ 100,000

For both tax and financial statement purposes, $100,000 was written off for the equipment. The write-off on the tax return was three years, while the write-off on the financial statements was five years. The faster write-off on the tax return resulted in lower taxable income than the income reported on the income statement during the first three years. During the last two years, the income statement income was lower than the tax return income.

In addition to temporary differences, the tax liability can be influenced by an **operating loss carryback** and/or **operating loss carryforward**. The tax code allows a corporation reporting an operating loss for income tax purposes in the current year to carry this loss back and forward to offset reported taxable income. The company may first carry an operating loss back three years in sequential order, starting with the earliest of the three years. If the taxable income for the past three years is not enough to offset the operating loss, then the remaining loss is sequentially carried forward 15 years and offset against future taxable income.

A company can elect to forgo a carryback and, instead, only carry forward an operating loss. A company would not normally forgo a carryback, because an operating loss carryback results in a definite and immediate income tax refund. A carryforward will reduce income taxes payable in future years to the extent of earned taxable income. A company could possibly benefit from forgoing a carryback if prospects in future years are good and an increase in the tax rate is anticipated.

Interperiod tax allocation should be used for all temporary differences. A temporary difference between the tax basis of an asset or liability and its reported amount in the financial statements will result in taxable or deductible amounts in future years when the reported amount of the asset or liability is recovered or settled, respectively.

A corporation reports deferred taxes in two classifications: a net current amount and a net noncurrent amount. The net current amount could result in a current asset or a current liability being reported. The net noncurrent amount could result in a noncurrent asset or a noncurrent liability being reported.

Classification as current or noncurrent is usually based on the classification of the asset or liability responsible for the temporary difference. For example, a deferred tax liability resulting from the excess of tax depreciation over financial reporting depreciation would be reported as a noncurrent liability. This is because the temporary difference is related to noncurrent assets (fixed assets).

When a deferred tax asset or liability is not related to an asset or liability, the deferred tax asset or liability is classified according to the expected reversal date of the temporary difference. For example, a deferred tax amount resulting from an operating loss carryforward would be classified based on the expected reversal date of the temporary difference.

There should be a valuation allowance against a deferred tax asset if sufficient uncertainty exists about a corporation's future taxable income. A valuation allowance reduces the deferred tax asset to its expected realizable amount. At the time that the valuation allowance is recognized, tax expense is increased.

A more likely than not criterion is used to measure uncertainty. If more likely than not a deferred asset will not be realized, a valuation allowance would be required.

Notice on the Cooper balance sheet (Chapter 6) that Cooper discloses deferred taxes in current assets and long-term liabilities. For many firms, the long-term liability, deferred taxes, has grown to a substantial amount, which often increases each year. This occurs because of the growth in the temporary differences that cause the timing difference. The Cooper amount increased substantially in 1995 for the long-term liability. This was caused by the increase to property, plant, and equipment. Cooper disclosed significant components of the Company's deferred tax (current asset) and long-term liability in the income tax footnote, as follows:

> Deferred income taxes reflect the net tax effects of temporary differences between the carrying amount of assets and liabilities for financial reporting purposes and the amounts used for income tax purposes. Significant components of the Company's deferred tax liabilities and assets as of December 31, 1995 and 1994 are as follows:

(Dollar amounts in thousands)	1995	1994
Deferred tax liabilities:		
Tax depreciation over book depreciation	$ 75,238	$65,638
Other	23,945	20,852
Total deferred tax liabilities	99,183	86,490
Deferred tax assets:		
Postretirement benefits other than pensions	48,163	46,119
Other	25,025	21,326
Total deferred tax assets	73,188	67,445
Net deferred tax liabilities	$ 25,995	$19,045

These amounts are included in the accompanying balance sheet captions:

(Dollar amounts in thousands)	1995	1994
Prepaid expenses and deferred income taxes	$ 10,661	$ 10,692
Deferred income taxes	36,656	29,737
Net deferred tax liabilities	$ 25,995	$ 19,045

Deferred taxes must be accounted for using the liability method, which focuses on the balance sheet. Deferred taxes are recorded at amounts at which they will be settled when underlying temporary differences reverse. Deferred taxes are adjusted for tax rate changes. A change in tax rates can result in a material adjustment to the deferred account and can substantially influence income in the year of the tax rate change.

Some individuals disagree with the concept of deferred taxes (interperiod tax allocation). It is uncertain that the deferred tax will be paid. If it will be paid (received), it is uncertain *when* it will be paid (or received). The deferred tax accounts are, therefore, often referred to as **soft accounts**.

Because of the uncertainty over whether (and when) a deferred tax liability (asset) will be paid (received), some individuals elect to exclude deferred tax liabilities and assets when performing analysis. (The liability amount is almost always more than any asset amount.) This book takes a conservative position that includes deferred taxes when computing the debt ratios. This is consistent with GAAP, which recognize deferred taxes.

Some revenue and expense items, referred to as **permanent differences**, never go on the tax return, but do go on the income statement. Examples would be premiums on life insurance and life insurance proceeds. Federal tax law does not allow these items to be included in expense and revenue, respectively. These items never influence either the tax expense or the tax liability, so they never influence the deferred tax accounts.

Minority Shareholders' Interest   The account, Minority Shareholders' Interest, results when the firm has consolidated another company of which it owns less than 100%. The proportion of the consolidated company that is not owned appears on the balance sheet just above stockholders' equity.

Some firms exclude the minority shareholders' interest when computing debt ratios because this amount does not represent a commitment to pay funds to outsiders. Other firms include the minority shareholders' interest when computing debt ratios because these funds came from outsiders and are part of the total funds that the firm uses. This book takes the conservative position of including minority shareholders' interest in the primary computation of debt ratios. (To review minority shareholders' interest, refer to the section of Chapter 3 on minority interest, pages 117-118.)

Redeemable Preferred Stock   Redeemable preferred stock is subject to mandatory redemption requirements or has a redemption feature outside the control of the issuer. Some redeemable preferred stock agreements require the firm to purchase certain amounts of the preferred stock on the open market. *Securities and Exchange Commission Accounting Series Release No. 268* dictates that redeemable preferred stock not be disclosed under shareholders' equity.

The nature of redeemable preferred stock leaves open to judgment how it should be handled when computing debt ratios. One view excludes it from debt and includes it in stockholders' equity, on the grounds that it does not represent a normal debt relationship. A conservative position includes it as debt when computing the debt ratios. This book uses the conservative approach and includes redeemable preferred stock in debt for the primary computation of debt ratios. (For a more detailed review, refer to the section of Chapter 3 that describes redeemable preferred stock, page 118.)

Debt/Equity Ratio

The **debt/equity ratio** is another computation that determines the entity's long-term debt-paying ability. This computation compares the total debt with the total shareholders' equity. The debt/equity ratio also helps determine how well creditors are protected in case of insolvency. From the perspective of long-term debt-paying ability, the lower this ratio is, the better the company's debt position.

In this book, the computation of the debt/equity ratio is conservative because all of the liabilities and near liabilities are included, and the shareholders' equity is understated to the extent that assets have a value greater than book value. This ratio should also be compared with industry averages and competitors. Compute the debt/equity ratio as follows:

$$\text{Debt/Equity Ratio} = \frac{\text{Total Liabilities}}{\text{Shareholders' Equity}}$$

Exhibit 8-5 shows the debt/equity ratio for Cooper for December 31, 1995, and December 31, 1994. Using a conservative approach to computing debt/equity, Exhibit 8-5 indicates that a smaller amount of funds came from outsiders than shareholders' equity provided. Also, the proportion of funds provided by outsiders decreased in 1995. The debt/equity ratio was 52.74% at the end of 1995, down from 57.04% at the end of 1994.

The debt ratio and the debt/equity ratio have the same objectives. Therefore, these ratios are alternatives to each other if computed in the manner recommended here. Because some financial services may be reporting the debt ratio and others may be reporting the debt/equity ratio, the reader should be familiar with both.

As indicated previously, a problem exists with the lack of uniformity in the way some ratios are computed. This especially occurs with the debt ratio and the debt/equity ratio. When comparing the debt ratio and the debt/equity ratio with industry ratios, try to determine how the industry ratios were computed. A reasonable comparison may not be possible because the financial sources sometimes do not indicate what elements of debt the computations include.

Debt to Tangible Net Worth Ratio

The **debt to tangible net worth ratio** also determines the entity's long-term debt-paying ability. This ratio also indicates how well creditors are protected in case of the firm's insolvency. As with the debt ratio and the

EXHIBIT 8-5   **COOPER TIRE & RUBBER COMPANY**
Debt/Equity
December 31, 1995 and 1994

	(Dollar amounts in thousands) 1995	1994
Total liabilities [Exhibit 8-4] [A]	$394,902	$377,654
Shareholders' equity [B]	748,799	662,077
Debt/equity ratio [A÷B]	52.74%	57.04%

debt/equity ratio, from the perspective of long-term debt-paying ability, it is better to have a lower ratio.

The debt to tangible net worth ratio is a more conservative ratio than either the debt ratio or the debt/equity ratio. It eliminates intangible assets, such as goodwill, trademarks, patents, and copyrights, because they do not provide resources to pay creditors—a very conservative position. Compute the debt to tangible net worth ratio as follows:

$$\text{Debt to Tangible Net Worth} = \frac{\text{Total Liabilities}}{\text{Shareholders' Equity} - \text{Intangible Assets}}$$

In this book, the computation of the debt to tangible net worth ratio is conservative. All of the liabilities and near liabilities are included, and the shareholders' equity is understated to the extent that assets have a value greater than book value.

Exhibit 8-6 shows the debt to tangible net worth ratios for Cooper for December 31, 1995, and December 31, 1994. Because Cooper does not list any intangible assets, no difference exists between the debt/equity ratio and its debt to tangible net worth ratio.

Other Long-Term Debt-Paying Ability Ratios

A number of additional ratios indicate perspective on the long-term debt-paying ability of a firm. This section describes some of these ratios.

The **current debt/net worth ratio** indicates a relationship between current liabilities and funds contributed by shareholders. The higher the proportion of funds provided by current liabilities, the greater the risk.

EXHIBIT 8-6 COOPER TIRE & RUBBER COMPANY
Debt to Tangible Net Worth Ratio
December 31, 1995 and 1994

	(Dollar amounts in thousands)	
	1995	1994
Total liabilities [Exhibit 8-4] [A]	$394,902	$377,654
Shareholders' equity	$748,799	$662,077
Less: Intangible assets	—	—
Adjusted shareholders' equity [B]	$748,799	$662,077
Debt to tangible net worth ratio [A÷B]	52.74%	57.04%

Another ratio, the **total capitalization ratio**, compares long-term debt to total capitalization. Total capitalization consists of long-term debt, preferred stock, and common shareholders' equity. The lower the ratio, the lower the risk. Cooper reported that long-term debt, as a percent of total capitalization, decreased to 9.3% at December 31, 1992, from 10.9% one year earlier.

Another ratio, the **fixed asset/equity ratio**, indicates the extent to which shareholders have provided funds in relation to fixed assets. Some firms subtract intangibles from shareholders' equity to obtain tangible net worth. This results in a more conservative ratio. The higher the fixed assets in relation to equity, the greater the risk.

Exhibit 8-7 indicates the trend in current liabilities, total liabilities, and stockholders' equity of firms in the United States between 1964 and 1995. It shows that there has been a major shift in the capital structure of firms, toward a higher proportion of debt in relation to total assets. This indicates a substantial increase in risk as management more frequently faces debt coming due. It also indicates that short-term debt is a permanent part of the financial structure of firms. This supports the decision to include short-term liabilities in the ratios determining long-term debt-paying ability (debt ratio, debt/equity ratio, and debt to tangible net worth ratio).

SPECIAL ITEMS THAT INFLUENCE A FIRM'S LONG-TERM DEBT-PAYING ABILITY

There are a number of special items that influence a firm's long-term debt-paying ability. These items are now reviewed.

Long-Term Assets Versus Long-Term Debt

The specific assets of the firm are important if the firm becomes unprofitable and the assets are sold. Therefore, consider the assets of the firm when determining the long-term debt-paying ability. The assets are insurance should the firm become unprofitable. The ability to analyze the assets, in relation to the long-term debt-paying ability, is limited, based on the information reported in the published financial statements. The statements do not extensively disclose market or liquidation values; they disclose only unrecovered cost for many items. The market value figure reported for some investments has been an exception.

A review of the financial statements is often of value if the firm liquidates or decides to reduce the scope of its operations. Examples of assets that may have substantial value would be land, timberlands, and investments.

When the Penn Central Company went bankrupt, it had substantial debt and operating losses. Yet because of assets that had substantial market values, creditors were repaid. In other cases, creditors receive nothing or only nominal amounts when a firm goes bankrupt.

EXHIBIT 8-7
Trends in Current Liabilities, Total Liabilities, and Owners' Equity, 1964-1995

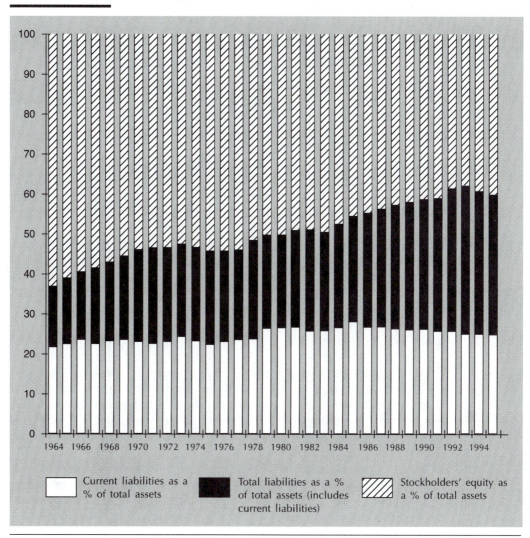

Source: Quarterly Financial Reports of Manufacturing, Mining, & Trading, Department of Commerce. Washington, DC: Government Printing Office.

Substantial assets that have a potential value higher than the book figures may also indicate an earnings potential that will be realized later. For example, knowing that a railroad owns land that contains millions or billions of tons of coal could indicate substantial profit potential, even if the coal is not economical to mine at the present time. In future years, as the price of competitive products such as oil and gas increase, the coal may become economical to mine. This happened in the United States in the late 1970s. Several railroads that owned millions or billions of tons of unmined coal found that the coal became very valuable as the price of oil and gas increased.

Long-Term Leasing

Earlier, this chapter explained the influence of long-term leasing in relation to the income statement. Now we will consider the influence of long-term leasing from the balance sheet perspective.

First, review some points made previously. The lessee classifies leases as either capital leases or operating leases. A capital lease is handled as if the lessee acquired the asset. The leased asset is classified as a fixed asset, and the related obligation is included in liabilities. Operating leases are not reflected on the balance sheet but in a footnote and on the income statement as rent expense.

Operating leases for a relatively long term (a type of long-term financing) should be considered in a supplemental manner as to their influence on the debt structure of the firms. Capital leases have already been considered in the debt ratios computed because the capital leases were part of the total assets and also part of the total liabilities on the balance sheet.

Cooper discloses capital leases included in property, plant, and equipment of $3,095,000 at December 31, 1995. The related liability for capital leases was $5,133,000.

The capitalized asset amount will not agree with the capitalized liability amount because the liability is reduced by payments and the asset is reduced by depreciation taken. Usually, a company depreciates capital leases faster than payments are made. This would result in the capitalized asset amount being lower than the related capitalized liability amount. On the original date of the capital lease, the capitalized asset amount and the capitalized liability amount are the same.

The Cooper footnote relating to long-term leases indicates the minimum future rentals under operating leases for years subsequent to December 31, 1995. These figures, shown below, do not include an amount for any possible contingent rentals because they are not practicable to estimate.

	Operating Leases
1996	$2,444,000
1997	1,428,000
1998	1,074,000
1999	676,000
2000	254,000
2001 and later	94,000
	$5,970,000

If these leases had been capitalized, the amount added to fixed assets and the amount added to liabilities would be the same at the time of the initial entry. As indicated previously, the amounts would not be the same, subsequently, because the asset is depreciated at some selected rate, while the liability is reduced as payments are made. As we observed for capital leases for Cooper at the end of 1995, $3,095,000 was under property, plant, and equipment, and $5,133,000 was under current liabilities and long-term liabilities. When incorporating the operating leases into the debt ratios, use the liability amount and assume that the asset and the liability amount would be the same since no realistic way exists to compute the difference.

It would not be realistic to include the total future rentals that relate to operating leases in the lease commitments footnote ($5,970,000) because part of the commitment would be an interest consideration. Earlier this chapter indicated that some firms estimate that one-third of the operating lease commitment is for interest. With a one-third estimate for interest, two-thirds is estimated for principal. For Cooper, this amount is $3,980,000 ($5,970,000 x 2/3). This amount can be added to fixed assets and long-term liabilities in order to obtain a supplemental view of the debt ratios that relate to the balance sheet. Exhibit 8-8 shows the adjusted debt ratio and debt/equity ratio for Cooper at the end of 1995; this increases the debt position by a modest amount. For some firms, the adjusted debt position would be materially higher than the unadjusted position.

EXHIBIT 8-8 **COOPER TIRE & RUBBER COMPANY**
Adjusted Debt Ratio and Debt/Equity Ratio Considering Operating Leases
December 31, 1995

(Dollar amounts in thousands)	1995
Adjusted debt ratio:	
Unadjusted total liabilities [Exhibit 8-4]	$ 394,902
Plus: Estimated for operating leases	
($5,970,000 x 2/3 = $3,980,000)	3,980
Adjusted liabilities [A]	$ 398,882
Unadjusted total assets	$1,143,701
Plus: Estimated for operating leases	3,980
Adjusted assets [B]	$1,147,681
Adjusted debt ratio [A÷B]	34.76%
Unadjusted debt ratio [Exhibit 8-4]	34.53%
Adjusted debt/equity:	
Adjusted liabilities (above) [A]	$ 398,882
Shareholders' equity [B]	748,799
Adjusted debt/equity [A÷B]	53.27%
Unadjusted debt/equity [Exhibit 8-5]	52.74%

Pension Plans

The Employee Retirement Income Security Act (ERISA) became law in 1974 and substantially influenced the administration of pension plans, while elevating their liability status for the firm. This act includes provisions requiring minimum funding of plans, minimum rights to employees upon termination of their employment, and the creation of a special federal agency, the Pension Benefit Guaranty Corporation (PBGC), to help fund employee benefits when pension plans are terminated. The PBGC receives a fee for every employee covered by a pension plan subject to the PBGC. The PBGC has the right to impose a lien against a covered firm of 30% of the firm's assets. This lien has the status of a tax lien and, therefore, ranks high among creditor claims. In practice, the PBGC has been reluctant to impose this lien except when a firm is in bankruptcy proceedings. This has resulted in the PBGC receiving a relatively small amount of assets when it has imposed the lien.

An important provision in a pension plan is the vesting provision. An employee vested in the pension plan is eligible to receive some pension benefits at retirement, regardless of whether the employee continues working for the employer. ERISA has had a major impact on reducing the vesting time. The original ERISA has been amended several times to increase the responsibility of firms regarding their pension plans.

In 1980, Congress passed the Multiemployer Pension Plan Amendment Act. Multiemployer pension plans are plans maintained jointly by two or more unrelated employers. This act provides for significant increased employer obligations for multiemployer pension plans and makes the PBGC coverage mandatory for multiemployer plans.

When a firm has a multiemployer pension plan, it normally covers union employees. Such a firm usually has other pension plans that cover nonunion employees. When disclosing a multiemployer pension plan, the firm normally includes the cost of the plan with the cost of the other pension plans. It is usually not practical to isolate the cost of these plans because of commingling. These plans operate usually on a pay-as-you-go basis, so no liability arises unless a payment has not been made. A potential **significant liability** arises if the company withdraws from the multiemployer plan. Unfortunately, the amount of this liability often cannot be ascertained from the pension footnote.

Ashland Coal Inc. included the following comment in a footnote with its 1994 annual report:

> Under the labor contract with the United Mine Workers of America (UMWA), Ashland Coal made payments of $1,293,000 in 1994, $475,000 in 1993, and $1,105,000 in 1992 into a multiemployer defined benefit pension plan trust established for the benefit of union employees. Payments are based on hours worked. Under the Multiemployer Pension Plan Amendments Act of 1980, a

contributor to a multiemployer pension plan may be liable, under certain circumstances, for its proportionate share of the plan's unfunded vested benefits (withdrawal liability). Ashland Coal has estimated its share of such amount to be $18,300,000 at December 31, 1994. Ashland Coal is not aware of any circumstances which would require it to reflect its share of unfunded vested pension benefits in its consolidated financial statements.

The Coal Industry Retiree Health Benefit Act of 1992 (Benefit Act) provides for the funding of medical and death benefits for certain retired members of the UMWA through premiums to be paid by assigned operators (former employers), transfers of monies from an overfunded pension trust established for the benefit of retired UMWA members, and transfers from the Abandoned Mine Lands Fund, which is funded by a federal tax on coal production. This funding arrangement commenced February 1, 1993.

Ashland Coal treats its obligation under the Benefit Act as a participation in a multiemployer plan and recognizes expense as premiums are paid. Ashland Coal recognized $296,000 in 1994 and $240,000 in 1993 in expense relative to premiums paid pursuant to the Benefit Act. The Company believes that the amount of its obligation under the Benefit Act is not significant. Under the prior funding arrangement for retirees now covered by the Benefit Act, Ashland Coal paid $609,000 in 1993 and $4,809,000 in 1992 into two multiemployer benefit trusts.

The financial influence of pension plans is one of the most difficult areas to consider in financial reporting, especially as related to long-term borrowing ability.

Defined Contribution Plan A company-sponsored pension plan is either a defined contribution plan or a defined benefit plan. A **defined contribution plan** defines the contributions of the company to the pension plan. Once this defined contribution is paid, the company has no further obligation to the pension plan. This type of plan shifts the risk to the employee as to whether the pension funds will grow to provide for a reasonable pension payment upon retirement. With this type of plan, which gained popularity during the 1980s, there is no problem of estimating the company's pension liability or pension expense. Thus, defined contribution plans do not present major financial reporting problems.

Firms should disclose the following for any defined contribution plan:

1. Description of the plan
2. The amount of cost recognized during the period

For firms with defined contribution plans, try to grasp the significance by doing the following:

1. For approximately a three-year period, compare pension expense with operating revenue. This will indicate the materiality of pension expense in relation to operating revenue.

2. For approximately a three-year period, compare pension expense with income before income taxes. This will indicate the materiality of pension expense in relation to income.

3. Note any balance sheet items. (There will usually not be a balance sheet item because the firm is paying on a pay-as-you-go basis.)

Exhibit 8-9 contains The Money Store statements of income and the footnote relating to a defined contribution plan. This information can be used to estimate the materiality of the defined contribution plan, as follows:

1. Comparison of pension expense with operating revenue:

	1995	1994	1993
Pension expense (A)	$ 3,479,000	$ 3,176,000	$ 1,509,000
Revenues (B)	$510,558,000	$330,470,000	$219,809,000
[A/B]	.68%	.96%	.69%

2. Comparison of pension expense with income before income taxes:

	1995	1994	1993
Pension expense (A)	$ 3,479,000	$ 3,176,000	$ 1,509,000
Income before income taxes (B)	$ 83,033,000	$ 53,027,000	$40,573,000
[A/B]	4.19%	5.99%	3.72%

3. Balance sheet items:
    No balance sheet items are disclosed.

Thus, pension expenses as a percentage of revenues were .68%, .96%, and .69% in 1995, 1994, and 1993, respectively. Pension expenses as a percentage of income before income taxes were 4.19%, 5.99%, and 3.72% in 1995, 1994, and 1993, respectively. Pension expense appears to be moderately material.

Defined Benefit Plan   A **defined benefit plan** defines the benefits to be received by the participants in the plan. For example, the plan may call for the participant to receive 40% of his or her average pay for the three years before retirement. This type of plan leaves the company with the risk of

EXHIBIT 8-9 **THE MONEY STORE**
Pension Footnote and Consolidated Statements of Income
1995 Annual Report

The Money Store Inc. and Subsidiaries

CONSOLIDATED STATEMENTS OF INCOME

	Years Ended December 31		
(Dollars in thousands)	1995	1994	1993
Revenues:			
Gain on sale of receivables	$353,995	$259,913	$159,576
Finance income, fees earned and other	156,563	70,557	60,233
	510,558	330,470	219,809
Expenses:			
Salaries and employee benefits	119,423	85,596	53,844
Other operating expenses	123,394	96,188	53,462
Provision for credit losses	90,723	52,600	42,746
Interest	93,985	43,059	29,184
	427,525	277,443	179,236
Income before income taxes	83,033	53,027	40,573
Income taxes	34,318	21,706	18,802
Net income	$ 48,715	$ 31,321	$ 21,771

Defined Contribution Plan

The Company has a defined contribution plan [401(k)] for all eligible employees. Contributions to the plan are in the form of employee salary deferrals which may be subject to employer matching contributions up to a specified limit. In addition, the Company may make an annual profit sharing contribution on behalf of its employees. The Company's contributions to the plan, net of reallocated forfeitures, amounted to $3,479,000, $3,176,000, and $1,509,000 for the years ended December 31, 1995, 1994, and 1993, respectively.

having sufficient funds in the pension fund to meet the defined benefit. This type of plan was the predominant type of plan prior to the 1980s. Most companies still have a defined benefit plan, partly because of the difficulties involved in switching to a defined contribution plan. Some companies have terminated their defined benefit plan by funding the obligations of the plan and starting a defined contribution plan. In some cases, this has resulted in millions of dollars being transferred to the company from the pension plan after the defined benefit plan obligations have been met.

A number of assumptions about future events must be made regarding a defined benefit plan. Some of these assumptions that relate to the future are interest rates, employee turnover, mortality rates, compensation, and pension benefits set by law. Assumptions about future events contribute materially to the financial reporting problems in the pension area. Two firms with the same plan may make significantly different assumptions, resulting in major differences in pension expense and liability.

Several terms should be understood in order to have a reasonable understanding of the financial reporting of defined benefit plans.

1. **Vested benefits and unvested benefits**. A **vested pension benefit** entitles the employee to a benefit, even if he or she leaves the firm prior to retirement. This benefit is usually due either at normal retirement age or after a minimum number of years of work. The typical pension plan requires several years of work with the firm before the employee receives a vested benefit, although an unvested benefit accrues. This means that the employee in the pension plan will lose rights if the employee leaves the firm prior to receiving a vested interest.

2. **Prior service cost**. A defined benefit plan, adopted or amended, often gives credit to employees for years of service provided before the date of adoption or amendment. The cost of taking on this added commitment is called the **prior service cost**.

3. **Accumulated benefit obligation**. This is the actuarial present value of benefits attributed by the pension benefit formula to employee service rendered before a specified date and based on employee service and compensation (if applicable) prior to that date. The interest rate used for the present value computation is very important. A high interest rate results in a low present value for the accumulated benefit obligation. This could give the appearance that the pension plan is overfunded when it is not. Too low an interest rate could give the appearance that the pension plan is underfunded.

4. **Projected benefit obligation**. This is the actuarial present value as of a date of all benefits attributed by the pension benefit formula to employee service rendered prior to that date. The projected benefit obligation is measured using assumptions as to future compensation levels if the pension benefit formula is based on those future compensation levels. For plans with flat-benefit or non-pay-related pension benefit formulas, the accumulated benefit obligation and the projected benefit obligation are the same. The interest rate used for the present value computation is very important since it is for the accumulated benefit obligation.

5. **Net periodic pension cost (expense)**. The amount of net periodic pension cost for a period equals the sum of the following six components:

    a.   Service cost (increases pension expense): The actuarial present value of benefits attributed by the pension benefit formula to services rendered by the employees during that period. (Future compensation levels must be considered if the plan benefit formula incorporates them.)

    b.   Interest cost (increases pension expense): The increase in the projected benefit obligation due to the passage of time. The assumed discount rate should reflect the rates at which pension benefits could be effectively settled.

    c.   Actual return on plan assets (decreases pension expense): The difference between the fair value of plan assets at the end of the period and the fair value at the beginning of the period, adjusted for contributions and payments of benefits during the period.

    d.   Amortization of unrecognized prior service cost (increases pension expense): Prior service cost is the cost of retroactive benefits granted in a plan amendment or at the initial adoption of the plan.

    e.   Amortization of net gains or losses (could increase or decrease pension expense): Gains and losses result from changes in the amount of either the projected benefit obligation or plan assets caused by differences between what was assumed would occur and what actually occurred or from changes in assumptions about the future of the plan.

    f.   Amortization of the unrecognized net obligation (and loss or cost) or unrecognized net asset (and gain) existing at the date of initial application of the pension accounting rules: The loss or gain associated with the unrecognized net obligation or unrecognized net asset at the beginning of the fiscal year in which pension accounting rules are first applied.

6.   **Balance sheet liabilities/assets**

    a.   A liability is recognized if the net periodic pension expense recognized as of the balance sheet date exceeds the amount funded to date.

    b.   An asset is recognized if the net periodic pension expense recognized as of the balance sheet date is less than the amount funded to date.

    c.   An additional balance sheet liability is recognized if the accumulated benefit obligation exceeds the fair market value of plan assets less the balance in the accrued pension liability account or plus the balance in the deferred pension asset account (a or b above).

If an additional liability is recognized, an equal amount is recognized as an intangible asset if the amount recognized does not exceed the amount of unrecognized prior service cost. If it does, the excess would be reported separately as a reduction of stockholders' equity.

Note that the additional balance sheet liability considers the accumulated benefit obligation, not the projected benefit obligation. Thus, any additional balance sheet liability is a very conservative estimate of the liability if the projected benefit obligation is greater than the accumulated benefit obligation.

7. **Footnote disclosure**. The required disclosures include the following:

   a. Description of the plan.
   b. The amount of the net periodic pension cost, including the components. (The detail of all six components of pension cost will usually only be disclosed when they are material.)
   c. A schedule reconciling the funded status of the plan with amounts reported in the statement of financial position.

For purposes of the disclosure regarding the reconciliation of the funded status of the plan with amounts reported in the firm's balance sheet, the disclosures are required to be presented in two groups:

1. Aggregate amounts for plans with assets in excess of the accumulated benefit obligation.

2. Aggregate amounts for plans that have an accumulated benefit obligation that exceeds plan assets.

For firms with defined benefit plans, try to grasp the significance by doing the following:

1. For approximately a three-year period, compare the pension expense with operating revenue. This will indicate the significance of pension expense in relation to operating revenue.

2. For approximately a three-year period, compare the pension expense with income before income taxes. This will indicate the materiality of expense in relation to income.

3. Compare the accumulated benefit obligations in relation to the plan assets at year-end. Observe the vested part of the accumulated benefit obligation.

4. Note the projected benefit obligations in relation to the plan assets. Observe the vested part of the projected benefit obligations.

5. Note the interest rate used to compute the actuarial present value of the accumulated benefit obligation and the projected benefit obligation. The higher the interest rate used, the lower the present value of the liability and the lower the immediate pension cost. Changes in this interest rate could significantly increase or decrease the present value of the liability and increase or decrease the pension cost. *The Wall Street Journal* included these comments in an article entitled "Pension Funds Boost Projected Returns Even Though Experts Take a Dim View."

> General Motors Corp., for example, was able to add $75 million to its first-quarter earnings largely by raising its annual pension earnings estimate to 11% from 10% . . . . International Business Machines Corp., for example, thinks it will earn 9% a year on its $26 billion pension fund. But if the computer maker made a more conservative long-term return forecast of, say, 8%, its pension costs would soar $228 million this year.[1]

6. Note the rate of compensation increase used in computing the projected benefit obligation. If the rate is too low, the projected benefit obligation is too low. If the rate is too high, the projected benefit obligation is too high.

7. Note the assumed rate of return on plan assets.

8. Note the unrecognized gains or losses. Unrecognized gains will reduce future pension cost, and unrecognized losses will increase future pension cost.

9. Note whether the unrecognized transition amount is an asset or liability. Amortization of an asset will reduce future pension cost. Amortization of a liability will increase future pension cost.

10. Note the unrecognized prior service cost. This amount will be amortized to pension expense in subsequent years.

11. Note the prepaid (accrued) pension cost. Keep in mind that the balance sheet account has been computed using the accumulated benefit obligation, which has not considered assumptions as to the future compensation levels. Consider the impact on the balance sheet account if the projected benefit obligation were considered instead of the accumulated benefit obligation.

Exhibit 8-10, pages 344-345, shows the Cooper pension footnote. We note that Cooper's pension plans are defined benefit plans.

EXHIBIT 8-10 COOPER TIRE & RUBBER COMPANY
Pension Footnote
1995 Annual Report

Pensions (Amounts in thousands)

The Company has defined benefit plans covering substantially all employees. The salary plan provides pension benefits based on an employee's years of service and average earnings for the five highest calendar years during the ten years immediately preceding retirement. The hourly plans provide benefits of stated amounts for each year of service. The Company's general funding policy is to contribute amounts deductible for federal income tax purposes.

Pension expense for 1995, 1994, and 1993 included the following components:

	1995	1994	1993
Service cost—benefits earned during period	$ 9,833	$ 9,769	$ 7,641
Interest cost on projected benefit obligation	20,374	17,485	16,327
Actual return on assets	(54,268)	1,565	(12,875)
Net amortization and deferral	38,966	(17,201)	(879)
Net periodic pension cost	$ 14,905	$ 11,618	$ 10,214

The plans' assets consist of cash, cash equivalents, and marketable securities. The funded status of the Company's plans at December 31, 1995 and 1994 was as follows:

	December 31, 1995		December 31, 1994	
	Plans for Which		Plans for Which	
	Assets Exceed Accumulated Benefits	Accumulated Benefits Exceed Assets	Assets Exceed Accumulated Benefits	Accumulated Benefits Exceed Assets
Actuarial present value of benefit obligations:				
Vested benefit obligation	$131,996	$108,028	$106,291	$86,629
Accumulated benefit obligation	$135,171	$111,320	$108,824	$88,350
Projected benefit obligation	$203,446	$112,845	$159,326	$90,310
Plans' assets at fair value	187,831	82,144	148,488	63,059
Projected benefit obligation in excess of plan assets	(15,615)	(30,701)	(10,838)	(27,251)
Unrecognized transition amount	5,175	2,723	5,814	3,172
Unrecognized prior service cost	—	8,014	173	10,498
Unrecognized net loss	33,093	15,895	26,344	9,707
Adjustment for minimum liability	—	(26,117)	—	(22,673)
Pension asset/(liability) recognized in the Balance Sheet	$ 22,653	$ (30,186)	$ 21,493	$(26,547)

EXHIBIT 8-10   (concluded)

The actual present value of benefit obligations in 1995 reflects changes in certain actuarial assumptions including demographics and decreases in the discount rate and the rate of increase in future compensation levels. The expected long-term rate of return on the plans' assets was ten percent in 1995, 1994, and 1993. The assumptions used to determine the status of the Company's plans at December 31 were as follows:

	1995	1994
Increase in future compensation levels	5.5%	6.0%
Discount rate	7.5	8.0

The information presented above includes an unfunded, nonqualified supplemental executive retirement plan covering certain employees whose participation in the qualified plan is limited by provisions of the Internal Revenue Code.

The Company sponsors several defined contribution plans for its employees. Substantially all employees are eligible to participate upon attaining minimum continuous service requirements. Participation is voluntary and participants' contributions are based on their compensation. The Company matches certain plan participant's contributions up to various limits. Company contributions are based on the lesser of (a) participants' contributions up to a specified percent of each participants' compensation, less any forfeitures, or (b) an amount equal to 15 percent of the Company's pre-tax earnings in excess of ten percent of stockholders' equity at the beginning of the year. Expense for these plans was $8,277, $7,485, and $6,027 for 1995, 1994, and 1993, respectively.

Observe the following relating to Cooper's defined benefit plans:

1. Pension expense in relation to operating revenue:

	1995	1994	1993
Pension expense [A]	$ 14,905,000	$ 11,618,000	$ 10,214,000
Operating revenue [B]	$1,493,622,000	$1,403,243,000	$1,193,648,000
Pension expense/ operating revenue [A/B]	1.00%	.83%	.86%

Cooper's pension expense increased in 1995 to 1.00% of operating revenue. A significant increase occurred in 1995 in relation to 1994.

2. Pension expense in relation to income before income taxes:

	1995	1994	1993
Pension expense [A]	$ 14,905,000	$ 11,618,000	$ 10,214,000
Income before income taxes [B]	$180,070,000	$208,119,000	$164,250,000
Pension expense/income before income taxes [A/B]	8.28%	5.58%	6.22%

Cooper's pension expense increased significantly in 1995 in relation to income before income taxes.

3. Comparison of accumulated benefit obligations in relation to the plan assets at December 31, 1995:

	Assets Exceed Accumulated Benefits	Accumulated Benefits Exceed Assets
Accumulated benefit obligation	$ 135,171,000	$111,320,000
Plan assets at fair value	187,831,000	82,144,000
Plan assets in excess (less) than accumulated benefit obligation	$ 52,660,000	$ (29,176,000)

In total, Cooper's plan assets exceed accumulated benefit obligations. Cooper does have some plans for which the accumulated benefits obligations exceed plan assets, but the excess for these plans does not appear to be material.

Approximately 97% of the accumulated benefit obligation is vested.

4. Comparison of projected benefit obligation in relation to the plan assets at December 31, 1995:

	Assets Exceed Projected Benefit Obligation	Projected Benefit Obligation Exceeds Assets
Projected benefit obligation	$203,446,000	$112,845,000
Plan assets at fair value	187,831,000	82,144,000
Plan assets in excess (less) than projected benefit obligation	$ (15,615,000)	$ (30,701,000)

Projected benefit obligations exceed plan assets at fair value. Approximately 76% of projected benefit obligations are vested.

5. The interest rate used to compute the actuarial present value of the projected benefit obligation was 7.5% in 1995 and 8% in 1994. These rates appear to be reasonable. According to the 1995 *Accounting Trends & Techniques*, most firms used a rate of 8 to 8.5% in 1994.[2]

6. The compensation rate of increase in computing the projected benefit obligation was 5.5% in 1995 and 6.0% in 1994. This rate appears to be reasonable. According to the 1995 *Accounting Trends & Techniques*, most firms used a rate of 4.5 to 5.5% in 1994.[3]

7. The assumed rate of return on plan assets was 10%. This rate is in line with the rate used by other firms (9.0%-10.0%).[4]

8. Unrecognized net losses totaled $48,988,000 at December 31, 1995, and $36,051,000 at December 31, 1994. These unrecognized net losses will increase subsequent pension expense.

9. Unrecognized transition amount totaled $7,898,000 at December 31, 1995. This amount will be amortized to pension expense in subsequent years.

10. Unrecognized prior service cost totaled $8,014,000 at December 31, 1995. This amount will be amortized to pension expense in subsequent years.

11. Balance sheet recognition of pension asset and pension liability has been $22,653,000 and $30,186,000, respectively. The asset appears to have been listed under other assets, and the liability appears to have been listed under other long-term liabilities.

    There is also a reduction in stockholders' equity of $9,167,000 for minimum pension liability. This indicates that the pension liability exceeds the unrecognized prior service cost.

Cooper sponsors several defined contribution plans for its employees. For these plans the expense for 1995, 1994, and 1993 was $8,277,000, $7,485,000, and $6,027,000, respectively. In relation to operating revenue, these amounts were .53%, .53%, and .50%, respectively, for 1995, 1994, and 1993. In relation to income before income taxes, these amounts were 4.60%, 3.60%, and 3.67%, respectively, for 1995, 1994, and 1993.

Pension costs, including defined contribution plans, have increased in recent years. This is especially the case in 1995 in relation to 1994. For Cooper, a subjective conclusion is that the pension plans are having an increasing influence on profitability and the debt position. Material pension cost could serve as a drag on future earnings. This could be a problem during a recession period if earnings are down but pension costs continue.

Employer's Accounting for Settlements and Curtailments Hundreds of companies have terminated their defined benefit plans because the plan assets exceeded accumulated plan benefits. Companies may keep the difference between the amount necessary to settle the accumulated plan benefits and the assets in the plan. They must meet requirements intended to protect the employee before they can obtain funds by curtailing a plan. Some companies have benefited by hundreds of millions of dollars by a termination.

McDonnell Douglas Corporation disclosed the following in a footnote in its 1994 annual report:

Note 15 (in Part)

MDC recorded a curtailment gain of $1.090 billion in the 1992 fourth quarter, reflecting the aforementioned termination of company-paid retiree health care for both current and future non-union retirees. The gain equaled the reduction in accrued retiree benefits, after providing as a liability the $385 million representing the aforementioned supplemental pension benefit. MDC recorded a curtailment gain of $70 million in 1993, reflecting a similar arrangement negotiated with the Southern California Professional Engineering Association for employees retiring after July 1, 1993.

Postretirement Benefits Other than Pensions

Some benefits other than pensions, such as medical insurance and life insurance contracts, accrue to employees upon retirement. These benefits can be substantial. Many firms have obligations in the millions of dollars. Prior to 1993 most firms did not have these obligations funded; therefore, for these firms, a potential for a significant liability existed.

Beginning in 1993, firms were required to accrue, or set up a reserve for, future postretirement benefits other than pensions (rather than deduct these costs when paid). Firms can usually spread the catch-up accrual costs over 20 years or take the charge in one lump sum. The amount involved is frequently material, so this choice can represent a major problem when comparing financial results of two or more firms. For some firms, the catch-up charge for medical insurance was so material that it resulted in a deficit in retained earnings or even a deficit to the entire stockholders' equity section.

Many firms reduce costs by changing their plans to limit health care benefits to retirees to a maximum fixed amount. This type of plan, in contrast to open-ended medical benefits, could materially reduce the firm's health care costs for retirees. Review the footnotes closely to determine how the firm records health care costs for retirees.

Exhibit 8-11 shows Cooper's footnote on postretirement benefits other than pensions. Review this footnote to form an opinion as to the materiality of the postretirement benefits expense and the materiality of the liability.

EXHIBIT 8-11 **COOPER TIRE & RUBBER COMPANY**
Postretirement Benefits Other than Pensions
Footnote—1995 Annual Report

(Dollar amounts in thousands)

The Company currently provides certain health care and life insurance benefits for its active and retired employees. If the Company does not terminate such benefits, or modify coverage or eligibility requirements, substantially all of the Company's United States employees may become eligible for these benefits upon retirement if they meet certain age and service requirements. The Company has reserved the right to modify or terminate such benefits at any time. In recent years, benefit changes have been implemented throughout the Company.

The Company continues to fund these benefit costs as claims are incurred. Postretirement benefits expense for 1995, 1994, and 1993 included the following components:

	1995	1994	1993
Service cost	$ 2,607	$ 3,022	$ 2,226
Interest cost	9,810	10,803	9,805
Amortization	(333)	261	—
	$12,084	$14,086	$12,031

The status of the Company's plans at December 31, 1995 and 1994 was as follows:

	1995	1994
Retirees	$ 71,077	$ 61,280
Fully eligible active plan participants	25,131	22,525
Other active plan participants	37,314	31,881
	133,522	115,686
Deferred gain	6,041	17,561
Postretirement benefits liability	$139,563	$133,247

These amounts are included in the accompanying balance sheet captions:

	1995	1994
Accrued liabilities	$ 6,600	$ 5,900
Postretirement benefits other than pensions	132,963	127,347
	$139,563	$133,247

The discount rate used in determining the APBO was 8.0 percent and 8.5 percent for 1995 and 1994, respectively. The increase in APBO is due primarily to the decrease in the assumption for the discount rate. At December 31, 1995, the assumed average annual rate of increase in the cost of health care benefits (health care cost trend rate) was 9.5 percent for 1996 declining by 2 percent per year through 2004 when the ultimate rate of 5.5 percent is attained. This trend rate assumption has a significant effect on the amounts reported above. A one percent increase in the health care cost

(continued)

EXHIBIT 8-11   (concluded)

trend rate would increase the APBO by $6,216 and the net periodic expense by $483 for the year.

   The Company has a Voluntary Employees' Beneficiary Trust and Welfare Benefits Plan (VEBA) to fund health benefits for eligible active and retired employees. The prefunded amount was $11,000 in 1995 and $9,900 in 1994.

Also observe the discount rate used to compute the accumulated postretirement benefit obligation and the assumed health care cost rate used for health care benefits.

   A review of Exhibit 8-11 indicates the following significant points relating to Cooper's postretirement benefits other than pensions:

1.   Postretirement benefits expense for 1995 was $12,084,000, while net sales was $1,493,622,000. Thus postretirement benefits expense was approximately 0.81% of net sales. This was a decline from approximately 1.00% of net sales in 1994.

2.   The footnote discloses a postretirement benefit liability recognized in the balance sheet of $139,563,000 and a prefunded amount of $11,000,000 at December 31, 1995 (net of $128,563,000). The postretirement benefits liability is included in the balance sheet captions accrued liabilities ($6,600,000) and postretirement benefits other than pensions ($132,963,000). This represents Cooper's single largest liability and appears to be very material.

3.   Cooper used a discount rate of 8.0% in determining the accumulated postretirement benefits obligation for 1995 and 1994 respectively. This discount rate is slightly less than the discount rate used for pensions.

4.   Apparently Cooper is making a significant effort to control the cost of health care benefits. The footnote reads: "At December 31, 1995, the assumed average annual rate of increase in the cost of health care benefits (health care cost trend rate) was 9.5 percent for 1996, declining by 1% percent per year through 2004 when the ultimate rate of 5.5 percent is attained. This trend rate assumption has a significant effect on the amounts reported above. A one percent increase in the health care cost trend rate would increase the accumulated postretirement benefit obligation by $6,216,000 and the net periodic expense by $483,000 for the year."

5.   The Cooper footnote states that the Company has reserved the right to modify or terminate such benefits at any time. The modification and/or termination of provisions makes it difficult

to evaluate this very substantial liability for postretirement benefits other than pensions.

Joint Ventures

A **joint venture** is an association of two or more businesses established
for a special purpose. Some joint ventures are in the form of partnerships
or other unincorporated forms of business. Others are in the form of corporations jointly owned by two or more other firms.

The accounting principles for joint ventures are flexible because of their
many forms. The typical problem concerns whether a joint venture should
be carried as an investment or consolidated. Some joint ventures are very
significant in relation to the parent firm. There is typically a question as
to whether the parent firm has control or only significant influence. When
the parent firm has control, it usually consolidates joint ventures by using
a pro rata share. Other joint ventures are usually carried in an investment
account by using the equity method. In either case, disclosure of significant
information often appears in a footnote.

When a firm enters into a joint venture, it frequently makes commitments such as guaranteeing a bank loan for the joint venture or a long-term
contract to purchase materials with the joint venture. This type of action
can give the company significant potential liabilities or commitments that
do not appear on the face of the balance sheet. This potential problem exists
with all joint ventures, including those that have been consolidated. To be
aware of these significant potential liabilities or commitments, read the
footnote that relates to the joint venture. Then consider this information in
relation to the additional liabilities or commitments to which the joint venture
may commit the firm.

LTV Corporation disclosed in a footnote to its 1994 annual report:

> LTV has guaranteed approximately $13 million per year through
> January 1999 for a joint venture's operating lease rental obliga-
> tion. The Company has guaranteed $5 million of debt of a
> company whose facilities are leased by the Company. The Com-
> pany does not believe it is practicable to estimate the fair value
> of the guarantees and does not believe exposure to loss is likely.

Contingencies

A **contingency** is an existing condition, situation, or set of circumstances
involving uncertainty as to possible gain or loss to an enterprise that will
ultimately be resolved when one or more future events occur or fail to occur.[5]

A contingency is characterized by an existing condition, uncertainty as
to the ultimate effect, and its resolution depending on one or more future
events. A loss contingency should be accrued if two conditions are met:[6]

1.   Information prior to issuance of the financial statements indicates that it is *probable* that an asset has been impaired or a liability has been incurred at the date of the financial statements.

2.   The amount of the *loss* can be *reasonably estimated*.

If a contingency loss meets one, but not both, of the criteria for recording and is, therefore, not accrued, disclosure by footnote is made when it is at *least reasonably possible* that there has been an impairment of assets or that a liability has been incurred. Examples of contingencies include warranty obligations and collectibility of receivables. If the firm guarantees the indebtedness of others, the contingency is usually disclosed in a footnote.

When examining financial statements, a footnote that describes contingencies should be closely reviewed for possible significant liabilities not disclosed on the face of the balance sheet.

No contingency footnote appears for Cooper at the end of 1995, indicating that the company does not have significant contingency problems that it considered necessary to disclose in a footnote. Practically all firms have addressed the contingency problem. Even the account, Allowance for Doubtful Accounts, has been recorded under the contingency standard.

The following covers gain contingencies:

1.   Contingencies that might result in gains usually are not reflected in the accounts, since to do so might be to recognize revenue prior to its realization.

2.   Adequate disclosure shall be made of contingencies that might result in gains, but care shall be exercised to avoid misleading implications as to the likelihood of realization.[7]

The footnotes of the firm should be reviewed for gain contingencies. Boise Cascade disclosed the following in the notes to its 1994 annual report:

At December 31, 1994, the Company had loss carryforwards for tax purposes of $513,427,000 expiring in 2007 through 2009. Additionally, the Company had income tax credits of $35,663,000 expiring in 1997 through 2008. The Company also had $79,615,000 of minimum tax credits, which may be carried forward indefinitely. The loss carryforwards and the minimum tax credits are realizable through future reversals of existing taxable temporary differences. Management believes that the income tax credits will be fully realized based on future reversals of existing taxable temporary differences, future earnings, or available tax planning strategies.

Financial Instruments with Off-Balance-Sheet Risk and Financial Instruments with Concentrations of Credit Risk

Credit and market risk for all financial instruments with off-balance-sheet risk require the following disclosure:

1. The face or contract amount.
2. The nature and terms including, at a minimum, a discussion of credit and market risk, cash requirements, and accounting policies.[8]

Disclosure is also required of the following regarding financial instruments with off-balance-sheet credit risk:

1. The amount of accounting loss the entity would incur if any party failed completely to perform according to the terms of the contract and the collateral or other security, if any, proved worthless.
2. The entity's policy of requiring collateral and a brief description of the collateral it currently holds.[9]

Accounting loss, a new term used in this SFAS, represents the worst-case loss, if everything related to a contract went wrong. This includes the possibility that a loss may occur from the failure of another party to perform according to the terms of a contract, as well as the possibility that changes in market prices may make a financial instrument less valuable or more troublesome.

In addition to requiring disclosure of matters relating to off-balance-sheet financial instruments, SFAS No. 105 requires disclosure of credit risk concentration. This disclosure includes information on the extent of risk from exposures to individuals or groups of counterparties in the same industry or region. The activity, region, or economic characteristic that identifies a concentration requires a narrative description. The provision of requiring disclosure of credit risk concentration can be particularly significant to small companies. Examples are a retail store whose receivables are substantially with local residents and a local bank with a loan portfolio concentrated with debtors dependent on the local tourist business.

Exhibit 8-12, page 354, presents financial instruments with off-balance-sheet risk and financial instruments with concentrations of credit risk for Nordson Corporation as disclosed in its 1995 annual report.

Disclosures About Fair Value of Financial Instruments

Disclosure is required about the fair value of financial instruments. This includes financial instruments recognized and not recognized in the balance sheet (both assets and liabilities). When estimating fair value is not

EXHIBIT 8-12 NORDSON CORPORATION
Off-Balance-Sheet Risk and Concentrations of Credit Risk
1995 Annual Report

Note 10 Financial Instruments (in Part)
Off-Balance-Sheet Risk and Concentrations of Credit Risk

The Company operates internationally and enters into transactions denominated in foreign currencies. As a result, the Company is subject to the transaction exposures that arise from exchange rate movements between the dates foreign currency transactions are recorded and the dates they are consummated. The Company enters into foreign currency forward exchange contracts to reduce these risks, and not for trading purposes. The maturities of these contracts are generally less than one year and usually less than 90 days. The contracts require the Company to buy or sell foreign currencies, usually in exchange for U.S. dollars. The following table summarizes, by currency, the contractual amounts of the Company's forward exchange contracts at October 29, 1995:

	Sell	Buy
	(In thousands)	
Contract amount:		
German marks	$25,265	$ 2,521
Japanese yen	25,030	10,861
French francs	6,152	—
Pound sterling	5,019	2,759
Other	14,030	3,960
Total	$75,496	$20,101

The Company is exposed to credit-related losses in the event of nonperformance by counterparties to financial instruments. The Company deposits cash and enters into forward exchange contracts with major banks throughout the world and invests in securities with strong credit ratings. The Company's customers represent a wide variety of industries and geographic regions. As of October 29, 1995, there were no significant concentrations of credit risk.

---

practicable, then descriptive information pertinent to estimating fair value should be disclosed.

The disclosure about fair value of financial instruments can be either in the body of the financial statements or in the footnotes.[10] This disclosure could possibly indicate significant opportunity or additional risk to the company. For example, long-term debt disclosed at a fair value above the carrying amount increases the potential for a loss.

Exhibit 8-13 presents the fair value of financial instruments for Nordson Corporation, as disclosed in its 1995 annual report.

EXHIBIT 8-13 **NORDSON CORPORATION**
Fair Value of Financial Instruments
1995 Annual Report

Note 10 Financial Instruments (in Part)

The carrying amounts and fair values of the Company's financial instruments, other than receivables and accounts payable, are as follows:

	Carrying Amount	Fair Value
	(In thousands)	
1995:		
Cash and cash equivalents	$ 359	$ 359
Marketable securities	1,225	1,227
Notes payable	(43,197)	(43,197)
Long-term debt	(15,622)	(15,556)
Forward exchange contracts	282	110
1994:		
Cash and cash equivalents	$ 4,578	$ 4,578
Marketable securities	6,486	6,493
Notes payable	(26,917)	(26,917)
Long-term debt	(17,680)	(16,280)
Forward exchange contracts	(873)	(882)

The following methods and assumptions were used by the Company in estimating the fair value of financial instruments:

— Cash, cash equivalents, and notes payable are valued at their carrying amounts due to the relatively short period to maturity of the instruments.

— Marketable securities are valued at quoted market prices.

— Long-term debt is valued by discounting future cash flows at currently available taxable rates for borrowing arrangements with similar terms and conditions.

— The fair value of forward exchange contracts is estimated using quoted exchange rates of comparable contracts. The carrying amounts are included in receivables.

At October 29, 1995, the Company had issued $5,290,000 of guarantees to support the term borrowing facilities of an unconsolidated affiliate. The fair value of these guarantees is not material.

SUMMARY

This chapter covered two approaches to a firm's long-term debt-paying ability. One approach considers the firm's ability to carry debt as

indicated by the income statement, and the other approach views it as
indicated by the balance sheet. The book ratios related to debt include the
following:

$$\text{Times Interest Earned} = \frac{\text{Recurring Earnings, Excluding Interest Expense, Tax Expense, Equity Earnings, and Minority Earnings}}{\text{Interest Expense, Including Capitalized Interest}}$$

$$\text{Fixed Charge Coverage} = \frac{\text{Recurring Earnings, Excluding Interest Expense, Tax Expense, Equity Earnings, and Minority Earnings + Interest Portion of Rentals}}{\text{Interest Expense, Including Capitalized Interest + Interest Portion of Rentals}}$$

$$\text{Debt Ratio} = \frac{\text{Total Liabilities}}{\text{Total Assets}}$$

$$\text{Debt/Equity Ratio} = \frac{\text{Total Liabilities}}{\text{Shareholders' Equity}}$$

$$\text{Debt to Tangible Net Worth} = \frac{\text{Total Liabilities}}{\text{Shareholders' Equity - Intangible Assets}}$$

QUESTIONS

Q 8-1.   Is profitability important to a firm's long-term debt-paying ability? Discuss.

Q 8-2.   List the two approaches to examining a firm's long-term debt-paying ability.
Discuss why each of these approaches gives an important view of a firm's
ability to carry debt.

Q 8-3.   What type of times interest earned ratio would be desirable? What type would
not be desirable?

Q 8-4.   Would you expect an auto manufacturer to finance a relatively high proportion
of its long-term funds from debt? Discuss.

Q 8-5.   Would you expect a telephone company to have a high debt ratio? Discuss.

Q 8-6.   Why should capitalized interest be added to interest expense when computing
times interest earned?

Q 8-7. Discuss how noncash charges for depreciation, depletion, and amortization can be used to obtain a short-run view of times interest earned.

Q 8-8. Why is it difficult to determine the value of assets?

Q 8-9. Is it feasible to get a precise measurement of the funds that could be available from long-term assets to pay long-term debts? Discuss.

Q 8-10. One of the ratios used to indicate long-term debt-paying ability compares total liabilities to total assets. What is the intent of this ratio? How precise is this ratio in achieving its intent?

Q 8-11. For a given firm, would you expect the debt ratio to be as high as the debt/equity ratio? Explain.

Q 8-12. Explain how the debt/equity ratio indicates the same relative long-term debt-paying ability as does the debt ratio, only in a different form.

Q 8-13. Why is it important to compare long-term debt ratios of a given firm with industry averages?

Q 8-14. How should lessees account for operating leases? Capital leases? Include both income statement and balance sheet accounts.

Q 8-15. A firm with substantial leased assets that have not been capitalized may be overstating its long-term debt-paying ability. Explain.

Q 8-16. Capital leases that have not been capitalized will decrease the times interest earned ratio. Comment.

Q 8-17. Indicate the status of pension liabilities under the Employee Retirement Income Security Act.

Q 8-18. Why is the vesting provision an important provision of a pension plan? How has the Employee Retirement Income Security Act influenced vesting periods?

Q 8-19. Indicate the risk to a company if it withdraws from a multiemployer pension plan or if the multiemployer pension plan is terminated.

Q 8-20. Operating leases are not reflected on the balance sheet, but they are reflected on the income statement in the rent expense. Comment on why an interest expense figure that relates to long-term operating leases should be considered when determining a fixed charge coverage.

Q 8-21. What portion of net worth can the federal government require a company to use to pay for pension obligations?

Q 8-22. Consider the debt ratio. Explain a position for including short-term liabilities in the debt ratio. Explain a position for excluding short-term liabilities from the debt ratio. Which of these approaches would be more conservative?

Q 8-23. Consider the accounts of bonds payable and reserve for rebuilding furnaces. Explain how one of these accounts could be considered a firm liability and the other could be considered a soft liability.

Q 8-24. Explain why deferred taxes that are disclosed as long-term liabilities may not result in actual cash outlays in the future.

Q 8-25.   A firm has a high current debt/net worth ratio in relation to prior years, competitors, and the industry. Comment on what this tentatively indicates.

Q 8-26.   Comment on the implications of relying on a greater proportion of short-term debt in relation to long-term debt.

Q 8-27.   When a firm guarantees a bank loan for a joint venture that it participates in and the joint venture is handled as an investment, then the overall potential debt position will not be obvious from the face of the balance sheet. Comment.

Q 8-28.   When examining financial statements, a footnote that describes contingencies should be reviewed closely for possible significant liabilities that are not disclosed on the face of the balance sheet. Comment.

Q 8-29.   There is a chance that a company may be in a position to have large sums transferred from the pension fund to the company. Comment.

Q 8-30.   Indicate why comparing firms for postretirement benefits other than pensions can be difficult.

Q 8-31.   Speculate on why the disclosure of the concentrations of credit risk is potentially important to the users of financial reports.

Q 8-32.   Comment on the significance of disclosing off-balance-sheet risk of accounting loss.

Q 8-33.   Comment on the significance of disclosing the fair value of financial instruments.

PROBLEMS

P 8-1.   Consider the following operating figures:

Net sales	$ 1,079,143
Cost and deductions:	
Cost of sales	792,755
Selling and administration	264,566
Interest expense, net	4,311
Income taxes	5,059
	1,066,691
	$ 12,452

Note: Depreciation expense totals $40,000.

Required   a.   Compute the times interest earned.
                    b.   Compute the cash basis times interest earned.

P 8-2. Jones Petro Company reports the following consolidated statement of income:

Operating revenues	$ 2,989
Costs and expenses:	
Cost of rentals and royalties	543
Cost of sales	314
Selling, service, administrative,	
and general expense	1,424
Total costs and expenses	2,281
Operating income	708
Other income	27
Other deductions (interest)	60
Income before income taxes	675
Income taxes	309
Income before outside shareholders' interests	366
Outside shareholders' interests	66
Net income	$ 300

Note: Depreciation expense totals $200; operating lease payments total $150; and preferred dividends total $50. Assume that 1/3 of operating lease payments is for interest.

Required   a. Compute the times interest earned.
           b. Compute the fixed charge coverage.

P 8-3. The Sherwill statement of consolidated income is as follows:

Net sales	$658
Other income	8
	666
Costs and expenses:	
Cost of products sold	418
Selling, general, and administrative expenses	196
Interest	16
	630
Income before income taxes and	
extraordinary charges	36
Income taxes	18
Income before extraordinary charge	18
Extraordinary charge—losses on tornado damage (net)	4
Net income	$ 14

Note: Depreciation expense totals $200; operating lease payments total $150; and preferred dividends total $50. Assume that 1/3 of operating lease payments is for interest.

Required   a. Compute the times interest earned.
           b. Compute the fixed charge coverage.

P 8-4.   Kaufman Company's balance sheet is as follows:

Assets
Current assets: $ 13,445
  Cash
  Short-term investments—at cost (approximate market)   5,239
  Trade accounts receivable, less allowance of $1,590   88,337
  Inventories—at lower-of-cost-(average method)-or-market:
    Finished merchandise   113,879
    Work in process, raw materials, and supplies   47,036
                                                                        160,915
  Prepaid expenses   8,221
     Total current assets   276,157
Other assets:
  Receivables, advances, and other assets   4,473
  Intangibles   2,324
     Total other assets   6,797
Property, plant, and equipment:
  Land   5,981
  Buildings   78,908
  Machinery and equipment   162,425
                                                                        247,314
  Less: Allowances for depreciation   106,067
     Net property, plant, and equipment   141,247
     Total assets $424,201

Liabilities and Shareholders' Equity
Current liabilities:
  Notes payable $ 2,817
  Trade accounts payable   23,720
  Pension, interest, and other accruals   33,219
  Taxes, other than income taxes   4,736
  Income taxes   3,409
     Total current liabilities   67,901
Long-term debt, 12% debentures   86,235
Deferred income taxes   8,768
Minority interest in subsidiaries   12,075
     Total liabilities   174,979
Shareholders' equity:
  Capital stock
  Serial preferred   9,154
  Common $5.25 par value   33,540
  Additional paid-in capital   3,506
  Retained earnings   203,712
                                                                        249,912
  Less: Cost of common shares in treasury   690
     Total shareholders' equity   249,222
     Total liabilities and shareholders' equity $424,201

Required a. Compute the debt ratio.
b. Compute the debt/equity ratio.
c. Compute the ratio of total debt to tangible net worth.
d. Comment on the amount of debt that Kaufman Company has.

P 8-5. Individual transactions often have a significant impact on ratios. This problem will consider the direction of such an impact.

Ratio Transaction	Times Interest Earned	Debt Ratio	Debt/ Equity Ratio	Debt to Tangible Net Worth
a. Purchase of buildings financed by mortgage.	$\frac{EBIT}{INT\ EXP}$	$\frac{T.\ LIAB +}{T.\ ASSETS}$		
b. Purchase of inventory on short-term loan at 1% over prime rate.	—	+		
c. Declaration and payment of cash dividend.	SAME	+		
d. Declaration and payment of stock dividend.	SAME	SAME		
e. Firm increases profits by cutting cost of sales.	+	—		
f. Appropriation of retained earnings.	0	0		
g. Sale of common stock.	0	↓ —		
h. Repayment of long-term bank loan.	↑ +	↓ —		
i. Conversion of bonds to common stock outstanding.	↑ +	↓ —		
j. Sale of inventory at greater than cost.	+	—		

Required Indicate the effect of each of the transactions on the ratios listed. Use + to indicate an increase, – to indicate a decrease, and 0 to indicate no effect. Assume an initial times interest earned of more than 1, and a debt ratio, debt/equity ratio, and a total debt to tangible net worth of less than 1.

P 8-6.   For the year ended June 30, 1996, A.E.G. Enterprises presented the following financial statements:

A.E.G. ENTERPRISES
Balance Sheet for June 30, 1996 (In thousands)

Assets

Current assets:		
Cash	$ 50,000	
Accounts receivable	60,000	
Inventory	106,000	
Total current assets		$ 216,000
Property, plant, and equipment	504,000	
Less: Accumulated depreciation	140,000	364,000
Patents and other intangible assets		20,000
Total assets		$ 600,000

Liabilities and Stockholders' Equity

Current liabilities:		
Accounts payable	$ 46,000	
Taxes payable	15,000	
Other current liabilities	32,000	
Total current liabilities		$ 93,000
Long-term debt		100,000
Stockholders' equity:		
Preferred stock ($100 par, 10% cumulative, 500,000 shares authorized and issued)		50,000
Common stock ($1 par, 200,000,000 shares authorized, 100,000,000 issued)		100,000
Premium on common stock		120,000
Retained earnings		137,000
Total liabilities and stockholders' equity		$ 600,000

A.E.G. ENTERPRISES
Income Statement
For the Year Ended June 30, 1996
(In thousands except earnings per share)

Sales		$ 936,000
Cost of sales		671,000
Gross profit		265,000
Operating expenses:		
Selling	$62,000	
General	41,000	103,000
Operating income		162,000
Other items:		
Interest expense		20,000
Earnings before provision for income tax		142,000
Provision for income tax		56,800
Net income		$ 85,200
Earnings per share		$ .83

Early in the new fiscal year, the officers of the firm formalized a substantial expansion plan. The plan will increase fixed assets by $190,000,000. In addition, extra inventory will be needed to support expanded production. The increase in inventory is purported to be $10,000,000.

The firm's investment bankers have suggested three alternative financing plans:

Plan A: Sell preferred stock at par.

Plan B: Sell common stock at $10 per share.

Plan C: Sell long-term bonds, due in 20 years, at par ($1,000), with a stated interest rate of 16%.

Required a. For the year ended June 30, 1996, compute:
1. Times interest earned
2. Debt ratio
3. Debt/equity ratio
4. Debt to tangible net worth ratio

b. Assuming the same financial results and statement balances, except for the increased assets and financing, compute the same ratios as in (a) under each financing alternative. Do not attempt to adjust retained earnings for the next year's profits.

c. Changes in earnings and number of shares will give the following earnings per share: Plan A—.73, Plan B—.69, Plan C—.73. Based on the information given, discuss the advantages and disadvantages of each alternative.

d. Why does the 10% preferred stock cost the company more than the 16% bonds?

P 8-7. Mr. Parks has asked you to advise him on the long-term debt-paying ability of Arodex Company. He provides you with the following ratios:

	1996	1995	1994
Times interest earned	8.2	6.0	5.5
Debt ratio	40%	39%	40%
Debt to tangible net worth	80%	81%	81%

Required a. Give the implications and the limitations of each item separately and then the collective influence one may draw from them about Arodex Company's long-term debt position.

b. What warnings should you offer Mr. Parks about the limitations of ratio analysis for the purpose stated here?

P 8-8. Allen Company and Barker Company are competitors in the same industry. Selected financial data from their 1996 statements are as follows:

Balance Sheet
December 31, 1996

	Allen Company	Barker Company
Cash	$ 10,000	$ 35,000
Accounts receivable	45,000	120,000
Inventory	70,000	190,000
Investments	40,000	100,000
Intangibles	11,000	20,000
Property, plant, and equipment, net	180,000	520,000
Total assets	$356,000	$985,000
Accounts payable	$ 60,000	$165,000
Bonds payable	100,000	410,000
Preferred stock, $1 par	50,000	30,000
Common stock, $10 par	100,000	280,000
Retained earnings	46,000	100,000
Total liabilities and capital	$356,000	$985,000

Income Statement
For the Year Ended December 31, 1996

	Allen Company	Barker Company
Sales	$ 1,050,000	$ 2,800,000
Cost of goods sold	725,000	2,050,000
Selling and administrative expenses	230,000	580,000
Interest expense	10,000	32,000
Income taxes	42,000	65,000
Net income	$ 43,000	$ 73,000

Industry averages:

Times interest earned	7.2 times per year
Debt ratio	40.3%
Debt/equity ratio	66.6%
Debt to tangible net worth	72.7%

Required a. Compute the following ratios for each company:
   1. Times interest earned
   2. Debt ratio
   3. Debt/equity ratio
   4. Debt to tangible net worth

   b. Is Barker Company in a position to take on additional long-term debt? Explain.

   c. Which company has the better long-term debt position? Explain.

P 8-9. The consolidated statement of earnings of Anonymous Corporation for the year ended December 31, 1996, is as follows:

Net sales	$ 1,550,010,000
Other income, net	10,898,000
	1,560,908,000
Cost and expenses:	
Cost of goods sold	1,237,403,000
Depreciation and amortization	32,229,000
Selling, general, and administrative	178,850,000
Interest	37,646,000
	1,486,128,000
Earnings from continuing operations before income taxes and equity earnings	74,780,000
Income taxes	37,394,000
Earnings from continuing operations before equity earnings	37,386,000
Equity in net earnings of unconsolidated subsidiaries and affiliated companies	27,749,000
Earnings from continuing operations	65,135,000
Earnings (losses) from discontinued operations, net of applicable income taxes	6,392,000
Net earnings	$ 71,527,000

Required

a. Compute the times interest earned for 1996.
b. Compute the times interest earned for 1996, including the equity income in the coverage.
c. What is the impact of excluding equity earnings in the coverage? Why should equity income be excluded from the times interest earned coverage?

P 8-10. The following are a number of terms that relate to pensions and a definition of the term. Match the appropriate definition with the term.

Term

1. Employee Retirement Income Security Act (ERISA)
2. Multiemployer pension plan
3. Defined contribution plan
4. Defined benefit plan
5. Vested pension plan
6. Prior service cost
7. Projected benefit obligation
8. Amortization of the unrecognized net obligation (and loss or cost) or unrecognized net asset (and gain) existing at the date of initial application of pension accounting rules.

Definition

a. Defines the benefits to be received by the participants in the plan.
b. A pension benefit that the employee is entitled to even if the employee leaves the firm prior to retirement.
c. The loss or gain associated with the unrecognized net obligation or unrecognized net asset at the beginning of the fiscal year in which pension accounting rules are first applied.
d. Federal pension law passed in 1974.
e. Credit given to employees for years of service provided before the date of adoption or amendment of the defined benefit plan.
f. Pension plan maintained jointly by two or more unrelated employers.
g. Defines the contributions of the company to the pension plan.
h. The actuarial present value as of a date of all benefits attributed by pension benefit formula to employee service rendered prior to that date; computed using assumptions as to future compensation levels if the pension benefit formula is based on those future compensation levels.

P 8-11.   Consecutive five-year balance sheets and income statements of Laura Gibson Corporation are as follows:

LAURA GIBSON CORPORATION
Balance Sheets
December 31, 1992 through December 31, 1996

(Dollars in thousands)	1996	1995	1994	1993	1992
Assets					
Current assets:					
Cash	$ 27,000	$ 26,000	$ 25,800	$ 25,500	$ 25,000
Accounts receivable, net	135,000	132,000	130,000	129,000	128,000
Inventories	128,000	130,000	134,000	132,000	126,000
Total current assets	290,000	288,000	289,800	286,500	279,000
Property, plant, and equipment, net	250,000	248,000	247,000	246,000	243,000
Intangibles	20,000	18,000	17,000	16,000	15,000
Total assets	$560,000	$554,000	$553,800	$548,500	$537,000
Liabilities and Stockholders' Equity					
Current liabilities:					
Accounts payable	$ 75,000	$ 76,000	$ 76,500	$ 77,000	$ 78,000
Income taxes	13,000	13,500	14,000	13,000	13,500
Total current liabilities	88,000	89,500	90,500	90,000	91,500
Long-term debt	170,000	168,000	165,000	164,000	262,000
Stockholders' equity	302,000	296,500	298,300	294,500	183,500
Total liabilities and stockholders' equity	$560,000	$554,000	$553,800	$548,500	$537,000

LAURA GIBSON CORPORATION
Statements of Earnings
Years Ended December 31, 1992-1996

(In thousands, except per share)	1996	1995	1994	1993	1992
Net sales	$920,000	$950,000	$910,000	$850,000	$800,000
Cost of goods sold	640,000	648,000	624,000	580,000	552,000
Gross profit	280,000	302,000	286,000	270,000	248,000
Selling and administrative expense	156,000	157,000	154,000	150,000	147,000
Interest expense	17,000	16,000	15,000	14,500	23,000
Earnings from continuing operations before income taxes	107,000	129,000	117,000	105,500	78,000
Income taxes	36,300	43,200	39,800	35,800	26,500
Earnings from continuing operations	70,700	85,800	77,200	69,700	51,500
Discontinued operations earnings (loss), net of taxes:					
From operations	(1,400)	1,300	1,400	1,450	1,600
On disposal	(900)	—	—	—	—
Earnings (loss) from discontinued operations	(2,300)	1,300	1,400	1,450	1,600
Net earnings	$ 68,400	$ 87,100	$ 78,600	$ 71,150	$ 53,100
Earnings (loss) per share:					
Continuing operations	$ 1.53	$ 1.69	$ 1.46	$ 1.37	$ 1.25
Discontinued operations	(.03)	.01	.01	.01	.01
Net earnings per share	$ 1.50	$ 1.70	$ 1.47	$ 1.38	$ 1.26

Note: Operating lease payments were as follows: 1996, $30,000; 1995, $27,000; 1994, $28,500; 1993, $30,000; 1992, $27,000. (Dollars in thousands)

Required   a. Compute the following for the years ended December 31, 1992-1996:
   1.   Times interest earned
   2.   Fixed charge coverage
   3.   Debt ratio
   4.   Debt/equity ratio
   5.   Debt to tangible net worth

   b. Comment on the debt position and the trends indicated in the long-term debt-paying ability.

Cases

CASE 8-1   Deferred Taxes? The Answer Is Yes!

GEORGIA POWER COMPANY
Position Paper on Accounting for Income Taxes
(Submitted to the Financial Accounting Standards Board)
Comprehensive Allocation

Comprehensive interperiod tax allocation is necessary to properly recognize the economic substance of a taxable transaction or event. Income taxes are an expense of doing business. It would be inconsistent with accrual accounting to not recognize the appropriate income tax expense at the time of a transaction, when the revenues and other expenses are recognized. The fact that the taxes are not currently payable does not eliminate the expense. If an asset is being depreciated at an accelerated rate for tax purposes, there is a clear economic event that must be recognized. In addition to a reduction in current taxes payable, part of the value of that asset has been consumed, and that fact must be recognized under accrual accounting. The current reduction in taxes payable is not income; it is simply the proceeds from the disposal of a portion of the asset. To recognize only the amount of taxes paid in a particular year would ignore the economic fact that income taxes are based on the separate revenue and expense transactions as measured by the tax laws.

Criticisms and concerns expressed in current articles and accounting literature have focused both on the complexities of current accounting requirements and the meaningfulness of the results of applying the requirements. Accrual accounting is obviously more complex than a listing of cash receipts and payments. However, *Concepts Statement No. 1*, "Objectives of Financial Reporting," states that information about enterprises' earnings based on accrual accounting generally provides a better indication of an enterprise's present and continuing ability to generate favorable cash flows than information limited to the financial effects of cash receipts and payments. Flow-through accounting or any method of partial allocation is inconsistent with accrual accounting.

Conceptual Definition

The Accounting Principles Board (APB) recognized that income taxes were an expense of doing business and that comprehensive tax allocation or accrual accounting was the most meaningful way to recognize this expense. However, the Board members had differing opinions on the conceptual definition of the balance sheet effect of tax allocations and selected the deferred method as a compromise. The deferred method properly dealt with the effect of income taxes on the income statement, but it gave only secondary consideration to the balance sheet effect. However, at the time of APB 11 the accounting profession was more concerned with the income statement.

Current accounting concepts place much more emphasis on the balance sheet. *Concepts Statement No. 3* states that deferred taxes, as defined under APB 11, do not meet the definition for proper elements of financial reporting. Deferred taxes must be defined as either liabilities or valuation accounts to be properly recorded on the balance sheet. This does not necessarily mean that the deferred method must be abandoned. It simply means that the balance sheet results must be defined under a different concept. For example, *Concepts Statement No. 3* states that some proponents of the deferred method hold that it is actually a variation of the net-of-tax method despite rejection of that method in Opinion 11. They view the deferred tax charges and credits as the separate display of the effects of interperiod tax allocation instead of as reductions of the related assets, liabilities, revenues, expenses, gains, and losses. They argue that separate display is necessary or desirable, but it is a matter of geography in financial statements rather than a matter of the nature of deferred income tax credits.

The APB could not agree on whether the tax effects of timing differences were liabilities or valuation accounts, and the reasons for this disagreement seem obvious. Not all timing differences are the same; some are liabilities (or assets), and some are valuations of other balance sheet accounts. The conceptual definition of a timing difference should be based on the economic substance of the particular timing difference.

Generally speaking, if an existing asset or liability is directly impacted by the timing difference, the tax effect of the timing difference should be considered a valuation of the asset or liability (but not necessarily netted against the asset or liability). If the timing difference is not related to an existing asset or liability, the tax effect of the timing difference would have to be evaluated based on the characteristics of an asset or a liability.

The valuation concept is based on the fact that taxability and tax deductibility are factors in the determination of the carrying amounts of individual assets and liabilities. *Concepts Statement No. 3* defines assets as a probable future economic benefits obtained or controlled by a particular entity as a result of past transactions or events. The Statement goes on to explain, "The common characteristics possessed by all assets and economic resources is service potential or future economic benefit, the capacity to provide services or benefits to the entities that use them. In a business enterprise, that service potential or future economic benefit eventually results in net cash inflows to the enterprise. That characteristic is the primary basis of the definition of assets in this Statement." Part of the value (future cash flow) of an asset is its tax deductibility. Any business person understands that an asset with a tax basis has more value than an asset with no tax basis. This fact was made explicitly clear with the provision of the Economic Recovery Tax Act of 1981, which allowed an enterprise to sell the tax benefits of an asset. When a portion of an asset's value has been consumed or sold, the future cash flow from that asset has been reduced. Under accrual accounting, financial statements should reflect this fact.

Concepts Statement No. 3 defines liabilities as a "probable future sacrifice of economic benefits arising from present obligations . . . as a result of past transactions or events." Since income taxes are based on separate revenue and expense transactions, the tax effects of timing differences do meet the definitions of assets and liabilities. A good example is an installment sale that is recognized for financial accounting in the period of the sale but included in taxable income of a later period when cash is collected. The past transaction is the sale which makes future tax payment a probable (but not certain). Certainly future taxes are dependent on future taxable income; however, for this one item there will be taxes payable, and the elimination of future taxable income will require future tax deductions or changes in the laws. This timing difference also could be viewed as a valuation of the receivable, and as explained above this would be the preferable treatment.

Presentation

The conceptual nature of the timing difference does not necessarily dictate the method of recording the timing difference. The tax effects of timing differences, which are in fact valuations of fixed assets, should be reported as a component of, or offset to, the fixed asset. The presentation would more properly reflect the future cash flows expected from the fixed asset. However, timing differences which are valuations of other assets or liabilities may be better recorded in a separate account similar to current deferred taxes, separated between current and noncurrent (see example of balance sheet presentation). This approach would avoid the problems of netting payables with future tax benefits or having other potentially misleading combinations. Furthermore, the adoption of the valuation concept would not necessarily change the current treatment of income taxes in the income statement. All income taxes (current and deferred) could still be recorded as tax expense.

Example Balance Sheet (In thousands)
Assets

Utility plant	$ 6,900,000
Less: Accumulated depreciation	1,500,000
Total	5,400,000
Less: Property-related accumulated deferred income taxes	700,000
Total	4,700,000

Current assets:	
Cash	540,000
Accounts receivable (net)	280,000
Materials and supplies	345,000
Total	1,165,000
Total assets	$ 5,865,000
Capitalization and Liabilities	
Capitalization:	
Common stock equity	$ 1,700,000
Preferred stock	550,000
Long-term debt	2,800,000
Total	5,050,000
Current liabilities:	
Accounts payable	250,000
Customer deposits	30,000
Taxes accrued	40,000
Current deferred income taxes	70,000
Miscellaneous	110,000
Total	500,000
Deferred income taxes	15,000
Accumulated deferred investment tax credits	300,000
Total capitalization and liabilities	$5,865,000

Tax Rate

Under either concept of interperiod tax allocation, an important issue is the tax rate to be used in calculating the tax timing difference. However, the conceptual nature of the timing difference should not dictate how the tax rate is determined. The tax impact of a transaction is determined at the time the transaction affects the tax return. Once an item has been reflected in the tax return, its economic impact is fixed, and this will not change regardless of changes in the income tax laws. Therefore, timing differences arising from transactions recognized first for tax purposes would be measured using the tax rate at that time. Timing differences arising from transactions recognized first for financial reporting purposes would be measured based on the tax rate expected to be in effect when the revenue or expense is to be reflected in the tax return. The economic impact of these timing differences would change if the tax rate changes. The tax rate change would be handled as would any other change in accounting estimate.

Discounting

In addition to the tax rate, another measurement question is whether the tax allocation balance should be discounted. The question normally arises when tax allocations are viewed as liabilities; however, the question is also relevant when using the valuation method. In APB Opinion No. 10, "Omnibus Opinion-1966 (Tax Allocation Accounts Discounting)," the Board concluded that pending further consideration of the broader aspects of discounting as it related to financial accounting in general, deferred taxes should not be discounted. The accounting profession (APB or FASB) has not yet reviewed the broad issue of discounting. Tax timing differences should not be considered independent of the broader issue. The FASB should defer this question until the completion of the Concepts Statement on accounting recognition and measurement.

Required

a. Should companies use the same financial reporting methods for their annual report as they use for their federal tax return? Discuss.

b. Explain why permanent differences between financial reporting of income and federal tax reporting of income exist.

c. Explain why a company may be reporting a revenue or expense item in a different period in its financial statements than in its federal tax return.

d. Critically comment on the following: Federal income tax expense should be recognized on the financial statements in the same period that the tax liability is incurred.

e. The Georgia Power position paper states: "Current accounting concepts place much more emphasis on the balance sheet. *Concepts Statement No. 3* states that deferred taxes, as defined under APB 11, do not meet the definition for proper elements of financial reporting. Deferred taxes must be defined as either liabilities or valuation accounts to be properly recorded on the balance sheet." How does the Georgia Power position paper propose to classify deferred taxes on the balance sheet?

f. An important issue to be resolved, if deferred taxes are to be recognized, is the tax rate. How should the tax rate be determined according to the Georgia Power position paper? In your opinion, do you agree with the determination of the tax rate as proposed by Georgia Power? Comment.

g. Discuss some practical reasons why many firms would prefer that deferred taxes not be part of GAAP.

h. Discuss some practical reasons why Georgia Power would prefer that deferred taxes be part of GAAP.

CASE 8-2   Expensing Interest Now and Later

Intel reported the following in its 1995 annual report:

Consolidated Statements of Income
Intel Corporation
Three Years Ended December 30, 1995

(In millions, except per-share amounts)	1995	1994	1993
Net revenues	$16,202	$11,521	$ 8,782
Cost of sales	7,811	5,576	3,252
Research and development	1,296	1,111	970
Marketing, general, and administrative	1,843	1,447	1,168
Operating costs and expenses	10,950	8,134	5,390
Operating income	5,252	3,387	3,392
Interest expense	(29)	(57)	(50)
Interest income and other, net	415	273	188
Income before taxes	5,638	3,603	3,530
Provision for taxes	2,072	1,315	1,235
Net income	$ 3,566	$ 2,288	$ 2,295
Earnings per common and common equivalent share	$ 4.03	$ 2.62	$ 2.60
Weighted average common and common equivalent shares outstanding	884	874	882

Notes to Consolidated Financial Statements (in Part)
Interest (in Part)

Interest expense capitalized as a component of construction costs was $46 million, $27 million, and $8 million for 1995, 1994, and 1993, respectively.

Required a. What is the amount of gross interest expense for 1995, 1994, and 1993?
 b. What is the interest expense reported on the income statement for 1995, 1994, and 1993?
 c. What was the amount of interest added to the cost of property, plant, and equipment during 1995, 1994, and 1993?
 d. When is capitalized interest recognized as an expense? Describe.
 e. What was the effect on income from capitalizing interest? Describe.

CASE 8-3   Consideration of Leases

Nordson Corporation included the following in its 1995 annual report:

Nordson Corporation
Consolidated Statement of Income

Years Ended October 29, 1995, October 30, 1994, and October 31, 1993

(In thousands except for per-share amounts)	1995	1994	1993
Sales	$581,444	$506,692	$461,557
Operating costs and expenses:			
Cost of sales	245,587	212,866	191,575
Selling and administrative expenses	251,913	219,422	202,608
Operating profit	83,944	74,404	67,374
Other income (expense):			
Interest expense	(4,553)	(4,392)	(6,426)
Interest and investment income	777	866	1,110
Other—net	474	(20)	190
	(3,302)	(3,546)	(5,126)
Income before income taxes and cumulative effect of accounting changes	80,642	70,858	62,248
Income taxes:			
Current	32,844	28,406	23,198
Deferred	(4,878)	(4,202)	(1,725)
	27,966	24,204	21,473
Income before cumulative effect of accounting changes	52,676	46,654	40,775
Cumulative effect of accounting changes	—	—	(4,784)
Net income	$ 52,676	$ 46,654	$ 35,991

Consolidated Balance Sheet, October 29, 1995 and October 30, 1994 (in Part)

(In thousands)	1995	1994
Assets		
Total current assets	$285,941	$250,307
Property, plant, and equipment, net	99,499	88,655
Intangible assets—net	31,768	29,900
Deferred income taxes	11,108	7,583
Other assets	6,394	4,499
Total assets	$434,710	$380,944

(In thousands)	1995	1994
Liabilities and Shareholders' Equity		
Total current liabilities	$155,379	$123,311
Long-term debt	12,663	15,212
Obligations under capital leases	4,471	4,042
Other liabilities	30,867	25,955
Total shareholders' equity	231,330	212,424
Total liabilities and shareholders' equity	$434,710	$380,944

Note 7. Leases

The Company has lease commitments expiring at various dates, principally for warehouse and office space, automobiles, and office equipment. Most leases contain renewal options and some contain purchase options.

The Company has an operating lease for office and manufacturing space owned by a partnership in which the Company is a partner. The lease ends in 2010 and contains a renewal option and an option to purchase the property at fair market value in 2000. Monthly rentals range from $57,000 to $98,000 and approximate market rates.

Rent expense for all operating leases was approximately $10,581,000 in 1995, $9,103,000 in 1994, and $8,740,000 in 1993.

Assets held under capitalized leases are included in property, plant, and equipment as follows:

	1995	1994
	(In thousands)	
Transportation equipment	$11,522	$ 9,797
Other	2,526	3,347
Total capitalized leases	14,048	13,144
Accumulated amortization	(6,078)	(5,852)
Net capitalized leases	$ 7,970	$ 7,292

At October 29, 1995, future minimum lease payments under noncancelable capitalized and operating leases are as follows:

	Capitalized Leases	Operating Leases
	(In thousands)	
Fiscal year ending:	$ 4,844	$ 9,092
1996	3,678	7,458
1997	2,048	5,716
1998	329	2,948
1999	23	2,557
Later years	18	14,348
Total minimum lease payments	10,940	$42,119
Less: Amount representing executory costs	1,321	
Net minimum lease payments	9,619	
Less: Amount representing interest	1,642	
Present value of net minimum lease payments	7,977	
Less: Current portion	3,506	
Long-term obligations at October 29, 1995	$ 4,471	

Required   a. Compute the following ratios for 1995:
1. Times interest earned
2. Fixed charge coverage
3. Debt ratio
4. Debt/equity ratio

b. Compute the debt ratio and the debt/equity ratio, considering operating leases.

c. Give your opinion of the significance of considering operating leases in the debt ratio and the debt/equity ratio.

CASE 8-4   Consider These Contingencies

Union Texas Petroleum Holdings, Inc. reported total revenues of $876,029,000, $769,595,000, and $696,663,000 in 1995, 1994, and 1993, respectively. Total assets at the end of 1995 were $1,836,818,000.

Footnote 15 of its 1995 annual report (10-K) follows:

Note 15. Contingencies

The Company and its subsidiaries and related companies are named defendants in a number of lawsuits and named parties in numerous governmental proceedings arising in the ordinary course of business.

While the outcome of such contingencies, lawsuits, or other proceedings against the Company cannot be predicted with certainty, management expects that such liability, to the extent not provided for through insurance or otherwise, will not have a material adverse effect on the financial statements of the Company.

Required   Discuss how to incorporate the contingency footnote into an analysis of Union Texas Petroleum.

CASE 8-5   Insight on Pensions and Postretirement Benefits

Fluor Corporation had total revenues of $9,301,384,000, $8,485,267,000 and $7,850,169,000 in 1995, 1994, and 1993, respectively. Total net earnings were $231,768,000, $192,399,000, and $166,800,000 in 1995, 1994, and 1993, respectively. Total assets were $3,228,906,000 and $2,824,768,000 at the year ended October 31, 1995, and 1994, respectively.

A footnote from the 1995 annual report follows:

Retirement Benefits

The company sponsors contributory and noncontributory defined contribution retirement and defined benefit pension plans for eligible employees. Contributions to defined contribution retirement plans are based on a percentage of the employee's compensation. Expense recognized for these plans of $69 million in 1995 and $67 million in both 1994 and 1993 is primarily related to domestic engineering and construction operations. Contributions to defined benefit pension plans are generally at the minimum annual amount required by applicable regulations. Payments to retired employees under these plans are generally based upon length of service and/or a percentage of qualifying compensation. The defined benefit pension plans are primarily related to international engineering and construction operations, U.S. craft employees and coal operations. Net periodic pension income for defined benefit pension plans includes the following components:

Dollars in thousands/Year Ended October 31	1995	1994	1993
Service cost incurred during the period	$ 12,385	$ 14,310	$ 11,528
Interest cost on projected benefit obligation	21,578	20,275	18,494
Income and gains on assets invested	(50,776)	(7,907)	(74,228)
Net amortization and deferral	11,198	(34,255)	39,295
Net periodic pension income	$ (5,615)	$ (7,577)	$ (4,911)

The following assumptions were used in the determination of net periodic cost:

Year Ended October 31	1995	1994	1993
Discount rates	7.75-9.25%	7.0-8.0%	8.5-9.5%
Rates of increase in compensation levels	4.0-6.25%	3.5-5.0%	5.0-6.0%
Expected long-term rates of return on assets	6.75-10.25%	6.0-10.0%	7.5-10.0%

The following table sets forth the funded status of the defined benefit pension plans:

Dollars in thousands/At October 31	1995	1994
Actuarial present value of benefit obligations:		
Vested benefit obligation	$ 253,444	$ 212,011
Nonvested benefit obligation	9,708	10,433
Accumulated benefit obligation	263,152	222,444
Plan assets at fair value (primarily listed stocks and bonds)	427,145	392,129
Projected benefit obligation	(307,759)	(263,038)
Plan assets in excess of projected benefit obligation	119,386	129,091
Unrecognized net loss (gain)	1,962	(13,682)
Unrecognized net asset at implementation	(18,590)	(20,640)
Pension asset recognized in the consolidated balance sheet	$ 102,758	$ 94,769

Amounts shown above at October 31, 1995 and 1994 exclude the projected benefit obligation of $117 million and $109 million, respectively, and an equal amount of associated plan assets relating to discontinued operations.

In recognition of the current interest rate environment, as of October 31, 1995, the company adjusted the discount rates used in the determination of its benefit obligations to 6.75-8.5 percent, the expected long-term rates of return to 5.75-9.5 percent, and the rates of salary increases to 3.25-5.5 percent.

Massey Coal Company ("Massey") participates in multiemployer defined benefit pension plans for its union employees. Pension expense related to these plans approximated $.5 million in each of the years ended October 31, 1995, 1994, and 1993. Under the Coal Industry Retiree Health Benefits Act of 1992, Massey is required to fund medical and death benefits of certain beneficiaries. Massey's obligation under the Act is estimated to aggregate $47 million at October 31, 1995, which will be recognized as expense as payments are assessed. The expense recorded for such benefits approximated $2 million for the year ended October 31, 1995, and $4 million in each of the years ended October 31, 1994 and 1993.

In addition to the company's defined benefit pension plans, the company and certain of its subsidiaries provide health care and life insurance benefits for certain retired employees. The health care and life insurance plans are generally contributory, with retiree contributions adjusted annually. Service costs are accrued currently.

The accumulated postretirement benefit obligation at October 31, 1995 and 1994 was determined in accordance with the current terms of the company's health care plans, together with relevant actuarial assumptions and health care cost trend rates projected at annual rates ranging from 11.3 percent in 1996 down to 5 percent in 2005 and beyond. The effect of a one-percent annual increase in these assumed cost trend rates would increase the accumulated postretirement benefit obligation and the aggregate of the annual service and interest costs by approximately 11 percent.

Net periodic postretirement benefit cost includes the following components:

Dollars in thousands/Year Ended October 31	1995	1994	1993
Service cost incurred during the period	$1,172	$1,352	$1,017
Interest cost on accumulated postretirement benefit obligation	4,899	4,153	4,633
Net periodic postretirement benefit cost	$6,071	$5,505	$5,650

The following table sets forth the plans' funded status and accumulated postretirement benefit obligation which has been fully accrued in the company's consolidated balance sheet:

Dollars in thousands/At October 31	1995	1994
Accumulated postretirement benefit obligation:		
Retirees	$51,787	$44,517
Fully eligible active participants	4,821	4,853
Other active plan participants	14,705	10,713
Unrecognized gain (loss)	(6,426)	3,667
Accrued postretirement benefit obligation	$64,887	$63,750

The discount rate used in determining the accumulated postretirement benefit obligation was 7.5 percent and 8.5 percent at October 31, 1995 and 1994, respectively: The above information does not include amounts related to benefit plans applicable to employees associated with certain contracts with the U.S. Department of Energy because the company is not responsible for the current or future funded status of these plans.

Required   a.   Determine the total pension cost (income) for 1995. Include contributory and noncontributory defined contribution retirement and defined benefit pension plans for eligible employees. Also include multiemployer defined benefit pension plans.

b.   Why is there income in 1995 relating to defined benefit pension plans?

c.   For defined benefit pension plans, compare the accumulated benefit obligation with the plan assets at fair value at October 31, 1995. Comment.

d.   For defined benefit pension plans, compare the projected benefit obligation with the plan assets at fair value at October 31, 1995.

e.   For defined benefit pension plans, what was the percentage of accumulated benefit obligation vested at October 31, 1995?

f.   For defined benefit pension plans, the discount rate used increased between 1994 and 1995. How did this influence the accumulated benefit obligation and the projected benefit obligation?

g.   For defined benefit pension plans, the assumption for rates of increase in compensation levels increased between 1994 and 1995. How did this influence the accumulated benefit obligation?

h.   For defined benefit pension plans, is the unrecognized transition amount an asset or liability? What impact will this have on future pension cost?

i.   Comment on significant aspects of the multiemployer defined benefit pension plans.

j.   For health care benefits, the accrued postretirement benefit obligation at October 31, 1995, was $64,887,000. Does this amount appear to be significant? (Give reasons for your opinion.)

k.   The company, to some extent, has protected itself from runaway future costs for health care and life insurance for retirees. How was this accomplished?

CASE 8-6   Retirement Plans Revisited

Lands' End, Inc. & Subsidiaries
Consolidated Statements of Operations

(In thousands, except per-share data)	For the Period Ended		
	February 2, 1996	January 27, 1995	January 28, 1994
Net sales	$1,031,548	$992,106	$869,975
Cost of sales	588,017	571,265	514,052
Gross profit	443,531	420,841	355,923
Selling, general, and administrative expenses	(392,484)	(357,516)	(285,513)
Charges from sale of subsidiary	(1,882)	(3,500)	—
Income from operations	49,165	59,825	70,410
Other income (expense):			
Interest expense	(2,771)	(1,769)	(359)
Interest income	253	307	346
Other	4,278	1,300	(527)
Total other income (expense), net	1,760	(162)	(540)
Income before income taxes and cumulative effect of change in accounting	50,925	59,663	69,870
Income tax provision	20,370	23,567	27,441
Net income before cumulative effect of change in accounting	30,555	36,096	42,429
Cumulative effect of change in accounting for income taxes	—	—	1,300
Net income	$ 30,555	$ 36,096	$ 43,729
Net income per share before cumulative effect of change in accounting	$ 0.89	$ 1.03	$ 1.18
Cumulative per share effect of change in accounting	—	—	0.04
Net income per share	$ 0.89	$ 1.03	$ 1.22

Lands' End, Inc. & Subsidiaries
Consolidated Balance Sheets (in Part)

(In thousands)	February 2, 1996	January 27, 1995
Total assets	$323,497	$297,612

A footnote from Lands' End 1996 annual report follows:

Note 7. Retirement Plan

The company has a retirement plan which covers most regular employees and provides for annual contributions at the discretion of the board of directors. Also included in the plan is a 401(k) feature that allows employees to make contributions, and the company matches a portion of those contributions. Total expense provided under this plan was $3.2 million, $3.5 million, and $3.7 million for the years ended February 2, 1996, January 27, 1995, and January 28, 1994, respectively.

As of October 1, 1995, the "Lands' End, Inc. Retirement Plan" was amended to allow certain participants to invest their elective contributions, employer matching contributions, and profit sharing contributions in a "Lands' End, Inc. Stock Fund" established primarily for investing in common stock of the company at the fair market value.

Required
a. In general, what type of plan does Lands' End have?
b. Give your opinion as to the materiality of the pension plans.
c. Give your opinion as to the control of pension expense.

CASE 8-7   Fair Value of Financial Instruments

Fluor Corporation included the following footnote in its 1995 annual report:

Fair Value of Financial Instruments

The estimated fair value of the company's financial instruments is as follows:

Dollars in thousands/At October 31	Carrying Amount	1995 Fair Value	Carrying Amount	1994 Fair Value
Assets				
Cash and cash equivalents	$292,934	$292,934	$374,468	$374,468
Marketable securities	137,758	137,758	117,618	119,555
Notes receivable including				
noncurrent portion	83,515	86,769	104,117	105,088
Long-term investments	30,990	32,127	15,811	16,616
Liabilities				
Commercial paper and notes payable	29,937	29,937	19,957	19,957
Long-term debt including current				
portion	27,248	28,420	62,367	64,405
Other noncurrent financial liabilities	2,572	2,572	2,691	2,691
Off-balance sheet financial instruments				
Foreign currency contract obligations	—	(2,146)	—	219
Letters of credit	—	572	—	740
Line of credit	—	997	—	1,384

Fair values were determined as follows:

The carrying amounts of cash and cash equivalents, short-term notes receivable, commercial paper and notes payable approximates fair value because of the short-term maturity of these instruments.

Marketable securities and long-term investments are based on quoted market prices for these or similar instruments.

Long-term notes receivable are estimated by discounting future cash flows using the current rates at which similar loans would be made to borrowers with similar credit ratings.

The fair value of long-term debt, including current portion, is estimated based on quoted market prices for the same or similar issues or on the current rates offered to the company for debt of the same maturities.

Other noncurrent financial liabilities consist primarily of deferred payments, for which cost approximates fair value.

Foreign currency contract obligations are estimated by obtaining quotes from brokers.

Letters of credit and line of credit amounts are based on fees currently charged for similar agreements or on the estimated cost to terminate or settle the obligations.

Additional information: **(Absolute dollars)**

	October 31, 1995	October 31, 1994
Total assets	$3,228,906,000	$2,824,768,000

	Year Ended October 31		
	1995	1994	1993
Earnings before taxes	$362,214,000	$303,299,000	$242,200,000

Required   Give your opinion as to the fair value of financial instruments in relation to carrying amount. Develop data to support your opinion.

Endnotes

1 "Pension Funds Boost Projected Returns Even Though Experts Take a Dim View," *The Wall Street Journal* (October 23, 1990), pp. C1, C12.

2 *Accounting Trends & Techniques* (Jersey City, NJ: American Institute of Certified Public Accountants, 1995), p. 342.

3 *Accounting Trends & Techniques*, p. 342.

4 *Accounting Trends & Techniques*, p. 342.

5 *Statement of Financial Accounting Standards No. 5*, "Accounting for Contingencies" (Stamford, CT: Financial Accounting Standards Board, 1975), paragraph 1.

6 *Statement of Financial Accounting Standards No. 5*, paragraph 8.

7 *Statement of Financial Accounting Standards No. 5*, paragraph 17.

8 *Statement of Financial Accounting Standards No. 105*, "Disclosure of Information About Financial Instruments with Off-Balance-Sheet Risk and Financial Instruments with Concentrations of Credit Risk" (Stamford, CT: Financial Accounting Standards Board, 1990), paragraph 17.

9 *Statement of Financial Accounting Standards No. 105*, paragraph 18.

10 *Statement of Financial Accounting Standards No. 107*, "Disclosure About Fair Value of Financial Instruments" (Stamford, CT: Financial Accounting Standards Board, 1991), paragraph 10.

9   Analysis of Profitability

PROFITABILITY IS THE ABILITY OF THE firm to generate earnings. Analysis of profit is of vital concern to stockholders since they derive revenue in the form of dividends. Further, increased profits can cause a rise in market price, leading to capital gains. Profits are also important to creditors because profits are one source of funds for debt coverage. Management uses profit as a performance measure.

In profitability analysis, absolute figures are less meaningful than earnings measured as a percentage of a number of bases: the productive assets, the owners' and creditors' capital employed, and sales.

PROFITABILITY MEASURES

The income statement contains several figures that might be used in profitability analysis. In general, the primary financial analysis of profit ratios should include only the types of income arising from the normal operations of the business. This excludes the following:

1. Discontinued operations
2. Extraordinary items
3. Cumulative effects of changes in accounting principles

Exhibit 4-3 in Chapter 4 illustrates an income statement with these items. Review this section on analysis in Chapter 4 before continuing with the discussion of profitability. Equity in earnings of nonconsolidated subsidiaries and the minority share of earnings are also important to the analysis of profitability. Chapter 4 covers these items, and Exhibits 4-5 and 4-9 illustrate the concepts.

Trend analysis should also consider only income arising from the normal operations of the business. An illustration will help justify this reasoning. XYZ Corporation had net income of $100,000 in Year 1 and $150,000 in Year 2. Year 2, however, included an extraordinary gain of $60,000. In reality, XYZ suffered a drop in profit from operating income.

Net Profit Margin

A commonly used profit measure is return on sales, often termed net profit margin. If a company reports that it earned 6% last year, this statistic usually means that its profit was 6% of sales. Calculate **net profit margin** as follows:

$$\text{Net Profit Margin} = \frac{\text{Net Income Before Minority Share of Earnings and Nonrecurring Items}}{\text{Net Sales}}$$

This ratio gives a measure of net income dollars generated by each dollar of sales. While it is desirable for this ratio to be high, competitive forces within an industry, economic conditions, use of debt financing, and operating characteristics such as high fixed costs will cause the net profit margin to vary between and within industries.

Exhibit 9-1 shows the net profit margin using the 1995 and 1994 figures for Cooper Tire & Rubber Company. This analysis shows that Cooper's net profit margin improved substantially.

Several refinements to the net profit margin ratio can make it more accurate than the ratio computation in this book. Numerator refinements include removing equity earnings from investments carried on the equity method and removing "other income" and "other expense" items from net income. These items do not relate to net sales (denominator). Therefore, they can cause a distortion in the net profit margin.

This book does not adjust the net profit margin ratio for these items because this often requires an advanced understanding of financial statements beyond the level intended. Also, this chapter covers operating income margin, operating asset turnover, and return on operating assets. These ratios provide a look at the firm's operations.

EXHIBIT 9-1 **COOPER TIRE & RUBBER COMPANY**
Net Profit Margin
For the Years Ended December 31, 1995 and 1994

(Dollar amounts in thousands)	1995	1994
Net income [A]	$ 112,820	$ 128,519
Net sales [B]	1,493,622	1,403,243
Net profit margin [A÷B]	7.55%	9.16%

When working the problems in this book, do not remove equity income or "other income" and "other expense" when computing the net profit margin unless otherwise instructed by the problem. In other analyses, if you elect to refine a net profit margin computation by removing equity income, then remove equity income using the gross amount since no tax or an insignificant amount of tax is paid on this income. If you remove "other income" and "other expense" items from net income, remove them net of the firm's tax rate. Both of these are reasonable approximations of the tax effect.

If you do not refine a net profit margin computation by removing equity income, at least observe whether the company has equity income. Equity income distorts the net profit margin on the high side. Substantial equity income results in a substantial distortion.

If you do not refine a net profit margin computation for "other income" and "other expense" items, at least observe whether the company has a net "other income" or a net "other expense." A net "other income" distorts the net profit margin on the high side, while a net "other expense" distorts the profit margin on the low side.

The Cooper statement can be used to illustrate the removal of other income. Exhibit 9-2 shows the net profit margin computed with the other income removed for 1995 and 1994. The adjusted computation results in the 1995 net profit margin being reduced by .16% and the 1994 net profit margin being reduced by .10%. Both of these reductions are likely to be considered immaterial.

EXHIBIT 9-2 **COOPER TIRE & RUBBER COMPANY**
Net Profit Margin (Revised Computation)
For the Years Ended December 31, 1995 and 1994

(Dollar amounts in thousands)	1995	1994
Net income	$ 112,820	$ 128,519
Tax rate:		
Provision for income taxes [A]	67,250	79,600
Income before income taxes [B]	180,070	208,119
Tax rate [A÷B]*	37.35%	38.25%
Other income	3,836	2,282
Other income x (1–tax rate)	2,403	1,409
Net income less net of tax other income [C]	110,417	127,110
Net sales [D]	1,493,622	1,403,243
Adjusted net profit margin [C÷D]	7.39%	9.06%

* The tax rate could also be determined from the income tax footnote.

Total Asset Turnover

Total asset turnover measures the activity of the assets and the ability of the firm to generate sales through the use of the assets. Compute **total asset turnover** as follows:

$$\text{Total Asset Turnover} = \frac{\textbf{Net Sales}}{\textbf{Average Total Assets}}$$

Exhibit 9-3 shows total asset turnover for Cooper for 1995 and 1994. The total asset turnover decreased from 1.45 to 1.37.

The total asset turnover computation has refinements that relate to assets (denominator) but do not relate to net sales (numerator). An example would be the exclusion of investments. This book does not make this refinement.

If the refinements are not made, observe the investment account and other assets that do not relate to net sales. The presence of these accounts distorts the total asset turnover on the low side (actual turnover is better than the computation indicates).

Return on Assets

Return on assets measures the firm's ability to utilize its assets to create profits by comparing profits with the assets that generate the profits. Compute the **return on assets** as follows:

$$\text{Return on Assets} = \frac{\textbf{Net Income Before Minority Share of Earnings and Nonrecurring Items}}{\textbf{Average Total Assets}}$$

EXHIBIT 9-3 **COOPER TIRE & RUBBER COMPANY**
Total Asset Turnover
For the Years Ended December 31, 1995 and 1994

(Dollar amounts in thousands)	1995	1994
Net sales [A]	$1,493,622	$1,403,243
Average total assets:		
Beginning of year	$1,039,731	$ 889,584
End of year	1,143,701	1,039,731
Total	2,183,432	1,929,315
Average [B]	$1,091,716	$ 964,658
Total asset turnover [A÷B]	1.37 times per year	1.45 times per year

Exhibit 9-4 shows the 1995 and 1994 return on assets for Cooper. The return on total assets for Cooper decreased slightly in 1995.

Theoretically, the best average would be based on month-end figures, which are not available to the outside user. Computing an average based on beginning and ending figures provides a rough approximation that does not consider the timing of interim changes in assets. Such changes might be related to seasonal factors.

However, even a simple average based on beginning and ending amounts requires two figures. Ratios for two years require three years of balance sheet data. Since an annual report only contains two balance sheets, obtaining the data for averages may be a problem. If so, ending balance sheet figures may be used consistently instead of averages for ratio analysis. Similar comments could be made about other ratios that utilize balance sheet figures.

DuPont Return on Assets

The net profit margin, the total asset turnover, and the return on assets are usually reviewed together because of the direct influence that the net profit margin and the total asset turnover have on return on assets. This book reviews these ratios together. When these ratios are reviewed together, it is called the DuPont return on assets.

The rate of return on assets can be broken down into two component ratios: the net profit margin and the total asset turnover. These ratios allow for improved analysis of changes in the return on assets percentage. E. I. DuPont de Nemours and Company developed this method of separating the rate of return ratio into its component parts. Compute the **DuPont return on assets** as follows:

$$\frac{\text{Net Income Before Minority Share of Earnings and Nonrecurring Items}}{\text{Average Total Assets}} = \frac{\text{Net Income Before Minority Share of Earnings and Nonrecurring Items}}{\text{Net Sales}} \times \frac{\text{Net Sales}}{\text{Average Total Assets}}$$

EXHIBIT 9-4 COOPER TIRE & RUBBER COMPANY
Return on Assets
For the Years Ended December 31, 1995 and 1994

(Dollar amounts in thousands)	1995	1994
Net income [A]	$ 112,820	$ 128,519
Average total assets [B]	1,091,716	964,658
Return on assets [A÷B]	10.33%	13.32%

Exhibit 9-5 shows the DuPont return on assets for Cooper for 1995 and 1994. Separating the ratio into the two elements allows for discussion of the causes for the increase in the percentage of return on assets. Exhibit 9-5 indicates that Cooper's return on assets decreased because of a decrease in net profit margin and a decrease in total asset turnover.

Interpretation Through DuPont Analysis

The following examples help to illustrate the use of this analysis:

	Return on Assets	=	Net Profit Margin	x	Total Asset Turnover
Year 1	10%	=	5%	x	2.0
Year 2	10%	=	4%	x	2.5

Example 1 shows how a more efficient use of assets can offset rising costs such as labor or materials.

	Return on Assets	=	Net Profit Margin	x	Total Asset Turnover
Firm A					
Year 1	10%	=	4.0%	x	2.5
Year 2	8%	=	4.0%	x	2.0
Firm B					
Year 1	10%	=	4.0%	x	2.5
Year 2	8%	=	3.2%	x	2.5

OIL   20%.   =   20%   x   1x

SUPERMARKET   20%   =   2%   x   10x

EXHIBIT 9-5 **COOPER TIRE & RUBBER COMPANY**
DuPont Return on Assets
For the Years Ended December 31, 1995 and 1994

Return on Assets*		=	Net Profit Margin	x	Total Asset Turnover
1995	10.33%	=	7.55%	x	1.37
1994	13.32%	=	9.16%	x	1.45

* There are some minor differences due to rounding.

Example 2 shows how a trend in return on assets can be better explained through the breakdown into two ratios. The two firms have identical returns on assets. Further analysis shows that Firm A suffers from a slowdown in asset turnover. It is generating fewer sales for the assets invested. Firm B suffers from a reduction in the net profit margin. It is generating less profit per dollar of sales.

Variation in Computation of DuPont Ratios Considering Only Operating Accounts

It is often argued that only operating assets should be considered in the return on asset calculation. Operating assets exclude construction in progress, long-term investments, intangibles, and the other assets category from total assets. Similarly, operating income—the profit generated by manufacturing, merchandising, or service functions—that equals net sales less the cost of sales and operating expenses should also be used instead of net income.

The operating ratios may give significantly different results from net earnings ratios if a firm has large amounts of nonoperating assets. For example, if a firm has heavy investments in unconsolidated subsidiaries, and if these subsidiaries pay large dividends, then other income may be a large portion of net earnings. The profit picture may not be as good if these earnings from other sources are eliminated by analyzing operating ratios. Since earnings from investments are not derived from the primary business, the lower profit figures that represent normal earnings will typically be more meaningful.

The DuPont analysis, considering only operating accounts, requires a computation of operating income and operating assets. Exhibit 9-6, page 392, shows the computations of operating income and operating assets for Cooper. This includes operating income for 1995 and 1994 and operating assets for 1995, 1994, and 1993.

Operating Income Margin

The **operating income margin** includes only operating income in the numerator. Compute the operating income margin as follows:

$$\text{Operating Income Margin} = \frac{\text{Operating Income}}{\text{Net Sales}}$$

Exhibit 9-7, page 392, indicates the operating income margin for Cooper in 1995 and 1994. It shows a significant decrease in 1995 in the operating income margin percentage.

EXHIBIT 9-6 COOPER TIRE & RUBBER COMPANY
Operating Income and Operating Assets
For the Years Ended December 31, 1995 and 1994

(Dollar amounts in thousands)	1995	1994	
Operating income:			
Net sales [A]	$1,493,622	$1,403,243	
Less operating expenses:			
Cost of products sold	1,242,895	1,125,978	
Selling, general, and administrative	73,796	68,748	
Total operating expenses [B]	$1,316,691	$1,194,726	
Operating income [A–B]	$ 176,931	$ 208,517	

	1995	1994	1993
Operating assets:			
Total assets [A]	$1,143,701	$1,039,731	$ 889,584
Less: Investments and			
other assets [B]	(34,241)	(35,419)	(29,618)
Operating assets [A–B]	$1,109,460	$1,004,312	$ 859,966

EXHIBIT 9-7 COOPER TIRE & RUBBER COMPANY
Operating Income Margin
For the Years Ended December 31, 1995 and 1994

(Dollar amounts in thousands)	1995	1994
Operating income [A]	$ 176,931	$ 208,517
Net sales [B]	1,493,622	1,403,243
Operating income margin [A÷B]	11.85%	14.86%

Operating Asset Turnover

This ratio measures the ability of operating assets to generate sales dollars. Compute **operating asset turnover** as follows:

$$\text{Operating Asset Turnover} = \frac{\textbf{Net Sales}}{\textbf{Average Operating Assets}}$$

Exhibit 9-8 shows the operating asset turnover for Cooper in 1995 and 1994. It indicates a decrease from 1.51 to 1.41. These are similar but slightly improved figures compared to those computed for the total asset turnover.

Return on Operating Assets

Adjusting for nonoperating items results in the following formula for **return on operating assets:**

$$\text{Return on Operating Assets} = \frac{\text{Operating Income}}{\text{Average Operating Assets}}$$

Exhibit 9-9 shows the return on operating assets for Cooper for 1995 and 1994. It indicates a decrease in the return on operating assets from 22.37% in 1994 to 16.74% in 1995.

EXHIBIT 9-8 **COOPER TIRE & RUBBER COMPANY**
Operating Asset Turnover
For the Years Ended December 31, 1995 and 1994

(Dollar amounts in thousands)	1995	1994
Net sales [A]	$ 1,493,622	$ 1,403,243
Average operating assets:		
Beginning of year	$ 1,004,312	$ 859,966
End of year	1,109,460	1,004,312
Total	2,113,772	1,864,278
Average [B]	$ 1,056,886	$ 932,139
Operating asset turnover [A÷B]	1.41 times per year	1.51 times per year

EXHIBIT 9-9 **COOPER TIRE & RUBBER COMPANY**
Return on Operating Assets
For the Years Ended December 31, 1995 and 1994

(Dollar amounts in thousands)	1995	1994
Operating income [A]	$ 176,931	$208,517
Average operating assets [B]	1,056,886	932,139
Return on operating assets [A÷B]	16.74%	22.37%

The return on operating assets can be viewed in terms of the DuPont analysis that follows:

Op. II Margin x Operat. asset Turn

Oper. ROA =

DuPont Return on Operating Assets	=	**Operating Income Margin**	x	**Operating Asset Turnover**

Exhibit 9-10 indicates the DuPont return on operating assets for Cooper for 1995 and 1994. This figure supports the conclusion that a decrease in operating income margin and a decrease in operating asset turnover both caused the decrease in return on operating assets.

Sales to Fixed Assets

This ratio measures the firm's ability to make productive use of its property, plant, and equipment by generating sales dollars. Since construction in progress does not contribute to current sales, it should be excluded from net fixed assets. This ratio may not be meaningful because of old fixed assets or a labor-intensive industry. In these cases, the ratio is substantially higher because of the low fixed asset base. Compute the **sales to fixed assets ratio** as follows:

$$\text{Sales to Fixed Assets} = \frac{\text{Net Sales}}{\begin{array}{c}\text{Average Net Fixed Assets}\\ \text{(Exclude Construction in Progress)}\end{array}}$$

Fixed Asset Turnover

Exhibit 9-11 shows the sales to fixed assets ratio for Cooper for 1995 and 1994. It declined substantially between 1994 and 1995. Analysts interested in Cooper should monitor this ratio closely in the future. It appears that sales increases have not kept pace with net fixed assets increases.

EXHIBIT 9-10 **COOPER TIRE & RUBBER COMPANY**
DuPont Analysis with Operating Accounts
For the Years Ended December 31, 1995 and 1994

	Return on Operating Assets*	=	Operating Income Margin	x	Operating Asset Turnover
1995:	16.74%	=	11.85%	x	1.41
1994:	22.37%	=	14.86%	x	1.51

* There are some minor differences due to rounding.

EXHIBIT 9-11 **COOPER TIRE & RUBBER COMPANY**
Sales to Fixed Assets
For the Years Ended December 31, 1995 and 1994

(Dollar amounts in thousands)	1995	1994
Net sales [A]	$ 1,493,622	$ 1,403,243
Net fixed assets:		
Beginning of year	$ 549,601	$ 527,949
End of year	678,876	549,601
Total	1,228,477	1,077,550
Average [B]	$ 614,239	$ 538,775
Sales to fixed assets [A÷B]	2.43 times per year	2.60 times per year

Return on Investment (ROI)

The **return on investment** applies to ratios measuring the income earned on the invested capital. These types of measures are widely used to evaluate enterprise performance. Since return on investment is a type of return on capital, this ratio measures the ability of the firm to reward those who provide long-term funds and to attract providers of future funds. Compute the return on investment as follows:

$$\text{Return on Investment} = \frac{\text{Net Income Before Minority Share of Earnings and Nonrecurring Items} + [(\text{Interest Expense}) \times (1 - \text{Tax Rate})]}{\text{Average (Long-Term Liabilities + Equity)}}$$

This ratio evaluates the earnings performance of the firm without regard to the way the investment is financed. It measures the earnings on investment and indicates how well the firm utilizes its asset base. Exhibit 9-12, page 396, shows the return on investment for Cooper for 1995 and 1994. From 1994 to 1995, this ratio decreased substantially, from 15.77% to 12.09%.

Return on Total Equity

The **return on total equity** measures the return to both common and preferred shareholders. Compute the return on total equity as follows:

$$\text{Return on Total Equity} = \frac{\text{Net Income Before Nonrecurring Items} - \text{Dividends on Redeemable Preferred Stock}}{\text{Average Total Equity}}$$

EXHIBIT 9-12   COOPER TIRE & RUBBER COMPANY
Return on Investment
For the Years Ended December 31, 1995 and 1994

(Dollar amounts in thousands)	1995	1994
Interest expense [A]	$ 697	$ 2,680
Net income	112,820	128,519
Tax rate (see footnote)	37.30%	38.20%
1–tax rate [B]	62.70%	61.80%
(Interest expense) x (1–tax rate) [AxB]	437	1,656
Net income + [(interest expense) x (1–tax rate)] [C]	$ 113,257	$ 130,175
Long-term liabilities and stockholders' equity:		
Beginning of year:		
Long-term liabilities	$ 226,046	$ 212,238
Total stockholders' equity	662,077	550,186
End of year:		
Long-term liabilities	236,534	226,046
Total stockholders' equity	748,799	662,077
Total	1,873,456	1,650,547
Average [D]	$ 936,728	$ 825,274
Return on investment [C÷D]	12.09%	15.77%

Preferred stock subject to mandatory redemption is termed **redeemable preferred stock**. The SEC requires that redeemable preferred stock be categorized separately from other equity securities because the shares must be redeemed in a manner similar to the repayment of debt. Most companies do not have redeemable preferred stock. For those firms that do, the redeemable preferred is excluded from total equity and considered part of debt. Similarly, the dividends must be deducted from income. They have not been deducted on the income statement, despite the similarity to debt and interest, because they are still dividends and payable only if declared.

Exhibit 9-13 shows the return on total equity for Cooper for 1995 and 1994. It decreased substantially from 21.20% in 1994 to 15.99% in 1995.

Return on Common Equity

This ratio measures the return to the common shareholder, the residual owner. Compute the **return on common equity** as follows:

$$\text{Return on Common Equity} = \frac{\text{Net Income Before Nonrecurring Items} - \text{Preferred Dividends}}{\text{Average Common Equity}}$$

EXHIBIT 9-13   **COOPER TIRE & RUBBER COMPANY**
Return on Total Equity
For the Years Ended December 31, 1995 and 1994

(Dollar amounts in thousands)	1995	1994
Net income [A]	$ 112,820	$ 128,519
Total equity:		
Beginning of year	$ 662,077	$ 550,186
End of year	748,799	662,077
Total	1,410,876	1,212,263
Average [B]	$ 705,438	$ 606,132
Return on total equity [A÷B]	15.99%	21.20%

The net income appears on the income statement. The preferred dividends appear most commonly on the statement of retained earnings. Common equity includes common capital stock and retained earnings less common treasury stock. This amount equals total equity minus the preferred capital and any minority interest included in the equity section.

Exhibit 9-14, page 398, shows the return on common equity for Cooper for 1995 and 1994. Cooper's return on common equity is the same as its return on total equity because it did not have preferred stock.

The Relationship Between Profitability Ratios

Technically, a ratio with a profit figure in the numerator and some type of "supplier of funds" figure in the denominator is a type of return on investment. Another frequently used measure is a variation of the return on total assets. Compute this return on total assets variation as follows:

$$\text{Return on Total Assets Variation} = \frac{\text{Net Income} + \text{Interest Expense}}{\text{Average Total Assets}}$$

This ratio includes the return to all suppliers of funds, both long and short term, by both creditors and investors. It differs from the return on assets ratio previously discussed because it adds back the interest. It differs from the return on investment in that it does not adjust interest for the income tax effect, it includes short-term funds, and it uses the average investment. It will not be discussed or utilized further here because it does not lend itself to DuPont analysis.

EXHIBIT 9-14   COOPER TIRE & RUBBER COMPANY
Return on Common Equity
For the Years Ended December 31, 1995 and 1994

(Dollar amounts in thousands)	1995	1994
Net income	$ 112,820	$ 128,519
Less: Preferred dividends	—	—
Adjusted income [A]	$ 112,820	$ 128,519
Total common equity:		
Beginning of year	$ 662,077	$ 550,186
End of year	748,799	662,077
Total	1,410,876	1,212,263
Average common equity [B]	$ 705,438	$ 606,132
Return on common equity [A÷B]	15.99%	21.20%

Rates of return have been calculated on a variety of bases. The interrelationship between these ratios is of importance in understanding the return to the suppliers of funds. Exhibit 9-15 displays a comparison of profitability measures for Cooper.

The return on assets measures the return to all providers of funds since total assets equal total liabilities and equity. This ratio will usually be the lowest since it includes all of the assets. The return on investment measures the return to long-term suppliers of funds, and it is usually higher than the return on assets because of the relatively low amount paid for short-term funds. This is especially true of accounts payable.

The rate of return on total equity will usually be higher than the return on investment because the rate of return on equity measures return only to

EXHIBIT 9-15   COOPER TIRE & RUBBER COMPANY
Comparison of Profitability Measures
For the Years Ended December 31, 1995 and 1994

	1995	1994
Return on assets	10.33%	13.32%
Return on investment	12.09%	15.77%
Return on total equity	15.99%	21.20%
Return on common equity	15.99%	21.20%

the shareholders. A profitable use of long-term sources of funds from creditors provides a higher return to shareholders than the return on investment. In other words, the profits made on long-term funds from creditors were greater than the interest paid for the use of the funds.

Common shareholders absorb the greatest degree of risk and, therefore, usually earn the highest return. For the return on common equity to be the highest, the return on funds obtained from preferred stockholders must be more than the funds paid to the preferred stockholders.

Gross Profit Margin

Gross profit equals the difference between net sales revenue and the cost of goods sold. The cost of goods sold is the beginning inventory plus purchases minus the ending inventory. It is the cost of the product sold during the period. Changes in the cost of goods sold, which represents such a large expense for merchandising and manufacturing firms, can have a substantial impact on the profit for the period. Comparing gross profit to net sales is termed the **gross profit margin.** Compute the gross profit margin as follows:

$$\text{Gross Profit Margin} = \frac{\text{Gross Profit}}{\text{Net Sales}}$$

This ratio should then be compared with industry data or analyzed by trend analysis. Exhibit 9-16 illustrates trend analysis. In this illustration, the gross profit margin has declined substantially over the three-year period. This could be attributable to a number of factors:

1. The cost of buying inventory has increased more rapidly than have selling prices.
2. Selling prices have declined due to competition.

EXHIBIT 9-16
Gross Profit Margin
For the Years Ended December 31, 1996, 1995, and 1994

	1996	1995	1994
Net sales [B]	$ 5,000,000	$ 4,500,000	$ 4,000,000
Less: Cost of goods sold	3,500,000	2,925,000	2,200,000
Gross profit [A]	$ 1,500,000	$ 1,575,000	$ 1,800,000
Gross profit margin [A÷B]	30.00%	35.00%	45.00%

3.   The mix of goods has changed to include more products with lower margins.

4.   Theft is occurring. If sales are not recorded, the cost of goods sold figure in relation to the sales figure is very high. If inventory is being stolen, the ending inventory will be low and the cost of goods sold will be high.

Gross profit margin analysis helps a number of users. Managers budget gross profit levels into their predictions of profitability. Gross profit margins are also used in cost control. Estimations utilizing gross profit margins can determine inventory levels for interim statements in the merchandising industries. Gross profit margins can also be used to estimate inventory involved in insured losses. In addition, gross profit measures are used by auditors and the Internal Revenue Service to judge the accuracy of accounting systems.

Gross profit margin analysis requires an income statement in multiple-step format. Otherwise the gross profit must be computed, which is the case with Cooper. Exhibit 9-17 presents Cooper's gross profit margin, which has decreased over the three-year period.

TRENDS IN PROFITABILITY

Exhibit 9-18 shows profitability trends for manufacturing for the period 1965-1995. Operating profit compared with net sales declined substantially over this period. Net income compared with net sales fluctuated substantially. This ratio recovered in recent years from a low in 1992. In general, there has been a decline in profitability. This decline in profitability probably occurred due to factors such as an increase in competition domestically and internationally. The decline in profitability indicates an increase in the risk of doing business.

SEGMENT REPORTING

Firms frequently operate in more than one line of business. When a firm is diversified in this manner, the results of operations of the individual segments may vary among one another. SFAS No. 14, "Financial Reporting for Segments of a Business Enterprise," requires disclosure on a segmented basis about such factors as sales, operating income, identifiable assets, aggregate depreciation, depletion and amortization, and capital expenditures. This statement also requires data on foreign operations by geographic area, export sales, and major customers. If a company operates predominantly or exclusively in a single industry, that industry must be identified.

EXHIBIT 9-17 **COOPER TIRE & RUBBER COMPANY**
Gross Profit Margin
For the Years Ended December 31, 1995, 1994, and 1993

(Dollar amounts in thousands)	1995	1994	1993
Net sales [B]	$1,493,622	$1,403,243	$1,193,648
Less: Cost of products sold	1,242,895	1,125,978	965,353
Gross profit [A]	$ 250,727	$ 277,265	$ 228,295
Gross profit margin [A÷B]	16.79%	19.76%	19.13%

EXHIBIT 9-18
Trends in Profitability
United States Manufacturing
1965-1995

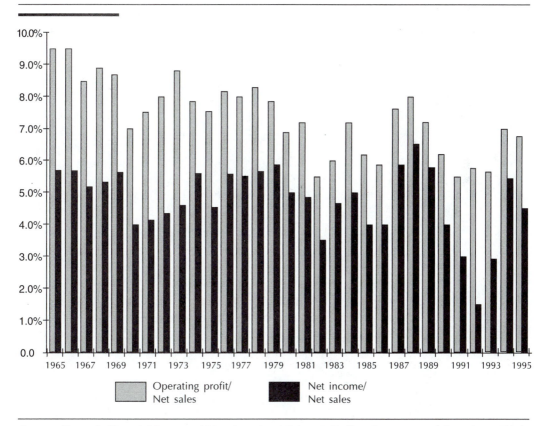

Source: Quarterly Financial Reports of Manufacturing, Mining, & Trading, Department of Commerce. Washington, DC: Government Printing Office.

Segment data can be analyzed both in terms of trends and ratios. Vertical and horizontal common-size analyses can be used for trends. Examples of ratios would be relating profits to sales or identifiable assets.

Segment trends would be of interest to management and investors. The maximum benefits from this type of analysis come when analyzing a non-integrated company in terms of product lines, especially with segments of relatively similar size.

Cooper does not report segment data. This means that it does not operate in more than one line of business or that lines of business beyond the major line are immaterial. The 1995 annual report of Ford Motor Company has been selected to illustrate segment reporting.

Exhibit 9-19 presents partial segment reporting (financial services) for Ford Motor Company for 1995, 1994, and 1993. These data should be

EXHIBIT 9-19 **FORD MOTOR COMPANY**
Segment Information (Note 17 in Part)
Financial Services

(Dollar amounts in millions)	1995	1994	1993
Revenue:			
United States	$ 21,383	$ 17,356	$ 14,102
Europe	3,144	2,336	1,673
All other	2,114	1,610	1,178
Total	$ 26,641	$ 21,302	$ 16,953
Income before income taxes:*			
United States	$ 2,822	$ 2,185	$ 2,311
Europe	493	419	285
All other	224	188	116
Total	$ 3,539	$ 2,792	$ 2,712
Net income:			
United States	$ 1,718	$ 1,119	$ 1,340
Europe	321	218	140
All other	44	58	41
Total	$ 2,083	$ 1,395	$ 1,521
Assets at December 31:			
United States	$ 137,154	$ 124,120	$ 117,290
Europe	20,237	16,507	12,132
All other	13,120	10,356	7,779
Total	$ 170,511	$ 150,983	$ 137,201

* Financial Services activities do not report operating income; income before income taxes is representative of operating income.

reviewed, and consideration should be given to using vertical and horizontal analyses and to computing ratios that appear meaningful. This type of review is illustrated in Exhibits 9-20 and 9-21.

Exhibit 9-20 presents some Ford Motor Company segment information in vertical common-size analysis. Revenue, income before income taxes, net income, and assets in the United States are analyzed in relation to the other segments in 1995, 1994, and 1993. Based on this analysis, the European segment and all other segments did well in 1995 vs. 1993.

A review of Exhibit 9-21 (segment information—ratio analysis), page 404, indicates that income before income taxes to revenue declined substantially from 1993 to 1995 in the United States. Income before income taxes to revenue also declined substantially in Europe. Net income to revenue declined substantially in the United States and all other segments. Net

EXHIBIT 9-20   **FORD MOTOR COMPANY**
Segment Information—Common-Size Analysis
Financial Services for the Years 1995, 1994, and 1993

	1995	1994	1993
Revenue:			
United States	80.26%	81.48%	83.18%
Europe	11.80	10.97	9.87
All other	7.94	7.56	6.95
Total	100.00%	100.00%	100.00%
Income before income taxes:*			
United States	79.74%	78.26%	85.21%
Europe	13.93	15.01	10.51
All other	6.33	6.73	4.28
Total	100.00%	100.00%	100.00%
Net income:			
United States	82.48%	80.22%	88.10%
Europe	15.41	15.63	9.20
All other	2.11	4.16	2.70
Total	100.00%	100.00%	100.00%
Assets at December 31:			
United States	80.44%	82.21%	85.49%
Europe	11.87	10.93	8.84
All other	7.69	6.86	5.67
Total	100.00%	100.00%	100.00%

* Financial Services activities do not report operating income; income before income taxes is representative of operating income.

EXHIBIT 9-21   FORD MOTOR COMPANY
Segment Information—Ratio Analysis
Financial Services for the Years 1995, 1994, and 1993

	1995	1994	1993
Income before income taxes* to revenue:			
United States	13.20%	12.59%	16.39%
Europe	15.68	17.94	17.04
All other	10.60	11.68	9.85
Net income to revenue:			
United States	8.03%	6.45%	9.50%
Europe	10.21	9.33	8.37
All other	2.08	3.60	3.48
Revenue to assets:			
United States	15.59%	13.98%	12.02%
Europe	15.54	14.15	13.79
All other	16.11	15.55	15.14
Income before income taxes* to assets:			
United States	2.06%	1.76%	1.97%
Europe	2.44	2.54	2.35
All other	1.71	1.82	1.49
Net income to assets:			
United States	1.25%	0.90%	1.14%
Europe	1.59	1.32	1.15
All other	0.34	0.56	0.53

* Financial Services activities do not report operating income; income before income taxes is representative of operating income.

income to revenue increased substantially in Europe. Revenue to assets increased substantially in all segments. Income before income taxes to assets increased moderately in all segments. Net income to assets increased moderately in the United States, increased substantially in Europe, and decreased substantially in all other segments.

GAINS AND LOSSES THAT BYPASS THE INCOME STATEMENT

There are a few gains and losses that are not reported on the income statement under GAAP. Some of these items are: (a) gains and losses from prior period adjustments, (b) unrealized declines in the market value of investments, and (c) foreign currency translation adjustments. The prior period adjustments are charged to retained earnings. The unrealized gains or losses in market value of investments and the foreign currency translation gains or losses are set up in separate accounts within stockholders' equity.

Gains and losses that bypass the income statement are potentially very significant. Therefore, the analyst should review the retained earnings account for prior period adjustments and look for separate accounts within stockholders' equity that represent unrealized gains or losses. When finding these items, consider them in your profitability analysis. You may want to change the income figure for the current year and prior years to accommodate these items. This would be done as a supplemental profitability analysis, in addition to your primary analysis.

Prior period adjustments result from certain changes in accounting principles, the realization of income tax benefits of preacquisition operating loss carryforwards of purchased subsidiaries, a change in accounting entity, and corrections of errors in prior periods.

Exhibit 9-22 includes an example of a prior period adjustment for Reeves Industries Inc. Reeves Industries reported that during 1994 the Company determined that the 1986 tax expense was understated by approximately $1,850,000 due to an error in the calculation of the 1986 tax provision.

Exhibit 9-23, page 406, includes an example of a net unrealized loss on noncurrent marketable equity securities. This represented a potential loss of $6,420,000 at December 31, 1995, for Overseas Shipholding Group, Inc. A loss could be recognized in a future income statement if the securities

EXHIBIT 9-22 **REEVES INDUSTRIES INC.**
Prior Period Adjustment
1994 Annual Report

Note 11 (in Part) Retained Earnings

During 1994 the Company determined that the 1986 tax expense was understated by approximately $1,850,000 due to an error in the calculation of the 1986 tax provision. Accordingly, during 1994, the Company recorded an adjustment to retained earnings and income taxes payable of $1,850,000. The adjustment is reflected in the Company's consolidated financial statements as if it occurred on December 31, 1991.

EXHIBIT 9-23   OVERSEAS SHIPHOLDING GROUP, INC.
Shareholders' Equity—Unrealized Loss
Annual Report—1995

(Dollars in thousands)	December 31, 1995	December 31, 1994
Common stock, par value $1 per share:		
Authorized—60,000,000 shares		
Issued—39,590,759 shares	$ 39,591	$ 39,591
Paid-in additional capital	93,687	93,599
Retained Earnings	707,220	737,583
	840,498	870,773
Less: Cost of treasury stock—		
3,363,243 and 3,380,838 shares	49,297	49,491
	791,201	821,282
Less: Net unrealized loss on noncurrent		
marketable equity securities	6,420	11,530
Total shareholders' equity	$784,781	$809,752

are sold, or management declares its intent to sell these securities. If management declares the intent to sell the securities, these investments will be classified under current assets in the future.

Exhibit 9-24 includes a shareholders' equity account that has been used for adjustments resulting from *translation* of foreign currency for the financial statements of Honeywell Inc. It indicates a positive balance of $140,900,000 at the end of 1995.

Most *translation* gains and losses are included in this shareholders' equity account. Thus, fluctuating exchange rates do not impact reported income. The exception is that *translation* gains and losses from a foreign entity that operates in a country experiencing high inflation are reported in the income statement. Exchange gains and losses resulting from foreign currency *transactions* are also included in the income statement.

INTERIM REPORTS    Un-audited

Interim reports are an additional source of information on profitability. These are reports that cover fiscal periods of less than one year. The SEC requires that limited financial data be provided on Form 10-Q. The SEC also

EXHIBIT 9-24   HONEYWELL INC.
Shareholders' Equity—Accumulated Translation Adjustment
Annual Report—1995

(Dollars in millions)	December 31, 1995	December 31, 1994
Common stock—$1.50 par value		
Authorized—250,000,000 shares		
Issued		
1995—188,126,704 shares	$ 282.2	
1994—188,286,000 shares		$ 282.4
Additional paid-in capital	481.3	446.9
Retained earnings	2,805.8	2,600.4
Treasury stock		
1995—61,306,251 shares	(1,650.2)	
1994—61,030,565 shares		(1,576.5)
Accumulated foreign currency translation	140.9	107.4
Pension liability adjustment	(19.9)	(5.9)
	$ 2,040.1	$ 1,854.7

requires that these companies disclose certain quarterly information in notes
to the annual report.

APB Opinion No. 28 provides the guidelines for interim financial reporting. The same reporting principles used for annual reports should be employed for interim reports, with the intent that the interim reporting be an
integral part of the annual report. For interim financial reports, timeliness
of data offsets lack of detail. Some data included are:

1. Income statement amounts:
    a. Sales or gross revenues
    b. Provision for income taxes
    c. Extraordinary items and tax effect
    d. Cumulative effect of an accounting change
    e. Net income
2. Earnings per share
3. Seasonal information
4. Significant changes in income tax provision or estimate
5. Disposal of segments of business and unusual items material to
    the period

6.   Contingent items

7.   Changes in accounting principles or estimates

8.   Significant changes in financial position

Interim reports contain more estimates in the financial data than in the annual reports. Interim reports are also unaudited. For these reasons, they are less reliable than annual reports.

Income tax expense is an example of a figure that can require considerable judgment and estimation for the interim period. The objective with the interim income tax expense is to use an annual effective tax rate, which may require considerable estimation. Some reasons for this are foreign tax credits and the tax effect of losses in an interim period.

Interim statements must disclose the seasonal nature of the activities of the firm. It is also recommended that firms that are seasonal in nature supplement their interim report by including information for twelve-month periods ended at the interim date for the current and preceding years.

Interim statements can help the analyst determine trends and identify trouble areas before the year-end report is available. The information obtained (such as a lower profit margin) may indicate that trouble is brewing.

SUMMARY

Profitability is the ability of a firm to generate earnings. It is measured relative to a number of bases, such as assets, sales, and investment. The ratios related to profitability covered in this chapter are listed below:

$$\text{Net Profit Margin} = \frac{\text{Net Income Before Minority Share of Earnings and Nonrecurring Items}}{\text{Net Sales}}$$

$$\text{Total Asset Turnover} = \frac{\text{Net Sales}}{\text{Average Total Assets}}$$

$$\text{Return on Assets} = \frac{\text{Net Income Before Minority Share of Earnings and Nonrecurring Items}}{\text{Average Total Assets}}$$

DuPont Return on Assets = Net Profit Margin x Total Asset Turnover

$$\text{Operating Income Margin} = \frac{\text{Operating Income}}{\text{Net Sales}}$$

$$\text{Operating Asset Turnover} = \frac{\text{Net Sales}}{\text{Average Operating Assets}}$$

$$\text{Return on Operating Assets} = \frac{\text{Operating Income}}{\text{Average Operating Assets}}$$

$$\begin{array}{c}\text{DuPont Return} \\ \text{on Operating Assets}\end{array} = \begin{array}{c}\text{Operating} \\ \text{Income} \\ \text{Margin}\end{array} \times \begin{array}{c}\text{Operating} \\ \text{Asset} \\ \text{Turnover}\end{array}$$

$$\text{Sales to Fixed Assets} = \frac{\text{Net Sales}}{\begin{array}{c}\text{Average Net Fixed Assets} \\ \text{(Exclude Construction in Progress)}\end{array}}$$

$$\text{Return on Investment} = \frac{\begin{array}{c}\text{Net Income Before Minority Share of} \\ \text{Earnings and Nonrecurring Items +} \\ \text{[(Interest Expense) x (1 - Tax Rate)]}\end{array}}{\text{Average (Long-Term Liabilities + Equity)}}$$

$$\text{Return on Total Equity} = \frac{\begin{array}{c}\text{Net Income Before Nonrecurring Items -} \\ \text{Dividends on Redeemable Preferred Stock}\end{array}}{\text{Average Total Equity}}$$

$$\text{Return on Common Equity} = \frac{\begin{array}{c}\text{Net Income Before Nonrecurring Items -} \\ \text{Preferred Dividends}\end{array}}{\text{Average Common Equity}}$$

$$\text{Gross Profit Margin} = \frac{\text{Gross Profit}}{\text{Net Sales}}$$

QUESTIONS

Q 9-1.   Profits might be compared to sales, assets, or owners' equity. Why might all three bases be used? Will trends in these ratios always move in the same direction?

Q 9-2.   What is the advantage of segregating extraordinary items in the income statement?

Q 9-3.   If profits as a percent of sales decline, what can be said about expenses?

Q 9-4.   Would you expect the profit margin in a quality jewelry store to differ from that of a grocery store? Comment.

Q 9-5.   The ratio return on assets has net income in the numerator and total assets in the denominator. Explain how each part of the ratio could cause return on assets to fall.

Q 9-6.   What is DuPont analysis, and how does it aid in financial analysis?

Q 9-7.   How does operating income differ from net income? How do operating assets differ from total assets? What is the advantage in removing nonoperating items from the DuPont analysis?

Q 9-8.   Why are equity earnings usually greater than cash flow generated from the investment? How can these equity earnings distort profitability analysis?

Q 9-9.   Explain how return on assets could decline, given an increase in net profit margin.

Q 9-10.   How is return on investment different from return on total equity? How does return on total equity differ from return on common equity?

Q 9-11.   What is meant by *return on investment?* What are some of the types of measures for return on investment? Why is the following ratio preferred?

$$\frac{\textbf{Net Income Before Minority Share of Earnings and Nonrecurring Items} + [(\textbf{Interest Expense}) \times (1 - \textbf{Tax Rate})]}{\textbf{Average (Long-Term Debt} + \textbf{Equity})}$$

Why is the interest multiplied by (1 - Tax Rate)?

Q 9-12.   G. Herrich Company and Thomas, Inc. are department stores. For the current year, they reported a net income after tax of $400,000 and $600,000, respectively. Is Thomas, Inc. a more profitable company than G. Herrich Company? Discuss.

Q 9-13.   Since interim reports are not audited, they are not meaningful. Comment.

Q 9-14.   Speculate on why APB Opinion No. 28 does not mandate full financial statements in interim reports.

Q 9-15.   a. Generally accepted accounting principles exclude some gains and losses from the income statement. List three types of gains and losses that are excluded from the income statement.
             b. Discuss the merit of including these items in your profitability analysis.

Q 9-16. Apple Tree Company disclosed an unrealized loss on noncurrent marketable equity securities in stockholders' equity at December 31, 1997, in the amount of $10,000,000. What is the significance of this disclosure?

Q 9-17. Indicate the difference between the reporting of gains and losses from the translation of foreign currency for the financial statements and the reporting of gains and losses resulting from foreign currency transactions.

PROBLEMS

P 9-1. Ahl Enterprise lists the following data for 1996 and 1995:

	1996	1995
Net income	$ 52,500	$ 40,000
Net sales	1,050,000	1,000,000
Average total assets	230,000	200,000
Average common equity	170,000	160,000

Required Calculate the net profit margin, return on assets, total asset turnover, and return on common equity for both years. Comment on the results. (For return on assets and total asset turnover, use end-of-year total assets; for return on common equity, use end-of-year common equity.)

P 9-2. Income statement data for Starr Canning Corporation are as follows:

	1996	1995
Sales	$ 1,400,000	$ 1,200,000
Cost of goods sold	850,000	730,000
Selling expenses	205,000	240,000
General expenses	140,000	100,000
Income tax expense	82,000	50,000

Required a. Prepare an income statement in comparative form, stating each item for both years as a percent of sales (vertical common-size analysis).
b. Comment on the findings in (a).

P 9-3. The balance sheet for Schultz Bone Company at December 31, 1996, had the following account balances:

Total current liabilities (non-interest-bearing)	$ 450,000
Bonds payable, 6% (issued in 1972; due in 2000)	750,000
Preferred stock, 5%, $100 par	300,000
Common stock, $10 par	750,000
Premium on common stock	150,000
Retained earnings	600,000

Income before income tax was $200,000, and income taxes were $80,000 for the current year.

Required   Calculate each of the following:
    a. Return on assets (using ending assets)
    b. Return on total equity (using ending total equity)
    c. Return on common equity (using ending common equity)
    d. Times interest earned

P 9-4.   Revenue and expense data for Vent Molded Plastics and for the plastics industry as a whole are as follows:

	Vent Molded Plastics	Plastics Industry
Sales	$462,000	100.3%
Sales returns	4,500	.3
Cost of goods sold	330,000	67.1
Selling expenses	43,000	10.1
General expenses	32,000	7.9
Other income	1,800	.4
Other expense	7,000	1.3
Income tax	22,000	5.5

Required   Convert the dollar figures for Vent Molded Plastics into percentages based on net sales. Compare these with the industry average, and comment on your findings.

P 9-5.   Day Ko Incorporated presented the following comparative income statements for 1996 and 1995:

	For the Years Ended	
	1996	1995
Net sales	$1,589,150	$1,294,966
Other income	22,334	20,822
	1,611,484	1,315,788
Costs and expenses:		
Material and manufacturing		
costs of products sold	651,390	466,250
Research and development	135,314	113,100
General and selling	526,680	446,110
Interest	18,768	11,522
Other	15,570	7,306
	1,347,722	1,044,288
Earnings before income taxes		
and minority equity	263,762	271,500
Provision for income taxes	114,502	121,740
Earnings before minority equity	149,260	149,760
Minority equity in earnings	11,056	12,650
Net earnings	$ 138,204	$ 137,110

Other relevant financial information follows:

	For the Years Ended	
	1996	**1995**
Average common shares issued	29,580	29,480
Total long-term debt	$ 209,128	$ 212,702
Total stockholders' equity		
(all common)	810,292	720,530
Total assets	1,437,636	1,182,110
Operating assets	1,411,686	1,159,666
Dividends per share	1.96	1.86
Stock price (December 31)	53 ³/₄	76 ¹/₈

Required   a.   How did 1996 net sales compare to 1995?
            b.   How did 1996 net earnings compare to 1995?
            c.   Calculate the following for 1996 and 1995:

1.	Net profit margin	7.	Operating asset turnover
2.	Return on assets (using		(using ending assets)
	ending assets)	8.	DuPont analysis with
3.	Total asset turnover		operating ratios
	(using ending assets)	9.	Return on investment (using
4.	DuPont analysis		ending liabilities and equity)
5.	Operating income margin	10.	Return on equity (using
6.	Return on operating assets		ending common equity)
	(using ending assets)		

            d.   Based on the above computations, summarize the trend in profitability for
                 this firm.

P 9-6.   Dorex, Inc. presented the following comparative income statements for 1996,
               1995, and 1994:

	For the Years Ended		
	1996	**1995**	**1994**
Net sales	$ 1,600,000	$ 1,300,000	$ 1,200,000
Other income	22,100	21,500	21,000
	1,622,100	1,321,500	1,221,000
Costs and expenses:			
Material and manufacturing			
costs of products sold	740,000	624,000	576,000
Research and development	90,000	78,000	71,400
General and selling	600,000	500,500	465,000
Interest	19,000	18,200	17,040
Other	14,000	13,650	13,800
	1,463,000	1,234,350	1,143,240

(continued)

	For the Years Ended		
	1996	**1995**	**1994**
Earnings before income taxes and minority equity	159,100	87,150	77,760
Provision for income taxes	62,049	35,731	32,659
Earnings before minority equity	97,051	51,419	45,101
Minority equity in earnings	10,200	8,500	8,100
Net earnings	$ 86,851	$ 42,919	$ 37,001

	For the Years Ended		
	1996	**1995**	**1994**
Other relevant financial information:			
Average common shares issued	29,610	29,100	28,800
Average long-term debt	$ 211,100	$ 121,800	$ 214,000
Average stockholders' equity (all common)	811,200	790,100	770,000
Average total assets	1,440,600	1,220,000	1,180,000
Average operating assets	1,390,200	1,160,000	1,090,000

Required   a.   Calculate the following for 1996, 1995, and 1994:

1. Net profit margin	7. Operating asset turnover
2. Return on assets	8. DuPont analysis with
3. Total asset turnover	operating ratios
4. DuPont analysis	9. Return on investment
5. Operating income margin	10. Return on total equity
6. Return on operating assets	

b.   Based on the above computations, summarize the trend in profitability for this firm.

P 9-7.   Selected financial data for Squid Company are as follows:

	1996	**1995**	**1994**
Summary of operations:			
Net sales	$ 1,002,100	$980,500	$900,000
Cost of products sold	520,500	514,762	477,000
Selling, administrative, and general expenses	170,200	167,665	155,700
Nonoperating income	9,192	8,860	6,500
Interest expense	14,620	12,100	11,250
Earnings before income taxes	287,588	277,113	249,550
Provision for income taxes	116,473	113,616	105,560
Net earnings	171,115	163,497	143,990

	1996	1995	1994
Financial information:			
Working capital	$ 190,400	$189,000	$180,000
Average property, plant,			
and equipment	302,500	281,000	173,000
Average total assets	839,000	770,000	765,000
Average long-term debt	120,000	112,000	101,000
Average shareholders' equity	406,000	369,500	342,000

Required

a. Compute the following for 1996, 1995, and 1994:

1.	Net profit margin	5.	Return on investment
2.	Return on assets	6.	Return on total equity
3.	Total asset turnover	7.	Sales to fixed assets
4.	DuPont analysis		

b. Discuss your findings in (a).

P 9-8. D. H. Muller Company presented the following income statement in its 1996 annual report:

(Dollars in thousands except per-share amounts)	For the Years Ended		
	1996	1995	1994
Net sales	$297,580	$256,360	$242,150
Cost of sales	206,000	176,300	165,970
Gross profit	91,580	80,060	76,180
Selling, administrative, and other expenses	65,200	57,200	56,000
Operating earnings	26,380	22,860	20,180
Interest expense	(5,990)	(5,100)	(4,000)
Other deductions, net	(320)	(1,100)	(800)
Earnings before income taxes, minority interests, and extraordinary items	20,070	16,660	15,380
Income taxes	(8,028)	(6,830)	(6,229)
Net earnings of subsidiaries applicable to minority interests	(700)	(670)	(668)
Earnings before extraordinary items	11,342	9,160	8,483
Extraordinary items:			
Gain on sale of investment, net of federal and state income taxes of $520	—	1,050	—
Loss due to damages to South American facilities, net of minority interest of $430	—	(1,600)	—
Net earnings	$ 11,342	$ 8,610	$ 8,483

(continued)

	1996	1995	1994
Earnings per common share:			
Earnings before extra-ordinary items	$ 2.20	$ 1.82	$ 1.65
Extraordinary items	—	(.06)	—
Net earnings	$ 2.20	$ 1.76	$ 1.65

The asset side of the balance sheet is summarized as follows:

(Dollars in thousands)	1996	1995	1994
Current assets	$ 89,800	$ 84,500	$ 83,100
Property, plant, and equipment	45,850	40,300	39,800
Other assets (including invest-ments, deposits, deferred charges, and intangibles)	10,110	12,200	13,100
Total assets	$145,760	$137,000	$136,000

Required

a. Based on these data, compute the following for 1996, 1995, and 1994:

1. Net profit margin
2. Return on assets (using total assets)
3. Total asset turnover (using total assets)
4. DuPont analysis
5. Operating income margin
6. Return on operating assets (using end-of-year operating assets)
7. Operating asset turnover (using end-of-year operating assets)
8. DuPont analysis with operating ratios
9. Gross profit margin

b. Discuss your findings.

P 9-9.   The following financial information is for A. Galler Company for 1996, 1995, and 1994:

	1996	1995	1994
Income before interest	$ 4,400,000	$ 4,000,000	$ 3,300,000
Interest expense	800,000	600,000	550,000
Income before tax	3,600,000	3,400,000	2,750,000
Tax	1,500,000	1,450,000	1,050,000
Net income	$ 2,100,000	$ 1,950,000	$ 1,700,000

	1996	1995	1994
Current liabilities	$ 2,600,000	$ 2,300,000	$ 2,200,000
Long-term debt	7,000,000	6,200,000	5,800,000
Preferred stock (14%)	100,000	100,000	100,000
Common equity	10,000,000	9,000,000	8,300,000

Required   a. For 1996, 1995, and 1994, determine the following:
1. Return on assets (using end-of-year total assets)
2. Return on investment (using end-of-year long-term liabilities and equity)
3. Return on total equity (using ending total equity)
4. Return on common equity (using ending common equity)

b. Discuss the trend in these profit figures.
c. Discuss the benefit from the use of long-term debt and preferred stock.

P 9-10.   Dexall Company recently had a fire in its store. Management must determine the inventory loss for the insurance company. Since the firm did not have perpetual inventory records, the insurance company has suggested that it might accept an estimate using the gross profit test. The beginning inventory, as determined from the last financial statements, was $10,000. Purchase invoices indicate purchases of $100,000. Credit and cash sales during the period were $120,000. Last year, the gross profit for the firm was 40%, which was also the industry average.

Required   a. Based on these data, estimate the inventory loss.
b. If the industry average gross profit was 50%, why might the insurance company be leery of the estimated loss?

P 9-11.   Transactions affect various financial statement amounts.

		Net Profit	Retained Earnings	Total Stock-holders' Equity
a.	A stock dividend is declared and paid.	0	✓ -	0
b.	Merchandise is purchased on credit.	0	0	0
c.	Marketable securities are sold above cost.	↑	↑	↑
d.	Accounts receivable are collected.	0	0	0
e.	A cash dividend is declared and paid.	0	—	—
f.	Treasury stock is purchased and recorded at cost.	0	0	—
g.	Treasury stock is sold above cost.	0	0	↑ +
h.	Common stock is sold.	0	0	↑ +
i.	A fixed asset is sold for less than book value.	—	—	—
j.	Bonds are converted into common stock.	0	0	+

Required   Indicate the effects of the transactions listed above on each of the following: net profit, retained earnings, total stockholders' equity. Use + to indicate an increase, - to indicate a decrease, and 0 to indicate no effect.

P 9-12.   Consecutive five-year balance sheets and income statements of Mary Lou Szabo Corporation are as follows:

MARY LOU SZABO CORPORATION
Balance Sheets
December 31, 1992, through December 31, 1996

(Dollars in thousands)	1996	1995	1994	1993	1992
Assets					
Current assets:					
Cash	$ 24,000	$ 25,000	$ 26,000	$ 24,000	$ 26,000
Accounts receivable, net	120,000	122,000	128,000	129,000	130,000
Inventories	135,000	138,000	141,000	140,000	137,000
Total current assets	279,000	285,000	295,000	293,000	293,000
Property, plant and equipment, net	500,000	491,000	485,000	479,000	470,000
Goodwill	80,000	85,000	90,000	95,000	100,000
Total assets	$859,000	$861,000	$870,000	$867,000	$863,000
Liabilities and Stockholders' Equity					
Current liabilities:					
Accounts payable	$180,000	$181,000	$181,500	$183,000	$184,000
Income taxes	14,000	14,500	14,000	12,000	12,500
Total current liabilities	194,000	195,500	195,500	195,000	196,500
Long-term debt	65,000	67,500	79,500	82,000	107,500
Redeemable preferred stock	80,000	80,000	80,000	80,000	—
Total liabilities	339,000	343,000	355,000	357,000	304,000
Stockholders' equity:					
Preferred stock	70,000	70,000	70,000	70,000	120,000
Common stock	350,000	350,000	350,000	350,000	350,000
Paid-in capital in excess of par, common stock	15,000	15,000	15,000	15,000	15,000
Retained earnings	85,000	83,000	80,000	75,000	74,000
Total stockholders' equity	520,000	518,000	515,000	510,000	559,000
Total liabilities and stockholders' equity	$859,000	$861,000	$870,000	$867,000	$863,000

MARY LOU SZABO CORPORATION
Statement of Earnings
Years Ended December 31, 1992-1996

(In thousands, except per share)	1996	1995	1994	1993	1992
Net sales	$980,000	$960,000	$940,000	$900,000	$880,000
Cost of goods sold	625,000	616,000	607,000	580,000	566,000
Gross profit	355,000	344,000	333,000	320,000	314,000
Selling and administrative expense	(240,000)	(239,000)	(238,000)	(239,000)	(235,000)
Interest expense	(6,500)	(6,700)	(8,000)	(8,100)	(11,000)
Earnings from continuing operations before income taxes	108,500	98,300	87,000	72,900	68,000
Income taxes	35,800	33,400	29,200	21,700	23,100
Earnings from continuing operations	72,700	64,900	57,800	51,200	44,900
Extraordinary loss, net of taxes	—	—	—	—	(30,000)
Net earnings	$ 72,700	$ 64,900	$ 57,800	$ 51,200	$ 14,900
Earnings (loss) per share:					
Continuing operations	$ 2.00	$ 1.80	$ 1.62	$ 1.46	$ 1.28
Extraordinary loss	—	—	—	—	(.85)
Net earnings per share	$ 2.00	$ 1.80	$ 1.62	$ 1.46	$ .43

Note: Dividends on preferred stock were as follows:

Redeemable preferred stock		Preferred stock	
1993-1996	$6,400	1993-1996	$ 6,300
		1992	$10,800

Required   a.   Compute the following for the years ended December 31, 1992-1996:
1. Net profit margin
2. Total asset turnover
3. Return on assets
4. DuPont return on assets
5. Operating income margin
6. Operating asset turnover
7. Return on operating assets
8. DuPont return on operating assets
9. Sales to fixed assets
10. Return on investment
11. Return on total equity
12. Return on common equity
13. Gross profit margin

Note: For ratios that call for using average balance sheet figures, compute the rate using average balance sheet figures and year-end balance sheet figures.

b.   Briefly comment on profitability and trends indicated in profitability. Also comment on the difference in results between using the average balance sheet figures and year-end figures.

Cases

CASE 9-1 Johnny's Self-Service Station

John Dearden and his wife, Patricia, have been taking an annual vacation to Stowe, Vermont, each summer. They like the area very much and would like to retire someday in this vicinity. While in Stowe during the summer, they notice a "for sale" sign in front of a self-service station. John is 55 and is no longer satisfied with commuting to work in New York City. He decides to inquire about the asking price of the station. He is aware that Stowe is considered a good vacation area during the entire year, especially when the ski season is in progress.

On inquiry, John determines that the asking price of the station is $70,000, which includes two pumps, a small building, and 1/8 acre of land.

John asks to see some financial statements and is shown profit and loss statements for 1996 and 1995 that have been prepared for tax purposes by a local accountant.

JOHNNY'S SELF-SERVICE STATION
Statement of Earnings
For the Years Ended December 31, 1996 and 1995

	1996	1995
Revenue	$185,060	$175,180
Expenses:		
Cost of goods sold	160,180	153,280
Depreciation (a)	1,000	1,000
Real estate and property taxes	1,100	1,050
Repairs and maintenance	1,470	1,200
Other expenses	680	725
Total expenses	164,430	157,255
Profit	$ 20,630	$ 17,925
(a) Building and equipment cost	$ 30,000	
Original estimated life	30 years	
Depreciation per year	$ 1,000	

John is also given an appraiser's report on the property. The land is appraised at $50,000, and the equipment and building are valued at $20,000. The equipment and building are estimated to have a useful life of ten years.

The station has been operated by Jeff Szabo without additional help. He estimates that if help were hired to operate the station, it would cost $10,000 per year. John Dearden anticipates that he will be able to operate the station without additional help. John Dearden intends to incorporate. The anticipated tax rate is 50%.

Required a. Determine the indicated return on investment if John Dearden purchases the station. Include only financial data that will be recorded on the books. Consider 1996 and 1995 to be representative years for revenue and expenses.

b. Determine the indicated return on investment if help were hired to operate the station.

c. Why is there a difference between the rates of return in part (a) and part (b)? Discuss.

d. Determine the cash flow for 1997 if Mr. Dearden serves as the manager and 1997 turns out to be the same as 1996. Do not include the cost of the hired help. No inventory is on hand at the date of purchase, but an inventory of $10,000 is on hand at the end of the year. There are no receivables or liabilities.

e. Indicate some other considerations that should be analyzed.

f. Should John purchase the station?

CASE 9-2 The Tale of the Segments

The segment information from the 1995 annual report of Procter & Gamble Company follows:

8. SEGMENT INFORMATION (in Part)

The Company has changed its segments for financial reporting purposes. All prior year amounts have been restated to reflect the following changes. Geographic segments are now aligned into four regions: North America— including the United States and Canada; Europe—including Europe, Middle East, and Africa; Asia; and Latin America.

Business segments now are aligned as follows:

Laundry and Cleaning: laundry, dishcare, hard surface cleaners and fabric conditioners. Representative brands include Ariel, Tide, Cascade, Dawn, Mr. Proper, Downy.

Paper: tissue/towel, feminine protection, and diapers. Representative brands include Bounty, Charmin, Always, Whisper, Pampers.

Beauty Care: hair care, deodorants, personal cleansing, skin care and cosmetics and fragrances. Representative brands include Pantene, Vidal Sassoon, Secret, Safeguard, Olay, Cover Girl.

Food and Beverage: coffee, peanut butter, juice, snacks, shortening and oil, baking mixes, and commercial services. Representative brands include Folgers, Jif, Sunny Delight, Pringles, Crisco, Duncan Hines.

Health Care: oral care, gastrointestinal, respiratory care, analgesics and pharmaceuticals. Representative brands include Crest, Scope, Metamucil, Vicks, Aleve.

The Company's operations are characterized by interrelated raw materials and manufacturing facilities and centralized research and staff functions. Accordingly, separate profit determination by segment is dependent upon assumptions regarding allocations.

Corporate items include interest income and expense, segment eliminations, and other general corporate income and expense. Corporate assets consist primarily of cash and cash equivalents.

			Geographic Segments				
(Millions of dollars except per-share amounts)		**North America**	**Europe, Middle East, and Africa**	**Asia**	**Latin America**	**Corporate**	**Total**
Net Sales	1995	$16,213	$11,019	$3,619	$2,184	$ 399	$33,434
	1994	15,147	9,739	3,134	2,256	20	30,296
	1993	15,100	10,336	2,775	1,990	232	30,433
Net Earnings Before	1995	1,871	687	203	215	(331)	2,645
Prior Year's Effect of	1994	1,710	563	145	145	(352)	2,211
Accounting Changes	1993[1]	1,500	494	161	107	(247)	2,015
Identifiable Assets	1995	11,375	7,446	3,311	1,305	4,688	28,125
	1994	10,699	5,576	2,690	1,302	5,268	25,535
	1993	10,809	5,486	2,375	1,067	5,198	24,935

[1]Excludes an after-tax charge for restructuring: North America–$1,223; Europe, Middle East, and Africa–$342; Asia–$53; Latin America–$50; and Corporate–$78. Total–$1,746.

		Business Segments						
		Laundry and Cleaning	**Paper**	**Beauty Care**	**Food and Beverage**	**Health Care**	**Corporate**	**Total**
Net Sales	1995	$10,224	$9,291	$6,507	$3,988	$3,025	$ 399	$33,434
	1994	9,838	8,282	5,912	3,261	2,983	20	30,296
	1993	10,013	8,307	5,562	3,343	2,976	232	30,434
Earnings Before	1995	1,695	1,131	736	513	360	(435)	4,000
Income Taxes and	1994	1,485	1,085	578	361	358	(521)	3,346
Accounting Changes	1993[1]	1,404	952	357	240	402	(301)	3,054
Identifiable Assets	1995	5,375	7,082	5,511	2,148	3,321	4,688	28,125
	1994	4,777	5,521	4,936	2,049	2,984	5,268	25,535
	1993	4,453	5,274	5,045	2,190	2,775	5,198	24,935
Capital	1995	608	731	341	150	295	21	2,146
Expenditures	1994	590	663	247	136	182	23	1,841
	1993	575	741	238	110	176	71	1,911
Depreciation	1995	279	500	189	108	144	33	1,253
and	1994	252	435	177	113	131	26	1,134
Amortization	1993	235	403	189	144	110	59	1,140

[1]Excludes a pre-tax for restructuring: Laundry and Cleaning–$559; Paper–$626; Beauty Care–$614; Food and Beverage–$450; Health Care–$333; and Corporate–$123. Total–$2,705.

Required   a. Perform vertical common-size analysis for 1995, 1994, and 1993. Use "total" as the base for geographic segments.
       1. Net sales
       2. Identifiable assets
   b. Perform horizontal common-size analysis, using 1993 as the base for business segments.
       1. Net sales
       2. Earnings before income taxes and accounting changes
       3. Capital expenditures
   c. Compute the following for 1995, 1994, and 1993 for business segments:
       1. Net sales/identifiable assets
       2. Earnings before income taxes and accounting changes/identifiable assets
   d. Comment on possible significant insights from the analysis in parts (a), (b), and (c).

CASE 9-3   Insights on Geographic Area

Hewlett-Packard Company and Subsidiaries presented the following note in their 1995 annual report:

Geographic Area Information

The company, operating in a single industry segment, designs, manufactures and services products and systems for measurement, computation, and communications.

Net revenue, earnings from operations and identifiable assets, classified by the major geographic areas in which the company operates, are:

(In millions)	1995	1994	1993
Net revenue			
United States:			
Unaffiliated customer sales	$ 13,963	$ 11,469	$ 9,346
Interarea transfers	5,728	4,653	4,249
	19,691	16,122	13,595
Europe:			
Unaffiliated customer sales	11,142	8,423	7,177
Interarea transfers	1,432	1,058	899
	12,574	9,481	8,076
Japan, Other Asia Pacific, Canada, Latin America:			
Unaffiliated customer sales	6,414	5,099	3,794
Interarea transfers	3,783	2,765	2,165
	10,197	7,864	5,959
Eliminations	(10,943)	(8,476)	(7,313)
	$ 31,519	$ 24,991	$ 20,317
Earnings from operations			
United States	$ 2,259	$ 1,472	$ 1,485
Europe	930	660	447
Japan, Other Asia Pacific, Canada, Latin America	1,240	824	630
Eliminations and corporate	(861)	(407)	(683)
	$ 3,568	$ 2,549	$ 1,879
Identifiable assets			
United States	$ 12,347	$ 9,848	$ 8,984
Europe	7,168	4,991	4,452
Japan, Other Asia Pacific, Canada, Latin America	5,854	4,052	3,056
Eliminations and corporate	(942)	676	244
	$ 24,427	$ 19,567	$ 16,736

Net revenue from sales to unaffiliated customers is based on the location of the customer. Interarea transfers are sales among HP affiliates principally made at market price, less an allowance primarily for subsequent manufacturing and/or marketing costs. Earnings from operations and identifiable assets are classified based on the location of the company's facilities.

Identifiable corporate assets, which are net of eliminations, comprise primarily cash and cash equivalents, property, plant and equipment, and other assets, and aggregate $4,343 million in 1995, $4,594 million in 1994 and $3,148 million in 1993.

Required

a. 1. Prepare horizontal common-size analysis for net revenue. Use 1993 as the base. (Do not include eliminations or interarea transfers.)
    2. Prepare horizontal common-size analysis for earnings from operations. Use 1993 as the base. (Do not include eliminations and corporate.)
    3. Prepare horizontal common-size analysis for identifiable assets. Use 1993 as the base. (Do not include eliminations and corporate.)

b. Calculate the earnings from operations/identifiable assets for 1995, 1994, and 1993. (Do not include eliminations and corporate.)

c. Comment on possible significant insights from the analysis in part (a) through (b).

CASE 9-4 Profitability Analysis

The consolidated statements of income and balance sheets are presented for Intel Corporation for 1995.

Consolidated Statements of Income
Three Years Ended December 30, 1995

(In millions, except per-share amounts)	1995	1994	1993
Net revenues	$ 16,202	$11,521	$ 8,782
Cost of sales	7,811	5,576	3,252
Research and development	1,296	1,111	970
Marketing, general, and administrative	1,843	1,447	1,168
Operating costs and expenses	10,950	8,134	5,390
Operating income	5,252	3,387	3,392
Interest expense	(29)	(57)	(50)
Interest income and other, net	415	273	188
Income before taxes	5,638	3,603	3,530
Provision for taxes	2,072	1,315	1,235
Net income	$ 3,566	$ 2,288	$ 2,295
Earnings per common and common equivalent share	$ 4.03	$ 2.62	$ 2.60
Weighted average common and common equivalent shares outstanding	884	874	882

Consolidated Balance Sheets
December 30, 1995 and December 31, 1994

(In millions, except per-share amounts)	1995	1994
Assets		
Current assets:		
Cash and cash equivalents	$ 1,463	$ 1,180
Short-term investments	995	1,230
Accounts receivable, net of allowance for		
doubtful accounts of $57 ($32 in 1994)	3,116	1,978
Inventories	2,004	1,169
Deferred tax assets	408	552
Other current assets	111	58
Total current assets	8,097	6,167
Property, plant, and equipment:		
Land and buildings	3,145	2,292
Machinery and equipment	7,099	5,374
Construction in progress	1,548	850
	11,792	8,516
Less: Accumulated depreciation	4,321	3,149
Property, plant, and equipment, net	7,471	5,367
Long-term investments	1,653	2,127
Other assets	283	155
Total assets	$ 17,504	$ 13,816
Liabilities and stockholders' equity		
Current liabilities:		
Short-term debt	$ 346	$ 517
Accounts payable	864	575
Deferred income on shipments to distributors	304	269
Accrued compensation and benefits	758	588
Accrued advertising	218	108
Other accrued liabilities	328	538
Income taxes payable	801	429
Total current liabilities	3,619	3,024
Long-term debt	400	392
Deferred tax liabilities	620	389
Put warrants	725	744
Commitments and contingencies		
Total liabilities	5,364	4,549
Stockholders' equity:		
Preferred stock, $.001 par value, 50 shares		
authorized; none issued	—	—
Common stock, $.001 par value, 1,400 shares		
authorized; 821 issued and outstanding in 1995		
(827 in 1994) and capital in excess of par value	2,583	2,306
Retained earnings	9,557	6,961
Total stockholders' equity	12,140	9,267
Total liabilities and stockholders' equity	$ 17,504	$ 13,816

Required a. Compute the following for 1995:
1. Net profit margin
2. Total asset turnover (using average total assets)
3. Return on assets (using average total assets)
4. Operating income margin
5. Return on operating assets (using average operating assets
6. Sales to fixed assets (using average net fixed assets)
7. Return on investment (using average long-term liabilities + equity)
8. Return on total equity (using average total equity)
9. Return on common equity (using average common equity)
10. Gross profit margin

10   Analysis for the Investor

CERTAIN TYPES OF ANALYSES PARTICULARLY CONCERN investors. While this chapter is not intended as a comprehensive guide to investment analysis, it will introduce certain types of analysis useful to the investor. In addition to the analysis covered in this chapter, an investor would also be interested in the liquidity, debt, and profitability ratios covered in prior chapters.

LEVERAGE AND ITS EFFECT ON EARNINGS

The use of debt, called *financial leverage*, has a significant impact on earnings. The existence of fixed operating costs, called *operating leverage*, also affects earnings. The higher the percentage of fixed operating costs, the greater the variation in income as a result of a variation in sales (revenue).

This book does not compute a ratio for operating leverage because it cannot be readily computed from published financial statements. This book does compute financial leverage because it is readily computed from published financial statements.

The expense of debt financing is interest, a fixed charge dependent on the amount of financial principal and the rate of interest. Interest is a contractual obligation created by the borrowing agreement. In contrast to dividends, interest must be paid regardless of whether the firm is in a highly profitable period or not. An advantage of interest over dividends is its tax deductibility. Because the interest is subtracted to calculate taxable income, income tax expense is reduced.

Definition of Financial Leverage and Magnification Effects

The use of financing with a fixed charge (such as interest) is termed **financial leverage**. Financial leverage is successful if the firm earns more on the borrowed funds than it pays to use them. It is not successful if the firm earns less on the borrowed funds than it pays to use them. Using financial leverage results in a fixed financing charge that can materially affect the earnings available to the common shareholders.

Exhibit 10-1 illustrates financial leverage and its magnification effects. In this illustration, earnings before interest and tax are $1,000,000. Further, the firm has interest expense of $200,000 and a tax rate of 40%. The statement illustrates the effect of leverage on the return to the common shareholder. At earnings before interest and tax (EBIT) of $1,000,000, the net income is $480,000. If EBIT increases by 10% to $1,100,000, as in the exhibit, the net income rises by 12.5%. This magnification is caused by the fixed nature of interest expense. While earnings available to pay interest rise, interest remains the same, thus leaving more for the residual owners. Note that since the tax rate remains the same, earnings before tax change at the same rate as earnings after tax. Hence, this analysis could be made with either profit figure.

If financial leverage is used, a rise in EBIT will cause an even greater rise in net income, and a decrease in EBIT will cause an even greater decrease in net income. Looking again at the statement for Dowell Company in Exhibit 10-1, when EBIT declined 20%, net income dropped from $480,000 to $360,000—a decline of $120,000, or 25%, based on the original $480,000. The use of financial leverage, termed **trading on the equity**, is only successful if the rate of earnings on borrowed funds exceeds the fixed charges.

EXHIBIT 10-1   **DOWELL COMPANY**
Financial Leverage
Partial Income Statement to Illustrate Magnification Effects

	Base Year Figures	20% Decrease in Earnings Before Interest and Tax	10% Increase in Earnings Before Interest and Tax
Earnings before interest and tax	$ 1,000,000	$ 800,000	$ 1,100,000
Interest	(200,000)	(200,000)	(200,000)
Earnings before tax	800,000	600,000	900,000
Income tax (40%)	(320,000)	(240,000)	(360,000)
Net income	$ 480,000	$ 360,000	$ 540,000
Percentage change in net income [A]		25.0%	12.5%
Percentage change in earnings before interest and tax [B]		20.0%	10.0%
Degree of financial leverage [A÷B]		1.25	1.25

Computation of the Degree of Financial Leverage

The degree of financial leverage is the multiplication factor by which the net income changes as compared to the change in EBIT. One way of computing it follows:

$$\frac{\text{\% Change Net Income}}{\text{\% Change EBIT}}$$

For Dowell Company:

$$\frac{12.5\%}{10.0\%} = 1.25, \text{ or } \frac{25.0\%}{20.0\%} = 1.25$$

The degree of financial leverage is 1.25. From a base EBIT of $1,000,000, any change in EBIT will be accompanied by 1.25 times that change in net income. If net income before interest and tax rises 4%, earnings to the shareholder will rise 5%. If net income before interest and tax falls 8%, earnings to the shareholder will decline 10%. The **degree of financial leverage** (DFL) can be computed more easily as follows:

$$\text{Degree of Financial Leverage} = \frac{\text{Earnings Before Interest and Tax}}{\text{Earnings Before Tax}}$$

Again referring to Dowell Company:

$$\begin{array}{l}\text{Degree of Financial Leverage at Earnings} \\ \text{Before Interest and Tax on \$1,000,000}\end{array} = \frac{\$1,000,000}{\$800,000} = 1.25$$

Note that the degree of financial leverage represents a particular base level of income. The degree of leverage may differ for other levels of income or fixed charges.

The degree of financial leverage formula will not work precisely when the income statement includes any of the following items:

1. Minority share of earnings
2. Equity income
3. Nonrecurring items
   a. Unusual or infrequent items
   b. Discontinued operations

    c.   Extraordinary items

    d.   Cumulative effect of change in an accounting principle

When any of these items are included, they should be eliminated from the numerator and denominator. The all-inclusive formula follows:

$$\text{Degree of Financial Leverage} = \frac{\begin{array}{c}\textbf{Earnings Before Interest, Tax, Minority}\\\textbf{Share of Earnings, Equity Income,}\\\textbf{and Nonrecurring Items}\end{array}}{\begin{array}{c}\textbf{Earnings Before Tax, Minority}\\\textbf{Share of Earnings, Equity Income,}\\\textbf{and Nonrecurring Items}\end{array}}$$

This formula results in the ratio by which earnings before interest, tax, minority share of earnings, equity income, and nonrecurring items will change in relation to a change in earnings before tax, minority share of earnings, equity income, and nonrecurring items. In other words, it eliminates the minority share of earnings, equity income, and nonrecurring items from the degree of financial leverage.

Exhibit 10-2 shows the degree of financial leverage for 1995 and 1994 for Cooper Tire & Rubber Company. The degree of financial leverage is 1.004 for 1995 and 1.013 for 1994. This is a very low degree of financial leverage. Therefore, the financial leverage at the end of 1995 indicates that as earnings before interest change, net income will change by 1.004 times that amount. If earnings before interest increases, the financial leverage will be favorable. If earnings before interest decrease, the financial leverage will be unfavorable. For Cooper, financial leverage is not a major factor because a leverage of 1.004 is very low. A conservative investor would look

EXHIBIT 10-2   **COOPER TIRE & RUBBER COMPANY**
Degree of Financial Leverage
Base Years 1995 and 1994

(Dollar amounts in thousands)	1995	1994
Income before income taxes [B]	$ 180,070	$ 208,119
Interest	697	2,680
Earnings before interest and income taxes [A]	$ 180,767	$ 210,799
Degree of financial leverage [A÷B]	1.004 or	1.013 or
	1.00	1.01

favorably on Cooper's low financial leverage. In periods of relatively low interest rates or declining interest rates, financial leverage looks more favorable than in periods of high interest rates or increasing interest rates.

Summary of Financial Leverage

Two things are important in looking at financial leverage as part of financial analysis. First, how high is the degree of financial leverage? This is a type of risk (or opportunity) measurement from the viewpoint of the shareholder. The higher the degree of financial leverage, the greater the multiplication factor. Second, does the financial leverage work for or against the owners?

EARNINGS PER COMMON SHARE

Earnings per share—the amount of income earned on a share of common stock during an accounting period—applies only to common stock and to corporate income statements. Nonpublic companies, because of cost-benefit considerations, do not have to report earnings per share. Because earnings per share receives much attention from the financial community, investors, and potential investors, it will be described in some detail.

Fortunately, we do not need to compute earnings per share. The company is required to present it at the bottom of the income statement. Per-share amounts for discontinued operations, extraordinary items, and the cumulative effect of an accounting change must be presented on the face of the income statement or in the notes to the financial statements. Earnings per share for recurring items is the most significant for primary analysis.

Computing earnings per share initially involves net income, preferred stock dividends declared and accumulated, and the weighted average number of shares outstanding, as follows:

$$\textbf{Earnings per Common Share} = \frac{\textbf{Net Income} - \textbf{Preferred Dividends}}{\substack{\textbf{Weighted Average Number of} \\ \textbf{Common Shares Outstanding}}}$$

Since earnings pertain to an entire period, they should be related to the common shares outstanding during the period. Thus, the denominator of the equation is the weighted average number of common shares outstanding.

To illustrate, assume that a corporation had 10,000 shares of common stock outstanding at the beginning of the year. On July 1, it issued 2,000 shares, and on October 1, it issued another 3,000 shares. The weighted average number of shares outstanding would be computed as follows:

Months Shares Are Outstanding	Shares Outstanding	x	Fraction of Year Outstanding	=	Weighted Average
January-June	10,000		6/12		5,000
July-September	12,000		3/12		3,000
October-December	15,000		3/12		3,750
					11,750

When the common shares outstanding increase as a result of a stock dividend or stock split, retroactive recognition must be given to these events for all comparative earnings per share presentations. Stock dividends and stock splits do not provide the firm with more funds; they only change the number of outstanding shares. Earnings per share should be related to the outstanding common stock after the stock dividend or stock split. In the weighted average common shares illustration, if we assume that a 2-for-1 stock split took place on December 31, the denominator of the earnings per share computation becomes 23,500 (11,750 × 2). The denominator of prior years' earnings per share computations would also be doubled. If we assume that net income is $100,000 and preferred dividends total $10,000 in this illustration, then the earnings per common share would be $3.83 [($100,000 − $10,000)/23,500].

The current earnings per share guidelines are in FASB Statement No. 128, "Earnings per Share." Statement No. 128 applies to financial statements issued for periods ending after December 15, 1997. Statement No. 128 replaced APB Opinion No. 15, "Earnings per Share." Comments relating to both sets of guidelines are included in the following paragraphs, since financial statements issued prior to December 15, 1997 will have used the guidelines in APB Opinion No. 15.

APB Opinion No. 15

Under APB Opinion No. 15, a corporation was required to compute three earnings per share numbers. These were:

1. Simple earnings per share (basic earnings per share computation).

2. Primary earnings per share (the numerator and denominator are subject to adjustments that consider potentially dilutive securities).

3. Fully diluted earnings per share (the numerator and denominator are subject to further adjustments that consider potentially dilutive securities, and the rules were more conservative than the rules for computing primary earnings per share).

Potentially dilutive securities are convertible securities, warrants, options, or other rights that upon conversion or exercise could in the aggregate dilute earnings per common share.

The corporation would either disclose the simple earnings per share or both the primary earnings per share and the fully diluted earnings per share, depending on the 3% test. If fully diluted earnings per share was 3% or more lower than simple earnings per share, the dual presentation was made. If fully diluted earnings per share was less than 3% lower than simple earnings per share, simple earnings per share was presented.

Exhibit 10-3 presents the earnings per share of Cooper Tire & Rubber Co. From this presentation, we can conclude that less than a 3% difference existed between Cooper's simple earnings per share and its fully diluted earnings per share.

Exhibit 10-4, page 436, presents the earnings per share of UtiliCorp United. The UtiliCorp United earnings per share reflects a complex capital structure, and we can conclude that a 3% or more difference existed between the company's simple earnings per share and its fully diluted earnings per share.

FASB Statement No. 128

Under FASB Statement No. 128, simple earnings per share is replaced by basic earnings per share. This is only a name change, since the computation is the same as for the simple earnings per share. The primary earnings per share computation is eliminated.

The fully diluted earnings per share is replaced by the diluted earnings per share. Diluted earnings per share is basically the same as the fully diluted earnings per share, except that the rules are less conservative. This usually results in a higher earnings per share for diluted earnings than for prior fully diluted earnings per share.

Corporations with only common stock present basic earnings per share for income from continuing operations and for net income on the face of the income statement. Other corporations present basic earnings per share

EXHIBIT 10-3 **COOPER TIRE & RUBBER COMPANY**
Earnings per Share
For the Years Ended December 31, 1995, 1994, and 1993

	1995	1994	1993
Net income per share	$1.35	$1.54	$1.22

EXHIBIT 10-4   **UTILICORP UNITED**
Earnings per Share
For the Years Ended December 31, 1995, 1994, and 1993

	1995	1994	1993
Earnings per common share:			
Primary	$1.72	$2.08	$1.95
Fully diluted	$1.71	$2.06	$1.92

and diluted earnings per share for income from continuing operations and for net income on the face of the income statement.

PRICE/EARNINGS RATIO

The **price/earnings (P/E) ratio** expresses the relationship between the market price of a share of common stock and that stock's current earnings per share. Compute the P/E ratio as follows:

$$\text{Price/Earnings Ratio} = \frac{\textbf{Market Price per Share}}{\textbf{Diluted Earnings per Share*}}$$

*Basic earnings per share if the company only presents basic earnings per share.

The text previously covered the use of diluted earnings per share. If used in the P/E ratio, diluted earnings per share will give a higher price/earnings ratio, a conservative computation of the ratio. Ideally, the P/E ratio should be computed using diluted earnings per share for continuing earnings per share. This gives an indication of what is being paid for a dollar of recurring earnings.

P/E ratios are available from many sources, such as the *Wall Street Journal* and *Standard & Poor's Industry Surveys.* Exhibit 10-5 shows the P/E ratio for Cooper for 1995 and 1994. The P/E ratio was 18.24 at the end of 1995 and 15.34 at the end of 1994. This indicates that the stock has been selling for about 18 times earnings. You can get a perspective on this ratio by comparing it to the average P/E for the industry and an average for all of the stocks on an exchange, such as the New York Stock Exchange. These averages will vary greatly over several years.

Investors view the P/E ratio as a gauge of future earning power of the firm. Companies with high growth opportunities generally have high P/E ratios; firms with low growth tend to have lower P/E ratios. However, investors may be wrong in their estimates of growth potential. One fundamental of investing is to be wiser than the market. An example would be buying a stock that has a relatively low P/E ratio when the prospects for the company are much better than reflected in the P/E ratio.

P/E ratios do not have any meaning when a firm has abnormally low profits in relation to the asset base or when a firm has losses. The P/E ratio in these cases would be abnormally high or negative.

PERCENTAGE OF EARNINGS RETAINED

The proportion of current earnings retained for internal growth is computed as follows:

$$\text{Percentage of Earnings Retained} = \frac{\text{Net Income} - \text{All Dividends}}{\text{Net Income}}$$

The percentage of earnings retained is better for trend analysis if nonrecurring items are removed. This indicates what is being retained of recurring earnings.

A problem occurs because the percentage of earnings retained implies that earnings represent a cash pool for paying dividends. Under accrual accounting, earnings do not represent a cash pool. Operating cash flow compared with cash dividends gives a better indication of the cash from operations and the dividends paid. Chapter 11 introduces this ratio.

EXHIBIT 10-5 **COOPER TIRE & RUBBER COMPANY**
Price/Earnings Ratio
December 31, 1995 and 1994

	1995	1994
Market price per common share (December 31, close) [A]	$ 24⅝	$ 23⅝
Earnings per share [B]	$ 1.35	$ 1.54
Price/earnings ratio [A÷B]	18.24	15.34

Many firms have a policy on the percentage of earnings that they want retained—for example, between 60% and 75%. In general, new firms, growing firms, and firms perceived as growth firms will have a relatively high percentage of earnings retained.

In the *Almanac of Business and Industrial Financial Ratios*, the percentage of earnings retained is called the *ratio of retained earnings to net income*. The phrase *retained earnings* as used in the ratio in the *Almanac* is a misnomer. Retained earnings in this ratio does not mean accumulated profits, but rather that portion of income retained in a single year. Hence, this ratio has two different names.

Exhibit 10-6 shows the percentage of earnings retained by Cooper, using 1995 and 1994 figures. Cooper retains a substantial proportion of its profits for internal use. It has been adding substantial production capacity.

DIVIDEND PAYOUT

The **dividend payout ratio** measures the portion of current earnings per common share being paid out in dividends. Compute the dividend payout ratio as follows:

$$\text{Dividend Payout} = \frac{\textbf{Dividends per Common Share}}{\textbf{Diluted Earnings per Share*}}$$

*Basic earnings per share if the company only presents basic earnings per share.

Earnings per share are diluted in the formula, because this is the most conservative viewpoint. Ideally, diluted earnings per share should not

---

EXHIBIT 10-6 **COOPER TIRE & RUBBER COMPANY**
Percentage of Earnings Retained
For the Years Ended December 31, 1995 and 1994

(Dollar amounts in thousands)	1995	1994
Net income [B]	$112,820	$128,519
Less: Dividends	22,584	19,234
Earnings retained [A]	$ 90,236	$109,285
Percentage of earnings retained [A÷B]	79.98%	85.03%

include nonrecurring items since directors normally look at recurring earnings to develop a stable dividend policy.

The dividend payout ratio has a similar problem as the percentage of earnings retained. Investors may assume that dividend payout implies that earnings per share represent cash. Under accrual accounting, earnings per share do not represent a cash pool.

Most firms hesitate to decrease dividends since this tends to have adverse effects on the market price of the company's stock. No rule of thumb exists for a correct payout ratio. Some stockholders prefer high dividends; others prefer to have the firm reinvest the earnings in hopes of higher capital gains. In the latter case, the payout ratio would be a relatively smaller percentage.

Exhibit 10-7 presents Cooper's 1995 and 1994 dividend payout ratios, which increased from 14.94% in 1994 to 20.00% in 1995. These are very conservative payout ratios. Often, to attract the type of stockholder who looks favorably on a low dividend payout ratio, a company must have a record of earning approximately 15% or better in return on common equity.

Industry averages of dividend payout ratios are available in *Standard & Poor's Industry Surveys*. Although no correct payout exists, even within an industry, the outlook for the industry often makes the bulk of the ratios in a particular industry similar.

The percentage of earnings retained and the dividend payout usually approximate the reciprocal of each other. An exception occurs when the company has a substantial amount of preferred stock. The percentage of earnings retained includes preferred dividends.

In general, new firms, growing firms, and firms perceived as growth firms have a relatively low dividend payout. Cooper would be considered a growing firm.

EXHIBIT 10-7 **COOPER TIRE & RUBBER COMPANY**
Dividend Payout
For the Years Ended December 31, 1995 and 1994

	1995	1994
Dividends per share [A]	$ .27	$ .23
Earnings per share [B]	$1.35	$1.54
Dividend payout ratio [A÷B]	20.00%	14.94%

DIVIDEND YIELD

The dividend yield indicates the relationship between the dividends per common share and the market price per common share. Compute the **dividend yield** as follows:

$$\text{Dividend Yield} = \frac{\textbf{Dividends per Common Share}}{\textbf{Market Price per Common Share}}$$

Exhibit 10-8 shows the dividend yield for Cooper for 1995 and 1994. The dividend yield has been steady and low.

Since total earnings from securities include both dividends and price appreciation, no rule of thumb exists for dividend yield. The yield depends on the firm's dividend policy and the market price. If the firm successfully invests the money not distributed as dividends, the price should rise. If the firm holds the dividends at low amounts to allow for reinvestment of profits, the dividend yield is likely to be low. A low dividend yield satisfies many investors if the company has a record of above average return on common equity. Investors that want current income prefer a high dividend yield.

BOOK VALUE PER SHARE

A figure frequently published in annual reports is book value per share, which indicates the amount of stockholders' equity that relates to each share of outstanding common stock. The formula for **book value per share** follows:

$$\text{Book Value per Share} = \frac{\textbf{Total Stockholders' Equity – Preferred Stock Equity}}{\textbf{Number of Common Shares Outstanding}}$$

EXHIBIT 10-8   COOPER TIRE & RUBBER COMPANY
Dividend Yield
December 31, 1995 and 1994

	1995	1994
Dividends per share [A]	$ .27	$ .23
Market price per share [B]	$ 24⁵⁄₈	$ 23⁵⁄₈
Dividend yield [A÷B]	1.10%	0.97%

Preferred stock equity should be stated at liquidation price, if other than book, because the preferred shareholders would be paid this value in the event of liquidation. Liquidation value is sometimes difficult to locate in an annual report. If this value cannot be found, the book figure that relates to preferred stock may be used in place of liquidation value. Exhibit 10-9 shows the book value per share for Cooper for 1995 and 1994.

The market price of the securities usually does not approximate the book value since assets are recorded at cost. These historical dollars reflect past unrecovered cost of the assets. The market value of the stock, however, reflects the potential of the firm as seen by the investor. For example, land will be valued at cost, and this asset value will be reflected in the book value. If the asset were purchased several years ago and is now worth substantially more, however, the market value of the stock may recognize this potential.

Book value is of limited use to the investment analyst since it is based on historical costs. When market value is below book value, investors view the company as lacking potential. A market value above book value indicates that investors view the company as having enough potential to be worth more than the unrecovered cost. Note that Cooper was selling materially above book value.

When investors are pessimistic about the prospects for stocks, the stocks sell below book value. On the other hand, when investors are optimistic about stock prospects, the stocks sell above book value.

STOCK OPTIONS

Corporations frequently provide stock options for employees and officers of the company, allowing them to purchase stock on favorable terms as an incentive to be more productive. A basic understanding of stock option

EXHIBIT 10-9 **COOPER TIRE & RUBBER COMPANY**
Book Value per Share
December 31, 1995 and 1994

	1995	1994
Stockholders' equity	$748,799,000	$662,077,000
Preferred stock (liquidation value)	—	—
Common equity [A]	$748,799,000	$662,077,000
Shares outstanding [B]	83,661,972	83,634,072
Book value per share [A÷B]	$8.95	$7.92

accounting is needed in order to assess the stock option disclosure of a company. There are two types of stock option plans: noncompensatory and compensatory.

A *noncompensatory plan* attempts to raise capital or encourage widespread ownership of the corporation's stock among officers and employees. Because the officers and employees purchase the stock at only a slight discount from the market price, there is not a substantial dilution of the position of existing stockholders.

A *compensatory plan* is available only to select individuals, such as officers of the company. These plans typically provide the potential for purchasing stock at a bargain rate.

Usually, the company records compensation only to the extent that the option price was below market price on the date the option was granted. When the option price is the market price on the date of grant, no compensation is recorded. Thus, many accountants feel that compensation from stock option plans is understated because the individual purchases the stock substantially below market at the date of exercise (the date that the options and cash are exchanged for stock).

When stock options are exercised, the additional funds improve the short-run liquidity of the firm and its long-term debt position. Any improvement is almost always immaterial, however, because of the relatively small amount of funds involved.

Stock options do not require a cash outlay by the company issuing them, but they are a form of potential dilution of the interest of stockholders. Extensive use of stock options would be of concern to existing and potential stockholders. The investor should consider the materiality of the number of stock options outstanding in relation to the number of outstanding shares of common stock, as follows:

$$\text{Materiality of Options} = \frac{\text{Stock Options Outstanding}}{\text{Number of Shares of Common Stock Outstanding}}$$

Ideally, only compensatory stock options should be included in the formula since these are the options that have the potential for material dilution of the position of existing stockholders. There may be a problem in identifying noncompensatory and compensatory options based on the footnote disclosure. The terms *noncompensatory* and *compensatory* are seldom used.

The Cooper footnote indicates that the company's stock option plans provide for granting options to key employees. These can likely be described as compensatory options, so all of them are included in our formula. Cooper had 541,175 options outstanding at December 31, 1995, at a price per share in the range of $5.09–$34.69. The market price of the stock at the close of the year was $24\frac{5}{8}$.

Exhibit 10-10 shows the materiality of stock options for Cooper in 1995 and 1994. In 1995, the materiality of options was .65%, as compared to .57% in 1994.

Many investors consider the materiality of options insignificant if it is below 5%. Because of the cash flow to the company when the options are exercised, a materiality of 5% is probably only 2% to 3% effective dilution.

Other factors related to stock options should be considered. First, the impact of stock options is already included in the denominator of the earnings per share computation. As the market price of the common shares increases, the dilutive impact on earnings per share is greater. Further dilution may also have a negative impact on market potential.

In October 1995, the FASB issued SFAS No. 123, "Accounting for Stock-Based Compensation." SFAS No. 123 establishes new fair value-based accounting for stock-based compensation. Because of significant opposition from industry, the FASB made the accounting under this new standard optional. Employers can stay on the old standard or adopt the new standard. Employers that stay on the old standard must comply with the disclosure requirements of SFAS No. 123. The disclosure includes net income and earnings per share as if the fair value-based method of accounting had been applied. This additional disclosure is in a footnote. For most companies this additional footnote was included for the first time with their 1996 annual report.

Certain companies with performance-based plans may recognize less compensation expense under SFAS No. 123 than under the old standard. These companies will likely adopt SFAS No. 123 in its entirety. Most companies are faced with additional compensation expense under SFAS No. 123. These companies will not likely implement SFAS No. 123 in its entirety, but only provide the footnote disclosure. The additional compensation expense could be substantial for some companies. An example would be a small high-tech company that is rewarding employees with substantial stock-based compensation.

EXHIBIT 10-10 **COOPER TIRE & RUBBER COMPANY**
Materiality of Options
December 31, 1995 and 1994

	1995	1994
Options outstanding at December 31 [A]	541,185	475,232
Number of common shares outstanding at December 31 [B]	83,661,972	83,634,072
Materiality of options [A÷B]	0.65%	0.57%

A review of the footnote under SFAS No. 123 could indicate that net income and earnings per share are much lower when stock-based compensation is considered. This could have a significant impact on analysis.

STOCK APPRECIATION RIGHTS

Some firms grant key employees stock appreciation rights instead of stock options or in addition to stock options. **Stock appreciation rights** give the employee the right to receive compensation in cash or stock (or a combination of these) at some future date, based on the difference between the market price of the stock at the date of exercise over a preestablished price.

The accounting for stock appreciation rights comes under FASB Interpretation No. 28, which directs that the compensation expense recognized each period be based on the difference between the quoted market value at the end of each period and the option price. This compensation expense is then reduced by previously recognized compensation expense on the stock appreciation right. For example, assume that the option price is $10.00 and the market value is $15.00 at the end of the first period of the stock appreciation right. Compensation expense would be recognized at $5.00 ($15.00 – $10.00) per share included in the plan. If 100,000 shares are in the plan, then the expense to be charged to the income statement would be $500,000 ($5.00 x 100,000 shares). If the market value is $12.00 at the end of the second period of the stock appreciation right, expenses are reduced by $3.00 per share. This is because the total compensation expense for the two years is $2.00 ($12.00 – $10.00). Since $5.00 of expense was recognized in the first year, $3.00 of negative compensation is considered in the second year in order to total $2.00 of expense. With 100,000 shares, the reduction to expenses in the second year would be $300,000 ($3.00 x 100,000 shares). Thus, stock appreciation rights can have a material influence on income, dictated by changing stock prices.

A company with outstanding stock appreciation rights describes them in a footnote to the financial statements. If the number of shares is known, a possible future influence on income can be computed, based on assumptions made regarding future market prices. For example, if the footnote discloses that the firm has 50,000 shares of stock appreciation rights outstanding, and the stock market price was $10.00 at the end of the year, the analyst can assume a market price at the end of next year and compute the compensation expense for next year. With these facts and an assumed market price of $15.00 at the end of next year, the compensation expense for next year can be computed to be $250,000 [($15.00 – $10.00) x 50,000 shares]. This potential charge to earnings should be considered as the stock is evaluated as a potential investment.

Stock appreciation rights tied to the future market price of the stock can represent a material potential drain on the company. Even a relatively small number of stock appreciation rights outstanding could be material. This should be considered by existing and potential stockholders. Some firms have placed limits on the potential appreciation in order to control the cost of appreciation rights.

Cooper has stock option plans that allow the issuance of stock appreciation rights. The Cooper footnote is not clear as to the number of appreciation rights outstanding.

SUMMARY

This chapter has reviewed certain types of analysis that particularly concern investors. Ratios relevant to this analysis include the following:

$$\text{Degree of Financial Leverage} = \frac{\text{Earnings Before Interest and Tax}}{\text{Earnings Before Tax}}$$

$$\text{All-Inclusive Degree of Financial Leverage} = \frac{\substack{\text{Earnings Before Interest, Tax, Minority} \\ \text{Share of Earnings, Equity Income,} \\ \text{and Nonrecurring Items}}}{\substack{\text{Earnings Before Tax, Minority} \\ \text{Share of Earnings, Equity Income,} \\ \text{and Nonrecurring Items}}}$$

$$\text{Basic Earnings per Common Share} = \frac{\text{Net Income} - \text{Preferred Dividends}}{\substack{\text{Weighted Average Number of} \\ \text{Common Shares Outstanding}}}$$

$$\text{Price/Earnings Ratio} = \frac{\text{Market Price per Share}}{\text{Diluted Earnings per Share}}$$

$$\text{Percentage of Earnings Retained} = \frac{\text{Net Income} - \text{All Dividends}}{\text{Net Income}}$$

$$\text{Dividend Payout} = \frac{\text{Dividends per Common Share}}{\text{Diluted Earnings per Share}}$$

$$\text{Dividend Yield} = \frac{\text{Dividends per Common Share}}{\text{Market Price per Common Share}}$$

$$\text{Book Value per Share} = \frac{\text{Total Stockholders' Equity} - \text{Preferred Stock Equity}}{\text{Number of Common Shares Outstanding}}$$

$$\text{Materiality of Options} = \frac{\text{Stock Options Outstanding}}{\text{Number of Shares of Common Stock Outstanding}}$$

QUESTIONS

Q 10-1. Give a simple definition of *earnings per share.*

Q 10-2. Assume that the corporation is a nonpublic company. Comment on the requirement for this firm to disclose earnings per share.

Q 10-3. Keller & Fink, a partnership, engages in the wholesale fish market. How would this company disclose earnings per share?

Q 10-4. Dividends on preferred stock total $5,000 for the current year. How would these dividends influence earnings per share?

Q 10-5. The denominator of the earnings per share computation includes the weighted average number of common shares outstanding. Why use the weighted average instead of the year-end common shares outstanding?

Q 10-6. Preferred dividends decreased this year because some preferred stock was retired. How would this influence the earnings per share computation this year?

Q 10-7. Retroactive recognition is given to stock dividends and stock splits on common stock when computing earnings per share. Why?

Q 10-8. Why do many firms try to maintain a stable percentage of earnings retained?

Q 10-9. Define *financial leverage.* What is its effect on earnings? When is the use of financial leverage advantageous and disadvantageous?

Q 10-10. Given a set level of earnings before interest and tax, how will a rise in interest rates affect the degree of financial leverage?

Q 10-11. Why is the price/earnings ratio considered a gauge of future earning power?

Q 10-12. Why does a relatively new firm often have a low dividend payout ratio? Why does a firm with a substantial growth record and/or substantial growth prospects often have a low dividend payout ratio?

Q 10-13. Why would an investor ever buy stock in a firm with a low dividend yield?

Q 10-14. Why is book value often meaningless? What improvements to financial statements would make it more meaningful?

Q 10-15. Why should an investor read the footnote concerning stock options? How might stock options affect profitability?

Q 10-16. Why can a relatively small number of stock appreciation rights prove to be a material drain on future earnings and cash of a company?

Q 10-17. Explain how outstanding stock appreciation rights could increase reported income in a particular year.

PROBLEMS

P 10-1. McDonald Company shows the following condensed income statement information for the current year:

Revenue from sales		$ 3,500,000
Cost of products sold		(1,700,000)
Gross profit		1,800,000
Operating expenses:		
Selling expenses	$425,000	
General expenses	350,000	(775,000)
Operating income		1,025,000
Other income		20,000
Interest		(70,000)
Operating income before income taxes		975,000
Taxes related to operations		(335,000)
Income from operations		640,000
Extraordinary loss (less applicable income taxes of $40,000)		(80,000)
Income before minority interest		560,000
Minority share of earnings		(50,000)
Net income		$ 510,000

Required Calculate the degree of financial leverage.

P 10-2. A firm has earnings before interest and tax of $1,000,000, interest of $200,000, and net income of $400,000 in Year 1.

Required a. Calculate the degree of financial leverage in base Year 1.

b. If earnings before interest and tax increase by 10% in Year 2, what will be the new level of earnings, assuming the same tax rate as in Year 1?

c. If earnings before interest and tax decrease to $800,000 in Year 2, what will be the new level of earnings, assuming the same tax rate as in Year 1?

P 10-3.   The following information was in the annual report of Rover Company:

	1995	1994	1993
Earnings per share	$ 1.12	$ 1.20	$ 1.27
Cash dividends per share (common)	$ .90	$ .85	$ .82
Market price per share	$ 12.80	$ 14.00	$ 16.30
Total common dividends	$ 21,700,000	$ 19,500,000	$ 18,360,000
Shares outstanding, end of year	24,280,000	23,100,000	22,500,000
Total assets	$ 1,280,100,000	$ 1,267,200,000	$ 1,260,400,000
Total liabilities	$ 800,400,000	$ 808,500,000	$ 799,200,000
Nonredeemable preferred stock	$ 15,300,000	$ 15,300,000	$ 15,300,000
Preferred dividends	$ 910,000	$ 910,000	$ 910,000
Net income	$ 31,200,000	$ 30,600,000	$ 29,800,000

Required   a. Based on these data, compute the following ratios for 1995, 1994, and 1993:
1. Percentage of earnings retained
2. Price/earnings ratio
3. Dividend payout
4. Dividend yield
5. Book value per share

b. Discuss your findings from the viewpoint of a potential investor.

P 10-4.   The following data relate to Edger Company:

	1995	1994	1993
Earnings per share	$ 2.30	$ 3.40	$ 4.54
Dividends per share (common)	$ 1.90	$ 1.90	$ 1.90
Market price, end of year	$ 41.25	$ 35.00	$ 29.00
Net income	$ 9,100,000	$ 13,300,000	$ 16,500,000
Total cash dividends	$ 6,080,000	$ 5,900,000	$ 6,050,000
Order backlog at year-end	$ 5,490,800,000	$ 4,150,200,000	$ 3,700,100,000
Net contracts awarded	$ 2,650,700,000	$ 1,800,450,000	$ 3,700,100,000

Note: The stock was selling at 120.5%, 108.0%, and 105.0% of book value in 1995, 1994, and 1993, respectively.

Required   a. Compute the following for 1995, 1994, and 1993:
1. Percentage of earnings retained
2. Price/earnings ratio

3. Dividend payout
4. Dividend yield
5. Book value per share

b. Comment on your results from (a). Include in your discussion the data on backlog and new contracts awarded.

P 10-5. Dicker Company has the following pattern of financial data for Years 1 and 2:

	Year 1	Year 2
Net income	$ 40,000	$ 42,000
Preferred stock (5%)	$450,000	$550,000
Weighted average number of common shares outstanding	38,000	38,000

Required Calculate earnings per share and comment on the trend.

P 10-6. Assume the following facts for the current year:

Common shares outstanding on January 1, 50,000 shares
July 1, 2-for-1 stock split
October 1, a stock issue of 10,000 shares

Required Compute the denominator of the earnings per share computation for the current year.

P 10-7. XYZ Corporation reported earnings per share of $2.00 in 1994. In 1995, XYZ Corporation reported earnings per share of $1.50. 2-for-1 stock splits were declared on July 1, 1995 and December 31, 1995.

Required Present the earnings per share for a two-year comparative income statement that includes 1995 and 1994.

P 10-8. Cook Company shows the following condensed income statement information for the year ended December 31, 1995:

Income before extraordinary gain	$30,000
Plus: Extraordinary gain, net of tax expense of $2,000	5,000
Net income	$35,000

The company declared dividends of $3,000 on preferred stock and $5,000 on common stock. At the beginning of 1995, 20,000 shares of common stock were outstanding. On July 1, 1995, the company issued 1,000 additional common shares. The preferred stock is not convertible.

Required a. Compute the earnings per share.
b. How much of the earnings per share appears to be recurring?

P 10-9.   Assume the following facts for the current year:

Net income	$200,000
Common dividends	$ 20,000
Preferred dividends (the preferred	
stock is *not* convertible)	$ 10,000
Common shares outstanding on January 1	20,000 shares
Common stock issued on July 1	5,000 shares
2-for-1 stock split on December 31	

Required   a.   Compute the earnings per share for the current year.
                b.   Earnings per share in the prior year was $8.00. Use the earnings per share
                    computed in part (a) and present a two-year earnings per share compari-
                    son for the current year and the prior year.

P 10-10.   Smith and Jones, Inc. is primarily engaged in the worldwide production,
processing, distribution, and marketing of food products. The following
information is extracted from its 1995 annual report:

	1995	1994
Earnings per share	$ 1.08	$ 1.14
Cash dividends per common share	$ .80	$ .76
Market price per common share	$ 12.94	$ 15.19
Common shares outstanding	25,380,000	25,316,000
Total assets	$ 1,264,086,000	$ 1,173,924,000
Total liabilities	$ 823,758,000	$ 742,499,000
Nonredeemable preferred stock	$ 16,600,000	$ 16,600,000
Preferred dividends	$ 4,567,000	$ 930,000
Net income	$ 32,094,000	$ 31,049,000

Required   a.   Based on these data, compute the following for 1995 and 1994:
                  1.   Percentage of earnings retained   4.   Dividend yield
                  2.   Price/earnings ratio   5.   Book value per share
                  3.   Dividend payout
                b.   Discuss your findings from the viewpoint of a potential investor.

P 10-11.   On December 31, 1995, Farley Camera, Inc. issues 5,000 stock appreciation
rights to its president to entitle her to receive cash for the difference between
the market price of its stock and a preestablished price of $20. The date of
exercise is December 31, 1998, and the required service period is the entire
three years. The market price fluctuates as follows: 12/31/96—$23.00;
12/31/97—$21.00; 12/31/98—$26.00.

Based on FASB Interpretation No. 28, Farley Camera accrued the following
compensation expense:

1996	$ 15,000
1997	$ (10,000)
1998	$ 25,000

Required   a. What is the executive's main advantage of receiving stock appreciation rights over stock options?

b. In 1996, a $15,000 expense is recorded. What is the offsetting account?

c. What is the financial impact on the company of the exercise of the stock appreciation rights in 1998? How does this impact affect financial statement analysis?

P 10-12a.   A company has only common stock outstanding.

Required   Answer the following multiple-choice question. Total shareholders' equity divided by the number of shares outstanding represents the:

1. Return on equity   3. Book value per share
2. Stated value per share   4. Price/earnings ratio

P 10-12b.   Maple Corporation's stockholders' equity at June 30, 1995 consisted of the following:

Preferred stock, 10%, $50 par value; liquidating value, $55 per share; 20,000 shares issued and outstanding	$1,000,000
Common stock, $10 par value; 500,000 shares authorized; 150,000 shares issued and outstanding	1,500,000
Retained earnings	500,000

Required   Answer the following multiple-choice question. The book value per share of common stock is:

1. $10.00   3. $13.33
2. $12.67   4. $17.65

P 10-13.   Consecutive five-year balance sheets and income statements of the Donna Szabo Corporation are as follows:

DONNA SZABO CORPORATION
Balance Sheets
December 31, 1991 through December 31, 1995

(Dollars in thousands)	1995	1994	1993	1992	1991
Assets					
Current assets:					
Cash	$ 26,000	$ 27,000	$ 29,000	$ 28,000	$ 27,000
Accounts receivable, net	125,000	126,000	128,000	130,000	128,000
Inventories	140,000	143,000	145,000	146,000	144,000
Total current assets	291,000	296,000	302,000	304,000	299,000
Property, plant, and equipment, net	420,000	418,000	417,000	418,000	415,000
Total assets	$711,000	$714,000	$719,000	$722,000	$714,000

(continued)

(Dollars in thousands)	1995	1994	1993	1992	1991
Liabilities and Stockholders' Equity					
Current liabilities:					
Accounts payable	$120,000	$122,000	$122,500	$124,000	$125,000
Income taxes	12,000	13,000	13,500	13,000	12,000
Total current liabilities	132,000	135,000	136,000	137,000	137,000
Long-term debt	90,000	65,000	67,000	68,000	69,000
Stockholders' equity:					
Preferred stock	49,000	76,000	80,000	82,000	75,000
Common stock	290,000	290,000	290,000	290,000	290,000
Paid-in capital in excess of par, common stock	70,000	70,000	70,000	70,000	70,000
Retained earnings	80,000	78,000	76,000	75,000	73,000
Total stockholders' equity	489,000	514,000	516,000	517,000	508,000
Total liabilities and stockholders' equity	$711,000	$714,000	$719,000	$722,000	$714,000

DONNA SZABO CORPORATION
Statement of Earnings
Years Ended December 31, 1991-1995

(In thousands, except per share)	1995	1994	1993	1992	1991
Net sales	$890,000	$870,000	$850,000	$935,000	$920,000
Cost of goods sold	(540,000)	(530,700)	(522,750)	(579,000)	(570,000)
Gross profit	350,000	339,300	327,250	356,000	350,000
Selling and administrative expense	(230,000)	(225,000)	(220,000)	(225,000)	(224,000)
Interest expense	(9,500)	(6,600)	(6,800)	(6,900)	(7,000)
Earnings from continuing operations before income taxes	110,500	107,700	100,450	124,100	119,000
Income taxes	(33,000)	(33,300)	(32,100)	(30,400)	(37,400)
Earnings from continuing operations	77,500	74,400	68,350	93,700	81,600
Extraordinary gains, net of taxes	20,000	—	—	—	—
Net earnings	$ 97,500	$ 74,400	$ 68,350	$ 93,700	$ 81,600
Earnings per share:					
Continuing operations	$2.67	$2.57	$2.36	$3.23	$2.81
Extraordinary gain	.69	—	—	—	—
Net earnings per share	$3.36	$2.57	$2.36	$3.23	$2.81

Note: Additional data:
1. Preferred stock dividends (in thousands):

1995	$3,920
1994	$6,100
1993	$6,400
1992	$6,600
1991	$6,000

2. Common shares outstanding, 29,000,000 (actual)
3. Stock options outstanding, 1,000,000 (actual)
4. Dividends per common share (actual):

1995	$3.16
1994	$2.29
1993	$2.10
1992	$2.93
1991	$2.80

5. Market price per common share (actual):

1995	$24.00
1994	$22.00
1993	$21.00
1992	$37.00
1991	$29.00

Required   a. Compute or determine the following for the years 1991-1995.
1. Degree of financial leverage
2. Earnings per common share
3. Price/earnings ratio
4. Percentage of earnings retained
5. Dividend payout
6. Dividend yield
7. Book value per share
8. Materiality of options

b. Comment on the investor perspective.

Cases

Micron Technology, Inc. and subsidiaries reported the following in its 1994 annual report:

MICRON TECHNOLOGY, INC.
Consolidated Balance Sheet (in Part)
(Amounts in millions)

	September 1, 1994	September 2, 1993
Shareholders' equity:		
Common stock, $0.10 par value; authorized, 150.0 million shares; issued and outstanding, 101.9 and 95.8 million shares	$ 10.2	$ 4.0
Additional paid-in capital	369.7	353.3
Retained earnings	670.8	282.5
Unamortized stock compensation	(1.4)	(0.3)
Total shareholders' equity	$1,049.3	$639.5

MICRON TECHNOLOGY, INC.
Consolidated Statements of Operations (in Part)
(Amounts in millions, except for per-share amounts)

Fiscal Year Ended	September 1, 1994	September 2, 1993	September 3, 1992
Net sales	$1,628.6	$828.3	$506.3
Operating income	620.1	165.9	13.7
Net income	400.5	104.1	6.6
Earnings per share:			
Primary	$3.83	$1.04	$0.07
Fully diluted	3.80	1.03	0.07
Number of shares used in per share calculation:			
Primary	104.5	100.2	97.3
Fully diluted	105.2	101.3	97.3

Note 1 (in Part)

On March 1, 1994, the company's board of directors announced a 5-for-2 stock split effected in the form of a stock dividend to shareholders of record as of April 1, 1994. A total of 60,942,448 additional shares were issued in conjunction with the stock split.

The company distributed cash in lieu of fractional shares resulting from the stock split. The company's par value of $0.10 per share remained unchanged. As a result, $6.1 million was transferred from additional paid-in capital to common stock. All historical shares and per-share amounts have been restated to reflect retroactively the stock split.

1993 Annual Report:

MICRON TECHNOLOGY, INC.
Consolidated Balance Sheet (in Part)
(Amounts in thousands)

	September 2, 1993	September 3, 1992
Shareholders' equity:		
Common stock, $0.10 par value; authorized, 100,000,000 shares; issued and outstanding, 40,099,156 and 38,336,565	$ 4,010	$ 3,834
Additional paid-in capital	353,277	327,179
Retained earnings	282,468	180,341
Unamortized stock compensation	(246)	(187)
Total shareholders' equity	$639,509	$511,167

MICRON TECHNOLOGY, INC.
Consolidated Statements of Operations (in Part)
(Amounts in thousands, except for per-share amounts)

Fiscal Year Ended	September 2, 1993	September 3, 1992	August 29, 1991
Net sales	$828,270	$506,300	$425,362
Operating income	165,946	13,716	11,761
Net income	104,065	6,626	5,079
Earnings per share:			
Primary	$2.60	$0.17	$0.13
Fully diluted	2.57	0.17	0.13
Number of shares used in per share calculations:			
Primary	40,070,000	38,912,000	37,821,000
Fully diluted	40,520,000	38,912,000	38,032,000

Required   a. The 1993 annual report indicated that 40,520,000 shares were used to compute the 1993 fully diluted earnings per share. The 1994 annual report indicated that 101,300,000 shares were used to compute the 1993 fully diluted earnings per share. Why the change in the number of shares? Show the calculation of the change in number of shares.

            b. What caused the change in reported fully diluted earnings per share in 1993 from $2.57 to $1.03? Show the calculation.

            c. Speculate on reasons for the stock split.

            d. How will the book value per share be affected by the stock split?

            e. For a stock split, the par or stated value of the stock is usually changed in proportion to the stock split, and no change is made to retained earnings, additional paid-in capital, or capital stock. How was this stock split handled?

CASE 10-2 View This Investment

Selected data from the 1995 annual report of Tyco International follows:

Consolidated Statement of Income
Year Ended June 30

(In thousands, except per-share data)	1995	1994	1993
Sales	$ 4,534,651	$ 4,076,383	$ 3,919,357
Costs and expenses:			
Cost of sales	3,313,301	3,003,194	2,909,947
Nonrecurring inventory charge	—	—	22,485
Selling, general, and administrative	735,917	682,568	682,520
Merger and transaction-related costs	37,170	—	—
Restructuring and severance charges	—	—	39,325
Interest	63,385	62,431	85,785
	4,149,773	3,748,193	3,740,062
Income before income taxes, extraordinary item, and cumulative effect of accounting changes	384,878	328,190	179,295
Income taxes	168,285	138,999	84,837
Income before extraordinary item and cumulative effect of accounting changes	216,593	189,191	94,458
Extraordinary item, net of taxes	(2,600)	—	(2,816)
Income before cumulative effect of accounting changes	213,993	189,191	91,642
Cumulative effect of accounting changes	—	—	(71,040)
Net income	$ 213,993	$ 189,191	$ 20,602
Income per share:			
Before extraordinary item and cumulative effect of accounting changes	$ 2.87	$ 2.56	$ 1.30
Extraordinary item	(.03)	—	(.04)
Cumulative effect of accounting changes	—	—	(.98)
Net income	$ 2.84	$ 2.56	$ .28
Common equivalent shares	75,509	73,770	72,316

Consolidated Balance Sheet

At June 30 (In thousands, except share data)	1995	1994
Current assets:		
Cash and cash equivalents	$ 66,021	$ 75,843
Receivables, less allowance for doubtful accounts of $29,554 in 1995 and $29,311 in 1994	527,946	515,160
Contracts in process	104,526	79,475
Inventories	592,158	517,068
Deferred income taxes	108,118	105,614
Prepaid expenses	53,132	54,904
	1,451,901	1,348,064
Property, plant, and equipment, net	658,471	609,873
Goodwill and other intangible assets	1,004,463	918,791
Reorganization value in excess of identifiable assets	108,801	115,201
Deferred income taxes	101,678	112,691
Other assets	56,147	39,978
Total assets	$ 3,381,461	$ 3,144,598
Current liabilities:		
Loans payable and current maturities of long-term debt	$ 84,387	$ 163,164
Accounts payable	417,395	332,004
Accrued expenses	423,387	382,576
Contracts in process—billings in excess of costs	75,546	63,324
Income taxes	72,370	73,301
Deferred income taxes	11,630	3,777
	1,084,715	1,018,146
Deferred income taxes	9,599	13,698
Long-term debt	506,417	588,491
Other liabilities	146,049	157,237
Commitments and contingencies	—	—
Shareholders' equity:		
Preferred stock, $1 par value, authorized 2,000 shares; none outstanding	—	—
Common stock, $.50 par value, authorized 180,000,000 shares; outstanding, 76,365,001 shares in 1995 and 71,084,293 shares in 1994, net of reacquired shares of 7,960,740 in 1995 and 7,600,747 in 1994	38,183	35,542
Capital in excess of par value, net of deferred compensation of $21,636 in 1995 and $9,318 in 1994	620,633	567,476
Currency translation adjustment	(9,451)	(40,874)
Retained earnings	985,316	804,882
	1,634,681	1,367,026
Total liabilities and shareholders' equity	$ 3,381,461	$ 3,144,598

Other selected data:

	June 30, 1995	June 30, 1994
Market price per share of common stock	$ 54	$ 45 $^{7}/_{8}$
Dividends paid	$ 24,335,000	$ 18,510,000
Dividends per share of common stock	40¢	40¢

Required   a.   Compute the following for 1995 and 1994:
  1.   Degree of financial leverage
  2.   Price/earnings ratio
  3.   Percentage of earnings retained
  4.   Dividend yield
  5.   Book value per share

b.   Comment on the ratios computed under (a).

CASE 10-3 Stock Option Plan

Selected data from the 1995 annual report of Amgen follows below and on page 461.

Stock option and purchase plans (in Part)

The Company's stock option plans provide for option grants designated as either nonqualified or incentive stock options. The options generally vest over a three- to five-year period and generally expire seven years from the date of grant. In general, stock option grants are set at the closing price of the Company's common stock on the date of grant. As of December 31, 1995, the Company had 26.3 million shares of common stock available for future grant under its stock option plans.

Most U.S. employees and certain employees outside the U.S. are eligible to receive a grant of stock options periodically with the number of shares generally determined by the employee's salary grade, performance level, and the stock price. In addition, certain management and professional-level employees normally receive a stock option grant upon hire. Non-employee directors of the Company receive a grant of stock options annually.

Stock option information with respect to all of the Company's stock option plans follows (in millions, except price information):

| | | Exercise Price | | |
	Shares	Low	High	Weighted Average
Balance, December 31, 1992, unexercised	30.2	$ 1.76	$ 38.88	$ 11.09
Granted	8.0	16.06	35.31	18.93
Exercised	(4.5)	1.76	30.50	4.62
Canceled	(0.6)	2.25	38.38	15.21
Balance, December 31, 1993, unexercised	33.1	$ 1.76	$ 38.88	$ 13.72
Granted	8.5	17.68	29.50	22.07
Exercised	(5.6)	1.93	28.00	6.95
Canceled	(1.0)	3.69	37.38	21.92
Balance, December 31, 1994, unexercised	35.0	$ 1.76	$ 38.88	$ 16.58
Granted	7.1	28.94	58.88	39.62
Exercised	(8.1)	1.93	38.88	12.87
Canceled	(1.0)	2.25	39.88	19.86
Balance, December 31, 1995, unexercised	33.0	$ 1.76	$ 58.88	$ 22.35

At December 31, 1995, stock options to purchase 15.7 million shares were exercisable.

Required   a.   Compute the materiality of options for 1995 and 1994. Comment on the significance of the options.

(continued on page 462)

Consolidated Balance Sheet
(In millions, except per-share data)

December 31	1995	1994
Assets Current assets:		
Cash and cash equivalents	$ 66.7	$ 211.3
Marketable securities	983.6	485.4
Trade receivables, net of allowance for doubtful accounts of $13.8 in 1995 and $13.3 in 1994	199.3	194.7
Inventories	88.8	98.0
Deferred tax assets, net	51.7	70.2
Other current assets	64.0	56.0
Total current assets	1,454.1	1,115.6
Property, plant, and equipment at cost, net	743.8	665.3
Investments in affiliated companies	95.7	82.3
Other assets	139.2	130.9
	$ 2,432.8	$ 1,994.1
Liabilities and Stockholders' Equity Current liabilities:		
Accounts payable	$ 54.4	$ 30.5
Commercial paper	69.7	99.7
Accrued liabilities	459.7	406.2
Total current liabilities	583.8	536.4
Long-term debt	177.2	183.4
Contingencies		
Stockholders' equity:		
Common stock and additional paid-in capital; $.0001 par value; 750.0 shares authorized; outstanding, 265.7 shares in 1995 and 264.7 shares in 1994	864.8	719.3
Retained earnings	807.0	555.0
Total stockholders' equity	1,671.8	1,274.3
	$ 2,432.8	$ 1,994.1

b. Comment on the influence to net income from the options granted.
c. Comment on the influence to earnings per share from the options granted.
d. Comment on the potential benefit to the employee from receiving these options.

CASE 10-4 Consideration of Stock Dividend

Selected data from the 1995 annual report of Mid Am, Inc. follows:

CONSOLIDATED STATEMENT OF CONDITION (in Part)

December 31 (Dollars in thousands)	1995	1994
Shareholders' Equity:		
Preferred stock, no par value		
Authorized, 2,000,000 shares		
Issued and outstanding, 1,422,744		
and 1,608,000 shares in 1995 and		
1994, respectively	$ 35,569	$ 40,200
Common stock, stated value of $3.33 per share		
Authorized, 35,000,000 shares		
Issued, 19,492,726 and 17,359,629 shares		
in 1995 and 1994, respectively	64,975	57,865
Surplus	91,723	75,624
Retained earnings	9,529	17,769
Treasury stock, 522,361 and 1,400 common		
shares in 1995 and 1994, respectively	(8,424)	(20)
Unrealized gains (losses) on securities available		
for sale	1,466	(6,186)
Commitments and contingencies (Notes 13 and 14)	—	—
	$194,838	$185,252

CONSOLIDATED STATEMENT OF EARNINGS (in Part)

Year Ended December 31 (Dollars in thousands, except per-share data)	1995	1994	1993
Net income	$ 24,967	$ 23,253	$ 24,681
Net income available to common shareholders	$ 22,216	$ 20,336	$ 21,763
Earnings per common share:			
Primary	$ 1.16	$ 1.07	$ 1.16
Fully diluted	$ 1.11	$ 1.03	$ 1.11

CONSOLIDATED STATEMENT OF CHANGES IN SHAREHOLDERS' EQUITY (in Part)

(Dollars in thousands, except for per-share data)	Preferred Stock	Common Stock	Surplus	Retained Earnings	Treasury Stock	Unrealized Gains (Losses) on Securities Available for Sale	Total Shareholders' Equity
Balances at December 31, 1994	$ 40,200	$ 57,865	$ 75,624	$ 17,769	$ (20)	$ (6,186)	$ 185,252
Net income for the year				24,967			24,967
Dividends declared:							
Preferred cash dividends				(2,751)			(2,751)
Common cash dividends of $.63 per share				(12,111)			(12,111)
10% common stock dividend (1,705,761 shares)		5,686	12,314	(18,000)			
Unrealized gains on securities available for sale						7,652	7,652
Treasury shares acquired					(9,197)		(9,197)
Treasury shares issued					793		793
Preferred stock conversions	(4,631)	1,358	3,273				
Fractional shares and other items		66	512	(345)			233
Balances at December 31, 1995	$ 35,569	$ 64,975	$ 91,723	$ 9,529	$ (8,424)	$ 1,466	$ 194,838

CONSOLIDATED STATEMENT OF CASH FLOWS (in Part)

Year Ended December 31 (Dollars in thousands)	1995	1994	1993
Financing Activities:			
Net increase (decrease) in demand deposits and savings accounts	$ 41,189	$ (43,066)	$ 99,768
Net increase in other time deposits	82,461	10,476	29,586
Net increase in federal funds purchased and securities sold under agreements to repurchase	7,412	8,363	17,729
Repayment of capitalized lease obligations and debt	(66,050)	(41,638)	(2,319)
Proceeds from issuance of long-term debt	49,021	79,002	19,358
Proceeds from issuance of common stock		1,893	4,749
Cash dividends paid	(14,862)	(13,638)	(11,692)
Cash paid to Colonial shareholders			(814)
Preferred stock conversions, fractional shares and other items	233	4	79
Treasury stock (net of reissuance of 793)	(8,404)	(655)	
Net Cash Provided by Financing Activities	$ 91,000	$ 741	$156,444

MID AM, INC. SUMMARY OF FINANCIAL DATA (in Part)

Years Ended December 31 (Dollars in thousands, except shares, per-share, and ratio data)	1995	1994	1993	1992	1991
Per Common Share Data:					
Cash dividends declared	$0.63	$0.59	$0.54	$0.50	$0.48
Shareholders' equity	8.40	7.61	7.76	7.29	6.41
Primary:					
Income before extraordinary item and change in accounting principle	1.16	1.07	1.16	0.95	0.42
Net income	1.16	1.07	1.16	1.03	0.44
Fully diluted:					
Income before extraordinary item and change in accounting principle	1.11	1.03	1.11	0.94	0.41
Net income	1.11	1.03	1.11	1.01	0.44

MID AM, INC. EIGHT-YEAR PERFORMANCE SUMMARY (UNAUDITED) (in Part)

Year	Net Income Pooled	Net Income Historic	Cash Dividends	Book Value	Stock Price	Total Market Equity $(000)
Data per Common Share						
1995	$1.16	$1.16	$0.63	$8.40	$16.41	$311,233
1994	1.07	1.28	0.59	7.61	13.52	232,631
1993	1.16	1.39	0.54	7.76	12.40	197,212
1992	1.03	1.30	0.50	7.29	10.74	166,126
1991	0.44	0.50	0.48	6.41	9.77	137,674
1990	0.73	1.01	0.48	6.01	8.01	103,111
1989	0.81	0.98	0.44	5.03	10.13	104,668
1988	0.85	0.82	0.38	4.87	7.35	75,909
Annual Growth 1995/94	8.41%		6.78%	10.38%	21.38%	33.79%
Average Growth 1995/88	13.39%		7.56%	8.29%	13.53%	23.01%

Year	Average Shares Outstanding (000)	Common Shares Traded (000)	Common Shareholders	Stock Dividends	Cash Dividend Payout Ratio	Year-End Price/Earnings Ratio
Common Stock Data (as originally reported)						
1995	19,205	4,377	8,208	10%	54.51%	14.36x
1994	15,623	3,500	7,899	10	52.23	11.62
1993	12,976	3,097	6,360		41.21	9.80
1992	9,968	1,903	5,543	10	39.92	9.70
1991	9,801	1,580	4,339		88.89	20.38
1990	8,745	1,491	4,379	10	46.76	8.51
1989	6,710	604	3,701	10	42.14	11.14
1988	5,533	264	3,301	5	36.12	9.77

Note 1. Accounting Policies (in Part)

The weighted average number of common shares outstanding for primary and fully diluted earnings per share computations were as follows:

Year Ended December 31	1995	1994	1993
Weighted average common shares outstanding—primary	19,205,000	19,046,000	18,736,000
Weighted average common shares outstanding—fully diluted	22,592,000	22,627,000	22,310,000

From 1992 Annual Report

CONSOLIDATED STATEMENT OF EARNINGS (in Part)

Year Ended December 31,
(Dollars in thousands, except per share data)

	1992	1991	1990
Income before extraordinary item and change in accounting principle	$ 14,619	$ 4,959	$ 9,548
Realization of operating loss carryforward		433	203
Cumulative effect of change in accounting principle	1,272		
Net income	$ 15,891	$ 5,392	$ 9,751
Net income available to common shareholders	$ 14,284	$ 5,392	$ 9,751
Earnings per Common Share			
Primary:			
Income before extraordinary item and change in accounting principle	$ 1.96	$ 0.76	$ 1.64
Realization of operating loss carryforward		0.07	0.03
Cumulative effect of change in accounting principle	0.19		
Net income	$ 2.15	$ 0.83	$ 1.67
Fully diluted:			
Income before extraordinary item and change in accounting principle	$ 1.88	$ 0.76	$ 1.64
Realization of operating loss carryforward		0.07	0.03
Cumulative effect of change in accounting principle	0.17		
Net income	$ 2.05	$ 0.83	$ 1.67

From library—*Standard & Poor's Daily Stock Price Record* (reviewed by year)

Data per Common Share

Year	Stock Price
1995	$16 $^{13}/_{32}$
1994	14 $^{7}/_{8}$
1993	15
1992	19 $^{1}/_{2}$
1991	19 $^{1}/_{2}$
1990	16
1989	22 $^{1}/_{4}$
1988	17 $^{3}/_{4}$

Required   a. Why is there a difference between the net income and net income available to common shareholders?

b. Is earnings per share computed using net income or net income available to common shareholders?

c. 1. How many shares of common stock were outstanding at December 31, 1995?
   2. What was the weighted average common shares for the year ended December 31, 1995?
   3. Which share number is used to compute earnings per share?

d. Which accounts were used to record the 10% common stock dividend?

e. 1. What was the percentage increase in total cash dividends paid between 1993 and 1995?
   2. What was the percentage increase in cash dividends declared per share between 1993 and 1995?
   3. Speculate on the difference in the increase between (1) and (2).

f. Speculate on the difference between the stock price disclosed in the 1995 annual report for 1988 and the stock price in the annual *Standard & Poor's Daily Stock Price Record* for 1988.

g. Consider the earnings per share reported in the consolidated statement of earnings for 1995 and the earnings per share disclosed in the eight-year performance summary. The primary earnings per share is equal to the pooled earnings under the eight-year performance summary.
   1. Speculate on what is intended by pooled earnings per share.
   2. Speculate on what is intended by historic earnings per share.

h. The 1992 annual report disclosed primary earnings per share for 1992 of $2.15. Why does the eight-year performance summary included in the 1995 annual report indicate a much lower earnings per share for 1992?

i. 1. Using primary earnings per share, compute the price/earnings ratio for the end of 1995.
   2. Using fully diluted earnings per share, compute the price/earnings ratio for the end of 1995.
   3. When computing the price/earnings ratio should the primary or fully diluted earnings per share be computed?

j. The eight-year performance summary shows a year-end price/earnings ratio of 14.36 for 1995. Compare this price/earnings ratio with your computations above. Speculate on why there is a difference.

CASE 10-5 Stock Split Revisited

Selected data from the 1995 annual report of Lands' End, Inc. follows:

LANDS' END, INC. & SUBSIDIARIES
Consolidated Statements of Operations (in Part)

	For the Period Ended		
(In thousands, except per-share data)	January 27, 1995	January 28, 1994	January 29, 1993
Net income	$ 36,096	$ 43,729	$ 33,500
Net income per share before cumulative effect of change in accounting	$ 1.03	$ 1.18	$ 0.92
Cumulative effect of change in accounting	—	.04	—
Net income per share	$ 1.03	$ 1.22	$ 0.92

Consolidated Balance Sheets (in Part)

(In thousands)	January 27, 1995	January 28, 1994
Shareholders' investment:		
Common stock, 40,221 and		
20,110 shares issued, respectively	$ 402	$ 201
Donated capital	8,400	8,400
Paid-in capital	25,817	24,888
Deferred compensation	(1,421)	(2,001)
Currency translation adjustment	284	246
Retained earnings	229,554	193,460
Treasury stock, 5,395 and 2,154		
shares at cost, respectively	(73,908)	(47,909)
Total shareholders' investment	$189,128	$177,285

Consolidated Statements of Shareholders' Investment

(In thousands)	For the Period Ended		
	January 27, 1995	January 28, 1994	January 29, 1993
Common Stock:			
Beginning balance	$ 201	$ 201	$ 201
2-for-1 stock split	201	—	—
Ending balance	$ 402	$ 201	$ 201
Donated Capital Balance	$ 8,400	$ 8,400	$ 8,400
Paid-in Capital:			
Beginning balance	$ 24,888	$ 24,857	$ 23,782
Tax benefit of stock options exercised	1,130	31	1,075
2-for-1 stock split	(201)	—	—
Ending balance	$ 25,817	$ 24,888	$ 24,857
Deferred Compensation:			
Beginning balance	$ (2,001)	$ (1,680)	$ (886)
Issuance of treasury stock	—	(564)	(985)
Amortization of deferred compensation	580	243	191
Ending balance	$ (1,421)	$ (2,001)	$ (1,680)
Foreign Currency Translation:			
Beginning balance	$ 246	$ —	$ —
Adjustment for the year	38	246	—
Ending balance	$ 284	$ 246	$ —
Retained Earnings:			
Beginning balance	$193,460	$153,324	$123,418
Net income	36,096	43,729	33,500
Cash dividends paid	—	(3,592)	(3,589)
Issuance of treasury stock	(2)	(1)	(5)
Ending balance	$229,554	$193,460	$153,324
Treasury Stock:			
Beginning balance	$ (47,909)	$ (45,714)	$ (28,283)
Purchase of treasury stock	(27,979)	(2,861)	(20,972)
Issuance of treasury stock	1,980	666	3,541
Ending balance	$ (73,908)	$ (47,909)	$ (45,714)
Total Stockholders' Equity	$189,128	$177,285	$139,388

Consolidated Statement of Cash Flows (in Part)

(In thousands)	For the Period Ended		
	January 27, 1995	January 28, 1994	January 29, 1993
Cash flows (used for) from financing activities:			
Proceeds from short-term and long-term debt	$ 7,539	$ 80	—
Payment of short-term and long-term debt	(40)	—	$(16,349)
Tax effect of exercise of stock options	1,130	31	1,075
Purchases of treasury stock	(27,979)	(2,861)	(20,972)
Issuance of treasury stock	1,978	101	2,551
Cash dividends paid to common shareholders	—	(3,592)	(3,589)
Net cash flows used for financing activities	$(17,372)	$(6,241)	$(37,284)

Note 1. Summary of significant accounting policies (in Part)

Net income per share

Net income per share is computed by dividing net income by the weighted average number of common shares outstanding during each period. After the 2-for-1 stock split, the weighted average common shares outstanding were 35.2 million, 35.9 million and 36.3 million (see Note 2) for fiscal years 1995, 1994, and 1993, respectively. Common stock equivalents include awards, grants, and stock options issued by the company. The common stock equivalents do not significantly dilute basic earnings per share.

Note 2. Shareholders' investment (in Part)

Capital Stock

Pursuant to shareholder approval in May 1994, the company increased its authorized common stock from 30 million shares of $0.01 par value to 160 million shares. Also, the company is authorized to issue 5 million shares of preferred stock, $0.01 par value. The company's board of directors has the authority to issue shares and to fix dividend, voting and conversion rights, redemption provisions, liquidation preferences, and other rights and restrictions of the preferred stock.

Ten-Year Consolidated Financial Summary (unaudited) (in Part)

(In thousands, except per share data)	1995	1994[2]	1993	1992
Per share of common stock:[1]				
Net income per share before cumulative effect of change in accounting	$1.03	$1.18	$0.92	$0.77
Cumulative effect of change in accounting	—	$0.04	—	—
Net income per share	$1.03	$1.22	$0.92	$0.77
Cash dividends per share	—	$0.10	$0.10	$0.10
Common shares outstanding	34,826	35,912	36,056	36,944

(1) Net income per share (pro forma 1986 and 1987) was computed after giving retroactive effect to the 108-for-1 stock split in August 1986, the 2-for-1 stock split in August 1987, the 2-for-1 stock split in May 1994, and assuming that the shares sold in the October 1986 initial public offering were issued at the beginning of fiscal 1986.

(2) Effective January 30, 1993, the company adopted Statement of Financial Accounting Standards (SFAS) No. 109, "Accounting for Income Taxes," which was recorded as a change in accounting principle at the beginning of fiscal 1994, with an increase to net income of $1.3 million or $0.04 per share.

Selected data from the 1993 annual report of Lands' End, Inc. follows:

Consolidated Balance Sheet (in Part)

(Dollars in thousands)	January 29, 1993	January 31, 1992
Shareholders' investment:		
Common stock, 20,110,294 shares issued	$ 201	$ 201
Donated capital	8,400	8,400
Paid-in capital	24,857	23,782
Deferred compensation	(1,680)	(886)
Retained earnings	153,324	123,418
Treasury stock, 2,082,035 and 1,638,840 shares at cost, respectively	(45,714)	(28,283)
Total shareholders' investment	$139,388	$126,632

Consolidated Statement of Operations (in Part)

(Dollars in thousands, except per share data)	January 29, 1993	January 31, 1992	January 31, 1991
Net income	$33,500	$28,732	$14,743
Net income per share	1.85	1.53	0.75

Required

a. The 1995 annual report discloses net income for the period ended January 29, 1993 of $33,500,000 and net income per share of $0.92 for this same period. The 1993 annual report discloses net income for the period ended January 29, 1993 of $33,500,000 and net income per share of $1.85 for this same period. Speculate on why the net income per share has changed.

b. 1. How many shares have been sold and paid for as of January 27, 1995?

2. How many shares have been bought back and not retired as of January 27, 1995?

3. How many shares are outstanding as of January 27, 1995?

c. Indicate the total cash dividend paid:
1. For the period ended January 27, 1995
2. For the period ended January 28, 1994
3. For the period ended January 29, 1993

d. Indicate the amount paid for the purchase of treasury stock:
1. For the period ended January 27, 1995
2. For the period ended January 28, 1994
3. For the period ended January 29, 1993

e. Indicate the total paid to stockholders:
1. For the period ended January 27, 1995
2. For the period ended January 28, 1994
3. For the period ended January 29, 1993

f. What common share number was used to compute earnings per share for 1995?

g. What is the par value of common stock?

11   Statement of Cash Flows

Quote the Banker, "Watch Cash Flow"

Once upon a midnight dreary as I pondered weak and weary
Over many a quaint and curious volume of accounting lore,
Seeking gimmicks (without scruple) to squeeze through some new
    tax loophole,
Suddenly I heard a knock upon my door,
    Only this, and nothing more.

Then I felt a queasy tingling and I heard the cash a-jingling
As a fearsome banker entered whom I'd often seen before.
His face was money-green and in his eyes there could be seen
Dollar-signs that seemed to glitter as he reckoned up the score.
    "Cash flow," the banker said, and nothing more.

I had always thought it fine to show a jet black bottom line,
But the banker sounded a resounding, "No,
Your receivables are high, mounting upward toward the sky;
Write-offs loom. What matters is cash flow."
    He repeated, "Watch cash flow."

Then I tried to tell the story of our lovely inventory
Which, though large, is full of most delightful stuff.
But the banker saw its growth, and with a mighty oath
He waved his arms and shouted, "Stop! Enough!
    Pay the interest, and don't give me any guff!"

Next I looked for non-cash items which could add ad infinitum
To replace the ever-outward flow of cash,
But to keep my statement black I'd held depreciation back,
And my banker said that I'd done something rash.
    He quivered, and his teeth began to gnash.

When I asked him for a loan, he responded, with a groan,
That the interest rate would be just prime plus eight,
And to guarantee my purity he'd insist on some security—
All my assets plus the scalp upon my pate.
    Only this, a standard rate.

Though my bottom line is black, I am flat upon my back.
My cash flows out and customers pay slow.
The growth of my receivables is almost unbelievable;
The result is certain—unremitting woe!
And I hear the banker utter an ominous low mutter,
  "Watch cash flow."

—Herbert S. Bailey, Jr.
Reprinted with permission

A REVIEW OF THE FUNDS STATEMENT

A statement that presented a flow of funds existed as early as 1862 in England and 1863 in the United States.[1] This is much later than the first issuance of a balance sheet and income statement. Thus, although the concept of issuing a statement that presented a flow of funds is over 100 years old, it is relatively new when compared with the balance sheet and income statement. A brief historical presentation will convey a perspective on the development of this statement.

The original funds statement accounted for the changes in cash in the bank, cash on hand, and stamps. The original statements emphasized the flow of cash, but they had many different formats. The Missouri Pacific Railway Company appears to have been the first organization to highlight changes in all balance sheet accounts when it presented a statement in 1893.[2] At the turn of the century, the United States Steel Corporation presentation began to provide subtotals for current assets and current liabilities, and the presentation reconciled to working capital (current assets less current liabilities).[3] By 1903, there were at least four conceptually different statements. The broad focal points of these statements presented the flow of funds as follows:[4]

1. Cash
2. Current assets
3. Working capital
4. All financial activities in a period

In the period from the 1910s to the late 1920s, an educator named H.A. Finney led a drive to present the statement using a format that showed the cause of a change in working capital.[5] Finney was successful, and the working capital approach became the dominant format for presenting the statement. Items that increased working capital were regarded as sources of funds, and items that decreased working capital were regarded as uses of funds.

The Accounting Principles Board addressed the presentation of the funds statement with the issuance of APB Opinion No. 3 in 1963. In general, this Opinion was vague and left a great deal of discretion as to the format of the statement. It did recommend that firms present a funds statement along with a balance sheet and income statement. At this time, the funds statement was usually titled the "Statement of Source and Application of Funds."

In 1971, APB Opinion No. 19 made the funds statement a **required statement** when a firm presents a balance sheet and income statement. Opinion No. 19 concluded that:

> When financial statements purporting to present both financial position (balance sheet) and results of operations (statement of income and retained earnings) are issued, a statement summarizing changes in financial position should also be presented as a basic financial statement for each period for which an income statement is presented.[6]

APB Opinion No. 19 gave the funds statement the title **statement of changes in financial position**. The guidelines for the presentation of the statement were still fairly flexible. Basically, the statement could take whatever form would give the most useful portrayal of the changes in financial position.

At the time of issuance of APB Opinion No. 19, two basic presentation formats existed for the statement: the working capital format and the cash and cash equivalents format. In 1971, the working capital format was the dominant approach. During the 1980s, the cash and cash equivalents format became the dominant format. Because change in presentation took place without guidance from an official standard, many presentation differences occurred, even among firms that used the same basic format.

Some brief comments are in order regarding why the dominant format was switched from the working capital concept to the cash concept. In 1973, the AICPA issued the "Report of the Study Group on the Objectives of Financial Statements." It stated that "an objective of financial statements is to provide information useful to investors and creditors for predicting, comparing, and evaluating potential cash flows to them in terms of amount, timing and related uncertainty."[7]

In 1978, the FASB issued *Statement of Financial Accounting Concepts No. 1*, "Objectives of Financial Reporting by Business Enterprises." Several of the objectives of financial reporting identified by Concept Statement No. 1 emphasized the importance of cash. For example, paragraph 39 stated that "since an enterprise's ability to generate favorable cash flows affects both its ability to pay dividends and interest and the market prices of its securities, expected cash flows to investors and creditors are related to expected cash flows to the enterprise in which they have invested or to which they have loaned funds."[8]

In December 1980, the FASB issued a Discussion Memorandum entitled "Reporting Funds Flows, Liquidity, and Financial Flexibility." Many of the respondents to the Discussion Memorandum favored the presentation of the funds statement on a cash basis. An important argument in its favor was that cash flows are a major consideration of investors and creditors. When a company presents its funds statement on a working capital basis, the cash flow may not be obvious. Thus, the effect on cash of large changes in working capital accounts, such as receivables and inventory, may go undetected.

In November 1981, the FASB issued an Exposure Draft as a follow-up to the December 1980 Discussion Memorandum. The Exposure Draft proposed focusing the funds statement on cash flow rather than on working capital. A FASB Statement typically follows an Exposure Draft, but this did not happen in this case because of the opposition to a required cash format. Additional time was allowed for discussion and research on the presentation of the funds statement. In 1984, the FASB issued *Statement of Financial Accounting Concepts, No. 5*, "Recognition and Measurement of Financial Statements of Business Enterprises." This Concepts Statement also emphasized the importance of cash flow, as did Concepts Statement No. 1.

Concepts Statement No. 5 recommended that a full set of financial statements for a period should show cash flows during the period. Paragraph 52 describes the role of information on the statement of cash flows as follows:

> It provides useful information about an entity's activities in generating cash through operations to repay debt, distribute dividends, or reinvest to maintain or expand operating capacity; about its financing activities, both debt and equity; and about its investing or spending of cash. Important uses of information about an entity's current cash receipts and payments include helping to assess factors such as the entity's liquidity, financial flexibility, profitability, and risk.[9]

In 1986, the FASB issued another Exposure Draft, followed in 1987 by FASB Statement No. 95, "Statement of Cash Flows," which superseded APB Opinion No. 19. Statement No. 95, effective in 1988, directed that the cash format be used, changed the title of the statement to the statement of cash flows, and required a fairly specific detailed format. By the time the standard was issued, most firms were using a cash format. Even these firms were affected by the change in the title of the statement and the specific presentation requirements.

Some nations require a statement of cash flows or funds flow, while others have no requirement for either cash or funds flow statements. Since the passage of FASB Statement No. 95, there has been an international trend to using the cash flow statement.

BASIC ELEMENTS OF THE STATEMENT OF CASH FLOWS

FASB Statement No. 95 directs that: (1) the statement be prepared on a cash basis; (2) the title be "The Statement of Cash Flows"; and (3) a fairly specific and detailed format be used. This statement allows the preparer to use a concept of cash that includes not only cash itself but also short-term, highly liquid investments. This is referred to as the "cash and cash equivalent" focus. The category cash and cash equivalents includes cash on hand, cash on deposit, and investments in short-term, highly liquid investments. The cash flow statement analysis explains the change in these focus accounts by examining all the accounts on the balance sheet other than the focus accounts.

Management may use the statement of cash flows to determine dividend policy, cash generated by operations, and investing and financing policy. Outsiders, such as creditors or investors, may use it to determine such things as the firm's ability to increase dividends, its ability to pay debt with cash from operations, and the percentage of cash from operations in relation to the cash from financing.

The statement of cash flows must report all transactions affecting cash flow. A company will occasionally have investing and/or financing activities that have no direct effect on cash flow. For example, a company may acquire land in exchange for common stock. This is an investing transaction (acquiring the land) and a financing transaction (issuing the common stock). The conversion of long-term bonds into common stock involves two financing activities with no effect on cash flow. Since transactions such as these will have future effects on cash flows, these transactions are to be disclosed in a separate schedule presented with the statement of cash flows.

The statement of cash flows classifies cash receipts and cash payments into operating, investing, and financing activities.[10] In brief, operating activities involve income statement items. Investing activities generally result from changes in long-term asset items. Financing activities generally relate to long-term liability and stockholders' equity items. A description of these activities and typical cash flows are as follows:

1. **Operating activities.** Operating activities include all transactions and other events that are not investing or financing activities. Cash flows from operating activities are generally the cash

effects of transactions and other events that enter into the determination of net income.

Typical cash inflows:
From sale of goods or services
From return on loans (interest)
From return on equity securities (dividends)

Typical cash outflows:
Payments for acquisitions of inventory
Payments to employees
Payments to governments (taxes)
Payments of interest expense
Payments to suppliers for other expenses

2.   **Investing activities.** Investing activities include lending money and collecting on those loans and acquiring and selling investments and productive long-term assets.

Typical cash inflows:
From receipts from loans collected
From sales of debt or equity securities of other corporations
From sale of property, plant, and equipment

Typical cash outflows:
Loans to other entities
Purchase of debt or equity securities of other entities
Purchase of property, plant, and equipment

3.   **Financing activities.** Financing activities include cash flows relating to liability and owners' equity.

Typical cash inflows:
From sale of equity securities
From sale of bonds, mortgages, notes, and other short- or long-term borrowings
Typical cash outflows:
Payment of dividends
Reacquisition of the firm's capital stock
Payment of amounts borrowed

The statement of cash flows presents cash flows from operating activities first, followed by investing activities and then financing activities. The individual inflows and outflows from investing and financing activities are presented separately. The operating activities section can be presented using the *direct method* or the *indirect method*. (The indirect method is sometimes referred to as the *reconciliation method*.) The direct method essentially presents the income statement on a cash basis, instead of an accrual basis.

The indirect method adjusts net income for items that affected net income but did not affect cash.

SFAS No. 95 encourages enterprises to present cash flows from operating activities using the direct method. However, if a company uses the direct method, the standard requires a reconciliation of net income to net cash provided by operating activities in a separate schedule. Many respondents to the Exposure Draft claimed that their accounting systems do not presently provide the information required by the direct method (e.g., cash collected from customers). For this reason, SFAS No. 95 permits the use of the indirect method. If a firm uses the indirect method, it must make a separate disclosure of interest paid and income taxes paid during the period. Exhibit 11-1, page 480-481, presents skeleton formats of a statement of cash flows using the direct method and the indirect method.

The 1986 SFAS Exposure Draft, "Statement of Cash Flows," indicates that:

> The principal advantage of the direct method is that it shows the operating cash receipts and payments. Knowledge of where operating cash flows came from and how cash was used in past periods may be useful in estimating future cash flows. The indirect method of reporting has the advantage of focusing on the differences between income and cash flow from operating activities.[11]

Exhibit 11-2, page 482, presents the 1995 Cooper Tire & Rubber Company Statement of Cash Flows. This statement presents cash from operations using the *indirect method*. The statement closely follows SFAS No. 95, but it does not separately disclose interest paid and income taxes paid during the period. Cooper has elected to disclose interest paid and income taxes paid in the footnotes to the financial statements.

In addition to reviewing the flow of funds on a yearly basis, reviewing a flow of funds for a three-year period may be helpful. This can be accomplished by adding a total column to the statement that represents the total of each item for the three-year period. This has been done for Cooper in Exhibit 11-2.

Some observations on the 1995 Cooper Statement of Cash Flows, considering the three-year period ended December 31, 1995, follow:

1. Net cash provided by operating activities was the major source of cash.

2. Net cash used in investing activities, specifically additions to property, plant, and equipment, was the major use of cash.

3. Payment of dividends was the major financing use of cash.

4. For the three-year period, net cash provided by operating activities was approximately equal to additions to property, plant, and equipment and dividends paid.

EXHIBIT 11-1   **JONES COMPANY EXAMPLE**
**Statement of Cash Flows—Comparison of Presentation
of Direct Method and Indirect Method
For the Year Ended December 31, 19XX**

	Direct Method
Cash flows from operating activities:	
Cash received from customers	$ 370,000
Cash paid to suppliers and employees	(310,000)
Interest received	10,000
Interest paid (net of amount capitalized)	(4,000)
Income taxes paid	(15,000)
Net cash provided by operating activities	51,000
Cash flows from investing activities:	
Capital expenditures	(30,000)
Proceeds from property, plant, and equipment disposals	6,000
Net cash used in investing activities	(24,000)
Cash flows from financing activities:	
Net proceeds from repayment of commercial paper	(4,000)
Proceeds from issuance of long-term debt	6,000
Dividends paid	(5,000)
Net cash used in financing activities	(3,000)
Net increase in cash and cash equivalents	24,000
Cash and cash equivalents at beginning of period	8,000
Cash and cash equivalents at end of period	$ 32,000
Reconciliation of net earnings to cash provided by operating activities:	
Net earnings	$ 40,000
Provision for depreciation	6,000
Provision for allowance for doubtful accounts	1,000
Deferred income taxes	1,000
Loss on property, plant, and equipment disposals	2,000
Changes in operating assets and liabilities:	
Receivables increase	(2,000)
Inventories increase	(4,000)
Accounts payable increase	5,000
Accrued income taxes increase	2,000
Net cash provided by operating activities	$ 51,000
Supplemental schedule of noncash investing and financing activities:	
Land acquired (investing) by issuing bonds (financing)	$ 10,000

EXHIBIT 11-1 (continued)

Indirect Method	
Operating activities:	
Net earnings	$ 40,000
Provision for depreciation	6,000
Provision for allowance for doubtful accounts	1,000
Deferred income taxes	1,000
Loss on property, plant, and equipment disposals	2,000
Changes in operating assets and liabilities:	
Receivables increase	(2,000)
Inventories increase	(4,000)
Accounts payable increase	5,000
Accrued income taxes increase	2,000
Net cash provided by operating activities	51,000
Cash flows from investing activities:	
Capital expenditures	(30,000)
Proceeds from property, plant, and equipment disposals	6,000
Net cash used in investing activities	(24,000)
Cash flows from financing activities:	
Net proceeds from repayment of commercial paper	(4,000)
Proceeds from issuance of long-term debt	6,000
Dividends paid	(5,000)
Net cash used in financing activities	(3,000)
Net increase in cash and cash equivalents	24,000
Cash and cash equivalents at beginning of period	8,000
Cash and cash equivalents at end of period	$ 32,000
Supplemental disclosure of cash flow information:	
Interest paid	$ 500
Income taxes paid	10,000
Supplemental schedule of noncash investing and financing activities:	
Land acquired (investing) and issuing bonds (financing)	$ 10,000

5. Total cash inflow from issuance of debt and from issuance of common stock were less than 9% of the net cash provided by operating activities.

6. Cash dividends were approximately 13.6% of net cash provided by operating activities.

EXHIBIT 11-2   **COOPER TIRE & RUBBER COMPANY**
Consolidated Statement of Cash Flows, with Three-Year Total
For Years Ended December 31, 1995, 1994, and 1993

	Total	1995	1994	1993
	(Dollar amounts in thousands)			
Operating activities:				
Net income	$ 343,549	$112,820	$128,519	$102,210
Adjustments to reconcile net income to net cash provided by operating activities:				
Depreciation and amortization	165,268	63,313	55,603	46,352
Deferred income taxes	28,865	9,356	8,983	10,526
Changes in operating assets and liabilities:				
Accounts receivable	(75,826)	(35,812)	(39,034)	(980)
Inventories and prepaid expenses	(71,956)	(20,159)	(6,174)	(45,623)
Accounts payable and accrued liabilities	13,950	2,052	24,698	(12,800)
Postretirement benefits other than pensions	22,885	6,315	8,170	8,400
Other	4,202	3,051	(828)	1,979
Net cash provided by operating activities	430,937	140,936	179,937	110,064
Investing activities:				
Property, plant, and equipment	(390,592)	(194,894)	(78,449)	(117,249)
Other	4,572	1,258	88	3,226
Net cash used in investing activities	(386,020)	(193,636)	(78,361)	(114,023)
Financing activities:				
Payment on debt	(56,784)	(5,117)	(18,349)	(33,318)
Issuance of debt	37,000	—	13,000	24,000
Issuance of common stock	1,471	303	493	675
Payment of dividends	(58,528)	(22,584)	(19,234)	(16,710)
Net cash used in financing activities	(76,841)	(27,398)	(24,090)	(25,353)
Changes in cash and short-term investments	(31,924)	(80,098)	77,486	(29,312)
Cash and short-term investments at beginning of period	55,111	103,285	25,799	55,111
Cash and short-term investments at end of period	$ 23,187	$ 23,187	$103,285	$ 25,799

A minority of companies have elected to present cash flow from operations using the direct method. The 1995 *Accounting Trends & Techniques* reports that of 600 survey companies presenting the cash flow statement in 1994, only 14 used the direct method.[12] As previously indicated, regardless of whether using the direct or indirect method, SFAS No. 95 requires that a reconciliation of net income to cash flow from operating activities be presented and that interest and income tax payments be disclosed.

Exhibit 11-3 presents the 1995 cash flow statement of Flowers Industries, with a total column for the three-year period. This firm presented the cash flows from operating activities using the direct method. Note the following with regard to Exhibit 11-3:

1. Net cash provided by operations represented the major source of cash for each year.

2. Capital expenditures represented the major outflow of cash each year under investing activities.

EXHIBIT 11-3 **FLOWERS INDUSTRIES**
Consolidated Statement of Cash Flows, with Three-Year Total
For Years Ended July 1, 1995, July 2, 1994, and July 3, 1993

(All dollar amounts in thousands)	Total	July 1, 1995	July 2, 1994	July 3, 1993
Cash flows from operating activities:				
Cash received from customers	$3,059,522	$1,117,262	$984,133	$958,127
Interest received	13,334	7,159	2,890	3,285
Other	13,954	5,890	3,646	4,418
Cash provided by operating activities	3,086,810	1,130,311	990,669	965,830
Cash paid to suppliers and employees	2,790,397	1,009,931	919,332	861,134
Interest paid	15,434	6,465	3,753	5,216
Income taxes paid	57,373	20,379	21,805	15,189
Cash disbursed for operating activities	2,863,204	1,036,775	944,890	881,539
Net cash provided by operating activities	223,606	93,536	45,779	84,291
Cash flows from investing activities:				
Purchase of property, plant, and equipment	(189,407)	(73,466)	(63,929)	(52,012)
Acquisition of business	(18,963)	(17,018)	(383)	(1,562)
Divestiture of business	23,179	22,679	—	500
Decrease in divestiture receivables	3,490	—	2,359	1,131
Escrow funds	4,835	4,835	—	—
Other	(244)	(1,845)	2,064	(463)
Net cash disbursed for investing activities	(177,110)	(64,815)	(59,889)	(52,406)
Cash flows from financing activities:				
Dividends paid	(87,982)	(31,257)	(29,102)	(27,623)
Purchase of treasury stock	(14,416)	(4,426)	(9,799)	(191)
Sale of note receivable with recourse	5,500	—	5,500	—
Increase in long-term notes payable	273,919	151,391	74,619	47,909
Payments of long-term notes payable	(205,943)	(132,351)	(19,012)	(54,580)
Net cash received from (disbursed for) financing activities	(28,922)	(16,643)	16,706	(28,985)
Net increase in cash and temporary investments	$ 17,574	$ 12,078	$ 2,596	$ 2,900

(continued)

EXHIBIT 11-3   **(continued)**

SCHEDULE 1 Schedule Reconciling Earnings to Net Cash Provided by Operating Activities

(All dollar amounts in thousands)	Total	July 1, 1995	July 2, 1994	July 3, 1993
Net income	$ 110,958	$ 42,301	$29,496	$39,161
Noncash expenses, revenues, losses, and gains included in income:				
Depreciation and amortization	103,851	36,604	34,110	33,137
Deferred income taxes	5,163	2,847	853	1,463
Changes in assets and liabilities, net of acquisitions and divestiture:				
(Increase) in accounts receivable	(18,503)	(5,510)	(7,723)	(5,270)
(Increase) decrease in inventories	(14,717)	(4,651)	(10,696)	630
(Increase) decrease in prepaid expenses	(137)	(86)	(678)	627
Increase in accounts payable	17,804	5,859	6,947	4,998
Increase (decrease) in accrued and other liabilities	19,187	16,172	(6,530)	9,545
	$ 223,606	$ 93,536	$45,779	$84,291

SCHEDULE 2 Schedule of Noncash Investing and Financial Activities

(All dollar amounts in thousands)	Total	July 1, 1995	July 2, 1994	July 3, 1993
Common stock receivable in connection with the exercise of employee stock options	$ 729	$ 663	$ 15	$ 51
Stock issued and held in escrow in connection with restricted stock awards and executive incentive award	7,272	—	3,299	3,973
Stock issued for acquisitions	24,486	18,946	3,425	2,115
Conversion of convertible subordinated debentures	47,241	—	—	47,241
Note receivable taken in divestiture of business	5,500	—	—	5,500
Undisbursed escrow funds available	2,161	2,161	—	—
Exercise of restricted stock award	535	535	—	—

3.   Cash dividends paid represented approximately 39.3% of cash provided by operations for the three-year period.

Exhibit 11-4 restates the 1995 cash flows for Flowers Industries, viewing inflows and outflows separately. Some observations regarding this exhibit follow:

1.   Approximately 86% of the total cash inflow came from operations.

EXHIBIT 11-4 **FLOWERS INDUSTRIES**
Statement of Cash Flows (Inflows and Outflows by Activity)
For Year Ended July 1, 1995

(All dollar amounts in thousands)	Inflows	Outflows	Inflow Percent	Outflow Percent
Cash flows from operating activities:				
Cash received from customers	$1,117,262		85.34	
Interest received	7,159		.55	
Other	5,890		.45	
Cash paid to suppliers and employees		$1,009,931		77.86
Interest paid		6,465		.50
Income taxes paid		20,379		1.57
Cash flows from operating activities	1,130,311	1,036,775	86.34	79.93
Cash flows from investing activities:				
Purchase of property, plant, and equipment		73,466		5.66
Acquisition of business		17,018		1.31
Divestiture of business	22,679		1.73	
Escrow funds	4,835		.37	
Other		1,845		.14
Cash flows from investing activities	27,514	92,329	2.10	7.11
Cash flows from financing activities:				
Dividends paid		31,257		2.41
Purchase of treasury stock		4,426		.34
Increase in long-term notes payable	151,391		11.56	
Payments of long-term notes		132,351		10.21
Cash flows from financing activities	151,391	168,034	11.56	12.96
Total cash	1,309,216	1,297,138	100.00	100.00
Total outflows	1,297,138			
Net increase in cash	$ 12,078			

2. Approximately 80% of the total cash outflows related to operations.

3. Capital expenditures represented approximately 6% of outflows.

4. Net borrowings provided approximately one-fifth the cash as net cash flows from operating activities.

5. Dividends paid represented approximately 2.4% of the total outflows.

FINANCIAL RATIOS AND THE STATEMENT OF CASH FLOWS

Financial ratios that relate to the statement of cash flows were slow in being developed. This was related to several factors. For one thing, most financial ratios traditionally related an income statement item(s) to a balance sheet item(s). This became the normal way of approaching financial analysis, and the statement of cash flows did not become a required statement until 1987. Thus, it took a while for analysts to become familiar with the statement.

Ratios have now been developed that relate to the cash flow statement. Some of these ratios are as follows:

1. Operating cash flow/current maturities of long-term debt and current notes payable
2. Operating cash flow/total debt
3. Operating cash flow per share
4. Operating cash flow/cash dividends

Operating Cash Flow/Current Maturities of Long-Term Debt and Current Notes Payable

The **operating cash flow/current maturities of long-term debt and current notes payable** is a ratio that indicates a firm's ability to meet its current maturities of debt. The higher this ratio, the better the firm's ability to meet its current maturities of debt. The higher this ratio, the better the firm's liquidity. This ratio relates to the liquidity ratios discussed in Chapter 7.

The formula for this ratio is:

$$\frac{\text{Operating Cash Flow}}{\text{Current Maturities of Long-Term Debt and Current Notes Payable}}$$

It is computed for Cooper for 1995 and 1994 in Exhibit 11-5. For Cooper, this ratio is very good.

Operating Cash Flow/Total Debt

The operating cash flow/total debt ratio indicates a firm's ability to cover total debt with the yearly cash flow. The higher the ratio, the

EXHIBIT 11-5   COOPER TIRE & RUBBER COMPANY
Operating Cash Flow/Current Maturities of Long-Term Debt and
Current Notes Payable
For the Years Ended December 31, 1995 and 1994

(Dollar amounts in thousands)	1995	1994
Operating cash flow [A]	$ 140,936	$179,937
Current maturities of long-term debt and current notes payable [B]	5,035	5,112
Operating cash flow/current maturities of long-term debt and current notes payable [A÷B]	27.99 times per year	35.20 times per year

better the firm's ability to carry its total debt. From a debt standpoint, this is considered to be important. It relates to the debt ratios presented in Chapter 8. It is a type of income view of debt, except that operating cash flow is the perspective instead of an income figure.

The operating cash flow amount in this ratio is the same cash flow amount that is computed for the operating cash flow/current maturities of long-term debt and current notes payable. The total debt figure is the same total debt amount that was computed in Chapter 8 for the debt ratio and the debt/equity ratio. For the primary computation of the operating cash flow/total debt ratio, all possible balance sheet debt items are included, as was done for the debt ratio and the debt/equity ratio. This is the more conservative approach to computing the ratio. In practice, many firms are more selective in what is included in debt. Some include only short-term liabilities and long-term items, such as bonds payable. The formula for **operating cash flow/total debt** is as follows:

$$\frac{\text{Operating Cash Flow}}{\text{Total Debt}}$$

The operating cash flow/total debt ratio is computed in Exhibit 11-6, page 488, for Cooper for the years ended December 31, 1995 and 1994. It indicates that cash flow is significant in relation to total debt in both years.

EXHIBIT 11-6   COOPER TIRE & RUBBER COMPANY
Operating Cash Flow/Total Debt
For the Years Ended December 31, 1995 and 1994

(Dollar amounts in thousands)	1995	1994
Operating cash flow [A]	$140,936	$179,937
Total debt [B]	394,902	377,654
Operating cash flow/total debt [A÷B]	35.69%	47.65%

Operating Cash Flow per Share

Operating cash flow per share indicates the funds flow per common share outstanding. It is usually substantially higher than earnings per share because depreciation has not been deducted.

In the short run, operating cash flow per share is a better indication of a firm's ability to make capital expenditure decisions and pay dividends than is earnings per share. This ratio should not be viewed as a substitute for earnings per share in terms of a firm's profitability. For this reason, SFAS No. 95 prohibits firms from reporting cash flow per share on the face of the statement of cash flows or elsewhere in its financials. However, it is a complementary ratio that relates to the ratios of relevance to investors (discussed in Chapter 10).

The **operating cash flow per share** formula is as follows:

$$\frac{\text{Operating Cash Flow - Preferred Dividends}}{\text{Common Shares Outstanding}}$$

The operating cash flow amount is the same figure that was used in the two previous cash flow formulas in this chapter. For common shares outstanding, use the shares that were used for the purpose of computing earnings per share on the most diluted basis. This figure is available when doing internal analysis. It is also in a firm's 10-K annual report. Some companies disclose these shares in the annual report. This share number cannot be computed from information in the annual report, except for very simple situations.

When these share amounts are not available, use the outstanding shares of common stock. This will result in an approximation of the operating cash flow per share. The advantage of using the number of shares used for earnings per share is that this results in an amount that can be compared to earnings per share, and it avoids distortions.

Operating cash flow per share is computed for Cooper for 1995 and 1994 in Exhibit 11-7. Operating cash flow per share was significantly more than earnings per share in both 1995 and 1994. Operating cash flow per share significantly decreased in 1995.

Operating Cash Flow/Cash Dividends

The operating cash flow/cash dividends ratio indicates a firm's ability to cover cash dividends with the yearly operating cash flow. The higher the ratio, the better the firm's ability to cover cash dividends. This ratio relates to the investor ratios discussed in Chapter 10.

The **operating cash flow/cash dividends** formula is as follows:

$$\frac{\textbf{Operating Cash Flow}}{\textbf{Cash Dividends}}$$

The operating cash flow amount is the same figure that was used in the three previous formulas in this chapter. Operating cash flow/cash dividends is computed for Cooper for 1995 and 1994 in Exhibit 11-8, page 490. It indicates a very high coverage of cash dividends in both 1995 and 1994. There was a decrease in the cash dividends coverage in 1995, but the coverage was still very high.

EXHIBIT 11-7 **COOPER TIRE & RUBBER COMPANY**
Operating Cash Flow per Share
For the Years Ended December 31, 1995 and 1994

	1995	1994
Operating cash flow	$140,936,000	$179,937,000
Less: Preferred dividends	—	—
Operating cash flow after preferred dividends [A]	$140,936,000	$179,937,000
Number of common shares based on the weighted average number of shares outstanding [B]	83,645,864	83,623,234
Operating cash flow per share [A÷B]	$1.68	$2.15

EXHIBIT 11-8   COOPER TIRE & RUBBER COMPANY
Operating Cash Flow/Cash Dividends
For the Years Ended December 31, 1995 and 1994

	1995	1994
	(Dollar amounts in thousands)	
Operating cash flow [A]	$140,936	$179,937
Cash dividends [B]	22,584	19,234
Operating cash flow/cash dividends [A÷B]	6.24 times per year	9.36 times per year

ALTERNATIVE CASH FLOW

There is no standard definition of cash flow. Often, cash flow is used to mean net income plus depreciation expense. This definition of cash flow could be used to compute the cash flow amount for the formulas introduced in this chapter. However, this is a narrow definition of cash flow, and it is considered less useful than the net cash flow from operating activities.

PROCEDURES FOR DEVELOPMENT OF THE STATEMENT OF CASH FLOWS

Cash inflows and outflows are determined by analyzing all balance sheet accounts other than the cash and cash equivalent accounts. The following account balance changes indicate cash inflows:

1.   Decreases in assets (e.g., the sale of land for cash)
2.   Increases in liabilities (e.g., the issuance of long-term bonds)
3.   Increases in stockholders' equity (e.g., the sale of common stock)

Cash outflows are indicated by the following account balance changes:

1.   Increases in assets (e.g., the purchase of a building for cash)
2.   Decreases in liabilities (e.g., retirement of long-term debt)
3.   Decreases in stockholders' equity (e.g., the payment of a cash dividend)

Transactions within any individual account may result in both a source and a use of cash. For example, the land account may have increased, but analysis may indicate that there was both an acquisition and a disposal of land.

Preparation of the statement of cash flows requires the following information:

1. The balance sheet for the current period
2. The balance sheet for the prior period
3. Income statement for the current period
4. Supplementary information from the balance sheet accounts, with the exception of the cash equivalent accounts

Steps in developing the statement of cash flows follow:

1. Compute the changes in the cash and cash equivalent accounts from the prior period to the end of the current period, which represents the net increase (decrease) in cash.

2. Compute the net change in each balance sheet account, except for cash and cash equivalent accounts. The explanation of why the cash and cash equivalent accounts changed is in the balance sheet accounts other than cash and cash equivalent accounts.

3. Determine the cash flows, the noncash investing and financing activities, and the effect of exchange rate changes,[13] using the net change in the balance sheet accounts, the income statement for the current period, and the supplementary information. Segregate the cash flows into cash flows from operating activities, cash flows from investing activities, and cash flows from financing activities.

4. Prepare the statement of cash flows.

Exhibit 11-9, page 492, contains the data needed for preparing a statement of cash flows for ABC Company for the year ended December 31, 1995. These data will be used to illustrate the preparation of the statement of cash flows.

Three techniques may be used to prepare the statement of cash flows: (1) the visual method, (2) the T-account method, and (3) the worksheet method. The visual method can be used only when the financial information is not complicated. When the financial information is complicated, either the T-account method or the worksheet method must be used. This book illustrates only the visual method because of the emphasis on using financial accounting information, not on preparing financial statements. For an explanation of the T-account method and the worksheet method, consult an intermediate accounting textbook.

EXHIBIT 11-9   **ABC COMPANY**
Financial Information for Statement of Cash Flows

Balance Sheet Information

	Balances		
Accounts	**December 31, 1994**	**December 31, 1995**	**Category**
Assets:			
Cash	$ 2,400	$ 3,000	Cash
Accounts receivable, net	4,000	3,900	Operating
Inventories	5,000	6,000	Operating
Total current assets	11,400	12,900	
Land	10,000	19,500	Investing
Equipment	72,000	73,000	Investing
Accumulated depreciation	(9,500)	(14,000)	Operating
Total assets	$83,900	$ 91,400	
Liabilities:			
Accounts payable	$ 4,000	$ 2,900	Operating
Taxes payable	1,600	2,000	Operating
Total current liabilities	5,600	4,900	
Bonds payable	35,000	40,000	Financing
Stockholders' Equity:			
Common stock, $10 par	36,000	39,000	Financing
Retained earnings	7,300	7,500	*
Total liabilities and stockholders' equity	$83,900	$ 91,400	

Income Statement Information
For the Year Ended December 31, 1995

		Category
Sales	$ 22,000	Operating
Operating expenses	17,500	Operating
Operating income	4,500	
Gain on sale of land	1,000	Investing
Income before tax expense	5,500	
Tax expense	2,000	Operating
Net income	$ 3,500	

Supplemental Information

		Category
(a)	Dividends declared and paid are $3,300.	Financing
(b)	Land was sold for $1,500.	Investing
(c)	Equipment was purchased for $1,000.	Investing
(d)	Bonds payable were retired for $5,000.	Financing
(e)	Common stock was sold for $3,000.	Financing
(f)	Operating expenses include depreciation expense of $4,500.	Operating
(g)	The land account and the bonds payable account increased by $10,000 because of a noncash exchange.	Investing and Financing

*Retained earnings is decreased by cash dividends, $3,300 (financing), and increased by net income, $3,500. Net income can be a combination of operating, investing, and financing activities. In this exhibit, all of the net income relates to operating activities, except for the gain on sale of land (investing).

Following the steps in developing the statement of cash flows, first compute the change in cash and cash equivalents. For ABC Company, this is the increase in the cash account of $600—the net increase in cash.

For the second step, compute the net change in each balance sheet account other than the cash account. The changes in the balance sheet accounts for ABC Company follow:

Assets:

Accounts receivable decrease	$ 100	Operating
Inventories increase	1,000	Operating
Land increase	9,500	Investing
Equipment increase	1,000	Investing
Accumulated depreciation increase (contra-asset—a change would be similar to a change in liabilities)	4,500	Operating

Liabilities:

Accounts payable decrease	1,100	Operating
Taxes payable increase	400	Operating
Bonds payable increase	5,000	Financing

Stockholders' equity:

Common stock increase	3,000	Financing
Retained earnings increase	200	*

*This is a combination of operating, financing, and investing activities.

For the third step, consider the changes in the balance sheet accounts along with the income statement for the current period and the supplementary information. The cash flows are segregated into cash flows from operating activities, cash flows from investing activities, and cash flows from financing activities. Noncash investing and/or financing activities should be shown in a separate schedule with the statement of cash flows.

To illustrate the direct and indirect methods of presenting operating activities, the ABC Company income statement is used, along with the relevant supplemental information and balance sheet accounts. For the direct approach, the income statement is adjusted to present the revenue and expense accounts on a cash basis. Exhibit 11-10, page 494, illustrates the accrual basis income statement adjusted to a cash basis. Exhibit 11-11, page 495, shows the statement of cash flows for ABC Company, using the direct approach for presenting cash flows from operations.

EXHIBIT 11-10 ABC COMPANY
Schedule of Change from Accrual Basis to Cash Basis Income Statement

	Accrual Basis	Adjustments*	Add (Subtract)	Cash Basis
Sales	$22,000	Decrease in receivables	100	$22,100
Operating expenses	17,500	Depreciation expense	(4,500)	
		Increase in inventories	1,000	
		Decrease in accounts payable	1,100	15,100
Operating income	4,500			7,000
Gain on sale of land	1,000	This gain is related to investing activities	(1,000)	-0-
Income before tax expense	5,500			7,000
Tax expense	2,000	Increase in taxes payable	(400)	1,600
Net income	$ 3,500			$ 5,400

*Adjustments are for noncash flow items in the income statement, changes in balance sheet accounts related to cash flow from operations, and the removal of gains and losses on the income statement that are related to investing or financing activities.

The noncash flow items in the income statement are removed from the account. For example, depreciation expense may be in the cost of goods sold, and this expense would be removed from the cost of goods sold.

Changes in balance sheet accounts related to cash flow from operations are adjusted to the related income statement account as follows:

Revenue accounts	$XXX
Add decreases in asset accounts and increases in liability accounts	+XXX
Deduct increases in asset accounts and decreases in liability accounts	-XXX
Cash inflow	$XXX
Expense accounts	
Add increases in asset accounts and decreases in liability accounts	+XXX
Deduct decreases in asset accounts and increases in liability accounts	-XXX
Cash outflow	$XXX

When the cash provided by operations is presented using the direct approach, the income statement accounts are usually described in terms of receipts or payments. For example, "sales" on the accrual basis income statement is usually described as "receipts from customers" when presented

EXHIBIT 11-11 ABC COMPANY
Direct Approach for Presenting Cash Flows from Operations
Statement of Cash Flows
For the Year Ended December 31, 1995

Cash flows from operating activities:		
Receipts from customers	$ 22,100	
Payments to suppliers	(15,100)	
Income taxes paid	(1,600)	
Net cash provided by operating activities		$ 5,400
Cash flows from investing activities:		
Proceeds from sale of land	1,500	
Purchase of equipment	(1,000)	
Net cash provided by investing activities		500
Cash flows from financing activities:		
Dividends declared and paid	(3,300)	
Retirement of bonds payable	(5,000)	
Proceeds from common stock	3,000	
Net cash used for financing activities		(5,300)
Net increase in cash		$ 600
Reconciliation of net income to net cash provided by operating activities:		
Net income		$ 3,500
Adjustments to reconcile net income to net cash provided by operating activities:		
Decrease in accounts receivable		100
Depreciation expense		4,500
Increase in inventories		(1,000)
Decrease in accounts payable		(1,100)
Gain on sale of land		(1,000)
Increase in taxes payable		400
Net cash provided by operating activities		$ 5,400
Supplemental schedule of noncash investing and financing activities:		
Land acquired by issuing bonds		$10,000

on a cash basis. For ABC Company, cash provided by operations, using the direct approach, follows:

Receipts from customers (from Exhibit 11-11)	$ 22,100
Payments to suppliers (from Exhibit 11-11)	(15,100)
Income taxes paid (from Exhibit 11-11)	(1,600)
Net cash provided by operating activities	$ 5,400

Exhibit 11-12 shows the statement of cash flows for ABC Company, using the indirect approach. To compute cash flows from operations, we start with net income and add back or deduct adjustments necessary to change the income on an accrual basis to income on a cash basis, after eliminating gains or losses that relate to investing or financing activities. Notice on the ABC Company schedule of change from accrual to cash basis income statement (Exhibit 11-10) that the adjustments include noncash flow items on the

EXHIBIT 11-12   ABC COMPANY
Indirect Approach for Presenting Cash Flows from Operations
Statement of Cash Flows
For the Year Ended December 31, 1995

Cash flows from operating activities:		
Net income	$ 3,500	
Add (deduct) items not affecting operating activities:		
Depreciation expense	4,500	
Decrease in accounts receivable	100	
Increase in inventories	(1,000)	
Decrease in accounts payable	(1,100)	
Increase in taxes payable	400	
Gain on sale of land	(1,000)	
Net cash provided by operating activities		$ 5,400
Cash flows from investing activities:		
Proceeds from sale of land	1,500	
Purchase of equipment	(1,000)	
Net cash provided by investing activities		500
Cash flows from financing activities:		
Dividends declared and paid	(3,300)	
Retirement of bonds payable	(5,000)	
Proceeds from common stock	3,000	
Net cash used for financing activities		(5,300)
Net increase in cash		$ 600
Supplemental disclosure of cash flow information:		
Cash paid during the year for:		
Interest net of amount capitalized		$ 0
Income taxes		1,600
Supplemental schedule of noncash investing and		
financing activities:		
Land acquired by issuing bonds		$10,000

income statement, changes in balance sheet accounts related to operations, and gains and losses on the income statement related to investing or financing activities.

Whether an adjustment should be added to or deducted from the net income (or loss) is sometimes confusing, partly because the additions and subtractions do not follow the same rules as were used on the schedule of change from accrual to cash basis income statement. For the indirect approach, follow these directions when adjusting the net income (or loss) to net cash flows from operating activities:

Net income (loss)	$ XXX
Noncash flow items:	
Add expense	+ XXX
Deduct revenues	- XXX
Changes in balance sheet accounts related to operations:*	
Add decreases in assets and increases	
in liabilities	+ XXX
Deduct increases in assets and decreases	
in liabilities	- XXX
Gains and losses on the income statement that	
are related to investing or financing activities:	
Add losses	+ XXX
Deduct gains	- XXX
Net cash provided by operating activities	$ XXX

*These are usually the current asset and current liability accounts.

The remaining changes in balance sheet accounts (other than those used to compute cash provided by operating activities) and the remaining supplemental information are used to determine the cash flows from investing activities and cash flows from financing activities. These accounts are also used to determine noncash investing and/or financing.

Some observations on the ABC Company statement of cash flows follow:

1.	Net cash provided by operating activities	$5,400
2.	Net cash provided by investing activities	$ 500
3.	Net cash used for financing activities	$5,300
4.	Net increase in cash	$ 600

When the operations section has been presented using the direct method, additional observations can be determined by preparing the statement of cash flows to present inflows and outflows separately. This has been done in Exhibit 11-13. Some observations from the summary of cash flows in Exhibit 11-13 follow:

Inflows:
1. Receipts from customers represent approximately 83% of total cash flow.
2. Proceeds from common stock sales approximate 11% of total cash inflow.
3. Proceeds from sales of land approximate 6% of total cash inflow.

Outflows:
1. Payments to suppliers represent approximately 58% of total cash outflow.
2. Retirement of bonds payable approximates 19% of total cash outflow.
3. Dividends paid approximate 13% of total cash outflow.

EXHIBIT 11-13 **ABC COMPANY**
Statement of Cash Flows
For the Year Ended December 31, 1995
(Inflows and Outflows by Activity—Inflows and Outflows Presented on Direct Basis)

	Inflows	Outflows	Inflow Percent	Outflow Percent
Operating activities:				
Receipts from customers	$ 22,100		83.1%	
Payments to suppliers		$15,100		58.1%
Income taxes paid		1,600		6.2
Cash flows from operating activities	22,100	16,700	83.1	64.3
Investing activities:				
Proceeds from sale of land	1,500		5.6	
Purchase of equipment		1,000		3.8
Cash flows from investing activities	1,500	1,000	5.6	3.8
Financing activities:				
Dividends declared and paid		3,300		12.7
Retirement of bonds payable		5,000		19.2
Proceeds from common stock	3,000		11.3	
Cash flows from financing activities	3,000	8,300	11.3	31.9
Total cash inflows/outflows	26,600	$26,000	100.0	100.0
Total cash outflows	26,000			
Net increase in cash	$ 600			

SUMMARY

This chapter has reviewed the development of the statement of cash flows. It is a required financial statement to be included with the balance sheet and income statement. The statement of cash flows should be reviewed for several time periods in order to determine the major sources of cash and the major uses of cash.

The ratios related to the statement of cash flows are the following:

$$\text{Operating Cash Flow/Current Maturities of Long-Term Debt and Current Notes Payable} = \frac{\text{Operating Cash Flow}}{\text{Current Maturities of Long-Term Debt and Current Notes Payable}}$$

$$\text{Operating Cash Flow/Total Debt} = \frac{\text{Operating Cash Flow}}{\text{Total Debt}}$$

$$\text{Operating Cash Flow per Share} = \frac{\text{Operating Cash Flow - Preferred Dividends}}{\text{Common Shares Outstanding}}$$

$$\text{Operating Cash Flow/Cash Dividends} = \frac{\text{Operating Cash Flow}}{\text{Cash Dividends}}$$

QUESTIONS

Q 11-1.   If a firm presents an income statement and a balance sheet, why is it necessary that a statement of cash flows also be presented?

Q 11-2.   When did the first funds statements appear? Relate the period a funds statement has been presented to the period that a balance sheet and income statement have been presented.

Q 11-3.   By 1903, at least four conceptually different statements were presented as the funds statement. List these four statements.

Q 11-4.   In what year did the statement of changes in financial position become required when a balance sheet and income statement are presented? In what year did the statement of cash flows become the required format (year standard passed)?

Q 11-5.   Indicate how each of the following influenced the selection of the format as the standard for presenting the funds statement.
  a. "Report of the Study Group on the Objectives of Financial Statements" (1973 AICPA).
  b. *Statement of Financial Accounting Concepts No. 1,* "Objectives of Financial Reporting by Business Enterprises" (1978 FASB Concept Statement).
  c. *Statement of Financial Accounting Concepts No. 5,* "Recognition and Measurement of Financial Statements of Business Enterprises" (1984 FASB Concept Statement).

Q 11-6.   Into what three categories are cash flows segregated on the statement of cash flows?

Q 11-7.   Using the descriptions of assets, liabilities, and stockholders' equity, summarize the changes to these accounts for cash inflows and changes to these accounts for cash outflows.

Q 11-8.   The land account may be used only to explain a use of cash, but not a source of cash. Comment.

Q 11-9.   Indicate the three techniques that may be used to complete the steps in developing the statement of cash flows.

Q 11-10.   There are two principal methods of presenting cash flow from operating activities—the direct method and the indirect method. Describe these two methods.

Q 11-11.   Depreciation expense, amortization of patents, and amortization of bond discount are examples of items that are added to net income when using the indirect method of presenting cash flows from operating activities. Amortization of premium on bonds and a reduction in deferred taxes are examples of items that are deducted from net income when using the indirect method of presenting cash flows from operating activities. Explain why these adjustments to net income are made to compute cash flows from operating activities.

Q 11-12.   What is the meaning of the term *cash* in the statement of cash flows?

Q 11-13.   What is the purpose of the statement of cash flows?

Q 11-14.   Why is it important to disclose certain noncash investing and financing transactions, such as exchanging common stock for land?

Q 11-15.   Would a write-off of uncollectible accounts against allowance for doubtful accounts be disclosed on a cash flow statement? Explain.

Q 11-16.   Fully depreciated equipment costing $60,000 was discarded, with no salvage value. What effect would this have on the statement of cash flows?

Q 11-17.   For the current year, a firm reported net income from operations of $20,000 on its income statement and an increase of $30,000 in cash from operations on the statement of cash flows. Explain some likely reasons for the greater increase in cash from operations than net income from operations.

Q 11-18.   A firm owed accounts payable of $150,000 at the beginning of the year and $250,000 at the end of the year. What influence will the $100,000 increase have on cash from operations?

Q 11-19.   A member of the board of directors is puzzled by the fact that the firm has had a very profitable year but does not have enough cash to pay its bills on time. Explain to the director how a firm can be profitable, yet not have enough cash to pay its bills and dividends.

Q 11-20.   Depreciation is often considered a major source of funds. Do you agree? Explain.

Q 11-21.   Pickerton started the year with $50,000 in accounts receivable. The firm ended the year with $20,000 in accounts receivable. How did this decrease influence cash from operations?

Q 11-22.   Aerco Company acquired equipment in exchange for $50,000 in common stock. Should this transaction be on the statement of cash flows?

Q 11-23.   Operating cash flow per share is a better indicator of profitability than is earnings per share. Do you agree? Explain.

Q 11-24.   Hornet Company had operating cash flow of $60,000 during a year in which it paid dividends of $11,000. What does this indicate about Hornet's dividend-paying ability?

PROBLEMS

P 11-1.   The following material relates to the Darrow Company:

		Cash Flows Classification			Effect on Cash		Noncash Transac-
Data		Operating Activity	Investing Activity	Financing Activity	Increase	Decrease	tions
a.	Net loss	_____	_____	_____	_____	_____	_____
b.	Increase in inventory	_____	_____	_____	_____	_____	_____
c.	Decrease in receivables	_____	_____	_____	_____	_____	_____
d.	Increase in prepaid insurance	_____	_____	_____	_____	_____	_____
e.	Issuance of common stock	_____	_____	_____	_____	_____	_____
f.	Acquisition of land using notes payable	_____	_____	_____	_____	_____	_____
g.	Purchase of land using cash	_____	_____	_____	_____	_____	_____
h.	Paid cash dividend	_____	_____	_____	_____	_____	_____

i.	Payment of income taxes	___	___	___	___	___	___
j.	Retirement of bonds using cash	___	___	___	___	___	___
k.	Sale of equipment for cash	___	___	___	___	___	___

Required   Place an X in the appropriate columns for each of the situations.

P 11-2.

Data	Cash Flows Classification			Effect on Cash		Noncash Transactions
	Operating Activity	Investing Activity	Financing Activity	Increase	Decrease	
a. Net income	✓	___	___	+	___	___
b. Paid cash dividend	___	___	✓	___	✓	___
c. Increase in receivables	✓	___	___	___	✓	___
d. Retirement of debt—paying cash	___	___	✓	___	✓	___
e. Purchase of treasury stock	___	___	✓	___	✓	___
f. Purchase of equipment	___	✓	___	___	✓	___
g. Sale of equipment	___	✓	___	+	___	___
h. Decrease in inventory	✓	___	___	+	___	___
i. Acquisition of land using common stock	___	___	___	___	___	✓
j. Retired bonds using common stock	___	___	___	___	___	✓
k. Decrease in accounts payable	✓	___	___	___	✓	___

Required   Place an X in the appropriate columns for each of the situations.

P 11-3. The BBB Company balance sheet and income statement follow:

BBB COMPANY
Balance Sheet
December 31, 1997 and 1996

	December 31	
	1997	1996
Assets		
Cash	$ 4,500	$ 4,000
Marketable securities	2,500	2,000
Accounts receivable	6,800	7,200
Inventories	7,500	8,000
Total current assets	21,300	21,200
Land	11,000	12,000
Equipment	24,000	20,500
Accumulated depreciation—equipment	(3,800)	(3,000)
Building	70,000	70,000
Accumulated depreciation—building	(14,000)	(12,000)
Total assets	$108,500	$108,700
Liabilities and Stockholders' Equity		
Accounts payable	$ 7,800	$ 7,000
Wages payable	1,050	1,000
Taxes payable	500	1,500
Total current liabilities	9,350	9,500
Bonds payable	30,000	30,000
Common stock, $10 par	32,000	30,000
Additional paid-in capital	21,000	19,200
Retained earnings	16,150	20,000
Total liabilities and stockholders' equity	$108,500	$108,700

BBB COMPANY
Income Statement
For the Year Ended December 31, 1997

Sales		$ 38,000
Operating expenses:		
Depreciation expense	$ 2,800	
Other operating expenses	35,000	37,800
Operating income		200
Gain on sale of land		800
Income before tax expense		1,000
Tax expense		500
Net income		$ 500

(continued)

Supplemental information:

Dividends declared and paid	$ 4,350
Land sold for cash	1,800
Equipment purchased for cash	3,500
Common stock sold for cash	3,800

Required

a. Prepare a statement of cash flows for the year ended December 31, 1997. (Present the cash flows from operations using the indirect method.)

b. Comment on the statement of cash flows.

P 11-4.   The income statement and other selected data for Frish Company is shown below:

FRISH COMPANY
Income Statement
For the Year Ended December 31, 1997

Net sales	$640,000
Expenses:	
Cost of goods sold	360,000
Selling and administrative expense	43,000
Other expense	2,000
Total expenses	405,000
Income before income tax	235,000
Income tax	92,000
Net income	$143,000

Other data:

a. Cost of goods sold, including depreciation expense of $15,000

b. Selling and administrative expense, including depreciation expense of $5,000

c. Other expense, representing amortization of goodwill, $3,000, and amortization of bond premium, $1,000

d. Increase in accounts receivable	$ 27,000
e. Increase in accounts payable	15,000
f. Increase in inventories	35,000
g. Decrease in prepaid expenses	1,000
h. Increase in accrued liabilities	3,000
i. Decrease in income taxes payable	10,000

Required

a. Prepare a schedule of change from accrual basis to cash basis income statement.

b. Using the schedule of change from accrual basis to cash basis income statement computed in (a), present the cash provided by operations using (1) the direct approach and (2) the indirect approach.

P 11-5.   The income statement and other selected data for Boyer Company are shown below:

BOYER COMPANY
Income Statement
For the Year Ended December 31, 1997

Sales		$ 19,000
Operating expenses:		
Depreciation expense	$ 2,300	
Other operating expenses	12,000	14,300
Operating income		4,700
Loss on sale of land		1,500
Income before tax expense		3,200
Tax expense		1,000
Net income		$ 2,200

Supplemental information:

a.	Dividends declared and paid	$ 800
b.	Land purchased	3,000
c.	Land sold	500
d.	Equipment purchased	2,000
e.	Bonds payable retired	2,000
f.	Common stock sold	1,400
g.	Land acquired in exchange for common stock	3,000
h.	Increase in accounts receivable	400
i.	Increase in inventories	800
j.	Increase in accounts payable	500
k.	Decrease in income taxes payable	400

Required   a.   Prepare a schedule of change from an accrual basis to a cash basis income statement.

b.   Using the schedule of change from accrual basis to cash basis income statement computed in (a), present the cash provided by operations, using (1) the direct approach and (2) the indirect approach.

P 11-6.   Sampson Company's balance sheet for December 31, 1997 as well as the income statement for the year ended December 31, 1997 follow on page 506.

SAMPSON COMPANY
Balance Sheet
December 31, 1997 and 1996

	1997	1996
Assets		
Cash	$ 38,000	$ 60,000
Net receivables	72,000	65,000
Inventory	98,000	85,000
Plant assets	195,000	180,000
Accumulated depreciation	(45,000)	(35,000)
Total assets	$358,000	$355,000
Liabilities and Stockholders' Equity		
Accounts payable	$ 85,000	$ 80,000
Accrued liabilities (related to cost of sales)	44,000	61,000
Mortgage payable	11,000	—
Common stock	180,000	174,000
Retained earnings	38,000	40,000
Total liabilities and stockholders' equity	$358,000	$355,000

SAMPSON COMPANY
Income Statement
For the Year Ended December 31, 1997

Net sales	$145,000
Cost of sales	108,000
Gross profit	37,000
Other expenses	6,000
Profit before taxes	31,000
Tax expense	12,000
Net income	$ 19,000

Other data:
1. Dividends paid in cash during 1997 were $21,000.
2. Depreciation is included in the cost of sales.
3. The change in the accumulated depreciation account is the depreciation expense for the year.

Required   a. Prepare the statement of cash flows for the year ended December 31, 1997, using the indirect method for net cash flow from operating activities.

b. Prepare the statement of cash flows for the year ended December 31, 1997, using the direct method for net cash flow from operating activities.

c. Comment on significant items disclosed in the statement of cash flows.

P 11-7.   Arrowbell Company is a growing company. Two years ago, it decided to expand in order to increase its production capacity. The company anticipates that the expansion program can be completed in another two years. Financial information for Arrowbell Company follows:

ARROWBELL COMPANY
Sales and Net Income

Year	Sales	Net Income
1993	$ 2,568,660	$145,800
1994	2,660,455	101,600
1995	2,550,180	52,650
1996	2,625,280	86,800
1997	3,680,650	151,490

ARROWBELL COMPANY
Balance Sheet
December 31, 1997 and 1996

	1997	1996
Assets		
Current assets:		
Cash	$ 250,480	$ 260,155
Accounts receivable (net)	760,950	690,550
Inventories at lower-of-cost-or-market	725,318	628,238
Prepaid expenses	18,555	20,250
Total current assets	1,755,303	1,599,193
Plant and equipment:		
Land, buildings, machinery, and equipment	3,150,165	2,646,070
Less: Accumulated depreciation	650,180	525,650
Net plant and equipment	2,499,985	2,120,420
Other assets:		
Cash surrender value of life insurance	20,650	18,180
Other	40,660	38,918
Total other assets	61,310	57,098
Total assets	$ 4,316,598	$ 3,776,711

(continued)

Liabilities and Stockholders' Equity

Current liabilities:

Notes and mortgages payable, current portion	$ 915,180	$ 550,155
Accounts payable and accrued liabilities	1,160,111	851,080
Total current liabilities	2,075,291	1,401,235
Long-term notes and mortgages payable, less current portion above	550,000	775,659
Total liabilities	2,625,291	2,176,894

Stockholders' equity:

Capital stock, par value $1.00; authorized, 800,000; issued and outstanding, 600,000 (1997 and 1996)	600,000	600,000
Paid in excess of par	890,000	890,000
Retained earnings	201,307	109,817
Total stockholders' equity	1,691,307	1,599,817
Total liabilities and stockholders' equity	$ 4,316,598	$ 3,776,711

ARROWBELL COMPANY
Statement of Cash Flows
For the Years Ended December 31, 1997 and 1996

	1997	1996
Cash flows from operating activities:		
Net income	$151,490	$ 86,800
Noncash expenses, revenues, losses, and gains included in income:		
Depreciation	134,755	102,180
Increase in accounts receivable	(70,400)	(10,180)
Increase in inventories	(97,080)	(15,349)
Decrease in prepaid expenses in 1997, increase in 1996	1,695	(1,058)
Increase in accounts payable and accrued liabilities	309,031	15,265
Net cash provided by operating activities	429,491	177,658
Cash flows from investing activities:		
Proceeds from retirement of property, plant, and equipment	10,115	3,865
Purchases of property, plant, and equipment	(524,435)	(218,650)
Increase in cash surrender value of life insurance	(2,470)	(1,848)
Other	(1,742)	(1,630)
Net cash used for investing activities	(518,532)	(218,263)

Cash flows from financing activities:

Retirement of long-term debt	(225,659)	(50,000)
Increase in notes and mortgages payable	365,025	159,155
Cash dividends	(60,000)	(60,000)
Net cash provided by financing activities	79,366	49,155
Net increase (decrease) in cash	$ (9,675)	$ 8,550

Required

a. Comment on the short-term debt position, including computations of current ratio, acid-test ratio, cash ratio, and operating cash flow/current maturities of long-term debt and current notes payable.

b. If you were a supplier to this company, what would you be concerned about?

c. Comment on the long-term debt position, including computations of the debt ratio, debt/equity, debt to tangible net worth, and operating cash flow/total debt. Review the statement of operating cash flows.

d. If you were a banker, what would you be concerned about if this company approached you for a long-term loan to continue its expansion program?

e. What should management consider doing at this point in regard to the company's expansion program?

P 11-8. The balance sheet for December 31, 1997, and income statement for the year ended December 31, 1997, of Bernett Company follow:

BERNETT COMPANY
Balance Sheet
December 31, 1997 and 1996

	1997	1996
Assets		
Cash	$ 5,000	$ 28,000
Accounts receivable, net	92,000	70,000
Inventory	130,000	85,000
Prepaid expenses	4,000	6,000
Land	30,000	10,000
Building	170,000	30,000
Accumulated depreciation	(20,000)	(10,000)
Total assets	$411,000	$219,000
Liabilities and Stockholders' Equity		
Accounts payable	$ 49,000	$ 44,000
Income taxes payable	5,000	4,000
Accrued liabilities	6,000	5,000
Bonds payable (current $10,000 at 12/31/97)	175,000	20,000
Common stock	106,000	96,000
Retained earnings	70,000	50,000
Total liabilities and stockholders' equity	$411,000	$219,000

BERNETT COMPANY
Income Statement
For the Year Ended December 31, 1997

Sales	$500,000
Less expenses:	
Cost of goods sold (includes depreciation of $4,000)	310,000
Selling and administrative expenses (includes depreciation of $6,000)	80,000
Interest expense	11,000
Total expenses	401,000
Income before taxes	99,000
Income tax expense	30,000
Net income	$ 69,000

Note: Cash dividends of $49,000 were paid during 1997.

The president of Bernett Company cannot understand why Bernett is having trouble paying current obligations. He notes that business has been very good, as sales have more than doubled, and the company achieved a profit of $69,000 in 1997.

Required   a. Prepare the statement of cash flows for 1997. (Present cash flows from operations, using the indirect approach.)

b. Comment on the statement of cash flows.

c. Compute the following liquidity ratios for 1997:
   1. Current ratio
   2. Acid-test ratio
   3. Operating cash flow/current maturities of long-term debt and current notes payable
   4. Cash ratio

d. Compute the following debt ratios for 1997:
   1. Times interest earned
   2. Debt ratio
   3. Operating cash flow/total debt

e. Compute the following profitability ratios for 1997:
   1. Return on assets (using average assets)
   2. Return on common equity (using average common equity)

f. Compute the following investor ratio for 1997: **Operating cash flow/ cash dividends**.

g. Give your opinion as to the liquidity of Bernett Company.

h. Give your opinion as to the debt position of Bernett Company.

i. Give your opinion as to the profitability of Bernett Company.

j. Give your opinion as to the investor ratio.

k. Give your opinion of the alternatives Bernett Company has in order to ensure that it can pay bills as they come due.

P 11-9. Zaro Company's balance sheet for December 31, 1997, and income statement for the year ended December 31, 1997, follow:

ZARO COMPANY
Balance Sheet
December 31, 1997 and 1996

	1997	1996
Assets		
Cash	$ 30,000	$ 15,000
Accounts receivable, net	75,000	87,000
Inventory	90,000	105,000
Prepaid expenses	3,000	2,000
Land	25,000	25,000
Building and equipment	122,000	120,000
Accumulated depreciation	(92,000)	(80,000)
Total assets	$253,000	$274,000
Liabilities and Stockholders' Equity		
Accounts payable	$ 25,500	$ 32,000
Income taxes payable	2,500	3,000
Accrued liabilities	5,000	5,000
Bonds payable (current $20,000 at 12/31/97)	90,000	95,000
Common stock	85,000	85,000
Retained earnings	45,000	54,000
Total liabilities and stockholders' equity	$253,000	$274,000

ZARO COMPANY
Income Statement
For the Year Ended December 31, 1997

Sales	$400,000
Less expenses:	
Cost of goods sold (includes depreciation of $5,000)	$280,000
Selling and administrative expenses (includes	
depreciation expenses of $7,000)	78,000
Interest expense	8,000
Total expenses	$366,000
Income before taxes	34,000
Income tax expense	14,000
Net income	$ 20,000

Note: Cash dividends of $29,000 were paid during 1997.

The president of Zaro Company cannot understand how the company was able to pay cash dividends that were greater than net income and at the same time increase the cash balance. He notes that business was down slightly in 1997.

Required

a. Prepare the statement of cash flows for 1997. (Present cash flows from operations, using the indirect approach.)

b. Comment on the statement of cash flows.

c. Compute the following liquidity ratios for 1997:
    1. Current ratio
    2. Acid-test ratio
    3. Operating cash flow/current maturities of long-term debt and current notes payable
    4. Cash ratio

d. Compute the following debt ratios for 1997:
    1. Times interest earned
    2. Debt ratio

e. Compute the following profitability ratios for 1997:
    1. Return on assets (use average assets)
    2. Return on common equity (use average common equity)

f. Give your opinion as to the liquidity of Zaro Company.

g. Give your opinion as to the debt position of Zaro Company.

h. Give your opinion as to the profitability of Zaro Company.

i. Explain to the president how Zaro Company was able to pay cash dividends that were greater than net income and at the same time increase the cash balance.

P 11-10. The Ladies Store presented the following statement of cash flows for the year ended December 31, 1997:

THE LADIES STORE
Statement of Cash Flows
For the Year Ended December 31, 1997

Cash received:	
From sales to customers	$150,000
From sales of bonds	100,000
From issuance of notes payable	40,000
From interest on bonds	5,000
Total cash received	295,000
Cash payments:	
For merchandise purchases	110,000
For purchase of truck	20,000
For purchase of investment	80,000
For purchase of equipment	45,000
For interest	2,000
For income taxes	15,000
Total cash payments	272,000
Net increase in cash	$ 23,000

Note: Depreciation expense was $15,000.

Required a. Prepare a statement of cash flows in proper form.
           b. Comment on the major flows of cash.

P 11-11. Answer the following multiple-choice questions:
  a. Which of the following could lead to cash flow problems?
      1. Tightening of credit by suppliers
      2. Easing of credit by suppliers
      3. Reduction of inventory
      4. Improved quality of accounts receivable
      5. Selling of bonds
  b. Which of the following would not contribute to bankruptcy of a profitable firm?
      1. Substantial increase in inventory
      2. Substantial increase in receivables
      3. Substantial decrease in accounts payable
      4. Substantial decrease in notes payable
      5. Substantial decrease in receivables

c. Which of the following current asset or current liability accounts is not included in the computation of cash flows from operating activities?
  1. Change in accounts receivable
  2. Change in inventory
  3. Change in accounts payable
  4. Change in accrued wages
  5. Change in notes payable to banks

d. Which of the following items is not included in the adjustment of net income to cash flows from operating activities?
  1. Increase in deferred taxes
  2. Amortization of goodwill
  3. Depreciation expense for the period
  4. Amortization of premium on bonds payable
  5. Proceeds from selling land

e. Which of the following represents an internal source of cash?
  1. Cash inflows from financing activities
  2. Cash inflows from investing activities
  3. Cash inflows from selling land
  4. Cash inflows from operating activities
  5. Cash inflows from issuing stock

f. How would revenue from services be classified?
  1. Investing inflow
  2. Investing outflow
  3. Operating inflow
  4. Operating outflow
  5. Financing outflow

g. What type of account is inventory?
  1. Investing
  2. Financing
  3. Operating
  4. Noncash
  5. Sometimes operating and sometimes investing

h. How would short-term investments in marketable securities be classified?
  1. Operating activities
  2. Financing activities
  3. Investing activities
  4. Noncash activities
  5. Cash and cash equivalents

P 11-12. The Szabo Company presented the following data with the 1997 financial statements:

SZABO COMPANY
Statement of Cash Flows
Years Ended December 31, 1997, 1996, and 1995

	1997	1996	1995
Increase (Decrease) in Cash:			
Cash flows from operating activities:			
Cash received from customers	$173,233	$176,446	$158,702
Cash paid to suppliers and employees	(150,668)	(157,073)	(144,060)
Interest received	132	105	89
Interest paid	(191)	(389)	(777)
Income taxes paid	(6,626)	(4,754)	(845)
Net cash provided by operations	15,880	14,335	13,109
Cash flows from investing activities:			
Capital expenditures	(8,988)	(5,387)	(6,781)
Proceeds from property, plant, and equipment disposals	1,215	114	123
Net cash used in investing activities	(7,773)	(5,273)	(6,658)
Cash flows from financing activities:			
Net increase (decrease) in short-term debt	—	5,100	7,200
Increase in long-term debt	4,100	3,700	5,200
Dividends paid	(6,050)	(8,200)	(8,000)
Purchase of common stock	(8,233)	(3,109)	(70)
Net cash used in financing activities	(10,183)	(2,509)	4,330
Net increase (decrease) in cash and cash equivalents	(2,076)	6,553	10,781
Cash and cash equivalents at beginning of year	24,885	18,332	7,551
Cash and cash equivalents at end of year	$ 22,809	$ 24,885	$ 18,332

Reconciliation of Net Income to Net Cash Provided by Operating Activities

	1997	1996	1995
Net income	$ 7,610	$ 3,242	$ 506
Provision for depreciation and amortization	12,000	9,700	9,000
Provision for losses on accounts receivable	170	163	140
Gain on property, plant, and equipment disposals	(2,000)	(1,120)	(1,500)
Changes in operating assets and liabilities:			
Accounts receivable	(2,000)	(1,750)	(1,600)
Inventories	(3,100)	(2,700)	(2,300)
Other assets	—	—	(57)
Accounts payable	—	5,100	7,200
Accrued income taxes	1,200	—	—
Deferred income taxes	2,000	1,700	1,720
Net cash provided by operating activities	$ 15,880	$ 14,335	$ 13,109

Required   a. Prepare a statement of cash flows with a three-year total column for 1995-1997.

             b. Comment on significant trends you detect in the statement prepared in (a).

             c. Prepare a statement of cash flows, with inflow/outflow for the year ended December 31, 1997.

             d. Comment on significant trends you detect in the statement prepared in (c).

P 11-13.   Consider the following data for three different companies:

	($000 Omitted)		
	Owens	Arrow	Alpha
Net cash provided (used) by:			
Operating activities	$ (2,000)	$2,700	$(3,000)
Investing activities	(6,000)	(600)	(400)
Financing activities	9,000	(400)	(2,600)
Net increase (decrease) in cash	$ 1,000	$1,700	$(6,000)

The patterns of cash flows for these firms differ. One firm is a growth firm that is expanding rapidly, another firm is in danger of bankruptcy, while the third firm is an older firm that is expanding slowly.

Required   Select the growth firm, the firm in danger of bankruptcy, and the firm that is the older firm expanding slowly. Explain your selection.

Cases

CASE 11-1 Cash Flow Tales

Osmonics included the following data in its 1995 annual report:

From the consolidated balance sheets:
Liabilities and Shareholders' Equity

(In thousands, except share amounts)	December 31 1995	December 31 1994
Current liabilities:		
Accounts payable	$ 12,247	$ 6,459
Notes payable and current portion of long-term debt (Note 7)	1,695	744
Accrued compensation and employee benefits	4,231	4,154
Reserve for discontinued operations	1,957	2,088
Other accrued liabilities	8,612	7,187
Total current liabilities	28,742	20,632
Long-term debt (Note 7)	12,441	14,050
Deferred income taxes (Note 10)	4,954	2,913
Other liabilities	450	689
Commitments and contingencies (Note 12)	—	—
Shareholders' equity:		
Common stock, $0.01 par value		
Authorized—20,000,000		
Issued— 1995: 12,773,184		
1994: 12,701,041	129	127
Capital in excess of par value	21,709	21,000
Retained earnings	52,620	41,408
Unrealized gain on marketable securities (Note 4)	3,694	1,038
Cumulative effect of foreign currency translation adjustments	319	178
Total shareholders' equity	78,471	63,751
Total liabilities and shareholders' equity	$125,058	$102,035

From the consolidated statements of income:	Year Ended December 31		
	1995	**1994**	**1993**
Net income per share	$.88	$.79	$.63
Average shares outstanding	12,745,000	12,668,000	12,624,000

Consolidated Statements of Cash Flows	Year Ended December 31		
	1995	**1994**	**1993**
Cash flows from operations:			
Net income	$11,212	$ 9,955	$ 7,895
Noncash items included in net income:			
Depreciation and amortization	3,222	3,048	3,080
Deferred income taxes	(91)	(341)	281
Gain on sale of land and investments	(810)	—	(499)
Changes in assets and liabilities (net of business acquisitions):			
Reserve for VAT tax	—	(1,605)	(1,030)
Accounts receivable	(4,232)	(1,463)	181
Inventories	(6,085)	(2,584)	2,785
Other current assets	(507)	1,475	(302)
Accounts payable and accrued liabilities	4,292	1,499	209
Reserve for deferred compensation	(432)	(78)	72
Reserves for losses of discontinued operations	—	—	(471)
Net cash provided (used) by operations	6,569	9,906	12,201
Cash flows from investing activities:			
Business acquisitions (net of cash acquired)	(5,380)	(673)	—
Purchase of investments	(6,633)	(17,467)	(15,253)
Maturities and sales of investments	13,228	11,225	8,680
Purchase of property and equipment	(12,568)	(3,435)	(3,257)
Proceeds from sale of subsidiary	—	—	613
Other	(315)	190	(111)
Net cash provided (used) for investing activities	(11,668)	(10,160)	(9,328)
Cash flows from financing activities:			
Notes payable and current debt	(299)	282	(376)
Reduction of long-term debt	(311)	(521)	(552)
Issuance of common stock	711	680	295
Net cash provided (used) in financing activities	101	441	(633)
Effect of exchange rate changes on cash	(94)	(444)	143
Increase (decrease) in cash and cash equivalents	(5,092)	(257)	2,383
Cash and cash equivalents—beginning of year	9,453	9,710	7,327
Cash and cash equivalents—end of year	$ 4,361	$ 9,453	$ 9,710

Required   a. Compute and comment on the following for 1995 and 1994:
1. Operating cash flow/current maturities of long-term debt and current notes payable
2. Operating cash flow/total debt
3. Operating cash flow per share
4. Operating cash flow/cash dividends

b. Comment on significant cash inflows and outflows.
c. Why is depreciation added to net income as part of the reconciliation of net income to net cash provided by operating activities?

CASE 11-2 Watch the Cash

The United States Surgical Corporation and subsidiaries presented the following statement of cash flows in its 1995 annual report:

	Year Ended December 31		
In thousands	**1995**	**1994**	**1993**
Cash flows from operating activities:			
Cash received from customers	$ 1,000,000	$ 913,100	$ 1,103,300
Cash paid to vendors, suppliers, and employees	(784,100)	(749,300)	(941,200)
Interest paid	(17,500)	(24,800)	(18,300)
Income taxes paid	(10,300)	(14,900)	(12,800)
Net cash provided by operating activities	188,100	124,100	131,000
Cash flows from investing activities:			
Additions to property, plant, and equipment	(33,600)	(47,000)	(216,400)
Acquisitions	(84,000)	—	—
Other assets	(18,100)	13,900	(30,000)
Net cash used in investing activities	(135,700)	(33,100)	(246,400)
Cash flows from financing activities:			
Long-term debt borrowings under credit agreements	2,407,300	3,483,900	2,614,400
Long-term debt repayments under credit agreements	(2,445,800)	(3,753,800)	(2,495,900)
Long-term debt issuance fees	(1,700)	(3,300)	(1,100)
Issuance of preferred stock, net	—	191,500	—
Common stock issued from stock plans	5,300	13,400	12,100
Dividends paid	(24,100)	(14,500)	(13,700)
Net cash (used in) provided by financing activities	(59,000)	(82,800)	115,800

(continued)

Effect of exchange rate changes	5,800	2,200	(2,000)
Net increase (decrease) in cash and cash equivalents	(800)	10,400	(1,600)
Cash and cash equivalents, beginning of year	11,300	900	2,500
Cash and cash equivalents, end of year	$ 10,500	$ 11,300	$ 900
Reconciliation of net income (loss) to net cash provided by operating activities:			
Net income (loss)	$ 79,200	$ 19,200	$(138,700)
Adjustments to reconcile net income (loss) to net cash provided by operating activities:			
Depreciation and amortization	91,700	89,400	83,200
Asset writedowns—restructuring	—	—	73,800
Adjustment of property, plant, and equipment reserves	18,600	22,300	17,400
Receivables—(increase) decrease	(23,900)	(3,300)	67,800
Inventories—(increase) decrease	(2,600)	7,400	(48,400)
Adjustment of inventory reserves	26,600	39,200	44,200
Other current assets—(increase)	(26,200)	(13,000)	(23,900)
Accounts payable and accrued liabilities —increase (decrease)	13,500	(42,500)	34,300
Income taxes payable and deferred —increase (decrease)	3,100	(2,900)	(24,300)
Income tax benefit from stock options exercised	8,200	1,100	14,400
Other assets—net	(100)	7,200	31,200
Total adjustments	108,900	104,900	269,700
Net cash provided by operating activities	$188,100	$124,100	$ 131,000

Required

a. Prepare the statement of cash flows, with a total column for the three-year period ended December 31, 1995. Do not include reconciliation of net income to net cash provided by operating activities.

b. Comment on significant cash flow items in the statement prepared in (a).

c. Prepare the statement of cash flows for 1995, with inflows separated from outflows. Present the data in dollars and percentages. Do not include reconciliation of net income to net cash provided by operating activities or the effect of exchange rate changes.

d. Comment on significant cash flow items in the statement prepared in (c).

CASE 11-3 Rapidly Expanding

The data for this case was extracted from the 1996 Annual Report of Best Buy Co., Inc.

Future Growth

Fiscal 1997 promises to be a challenging year for all retailers. A more cautious consumer outlook and higher levels of consumer debt may signal a softer retail environment during the first half of this fiscal year. Also, increased competition in the PC industry and the anticipated slowdown of personal computer sales will mean additional pressure on sales and margins. The initiatives we have implemented in major appliances and ESP sales will help offset this anticipated slowdown.

In addition, we intend to moderate overall new store growth and open 20 to 25 new retail locations. Half of these stores are expected to open in the new markets of Philadelphia, Pennsylvania, and Tampa, Florida. The remainder will increase our presence in existing markets where we have established advertising, administrative, regional management and distribution leverage. We intend to finance this expansion with internally generated funds.

This more conservative store expansion will allow us to refine our stores' operations and focus our retail efforts on our four major categories of product specialization. Our plan is to simplify our retail procedures while improving our level of customer service. We will strengthen the training programs for our retail personnel to prepare them for the challenges ahead. A well-trained sales force will help us attract and retain customers while enhancing our market position. Our store teams will be more actively engaged in the presentation of new product technologies, technical services, appropriate product accessories, ESPs, and classroom training. This will enhance consumers' knowledge and their shopping experience. We intend to improve overall product in-stock by establishing improved standards of inventory management.

Our Strategy

We believe that our retail strategy is right for today's consumer and expect to improve our execution in all our product categories. Fiscal 1996 was a challenging year for retail, and we thank our employees, shareholders and vendor partners for their continued commitment and support. We are confident that the initiatives we are implementing will result in strengthened execution of our retail strategy and market-leading position as we enter our 30th year of business.

Richard M. Schulze
Founder, Chairman & CEO

Bradbury H. Anderson
President & COO

Selected Consolidated Financial and Operating Data
(Dollars in thousands, except per-share amounts)

Fiscal Period	1996[1]	1995	1994[2]	1993	1992
Statement of Earnings Data:					
Revenues	$7,217,448	$5,079,557	$3,006,534	$1,619,978	$929,692
Gross profit	936,571	690,393	456,925	284,034	181,062
Selling, general, and administrative expenses	813,988	568,466	379,747	248,126	162,286
Operating income	122,583	121,927	77,178	35,908	18,776
Earnings before cumulative effect of accounting change	48,019	57,651	41,710	19,855	9,601
Net earnings	48,019	57,651	41,285	19,855	9,601
Per-Share Data:					
Earnings before cumulative effect of accounting change	$ 1.10	$ 1.33	$ 1.01	$ .57	$ .33
Net earnings	1.10	1.33	1.00	.57	.33
Common stock price: High	29 5/8	45 1/4	31 7/16	15 23/32	11 25/32
Low	12 3/4	22 1/8	10 27/32	4 23/32	2 21/32
Weighted average shares outstanding (000s)	43,640	43,471	41,336	34,776	28,848
Operating and Other Data:					
Comparable stores sales increase[3]	5.5%	19.9%	26.9%	19.4%	14.0%
Number of stores (end of period)	251	204	151	111	73
Average revenues per store[4]	$ 31,100	$ 28,400	$ 22,600	$ 17,600	$ 14,300
Gross profit percentage	13.0%	13.6%	15.2%	17.5%	19.5%
Selling, general, and administrative expense percentage	11.3%	11.2%	12.6%	15.3%	17.5%
Operating income percentage	1.7%	2.4%	2.6%	2.2%	2.0%
Inventory turns[5]	4.8x	4.7x	5.0x	4.8x	5.1x
Balance Sheet Data (at period end):					
Working capital	$ 585,855	$ 609,049	$ 362,582	$ 118,921	$126,817
Total assets	1,890,832	1,507,125	952,494	439,142	337,218
Long-term debt, including current portion	229,855	240,965	219,710	53,870	52,980
Convertible preferred securities	230,000	230,000	—	—	—
Shareholders' equity	431,614	376,122	311,444	182,283	157,568

This table should be read in conjunction with the Management's Discussion and Analysis of Financial Condition and Results of Operations and the Consolidated Financial Statements and Notes thereto.

(1) Fiscal 1996 contained 53 weeks. All other periods presented contained 52 weeks.
(2) During fiscal 1994, the Company adopted FAS 109, resulting in a cumulative effect adjustment of ($425) or ($.01) per share.
(3) Comparable stores are stores open at least 14 full months.
(4) Average revenues per store are based upon total revenues for the period divided by the weighted average number of stores open during such period.
(5) Inventory turns are calculated based upon a rolling 12-month average of inventory balances.

MANAGEMENT'S DISCUSSION & ANALYSIS OF FINANCIAL CONDITION AND RESULTS OF OPERATIONS (IN PART)

Liquidity and Capital Resources

The Company has funded the retail growth and the increase in distribution capacity in the last two years through a combination of long-term financing, working capital, and cash flow from operations. In fiscal 1995, the Company issued $230 million of 6½% monthly income convertible preferred securities which mature in November 2024. The Company also entered into a master lease facility which has provided over $125 million in financing for retail store and distribution center development in fiscal 1995 and 1996. The funds from these two long-term financings and the increase in the Company's credit facility to $550 million in fiscal 1996, have supported the Company's growth. The proceeds from the $150 million note offering in October 1993 were also used to support much of the Company's expansion and growth in fiscal 1995. In fiscal 1994, the $86 million in proceeds from a Common Stock offering and the proceeds of the 1993 note offering were used to provide the financing necessary for business expansion that year. Cash flow from operations, before changes in working capital, improved to over $100 million in fiscal 1996, an increase from the $97 million in fiscal 1995 and $65 million in fiscal 1994.

Over the past two fiscal years, the Company has developed 50 new and relocated stores in order to secure the desired store locations and assure timely completion of the stores. The Company also built two of the brown goods distribution centers opened in the last two years, including the Company's newest 780,000 square foot distribution center in Findlay, Ohio, opened in September 1995. Interim financing for these properties was provided either through working capital or the Company's master lease agreement. The Company's practice is to lease rather than own real estate, and for those sites developed using working capital, it is the Company's intention to enter into sale/leaseback transactions and recover the cost of development. The costs of this development are classified in the balance sheet as recoverable costs from developed properties. Proceeds from the sale of properties were nearly $90 million in fiscal 1996 and $43 million in fiscal 1995. In fiscal 1994, the Company sold 17 store locations for an aggregate of $44 million in a single sale/leaseback transaction. At fiscal 1996 year end, the Company had approximately $125 million in recoverable costs related to developed properties. A difficult credit market for retail real estate has delayed the sale of certain of these properties, the majority of which were opened late in fiscal 1996. These properties are expected to be sold and leased back during fiscal 1997.

Current assets increased to $1.6 billion at March 2, 1996, compared to $1.2 billion at February 25, 1995, primarily as a result of the increased inventory levels necessary to support the larger stores and higher sales volumes. The 47 new stores added approximately $160 million in inventory. Inventory turns were 4.8 times in fiscal 1996, comparable to the prior year. Increases in trade payables and secured inventory financing arrangements at year-end supported most of the increase in inventory. Higher business volumes in February 1996 as compared to February 1995 resulted in higher year-end receivables. The Company sells the receivables from sales on the Company's private label credit card, without recourse, to an unrelated third party. An increase in recoverable costs from developed properties also contributed to the increase in current assets.

The Company's revolving credit facility provides for borrowings of $250 million throughout the year and an increase to $550 million on a seasonal basis from July through December. Borrowings under the facility are unsecured and are limited to certain percentages of inventories. The underlying agreement requires that the maximum balance outstanding be reduced to $50 million for a period of 45 days, following the holiday season. This facility expires in June 1998. The Company also has $185 million available, increasing to $310 million on a seasonal basis, under an inventory financing facility provided by a commercial credit corporation.

The Company's expansion plans for fiscal 1997 reflect management's expectations for a slowing economy and the Company's desire to fund growth with internally generated funds. The Company plans to open approximately 20 to 25 new stores, including entry into the new major markets of Philadelphia, Pennsylvania, in May and Tampa, Florida, in the third quarter. The remainder of the new stores opened will be in existing markets. The Company also intends to remodel or relocate ten stores to larger facilities during fiscal 1997. Only six of the new and relocated stores are expected to be developed by the Company. Management believes the Company's existing distribution facilities are adequate to support the planned expansion and operations in fiscal 1997.

Each new store requires approximately $3.0 to $4.0 million in working capital for merchandise inventory (net of vendor financing), fixtures, and leasehold improvements. Management expects that there will be adequate funds available, including funds generated from the sale of developed property owned at the end of fiscal 1996, to finance the $80 million in planned capital expenditures in addition to the anticipated property development in fiscal 1997.

Management believes that funds available from the Company's revolving credit facility, inventory financing programs and expected vendor terms, along with cash on hand and anticipated cash flow from operations, will be sufficient to support planned store expansion and the increased assortment in the appliance category in the coming year.

Consolidated Balance Sheets
(Dollars in thousands, except per-share amounts)

	March 2, 1996	February 25, 1995
Assets		
Current assets:		
Cash and cash equivalents	$ 86,445	$ 144,700
Receivables	121,438	84,440
Recoverable costs from developed properties	126,237	86,222
Merchandise inventories	1,201,142	907,677
Deferred income taxes	20,165	15,022
Prepaid expenses	5,116	2,606
Total current assets	1,560,543	1,240,667
Property and equipment:		
Land and buildings	16,423	13,524
Leasehold improvements	131,289	93,889
Furniture, fixtures, and equipment	266,582	191,084
Property under capital leases	29,421	27,096
	443,715	325,593
Less accumulated depreciation and amortization	132,676	88,116
Net property and equipment	311,039	237,477
Other assets:		
Deferred income taxes	7,204	9,223
Other assets	12,046	19,758
Total other assets	19,250	28,981
Total assets	$ 1,890,832	$ 1,507,125

(continued)

	March 2, 1996	February 25, 1995
Liabilities and Shareholders' Equity		
Current liabilities:		
Accounts payable	$ 673,852	$ 395,337
Obligations under financing arrangements	93,951	81,755
Accrued salaries and related expenses	26,890	23,785
Accrued liabilities	125,582	77,102
Deferred service plan revenue and warranty reserve	30,845	24,942
Accrued income taxes		14,979
Current portion of long-term debt	23,568	13,718
Total current liabilities	974,688	631,618
Deferred service plan revenue and warranty reserve, long-term	48,243	42,138
Long-term debt	206,287	227,247
Convertible preferred securities of subsidiary	230,000	230,000
Shareholders' equity:		
Preferred stock, $1.00 par value: Authorized—400,000 shares; Issued and outstanding—none	—	—
Common stock, $.10 par value: Authorized—120,000,000 shares; Issued and outstanding—42,842,000 and 42,216,000 shares, respectively	4,284	4,221
Additional paid-in capital	236,392	228,982
Retained earnings	190,938	142,919
Total shareholders' equity	431,614	376,122
Total liabilities and shareholders' equity	$ 1,890,832	$ 1,507,125

Consolidated Statement of Earnings
(Dollars in thousands, except per-share amounts)

For the Fiscal Years Ended	March 2, 1996	February 25, 1995	February 26, 1994
Revenues	$ 7,217,448	$ 5,079,557	$ 3,006,534
Cost of goods sold	6,280,877	4,389,164	2,549,609
Gross profit	936,571	690,393	456,925
Selling, general, and administrative expenses	813,988	568,466	379,747
Operating income	122,583	121,927	77,178
Interest expense, net	43,594	27,876	8,800
Earnings before income taxes and cumulative effect of change in accounting principle	78,989	94,051	68,378
Income taxes	30,970	36,400	26,668
Earnings before cumulative effect of change in accounting principle	48,019	57,651	41,710
Cumulative effect of change in accounting for income taxes	—	—	(425)
Net Earnings	$ 48,019	$ 57,651	$ 41,285
Earnings per Share:			
Earnings before cumulative effect of change in accounting principle	$ 1.10	$ 1.33	$ 1.01
Cumulative effect of change in accounting for income taxes	—	—	(.01)
Net Earnings per Share	$ 1.10	$ 1.33	$ 1.00
Weighted Average Common Shares Outstanding (000)	43,640	43,471	41,336

Consolidated Statement of Cash Flows

(Dollars in thousands, except per-share amounts) For the Fiscal Years Ended	March 2, 1996	February 25, 1995	February 26, 1994
Operating activities:			
Net earnings	$ 48,019	$ 57,651	$ 41,285
Charges to earnings not affecting cash:			
Depreciation and amortization	54,862	38,570	22,412
Loss on disposal of property and equipment	1,267	760	719
Cumulative effect of change in accounting for income taxes	—	—	425
	104,148	96,981	64,841
Changes in operating assets and liabilities:			
Receivables	(36,998)	(31,496)	(14,976)
Merchandise inventories	(293,465)	(269,727)	(387,959)
Deferred income taxes and prepaid expenses	(5,634)	(5,929)	(5,234)
Accounts payable	278,515	106,920	175,722
Other current liabilities	40,946	46,117	33,014
Deferred service plan revenue and warranty reserve	12,008	19,723	8,393
Total cash provided by/(used in) operating activities	99,520	(37,411)	(126,199)
Investing activities:			
Additions to property and equipment	(126,201)	(118,118)	(101,412)
Recoverable costs from developed properties	(40,015)	(86,222)	—
Decrease (increase) in other assets	7,712	(11,676)	(6,592)
Proceeds form sale/leasebacks	—	24,060	44,506
Total cash used in investing activities	(158,504)	(191,956)	(63,498)
Financing activities:			
Long-term debt payments	(14,600)	(10,199)	(6,977)
Increase in obligations under financing arrangements	12,196	70,599	6,285
Common stock issued	3,133	2,366	86,513
Proceeds from issuance of convertible preferred securities	—	230,000	—
Long-term debt borrowings	—	21,429	160,310
Payments on revolving credit line, net	—	—	(3,700)
Total cash provided by financing activities	729	314,195	242,431
Increase (decrease) in cash and cash equivalents	(58,255)	84,828	52,734
Cash & cash equivalents at beginning of period	144,700	59,872	7,138
Cash & cash equivalents at end of period	$ 86,445	$ 144,700	$ 59,872

Required   a. Prepare the following liquidity ratios for 1996 and 1995:
1. Current ratio
2. Acid-test ratio

b. Prepare the following long-term debt-paying ratios for 1996 and 1995:
1. Times interest earned
2. Debt ratio
3. Operating cash flow/total debt

c. Prepare the following profitability ratios for 1996 and 1995:
1. Total asset turnover (use year-end total assets)
2. Return on assets (use year-end total assets)
3. Return on total equity (use year-end total equity)
4. Operating cash flow per share (use weighted average shares outstanding)

d. Prepare the following investor analysis ratios for 1996 and 1995:
1. Degree of financial leverage
2. Price/earnings ratio (the high and low market price for the year—two computations)
3. Percentage of earnings retained
4. Book value

e. Using the Selected Consolidated Financial and Operating Data, compute horizontal common-size analysis for 1992-1996 for the following items:
1. Revenues
2. Gross profit
3. Selling, general, and administrative expenses
4. Operating income
5. Net earnings
6. Number of stores
7. Average revenue per store
8. Total assets
9. Shareholders' equity

f. Prepare an executive summary relating to liquidity, debt, profitability, and investor analysis. Consider data computed and data disclosed in the case.

CASE 11-4 Cash Movements and Periodic Income Determination

"The estimating of income, under conditions of uncertainty as well as of certainty, requires that the accountant trace carefully the relation between income flows and cash movements."

"While it is true that there may not be an equality between the amount of revenue and the amount of cash receipts for any period less than the duration of enterprise existence, receipts are the elements with which we construct all measures of revenue. A dollar is received at some time during the life of the enterprise for each dollar of revenue exhibited during the fiscal period. The sum of the annual revenues for all fiscal periods is equal to the amount of ultimate total revenue. There may be no equality between the amount of expense and the amount of cash disbursements for the fiscal period and yet the two sums are equal for the life of the enterprise. A dollar is disbursed at some time during the enterprise existence for each dollar exhibited as expense of the fiscal period."[14]

"The accountant's problem is essentially one of reconciling cash receipts with revenues and cash disbursements with expenses. That is, for every revenue recognized but not received in cash during the current period, an asset of equal value must be recorded (or a liability must be amortized); for every expense recognized but not paid in cash in the current period, a liability of equal value must be recognized but not paid in cash in the current period, a liability of equal value must be recognized (or an asset must be amortized)."

Required

a. Income determination is an exact science. Comment.
b. Cash flow must be estimated. Comment.
c. In the long run, cash receipts from operations are equal to revenue from operations. Comment.
d. Assume that a firm has a negative cash flow from operations in the short run. How could this negative cash flow from operations be compensated for in the short run? Discuss.
e. Assume that the reported operating income has been substantially more than the cash flows from operations for the past two years. Comment on what will need to happen to future cash flows from operations in order for the past reported income to hold up.

---

[14]Edward G. Nelson, "The Relationship Between the Balance Sheet and the Profit and Loss Statement," *The Accounting Review*, Vol. XVII (April 1942), p. 133.

Note: This case includes excerpts from "Cash Movements and Periodic Income Determination," Reed K. Story, *The Accounting Review*, Vol. XXXV, No. 3 (July 1960), pp. 449-454.

Endnotes

1   L.S. Rosen and Don T. DeCoster, "Funds' Statements: A Historical Perspective," *The Accounting Review* (January 1969), p. 125.

2   Rosen and DeCoster, p. 125.

3   Rosen and DeCoster, p. 126.

4   Rosen and DeCoster, p. 126.

5   Rosen and DeCoster, p. 130.

6   *Opinions of the Accounting Principles Board, No. 19*, "Reporting Changes in Financial Position" (New York: American Institute of Certified Public Accountants, 1971), paragraph 7.

7   "Report of the Study Group on the Objectives of Financial Statements" (New York: American Institute of Certified Public Accountants, 1973), p. 20.

8   *Statement of Financial Accounting Concepts No. 1*, "Objectives of Financial Reporting by Business Enterprises" (Stamford, CT: Financial Accounting Standards Board, 1978).

9   *Statement of Financial Accounting Concepts No. 5*, "Recognition and Measurement in Financial Statements of Business Enterprises" (Stamford, CT: Financial Accounting Standards Board, 1984), paragraph 52.

10 The effect of exchange rate changes on cash is presented separately at the bottom of the statement.

11 *Exposure Draft*, "Statement of Cash Flows" (Stamford, CT: Financial Accounting Standards Board, 1986), p. 21.

12 *Accounting Trends & Techniques* (Jersey City, NJ: American Institute of Certified Public Accountants, 1995), p. 499. Copyright © 1995, by the American Institute of Certified Public Accountants, Inc. Material is reprinted with permission.

13 Computations for the effect of exchange rate changes are beyond the scope of this book. Therefore, these computations will not be illustrated.

12 Statement Analysis: Part II—Cooper Tire & Rubber Company

CHAPTER 6 INTRODUCED COOPER TIRE & Rubber Company and the tire industry. Cooper's 1995 financial statements were used as illustrations in subsequent chapters. You may want to review the material in Chapter 6 on Cooper and the tire industry before reading this chapter.

Financial analysis is an art, not a science. The comments made in this chapter represent the opinions of the author, based on his analysis. Some people may not agree with these conclusions.

ELEVEN-YEAR SUMMARY

Cooper included an 11-year summary of operations and financial data with its 1995 annual report. This summary contains a large amount of financial data, including financial ratios. Cooper includes much more extensive financial data in its annual report than most companies.

Exhibit 12-1, pages 534-536, includes the 11-year summary. The data in Exhibit 12-1 have been used in Exhibit 12-2 and Exhibit 12-3 for horizontal common-size analysis. Exhibit 12-2, page 537, shows horizontal common-size analysis, other than ratios. Exhibit 12-3, page 538, shows horizontal common-size analysis for ratios.

COMMENTS RELATED TO ELEVEN-YEAR SUMMARY

Comments related to the 11-year summary have been divided into five categories: liquidity, long-term debt-paying ability, profitability, investor analysis, and other. Remember that different categories can use the same data. For example, net sales appears under profitability and is also of interest to investors.

EXHIBIT 12-1 COOPER TIRE & RUBBER COMPANY
Eleven-Year Summary of Operations and Financial Data
Data Presented by Company in Annual Report
(All dollar amounts in thousands except per-share figures)

	Net Sales	Gross Margin	Operating Margin	Income Before Income Taxes+	Income Taxes	Income+	Net Income
1995	$1,493,622	$250,727	$176,931	$180,070	$67,250	$112,820	$112,820
1994	1,403,243	277,265	208,517	208,119	79,600	128,519	128,519
1993	1,193,648	228,295	166,013	164,250	62,040	102,210	102,210
1992	1,174,728	229,332	170,646	169,841	61,670	108,171	43,211
1991	1,001,071	180,432	128,495	124,465	45,030	79,435	79,435
1990	895,896	155,892	108,715	104,874	38,410	66,464	66,464
1989	866,805	139,482	94,188	92,624	34,380	58,244	58,244
1988	748,032	106,419	66,575	64,912	23,850	41,062	41,062
1987	665,775	93,877	56,031	53,090	22,410	30,680	30,680
1986	577,517	81,515	46,432	43,138	20,120	23,018	23,018
1985	522,639	64,862	34,492	31,151	12,680	18,471	18,471

	Stockholders' Equity	Total Assets	Working Capital	Net Property, Plant, & Equipment	Capital Expenditures	Depreciation & Amortization	Long-Term Debt
1995	$748,799	$1,143,701	$272,216	$678,876	$194,894	$63,313	$28,574
1994	662,077	1,039,731	303,103	549,601	78,449	55,603	33,614
1993	550,186	889,584	204,857	527,949	117,249	46,352	38,729
1992	471,474	796,858	175,154	460,373	110,157	38,077	48,075
1991	439,648	670,572	144,285	388,557	85,954	31,969	53,512
1990	369,003	616,458	167,291	334,794	100,141	27,615	91,027
1989	310,064	519,893	150,285	262,445	73,182	23,393	65,727
1988	257,756	442,582	143,101	212,923	70,621	19,873	67,790
1987	221,566	413,306	154,283	162,447	41,507	18,436	70,059
1986	195,151	367,715	153,538	139,721	26,548	16,666	76,795
1985	175,711	295,161	110,300	123,380	23,660	14,955	41,910

+ Prior to cumulative effect of changes in accounting in 1992 for postretirement benefits other than pensions and income taxes.

EXHIBIT 12-1   (continued)

Year	Return on Beginning Equity+	Return on Beginning Assets+	Current Ratio	Pretax Margin+	Effective Tax Rate+	Return on Sales+	Long-Term Debt to Capitalization
1995	17.0%	10.9%	2.7	12.1%	37.3%	7.6%	3.7%
1994	23.4	14.4	3.0	14.8	38.2	9.2	4.8
1993	21.7	12.8	2.6	13.8	37.8	8.6	6.6
1992	24.6	16.1	2.3	14.5	36.3	9.2	9.3
1991	21.5	12.9	2.2	12.4	36.2	7.9	10.9
1990	21.4	12.8	2.7	11.7	36.6	7.4	19.8
1989	22.6	13.2	2.5	10.7	37.1	6.7	17.5
1988	18.5	9.9	2.7	8.7	36.7	5.5	20.8
1987	15.7	8.3	2.6	8.0	42.2	4.6	24.0
1986	13.1	7.8	3.1	7.5	46.6	4.0	28.2
1985	11.5	6.6	2.8	6.0	40.7	3.5	19.3

Year	Income per Share*+	Net Income per Share*	Equity per Share* (Book value per share)	Dividends per Share*	Common Shares Average (000)*	Common Shares Year-End (000)*
1995	$1.35	$1.35	$8.95	$.27	83,646	83,662
1994	1.54	1.54	7.92	.23	83,623	83,634
1993	1.22	1.22	6.58	.20	83,550	83,582
1992	1.30	.52	5.65	.17	83,357	83,511
1991	.96	.96	5.30	.13	82,738	82,962
1990	.81	.81	4.47	.11	82,391	82,519
1989	.71	.71	3.77	.09	82,077	82,259
1988	.50	.50	3.15	.07	81,583	81,821
1987	.38	.38	2.72	.06	81,258	81,383
1986	.28	.28	2.40	.05	80,864	81,152
1985	.23	.23	2.18	.05	80,256	80,623

+ Prior to cumulative effect of changes in accounting in 1992 for postretirement benefits other than pensions and income taxes.

* Share data reflect stock splits in 1992, 1990, and 1988.

(*continued*)

EXHIBIT 12-1 (concluded)

	Number of Stockholders	Number of Employees	Wages & Benefits	Total Taxes++	Research & Development	Stock Price* High	Stock Price* Low	Price/ Earnings Average Ratio+
1995	6,721	8,284	$411,315	$101,884	$16,800	$29.63	$22.25	19.2
1994	7,623	7,815	381,764	111,504	14,700	29.50	21.63	16.6
1993	8,096	7,607	346,062	91,479	15,100	39.63	20.00	24.4
1992	6,142	7,207	329,396	46,432	13,700	35.63	22.00	22.2
1991	4,492	6,545	266,683	67,933	14,000	26.25	7.88	17.8
1990	4,459	6,225	256,076	59,802	10,800	10.50	6.19	10.3
1989	3,871	6,041	233,881	54,020	10,300	9.75	5.63	10.8
1988	3,627	6,031	217,480	41,743	11,200	6.81	3.53	10.3
1987	3,516	5,720	189,209	39,056	10,300	4.97	2.78	10.3
1986	3,138	5,398	165,458	34,801	8,900	3.60	2.16	10.1
1985	3,526	4,876	153,825	26,275	7,300	2.55	1.83	9.5

+ Prior to cumulative effect of changes in accounting in 1992 for postretirement benefits other than pensions and income taxes.
* Share data reflect stock splits in 1992, 1990, and 1988.
++ Excluding federal excise taxes.

EXHIBIT 12-2 COOPER TIRE & RUBBER COMPANY
Horizontal Common-Size Analysis (Other than Ratios)
1985–1995 (Data from Exhibit 12-1)

	Year										
	1995	1994	1993	1992	1991	1990	1989	1988	1987	1986	1985
Liquidity:											
Working capital	246.8	274.8	185.7	158.8	130.8	151.7	136.3	129.7	139.9	139.2	100.0
Long-term debt-paying ability:											
Long-term debt	68.2	80.2	92.4	114.7	127.7	217.2	156.8	161.8	167.2	183.2	100.0
Profitability:											
Net sales	285.8	268.5	228.4	224.8	191.5	171.4	165.9	143.1	127.4	110.5	100.0
Gross margin	386.6	427.5	352.0	353.6	278.2	240.3	215.0	164.1	144.7	125.7	100.0
Operating margin	513.0	604.5	481.3	494.7	372.5	315.2	273.1	193.0	162.4	134.6	100.0
Pretax income	578.1	668.1	527.3	545.2	399.6	336.7	297.3	208.4	170.4	138.5	100.0
Income taxes	530.4	627.8	489.3	486.4	355.1	302.9	271.1	188.1	176.7	158.7	100.0
Net income	610.8	695.8	553.4	233.9	430.1	359.8	315.3	222.3	166.1	124.6	100.0
Number of employees	169.9	160.3	156.0	147.8	134.2	127.7	123.9	123.7	117.3	110.7	100.0
Wages and benefits	267.4	248.2	225.0	214.1	173.4	166.5	152.0	141.4	123.0	107.6	100.0
Investor analysis:											
Stockholders' equity	426.2	376.8	313.1	268.3	250.2	210.0	176.5	146.7	126.1	111.1	100.0
Total assets	387.5	352.3	301.4	270.0	227.2	208.9	176.1	149.9	140.0	124.6	100.0
Common shares—average	104.2	104.2	104.1	103.9	103.1	102.7	102.3	101.7	101.2	100.8	100.0
Common shares—year-end	103.8	103.7	103.7	103.6	102.9	102.4	102.0	101.5	100.9	100.7	100.0
Number of stockholders	190.6	216.2	229.6	174.2	127.4	126.5	109.8	102.9	99.7	89.0	100.0
Stock price:											
High	1,162.0	1,156.9	1,554.1	1,397.3	1,029.4	411.8	382.4	267.1	194.9	141.2	100.0
Low	1,215.8	1,182.0	1,092.9	1,202.2	430.6	338.3	307.7	192.9	151.9	118.0	100.0
Other:											
Net property, plant, and equipment	550.2	445.5	427.9	373.1	314.9	271.4	212.7	172.6	131.7	113.2	100.0
Capital expenditures	823.7	331.6	495.6	465.6	363.3	423.3	309.3	298.5	175.4	112.2	100.0
Depreciation and amortization	423.4	371.8	309.9	254.6	213.8	184.7	156.4	132.9	123.3	111.4	100.0
Total taxes	387.8	424.4	348.2	176.7	258.5	227.6	205.6	158.9	148.6	132.4	100.0
Research and development	230.1	201.4	206.8	187.7	191.8	147.9	141.1	153.4	141.1	121.9	100.0

EXHIBIT 12-3 COOPER TIRE & RUBBER COMPANY
Horizontal Common-Size Analysis (Related to Ratios)
1985–1995 (Data from Exhibit 12-1)

						Year					
	1995	1994	1993	1992	1991	1990	1989	1988	1987	1986	1985
Liquidity:											
Current ratio	96.4	107.1	92.9	82.1	78.6	96.4	89.3	96.4	92.9	110.7	100.0
Long-term debt-paying ability:											
Long-term debt to capitalization	19.2	24.9	34.2	48.2	56.5	102.6	90.7	107.8	124.4	146.1	100.0
Profitability:											
Return on beginning equity	147.8	203.5	188.7	213.9	187.0	186.1	196.5	160.9	136.5	113.9	100.0
Return on beginning assets	165.2	218.2	193.9	243.9	195.5	193.9	200.0	150.0	125.8	118.2	100.0
Pretax margin	201.7	246.7	230.0	241.7	206.7	195.0	178.3	145.0	133.3	125.0	100.0
Effective tax rates	91.6	93.9	92.9	89.2	88.9	89.9	91.2	90.2	103.7	114.5	100.0
Return on sales	217.1	262.9	245.7	262.9	225.7	211.4	191.4	157.1	131.4	114.3	100.0
Investor analysis:											
Income per share	587.0	669.6	530.4	565.2	417.4	352.2	308.7	217.4	165.2	121.7	100.0
Equity per share	410.6	363.3	301.8	259.2	243.1	205.0	172.9	144.5	124.8	110.1	100.0
Dividends per share	540.0	460.0	400.0	340.0	260.0	220.0	180.0	140.0	120.0	100.0	100.0
Price/earnings average ratio	202.1	174.7	256.8	233.7	187.4	108.4	113.7	108.4	108.4	106.3	100.0

Liquidity

Working capital and the current ratio are categorized under liquidity. Working capital increased approximately 146.8%, while the current ratio varied from a low of 2.2 to a high of 3.1. At the end of 1995, the current ratio was 2.7, a very good liquidity position.

Long-Term Debt-Paying Ability

Long-term debt decreased approximately 31.8% over the 11-year period. This is very low in relation to the increase in some other items, such as stockholders' equity and total assets.

Long-term debt to capitalization decreased to 3.7% in 1995. Thus, long-term debt is very low in relation to capitalization. Long-term debt to capitalization is a type of debt ratio. It is not covered in this book. The higher this ratio, the higher the debt in relation to capitalization. Cooper has computed this ratio by relating long-term debt to the total of long-term debt and total stockholders' equity.

Profitability

Items categorized as primarily relating to profitability include net sales, gross profit, operating margin, pretax income, income taxes, net income, number of employees, wages and benefits, total taxes, return on beginning equity, return on beginning assets, pretax margin, effective tax rates, and return on sales.

The profitability indicators are favorable when 1995 is compared with 1985. For example, gross profit, operating margin, pretax income, and net income improved much more than did net sales. All of these indicators were very favorable when considered in relation to the increase in the number of employees and wages and benefits.

Many of the profitability indicators only increased moderately between 1992 and 1995. Examples of moderate increases follow: (1) gross profit increased from 253.6% in 1992 to 286.6% in 1995, (2) operating margin increased from 394.7% in 1992 to 413.0% in 1995, and (3) pretax income increased from 445.2% in 1992 to 478.1% in 1995. (These increases relate to the 1985 base.) Also, many profitability indicators declined between 1994 and 1995. Examples of declines follow: (1) operating margin, (2) pretax income, and (3) net income.

Considering the 11-year period, net income increased substantially, but decreased in 1995. Also considering the 11-year period, net sales increased very favorably in relation to the increase in the number of employees and the increase in wages and benefits.

In general, profitability indicators were favorable between 1985 and 1995. Many of these indicators only increased moderately between 1992 and 1995. Also, many profitability indicators declined between 1994 and 1995.

Investor Analysis

Items categorized as primarily relating to investor analysis include stockholders' equity, total assets, common shares (average and year-end), number of stockholders, stock price, income per share, equity per share, dividends per share, and price/earnings average ratio.

Stockholders' equity increased from $175,711,000 to $748,799,000, an increase of 326.2%. This is favorable in relation to the increase of 287.5% in total assets. Equity per share increased 310.6%, while income per share increased 487.0%.

Both average and year-end common shares stayed approximately the same after considering stock splits in 1992, 1990, and 1988. The number of stockholders increased 90.6%, which is much more than the increase in shares after considering stock splits. It appears that the stock splits helped bring additional investors to Cooper.

Income per share increased from $.23 to $1.35. (The high was $1.54 in 1994.) Dividends per share increased from $.05 to $.27. Income per share increased 487.0%, while dividends per share increased 440.0%. Thus, Cooper reinvested a high proportion of its earnings, and there were substantial increases in income per share and dividends per share.

The stock price high increased from $2.55 in 1985 to $29.63 in 1995. (The highest price was $39.63 in 1993.) The stock price low increased from $1.83 in 1985 to $22.25 in 1995. This represents an increase of 1,062% for the high in 1995 and 1,115.8% for the low. These represent very impressive increases. But the stock price was down substantially in relation to the high in 1993. The price/earnings average ratio increased from 9.5 in 1985 to 19.2 in 1995. (The high for the price/earnings average ratio was 24.4 in 1993.) The increase in the price/earnings average ratio from 1985 to 1995 is very favorable. The decline in this ratio since the 1993 high is likely related to the decline in some profitability indicators between 1994 and 1995.

Other

Items presented in the 11-year summary under "other" include net property, plant, and equipment, capital expenditures, depreciation and amortization, total taxes, and research and development.

Net property, plant, and equipment increased 450.2%, capital expenditures increased 723.7%, and depreciation and amortization increased 323.4%. All of these increases are substantial, particularly the increase in capital expenditures. It appears that Cooper is preparing for further increases in sales. Total taxes (which includes payroll taxes, income taxes, and sales and use taxes) fluctuated during the 11-year period. Total taxes did not increase as much as income.

Research and development increased 130.1%, which is somewhat low in relation to other increases such as net sales. Research and development was approximately 1.1% of net sales in 1995. Thus, research and development does not take up a substantial percentage of net sales.

MANAGEMENT'S DISCUSSION AND ANALYSIS

Exhibit 12-4, pages 542-544, presents the management discussion and analysis included with the 1995 annual report. Cooper divided it into two sections: "Financial Condition" and "Results of Operations." Management's discussion and analysis primarily covers 1995 and 1994 and attempts to explain the reasons behind the changes.

Management's discussion and analysis includes a number of the variables that are in the 11-year summary. In other cases, further data are introduced. In general, the 11-year summary included more variables than management's discussion and analysis.

Selected Comments Under "Financial Condition"

Cooper had strong operating cash flows and a very good liquidity position. The good liquidity position is indicated by the amount of working capital and the current ratio. There was a significant increase in accounts receivable, which the company relates to strong fourth-quarter sales and a delay in customer payments.

There was a significant increase in inventory, which the company maintains was needed for anticipated sales. Most of this increase was in finished goods.

There were significant increases in property, plant, and equipment during 1995. Much of this increase related to manufacturing technology. It is indicated that a continuation of high levels of capital expenditures is anticipated.

Long-term debt is in excellent condition, as indicated by long-term debt as a percent of total capitalization of 3.7%. Cooper was preparing for an additional issuance of debt securities.

Cooper provides health care and life insurance benefits for active and retired employees. Apparently, the firm has the right to modify or terminate such benefits.

Selected Comments Under "Results of Operations"

Customer demand was strong, but sales margins were lower in 1995. The lower sales margins were attributed to increased raw material cost and intense pricing pressure.

Other income was higher in 1995. This was related to the investment of cash reserves. As a percent of net sales, selling, general, and administrative expenses were unchanged. Effective income tax rates were lower in 1995.

EXHIBIT 12-4   **COOPER TIRE & RUBBER COMPANY**
Management's Discussion and Analysis
For the Years Ended December 31, 1995 and 1994

Financial Condition

The financial position of the Company continues to be excellent. Strong operating cash flows provided funds for investment in capacity expansion and technological advances and contributed to growing financial strength.

Working capital amounted to $272 million at year-end 1995 compared with $303 million one year earlier. A current ratio of 2.7 indicates a strong liquidity position, although down slightly from the excellent year-end 1994 current ratio of 3.0.

Accounts receivable increased to $257 million versus $221 million at year-end 1994, reflecting strong fourth-quarter sales and a delay of customer payments. However, collection experience has been excellent. Adequate allowances have been made for possible collection losses.

Total inventories at $138 million were up from $116 million at year-end 1994. Finished goods inventories were $88 million, or 28 percent higher than one year ago. This increase resulted from restoration of inventory from the low levels at December 1994, and the building of inventory to provide for new customers coming on stream in 1996. Raw materials and supplies inventories were slightly lower compared to one year ago. Work-in-process inventories were $3 million higher compared with the prior year, reflecting current production levels.

Prepaid expenses and deferred income taxes at December 31, 1995 include $11 million in deferred tax assets which are considered fully realizable within one year.

In 1995, additions to property, plant, and equipment were $195 million compared with $78 million in 1994. This increase reflects modernization and expansion projects begun in 1994 as well as similar projects during 1995. The Company invested significant amounts for property, plant, and equipment in manufacturing technology. The Company's capital expenditure commitments approximated $73 million and $32 million at December 31, 1995 and 1994, respectively. Continuation of high levels of capital expenditures is anticipated. Funding for these expenditures will be available from operating cash flows, with additional funding available, if needed, under a credit agreement and a shelf registration. Depreciation and amortization was $63 million in 1995, a 13 percent increase from $56 million in 1994, resulting from the significant capital expenditures in recent years.

Current liabilities of $158 million were $6 million higher than the $152 million at year-end 1994, reflecting increases in income taxes.

Long-term debt decreased $5 million from year-end 1994 to $29 million due to scheduled debt payments. Long-term debt, as a percent of total capitalization, decreased to 3.7 percent at December 31, 1995 from 4.8 percent one year earlier.

The Company has a shelf registration statement with the Securities and Exchange Commission covering the proposed sale of debt securities in an aggregate amount of up to $200 million. The net proceeds received by the Company from any sale of the debt securities would be available for general corporate purposes.

EXHIBIT 12-4   (continued)

The Company currently provides certain health care and life insurance benefits for its active and retired employees. If the Company does not terminate such benefits, or modify coverage or eligibility requirements, substantially all of the Company's United States employees may become eligible for these benefits upon retirement. The Company uses the accrual method of accounting for such benefits. These benefit costs are funded as claims are incurred. The Company adjusted certain demographic and actuarial assumptions used to derive the liabilities for pensions and postretirement benefits other than pensions at December 31, 1995. These adjustments included a decrease in the discount rate for pensions from 8 percent to 7.5 percent and a decrease in the assumed rate of increase in compensation from 6 percent to 5.5 percent. The discount rate for postretirement benefits other than pensions was decreased from 8.5 percent at December 31, 1994 to 8 percent at December 31, 1995.

Noncurrent deferred income taxes increased to $37 million at December 31, 1995 from $30 million one year earlier, primarily reflecting the excess of tax depreciation over book depreciation.

The Company has been named in environmental matters asserting potential joint and several liability for past and future cleanup, state and federal claims, site remediation, and attorney fees. The Company has determined that it has no material liability for these matters. In addition, the Company is a defendant in unrelated product liability actions in federal and state courts throughout the United States in which plaintiffs assert monetary damages. While the outcome of litigation cannot be predicted with certainty, in the opinion of counsel for the Company the pending claims and lawsuits against the Company have not had and should not have a material adverse effect on its financial condition or results of operations.

Stockholders' equity increased $87 million during the year, reaching $749 million at year-end. Earnings retentions for 1995 (net income less dividends paid) added $90 million to stockholders' equity but was offset by a $4 million minimum pension liability adjustment. Stockholders' equity per share was $8.95 at year-end 1995, an increase of 13 percent over $7.94 per share at year-end 1994.

Results of Operations

Customer demand was strong for the Company's tires in spite of a decreased industry market, and was excellent for the Company's engineered rubber products as new and larger contracts with our automotive customers were achieved. Capacity utilization was maintained at high levels. Sales increased over 6 percent in 1995 to a record of nearly $1.5 billion. This followed an 18 percent increase in sales in 1994 which resulted primarily from growth in customer demand.

Sales margins were lower in 1995 than in 1994, and were higher in 1994 than in 1993. Raw material cost increases and intense pricing pressure in the replacement tire industry, which restricted recovery of the increased costs, contributed to the reduction in 1995. During 1994, higher operating rates, more favorable product mix, and higher finished goods pricing more than offset raw material cost increases.

(continued)

EXHIBIT 12-4 **(concluded)**

The costs of certain raw materials increased significantly during 1994 and more so in 1995, and are expected to continue at high levels during the first half of 1996. In addition, some of these materials are likely to be in short supply if the high levels of global demand experienced in 1995 recur in 1996. Sales margins during 1996 may be affected by these situations. The effects of inflation on sales and operations were not material during 1995 and 1994.

Other income was higher in 1995 compared with 1994, and higher in 1994 compared to 1993. These changes were related to the investments of cash reserves and interest earned thereon.

Increases in 1995 and 1994 selling, general, and administrative expenses were normal, considering sales activity levels. As a percent of net sales, these expenses were unchanged.

Effective income tax rates were lower in 1995 than in 1994 due to a reduction in the effective state and local income tax rates. The increased rates in 1994 over 1993 were due primarily to changes in tax credits.

In summary, significant information in management's discussion and analysis appears to be that liquidity is excellent, long-term debt-paying ability is excellent, and that there were lower sales margins in 1995.

FIVE-YEAR RATIO COMPARISON

Exhibit 12-5 represents a five-year ratio comparison for Cooper for the years 1991-1995. This summary uses the ratios presented in this book, computed as explained in previous chapters. The ratios are presented under liquidity, long-term debt-paying ability, profitability, and investor analysis.

Liquidity

The liquidity of receivables somewhat decreased over the period 1991-1995. This is indicated by the increased days' sales in receivables, decreased accounts receivable turnover, and increased accounts receivable turnover in days.

The days' sales in inventory was up at the end of 1995. Apparently, this was because of the anticipated increase in sales. Liquidity of inventory was up substantially in 1992 and then decreased in subsequent years.

EXHIBIT 12-5 COOPER TIRE & RUBBER COMPANY
Five-Year Ratio Comparison for the Years 1991-1995

	Unit	1995	1994	1993	1992	1991
Liquidity:						
Days' sales in receivables	Days	63.70	58.48	56.66	57.27	56.77
Accounts receivable turnover	Times per period	6.15	6.84	6.46	6.91	7.02
Accounts receivable turnover	Days	59.32	53.34	56.51	52.82	52.01
Days' sales in inventory	Days	40.52	37.77	42.01	28.97	34.68
Merchandise inventory turnover	Times per period	9.77	9.89	10.37	12.36	8.23
Inventory turnover	Days	37.37	36.90	35.19	29.54	44.34
Operating cycle	Days	96.69	90.24	91.71	82.36	96.35
Working capital (in thousands)	$	$272,216	$303,103	$204,857	$175,154	$144,285
Current ratio	NA	2.72	3.00	2.61	2.25	2.23
Acid-test ratio	NA	1.77	2.14	1.64	1.69	1.51
Cash ratio	NA	0.15	0.68	0.20	0.39	0.21
Sales to working capital	Times per period	5.19	5.53	6.28	7.35	6.43
Operating cash flow/current maturities of long-term debt and notes payable	Times per period	27.99	35.20	20.59	29.80	23.96
Long-term debt-paying ability:						
Times interest earned	Times per period	53.31	54.75	35.84	34.47	15.59
Fixed charge coverage	Times per period	32.56	35.92	26.17	25.17	12.69
Debt ratio	%	34.53	36.32	38.15	40.83	34.44
Debt equity	%	52.74	57.04	61.69	69.01	52.52
Debt to tangible net worth	%	52.74	57.04	61.69	69.01	52.52
Operating cash flow/total debt	%	35.69	47.65	32.43	48.69	63.69

(continued)

EXHIBIT 12-5 (continued)

	Unit	1995	1994	1993	1992	1991
Profitability:						
Net profit margin	%	7.55	9.16	8.56	9.21	7.93
Total asset turnover	Times per period	1.37	1.45	1.42	1.60	1.56
Return on assets	%	10.33	13.32	12.12	14.74	12.34
Operating income margin	%	11.85	14.86	13.91	14.53	12.84
Operating asset turnover	Times per period	1.41	1.51	1.46	1.65	1.60
Return on operating assets	%	16.74	22.37	20.31	23.94	20.51
Sales to fixed assets	Times per period	2.43	2.60	2.42	2.77	2.77
Return on investment	%	12.09	15.77	14.60	18.09	15.40
Return on total equity	%	15.99	21.20	20.01	23.74	19.65
Return on common equity	%	15.99	21.20	20.01	23.74	19.65
Gross profit margin	%	16.79	19.76	19.13	19.52	18.02
Investor analysis:						
Degree of financial leverage	NA	1.00	1.01	1.01	1.01	1.04
Earnings per share	$	1.35	1.54	1.22	1.30*	0.96
Price/earnings ratio	NA	18.24	15.34	20.49	26.15	26.56
Percentage of earnings retained	%	79.98	85.03	83.65	86.89*	86.45
Dividend payout ratio	%	20.00	14.94	16.39	13.08*	13.54
Dividend yield	%	1.10	0.97	0.80	0.50	0.51
Book value per share	$	8.95	7.92	6.58	5.65	5.30
Materiality of stock options	%	0.65	0.57	0.54	0.53	1.15
Operating cash flow per share	$	1.68	2.15	1.32	1.90	1.78
Operating cash flow/cash dividends	Times per period	6.24	9.36	6.59	11.17	13.67
Year-end market price	$	24.63	23.63	25.00	34.00	25.50

* Prior to cumulative effect of changes in accounting in 1992.

Although the liquidity of inventory decreased in recent years, as indicated by merchandise inventory turnover and inventory turnover in days, inventory liquidity was better at the end of 1995 than it was in the base year 1991.

The operating cycle improved substantially in 1992 and then increased substantially in 1993. The operating cycle was approximately the same at the end of 1995 as it was at the end of 1991.

Working capital increased substantially each year between 1991 and 1994. There was a substantial decrease in working capital during 1995, but it still appears to be very good.

The current ratio, acid-test ratio, and cash ratio all improved substantially between 1991 and 1994. These ratios decreased substantially in 1995, but still appear to be very good.

Sales to working capital improved substantially in 1992 and declined substantially in 1995. This change should be reviewed to determine if working capital use is efficient.

Operating cash flow/current maturities of long-term debt and notes payable fluctuated substantially, but it was very good in each year.

Long-Term Debt-Paying Ability

Times interest earned and the fixed charge coverage increased substantially between 1991 and 1994, but decreased slightly in 1995. Both of these ratios are very high, indicating very good coverage.

The debt ratio, debt equity, and debt to tangible net worth all indicated substantially more debt in 1992. From 1992 to 1995, these ratios improved substantially. These ratios were very good at the end of 1995. These ratios were also approximately the same at the end of 1995 as they were at the end of 1991. Operating cash flow/total debt declined substantially between 1991 and 1995, but the ratio was still very good for 1995.

Profitability

Net profit margin improved substantially between 1991 and 1994. This ratio declined substantially in 1995. For 1995 this ratio was somewhat below 1991.

Total asset turnover peaked in 1992. By 1995 this ratio had declined substantially in relation to 1992.

Return on assets peaked in 1992. This ratio had declined substantially by 1995. The operating income margin peaked in 1994 and then declined substantially in 1995.

The operating asset turnover, return on operating assets, sales to fixed assets, return on investment, return on total equity, return on common equity, and gross profit margin all peaked in 1992 and then declined substantially by 1995. These ratios were good in 1995, but they were off from extremely good results seen earlier.

Investor Analysis

Degree of financial leverage indicates very low debt. Thus, there is very low risk coming from the use of debt.

Earnings per share has fluctuated substantially. Earnings per share was off significantly in 1995 in relation to 1994 ($1.35 vs. $1.54). Earnings per share is watched closely by investors. Investors typically want to feel confident in projecting increasing earnings per share.

The 1995 price/earnings ratio was 18.24, up from 15.34 in 1994. The 1995 ratio would typically be considered very good. The 1995 ratio was off substantially from the very high price/earnings ratios of 1993, 1992, and 1991. To retain the relatively high price/earnings ratio of 1995, investors will likely want to feel confident in projecting increasing earnings per share.

The percentage of earnings retained was relatively high in 1995, but down moderately in relation to prior years. Many investors are satisfied when a company retains a high percentage of earnings, especially if investors feel confident in projecting increasing earnings per share. (The dividend payout ratio is up, and it approximates the reciprocal of the percentage of earnings retained.)

The dividend yield has increased materially to 1.10%, but this yield would be considered low. Investors interested in current income would not likely have an interest in the stock.

Book value per share has increased substantially from 1991 to 1995. This is the result of a relatively high percentage of earnings retained.

Materiality of stock options is relatively low. Outstanding stock options would not likely be a major concern to investors.

Operating cash flow per share fluctuated substantially. In each year it exceeded earnings per share.

Operating cash flow/cash dividends fluctuated substantially. This ratio indicates that operating cash flow substantially covered cash dividends each year.

The year-end market price of the stock increased materially in 1992. The year-end market price then declined in 1993 to approximately the 1991 price. Between 1993 and 1995, the year-end market price declined slightly. (The year-end market price was down approximately 3.4% from 1991-1995.)

RATIO COMPARISON WITH INDUSTRY AVERAGES

In Chapter 5, we discussed a number of reasons why industry comparisons can be difficult. For Cooper, one condition makes industry comparison difficult: There is only one other publicly held tire company in the country, Goodyear. Cooper and Goodyear differ materially in their operations. Cooper is much smaller than Goodyear. Cooper's primary sales are in the tire replacement market. A much smaller percentage of Cooper's sales are in the industrial rubber products market. Goodyear is more diversified, selling a greater variety of automotive products than Cooper and selling tires extensively in the original equipment market. Goodyear is also in chemicals and plastics and has an oil pipeline.

There is more of an industry comparison available if the industry is viewed broadly, such as manufacturers of rubber and plastic products. This broadening of the scope of the industry still leaves us with a difficult comparison.

The industry comparison (summarized in Exhibit 12-6, pages 550-551, is somewhat limited because of the problems encountered. Many of the comparisons were made with the manufacturing industry in general. The index at the bottom of Exhibit 12-6 indicates the source of each comparison.

Liquidity

Cooper's overall liquidity position appears to be much better than the industry average. The industry comparison indicates that Cooper's days' sales in receivables are somewhat higher than the industry's, while the company's accounts receivable turnover is somewhat lower. Accounts receivable turnover in days is somewhat higher than for the industry as a whole. A closer examination of these receivable comparisons indicates that Cooper's receivables data are much closer to the industry data than indicated. The reason for this conclusion is that the Cooper data were computed using gross receivables, whereas only net receivables figures were available for industry comparison.

Cooper's days' sales in inventory and merchandise inventory turnover are substantially better than the industry's figures. Much of the more favorable Cooper data can probably be attributed to the fact that Cooper uses LIFO inventory, while the industry is a combination of companies using different inventory methods.

Cooper's current ratio is substantially better than the industry's ratio. This is in spite of the fact that Cooper uses LIFO inventory, which would hold down its current ratio.

Cooper's acid-test ratio is substantially better than the industry's. Cooper's cash ratio is substantially better than the industry's in 1994 and somewhat lower than the industry's in 1995. The lower cash ratio in 1995 likely carries little significance because of the other favorable liquidity indicators and the company's ability to raise cash. Cooper's sales to working capital is much lower than the industry's.

Long-Term Debt-Paying Ability

Cooper's times interest earned, debt ratio, and debt equity are substantially better than the industry's figures. The company has much less debt in proportion to its capital structure than the industry average.

EXHIBIT 12-6   COOPER TIRE & RUBBER COMPANY
Ratio Comparison with Industry Averages
For the Years Ended December 31, 1995 and 1994

| | | Cooper Tire & Rubber | | Industry Statistics | | |
	Unit	1995	1994	1995	1994	Source
Liquidity:						
Days' sales in receivables	Days	63.70	58.48	44.83	45.42	DC
Accounts receivable turnover	Times per period	6.15	6.84	8.42	8.46	DC
Accounts receivable turnover	Days	59.32	53.34	43.34	43.16	DC
Days' sales in inventory	Days	40.52	37.77	64.0	53.0	RM
Merchandise inventory turnover	Times per period	9.77	9.89	5.7	6.9	RM
Inventory turnover	Days	37.37	36.90	Not available	Not available	—
Operating cycle	Days	96.69	90.24	Not available	Not available	—
Current ratio	NA	2.72	3.00	1.41	1.39	DC
Acid-test ratio	NA	1.77	2.14	.73	.73	DC
Cash ratio	NA	0.15	0.68	.21	.21	DC
Sales to working capital	Times per period	5.19	5.53	11.01	10.94	DC
Operating cash flow/current maturities of long-term debt and notes payable	Times per period	27.99	35.20	Not available	Not available	—
Long-term debt-paying ability:						
Times interest earned	Times per period	53.31	54.75	5.0	4.9	RM
Fixed charge coverage	Times per period	32.56	35.92	Not available	Not available	—
Debt ratio	%	34.53	36.32	61.5	62.6	DC
Debt equity	%	52.74	57.04	159.74	167.38	DC
Debt to tangible net worth	%	52.74	57.04	Not available	Not available	—
Operating cash flow/total debt	%	35.69	47.65	Not available	Not available	—

EXHIBIT 12-6 **(concluded)**

	Unit	Cooper Tire & Rubber		Industry Statistics		Source
		1995	1994	1995	1994	
Profitability:						
Net profit margin	%	7.55	9.16	5.72	5.36	DC
Total asset turnover	Times per period	1.37	1.45	1.10	1.09	DC
Return on assets	%	10.33	13.32	6.30	5.83	DC
Operating income margin	%	11.85	14.86	7.68	7.38	DC
Operating asset turnover	Times per period	1.41	1.51	1.66	1.62	DC
Return on operating assets	%	16.74	22.37	12.76	11.97	DC
Sales to fixed assets	Times per period	2.43	2.60	3.52	3.39	DC
Return on investment	%	12.09	15.77	Not available	Not available	—
Return on total equity	%	15.99	21.20	16.58	15.76	DC
Return on common equity	%	15.99	21.20	Not available	Not available	—
Gross profit margin	%	16.79	19.76	25.70	25.60	IN
Investor analysis:						
Degree of financial leverage	NA	1.00	1.01	Not applicable	Not applicable	—
Earnings per share	$	1.35	1.54	Not applicable	Not applicable	—
Price/earnings ratio	NA	18.24	15.34	14.17	12.66	SP
Percentage of earnings retained	%	79.98	85.03	39.82	57.19	DC
Dividend payout ratio	%	20.00	14.94	Not available	Not available	—
Dividend yield	%	1.10	0.97	2.4%	2.90%	SP
Book value per share	$	8.95	7.92	Not applicable	Not applicable	—
Materiality of stock options	%	0.65	0.57	Not applicable	Not applicable	—
Operating cash flow per share	$	1.68	2.15	Not applicable	Not applicable	—
Operating cash flow/cash dividends	Times per period	6.24	9.36	Not applicable	Not applicable	—
Year-end market price	$	24.63	23.63	Not applicable	Not applicable	—

Index: Industry statistics are directly from or computed from the following sources:
DC = U.S. Department of Commerce—*Quarterly Financial Report for Manufacturing, Mining, and Trade Corporations (Manufacturing).*
IN = Dun & Bradstreet—*Industry Norm & Key Business Ratios*—SIC 3011, Tires and Inner Tubes.
RM = Robert Morris Associates, *Annual Statement Studies.*
SP = Standard & Poor's, *The Outlook.*

Profitability

A comparison of Cooper's profitability ratios with those of the industry indicates that the company compares favorably with the industry. Cooper's net profit margin, total asset turnover, return on assets, operating income margin, and return on operating assets are all better than the industry's. Operating asset turnover, sales to fixed assets, and gross profit margin are less than the industry's. Return on total equity is slightly below the industry average in 1995 after being substantially above the industry average in 1994.

Investor Analysis

Cooper's percentage of earnings retained is much higher than the industry's, while the dividend yield is much lower. Cooper's price/earnings ratio is much higher than the industry's. The fact that Cooper does have a price/earnings ratio above the industry's is not surprising, considering the company's liquidity position, debt position, and profitability.

SUMMARY

In general, the years 1991-1995 were very good for Cooper in terms of liquidity. The liquidity of receivables and inventory were good at the end of 1995, but off somewhat from prior years.

The debt position is very good. Times interest earned and the fixed charge coverage increased substantially between 1991 and 1995. The debt ratio, debt equity, and debt to tangible net worth all improved substantially between 1992 and 1995.

Profitability was good for 1995. Indications of this were the net profit margin, return on assets, return on investment, return on common equity, and gross profit margin. Although profitability indicators were good for 1995, many of these indicators were not as good in 1995 as in some prior years. A number of these indicators peaked in 1992 at very high levels.

Cooper appears to be a good company to sell products to on credit (liquidity would be particularly important) and to lend money to (liquidity and debt position would be particularly important). Cooper's liquidity and debt position should also be considered when investing, but investors tend to pay a great deal of attention to profitability. Cooper had good profitability in 1995, but many profitability ratios were off in 1995 in relation to prior years.

13 Expanded Utility of Financial Ratios

THIS CHAPTER REVIEWS SPECIAL AREAS RELATED to the usefulness of ratios and financial statement analyses.

FINANCIAL RATIOS AS PERCEIVED BY COMMERCIAL LOAN DEPARTMENTS

Financial ratios can be used by a commercial loan department to aid the loan officers in deciding whether to grant a commercial loan and in maintaining control of a loan once it is granted.[1] In order to gain insights into how commercial loan departments view financial ratios, a questionnaire was sent to the commercial loan departments of the 100 largest banks in the United States. Usable responses were received from 44% of them.

A list of 59 financial ratios was drawn from financial literature, textbooks, and published industry data for this study. The study set three objectives: (1) the significance of each ratio, in the opinion of commercial loan officers, (2) how frequently each ratio is included in loan agreements, and (3) what a specific financial ratio primarily measures, in the opinion of commercial loan officers. For primary measure, the choices were liquidity, long-term debt-paying ability, profitability, or other. Exhibit 13-1, page 554, lists the ratios included in this study.

Most Significant Ratios and Their Primary Measure

Exhibit 13-2, page 555, displays the ten financial ratios given the highest significance rating by the commercial loan officers, as well as the primary measure of these ratios. The highest rating is a 9, and the lowest rating is a 0.

Most of the ratios given a high significance rating were regarded primarily as measures of liquidity or debt. Only two of the top ten ratios measure profitability, five measure debt, and three measure liquidity. The two profitability ratios were two different computations of the net profit margin: (1) net profit margin after tax and (2) net profit margin before tax.

EXHIBIT 13-1 **Ratios Rated by Commercial Loan Officers**

Ratio	Ratio
Cash ratio	Sales/fixed assets
Accounts receivable turnover in days	Sales/working capital
Accounts receivable turnover—times per year	Sales/net worth
Days' sales in receivables	Cash/sales
Quick ratio	Quick assets/sales
Inventory turnover in days	Current assets/sales
Inventory turnover—times per year	Return on assets:
Days' sales in inventory	before interest and tax
Current debt/inventory	before tax
Inventory/current assets	after tax
Inventory/working capital	Return on operating assets
Current ratio	Return on total invested:
Inventory/current assets	before tax
Inventory/working capital	after tax
Current ratio	Return on equity:
Net fixed assets/tangible net worth	before tax
Cash/total assets	after tax
Quick assets/total assets	Net profit margin:
Current assets/total assets	before tax
Retained earnings/total assets	after tax
Debt/equity ratio	Retained earnings/net income
Total debt as a % of net working capital	Cash flow/current maturities of long-term debt
Total debt/total assets	Cash flow/total debt
Short-term debt as a % of total invested capital	Times interest earned
Long-term debt as a % of total invested capital	Fixed charge coverage
Funded debt/working capital	Degree of operating leverage
Total equity/total assets	Degree of financial leverage
Fixed assets/equity	Earnings per share
Common equity as a % of total invested capital	Book value per share
Current debt/net worth	Dividend payout ratio
Net worth at market value/total liabilities	Dividend yield
Total asset turnover	Price/earnings ratio
Sales/operating assets	Stock price as a % of book value

Two of the top three ratios were measures of debt, and the other was a measure of liquidity. The debt/equity ratio was given the highest significance rating, with the current ratio second highest. We can assume that the financial ratios rated most significant by commercial loan officers would have the greatest influence on a loan decision.

EXHIBIT 13-2 Commercial Loan Departments—Most Significant Ratios and Their Primary Measures

Ratio	Significance Rating	Primary Measure
Debt/equity	8.71	Debt
Current ratio	8.25	Liquidity
Cash flow/current maturities of long-term debt	8.08	Debt
Fixed charge coverage	7.58	Debt
Net profit margin after tax	7.56	Profitability
Times interest earned	7.50	Debt
Net profit margin before tax	7.43	Profitability
Degree of financial leverage	7.33	Debt
Inventory turnover in days	7.25	Liquidity
Accounts receivable turnover in days	7.08	Liquidity

Ratios Appearing Most Frequently in Loan Agreements

A commercial bank may elect to include a ratio as part of a loan agreement. This would be a way of using ratios to control an outstanding loan. Exhibit 13-3, page 556, contains a list of the ten financial ratios that appear most frequently in loan agreements, along with an indication of what each ratio primarily measures. For the two ratios that do not have a primary measure indicated, there was no majority opinion as to what the ratio primarily measured. Six of the ratios that appear most frequently in loan agreements primarily measure debt, two primarily measure liquidity, and none primar-ily measure profitability.

The two top ratios, debt/equity and current ratio, were given the highest significance rating. The dividend payout ratio was the third most likely ratio to appear in loan agreements, but it was not rated as a highly significant ratio. Logically, this ratio appears in loan agreements as a means of controlling outflow of cash for dividends.

FINANCIAL RATIOS AS PERCEIVED BY CORPORATE CONTROLLERS

To get the views of corporate controllers on important issues relating to financial ratios, a questionnaire was sent to the controllers of the

EXHIBIT 13-3   Commercial Loan Departments—Ratios Appearing Most Frequently in Loan Agreements

Ratio	Percentage of Banks Including Ratio in 26% or More of Their Loan Agreements	Primary Measure
Debt/equity	92.5	Debt
Current ratio	90.0	Liquidity
Dividend payout ratio	70.0	*
Cash flow/current maturities of long-term debt	60.3	Debt
Fixed charge coverage	55.2	Debt
Times interest earned	52.6	Debt
Degree of financial leverage	44.7	Debt
Equity/assets	41.0	*
Cash flow/total debt	36.1	Debt
Quick ratio	33.3	Liquidity

* No majority primary measure indicated in this survey.

companies included in the *Fortune 500* list of the largest industrials.[2] The study excluded companies 100% owned or controlled by another firm. The survey received a usable response rate of 19.42%. The questionnaire used the same ratios used for the commercial loan department survey. Three objectives of this study were the determination of: (1) the significance of a specific ratio as perceived by controllers, (2) which financial ratios are included as corporate objectives, and (3) the primary measure of each ratio.

Most Significant Ratios and Their Primary Measure

Exhibit 13-4 displays the ten financial ratios given the highest significance rating by the corporate controllers, along with the primary measure of these ratios. The highest rating is a 9 and the lowest is a 0.

The financial executives gave the profitability ratios the highest significance ratings. The highest rated debt ratio was debt/equity, while the highest rated liquidity ratio was the current ratio. In comparing the responses of the commercial loan officers and the controllers, the controllers rate the profitability ratios as having the highest significance,

EXHIBIT 13-4 **Corporate Controllers—Most Significant Ratios and Their Primary Measures**

Ratio	Significance Rating	Primary Measure
Earnings per share	8.19	Profitability
Return on equity after tax	7.83	Profitability
Net profit margin after tax	7.47	Profitability
Debt/equity ratio	7.46	Debt
Net profit margin before tax	7.41	Profitability
Return on total invested capital after tax	7.20	Profitability
Return on assets after tax	6.97	Profitability
Dividend payout ratio	6.83	Other*
Price/earnings ratio	6.81	Other*
Current ratio	6.71	Liquidity

* Primary measure indicated to be other than liquidity, debt, or profitability. The ratios rated this way tend to be related to stock analysis.

while the commercial loan officers rate the debt and liquidity ratios highest.

Key Financial Ratios Included as Corporate Objectives

Many firms have selected key financial ratios to be included as part of their corporate objectives. The next section of the survey was designed to determine what ratios the firms used in their corporate objectives. Exhibit 13-5, page 558, lists the ten ratios most likely to be included in corporate objectives according to the controllers. Nine of the ratios included in Exhibit 13-5 were also included in Exhibit 13-4. One ratio, accounts receivable turnover in days, appears in the top ten ratios in relation to corporate objectives but not in the top ten significant ratios. One ratio, the price/earnings ratio, appears in the top ten ratios in relation to significance but not in the top ten ratios used for corporate objectives.

Logically, there would be a high correlation between the ratios rated as highly significant and those included in corporate objectives. The debt/equity ratio and the current ratio are rated higher on the objectives list than on the significance list. This makes sense since a firm has to have some balance in its objectives between liquidity, debt, and profitability.

EXHIBIT 13-5   Ratios Appearing in Corporate Objectives and Their Primary Measures

Ratio	Percentage of Firms Indicating That the Ratio Was Included in Corporate Objectives	Primary Measure
Earnings per share	80.6	Profitability
Debt/equity ratio	68.8	Debt
Return on equity after tax	68.5	Profitability
Current ratio	62.0	Liquidity
Net profit margin after tax	60.9	Profitability
Dividend payout ratio	54.3	Other
Return on total invested capital after tax	53.3	Profitability
Net profit margin before tax	52.2	Profitability
Accounts receivable turnover in days	47.3	Liquidity
Return on assets after tax	47.3	Profitability

FINANCIAL RATIOS AS PERCEIVED BY CERTIFIED PUBLIC ACCOUNTANTS

A research study performed in 1984 dealt with financial ratios as perceived by certified public accountants (CPAs).[3] A questionnaire was sent to one-third of the members of The Ohio Society of Certified Public Accountants who were registered as a partner in a CPA firm. A total of 495 questionnaires were sent and the usable response rate was 18.8%.

This questionnaire used the same ratios as were used for the commercial loan department and corporate controllers. The specific objectives of this study were to determine the following from the viewpoint of the CPA:

1. The specific financial ratios that CPAs view primarily as a measure of liquidity, debt, and profitability.

2. The relative importance of the financial ratios viewed as a measure of liquidity, debt, or profitability.

Exhibit 13-6 displays the ten financial ratios given the highest significance rating by the CPAs and the primary measure of these ratios. The highest rating is a 9 and the lowest is a 0.

The CPAs gave the highest significance rating to two liquidity ratios—the current ratio and the accounts receivable turnover in days. The

EXHIBIT 13-6 CPAs—Most Significant Ratios and Their Primary Measures

Ratio	Significance Rating	Primary Measure
Current ratio	7.10	Liquidity
Accounts receivable turnover in days	6.94	Liquidity
After-tax return on equity	6.79	Profitability
Debt/equity ratio	6.78	Debt
Quick ratio (acid test)	6.77	Liquidity
Net profit margin after tax	6.67	Profitability
Net profit margin before tax	6.63	Profitability
Return on assets after tax	6.39	Profitability
Return on total invested capital after tax	6.30	Profitability
Inventory turnover in days	6.09	Liquidity

highest rated profitability ratio was after-tax return on equity, and the highest rated debt ratio was debt/equity.

FINANCIAL RATIOS AS PERCEIVED BY CHARTERED FINANCIAL ANALYSTS[4]

Exhibit 13-7, page 560, displays the ten financial ratios given the highest significance rating by chartered financial analysts (CFAs) and the primary measure of these ratios. Again, the highest rating is a 9 and the lowest rating is a 0.

The surveyed CFAs gave the highest significance ratings to profitability ratios, with the exception of the price/earnings ratio. Return on equity after tax received the highest significance by a wide margin. Four of the next five most significant ratios were also profitability ratios—earnings per share, net profit margin after tax, return on equity before tax, and net profit margin before tax.

The price/earnings ratio—categorized by the analysts as an "other" measure—received the second highest significance rating. CFAs apparently view profitability and what is being paid for those profits before turning to liquidity and debt.

The two highest rated debt ratios were fixed charge coverage and times interest earned, rated 7th and 10th, respectively. Both of these ratios indicate a firm's ability to carry debt. The highest rated debt ratio relating to the balance sheet was the debt/equity ratio, rated as the 11th most significant.

EXHIBIT 13-7 **Chartered Financial Analysts—Most Significant Ratios and Their Primary Measures**

Ratio	Significance Rating	Primary Measure
Return on equity after tax	8.21	Profitability
Price/earnings ratio	7.65	*
Earnings per share	7.58	Profitability
Net profit margin after tax	7.52	Profitability
Return on equity before tax	7.41	Profitability
Net profit margin before tax	7.32	Profitability
Fixed charge coverage	7.22	Debt
Quick ratio	7.10	Liquidity
Return on assets after tax	7.06	Profitability
Times interest earned	7.06	Debt

* Primary measure indicated to be other than liquidity, debt, or profitability. The ratios rated this way tend to be related to stock analysis.

Surprisingly, more significance was placed on debt ratios relating to the ability to carry debt than on those relating to the ability to meet debt obligations.

The highest rated liquidity ratio was the acid-test ratio, rated 8th. The second highest liquidity ratio was the current ratio, rated 20th.[5]

FINANCIAL RATIOS USED IN ANNUAL REPORTS

Financial ratios are used to interpret and explain financial statements.[6] Used properly, they can be effective tools in evaluating a company's liquidity, debt position, and profitability. Probably no tool is as effective in evaluating where a company has been financially and projecting its financial future as the proper use of financial ratios.

A firm can use its annual report effectively to relate financial data by the use of financial ratios. To determine how effectively firms use ratios to communicate financial data, the annual reports of 100 firms identified in the *Fortune 500* industrial companies in 1979 were reviewed in a research study in 1981. The 100 firms represented the first 20 of each 100 in the *Fortune 500* list. The objective of this research project was to determine: (1) which financial ratios were frequently reported in annual reports, (2) where the ratios were disclosed in the annual reports, and

(3) what computational methodology was used to compute these ratios.

Exhibit 13-8 indicates the ratios disclosed most frequently in the annual reports reviewed and the section of the annual report where the ratios were located. The locations were the president's letter, management discussion, management highlights, financial review, and financial summary. In many cases, the same ratio was located in several sections, so the numbers under the sections in Exhibit 13-8 do not add up to the total number of annual reports where the ratio was included.

Seven ratios appeared more than 50% of the time in one section or another. These ratios and the number of times found were earnings per share (100), dividends per share (98), book value per share (84), working capital (81), return on equity (62), profit margin (58), and effective tax rate (50). The current ratio was found 47 times, and the next ratio in order of disclosure, the debt/capital ratio, appeared 23 times. From this listing, we can conclude that

EXHIBIT 13-8   Ratios Disclosed Most Frequently in Annual Reports*

Ratio	Number Included	President's Letter	Management Discussion	Management Highlights	Financial Review	Financial Summary
Earnings per share	100	66	5	98	45	93
Dividends per share	98	53	10	85	49	88
Book value per share	84	10	3	53	18	63
Working capital	81	1	1	50	23	67
Return on equity	62	28	3	21	23	37
Profit margin	58	10	3	21	23	35
Effective tax rate	50	2	1	2	46	6
Current ratio	47	3	1	16	12	34
Debt/capital	23	9	0	4	14	23
Return on capital	21	6	2	8	8	5
Debt/equity	19	5	0	3	8	8
Return on assets	13	4	1	2	5	10
Dividend payout	13	3	0	0	6	6
Gross profit	12	0	1	0	11	3
Pretax margin	10	2	0	3	6	6
Total asset turnover	7	1	0	0	4	4
Price/earnings ratio	7	0	0	0	1	6
Operating margin	7	1	0	2	6	1
Labor per hour	5	0	2	2	2	2

* Numbers represent both absolute numbers and percentages since a review was made of the financial statements of 100 firms.

profitability ratios and ratios related to investing were the most popular. Exhibit 13-8 excludes ratios not disclosed at least five times.

Logically, profitability ratios and ratios related to investing were the most popular for inclusion in the annual report. Including ratios related to investing in the annual report makes sense because one of the annual report's major objectives is to inform stockholders.

A review of the methodology used indicated that wide differences of opinion exist on how some of the ratios should be computed. This is especially true of the debt ratios. The two debt ratios most frequently disclosed were the debt/capital ratio and the debt/equity ratio. This book does not cover the debt/capital ratio. It is similar to the debt/equity ratio, except that the denominator includes sources of capital, in addition to stockholders' equity.

The annual reports disclosed the debt/capital ratio 23 times and used 11 different formulas. One firm used average balance sheet amounts between the beginning and the end of the year, while 22 firms used ending balance sheet figures. The debt/equity ratio was disclosed 19 times, and 6 different formulas were used. All firms used the ending balance sheet accounts to compute the debt/equity ratio.

In general, no major effort is being made to explain financial results by the disclosure of financial ratios in annual reports. Several financial ratios that could be interpreted as important were not disclosed or were disclosed very infrequently. This is particularly important for ratios that cannot be reasonably computed by outsiders because of a lack of data such as accounts receivable turnover.

At present, no regulatory agency such as the SEC or the FASB accepts responsibility for determining either the content of financial ratios or the format of presentation for annual reports, except for the ratio earnings per share. Many practical and theoretical issues relate to the computation of financial ratios. As long as each firm can exercise its opinion as to the practical and theoretical issues, there will be a great divergence of opinion on how a particular ratio should be computed.

DEGREE OF CONSERVATISM AND QUALITY OF EARNINGS

A review of financial statements, including the footnotes, indicates their conservatism in regard to accounting policies. Accounting policies that result in the slowest reporting of income are the most conservative. When a firm has conservative accounting policies, it is said that its earnings are of high quality. This section reviews a number of areas that often indicate a firm's degree of conservatism in reporting income.

Inventory

Under inflationary conditions, the matching of current cost against the current revenue results in the lowest income for a period of time. The LIFO inventory method follows this procedure. FIFO, the least conservative method, uses the oldest costs and matches them against revenue. Other inventory methods fall somewhere between the results of LIFO and FIFO.

For a construction firm that has long-term contracts, the two principal accounting methods that relate to inventory are the completed-contract method and the percentage-of-completion method. The conservative completed-contract method recognizes all of the income when the contract is completed; the percentage-of-completion method recognizes income as work progresses on the contract.

Fixed Assets

Two accounting decisions related to fixed assets can have a significant influence on income: the method of depreciation and the period of time selected to depreciate an asset.

The conservative methods, sum-of-the-years'-digits and declining-balance, recognize a large amount of depreciation in the early years of the assets. The straight-line method, the least conservative method, recognizes depreciation in equal amounts over each year of the asset's life.

Sometimes a material difference in the asset lives used for depreciation occurs between firms. Comparing the lives used for depreciation for similar firms can be a clue as to how conservative the firms are in computing depreciation. The shorter the period of time used, the lower the income.

Intangible Assets

Intangible assets include goodwill, patents, and copyrights. Research and development (R&D) costs are a type of intangible asset, but they are expensed as incurred. The shorter the period of time used to recognize the cost of the intangible asset, the more conservative the accounting.

Some firms spend very large sums on R&D, and others spend little or nothing. Because of the requirement that R&D costs be expensed in the period incurred, the income of a firm that does considerable research is reduced substantially in the period that the cost is incurred. This results in more conservative earnings.

Intangible assets must be amortized over 40 years or fewer, unless they were acquired prior to 1970. Intangibles that have a legal or economic life shorter than 40 years should be amortized over the shorter period.

The intangible asset, goodwill, results when a firm buys another firm and pays a price greater than the value of the identifiable assets. Conservative firms expense goodwill over a relatively short period of time such as five years. Other firms use the maximum time allowed of 40 years.

Pensions

Two points relating to pensions should be examined when the firm has a defined benefit plan. One is the assumed discount rate used to compute the actuarial present value of the accumulated benefit obligation and the projected benefit obligation. The higher the interest rate used, the lower the present value of the liability and the lower the immediate pension cost. The other item is the rate of compensation increase used in computing the projected benefit obligations. If the rate is too low, the projected benefit obligation is too low. If the rate is too high, the projected benefit obligation is too high.

Leases

A firm with extensive assets accounted for as operating leases result in a more favorable income than a similar firm with capital leases or one that has financed its assets with debt. Examine the footnote that describes the firm's lease obligations. An immaterial amount of operating leases is conservative as to the effect of leases on income.

FORECASTING FINANCIAL FAILURE

There have been many academic studies on the use of financial ratios to forecast financial failure. Basically, these studies try to isolate individual ratios or combinations of ratios that can be observed as trends that may forecast failure.

A reliable model that can be used to forecast financial failure can also be used by management to take preventive measures. Such a model can aid investors in selecting and disposing of stocks. Banks can use it to aid in lending decisions and in monitoring loans. Firms can use it in making credit decisions and in monitoring accounts receivable. In general, many sources can use such a model to improve the allocation and control of resources. A model that forecasts financial failure can also be valuable to an auditor. It can aid in the determination of audit procedures and in making a decision as to whether the firm will remain as a going concern.

Financial failure can be described in many ways. It can mean liquidation, deferment of payments to short-term creditors, deferment of payments of interest on bonds, deferment of payments of principal on bonds, or the omission of a preferred dividend. One of the problems in examining the literature on forecasting financial failure is that different authors use different criteria to indicate failure. When reviewing the literature, always determine the criteria used to define financial failure.

This book reviews two of the studies that deal with predicting financial failure. Based on the number of references to these two studies in the literature, they appear to be particularly significant on the subject of forecasting financial failure.

Univariate Model

William Beaver reported his univariate model in a study published in *The Accounting Review* in October 1968.[7] A univariate model uses a single variable. Such a model would use individual financial ratios to forecast financial failure. The Beaver study classified a firm as failed when any one of the following events occurred in the 1954-1964 period: bankruptcy, bond default, an overdrawn bank account, or nonpayment of a preferred stock dividend.

Beaver paired 79 failed firms with a similar number of successful firms drawn from *Moody's Industrial Manuals*. For each failed firm in the sample, a successful one was selected from the same industry. The Beaver study indicated that the following ratios were the best for forecasting financial failure (in the order of their predictive power):

1. Cash flow/total debt
2. Net income/total assets (return on assets)
3. Total debt/total assets (debt ratio)

Beaver speculated as to the reason for these results:

> My interpretation of the finding is that the cash flow, net income, and debt positions cannot be altered and represent permanent aspects of the firm. Because failure is too costly to all involved, the permanent, rather than the short-term, factors largely determine whether or not a firm will declare bankruptcy or default on a bond payment.[8]

Assuming that the ratios identified by Beaver are valid in forecasting financial failure, it would be wise to pay particular attention to trends in these ratios when following a firm. Beaver's reasoning for seeing these ratios as valid in forecasting financial failure appears to be very sound.

These three ratios for Cooper for 1995 have been computed earlier. Cash flow/total debt was 35.69%, which appears to be good. Net income/total assets (return on assets) was 10.33%, which appears to be good. The debt ratio was 34.53%, which is very good. Thus, Cooper appears to have minimal risk of financial failure.

The Beaver study also computed the mean values of 13 financial statement items for each year before failure. Several important relationships were indicated among the liquid asset items.[9]

1.   Failed firms have less cash but more accounts receivable.

2.   When cash and receivables are added together, as they are in quick assets and current assets, the differences between failed and successful firms is obscured because the cash and receivables differences are working in opposite directions.

3.   Failed firms tend to have less inventory.

These results indicate that particular attention should be paid to three current assets when forecasting financial failure: cash, accounts receivable, and inventory. The analyst should be alert for low cash and inventory and high accounts receivable.

Multivariate Model (REGRESSION MODEL)

Edward I. Altman developed a multivariate model to predict bankruptcy.[10] His model uses five financial ratios weighted in order to maximize the predictive power of the model. The model produces an overall discriminant score, called a **Z score.** The Altman model is as follows:

$$Z = .012\ X_1 + .014\ X_2 + .033\ X_3 + .006\ X_4 + .010\ X_5$$

X_1 = **Working Capital/Total Assets**

This computation is a measure of the net liquid assets of the firm relative to the total capitalization.

X_2 = **Retained Earnings (balance sheet)/Total Assets**

This variable measures cumulative profitability over time.

X_3 = **Earnings Before Interest and Taxes/Total Assets**

This variable measures the productivity of the firm's assets, abstracting any tax or leverage factors.

X_4 = **Market Value of Equity/Book Value of Total Debt**

This variable measures how much the firm's assets can decline in value before the liabilities exceed the assets and the firm becomes insolvent. Equity is measured by the combined market value of all shares of stock, preferred and common, while debt includes both current and long-term debts.

X_5 = **Sales/Total Assets**

This variable measures the sales-generating ability of the firm's assets.
When computing the Z score, the ratios are expressed in absolute percentage terms. Thus, X_1 (working capital/total assets) of 25% is noted as 25.

The Altman model was developed using manufacturing companies whose asset size was between $1 million and $25 million. The original sample by Altman and the test samples used the period 1946-1965. The model's accuracy in predicting bankruptcies in more recent years (1970-1973) was reported in a 1974 article.[11] Not all of the companies included in the test were manufacturing companies, although the model was initially developed by using only manufacturing companies.

With the Altman model, the lower the Z score, the more likely that the firm will go bankrupt. By computing the Z score for a firm over several years, it can be determined if the firm is moving toward a more likely or less likely position in regard to bankruptcy. In the more recent study that covered the period 1970-1973, a Z score of 2.675 was established as a practical cutoff point. Firms that scored below 2.675 are assumed to have characteristics similar to those of past failures.[12] Current GAAP recognizes more liabilities than the GAAP used at the time of this study. Thus, we would expect firms to score somewhat less than in the time period 1970-1973. The Altman model is substantially less significant if there is no firm market value for the stock (preferred and common), because variable X_4 in the model requires that the market value of the stock be determined.

The Z score for Cooper at the end of 1995 follows:

$$
\begin{aligned}
Z = \; & .012 \text{ (working capital/total assets)} \\
+ \; & .014 \text{ (retained earnings [balance sheet]/total assets)} \\
+ \; & .033 \text{ (earnings before interest and taxes/total assets)} \\
+ \; & .006 \text{ (market value of equity/book value of total debt)} \\
+ \; & .010 \text{ (sales/total assets)}
\end{aligned}
$$

$$
\begin{aligned}
Z = \; & .012 \text{ ([\$430,584,000 - \$158,368,000]/\$1,143,701,000)} \\
+ \; & .014 \text{ (\$672,373,000/\$1,143,701,000)} \\
+ \; & .033 \text{ ([\$180,070,000 + \$697,000]/\$1,143,701,000)} \\
+ \; & .006 \text{ ([83,661,972 x \$24.63]/[\$158,368,000 + \$28,574,000} \\
& \quad + \$132,963,000 + \$38,341,000 + \$36,656,000]) \\
+ \; & .010 \text{ (\$1,493,622,000/\$1,143,701,000)}
\end{aligned}
$$

$$
\begin{aligned}
Z = \; & .012 \text{ (23.80)} \\
+ \; & .014 \text{ (58.79)} \\
+ \; & .033 \text{ (15.81)} \\
+ \; & .006 \text{ (521.80)} \\
+ \; & .010 \text{ (130.60)}
\end{aligned}
$$

$$Z = .29 + .82 + .52 + 3.13 + 1.31$$

$$Z = 6.07$$

The Z score for Cooper at the end of 1995 was 6.07. Considering that higher scores are better and that companies with scores below 2.675 are assumed to have characteristics similar to those of past failures, Cooper is a very healthy company.

There are many academic studies on the use of ratios to forecast financial failure. These studies help substantiate that firms with weak ratios are more likely to go bankrupt than firms with strong ratios. Since no conclusive model has yet been developed, the best approach is probably an integrated one. As a supplemental measure, it may also be helpful to compute some of the ratios that appear useful in forecasting financial failure.

ANALYTICAL REVIEW PROCEDURES

Statement of Auditing Standards No. 23, "Analytical Review Procedures," provides guidance for the use of such procedures in audits. The objective of analytical review procedures is to isolate significant fluctuations and unusual items in operating statistics.

Analytical review procedures may be performed at various times, including the planning stage, during the audit itself, and near the completion of the audit. Some examples of analytical review procedures that may lead to special audit procedures follow:

1. Horizontal common-size analysis of the income statement may indicate that an item, such as selling expenses, is abnormally high for the period. This could lead to a close examination of the selling expenses.

2. Vertical common-size analysis of the income statement may indicate that cost of goods sold is out of line in relation to sales, in comparison with prior periods.

3. A comparison of accounts receivable turnover with the industry data may indicate that receivables are turning over much slower than is typical for the industry. This may indicate that receivables should be analyzed closely.

4. Cash flow in relation to debt may have declined significantly, indicating a materially reduced ability to cover debt from internal cash flow.

5. The acid-test ratio may have declined significantly, indicating a materially reduced ability to pay current liabilities with current assets less inventories.

When the auditor spots a significant trend in a statement or ratio, follow-up procedures should be performed to determine the reason. Such an investigation can lead to significant findings.

MANAGEMENT'S USE OF ANALYSIS

Management can use financial ratios and common-size analysis as aids in many ways. Analysis can indicate the relative liquidity, debt, and profitability of a firm. Analysis can also indicate how investors perceive the firm and can help detect emerging problems and strengths in a firm. As indicated previously, financial ratios can also be used as part of the firm's corporate objectives. Using financial ratios in conjunction with the budgeting process can be particularly helpful. An objective of the budgeting process is the determination of the firm's game plan. The budget can consist of an overall comprehensive budget and many separate budgets, such as a production budget.

The comprehensive budget relating to financial statements indicates how a firm plans to get from one financial position (balance sheet) to another. The income statement details how the firm changed internally from one balance sheet position to another in terms of revenue and expenses. The statement of cash flows indicates how the firm's cash changed from one balance sheet to another.

A proposed comprehensive budget should be compared with financial ratios that have been agreed upon as part of the firm's corporate objectives. For example, if corporate objectives include a current ratio of 2:1, a debt equity of 40%, and a return on equity of 15%, then the proposed comprehensive budget should be compared with these corporate objectives before accepting the budget as the firm's overall game plan. If the proposed comprehensive budget will not result in the firm achieving its objectives, management should attempt to change the game plan in order to achieve its objectives. If management cannot change the proposed comprehensive budget satisfactorily to achieve the corporate objectives, they should know this when the comprehensive budget is accepted.

USE OF LIFO RESERVES

A firm that uses LIFO usually discloses a LIFO reserve account in a footnote or on the face of the balance sheet. If a LIFO reserve account is not disclosed, there is usually some indication of an amount that approximates current cost. In its 1995 annual report, Cooper disclosed in a footnote under the LIFO method, "Inventories have been reduced by approximately $76,309,000 and $64,653,000 at December 31, 1995 and 1994, respectively, from current cost which would be reported under the first-in, first-out method."

This information can be used to improve the analysis of inventory and (in general) the analysis of liquidity, debt, and profitability. Supplemental analysis using this additional inventory information can be particularly significant when there has been substantial inflation.

The disclosure is usually limited as to differences in profit figures when using LIFO or FIFO. A primary reason for this is that the Internal Revenue Service objects to a firm's using LIFO and then disclosing details on what profits would have been, based on some other inventory method. When a net income figure is not disclosed, based on inventory at approximate current costs, it usually can be approximated.

For Cooper, an approximation of the increase or decrease in income if inventory is at approximate current costs could be computed by comparing the change in inventory, net of any tax effect. For 1995, compute the approximation of the income if the inventory were at approximate current costs as follows:

1995 net income		$112,820,000
Net increase in inventory reserve:		
1995	$76,309,000	
1994	(64,653,000)	
(a)	$11,656,000	

(b) Effective tax rate—federal income taxes
(Effective tax rate could be approximated by comparing provision for income taxes to income before income taxes)

$$\frac{\$\ 67,250,000}{\$180,070,000} = 37.35\%$$

(c) Increase in taxes [a x b] = $4,353,516
(d) Net increase in income [a − c]

	$11,656,000 − $4,353,516	7,302,484
Approximate income for 1995 if inventory had been valued at approximate current cost		$120,122,484

This type of computation can be made for each year. The approximate new income figures can then be considered and reviewed over a series of years to obtain an idea of what net income would have been if inventory had been computed using a method that approximated inventory costs closer to current costs. Some analysts would consider this adjusted income amount to be more realistic than the unadjusted amount. Others would consider the unadjusted income to be more realistic from an operating basis because it usually represents a better matching of current costs against revenue.

Specific liquidity and debt ratios can be recomputed, taking into consideration the adjusted inventory figure. To make these computations, add the gross inventory reserve to the inventory disclosed in current assets. Add the approximate additional taxes to the current liabilities.

Estimate the additional tax figure by multiplying the gross LIFO reserve by the effective tax rate. This tax figure relates to the additional income that would have been reported in the current year and all prior years, if the higher inventory amounts had been reported. The additional tax amount is a deferred tax amount that is added to current liabilities, to be conservative. The difference between the additional inventory amount and the additional tax amount is added to retained earnings because it represents the total prior influence on net income. The adjusted figures for Cooper at the end of 1995 follow:

Inventory:	
As disclosed on the balance sheet	$137,964,000
Increase in inventory	76,309,000
	$214,273,000
Deferred current tax liability:	
Effective tax rate (37.35%) x increase in inventory	
($76,309,000)	$ 28,501,412
Retained earnings:	
As disclosed on the balance sheet	$672,373,000
Increase in retained earnings	
($76,309,000 – $28,501,412)	47,807,588
	$720,180,588

An adjusted cost of goods sold can also be estimated, using the change in the inventory reserve. A net increase in the inventory reserve would reduce the cost of goods sold. A net decrease in inventory reserve would increase the cost of goods sold.

Cooper reported cost of goods sold of $1,242,895,000 and an increase in inventory reserve of $11,656,000 in 1995. The increase in inventory reserve is deducted from the cost of goods sold, resulting in an adjusted cost of goods sold of $1,231,239,000. The adjusted cost of goods sold could be used when computing several ratios, such as days' sales in inventory. This refinement of the cost of goods sold usually has an immaterial influence on the ratios because the change in inventory reserve is usually immaterial in relation to the cost of goods sold figure. Therefore, this refinement to the cost of goods sold is not used in the illustrations and problems in this book.

Exhibit 13-9, page 572, displays selected liquidity, debt, and profitability ratios for Cooper, comparing the adjusted ratio with the prior computation. The ratios that relate to inventory are not as favorable when considering the LIFO disclosure as when not considering the LIFO disclosure. Working capital is more favorable, and the current ratio is slightly less favorable. The acid-test and cash ratios are less favorable. The balance sheet-related debt ratios (debt ratio and debt/equity) are approximately the same when considering the LIFO disclosure. The income statement-related debt ratio of times interest earned is slightly more favorable. The profitability ratios are approximately the same when considering the LIFO disclosure. Net profit margin, return on assets, and return on total equity are slightly improved, while total asset turnover is lower.

The adjusted liquidity, debt, and profitability ratios could be considered to be more realistic than the prior computations because of the use of a realistic inventory amount. This is particularly true for the ratios that relate to inventory. For many of the ratios, we cannot generalize about whether the ratio will improve or decline when the LIFO reserve is used. For example, if the current ratio is above 2.00, then it may not improve when the LIFO reserve is considered, especially if the firm has a high tax rate. When the current ratio is low and/or the tax rate is low, then the current ratio will likely improve.

EXHIBIT 13-9   **COOPER TIRE & RUBBER COMPANY**
Selected Liquidity, Debt, and Profitability Considering LIFO
Disclosure for the Year Ended December 31, 1995

	1995 Considering LIFO Disclosure	1995 Prior Computations
Liquidity:		
Days' sales in inventory	63.52 days	40.52 days
Inventory turnover	6.23 times per year	9.77 times per year
Inventory turnover in days	58.62 days	37.37 days
Operating cycle	117.94 days	96.69 days
Working capital	$320,023,588	$272,216,000
Current ratio	2.71	2.72
Acid-test ratio	1.50	1.77
Cash ratio	.12	.15
Debt:		
Debt ratio	34.70%	34.53%
Debt/equity	53.15%	52.74%
Times interest earned	56.75 times per year	53.31 times per year
Profitability:		
Net profit margin	8.04%	7.55%
Total asset turnover	1.29 times per year	1.37 times per year
Return on assets	10.34%	10.33%
Return on total equity	16.02%	15.99%

GRAPHING FINANCIAL INFORMATION

It has become very popular to use graphs in annual reports to present financial information. Graphs make it easier to grasp key financial information. Graphs can be a better communicative device than a written report or a tabular presentation because they communicate by means of pictures and, thus, create more immediate mental images.

There are many forms of graphs. Some popular forms used by accountants are line, column, bar, and pie graphs. These forms will be briefly described here, but a detailed description of these and other forms can be found in reference books and articles.[13]

The **line graph** uses a set of points connected by a line to show change over time. It is important for the vertical axis to start at zero and that it not be broken. Not starting the vertical axis at zero and/or breaking the vertical axis can result in a very misleading presentation. Exhibit 13-10, page 574, illustrates a line graph.

A **column graph** has vertical columns. As in a line graph, it is important that the vertical axis start at zero and that it not be broken. A column graph is often the best form of graph for presenting accounting data. Exhibit 13-11, page 574, presents a column graph.

A **bar graph** is similar to a column graph, except that the bars are horizontal. Exhibit 13-12, page 575, illustrates a bar graph.

A **pie graph** is divided into segments. This type of graph makes a comparison of the segments, which must add up to a total or to 100%. A pie graph can mislead if it creates an optical illusion. Also, some accounting data do not fit on a pie graph. Exhibit 13-13, page 575, illustrates a pie graph.

SUMMARY

This chapter reviewed special areas related to financial statements. It was noted that commercial loan departments give a high significance rating to selected ratios that primarily measure liquidity or debt. The debt/equity ratio received the highest significance rating, and the current ratio was the second highest rated by the commercial loan officers. A commercial bank may elect to include a ratio as part of a loan agreement. The two ratios most likely to be included in a loan agreement are the debt/equity and the current ratio.

Financial executives give the profitability ratios the highest significance ratings. They rate earnings per share and return on investment the highest. Many firms have selected key financial ratios, such as profitability ratios, to be included as part of their corporate objectives.

EXHIBIT 13-10   UNITED DOMINION REALTY TRUST
Line Graph—1995 Annual Report

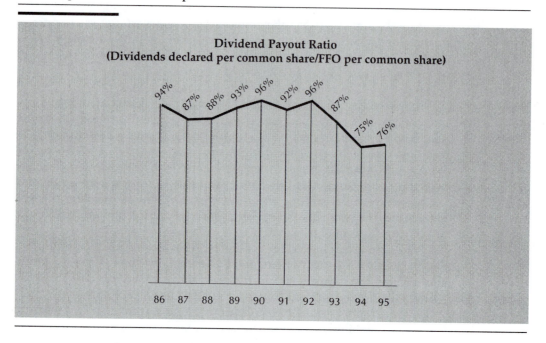

Dividend Payout Ratio
(Dividends declared per common share/FFO per common share)

EXHIBIT 13-11   TRIBUNE COMPANY
Column Graph—1995 Annual Report

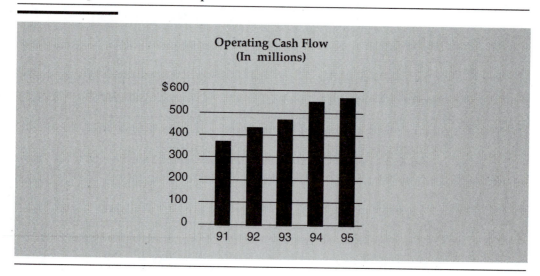

Operating Cash Flow
(In millions)

EXHIBIT 13-12 **FLOWERS INDUSTRIES, INC.**
Bar Graph—1995 Annual Report

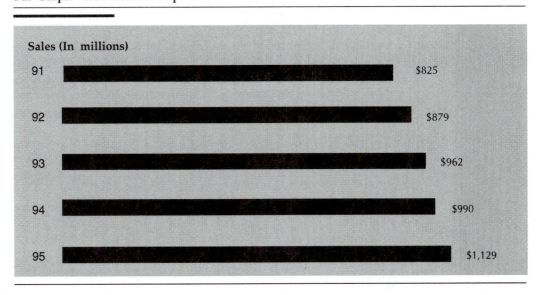

EXHIBIT 13-13 **NOVELL**
Pie Graph—1995 Annual Report

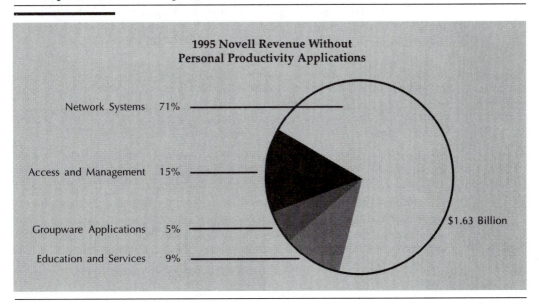

Certified public accountants give the highest significance rating to two liquidity ratios: the current ratio and the accounts receivable turnover in days. The highest rated profitability ratio was the after-tax net profit margin, while the highest rated debt ratio was debt/equity.

A firm could use its annual report to relate financial data effectively by the use of financial ratios. In general, no major effort is being made to explain financial results by the disclosure of financial ratios in annual reports. A review of the methodology used to compute the ratios disclosed in annual reports indicated that wide differences of opinion exist on how many of the ratios should be computed.

A review of the financial statements, including the footnotes, indicates the conservatism of the statements in terms of accounting policies. When a firm has conservative accounting policies, it is said that its earnings are of high quality.

There have been many academic studies on the use of financial ratios to forecast financial failure. No conclusive model has yet been developed to forecast financial failure.

Auditors use financial analysis as part of their analytical review procedures. By using financial analysis, they can detect significant fluctuations and unusual items in operating statistics. This can result in a more efficient and effective audit.

Management can use financial analysis in many ways to manage a firm more effectively. A particularly effective use of financial analysis is to integrate ratios that have been accepted as corporate objectives into comprehensive budgeting.

It has become very popular to use graphs in annual reports to present financial information. Graphs make it easier to grasp key financial information. Graphs can communicate better than a written report or a tabular presentation.

QUESTIONS

Q 13-1.   Commercial loan officers regard profitability financial ratios as very significant. Comment.

Q 13-2.   Which two financial ratios do commercial loan officers regard as the most significant? Which two financial ratios appear most frequently in loan agreements?

Q 13-3.   The commercial loan officers did not list the dividend payout ratio as a highly significant ratio, but they indicated that the dividend payout ratio was a ratio that appeared frequently in loan agreements. Speculate on the reason for this apparent inconsistency.

Q 13-4.   Corporate controllers regard profitability financial ratios as very significant. Comment.

Q 13-5. List the top five financial ratios included in corporate objectives according to the study reviewed in this book. Indicate what each of these ratios primarily measures.

Q 13-6. CPAs regard which two financial ratios as the most significant? The highest rated profitability ratio? The highest debt ratio?

Q 13-7. Financial ratios are used extensively in annual reports to interpret and explain financial statements. Comment.

Q 13-8. List the sections of annual reports where ratios are most frequently located, in order of use.

Q 13-9. According to a study of annual reports reviewed in this chapter, what type or types of financial ratios are most likely to be included in annual reports? Speculate on the probable reason for these ratios appearing in annual reports.

Q 13-10. The study of annual reports reviewed in this chapter showed that earnings per share was disclosed in every annual report. Why?

Q 13-11. The study of annual reports reviewed in this chapter indicated that wide differences of opinion exist on how many ratios should be computed. Comment.

Q 13-12. What type of accounting policies are described as conservative?

Q 13-13. Indicate which of the following accounting policies are conservative by placing an X under *Yes* or *No*. Assume inflationary conditions exist.

	Conservative	
	Yes	No
a. LIFO inventory	_____	_____
b. FIFO inventory	_____	_____
c. Completed-contract method	_____	_____
d. Percentage-of-completion method	_____	_____
e. Accelerated depreciation method	_____	_____
f. Straight-line depreciation method	_____	_____
g. A relatively short estimated life for a fixed asset	_____	_____
h. Short period for expensing intangibles	_____	_____
i. Amortization of goodwill over 40 years	_____	_____
j. High interest rate used to compute the present value of accumulated benefit obligation	_____	_____
k. High rate of compensation increase used in computing the projected benefit obligation	_____	_____
l. Extensive assets accounted for as operating leases	_____	_____

Q 13-14.   All firms are required to expense R&D costs incurred each period. Some firms spend very large sums on R&D, while others spend little or nothing on this area. Why is it important to observe whether a firm has substantial or immaterial R&D expenses?

Q 13-15.   Indicate some possible uses of a reliable model that can be used to forecast financial failure.

Q 13-16.   Describe what is meant by a firm's *financial failure.*

Q 13-17.   According to the Beaver study, which ratios should be watched most closely, in order of their predictive power?

Q 13-18.   According to the Beaver study, three current asset accounts should be paid particular attention in order to forecast financial failure. List each of these accounts and indicate whether they should be abnormally high or low.

Q 13-19.   What does a Z score below 2.675 indicate, according to the Altman model?

Q 13-20.   Indicate a practical problem with computing a Z score for a closely held firm.

Q 13-21.   No conclusive model has been developed to forecast financial failure. This indicates that financial ratios are not helpful in forecasting financial failure. Comment.

Q 13-22.   You are the auditor of Piedmore Corporation. You determine that the accounts receivable turnover has been much slower this period than in prior periods and that it is also materially lower than the industry average. How might this situation affect your audit plan?

Q 13-23.   You are in charge of preparing a comprehensive budget for your firm. Indicate how financial ratios can help determine an acceptable, comprehensive budget.

Q 13-24.   List four popular forms of graphs used by accountants.

Q 13-25.   List two things that can make a line graph misleading.

Q 13-26.   Indicate two possible problems with a pie graph for accounting data.

Q 13-27.   The surveyed CFAs gave the highest significance rating to which type of financial ratio?

Q 13-28.   CFAs gave liquidity ratios a high significance rating. Comment.

PROBLEMS

P 13-1.

Required   Answer the following multiple-choice questions.

a.   Footnotes to financial statements are beneficial in meeting the disclosure requirements of financial reporting. The footnotes should not be used to
1.   Describe significant accounting policies.
2.   Describe depreciation methods employed by the company.
3.   Describe principles and methods peculiar to the industry in which the company operates when these principles and methods are predominately followed in that industry.
4.   Disclose the basis of consolidation for consolidated statements.
5.   Correct an improper presentation in the financial statements.

b. Which one of the following would be a source of funds under a cash concept of funds, but would not be listed as a source under the working capital concept?
   1. Sale of stock
   2. Sale of machinery
   3. Sale of treasury stock
   4. Collection of accounts receivable
   5. Proceeds from long-term bank borrowing

c. The concept of conservatism is often considered important in accounting. The application of this concept means that in the event some doubt occurs as to how a transaction should be recorded, it should be recorded, so as to
   1. Understate income and overstate assets.
   2. Overstate income and overstate assets.
   3. Understate income and understate assets.
   4. Overstate income and understate assets.
   5. The concept relates to the content of the president's letter that accompanies the statements, not to the statements themselves.

d. Early in a period in which sales were increasing at a modest rate and plant expansion and start-up costs were occurring at a rapid rate, a successful business would likely experience
   1. Increased profits and increased financing requirements because of an increasing cash shortage.
   2. Increased profits and decreased financing requirements because of an increasing cash surplus.
   3. Increased profits and no change in financing requirements.
   4. Decreased profits and increased financing requirements because of an increasing cash shortage.
   5. Decreased profits and decreased financing requirements because of an increasing cash surplus.

e. Which of the following ratios would best disclose effective management of working capital by a given firm relative to other firms in the same industry?
   1. A high rate of financial leverage relative to the industry average.
   2. A high number of days' sales uncollected relative to the industry average.
   3. A high turnover of net working capital relative to the industry average.
   4. A high number of days' sales in inventory relative to the industry average.
   5. A high proportion of fixed assets relative to the industry average.

f. Stock options are frequently provided to officers of companies. Exercised stock options would
   1. Improve the debt/equity ratio
   2. Improve earnings per share
   3. Improve the ownership interest of existing stockholders
   4. Improve the total asset turnover
   5. Improve the net profit margin

P 13-2.

Required   Answer the following multiple-choice questions.

a. If business conditions are stable, a decline in the number of days' sales outstanding from one year to the next (based on a company's accounts receivable at year-end) might indicate
    1. A stiffening of the company's credit policies.
    2. That the second year's sales were made at lower prices than the first year's sales.
    3. That a longer discount period and a more distant due date were extended to customers in the second year.
    4. A significant decrease in the volume of sales of the second year.

b. Trading on the equity (financial leverage) is likely to be a good financial strategy for stockholders of companies having
    1. Cyclical high and low amounts of reported earnings.
    2. Steady amounts of reported earnings.
    3. Volatile fluctuation in reported earnings over short periods of time.
    4. Steadily declining amounts of reported earnings.

c. The ratio of total cash, trade receivables, and marketable securities to current liabilities is
    1. The acid-test ratio
    2. The current ratio
    3. Significant if the result is 2 to 1 or below
    4. Meaningless

d. The times interest earned ratio is a primary measure of
    1. Liquidity
    2. Long-term debt-paying ability
    3. Activity
    4. Profitability

e. The calculation of the number of times bond interest is earned involves dividing
    1. Net income by annual bond interest expense.
    2. Net income plus income taxes by annual bond interest expense.
    3. Net income plus income taxes and bond interest expense by annual bond interest expense.
    4. Sinking fund earnings by annual bond interest expense.

P 13-3.   Thorpe Company is a wholesale distributor of professional equipment and supplies. The company's sales have averaged about $900,000 annually for the three-year period 1996-1998. The firm's total assets at the end of 1998 amounted to $850,000.

  The president of Thorpe Company has asked the controller to prepare a report that summarizes the financial aspects of the company's operations for the past three years. This report will be presented to the board of directors at its next meeting.

In addition to comparative financial statements, the controller has decided to present a number of relevant financial ratios that can assist in the identification and interpretation of trends. At the request of the controller, the accounting staff has calculated the following ratios for the three-year period 1996-1998:

Ratio	1996	1997	1998
Current ratio	2.00	2.13	2.18
Acid-test (quick) ratio	1.20	1.10	0.97
Accounts receivable turnover	9.72	8.57	7.13
Inventory turnover	5.25	4.80	3.80
Percent of total debt to total assets	44.00%	41.00%	38.00%
Percent of long-term debt to total assets	25.00%	22.00%	19.00%
Sales to fixed assets (fixed asset turnover)	1.75	1.88	1.99
Sales as a percent of 1996 sales	100.00%	103.00%	106.00%
Gross profit percentage	40.0%	33.6%	38.5%
Net income to sales	7.8%	7.8%	8.0%
Return on total assets	8.5%	8.6%	8.7%
Return on stockholders' equity	15.1%	14.6%	14.1%

In preparing his report, the controller has decided first to examine the financial ratios independently of any other data to determine if the ratios themselves reveal any significant trends over the three-year period.

Required   a. The current ratio is increasing, while the acid-test (quick) ratio is decreasing. Using the ratios provided, identify and explain the contributing factor(s) for this apparently divergent trend.

b. In terms of the ratios provided, what conclusion(s) can be drawn regarding the company's use of financial leverage during the 1996-1998 period?

c. Using the ratios provided, what conclusion(s) can be drawn regarding the company's net investment in plant and equipment?

CMA Adapted

P 13-4.   L. Konrath Company is considering extending credit to D. Hawk Company. Konrath estimated that sales to D. Hawk Company would amount to $2,000,000 each year. L. Konrath Company, a wholesaler, sells throughout the Midwest. D. Hawk Company, a retail chain operation, has a number of stores in the Midwest. L. Konrath Company has had a gross profit of approximately 60% in recent years and expects to have a similar gross profit on the D. Hawk Company order. The D. Hawk Company order is approximately 15% of L. Konrath Company's present sales. Data from recent statements of D. Hawk Company follow:

	1996	1997	1998
	(In millions)		
Assets			
Current assets:			
Cash	$ 2.6	$ 1.8	$ 1.6
Government securities (cost)	.4	.2	—
Accounts and notes			
receivable (net)	8.0	8.5	8.5
Inventories	2.8	3.2	2.8
Prepaid assets	.7	.6	.6
Total current assets	14.5	14.3	13.5
Property, plant, and equipment (net)	4.3	5.4	5.9
Total assets	$18.8	$19.7	$19.4
Liabilities and Equities			
Current liabilities	$ 6.9	$ 8.5	$ 9.3
Long-term debt, 6%	3.0	2.0	1.0
Total liabilities	9.9	10.5	10.3
Shareholders' equity	8.9	9.2	9.1
Total liabilities and equities	$18.8	$19.7	$19.4
Income			
Net sales	$24.2	$24.5	$24.9
Cost of goods sold	16.9	17.2	18.0
Gross margin	7.3	7.3	6.9
Selling and administrative expenses	6.6	6.8	7.3
Earnings (loss) before taxes	.7	.5	(.4)
Income taxes	.3	.2	(.2)
Net income	$ .4	$ .3	$ (.2)

Required

a. Calculate the following for D. Hawk Company for the year 1998:
  1. Rate of return on total assets
  2. Acid-test ratio
  3. Return on sales
  4. Current ratio
  5. Inventory turnover

b. As part of the analysis to determine whether or not Konrath should extend credit to Hawk, assume the ratios at the top of the next page were calculated from Hawk Company statements. For each ratio, indicate whether it is a favorable, unfavorable, or neutral statistic in the decision to grant Hawk credit. Briefly explain your choice in each case.

Ratio	1996	1997	1998
Rate of return on total assets	1.96%	1.12%	(.87)%
Return on sales	1.69%	.99%	(.69)%
Acid-test ratio	1.73	1.36	1.19
Current ratio	2.39	1.92	1.67
Inventory turnover (times per year)	4.41	4.32	4.52
Equity relationships:			
Current liabilities	36.0%	43.0%	48.0%
Long-term liabilities	16.0	10.5	5.0
Shareholders	48.0	46.5	47.0
	100.0%	100.0%	100.0%
Asset relationships:			
Current assets	77.0%	72.5%	69.5%
Property, plant, and equipment	23.0	27.5	30.5
	100.0%	100.0%	100.0%

c. Would you grant credit to D. Hawk Company? Support your answer with facts given in the problem.

d. What additional information, if any, would you want before making a final decision?

CMA Adapted

P 13-5.   Your company is considering the possible acquisition of Growth Inc. Financial statements of Growth Inc. follow:

GROWTH INC.
Statement of Income
Years Ended December 31, 1998, 1997, and 1996

	1998	1997	1996
Revenues	$578,530	$523,249	$556,549
Costs and expenses:			
Cost of products sold	495,651	457,527	482,358
Selling, general, and administrative	35,433	30,619	29,582
Interest and debt expense	4,308	3,951	2,630
	535,392	492,097	514,570
Income before income taxes	43,138	31,152	41,979
Provision for income taxes	20,120	12,680	17,400
Net income	$ 23,018	$ 18,472	$ 24,579
Net income per share	$2.27	$1.85	$2.43

GROWTH INC.
Balance Sheet
December 31, 1998 and 1997

	1998	1997
Assets		
Current assets:		
Cash	$ 64,346	$ 11,964
Accounts receivable, less allowance		
of $750 for doubtful accounts	99,021	83,575
Inventories, FIFO	63,414	74,890
Prepaid expenses	834	1,170
Total current assets	227,615	171,599
Investments and other assets	379	175
Property, plant, and equipment:		
Land and land improvements	6,990	6,400
Buildings	63,280	59,259
Machinery and equipment	182,000	156,000
	252,270	221,659
Less: Accumulated depreciation	110,000	98,000
Net property, plant, and equipment	142,270	123,659
Total assets	$370,264	$295,433
Liabilities and Stockholders' Equity		
Current liabilities:		
Accounts payable	$ 32,730	$ 26,850
Federal income taxes	5,300	4,800
Accrued liabilities	30,200	24,500
Current portion of long-term debt	5,500	5,500
Total current liabilities	73,730	61,650
Long-term debt	76,750	41,900
Other long-term liabilities	5,700	4,300
Deferred federal income taxes	16,000	12,000
Total liabilities	172,180	119,850
Stockholders' equity:		
Capital stock	44,000	43,500
Retained earnings	154,084	132,083
Total stockholders' equity	198,084	175,583
Total liabilities and stockholders' equity	$370,264	$295,433

Partial footnotes:

Under the LIFO method, inventories have been reduced by approximately $35,300 and $41,100 at December 31, 1998 and 1997, respectively, from current cost, which would be reported under the first-in, first-out method.

The effective tax rates were 36.6%, 30.7%, and 31.4%, respectively, for the years ended December 31, 1998, 1997, and 1996.

Required   a. Compute the following for 1998, without considering the LIFO reserve:

Liquidity
1.   Days' sales in inventory
2.   Merchandise inventory turnover
3.   Inventory turnover in days
4.   Operating cycle
5.   Working capital
6.   Current ratio
7.   Acid-test ratio
8.   Cash ratio

Debt
1.   Debt ratio
2.   Debt/equity ratio
3.   Times interest earned

Profitability
1.   Net profit margin
2.   Total asset turnover
3.   Return on assets
4.   Return on total equity

b. Compute the ratios in part (a) considering the LIFO reserve.

c. Comment on the apparent liquidity, debt, and profitability, considering both sets of ratios.

P 13-6.

Required   For each of the following numbered items, you are to select the lettered item(s) that indicate(s) its effect(s) on the corporation's statements. If more than one effect is applicable to a particular item, be sure to indicate *all* applicable letters. (Assume that the state statutes do not permit declaration of nonliquidating dividends except from earnings.)

Item	Effect
1. Declaration of a cash dividend due in one month on noncumulative preferred stock.	a. Reduces working capital b. Increases working capital c. Reduces current ratio d. Increases current ratio
2. Declaration and payment of an ordinary stock dividend.	e. Reduces the dollar amount of total capital stock f. Increases the dollar amount of total capital stock
3. Receipt of a cash dividend, not previously recorded, on stock of another corporation.	g. Reduces total retained earnings h. Increases total retained earnings
4. Passing of a dividend on cumulative preferred stocks.	i. Reduces equity per share of common stock
5. Receipt of preferred shares as a dividend on stock held as a temporary investment. This was not a regularly recurring dividend.	j. Reduces equity of each common stockholder
6. Payment of dividend mentioned in 1.	
7. Issue of new common shares in a 5-for-1 stock split.	

P 13-7.   Argo Sales Corporation has in recent prior years maintained the following relationships among the data on its financial statements:

Gross profit rate on net sales	40%
Net profit rate on net sales	10%
Rate of selling expenses to net sales	20%
Accounts receivable turnover	8 per year
Inventory turnover	6 per year
Acid-test ratio	2 to 1
Current ratio	3 to 1
Quick-asset composition: 8% cash, 32% marketable securities, 60% accounts receivable	
Asset turnover	2 per year
Ratio of total assets to intangible assets	20 to 1
Ratio of accumulated depreciation to cost of fixed assets	1 to 3
Ratio of accounts receivable to accounts payable	1.5 to 1
Ratio of working capital to stockholders' equity	1 to 1.6
Ratio of total debt to stockholders' equity	1 to 2

The corporation had a net income of $120,000 for 1998, which resulted in earnings of $5.20 per share of common stock. Additional information includes the following:

Capital stock authorized, issued (all in 1970), and outstanding:
   Common, $10 per share par value, issued at 10% premium.
   Preferred, 6% nonparticipating, $100 per share par value, issued at a 10% premium.
Market value per share of common at December 31, 1998: $78.
Preferred dividends paid in 1998: $3,000.
Times interest earned in 1998: 33.
The amounts of the following were the same at December 31, 1998, as at January 1, 1998: inventory, accounts receivable, 5% bonds payable—due 2000, and total stockholders' equity.
All purchases and sales were on account.

Required a. Prepare in good form the condensed balance sheet and income statement for the year ending December 31, 1998, presenting the amounts you would expect to appear on Argo's financial statements (ignoring income taxes). Major captions appearing on Argo's balance sheet are Current assets, Fixed assets, Intangible assets, Current liabilities, Long-term liabilities, and Stockholders' equity. In addition to the accounts divulged in the problem, you should include accounts for Prepaid expenses, Accrued expenses, and Administrative expenses. Supporting computations should be in good form.
  b. Compute the following for 1998 (show your computations):
     1. Rate of return on stockholders' equity
     2. Price/earnings ratio for common stock
     3. Dividends paid per share of common stock
     4. Dividends paid per share of preferred stock
     5. Yield on common stock

CMA Adapted

P 13-8. Warford Corporation was formed five years ago through a public subscription of common stock. Lucinda Street, who owns 15% of the common stock, was one of the organizers of Warford and is its current president. The company has been successful but currently is experiencing a shortage of funds. On June 10, Street approached Bell National Bank, asking for a 24-month extension on two $30,000 notes, which are due on June 30, 1998, and September 30, 1998. Another note of $7,000 is due on December 31, 1998, but she expects no difficulty in paying this note on its due date. Street explained that Warford's cash flow problems are due primarily to the company's desire to finance a $300,000 plant expansion over the next two fiscal years through internally generated funds.

The commercial loan officer of Bell National Bank requested financial reports for the last two fiscal years. These reports are reproduced below:

WARFORD CORPORATION
Statement of Financial Position
March 31

Assets:	1997	1998
Cash	$ 12,500	$ 16,400
Notes receivable	104,000	112,000
Accounts receivable (net)	68,500	81,600
Inventories (at cost)	50,000	80,000
Plant and equipment (net of depreciation)	646,000	680,000
Total assets	$881,000	$970,000

Liabilities and Owners' Equity:	1997	1998
Accounts payable	$ 72,000	$ 69,000
Notes payable	54,500	67,000
Accrued liabilities	6,000	9,000
Common stock (60,000 shares, $10 par)	600,000	600,000
Retained earnings**	148,500	225,000
Total liabilities and owners' equity	$881,000	$970,000

** Cash dividends were paid at the rate of $1.00 per share in fiscal year 1997 and $1.25 per share in fiscal year 1998.

WARFORD CORPORATION
Income Statement
For the Fiscal Years Ended March 31, 1997 and 1998

	1997	1998
Sales	$ 2,700,000	$ 3,000,000
Cost of goods sold*	1,720,000	1,902,500
Gross profit	980,000	1,097,500
Operating expenses	780,000	845,000
Net income before taxes	200,000	252,500
Income taxes (40%)	80,000	101,000
Income after taxes	$ 120,000	$ 151,500

* Depreciation charges on the plant and equipment of $100,000 and $102,500 for fiscal years ended March 31, 1997 and 1998, respectively, are included in cost of goods sold.

Required   a. Calculate the following items for Warford Corporation:
           1. Current ratio for fiscal years 1997 and 1998
           2. Acid-test (quick) ratio for fiscal years 1997 and 1998
           3. Inventory turnover for fiscal year 1998
           4. Return on assets for fiscal years 1997 and 1998

5.   Percentage change in sales, cost of goods sold, gross profit, and net income after taxes from fiscal year 1997 to 1998

b.   Identify and explain what other financial reports and/or financial analyses might be helpful to the commercial loan officer of Bell National Bank in evaluating Street's request for a time extension on Warford's notes.

c.   Assume that the percentage changes experienced in fiscal year 1998, as compared with fiscal year 1997 for sales, cost of goods sold, gross profit, and net income after taxes, will be repeated in each of the next two years. Is Warford's desire to finance the plant expansion from internally generated funds realistic? Explain.

d.   Should Bell National Bank grant the extension on Warford's notes, considering Street's statement about financing the plant expansion through internally generated funds? Explain.

CMA Adapted

P 13-9.   The following data apply to items (a) through (g):

JOHANSON COMPANY
Statement of Financial Position
December 31, 1997 and 1998

(In thousands)	1997	1998
Assets		
Current assets:		
Cash and temporary investments	$ 380	$ 400
Accounts receivable (net)	1,500	1,700
Inventories	2,120	2,200
Total current assets	4,000	4,300
Long-term assets:		
Land	500	500
Building and equipment (net)	4,000	4,700
Total long-term assets	4,500	5,200
Total assets	$ 8,500	$ 9,500
Liabilities and Equities		
Current liabilities:		
Accounts payable	$ 700	$ 1,400
Current portion of long-term debt	500	1,000
Total current liabilities	1,200	2,400
Long-term debt	4,000	3,000
Total liabilities	5,200	5,400
Stockholders' equity:		
Common stock	3,000	3,000
Retained earnings	300	1,100
Total stockholders' equity	3,300	4,100
Total liabilities and equities	$ 8,500	$ 9,500

JOHANSON COMPANY
Statement of Income and Retained Earnings
For the Year Ended December 31, 1998

(In thousands)

Net sales		$28,800
Less: Cost of goods sold	$15,120	
Selling expenses	7,180	
Administrative expenses	4,100	
Interest	400	
Income taxes	800	27,600
Net income		1,200
Retained earnings, January 1		300
Subtotal		1,500
Cash dividends declared and paid		400
Retained earnings, December 31		$ 1,100

Required   Answer the following multiple-choice questions.

a. The acid-test ratio for 1998 is
   1.   1.1 to 1   4.   .2 to 1
   2.   .9 to 1   5.   .17 to 1
   3.   1.8 to 1

b. The average number of days' sales outstanding in 1998 is
   1.   18 days   4.   4.4 days
   2.   360 days   5.   80 days
   3.   20 days

c. The times interest earned ratio for 1998 is
   1.   3.0 times   4.   2.0 times
   2.   1.0 times   5.   6.0 times
   3.   72.0 times

d. The asset turnover in 1998 is
   1.   3.2 times   4.   1.1 times
   2.   1.7 times   5.   .13 times
   3.   .4 times

e. The inventory turnover in 1998 is
   1.   13.6 times   4.   7.0 times
   2.   12.5 times   5.   51.4 times
   3.   .9 times

f. The operating income margin in 1998 is
   1.   2.7%   4.   95.8%
   2.   91.7%   5.   8.3%
   3.   52.5%

g. The dividend payout ratio in 1998 is
   1.   100%   4.   8.8%
   2.   36%   5.   33.3%
   3.   20%

CMA Adapted

P 13-10. The statement of financial position for Paragon Corporation at November 30, 1998, the end of its current fiscal year, is presented below. The market price of the company's common stock was $4 per share on November 30, 1998.

Assets		(In thousands)	
Current assets:			
Cash		$ 6,000	
Accounts receivable	$ 7,000		
Less: Allowance for doubtful accounts	400	6,600	
Merchandise inventory		16,000	
Supplies on hand		400	
Prepaid expenses		1,000	
Total current assets			$ 30,000
Property, plant, and equipment:			
Land		27,500	
Building	36,000		
Less: Accumulated depreciation	13,500	22,500	
Total property, plant, and equipment			50,000
Total assets			$ 80,000
Liabilities and Stockholders' Equity			
Current liabilities:			
Accounts payable		$ 6,400	
Accrued interest payable		800	
Accrued income taxes payable		2,200	
Accrued wages payable		600	
Deposits received from customers		2,000	
Total current liabilities			$ 12,000
Long-term debt:			
Bonds payable—20-year, 8% convertible debentures due December 1, 2004 (Note 1)		20,000	
Less: Unamortized discount		200	19,800
Total liabilities			31,800
Stockholders' equity:			
Common stock—authorized 40,000,000 shares of $1 par value; 20,000,000 shares issued and outstanding		20,000	
Paid-in capital in excess of par value		12,200	
Total paid-in capital		32,200	
Retained earnings		16,000	
Total stockholders' equity			48,200
Total liabilities and stockholders' equity			$ 80,000

All items are to be considered independent of one another, and any transactions given in the items are to be considered the only transactions to affect Paragon Corporation during the just-completed current or coming fiscal year. Average balance sheet account balances are used in computing ratios involving income statement accounts. Ending balance sheet account balances are used in computing ratios involving only balance sheet items.

Required   a.   If Paragon paid back all of the deposits received from customers, its current ratio would be

1.	2.50 to 1.00	4.	3.00 to 1.00
2.	2.80 to 1.00	5.	2.29 to 1.00
3.	2.33 to 1.00		

b.   If Paragon paid back all of the deposits received from customers, its quick (acid-test) ratio would be

1.	1.06 to 1.00	4.	1.26 to 1.00
2.	1.00 to 1.00	5.	1.20 to 1.00
3.	0.88 to 1.00		

c.   A 2-for-1 common stock split by Paragon would

1. Result in each $1,000 bond being convertible into 600 new shares of Paragon common stock.
2. Decrease the retained earnings due to the capitalization of retained earnings.
3. Not affect the number of common shares outstanding.
4. Increase the total paid-in capital.
5. Increase the total stockholders' equity.

d.   Paragon Corporation's building is being depreciated using the straight-line method, salvage value of $6,000,000, and life of 20 years. The number of years the building has been depreciated by Paragon as of November 30, 1998, is

1.	7.5 years	4.	15.0 years
2.	12.5 years	5.	None of these
3.	9.0 years		

e.   Paragon's book value per share of common stock as of November 30, 1998, is

1.	$4.00	4.	$2.41
2.	$1.61	5.	None of these
3.	$1.00		

f. If, during the current fiscal year ending November 30, 1998, Paragon
    had sales of $90,000,000 with a gross profit of 20% and an inventory
    turnover of five times per year, the merchandise inventory balance on
    December 1, 1997, was

    1. $14,400,000   4. $20,000,000
    2. $12,800,000   5. $16,000,000
    3. $18,000,000

g. If Paragon has a payout ratio of 80% and declared and paid $4,000,000 of
    cash dividends during the current fiscal year ended November 30, 1998,
    the retained earnings balance on December 1, 1997, was

    1. $20,000,000   4. $11,000,000
    2. $17,000,000   5. None of these
    3. $15,000,000

CMA Adapted

P 13-11.   Calcor Company has been a wholesale distributor of automobile parts for
domestic automakers for 20 years. Calcor has suffered through the recent
slump in the domestic auto industry, and its performance has not rebounded
to the levels of the industry as a whole.

Calcor's single-step income statement for the year ended November 30,
1998, is presented below:

CALCOR COMPANY
Income Statement
For the Year Ended November 30, 1998 (Thousands omitted)

Net sales	$8,400
Expenses:	
Cost of goods sold	6,300
Selling expense	780
Administrative expense	900
Interest expense	140
Total	8,120
Income before income taxes	280
Income taxes	112
Net income	$ 168

Calcor's return on sales before interest and taxes was 5% in fiscal 1998
compared to the industry average of 9%. Calcor's turnover of average assets
of four times per year and return on average assets before interest and taxes
of 20% are both well below the industry average.

Joe Kuhn, president of Calcor, wishes to improve these ratios and raise them nearer to the industry averages. He established the following goals for Calcor Company for fiscal 1999:

Return on sales before interest and taxes   8%
Turnover of average assets   5 times per year
Return on average assets before interest and taxes 30%

For fiscal 1999, Kuhn and the rest of Calcor's management team are considering the following actions, which they expect will improve profitability and result in a 5% increase in unit sales:

1. Increase selling prices 10%.

2. Increase advertising by $420,000 and hold all other selling and administrative expenses at fiscal 1998 levels.

3. Improve customer service by increasing average current assets (inventory and accounts receivable) by a total of $300,000, and hold all other assets at fiscal 1998 levels.

4. Finance the additional assets at an annual interest rate of 10% and hold all other interest expense at fiscal 1998 levels.

5. Improve the quality of products carried; this will increase the units of goods sold by 4%.

6. Calcor's 1999 effective income tax rate is expected to be 40%— the same as in fiscal 1998.

Required   a. Prepare a single-step pro forma income statement for Calcor Company for the year ended November 30, 1999, assuming that Calcor's planned actions would be carried out, and that the 5% increase in unit sales would be realized.

b. Calculate the following ratios for Calcor Company for the 1998-1999 fiscal year and state whether Kuhn's goal would be achieved:
1. Return on sales before interest and taxes
2. Turnover of average assets
3. Return on average assets before interest and taxes

c. Would it be possible for Calcor Company to achieve the first two of Kuhn's goals without achieving his third goal of a 30% return on average assets before interest and taxes? Explain your answer.

CMA Adapted

P 13-12.   The following data are for the A, B, and C Companies.

Variables	Company		
	A	B	C
Current assets	$150,000	$170,000	$180,000
Current liabilities	$ 60,000	$ 50,000	$ 30,000
Total assets	$300,000	$280,000	$250,000
Retained earnings	$ 80,000	$ 90,000	$ 60,000
Earnings before interest and taxes	$ 70,000	$ 60,000	$ 50,000
Market price per share	$ 20.00	$ 18.75	$ 16.50
Number of shares outstanding	9,000	9,000	9,000
Book value of total debt	$ 30,000	$ 50,000	$ 80,000
Sales	$430,000	$400,000	$200,000

Required   a. Compute the Z score for each company.

b. According to the Altman model, which of these firms is most likely to experience financial failure?

P 13-13.   The General Company financial statements for 1998 follow:

GENERAL COMPANY
Statement of Income
Years Ended December 31

	1998	1997	1996
Net sales	$860,000	$770,000	$690,000
Cost and expenses:			
Cost of products sold	730,000	630,000	580,000
Selling, general, and administrative	46,000	40,000	38,000
Interest and debt expense	4,000	3,900	6,500
	780,000	673,900	624,500
Income before income taxes	80,000	96,100	65,500
Provision for income taxes	33,000	24,000	21,000
Net income	$ 47,000	$ 72,100	$ 44,500
Net income per share	$2.67	$4.10	$2.54

GENERAL COMPANY
Balance Sheet
December 31, 1998

	1998	1997
Assets		
Current assets:		
Cash	$ 48,000	$ 39,000
Accounts receivable, less allowance for doubtful accounts of $2,000 in 1998 and $1,400 in 1997	125,000	121,000
Inventories	71,000	68,000
Prepaid expenses	2,500	2,200
Total current assets	246,500	230,200
Property, plant, and equipment:		
Land and land improvements	12,000	10,500
Buildings	98,000	89,000
Machinery and equipment	303,000	247,000
	413,000	346,500
Less: Accumulated depreciation	165,000	144,000
Net property, plant, and equipment	248,000	202,500
Total assets	$ 494,500	$ 432,700
Liabilities and Stockholders' Equity		
Current liabilities:		
Accounts payable	$ 56,000	$ 50,000
Income taxes	3,700	3,600
Accrued liabilities	34,000	28,000
Total current liabilities	93,700	81,600
Long-term debt	63,000	64,000
Other long-term liabilities	16,000	6,800
Deferred federal income taxes	27,800	24,000
Total liabilities	200,500	176,400
Stockholders' equity:		
Capital stock	46,000	45,000
Retained earnings	248,000	211,300
Total stockholders' equity	294,000	256,300
Total liabilities and stockholders' equity	$ 494,500	$ 432,700

GENERAL COMPANY
Statement of Cash Flows
Years Ended December 31

	1998	1997	1996
Operating activities:			
Net income	$ 47,000	$ 72,100	$ 44,500
Adjustments to reconcile net income to net cash provided by operating activities:			
Depreciation and amortization	21,000	20,000	19,000
Deferred taxes	3,800	2,500	2,000
Increase in accounts receivable	(4,000)	(3,000)	(3,000)
Decrease (increase) in inventories	(3,000)	(2,500)	1,000
Decrease (increase) in prepaid expenses	(300)	(200)	100
Increase (decrease) in accounts payable	6,000	5,000	(1,000)
Increase (decrease) in income taxes	100	300	(100)
Increase (decrease) in accrued liabilities	6,000	3,000	(1,000)
Net cash provided by operating activities	76,600	97,200	61,500
Investing activities:			
Additions to property, plant, and equipment	(66,500)	(84,400)	(52,500)
Financing activities:			
Payment on long-term debt	(1,000)	(2,000)	(1,500)
Issuance of other long-term liabilities	9,200	1,000	(1,000)
Issuance of capital stock	1,000	—	—
Dividend paid	(10,300)	(9,800)	(9,500)
Net cash used in financing activities	(1,100)	(10,800)	(12,000)
Increase (decrease) in cash	9,000	2,000	(3,000)
Cash at beginning of year	39,000	37,000	40,000
Cash at end of year	$ 48,000	$ 39,000	$ 37,000

Note: The market price of the stock at the end of 1998 was $30.00 per share. There were 23,000 common shares outstanding at December 31, 1998.

Required　　a.　Compute the Z score of the General Company at the end of 1998.
　　　　　　b.　According to the Altman model, does the Z score of the General Company indicate a high probability of financial failure?

P 13-14.

LIFO reserves: Rhodes Company
Reported year for analysis, 1998

1998 net income as reported	$ 90,200,000
1998 inventory reserve	50,000,000
1997 inventory reserve	46,000,000
1998 income taxes	55,000,000
1998 income before income taxes	145,200,000

Required　　Compute the approximate income if inventory had been valued at approximate current cost.

P 13-15.

LIFO reserves: Lion Company
Reported year for analysis, 1997

1997 net income as reported	$ 45,000,000
1997 inventory reserve	20,000,000
1996 inventory reserve	28,000,000
1997 income taxes	14,000,000
1997 income before income taxes	59,000,000

Required　　Compute the approximate income if inventory had been valued at approximate current cost.

P 13-16.　　An airline presented this graph with its annual report:

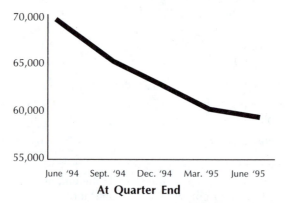

Required　　Indicate the misleading feature in this graph.

Cases

CASE 13-1 What Position?

Seaway Food Town, Inc. presented this data in its 1995 annual report:

SEAWAY FOOD TOWN, INC.
CONSOLIDATED STATEMENTS OF INCOME
Years Ended August 26, 1995, August 27, 1994, and August 28, 1993

(Dollars in thousands, except per share data)	1995	1994	1993
Net sales	$559,244	$546,193	$566,883
Cost of merchandise sold	418,128	409,305	428,478
Gross profit	141,116	136,888	138,405
Selling, general, and administrative expenses	131,267	129,921	133,175
Operating profit	9,849	6,967	5,230
Interest expense	(4,469)	(4,410)	(4,660)
Other income—net	1,815	1,169	1,133
Income before income taxes, extraordinary item, and cumulative effect	7,195	3,726	1,703
Provision for income taxes	2,715	1,288	580
Income before extraordinary item and cumulative effect	4,480	2,438	1,123
Extraordinary item—losses from early extinguishment of debt, less applicable income taxes of $63 (Note 2)	—	(123)	—
Cumulative effect of change in accounting for income taxes (Note 3)	—	(256)	—
Net income	$ 4,480	$ 2,059	$ 1,123
Per common share:			
Income before extraordinary item and cumulative effect	$2.04	$1.06	$.48
Extraordinary item	—	(.06)	—
Cumulative effect of change in accounting for income taxes	—	(.11)	—
Net income	$2.04	$ .89	$.48

SEAWAY FOOD TOWN, INC.
CONSOLIDATED BALANCE SHEETS
August 26, 1995 and August 27, 1994
(Dollars in thousands, except per-share data)

	1995	1994
Assets		
Current assets:		
Cash and cash equivalents	$ 7,402	$ 7,137
Income tax recoverable	—	600
Notes and accounts receivable, less allowance of $450 for doubtful accounts	6,587	5,627
Merchandise inventories	44,064	44,749
Prepaid expenses	1,371	1,272
Deferred income taxes	4,211	4,036
Total current assets	63,635	63,421
Other assets	6,366	6,436
Property and equipment, at cost:		
Land	4,160	4,202
Buildings and improvements	65,983	62,453
Leasehold improvements	28,921	26,005
Equipment	89,356	92,165
	188,420	184,825
Less accumulated depreciation and amortization	104,420	99,479
Net property and equipment	84,000	85,346
	$154,001	$155,203
Liabilities and shareholders' equity		
Current liabilities:		
Accounts payable—trade	$ 38,889	$ 36,318
Income taxes	1,027	407
Accrued liabilities:		
Insurance	5,521	5,027
Payroll	2,994	2,766
Taxes, other than income	2,352	2,434
Other	3,213	4,191
	14,080	14,418
Long-term debt due within one year	3,553	3,341
Total current liabilities	57,549	54,484
Long-term debt	48,399	55,060
Deferred income taxes	5,276	5,495
Deferred other	2,046	2,579
Total liabilities	113,270	117,618
Shareholders' equity:		
Serial preferred stock, without par value: 300,000 shares authorized, none issued	—	—
Common stock, without par value (stated value $2 per share): 6,000,000 shares authorized, 2,193,352 shares outstanding (2,242,373 shares in 1994)	4,387	4,485
Capital in excess of stated value	680	434
Retained earnings	35,664	32,666
Total shareholders' equity	40,731	37,585
	$154,001	$155,203

1. Significant Accounting Policies (in Part)

Inventories—Meat, produce, and drug inventories are valued at the lower of cost, using the first-in, first-out (FIFO) method, or market. All other merchandise inventories are valued at the lower of cost, using the last-in, first-out (LIFO) method, or market. Inventories have been reduced by $18,157,000 and $17,576,000 at August 26, 1995, and August 27, 1994, respectively, from amounts which would have been reported under the FIFO method (which approximates current cost).

During 1995 and 1994, merchandise inventory quantities were reduced. These reductions resulted in liquidations of the LIFO inventory quantities carried at lower costs prevailing in prior years as compared with costs of 1995 and 1994 purchases, the effect of which increased consolidated net income by approximately $89,000 ($.04 per share) in 1995 and $75,000 ($.03 per share) in 1994.

Other data:

a. Net cash provided by operating activities $19,829,000, $16,183,000, and $16,534,000 for 1995, 1994, and 1993, respectively.

b. Market Price of common stock:
   1. August 26, 1995, $16.25
   2. August 27, 1994, $10.50

Required

a. LIFO inventory liquidation increased income in 1995 and 1994. Determine the amount by which income was increased in 1995 and 1994 because of LIFO inventory.

b. Determine the change in net income, in comparison with the reported net income, if FIFO had been used for all inventory.

c. Compute the following for 1995, with no adjustment for LIFO reserve:
   1. Days' sales in inventory
   2. Working capital
   3. Current ratio
   4. Acid-test ratio
   5. Debt ratio

d. Compute the measures in (c) considering the LIFO reserve. (Eliminate the LIFO reserve.)
   1. Days' sales in inventory
   2. Working capital
   3. Current ratio
   4. Acid-test ratio
   5. Debt ratio

e. Comment on the different results of the ratios computed in (c) and (d).

f. Compute the following for 1995 (use the financial statements as published):
   1. Cash flow/total debt
   2. Net income/total assets
   3. Debt ratio
   Assuming that these ratios are valid in forecasting financial failure, give your opinion as to the financial position of this company.

g. Compute the Z score for 1995. Comment.

Endnotes

1   C. H. Gibson, "Financial Ratios as Perceived by Commercial Loan Officers," *Akron Business and Economic Review* (Summer 1983), pp. 23-27.

2   The basis of the comments in this section is a study by Dr. Charles Gibson in 1981. The research was done under a grant from the Deloitte Haskins & Sells Foundation.

3   C. H. Gibson, "Ohio CPA's Perceptions of Financial Ratios," *The Ohio CPA Journal* (Autumn 1985), pp. 25-30.© 1985. Reprinted with permission of *The Ohio CPA Journal*.

4   C. H. Gibson, "How Chartered Financial Analysts View Financial Ratios," *Financial Analysts Journal* (May-June 1987), pp. 74-76.

5   Gibson, "How Chartered Financial Analysts View Financial Ratios," pp. 74-76.

6   C. H. Gibson, "Financial Ratios in Annual Reports," *The CPA Journal* (September 1982), pp. 18-29.

7   W. H. Beaver, "Alternative Accounting Measures as Predictors of Failure," *The Accounting Review* (January 1968), pp. 113-122.

8   Beaver, p. 117.

9   Beaver, p. 119.

10   E. I. Altman, "Financial Ratios, Discriminant Analysis and the Prediction of Corporate Bankruptcy," *Journal of Finance* (September 1968), pp. 589-609.

11   Edward I. Altman and Thomas P. McGough, "Evaluation of a Company as a Going Concern," *The Journal of Accountancy* (December 1974), pp. 50-57.

12   Altman and McGough, p. 52.

13   Suggested reference sources:

Anker V. Andersen, "Graphing Financial Information: How Accountants Can Use Graphs to Communicate," National Association of Accountants (1983), p. 50.

Edward Bloches, Robert P. Moffie, and Robert W. Smud, "How Best to Communicate Numerical Data," *The Internal Auditor* (February 1985), pp. 38-42.

Charles H. Gibson and Nicholas Schroeder, "Improving Your Practice— Graphically," *The CPA Journal* (August 1990), pp. 28-37.

Johnny R. Johnson, Richard R. Rice, and Roger A. Roemmich, "Pictures That Lie: The Abuse of Graphs in Annual Reports," *Management Accounting* (October 1980), pp. 50-56.

Calvin F. Schmid and Stanton E. Schmid, *Handbook of Graphic Presentation*, 2d ed. (New York: Ronald Press, 1979), p. 308.

14   Impact of Changing Prices on Financial Statements

TRADITIONAL FINANCIAL STATEMENTS ARE NOT DESIGNED to account for distortions created by changing prices. The distortion that changing prices can create has generated years of debate. This chapter introduces constant dollar accounting and current cost, both of which will be discussed in general terms.

CONSTANT DOLLAR ACCOUNTING (PRICE-LEVEL)

Constant dollar accounting (formerly termed *price-level accounting*) is a method of reporting financial statement elements in dollars having similar purchasing power. It measures general changes in prices of goods and services.

Financial statements are adjusted for inflation, using constant dollar (price-level) accounting, to represent the purchasing power of the historical dollars. Usually the adjustment is to the most recent year-end, using the balance sheet date. The adjustment could be to any date selected. To adjust the statements, accounts on the balance sheet are classified as monetary or nonmonetary. **Monetary accounts** are stated in terms of a fixed or determinable amount to be received or paid. **Nonmonetary accounts** are stated in terms of the purchasing power at the time when the original transaction occurred.

Monetary accounts on the balance sheet do not need to be adjusted if the adjustment is to the balance sheet date because they have fixed dollar balances in terms of current purchasing power as of the balance sheet date. However, a gain or loss in purchasing power does need to be computed for monetary items. A loss in purchasing power arises from holding monetary assets, and a gain in purchasing power arises from holding monetary liabilities during a period of inflation. As an example, $10,000 in cash held for a year, while the inflation rate is 5%, results in a $500 loss in purchasing power if the restatement is to the year-end. The $10,000 in cash is automatically stated in terms of the new purchasing power. In other words, the

$10,000 will now buy fewer goods. A $10,000 note payable on the balance sheet for a year, when the inflation rate is 5%, results in a $500 gain in purchasing power, although the note payable of $10,000 is automatically stated in terms of the new purchasing power at year-end.

The computation of gain or loss in purchasing power is more complicated than described previously. The purchasing power gain (loss) on monetary items requires a reconciliation of the beginning and ending balances of the net monetary amount. A restatement ratio is applied to the beginning balance and each reconciling amount. The restatement amount is compared with the year-end net monetary items to determine the purchasing power gain (loss). An example reconciliation follows:

	Historical Cost	**Conversion**	**Adjusted Basis**
Net monetary position, beginning of year	$XXXX	X $\dfrac{\text{Price Index Converting to}}{\text{Price Index Beginning of Year}}$ =	$XXXX
Add monetary inflows: Individual monetary inflows	XXXX	X $\dfrac{\text{Price Index Converting to}}{\text{Price Index at Time of Monetary Flow}}$ =	XXXX
Total inflows	XXXX		XXXX
Subtract monetary outflows: Individual monetary outflows	XXXX	X $\dfrac{\text{Price Index Converting to}}{\text{Price Index at Time of Monetary Flow}}$ =	XXXX
Total outflows	XXXX		XXXX
Net monetary position, end of year	(A) $XXXX		XXXX (A) XXXX
Purchasing power gain (loss) (place at the bottom of the income statement)			$XXXX

To restate financial statements into constant dollars, it is necessary to measure a change in the price of a "basket of goods" from one period to the next. The U.S. government puts together a number of different baskets of goods and computes indexes for them. The one that accountants typically use is the Consumer Price Index for all Urban Consumers (CPI-U). The CPI-U reflects the average change in the retail prices of a broad group of consumer goods.

Nonmonetary accounts do need to be adjusted in terms of the new purchasing power. Adjustment to the nonmonetary accounts indirectly affects the income statement because the income statement reflects figures computed from the adjusted amounts. For example, if the building account has been adjusted upward for inflation, the depreciation expense increases on the income statement. To illustrate, if a building were purchased for $100,000 when the price level was 100, and the level is now 150, then the building would be presented at $150,000 and depreciation based thereon.

Compute comprehensive constant dollar restatements by applying the following formula to nonmonetary items:

$$\text{Historical Cost} \quad \times \quad \frac{\text{Price Index Converting to}}{\text{Price Index at Time of Original Transaction}} \quad = \quad \text{Adjusted Amount}$$

The following are some monetary and nonmonetary accounts:

Monetary
　Assets:
　　Cash
　　Accounts receivable (net of allowance account)
　　Notes receivable
　　Advances to employees
　Liabilities:
　　Accounts payable
　　Notes payable
　　Accrued expenses payable
　　Bonds payable

Nonmonetary
　Assets:
　　Inventories
　　Property, plant, and equipment
　　Patents, trademarks, goodwill
　Liabilities:
　　Deferred income (if to furnish goods and services)
　Owners' equity:
　　Minority interest
　　Preferred stock
　　Common stock

Hawkeye Company will be used to illustrate how the traditional financial statements would be adjusted for constant dollar accounting on a comprehensive basis. For the Hawkeye Company statements, the price index converted "to" is the end-of-year index. Alternatively, any date could have been selected. Exhibits 14-1 and 14-2 initially present the Hawkeye Company statements, based on current GAAP. Exhibits 14-3, 14-4, and 14-5 (pages 608, 609, and 610, respectively) show the statements adjusted on a constant dollar basis.

Additional information:

1. The general price index in effect on the following dates is:

December 31, 1997	100
December 31, 1998	120
Average index for 1998	110

2. The December 31, 1997 inventory is at an index of 100. The increase in inventory came when the index was 110. LIFO inventory is used.

3. There were no disposals of plant and equipment during 1998. The increase in plant and equipment came on January 1, 1998 when the price index was 100. No depreciation is taken in the year of acquisition. The remainder of the fixed assets was purchased on December 31, 1980 when the price index was 50.

4. The price index was 115 when capital stock of $10,000 was sold in 1998. Prior capital stock of $110,000 was sold when the price

EXHIBIT 14-1 **HAWKEYE COMPANY**
Statement of Earnings
For the Year Ended December 31, 1998

Sales		$350,000
Cost of goods sold:		
Inventory, January 1, 1998	$ 30,000	
Net purchases	150,000	
Total inventory available	180,000	
Less: Inventory, December 31, 1998	50,000	130,000
Gross profit		220,000
Operating expenses (including depreciation of $10,000)		120,000
Operating profit		100,000
Less: Interest expense		8,000
Income before income taxes		92,000
Less: Income taxes		50,000
Net income		$ 42,000

EXHIBIT 14-2   **HAWKEYE COMPANY**
Balance Sheet
December 31, 1997 and 1998

		1997		1998
Assets				
Current assets:				
Cash		$ 45,000		$ 25,000
Accounts receivable (net)		35,000		30,000
Inventory		30,000		50,000
Total current assets		110,000		105,000
Property, plant, and equipment	$140,000		$180,000	
Less: Accumulated depreciation	30,000	110,000	40,000	140,000
Total assets		$220,000		$245,000
Liabilities and Stockholders' Equity				
Current liabilities:				
Accounts payable		$ 40,000		$ 15,000
Accrued payroll		5,000		10,000
Notes payable		40,000		40,000
Total current liabilities		85,000		65,000
Stockholders' equity:				
Capital stock	$120,000		$130,000	
Retained earnings	15,000		50,000	
Total stockholders' equity		135,000		180,000
Total liabilities and stockholders' equity		$220,000		$245,000

index was 50, while the price index was 100 when capital stock of $10,000 was sold.

5. Assume an average price index for sales, purchases, and operating expenses. (This does not include depreciation.)

6. Income taxes and interest expenses were paid on December 31, 1998.

7. Dividends of $7,000 were paid on December 31, 1998.

8. Assume that the December 31, 1997 retained earnings balance of $15,000 can be converted at December 31, 1998, using the computation, $15,000 x 120/100. The first year that a company prepares a constant dollar statement, the opening retained earnings amount is usually forced (not computed directly). The alternative would be to compute retained earnings for each year since the company went into business.

EXHIBIT 14-3 **HAWKEYE COMPANY**
Computation of Purchasing Power Gain or Loss
For the Year Ended December 31, 1998

Schedule 1 Monetary Position at the Beginning and End of the Year

	Jan. 1, 1998	Dec. 31, 1998
Monetary assets:		
Cash	$45,000	$ 25,000
Accounts receivable	35,000	30,000
Total monetary assets	80,000	55,000
Monetary liabilities:		
Accounts payable	40,000	15,000
Accrued payroll	5,000	10,000
Notes payable	40,000	40,000
Total monetary liabilities	85,000	65,000
Net monetary position	$ (5,000)	$(10,000)

Schedule 2 Change in Monetary Position and Purchasing Power Gain or Loss Between January 1, 1998 and December 31, 1998

	Historical Cost	Price Index	Adjusted Basis
Net monetary position, January 1, 1998	$ (5,000)	120/100	$ (6,000)
Add monetary inflows:			
Sales	350,000	120/110	381,818
Sales of stock	10,000	120/115	10,435
Total inflows	360,000		392,253
Subtract monetary outflows:			
Purchase of inventory	150,000	120/110	163,636
Operating expenses (excluding depreciation)	110,000	120/110	120,000
Interest expense	8,000	120/120	8,000
Income taxes paid	50,000	120/120	50,000
Purchase of fixed assets	40,000	120/100	48,000
Dividends	7,000	120/120	7,000
Total outflows	365,000		396,636
Net monetary position, December 31, 1998 (A)	$ (10,000)		(10,383)
			(A)(10,000)
Purchasing power gain (loss) (place at the bottom of the income statement)			$ 383

EXHIBIT 14-4   **HAWKEYE COMPANY**
Computation of Constant Dollar Adjusted Statement of Earnings
For the Year Ended December 31, 1998

	Historical Cost	Price Index	Adjusted Basis
Sales	$ 350,000	120/110	$ 381,818
Cost of goods sold:			
Inventory, January 1, 1998	30,000	120/100	36,000
Net purchases	150,000	120/110	163,636
Total inventory available	180,000		199,636
Less: Inventory, December 31, 1998	50,000	30,000 x 120/100	(36,000)
		20,000 x 120/110	(21,818)
Cost of goods sold	130,000		141,818
Gross profit	220,000		240,000
Operating expenses:			
General expenses	(110,000)	120/110	(120,000)
Depreciation	(10,000)	120/50	(24,000)
Operating profit	100,000		96,000
Less: Interest expense	8,000	120/120	8,000
Income before income taxes	92,000		88,000
Less: Income taxes	50,000	120/120	50,000
Earnings before purchasing power gain	42,000		38,000
Purchasing power gain			383
Net income	$ 42,000		$ 38,383

For financial statement analysis, we must be aware of the impact that constant dollar accounting has on the resulting financial statements. The Hawkeye Company illustration shows how the income statement and balance sheet would be adjusted for constant dollar accounting. (The adjustments to these statements do not change the statement of cash flows.) However, these statements do not represent a general case from which conclusions can be drawn that would apply to all companies. The extent of the impact depends on several factors: the rates of inflation, the length of time that the monetary assets and liabilities have been held, and the mixture of monetary and nonmonetary accounts found on the statements.

If there were no inflation, there would be no difference between historical cost statements and constant dollar statements. The greater the inflation,

EXHIBIT 14-5   **HAWKEYE COMPANY**
Computation of Constant Dollar Adjusted Balance Sheet
December 31, 1998

	Historical Cost	Price Index	Adjusted Basis
Assets			
Current assets:			
Cash	$ 25,000		$ 25,000
Accounts receivable (net)	30,000		30,000
Inventory	50,000	30,000 x 120/100	36,000
		20,000 x 120/110	21,818
Total current assets	105,000		112,818
Property, plant, and equipment	180,000	140,000 x 120/50	336,000
		40,000 x 120/100	48,000
Less: Accumulated depreciation	(40,000)	40,000 x 120/50	(96,000)
Net property, plant, and equipment	140,000		288,000
Total assets	$ 245,000		$ 400,818
Liabilities and Stockholders' Equity			
Current liabilities:			
Accounts payable	$ 15,000		$ 15,000
Accrued payroll	10,000		10,000
Notes payable	40,000		40,000
Total current liabilities	65,000		65,000
Stockholders' equity:			
Capital stock	130,000	110,000 x 120/50	264,000
		10,000 x 120/100	12,000
		10,000 x 120/115	10,435
Retained earnings	50,000	15,000 x 120/100	18,000
		(42,000 Earnings)	38,383
		(7,000 Dividends)	(7,000)
Total stockholders' equity	180,000		335,818
Total liabilities and stockholders' equity	$ 245,000		$ 400,818

the greater the difference between historical cost statements and constant dollar statements. This also applies to the length of time that the nonmonetary assets and liabilities have been held.

Because the effects of general price-level changes can vary greatly from firm to firm, it is difficult to generalize. Some firms will actually have an increase in income; others, a decrease. The following comments briefly describe some of the effects on financial statements. These comments assume that the price index converted "to" is the end-of-year index.

From a short-term analysis view, the working capital and the current ratio have increased, principally because of the higher inventory amount in current assets. The acid-test ratio would change very little or not at all, because the computation excludes the inventory account. Current asset and current liability accounts would essentially be monetary, except for inventory, prepaids, and marketable securities. We can conclude that the short-term debt-paying ability would usually show an improvement, based on the constant dollar statement, because of the improved working capital and current ratio. This improvement comes essentially from the increase in inventory. The improvement in the indicated short-term debt-paying ability will be particularly significant for a firm that uses LIFO.

A firm that has a large investment in productive fixed assets would find that inflation can have a material influence on the adjusted statement. The fixed assets would increase on the balance sheet, so there would be a larger depreciation expense on the income statement. This would result in decreased earnings and earnings per share. Net income to sales will decrease, as would return on assets and owners' equity. The debt to equity ratio would improve—the adjusted figures would indicate that a smaller proportion of the financing has come from debt than the historical statements indicated. The improvement in the debt/equity ratio would be offset by a reduced times interest earned ratio. In summary, the profitability of the firm would decrease, and the long-term debt position would improve, according to the times interest earned, but a smaller proportion of assets would be financed by debt.

A firm that has a large proportion of its financing in debt would find that inflation can also have a material impact on the adjusted statements. This type of firm would have a large monetary gain from holding the monetary liabilities, which would result in an improved profit picture and an improved long-term debt position, both in terms of times interest earned and debt to equity.

Some firms will have a mixture of a large investment in productive fixed assets and a large proportion of their financing in debt. Such firms would often have a net gain from the restatement because of the large purchasing power gain on monetary liabilities. This would be the case for the typical public utility. This type of firm would show an improved long-term debt position. The times interest earned and the debt ratios would also be improved.

CURRENT COST ACCOUNTING

Current cost is equal to the current replacement cost of the same asset owned, adjusted for the value of any operating advantages or disadvantages. Current cost information attempts to reflect the current value of certain balance sheet items. It measures specific changes in the prices of goods and services.

Under current cost accounting, such nonmonetary accounts as inventory and fixed assets are reported on the balance sheet at their current cost. On the income statement, the cost of goods sold and depreciation expense are also measured at current cost. The comprehensive current cost approach also recognizes income as the value of nonmonetary assets changes. This change, termed a *holding gain,* is unrealized until the asset is sold (as with inventory) or its use recognized (as with fixed assets) and then realized at that point. Unrealized holding gains occur on the unsold portion of inventory and the undepreciated portion of fixed assets.

The Hawkeye Company illustration will now be continued on a current cost basis in Exhibits 14-6, 14-7, and 14-8.

EXHIBIT 14-6 **HAWKEYE COMPANY**
Summary of Unrealized and Realized Holding Gains
For the Year Ended December 31, 1998

	Historical Cost	Current Cost	Difference
Inventory, 1/1/98	$ 30,000	$ 35,000	$ 5,000
Inventory, 12/31/98	50,000	60,000	10,000
Cost of goods sold	130,000	150,000	20,000
Property, plant, and equipment (net), 1/1/98	110,000	154,000	44,000
Property, plant, and equipment (net), 12/31/98	140,000	210,000	70,000
Depreciation expense	10,000	18,000	8,000

	Inventory	Property, Plant, and Equipment	Total
Unrealized gains:			
at 1/1/98	$ 5,000	$ 44,000	$ 49,000
at 12/31/98	10,000	70,000	80,000
Increase in unrealized gains	5,000	26,000	31,000
Realized gains	20,000	8,000	28,000
Increase in current cost of assets held during the year (total holding gain)	$ 25,000	$ 34,000	$ 59,000

EXHIBIT 14-7 **HAWKEYE COMPANY**
Current Cost Statement of Earnings and Retained Earnings
For the Year Ended December 31, 1998

Sales	$350,000
Cost of goods sold	150,000
Gross profit	200,000
Operating expenses	(110,000)
Depreciation	(18,000)
Operating profit	72,000
Less: Interest expense	8,000
Income before income taxes	64,000
Less: Income taxes	50,000
Current cost income before holding gains	14,000
Realized holding gains	28,000
Unrealized holding gains	31,000
Current cost net income	73,000
Retained earnings, January 1, 1998	64,000
	137,000
Cash dividends	7,000
Retained earnings, December 31, 1998	$130,000

EXHIBIT 14-8 **HAWKEYE COMPANY**
Current Cost Balance Sheet
December 31, 1997 and 1998

	1997		1998	
Assets				
Current assets:				
Cash		$ 45,000		$ 25,000
Accounts receivable (net)		35,000		30,000
Inventory		35,000		60,000
Total current assets		115,000		115,000
Property, plant, and equipment	$196,000		$270,000	
Less: Accumulated depreciation	42,000	154,000	60,000	210,000
Total assets		$ 269,000		$325,000
Liabilities and Stockholders' Equity				
Current liabilities:				
Accounts payable		$ 40,000		$ 15,000
Accrued payroll		5,000		10,000
Notes payable		40,000		40,000
Total current liabilities		85,000		65,000
Stockholders' equity:				
Capital stock		120,000		130,000
Retained earnings		64,000		130,000
Total stockholders' equity		184,000		260,000
Total liabilities and stockholders' equity		$ 269,000		$325,000

Consider the following additional information when referring to Exhibit 14-1 and Exhibit 14-2:

1. The cost of goods sold on a current cost basis at different dates during the year is $150,000. The current cost of the inventory at the end of 1998 is $60,000; at the beginning of 1998, $35,000.

2. The current cost of the property, plant, and equipment at the end of 1998, excluding depreciation, is $270,000; the net current cost is $210,000. The current cost of the property, plant, and equipment at the beginning of 1998, excluding depreciation, is $196,000; the net current cost is $154,000. Depreciation expense on a current cost basis is $18,000.

3. All other expenses are the same on a historical and a current cost basis.

As with constant dollar accounting, the increased value of inventory improves the liquidity picture. The profitability situation must be viewed carefully. The higher cost of goods sold and depreciation expense cause current cost income before holding gains to drop, often sharply. However, for some firms (such as high-technology firms), the cost of replacing inventory, plant, and equipment can actually be less than the historical cost. Holding gains included in profitability analysis may improve the profit picture substantially, even if the firm is not a high-technology firm. Part of the holding gains, however, is as yet unrealized. The long-term debt-paying ability may look mixed, as debt to equity may increase or decrease; but times interest earned will decrease because it is measured before any type of holding gains.

FINANCIAL REPORTING AND CHANGING PRICES

Based on SFAS No. 33, "Financial Reporting and Changing Prices," companies experimented with constant dollar and current cost accounting in the period from 1979-1986. These data were presented as supplementary information in published annual reports and were unaudited.

David Masso, a FASB member, dissented to the 1986 elimination of these disclosures. Masso stated:

The basic proposition underlying Statement No. 33—that inflation causes historical cost financial statements to show illusory profits and mask erosion of capital—is virtually undisputed. Specific price changes are inextricably linked to general inflation, and the combination of general and specific price changes seriously reduces the relevance, the representational faithfulness, and the comparability of historical cost financial statements.

Although the current inflation rate in the United States is relatively low in the context of recent history, its compound effect through time is still highly significant. High inflation rates prevail in many countries where U.S. corporations operate. Rates from country to country vary from time to time. Those distortive influences on financial statements will now go materially unmeasured and undisclosed.

Although SFAS No. 33 had obvious shortcomings, it was a base on which to build, it represented years of due process—research, debate, deliberations, decisions—and application experience. As last amended, it had made significant progress in eliminating alternative concepts and methodologies. Its recision means that much of that due process and application experience will have to be repeated in response to a future inflation crisis. That will entail great cost in terms of time, money, and creative talent; and because due process does not permit quick reaction to crises, it risks loss of credibility for the Board and loss of initiative in private sector standard setting.[1]

Some real estate companies have attempted to reflect value by disclosing current value in addition to the conventional accounting. Further comments on this are in Chapter 15.

Many companies include comments in their management discussion and analysis relating to inflation. Examples from 1995 annual reports follow:

Norfolk Southern
Inflation

Generally accepted accounting principles require the use of historical cost in preparing financial statements. This approach disregards the effects of inflation on the replacement cost of property. NS, a capital-intensive company, has approximately $13.6 billion invested in such assets. The replacement cost of these assets, as well as the related depreciation expense, would be substantially greater than the amounts reported on the basis of historical cost.

Orange and Rockland Utilities, Inc.
Effects of Inflation

The Company's utility revenues are based on rate regulation, which provides for recovery of operating costs and a return on rate base.

Inflation affects the Company's construction costs, operating expenses, and interest charges and can impact the Company's financial performance if rate relief is not granted on a timely basis. Financial statements, which are prepared in accordance with generally accepted accounting principles, report operating results in terms of historic costs and do not generally recognize the impact of inflation.

Mid Am, Inc.
Effects of Inflation

The effect of inflation on financial institutions differs from the impact on nonfinancial institutions. Financial institutions, as financial intermediaries, have assets and liabilities which may move in concert with inflation. This is especially true for financial institutions with a high percentage of rate-sensitive interest-earning assets and interest-bearing liabilities. A financial institution can reduce the impact of inflation by managing its interest rate sensitivity gap.

HFS Incorporated
Impact of Inflation

The primary source of revenue of the Company is based on a percentage of the franchised lodging facilities' gross room revenue and franchised real estate brokerage offices' gross commission revenue. As a result, the Company's revenue (excluding those changes attributable to a change in the number of franchises) is expected to change consistent with the trend of the consumer price index. The Company does not believe that inflation would have an unfavorable impact on its operations.

Nordson Corporation
Effects of Foreign Currency and Inflation (in Part)

Inflation puts pressure on profit margins because the ability to pass cost increases onto customers is restricted by competitive pricing. Although inflation has been modest in recent years, and its effect is not material for the years covered by the financial statements, Nordson continues to seek ways to minimize the impact of inflation through efforts to achieve greater productivity.

SUMMARY

Changing prices, both constant dollar and current cost, can have a major impact on all aspects of a firm's financial position and profitability. Although comprehensive accounting for changing prices is not now required, the reviewer of financial statements should have a reasonable understanding of how changing prices can affect the financial statements.

QUESTIONS

Q 14-1.   In what way are traditional financial statements not designed to account for changing prices?

Q 14-2.   Differentiate between current cost and constant dollar accounting.

Q 14-3.   Which changing price adjustments measure specific changes in prices, and which measure general changes in the level of prices?   Are these changes necessarily at the same rate?

Q 14-4.   What is meant by a *monetary account?*   Give an example of a monetary asset and a monetary liability.

Q 14-5.   What is meant by a *nonmonetary account?*   Give an example of a nonmonetary asset and a nonmonetary liability.

Q 14-6.   Why is there a loss in purchasing power from holding monetary assets and a gain in purchasing power from holding monetary liabilities during an inflationary period?

Q 14-7.   Why do nonmonetary accounts need to be adjusted to state these accounts in terms of their new purchasing power for constant dollar statements?

Q 14-8.   When statements are adjusted for general price-level changes, one often finds that the amount of working capital and the current ratio have improved. Often, these results come from the change in inventory.   Explain.

Q 14-9.   What influence will a large investment in productive fixed assets have on constant dollar statements during a time of inflation?

Q 14-10.   What influence will a large proportion of debt have on constant dollar statements during a time of inflation?

Q 14-11.   Explain how depreciation expense and the cost of goods sold change under current cost accounting.

Q 14-12.   What is meant by the term *holding gains?*   Differentiate between realized and unrealized holding gains.

Q 14-13.   Assume that land had been purchased for $20,000 and that the general price level increased by 60% since the acquisition.   Answer the following:

a.   What is the historical cost of the land?
b.   If constant dollar statements are prepared, what figure is used for land?
c.   If current cost statements are prepared, will the figure be higher or lower than the constant dollar figure?

Q 14-14.   What is the major current asset account affected by constant dollar accounting? How does inflation affect days' sales in inventory and the current ratio?

Q 14-15.   During the past fiscal year, Burger Company had a net monetary balance of assets over liabilities. Prices rose by 10%. Would this condition give rise to a purchasing power gain or loss? Explain.

Q 14-16.   Current cost income is always lower than constant dollar income. Discuss.

Q 14-17.   How does inflation affect return on net assets?

Q 14-18.   What does an inflation-adjusted price/earnings ratio indicate to the investor?

Q 14-19.   Inflation-adjusted dividend payout ratios sometimes exceed 1 to 1. What does this indicate?

Q 14-20.   The conventional statements reflect depreciation computed on a historical cost basis. One of the basic assumptions under which financial statements are prepared is the going concern assumption. Comment on how there can be a possible conflict between computing depreciation based on historical cost and the going concern assumption during a long period of inflation.

Q 14-21.   Accountants normally rely on objective data to give them a cost basis for recorded transactions. Will current cost data be as objective as traditional historical data? Comment.

Q 14-22.   During a period of inflation, which of the following items would result in a purchasing power gain, a purchasing power loss, or neither?

a.   Bonds payable
b.   Accounts payable
c.   Cash
d.   Notes receivable
e.   Land

Q 14-23.   "When prices are going up, they all go up." Comment on this statement and give an example to illustrate your comment.

PROBLEMS

P 14-1.   XYZ, Inc. presented the following simplified balance sheet comparison in 1998:

	December	
	1998	**1997**
Assets		
Cash	$ 60,000	$ 30,000
Receivables	70,000	35,000
Inventory	120,000	90,000
Total current assets	250,000	155,000
Plant, property, and equipment, net	150,000	145,000
Total assets	$400,000	$300,000
Liabilities and Stockholders' Equity		
Current liabilities	$ 90,000	$ 60,000
Long-term debt	100,000	60,000
Stockholders' equity	210,000	180,000
Total liabilities and stockholders' equity	$400,000	$300,000

The change in monetary accounts came from transactions that occurred evenly throughout the year. The relevant price indices follow:

	1998	**1997**
Year-end	250	225
Year average	240	220

Required   a.   Separate the accounts into monetary and nonmonetary.
             b.   Compute the purchasing power gain or loss in year-end 1998 dollars.

P 14-2.   Integrated Electronics is a retailing operation with leased facilities. The company's maverick accountant elected to experiment with current cost in the first year of business. At the start of the first year, 1998, the company purchased $1,000,000 in inventory and at the end of the year held an inventory of $600,000 on a historical cost basis and $875,000 on a current cost basis. When the inventory was sold, the current cost was $550,000. Sales for the year, incurred evenly, were $800,000. Other expenses, including rent, were $100,000 on both a current cost and historical basis.

Required   Prepare a comprehensive current cost income statement. Ignore tax effects.

P 14-3.   Arrow Company's primary financial statements report financial information on the basis of prices that were in effect when the transactions occurred (historical costs). The following information has been prepared to portray certain aspects of changing prices:

	As Reported (Historical Cost)		Adjusted for Changes in Specific Prices (Current Cost)	
Net sales		$380,000		$380,000
Cost of goods sold	$160,000		$180,000	
Depreciation	19,000		27,000	
Other operating expense	120,000		120,000	
Income tax expense	30,000		30,000	
Total expenses		329,000		357,000
Income from continuing operations		$ 51,000		$ 23,000

	Inventory	Property, Plant, and Equipment
Current cost:		
Specific price (current cost) at year-end	$105,000	$205,000
Increase (decrease) in current costs:		
Increase in specific prices	$ 23,000	$ 44,000
Effect of increase in general price level	12,400	28,000
Excess of increase in specific prices over increase in the general price level	$ 10,600	$ 16,000

Required

a. The inflation footnote discloses current cost of properties of $205,000, while the balance sheet discloses plant and properties of $143,000. Indicate the cause of the difference between these two figures.

b. The inflation footnote discloses depreciation as reported (historical cost) at $19,000 and specific prices (current cost) at $27,000. Indicate the cause of the difference between these two figures.

c. In calculating the current cost of properties, the company relied on published price indexes, so the current cost relates to assets owned by the company rather than technologically different or superior assets that may be available. Among other important considerations, potential improvements in manufacturing efficiencies and cost savings are not reflected in the adjusted income statement. Does this imply that the income from continuing operations adjusted for changes in specific prices ($23,000) is overstated or understated? Discuss.

d. Is the dollar amount of the inventory reported on the balance sheet more or less than the inventory at current cost amounts? Explain.

e. Using current cost, would you expect the working capital and current ratio to be higher than when historical cost is used? Why?

    f.   The historical cost of products sold was $160,000, and the current cost of products sold was $180,000.
1. Indicate reasons for the difference.
2. Speculate on why the historical cost of products sold was similar to the current cost of products sold.

    g. For this company, is the effect of general prices on inventories and properties held during the year greater or less than the effect of specific prices of inventories and properties? Discuss.

P 14-4.   Excerpts from the trial balance of Smolen Company as of December 31, 1998 include the following accounts:

Inventory, LIFO	$ 60,000
Notes receivable	150,000
Bonds payable	175,000
Depreciation expense—plant and equipment	20,000
Sales	350,000
Land	280,000
Plant and equipment	500,000
Notes payable	80,000

During 1998, the average price index was 130. At December 31, 1998, the price index was 136. The plant and equipment was purchased in 1990 when the index was 110. The LIFO inventory was built up during 1992 when the average index was 114. The land was purchased in 1990 when the index was 109.

Required   a. At what amounts would these accounts be presented in constant dollar financial statements in 1998 average-for-year dollars?

    b. At what amounts would these accounts be presented in constant dollar financial statements in 1998 end-of-year dollars?

P 14-5.   Presented below are selected price indices:

December 31, 1998	180
Average 1998	175
July 1, 1987	160
January 20, 1980	140
July 20, 1979	138

Selected accounts at December 31, 1998:
Cash
Trucks (purchased July 1, 1984)
Land (purchased January 20, 1980)
Common stock (issued July 20, 1979)

Depreciation (on trucks purchased July 1, 1984)
Sales
Accounts payable (relate to purchases in 1998)
Purchases
Interest expense (incurred evenly through 1998)

Required   a. Indicate the numerator and the denominator for each account to adjust for constant dollar presentation at December 31, 1998 in end-of-year dollars.
             b. Indicate the numerator and the denominator for each account to adjust for constant dollar presentation at December 31, 1998 in average-for-year dollars.

P 14-6.   Gossett Company showed the following cost of goods sold for 1998:

Inventory, December 31, 1997	$20,000
Purchases	60,000
Cost of goods available for sale	80,000
Less: Inventory, December 31, 1998	12,000
Cost of goods sold	$68,000

The current cost of the inventory was $5.00 at December 31, 1997 and $5.50 at December 31, 1998. The company uses a LIFO cost flow assumption. The December 31, 1997 inventory consisted of 5,000 units purchased on October 1, 1980. The December 31, 1998 inventory consisted of 3,000 units purchased on October 1, 1980. Purchases of 11,430 units were made during 1998.
The price index was as follows:

December 31, 1997	160
December 31, 1998	170
Average 1998	165
October 1, 1980	140

Required   a. Determine the current cost of inventory at December 31, 1997.
             b. Determine the current cost of inventory at December 31, 1998.
             c. Determine the cost of goods sold on a current cost basis.
             d. Determine the constant dollar inventory at December 31, 1997 using average 1998 dollars.
             e. Determine the constant dollar inventory at December 31, 1998 using average 1998 dollars.
             f. Determine the cost of goods sold on a constant dollar basis, using average 1998 dollars.

P 14-7.   Arrow Company is preparing a constant dollar balance sheet for December 31, 1998. The following are selected accounts and their amounts:

Cash	$ 20,000	
Accounts receivable (net)	30,000	(originated when the index was 140)
Inventory	40,000	(originated when the index was 110)
Plant and equipment	100,000	(originated when the index was 100)
Accounts payable	15,000	(originated when the index was 145)
Bonds payable	100,000	(originated when the index was 100)

The average price index for the year was 160, and the end-of-year index was 165.

Required a. Compute the amounts that would appear in the constant dollar balance sheet at the average price index for the year.

  b. Compute the amounts that would appear in the constant dollar balance sheet at the end-of-year price index.

P 14-8. Quickie Rice Company sells Rice-O-Matic, a device that reduces the time required to prepare rice. Inventory at the beginning of the accounting period was one unit at $35. Two more units were purchased during the period, the first at $39, and the second at $43. One unit was sold at $65. Replacement cost at the end of the accounting period was $46.

Required The following questions relate to Quickie Rice Company.

  a. What is the ending inventory under LIFO?
    1. $82
    2. $78
    3. $74
    4. None of the above

  b. What is the gross profit under FIFO?
    1. $30
    2. $26
    3. $22
    4. None of the above

  c. What is the unrealized holding period gain under LIFO?
    1. $10
    2. $12
    3. $18
    4. None of the above

  d. What is the comprehensive income (income including both conventional income and unrealized holding period gains) under FIFO?
    1. $30
    2. $40
    3. $48
    4. None of the above

CFA Adapted

Endnotes

1   *Statement of Financial Accounting Standards No. 89*, "Financial Reporting and Changing Prices" (Stamford, CT: Financial Accounting Standards Board, 1986), paragraph 4.

15 Statement Analysis for Special Industries: Banks, Utilities, Oil and Gas, Transportation, Insurance, Real Estate Companies

THE PRECEDING CHAPTERS COVERED MATERIAL MOST applicable to manufacturing, retailing, wholesaling, and service industries. This chapter problems in analyzing six specialized industries: banks, electric utilities, oil and gas, transportation, insurance, and real estate companies. The chapter notes the differences in statements and suggests changes or additions to analysis.

BANKS

Banks operate under either a federal or state charter. National banks are required to submit uniform accounting statements to the Comptroller of the Currency. State banks are controlled by their state banking departments. In addition, the Federal Deposit Insurance Corporation and the Board of Governors of the Federal Reserve System receive financial and operating statements from all members of the Federal Reserve System. Member banks are required to keep reserves with their district Federal Reserve bank. State banking laws also dictate the geographical area within which a bank may function. The range runs from within one county to interstate.

Banking systems usually involve two types of structures: individual banks and bank holding companies. **Bank holding companies** consist of a parent that owns one or many banks. Additionally, the holding company may own bank-related financial services and nonfinancial subsidiaries. In financial statement analysis, we must determine the extent of the business generated by banking services. In order for the specific industry ratios to be meaningful, a large proportion of the services should be bank related.

Exhibit 15-1, pages 627-631, presents part of the 1995 annual report of Huntington Bancshares Incorporated. Located in Columbus, Ohio, Huntington Bancshares Incorporated has offices throughout Ohio and has purchased several banks in Michigan, Indiana, Kentucky, West Virginia, and Florida. It also has nonbanking services in approximately fourteen states.

Balance Sheet

The balance sheet of a commercial bank is sometimes termed the *report of condition*. Two significant differences exist between the traditional balance sheet and that of a bank. First, the accounts of banks may seem the opposite of those of other types of firms. Checking accounts or demand deposits are liabilities to a bank, since it owes the customers money in these cases. Similarly, loans to customers are assets—receivables. Further, the balance sheet accounts are not subdivided into current and noncurrent accounts.

Some banks provide a very detailed disclosure of their assets and liabilities. Other banks provide only general disclosure. The quality of review that can be performed can be no better than the disclosure.

Representative assets of a bank may include cash on hand or due from other banks, investment securities, loans, bank premises, and equipment. Closely review the disclosure of a bank's assets. This review may indicate risk or opportunity. For example, a review of the assets may indicate that the bank has a substantial risk if interest rates increase. The general rule is that for 20-year fixed obligations, a gain or loss of 8% of principal arises when interest rates change by 1%. Thus, an investment of $100,000,000 in 20-year bonds would lose approximately $32,000,000 in principal if interest rates increased by 4%. A similar example would be a bank that holds long-term fixed-rate mortgages. The value of these mortgages could decline substantially if interest rates increased. Many bank annual reports do not disclose the amount of fixed-rate mortgages.

For debt and equity investments, review the stockholders' equity section of the balance sheet to determine if significant unrealized gains (losses) exist. For Huntington Bancshares, net unrealized gains (losses) on securities available for sale were gains in 1995 of $40,972,000, and losses in 1994 of $63,289,000.

In recent years, Less Developed Country (LDC) loans have become a national issue. In general, LDC loans are perceived as being more risky than domestic loans. Huntington Bancshares apparently did not have LDC loans at December 31, 1995.

As part of the review of assets, review the disclosure that describes related-party loans. Observe the materiality and the trend of these loans. Footnote 4 in the Huntington Bancshares annual report indicates related-party loans totaling $142,638,000 at December 31, 1995, an increase from $98,225,000 at December 31, 1994.

Review the disclosure of allowance for loan losses. It may indicate a significant change and/or significant losses charged. Huntington Bancshares disclosed allowance for loan losses of $194,456,000, $200,492,000, and $211,835,000 at December 31, 1995, 1994, and 1993, respectively.

EXHIBIT 15-1 **HUNTINGTON BANCSHARES INCORPORATED**
Selected Data from 1995 Annual Report
Consolidated Statements of Income

(In thousands of dollars, except per-share amounts) Year Ended December 31	**1995**	**1994**	**1993**
Interest and fee income			
Loans	$ 1,156,446	$ 975,604	$ 896,932
Securities			
Taxable	281,633	198,594	254,795
Tax-exempt	8,099	13,663	20,268
Mortgages held for sale	9,807	25,886	60,188
Other	5,911	5,974	4,128
Total interest income	1,461,896	1,219,721	1,236,311
Interest expense			
Deposits	425,631	294,780	317,545
Short-term borrowings	212,110	106,646	89,444
Long-term debt	99,592	62,245	33,122
Total interest expense	737,333	463,671	440,111
Net interest income	724,563	756,050	796,200
Provision for loan losses	28,721	15,284	79,294
Net interest income after provision for loan losses	695,842	740,766	716,906
Total non-interest income	248,390	222,314	293,365
Total non-interest expense	(565,784)	(596,606)	(646,480)
Income before income tax expense	378,448	366,474	363,791
Provision for income taxes	133,959	123,881	126,879
Net income	$ 244,489	$ 242,593	$ 236,912
Per common share[1]			
Net income	$1.78	$1.78	$1.76
Cash dividends	$ .78	$ .68	$ .56
Average common shares outstanding	137,702,243	136,209,760	134,729,322

[1]Restated for the five percent stock dividend distributed July 31, 1995.

(continued)

EXHIBIT 15-1   (continued)
Consolidated Balance Sheets

(In thousands of dollars)	1995	1994
Assets		
Cash and due from banks	$ 860,958	$ 885,327
Interest-bearing deposits in banks	284,393	3,059
Trading account securities	12,924	9,427
Federal funds sold and securities purchased under resale agreements	197,531	5,329
Mortgages held for sale	159,705	138,997
Securities available for sale—at fair value	4,721,144	3,304,493
Investment securities—fair value, $69,196 and $474,147, respectively	67,604	475,692
Total loans	13,261,667	12,264,436
Less allowance for loan losses	194,456	200,492
Net loans	13,067,211	12,063,944
Premises and equipment	296,465	288,793
Customers' acceptance liability	56,926	53,883
Accrued income and other assets	529,737	541,696
Total Assets	$20,254,598	$17,770,640
Liabilities and Shareholders' Equity		
Demand deposits		
Non-interest-bearing	$ 2,088,074	$ 2,169,095
Interest-bearing	2,772,845	2,646,785
Savings deposits	2,207,378	2,227,406
Certificates of deposit of $100,000 or more	909,403	605,763
Other domestic time deposits	4,384,949	3,909,061
Foreign time deposits	273,933	406,957
Total deposits	12,636,582	11,965,067
Short-term borrowings	3,514,773	2,898,201
Bank acceptances outstanding	56,926	53,883
Long-term debt	2,103,024	1,214,052
Accrued expenses and other liabilities	424,428	227,617
Total Liabilities	18,735,733	16,358,820
Shareholders' equity		
Preferred stock—authorized 6,617,808 shares; none outstanding		
Common stock—without par value; authorized 200,000,000 shares; issued and outstanding—141,402,769 and 131,119,504 shares, respectively	1,056,209	912,318
Less 8,351,978 and 904,739 treasury shares, respectively	(180,632)	(16,577)
Capital surplus	235,802	215,084
Net unrealized gains (losses) on securities available for sale	40,972	(63,289)
Retained earnings	366,514	364,284
Total Shareholders' Equity	1,518,865	1,411,820
Total Liabilities and Shareholders' Equity	$20,254,598	$17,770,640

EXHIBIT 15-1 (continued)
Consolidated Statement of Cash Flows

(In thousands of dollars)	1995	1994	1993
Operating Activities			
Net income	$ 244,489	$ 242,593	$ 236,912
Adjustments to reconcile net income to net cash provided by operating activities			
Provision for loan losses	28,721	15,284	79,294
Provision for depreciation and amortization	68,763	84,215	127,459
Deferred income tax expense (benefit)	26,694	57,329	(30,412)
(Increase) decrease in trading account securities	(3,497)	12,537	(20,681)
(Increase) decrease in mortgages held for sale	(20,708)	893,341	(288,296)
Gain on sale of subsidiary	(8,939)	—	—
Net gains on sales of securities	(9,056)	(2,594)	(27,189)
(Increase) decrease in accrued income receivable	(23,331)	(247)	3,924
Net increase in other assets	(37,053)	(59,397)	(63,791)
Increase (decrease) in accrued expenses	112,963	(22,033)	(8,775)
Net increase (decrease) in other liabilities	879	(46,649)	48,157
Net cash provided by operating activities	379,925	1,174,379	56,602
Investing Activities			
(Increase) decrease in interest-bearing deposits in banks	(281,334)	9,551	152,077
Proceeds from:			
Maturities and calls of investment securities	82,082	86,027	308,654
Maturities and calls of securities available for sale	216,878	317,031	542,062
Sales of investment securities	—	—	252,590
Sales of securities available for sale	2,653,545	2,316,843	2,306,111
Purchases of:			
Investment securities	(2,660)	(230,676)	(239,164)
Securities available for sale	(3,719,144)	(2,146,362)	(2,956,527)
Proceeds from sales of loans	306,105	—	—
Net loan originations, excluding sales	(1,267,185)	(1,187,428)	(959,314)
Proceeds from disposal of premises and equipment	2,902	1,200	13,035
Purchases of premises and equipment	(33,429)	(25,938)	(56,820)
Proceeds from sales of other real estate	30,133	44,484	24,169
Net cash received (paid) from purchase/sale of subsidiaries	165,803	2,670	(13,173)
Net cash used for investing activities	(1,846,304)	(812,598)	(626,300)
Financing Activities			
Increase (decrease) in total deposits	397,675	(240,219)	(300,206)
Increase (decrease) in short-term borrowings	620,369	(303,287)	517,008
Proceeds from issuance of long-term debt	1,095,220	475,000	560,961
Payment of long-term debt	(206,166)	(26,415)	(278,611)
Dividends paid on common stock	(105,520)	(87,545)	(61,892)
Acquisition of treasury stock	(204,645)	(73,634)	(36,795)
Proceeds from issuance of treasury stock	37,279	39,896	22,594
Net cash provided by (used for) financing activities	1,634,212	(216,204)	423,059
Change in cash and cash equivalents	167,833	145,577	(146,639)
Cash and cash equivalents at beginning of year	890,656	745,079	891,718
Cash and cash equivalents at end of year	$ 1,058,489	$ 890,656	$ 745,079

Note: Huntington Bancshares made interest payments of $667,712, $451,694, and $430,701 in 1995, 1994, and 1993, respectively. Federal income tax payments were $100,039 in 1995, $97,775 in 1994, and $155,457 in 1993.

(continued)

EXHIBIT 15-1   (continued)
Consolidated Average Balances and Interest Rates (Annual Data)
(Note: In the annual report this statement was presented for 1990-1995.)

Fully Tax Equivalent Basis[1]	1995			1994		
(In millions of dollars)	Average Balance	Interest Income/ Expense	Yield/ Rate	Average Balance	Interest Income/ Expense	Yield/ Rate
Assets						
Interest-bearing deposits in banks	$ 21	$ 1.3	5.99%	$ 4	$ .3	7.57%
Trading account securities	23	1.7	7.29	14	.9	6.16
Federal funds sold and securities						
purchased under resale agreements	46	3.0	6.45	115	5.0	4.32
Mortgages held for sale	130	9.8	7.58	367	25.9	7.06
Securities						
Taxable	4,191	281.6	6.72	3,217	198.6	6.17
Tax exempt	124	12.6	10.30	190	20.5	10.80
Total securities	4,315	294.2	6.82	3,407	219.1	6.43
Loans						
Commercial	4,049	341.1	8.43	3,565	302.2	8.48
Real estate						
Construction	339	29.1	8.58	298	23.1	7.75
Mortgage	3,070	256.6	8.36	2,786	220.3	7.91
Consumer	4,892	434.3	8.88	4,316	354.2	8.21
Lease financing	731	57.1	7.81	556	40.8	7.34
Total loans	13,081	1,118.2	8.55	11,521	940.6	8.16
Allowance for loan losses/loan						
fees	200	40.4		212	37.4	
Net loans	12,881	1,158.6	8.86	11,309	978.0	8.49
Total earning assets	17,616	$1,468.6	8.34	15,428	$1,229.2	7.97
Cash and due from banks	780			741		
All other assets	852			793		
Total Assets	$19,048			$16,750		
Liabilities and Shareholders' Equity						
Demand deposits:						
Non-interest-bearing	$ 2,179			$ 2,116		
Interest-bearing	2,539	$ 62.2	2.45%	2,713	$ 59.9	2.21%
Savings deposits	2,053	56.4	2.75	2,281	49.0	2.15
Certificates of deposit of $100,000 or						
more	812	47.1	5.80	607	25.6	4.22
Other domestic time deposits	4,383	242.9	5.54	3,523	148.1	4.20
Foreign time deposits	261	17.0	6.50	286	12.2	4.25
Total deposits	12,227	425.6	3.48	11,526	294.8	3.13
Short-term borrowings	3,491	212.1	6.08	2,629	106.7	4.06
Long-term debt	1,424	99.6	7.00	928	62.2	6.71
Interest-bearing liabilities	14,963	$ 737.3	4.93	12,967	$ 463.7	3.58
All other liabilities	403			264		
Shareholders' equity	1,503			1,403		
Total Liabilities and Shareholders' Equity	$19,048			$16,750		

EXHIBIT 15-1   (concluded)

	1995		1994	
	Interest Income/ Expense	Yield/ Rate	Interest Income/ Expense	Yield/ Rate
Net interest rate spread		3.41%		4.39%
Impact of non-interest-bearing funds on margin		.74		.57
Net Interest Income/Margin	$731.3	4.15	$765.5	4.96

[1] Fully tax equivalent yields are calculated assuming a 35% tax rate. Average loan balances include nonaccruing loans. Loan income includes cash received on nonaccruing loans.

Review the footnotes and Management's Discussion and Analysis for disclosure of nonperforming assets. In general, **nonperforming assets** are those for which the bank is not receiving income or is receiving reduced income. The categories of nonperforming assets are nonaccrual loans, renegotiated loans, and other real estate. *Nonaccrual loans* are loans for which payments have fallen significantly behind, so that the bank has stopped accruing interest income on these loans. *Renegotiated loans* are loans that the bank has renegotiated with a customer because the customer has had trouble meeting the terms of the original loan. For example, a loan in the amount of $10,000,000 and 10% interest may come due. The customer who cannot pay may be allowed to renegotiate the loan with the bank, reducing the principle to $8,000,000 and the interest rate to 6% and gaining a five-year extension. Under current GAAP, no immediate loss will be taken by the bank on the renegotiated loan if the projected cash flow under the renegotiated loan will cover the current book value of the loan. In the example, the projected cash flow comes to $10,400,000 ($8,000,000 in principal and $480,000 in interest each year for five years). Since this covers the current book figure of $10,000,000, no immediate loss will be recognized. In addition to other factors, banks should consider renegotiated loans when they adjust the loan loss reserve.

Other real estate usually consists of real estate the bank has taken when it foreclosed on a loan. For example, the bank may have made a loan to a company for a hotel and accepted a mortgage on the hotel as collateral. If the bank must foreclose on the loan, it may take possession of the hotel. The bank would want to sell the hotel, but it may be necessary to hold and operate the hotel for a relatively long period of time before a buyer can be found.

The amount and trend of nonperforming assets should be observed closely. This can be an early indication of troubles to come. For example, a significant increase in nonperforming assets late in the year may have had an insignificant effect on the past year's profits, but it could indicate a significant negative influence on the future year's profits.

Huntington Bancshares discloses nonperforming assets for 1995 in Management's Discussion and Analysis. The disclosure indicates that nonperforming assets significantly decreased at the end of 1995 in comparison with prior years. This is a very positive indicator of the quality of the assets.

Typical liabilities of a bank include savings, time and demand deposits, loan obligations, and long-term debt. Closely review the disclosure of liabilities for favorable or unfavorable trends. For example, a decreasing amount in savings deposits would indicate that the bank is losing one of its cheapest sources of funds.

As part of the review of liabilities, look for a footnote that describes commitments and contingent liabilities. This footnote may reveal significant additional commitments and contingent liabilities. Huntington Bancshares discloses significant commitments to extend credit. They also have standby letters of credit and commercial letters of credit.

The stockholders' equity of a bank resembles that of other types of firms, except that the total stockholders' equity is usually very low in relation to total assets. A general guide for many years was that a bank's stockholders' equity should be approximately 10% of total assets, but very few banks in recent years have had that much stockholders' equity. Currently, stockholders' equity of 6%-7% would probably be considered favorable. In general, the lower the proportion of stockholders' equity in relation to total assets, the greater the risk of failure. A higher stockholders' equity in relation to total assets would probably improve safety, but the bank would perhaps be less profitable because of the additional capital requirement.

As part of the analysis of stockholders' equity, review the statement of stockholders' equity and the related footnotes for any significant changes. For Huntington Bancshares, there was a 5% stock dividend and a substantial increase in treasury shares during 1995.

The current approach by bank regulators is not only to view the adequacy of stockholders' equity in relation to total assets, but also to view capital in relation to risk-adjusted assets. New guidelines establishing minimum standards for risk-based capital were implemented in 1992. Huntington Bancshares discloses risk-based capital ratios in Management's Discussion and Analysis. Huntington Bancshares discloses that its "regulatory capital ratios exceeded the levels established for 'well-capitalized' institutions."

Income Statement

A bank's principal revenue source is usually interest income from loans and investment securities. The principal expense is usually interest expense on deposits and other debt. The difference between interest income and interest expense is termed *net interest income* or *net interest margin*.

The net interest margin is important to the profitability of a bank. Usually, falling interest rates are positive for a bank's interest margin because the bank will be able to reduce the interest rate that it pays for deposits before the average rate of return earned on loans and investments declines. Increasing interest rates are usually negative for a bank's interest margin because the bank will need to increase the interest rate on deposits, which is usually done before rates on loans and investments are adjusted.

Bank income statements include a separate section for other income. Typical other income includes trust department fees, service charges on deposit accounts, trading account profits (losses), and securities transactions.

The importance of other income has substantially increased for banks. For example, service charges have increased in importance in recent years since many banks have set service charges at a level to make the service profitable. This has frequently been the result of improved cost analysis. In addition, banks have been adding nontraditional sources of income, such as mortgage banking, sales of mutual funds, sales of annuities, and computer services for other banks and financial institutions.

Non-interest income increased substantially in 1995 for Huntington Bancshares. Huntington Bancshares disclosed in Management's Discussion and Analysis that it "achieved broadbased growth in non-interest income during the year just ended, with all categories but mortgage banking income showing improvement."

Expenses other than interest expense include such items as salaries and commissions, provision for loan losses (disclosed separately in the Huntington Bancshares statement), and provision for real estate losses. Investors should pay close attention to the provision for loan losses. An increase in the loan loss provision could indicate a problem with asset quality.

The provision for loan losses was $28,721,000 in 1995 for Huntington Bancshares. This was a substantial increase over 1994, but much less than 1993.

Ratios for Banks

Because of the vastly different accounts and statement formats, few of the traditional ratios are appropriate for banks. Exceptions include return on assets, return on equity, and most of the investment-related ratios. The following sections present meaningful ratios for bank analysis, but this is not a comprehensive treatment. The Bank Administration Institute, in its annual *Index of Bank Performance*, includes 43 ratios and growth statistics. The investment firm of Keefe, Bruyette & Woods, Inc., in its *Bankbook Report on Performance*, lists 21 financial ratios. Both are excellent sources of industry averages for banks.

Earning Assets to Total Assets   Earning assets includes loans, leases, investment securities, and money market assets. It excludes cash and nonearning deposits plus fixed assets. This ratio shows how well bank management puts bank assets to work. High-performance banks have a high ratio.

Banks typically present asset data on an average annual basis. Huntington Bancshares provides a schedule of average balances in its annual report. This schedule is used for the average total assets in computing earning assets to total assets. Exhibit 15-2 presents Huntington Bancshares' earning assets to total assets ratio, which has increased slightly between 1994 and 1995.

Return on Earning Assets   Return on earning assets, computed by dividing net income by average earning assets, is a profitability measure to be viewed in conjunction with return on assets and return on equity. Exhibit 15-3 presents this ratio for Huntington Bancshares; the ratio decreased moderately in 1995.

Interest Margin to Average Earning Assets   This is a key determinant of bank profitability, for it provides an indication of management's ability to control the spread between interest income and interest expense. Exhibit 15-4 presents this ratio for Huntington Bancshares and indicates a decline in profitability.

Loan Loss Coverage Ratio   The loan loss coverage ratio, computed by dividing pretax income plus provision for loan losses by net charge-offs, helps determine the asset quality and the level of protection of loans. Exhibit 15-5 presents this ratio for Huntington Bancshares. This ratio decreased moderately in 1995.

Equity Capital to Total Assets   This ratio, also called *funds to total assets*, measures the extent of equity ownership in the bank. This ownership provides the cushion against the risk of using debt and leverage. Exhibit 15-6 presents this ratio, computed by using average figures, for Huntington Bancshares. This ratio declined in 1995 to 7.89% from 8.38% in 1994. Both of these ratios appear to be very good.

EXHIBIT 15-2 **HUNTINGTON BANCSHARES INCORPORATED**
Earning Assets to Total Assets
1995 and 1994

(In millions of dollars)	1995	1994
Average earning assets [A]	$17,616	$15,428
Average total assets [B]	$19,048	$16,750
Earning assets to total assets [A÷B]	92.48%	92.11%

EXHIBIT 15-3 HUNTINGTON BANCSHARES INCORPORATED
Return on Earning Assets
For the Years Ended December 31, 1995 and 1994

(In thousands of dollars)	1995	1994
Net income [A]	$ 244,489	$ 242,593
Average earning assets [B]	$17,616,000	$15,428,000
Return on earning assets [A÷B]	1.39%	1.57%

EXHIBIT 15-4 HUNTINGTON BANCSHARES INCORPORATED
Interest Margin to Average Earning Assets
For the Years Ended December 31, 1995 and 1994

(In thousands of dollars)	1995	1994
Interest margin [A]	$ 724,563	$ 756,050
Average earning assets [B]	$17,616,000	$15,428,000
Interest margin to average earning assets [A÷B]	4.11%	4.90%

EXHIBIT 15-5 HUNTINGTON BANCSHARES INCORPORATED
Loan Loss Coverage Ratio
For the Years Ended December 31, 1995 and 1994

(In thousands of dollars)	1995	1994
Pretax income	$ 378,448	$ 366,474
Provision for loan losses	28,721	15,284
[A]	$ 407,169	$ 381,758
Net charge-offs [B]	$ 41,584	$ 28,020
Loan loss coverage ratio [A÷B]	9.79 times per year	13.62 times per year

EXHIBIT 15-6 HUNTINGTON BANCSHARES INCORPORATED
Equity Capital to Total Assets
For the Years Ended December 31, 1995 and 1994

(In millions of dollars)	1995	1994
Average equity [A]	$ 1,503	$ 1,403
Average total assets [B]	$19,048	$16,750
Equity capital to total assets [A÷B]	7.89%	8.38%

Deposits Times Capital   The ratio of deposits times capital concerns both depositors and stockholders. To some extent, it is a type of debt/ equity ratio, indicating a bank's debt position.   More capital implies a greater margin of safety, while a larger deposit base gives a prospect of higher return to shareholders, since more money is available for investment purposes. Exhibit 15-7 presents this ratio for Huntington Bancshares, based on average figures. Deposits times capital decreased slightly in 1995.

Loans to Deposits   Average total loans to average deposits is a type of asset to liability ratio. Loans make up a large portion of the bank's assets, and its principal obligations are the deposits that can be withdrawn on request—within time limitations. This is a type of debt coverage ratio, and it measures the position of the bank with regard to taking risks. Exhibit 15-8 shows this ratio for Huntington Bancshares. Loans to deposits increased moderately in 1995, indicating an increase in risk from a debt standpoint.

ELECTRIC UTILITIES

Electric utilities render a unique service on which the public depends. Electric utilities are basically monopolies subject to government regulation, including strict rate regulation. In recent years, laws have been enacted that greatly reduce the monopoly aspect. In general, the comments in this book that relate to electric utilities also apply to other utilities, such as gas utilities.

Services of electric utilities are consumed in the home or at the business premises. In general, substitute services are not available, rates have been determined primarily by regulatory agencies rather than by competition, and service areas have been small and localized. However, competition in rates and the size of service areas have increased substantially.

Uniformity of accounting is prescribed by the Federal Energy Regulatory Commission for interstate electric and gas companies and by the Federal Communications Commission for telephone and telegraph companies, as well as by state regulatory agencies.

Financial Statements

Balance sheets for utilities differ from business balance sheets mainly in the order accounts for utilities are presented. Plant and equipment

EXHIBIT 15-7 **HUNTINGTON BANCSHARES INCORPORATED**
Deposits Times Capital
For the Years Ended December 31, 1995 and 1994

(In millions of dollars)	1995	1994
Average deposits [A]	$12,227	$11,526
Average stockholders' equity [B]	$ 1,503	$ 1,403
Deposits times capital [A÷B]	8.14 times per year	8.22 times per year

are the first assets listed, followed by investments and other assets, current assets, and deferred charges. Under liabilities and equity, the first section is capitalization, followed by noncurrent liabilities (such as defueling and decommissioning liability, pension liability, and postemployment benefits), and other. The capitalization section usually includes all sources of long-term capital, such as common stock, preferred stock, and long-term debt.

The income statement for utilities is set up by operating revenues, less operating expenses to arrive at net operating income. Net operating income is adjusted by other income (deductions) to arrive at income before interest charges. Interest charges are then deducted to arrive at net income.

Exhibit 15-9, pages 638-642, presents a substantial part of the 1995 annual report of Public Service Company of Colorado. Review Exhibit 15-9 to become familiar with the form of electric utility financial statements.

EXHIBIT 15-8 **HUNTINGTON BANCSHARES INCORPORATED**
Loans to Deposits
For the Years Ended December 31, 1995 and 1994

(In millions of dollars)	1995	1994
Average total loans [A]	$12,881	$11,309
Average deposits [B]	$12,227	$11,526
Loans to deposits [A÷B]	105.35%	98.12%

EXHIBIT 15-9 PUBLIC SERVICE COMPANY OF COLORADO AND SUBSIDIARIES
Electric Utility Company
Selected Financial Data

Consolidated Statements of Income

Public Service Company of Colorado and Subsidiaries	Years Ended December 31, 1995, 1994, & 1993 (In thousands of dollars, except per-share data)		
	1995	1994	1993
Operating Revenues:			
Electric	$ 1,449,096	$ 1,399,836	$ 1,337,053
Gas	624,585	624,922	628,324
Other	36,920	32,626	33,308
	2,110,601	2,057,384	1,998,685
Operating Expenses:			
Fuel used in generation	181,995	198,118	194,918
Purchased power	481,958	437,087	396,953
Gas purchased for resale	392,680	397,877	384,393
Other operating expenses	350,093	369,094	376,686
Maintenance	64,069	67,097	76,229
Defueling and decommissioning (Note 2)	—	43,376	—
Depreciation and amortization	141,380	139,035	140,804
Taxes (other than income taxes)	81,319	86,408	86,775
Income taxes (Note 13)	95,357	48,500	60,994
	1,788,851	1,786,592	1,717,752
Operating Income	321,750	270,792	280,933
Other Income and Deductions:			
Allowance for equity funds used during construction	3,782	3,140	8,119
Gain on sale of WestGas Gathering, Inc. (Note 4)	—	34,485	—
Miscellaneous income and deductions—net	(2,770)	(6,014)	(1,355)
	1,012	31,611	6,764
Interest Charges:			
Interest on long-term debt	85,832	89,005	98,089
Amortization of debt discount and expense less premium	3,278	3,126	2,018
Other interest	58,109	44,021	34,778
Allowance for borrowed funds used during construction	(3,313)	(4,018)	(4,548)
	143,906	132,134	130,337
Net Income	178,856	170,269	157,360
Dividend Requirements on Preferred Stock	11,963	12,014	12,031
Earnings Available for Common Stock	$ 166,893	$ 158,255	$ 145,329
Shares of Common Stock Outstanding (Thousands):			
Year-end	63,358	62,155	60,457
Weighted average	62,932	61,547	59,695
Earnings per Weighted Average Shares of Common Stock Outstanding	$2.65	$2.57	$2.43
Dividends per Share of Common Stock:			
Paid	$2.03	$2.00	$2.00
Declared	$2.04	$2.00	$2.00

EXHIBIT 15-9   (continued)

Consolidated Balance Sheets
Public Service Company of Colorado and Subsidiaries

December 31, 1995 and 1994

(In thousands of dollars)

Assets	1995	1994
Property, Plant, and Equipment, at Cost:		
Electric	$ 3,751,321	$ 3,641,711
Gas	989,215	867,239
Steam and other	88,446	86,458
Common to all departments	380,809	369,070
Construction in progress	192,580	187,577
	5,402,371	5,152,055
Less: Accumulated depreciation	1,921,659	1,860,653
Total Property, Plant, and Equipment	3,480,712	3,291,402
Investments, at Cost	24,282	18,202
Current Assets:		
Cash and temporary cash investments	14,693	5,883
Accounts receivable, less reserve for uncollectible accounts ($3,630 at December 31, 1995; $3,173 at December 31, 1994)	124,731	163,465
Accrued unbilled revenues (Note 1)	96,989	86,106
Recoverable purchased gas and electric energy costs—net (Note 1)	—	37,979
Materials and supplies, at average cost	56,525	67,600
Fuel inventory, at average cost	35,654	31,370
Gas in underground storage, at cost (LIFO)	44,900	42,355
Current portion of accumulated deferred income taxes (Note 13)	19,229	20,709
Regulatory assets recoverable within one year (Note 1)	40,247	39,985
Prepaid expenses and other	35,619	16,312
Total Current Assets	468,587	511,764
Deferred Charges:		
Regulatory assets (Note 1)	321,797	335,893
Unamortized debt expense	10,460	11,073
Other	48,457	39,498
Total Deferred Charges	380,714	386,464
Total Assets	$ 4,354,295	$ 4,207,832

The accompanying Notes to Consolidated Financial Statements are an integral part of these financial statements.

(continued)

EXHIBIT 15-9   (continued)

| | (In thousands of dollars) | |
Capital and Liabilities	1995	1994
Common Equity (Note 5):		
Common stock	$ 997,106	$ 959,268
Retained earnings	346,539	308,214
Total Common Equity	1,343,645	1,267,482
Preferred Stock (Note 5):		
Not subject to mandatory redemption	140,008	140,008
Subject to mandatory redemption at par	41,289	42,665
Long-Term Debt (Note 6)	1,195,553	1,155,427
	2,720,495	2,605,582
Noncurrent Liabilities:		
Defueling and decommissioning liability (Note 2)	23,115	40,605
Employees' postretirement benefits other than pensions (Note 11)	51,704	42,106
Employees' postemployment benefits (Note 11)	23,500	20,975
Total Noncurrent Liabilities	98,319	103,686
Current Liabilities:		
Notes payable and commercial paper (Note 7)	288,050	324,800
Long-term debt due within one year	82,836	25,153
Preferred stock subject to mandatory redemption within one year (Note 5)	2,576	2,576
Accounts payable	156,109	177,031
Dividends payable	35,284	34,078
Recovered purchased gas and electric energy costs—net (Note 1)	9,508	—
Customers' deposits	17,462	17,099
Accrued taxes	55,393	54,148
Accrued interest	32,071	32,265
Current portion of defueling and decommissioning liability (Note 2)	24,055	36,365
Other	78,451	62,640
Total Current Liabilities	781,795	766,155
Deferred Credits:		
Customers' advances for construction	99,519	96,442
Unamortized investment tax credits	113,184	118,532
Accumulated deferred income taxes (Note 13)	508,143	485,668
Other	32,840	31,767
Total Deferred Credits	753,686	732,409
Commitments and Contingencies (Notes 2 and 9)		
Total Capital and Liabilities	$ 4,354,295	$ 4,207,832

EXHIBIT 15-9   (continued)

Consolidated Statements of Cash Flows Public Service Company of Colorado and Subsidiaries	Years Ended December 31, 1995, 1994, & 1993 (In thousands of dollars)		
	1995	**1994**	**1993**
Operating Activities:			
Net income	$ 178,856	$ 170,269	$ 157,360
Adjustments to reconcile net income to net cash			
provided by operating activities (Note 1):			
Depreciation and amortization	145,370	142,843	143,940
Defueling and decommissioning expenses	—	43,376	—
Gain on sale of WestGas Gathering, Inc.	—	(34,485)	—
Amortization of investment tax credits	(5,348)	(5,799)	(4,917)
Deferred income taxes	39,170	34,234	33,435
Allowance for equity funds used during construction	(3,782)	(3,140)	(8,119)
Change in accounts receivable	38,734	(16,281)	(3,813)
Change in inventories	4,246	10,007	(25,378)
Change in other current assets	7,618	(1,695)	(14,619)
Change in accounts payable	(20,922)	(35,364)	31,909
Change in other current liabilities	24,230	(39,730)	(5,439)
Change in deferred amounts	(20,385)	(33,920)	(17,483)
Change in noncurrent liabilities	(5,367)	15,321	(14,759)
Other	3,279	92	7,762
Net Cash Provided by Operating Activities	385,699	245,728	279,879
Investing Activities:			
Construction expenditures	(285,516)	(317,138)	(293,515)
Allowance for equity funds used during construction	3,782	3,140	8,119
Proceeds from sale of WestGas Gathering, Inc.	—	87,000	—
Proceeds from disposition of property, plant, and equipment	2,470	49,438	43,120
Purchase of other investments	(10,249)	(955)	(5,660)
Sale of other investments	4,898	1,148	8,678
Net Cash Used in Investing Activities	(284,615)	(177,367)	(239,258)
Financing Activities:			
Proceeds from sale of common stock (Note 1)	28,030	38,086	47,894
Proceeds from sale of long-term notes and bonds (Note 1)	101,860	250,068	257,913
Redemption of long-term notes and bonds	(44,713)	(281,835)	(274,829)
Short-term borrowings—net	(36,750)	47,925	26,249
Redemption of preferred stock	(1,376)	(213)	(200)
Dividends on common stock	(127,352)	(122,531)	(118,732)
Dividends on preferred stock	(11,973)	(12,016)	(12,033)
Net Cash Used in Financing Activities	(92,274)	(80,516)	(73,738)
Net Increase (Decrease) in Cash and Temporary Cash Investments	8,810	(12,155)	(33,117)
Cash and Temporary Cash Investments at Beginning of Year	5,883	18,038	51,155
Cash and Temporary Cash Investments at End of Year	$ 14,693	$ 5,883	$ 18,038

(continued)

EXHIBIT 15-9   (concluded)

Selected Partial Footnote

Allowance of funds used during construction (AFDC)

AFDC, as defined in the system of accounts prescribed by the FERC and the CPUC, represents the net cost during the period of construction of borrowed funds used for construction purposes, and a reasonable rate on funds derived from other sources. AFDC does not represent current cash earnings. The Company capitalizes AFDC as a part of the cost of utility plant. The AFDC rates or ranges of rates used during 1995, 1994, and 1993 were 7.97%, 6.81%-8.75%, and 10.21%, respectively.

Inventories are not a problem for electric utilities. Traditionally, receivables have not been a problem because the services are essential and could be cut off for nonpayment and because often a prepayment is required of the customer. In recent years, receivables have been a problem for some electric utilities because some utility commissions have ruled that services could not be cut off during the winter.

A few accounts on the financial statements of an electric utility are particularly important to the understanding of the statements. On the balance sheet, practically all utilities have a construction work in progress account. Exhibit 15-9 discloses that Public Service Company of Colorado had construction work in progress of $192,580,000 and $187,577,000 in 1995 and 1994, respectively.

Electric utilities that have substantial construction work in progress are usually viewed as being more risky investments than electric utilities that do not. Most utility commissions allow no construction work in progress or only a small amount in the rate base. Therefore, the utility rates essentially do not reflect the construction work in progress.

The utility intends to have the additional property and plant considered in the rate base when the construction work is completed. However, the utility commission may not allow all of this property and plant in the rate base. If the commission rules that inefficiency caused part of the cost, it may disallow the cost. The commission may also disallow part of the cost on the grounds that the utility used bad judgment and provided for excess capacity. Costs disallowed are in effect charged to the stockholders, as future income will not include a return on disallowed cost. In the long run, everybody pays for inefficiency and excess capacity because disallowed costs are a risk that can drive the stock price down and interest rates up for the utility. This increases the cost of capital for the utility, which in turn may force utility rates up.

For the costs allowed, the risk exists that the utility commission will not allow a reasonable rate of return. It is important to observe what proportion of total property and plant is represented by construction work in progress. Also, be familiar with the political climate of the utility commission that will be ruling on the construction work in progress costs.

The income statement accounts—allowance for equity funds and allowance for borrowed funds used during construction—relate to construction work in progress costs on the balance sheet. Both of these accounts, sometimes jointly referred to as the allowance for funds used during construction, are added to construction work in progress costs.

The account—Allowance for Equity Funds Used During Construction—represents an assumed rate of return on equity funds used for construction. The account—Allowance for Borrowed Funds Used During Construction—represents the cost of borrowed funds that are used for construction.

By increasing the balance sheet account, Construction Work in Progress, for an assumed rate of return on equity funds, the utility builds into the cost base an amount for an assumed rate of return on equity funds. As explained previously, the utility commission may not accept this cost base. The costs that have been added into the cost base have also been added to income, through the allowance for equity funds. Sometimes the account—Allowance for Equity Funds Used During Construction—represents a significant portion of the utility's net income.

The income statement account—Allowance for Borrowed Funds Used During Construction—charges to the balance sheet account, Construction in Progress, the interest on borrowed funds used for Construction in Progress. Thus, this interest is added to the cost base.

Utilities with substantial construction work in progress can have significant cash flow problems. Their reported net income can be substantially higher than the cash flow related to the income statement. Sometimes these utilities issue additional bonds and stocks to obtain funds to pay dividends.

Exhibit 15-9 discloses that Public Service Company of Colorado had a relatively immaterial construction work in progress at the end of 1995. Exhibit 15-9 also shows a relatively immaterial allowance for equity funds used during construction and allowance for borrowed funds used during construction throughout 1995. This indicates that the company's quality of earnings is relatively good.

Ratios for Electric Utilities

Because of the vastly different accounts and statement formats, few of the traditional ratios are appropriate for electric utilities. Exceptions are the return on assets, return on equity, debt/equity, and times interest earned. Investor-related ratios are also of value in analyzing utilities. For example, the cash flow per-share ratio can be a particularly important indicator of the utility's ability to maintain and increase dividends. Standard & Poor's *Industry Survey* is a good source for composite industry data on utilities.

Operating Ratio   The operating ratio measures efficiency by comparing operating expenses to operating revenues. A profitable utility holds this ratio low. A vertical common-size analysis of the income statement will aid in conclusions regarding this ratio. Exhibit 15-10 presents the operating ratio for the Public Service Company of Colorado. This ratio decreased substantially in 1995, thus having a positive influence on profitability.

Funded Debt to Operating Property   A key ratio, the comparison of funded debt to net fixed operating property, is sometimes termed *LTD* (long-term debt) to *net property* because funded debt is long-term debt. Operating property consists of property and plant less the allowance for depreciation. Construction in progress is included since it has probably been substantially funded by debt. This ratio measures debt coverage and indicates how funds are supplied. It resembles debt to total assets, with only specialized debt and the specific assets that generate the profits to cover the debt charges. Exhibit 15-11 presents funded debt to operating property for the Public Service Company of Colorado. This ratio decreased in 1995, indicating a less risky debt position.

Percent Earned on Operating Property   This ratio, sometimes termed *earnings on net property*, relates net earnings to the assets primarily intended to generate earnings—net property and plant. Exhibit 15-12 presents this ratio for the Public Service Company of Colorado. Note that this ratio increased in 1995, which is a favorable trend.

EXHIBIT 15-10 **PUBLIC SERVICE COMPANY OF COLORADO**
Operating Ratio
For the Years Ended December 31, 1995 and 1994

(In thousands of dollars)	1995	1994
Operating expenses [A]	$1,788,851	$1,786,592
Operating revenue [B]	$2,110,601	$2,057,384
Operating ratio [A÷B]	84.76%	86.84%

Operating Revenue to Operating Property   This ratio is basically an operating asset turnover ratio. In public utilities, the fixed plant is often much larger than the expected annual revenue, and this ratio will be less than 1. Exhibit 15-13 presents this ratio for the Public Service Company of Colorado, which indicates a decrease in the operating revenue to operating property and represents an unfavorable trend.

EXHIBIT 15-11   PUBLIC SERVICE COMPANY OF COLORADO
Funded Debt to Operating Property
For the Years Ended December 31, 1995 and 1994

(In thousands of dollars)	1995	1994
Funded debt [A]	$1,195,553	$1,155,427
Operating property [B]	$3,480,712	$3,291,402
Funded debt to operating property [A÷B]	34.35%	35.10%

EXHIBIT 15-12   PUBLIC SERVICE COMPANY OF COLORADO
Percent Earned on Operating Property
For the Years Ended December 31, 1995 and 1994

(In thousands of dollars)	1995	1994
Net income [A]	$ 143,906	$ 132,134
Operating property [B]	$3,480,712	$3,291,402
Percent earned on operating property [A÷B]	4.13%	4.01%

EXHIBIT 15-13   PUBLIC SERVICE COMPANY OF COLORADO
Operating Revenue to Operating Property
For the Years Ended December 31, 1995 and 1994

(In thousands of dollars)	1995	1994
Operating revenue [A]	$2,110,601	$2,057,384
Operating property [B]	$3,480,712	$3,291,402
Operating revenue to operating property [A÷B]	60.64%	62.51%

OIL AND GAS

Oil and gas companies' financial statements are affected significantly by the method they choose to account for costs associated with exploration and production. The method chosen is some variation of the successful-efforts or full-costing methods, which will be explained along with their effects on the financial statements. The financial statements of oil and gas companies are also unique because they are required to disclose, in a footnote, supplementary information on oil and gas exploration, development, and production activities. This requirement will be explained in this section.

Cash flow is important to all companies, but particularly to oil and gas companies. Therefore, cash flow must be part of the analysis of an oil or gas company. In addition, most of the traditional financial ratios apply to oil and gas companies. This section will not cover special ratios that relate to oil and gas companies.

The 1995 financial statements of Chevron Corporation will be used to illustrate oil and gas financial statements. Chevron's major business is energy, principally petroleum.

Successful Efforts Versus Full Cost

A variation of one of two costing methods is used by an oil or gas company to account for exploration and production costs: the successful-efforts method and the full-costing method.

The successful-efforts method places only exploration and production costs of successful wells on the balance sheet under property, plant, and equipment. Exploration and production costs of unsuccessful (or dry) wells are expensed when it is determined that there is a dry hole. With the full-costing method, exploration and production costs of all the wells (successful and unsuccessful) are placed on the balance sheet under property, plant, and equipment.

Under both methods, exploration and production costs placed on the balance sheet are subsequently amortized as expense to the income statement. Amortization costs that relate to natural resources are called *depletion expense*.

The costing method used for exploration and production can have a very significant influence on the balance sheet and the income statement. Under both methods, exploration and production costs are eventually expensed, but a significant difference exists in the timing of the expense.

In theory, the successful-efforts method takes the position that a direct relationship exists between costs incurred and specific reserves discovered.

These costs should be placed on the balance sheet. Costs associated with unsuccessful efforts are a period expense and should be charged to expense. In theory, the full-costing method takes the position that the drilling of all wells, successful and unsuccessful, is part of the process of finding successful wells. Therefore, all of the cost should be placed on the balance sheet.

In practice, the decision to use the successful-efforts method or the full-costing method is probably not significantly influenced by theory, but by practicalities. Most relatively small oil and gas companies select a variation of the full-costing method. This results in a much larger balance sheet. In the short run it also usually results in higher reported profits. Small oil companies speculate that the larger balance sheet and the increased reported profits can be used to influence some banks and limited partners, which the small companies tend to use as sources of funds.

Large oil and gas companies tend to select a variation of the successful-efforts method. This results in a lower balance sheet amount and lower reported income in the short run. The large companies usually depend on bonds and stock as their primary sources of outside capital. Investors in bonds and stock are not likely to be influenced by the larger balance sheet and higher income that results from capitalizing dry wells.

The method used can have a significant influence on the balance sheet and the income statement. The successful-efforts method is more conservative.

Supplementary Information on Oil and Gas Exploration, Development, and Production Activities

As part of your review of an oil or gas company, note the method used to account for exploration and production costs. *Statement of Financial Accounting Standards No. 69* establishes comprehensive disclosures for oil- and gas-producing activities. Review Exhibit 15-14, pages 648-650, for a brief summary of the supplementary information presented by Chevron Corporation. Chevron uses the successful-efforts method to account for the cost of oil and gas wells.

Cash Flow

Monitoring cash flow can be particularly important when following an oil or gas company. The potential for a significant difference exists between the reported income and cash flow from operations. One reason is that large sums can be spent for exploration and development, years in advance of revenue from the found reserves. The other reason is that there can be significant differences between when expenses are deducted on the financial statements and when they are deducted on the tax return. Therefore, observe the operating cash flow.

EXHIBIT 15-14   CHEVRON CORPORATION
Supplemental Information on Oil- and Gas-Producing Activities—Unaudited
1995 Annual Report

Note: This exhibit only includes a small part of the supplemental information on oil- and gas-producing activities of Chevron Corporation. The total disclosure consists of six pages in the Chevron Corporation 1995 annual report. The tables were introduced with the following comment:

In accordance with *Statement of Financial Accounting Standards No. 69,* "Disclosures About Oil and Gas Producing Activities" (SFAS 69), this section provides supplemental information on oil and gas exploration and producing activities of the company in six separate tables. The first three tables provide historical cost information pertaining to costs incurred in exploration, property acquisitions, and development; capitalized costs; and results of operations. Tables IV through VI present information on the company's estimated net proved reserve quantities, standardized measure of estimated discounted future net cash flows related to proved reserves, and changes in estimated discounted future net cash flows. The Africa geographic area includes activities principally in Nigeria, Angola, Zaire, and Congo. The "other" geographic category includes activities in Australia, the United Kingdom North Sea, Canada, Papua New Guinea, China, and other countries. Amounts shown for affiliated companies are Chevron's 50 percent equity share in each of P.T. Caltex Pacific Indonesia (CPI), an exploration and production company operating in the Republic of Kazakstan, which began operations in April 1993.

Additional comments relating to Tables I–VI.

Table I—Costs Incurred in Exploration, Property Acquisitions, and Development
(This table details the costs incurred in exploration, property acquisition, and development for 1995, 1994, and 1993.)

Table II—Capitalized Costs Related to Oil- and Gas-Producing Activities
(This table details the capitalized costs related to oil- and gas-producing activities for 1995, 1994, and 1993.)

Table III—Results of Operations for Oil- and Gas-Producing Activities
(This table details the company's results of operations from oil- and gas-producing activities for the years 1995, 1994, and 1993.)

Table IV—Reserve Quantities Information
This table was introduced with the following comment:

The Company's estimated net proved underground oil and gas reserves and changes thereto for the years 1995, 1994, and 1993 are shown in the following table. Proved reserves are estimated by the company's asset teams composed of earth scientists and reservoir engineers. These proved reserve estimates are reviewed annually by the corporation's reserves advisory committee to ensure that rigorous professional standards and the reserves definitions prescribed by the Securities and Exchange Commission are consistently applied throughout the company.

Proved reserves are the estimated quantities that geologic and engineering data demonstrate with reasonable certainty to be recoverable in future years from known

EXHIBIT 15-14 (continued)

reservoirs under existing economic and operating conditions. Due to the inherent uncertainties and the limited nature of reservoir data, estimates of underground reserves are subject to change over time as additional information becomes available.

Proved reserves do not include additional quantities removable beyond the term of the lease or contract unless renewal is reasonably certain, or that may result from extensions of currently proved areas, or from application of secondary or tertiary recovery processes not yet tested and determined to be economic.

Proved developed reserves are the quantities expected to be recovered through existing wells with existing equipment and operating methods.

"Net" reserves exclude royalties and interests owned by others and reflect contractual arrangements and royalty obligations in effect at the time of the estimate.

Proved reserves for Tengizchevroil (TCO), the company's 50-percent-owned affiliate in Kazakstan, do not include reserves that will be produced when a dedicated export system is in place.

Table V—Standardized Measure of Discounted Future Net Cash Flows Related to Proved Oil and Gas Reserves
(This table details the standardized measure of discounted future net cash flows related to proved oil and gas reserves for 1995, 1994, and 1993. Chevron provided the following comment as an introduction to Table V.)

The standardized measure of discounted future net cash flows, related to the above proved oil and gas reserves, is calculated in accordance with the requirements of SFAS 69. Estimated future cash inflows from production are computed by applying year-end prices for oil and gas to year-end quantities of estimated net proved reserves. Future price changes are limited to those provided by contractual arrangements in existence at the end of each reporting year. Future development and production costs are those estimated future expenditures necessary to develop and produce year-end estimated proved reserves based on year-end cost indices, assuming continuation of year-end economic conditions. Estimated future income taxes are calculated by applying appropriate year-end statutory tax rates. These rates reflect allowable deductions and tax credits and are applied to estimated future pre-tax net cash flows, less the tax basis of related assets. Discounted future net cash flows are calculated using 10 percent midperiod discount factors. This discounting requires a year-by-year estimate of when the future expenditures will be incurred and when the reserves will be produced.

The information provided does not represent management's estimate of the company's expected future cash flows or value of proved oil and gas reserves. Estimates of proved reserve quantities are imprecise and change over time as new information becomes available. Moreover, probable and possible reserves, which may become proved in the future, are excluded from the calculations. The arbitrary valuation prescribed under SFAS 69 requires assumptions as to the timing and amount of future development and production costs. The calculations are made as of December 31 each year and should not be relied upon as an indication of the company's future cash flows or value of its oil and gas reserves.

(continued)

EXHIBIT 15-14   (concluded)

Table VI—Changes in the Standardized Measure of Discounted Future Net Cash Flows from Proved Reserves

(This table details information for 1995, 1994, and 1993. Chevron provided the following comment at the bottom of Table VI.)

The changes in present values between years, which can be significant, reflect changes in estimated proved reserve quantities and prices and assumptions used in forecasting production volumes and costs. Changes in the timing of production are included with "Revisions of previous quantity estimates." The 1995 changes reflected higher year-end crude oil and natural gas prices and quantity increases in crude oil and natural gas reserves.

Cash from operating activities for a three-year period will be disclosed on the statement of cash flows. For Chevron, net cash provided by operating activities was $4,075,000,000, $2,896,000,000, and $4,221,000,000 for 1995, 1994, and 1993, respectively. Net income for Chevron was $930,000,000, $1,693,000,000, and $1,265,000,000 for 1995, 1994, and 1993, respectively.

TRANSPORTATION

Three components of the transportation industry will be discussed: air carriers, railroads, and the motor carrier industry. The Civil Aeronautics Board, which requires the use of a uniform system of accounts and reporting, regulates interstate commercial aviation. The Interstate Commerce Commission, which also has control over a uniform system of accounts and reporting, regulates interstate railroads. The Interstate Commerce Commission also regulates interstate motor carriers whose principal business is transportation services.

Financial Statements

The balance sheet format for air carriers, railroads, and motor carriers resembles that for manufacturing or retailing firms. As in a heavy manufacturing firm, property and equipment make up a large portion of assets. Also, supplies and parts comprise the basic inventory items. The income statement format resembles that of a utility. The system of accounts provides for the grouping of all revenues and expenses in terms of both major natural objectives and functional activities. There is no cost of goods sold calculation; rather, there is operating income: revenue (categorized) minus operating expenses. In essence, the statements are a prescribed, categorized form of single-step income statement. They cannot be converted to multiple-step format.

Ratios

Most of the traditional ratios also apply in the transportation field. Exceptions are inventory turnovers (because there is no cost of goods sold) and gross profit margin. The ratios discussed in the subsections that follow are especially suited to transportation. They are derived from the 1995 statement of income and balance sheet for Delta Air Lines, Inc., presented in Exhibit 15-15, pages 652-654.

The traditional sources of industry averages cover transportation. The federal government accumulates numerous statistics for regulated industries, including transportation. An example is the Interstate Commerce Commission's *Annual Report* on transport statistics in the United States.

For the motor carrier industry, a particularly good source of industry data is the annual publication *Financial Analysis of the Motor Carrier Industry*, published by the American Trucking Association, Inc., 1616 P Street, NW, Washington, DC 20036. This publication includes an economic and industry overview, distribution of revenue by carrier type, and industry issues. It also includes definitions of terminology that relate to the motor carrier industry.

There are hundreds of motor carrier firms, most of which are relatively small. The American Trucking Association compiles data by composite carrier groups. For example, Group A includes composite data for several hundred general freight carriers with annual revenues of less than $5 million. One of the groups includes composite data for the publicly held carriers of general freight.

The very extensive composite data in the American Trucking Association publication include industry total dollars for the income statement and balance sheet. It also includes vertical common-size analyses for the income statement and the balance sheet. This publication also includes approximately 36 ratios and other analytical data, such as total tons.

Operating Ratio The operating ratio is computed by comparing operating expense to operating revenue. It measures cost and should be kept low, but external conditions, such as the level of business activity, may affect this ratio. Operating revenues vary from year to year because of differences in rates, classification of traffic, volume of traffic carried, and

EXHIBIT 15-15   **DELTA AIR LINES, INC.**
Air Transportation
Selected Financial Data

Consolidated Balance Sheets
June 30, 1995 and 1994

Assets	1995	1994
	(In millions of dollars)	
Current Assets:		
Cash and cash equivalents	$ 1,233	$ 1,302
Short-term investments	529	408
Accounts receivable, net of allowance for uncollectible		
accounts of $29 at June 30, 1995, and $50 at June 30, 1994	755	886
Maintenance and operating supplies, at average cost	68	67
Deferred income taxes	234	336
Prepaid expenses and other	195	224
Total current assets	3,014	3,223
Property and Equipment:		
Flight equipment	9,288	9,063
Less: Accumulated depreciation	4,209	3,880
	5,079	5,183
Flight equipment under capital leases	537	173
Less: Accumulated amortization	99	142
	438	31
Ground property and equipment	2,442	2,398
Less: Accumulated depreciation	1,354	1,250
	1,088	1,148
Advance payment for equipment	331	241
	6,936	6,603
Other Assets:		
Marketable equity securities	398	351
Deferred income taxes	506	560
Investments in associated companies	265	219
Cost in excess of net assets acquired, net of accumulated		
amortization of $75 at June 30, 1995, and $66 at June 30, 1994	274	283
Leasehold and operating rights, net of accumulated amortization		
of $165 at June 30, 1995, and $135 at June 30, 1994	177	207
Other	573	450
	2,193	2,070
	$12,143	$11,896

EXHIBIT 15-15 (continued)

Liabilities and Stockholders' Equity	1995	1994
	(In millions of dollars, except per-share data)	
Current Liabilities:		
Current maturities of long-term debt	$ 151	$ 227
Current obligations under capital leases	61	11
Accounts payable and miscellaneous accrued liabilities	1,578	1,552
Air traffic liability	1,143	1,247
Accrued rent	235	195
Accrued vacation pay	167	196
Transportation tax payable	106	108
Total current liabilities	3,441	3,536
Noncurrent Liabilities:		
Long-term debt	2,683	3,142
Postretirement benefits	1,714	1,641
Accrued rent	556	541
Capital leases	438	86
Other	395	395
	5,786	5,805
Deferred Credits:		
Deferred gain on sale and leaseback transactions	860	923
Manufacturers and other credits	109	63
	969	986
Commitments and Contingencies (Notes 7, 8, 9, and 11)		
Employee Stock Ownership Plan Preferred Stock:		
Series B ESOP Convertible Preferred Stock, $1.00 par value, $72 stated and liquidation value; issued and outstanding 6,786,632 shares at June 30, 1995, and 6,878,292 shares at June 30, 1994	489	495
Less: Unearned compensation under employee stock ownership plan	369	393
	120	102
Stockholders' Equity:		
Series C Convertible Preferred Stock, $1.00 par value, $50,000 liquidation preference; issued and outstanding 23,000 shares at June 30, 1995 and 1994	—	—
Common stock, $3.00 par value; authorized 150,000,000 shares; issued 54,537,103 shares at June 30, 1995, and 54,469,491 shares at June 30, 1994	164	163
Additional paid-in capital	2,016	2,013
Accumulated deficit	(184)	(490)
Net unrealized gain on marketable securities	83	53
Less: Treasury stock at cost, 3,721,093 shares at June 30, 1995, and 4,016,219 shares at June 30, 1994	(252)	(272)
	1,827	1,467
	$12,143	$11,896

(continued)

EXHIBIT 15-15   (concluded)

Consolidated Statements of Operations
For the Years Ended June 30, 1995, 1994, and 1993

	1995	1994	1993
	(In millions of dollars, except per-share data)		
Operating Revenues:			
Passenger	$ 11,303	$ 11,252	$ 10,899
Cargo	565	551	534
Other, net	326	274	224
Total operating revenues	12,194	12,077	11,657
Operating Expenses:			
Salaries and related costs	4,354	4,589	4,798
Aircraft fuel	1,370	1,411	1,592
Passenger commissions	1,195	1,255	1,074
Aircraft rent	671	732	729
Depreciation and amortization	622	678	735
Other selling expenses	618	614	569
Contracted services	556	457	450
Passenger service	443	522	542
Facilities and other rent	436	380	356
Aircraft maintenance materials and outside repairs	430	418	465
Landing fees	266	261	262
Restructuring charges	—	526	82
Other	572	681	578
Total operating expenses	11,533	12,524	12,232
Operating Income (Loss)	661	(447)	(575)
Other Income (Expenses):			
Interest expense	(292)	(304)	(239)
Interest capitalized	30	33	62
Interest income	95	57	22
Gain on disposition of flight equipment	—	2	65
Miscellaneous income (expense), net	—	(1)	14
	(167)	(213)	(76)
Income (Loss) Before Income Taxes and Cumulative Effect of Accounting Changes	494	(660)	(651)
Income Taxes (Provided) Credited, Net	(200)	251	236
Income (Loss) Before Cumulative Effect of Accounting Changes	294	(409)	(415)
Cumulative Effect of Accounting Changes, Net of Tax	114	—	(587)
Net Income (Loss)	408	(409)	(1,002)
Preferred Stock Dividends	(88)	(110)	(110)
Net Income (Loss) Attributable to Common Stockholders	$ 320	$ (519)	$ (1,112)
Primary Income (Loss) Per Common Share:			
Before cumulative effect of accounting changes	$ 4.07	$ (10.32)	$ (10.54)
Cumulative effect of accounting changes	2.25	—	(11.78)
	$ 6.32	$ (10.32)	$ (22.32)
Fully Diluted Income (Loss) Per Common Share:			
Before cumulative effect of accounting changes	$ 4.01	$ (10.32)	$ (10.54)
Cumulative effect of accounting changes	1.42	—	(11.78)
	$ 5.43	$ (10.32)	$ (22.32)

the distance traffic is transported. Operating expenses change because of variations in the price level, traffic carried, the type of service performed, and the effectiveness of operating and maintaining the properties. Common-size analysis of revenues and expenses is needed to explain changes in the operating ratio.

Exhibit 15-16 presents the operating ratio for Delta Air Lines, Inc. Notice that the operating ratio indicates more operating expenses than operating revenues in 1994 and a substantial improvement in 1995. The operating ratio can dramatically affect the profitability of a carrier. In fact, Delta went from an operating loss in 1994 of $447,000,000 to an operating income in 1995 of $661,000,000.

Long-Term Debt to Operating Property Because of the transportation companies' heavy investment in operating assets, such as equipment, the long-term ratios increase in importance. Long-term borrowing capacity is also a key consideration. The ratio of long-term debt to operating property ratio gives a measure of the sources of funds with which property is obtained. It also measures borrowing capacity. *Operating property* is defined as long-term property and equipment. Exhibit 15-17, on page 656, presents this ratio for Delta Air Lines. For Delta, the long-term debt to operating property ratio decreased in 1995 to 45.00% from 48.89%. These are relatively high numbers in relation to recent prior years.

Operating Revenue to Operating Property This ratio measures turn-over of operating assets. The objective is to generate as many dollars in revenue per dollar of property as possible. Exhibit 15-18, on page 656, presents this ratio for Delta Air Lines. The operating revenue to operating property decreased moderately between 1994 and 1995.

EXHIBIT 15-16 **DELTA AIR LINES, INC.**
Operating Ratio
For the Years Ended December 31, 1995 and 1994

(In millions of dollars)	1995	1994
Operating expense [A]	$11,533	$12,524
Operating revenue [B]	$12,194	$12,077
Operating ratio [A÷B]	94.58%	103.70%

EXHIBIT 15-17   **DELTA AIR LINES, INC.**
Long-Term Debt to Operating Property
For the Years Ended December 31, 1995 and 1994

(In millions of dollars)	1995	1994
Long-term debt	$ 2,683	$ 3,142
Capital leases	438	86
[A]	$ 3,121	$ 3,228
Operating property [B]	$ 6,936	$ 6,603
Long-term debt to operating property [A÷B]	45.00%	48.89%

Per-Mile, Per-Person, and Per-Ton Passenger Load Factors   For transportation companies, additional insight can be gained by looking at revenues and expenses on a per unit of usage basis. Examples would be per mile of line or per ten miles for railroads, or a per passenger mile for air carriers. Although this type of disclosure is not required, it is often presented in highlights.

This type of disclosure is illustrated in Exhibit 15-19, which shows statistics for Delta Air Lines. Statistics in Exhibit 15-19 are available for revenue passengers enplaned, available seat miles, revenue passenger miles, operating revenue per available seat mile, passenger mile yield, operating cost per available seat mile, passenger load factor, breakeven passenger load factor, available ton miles, revenue ton miles, and cost per available ton mile.

EXHIBIT 15-18   **DELTA AIR LINES, INC.**
Operating Revenue to Operating Property
For the Years Ended December 31, 1995 and 1994

(In millions of dollars)	1995	1994
Operating revenue [A]	$12,194	$12,077
Operating property [B]	$ 6,936	$ 6,603
Operating revenue to operating property [A÷B]	1.76 times per year	1.83 times per year

EXHIBIT 15-19 **DELTA AIR LINES, INC.**
Other Financial and Statistical Data
For the Years Ended June 30, 1995, 1994, 1993, and 1992

(This represents four years from an eleven-year summary)

(Dollar amounts in millions, except per-share figures)	For the Years Ended June 30			
	1995	1994[1]	1993[2]	1992
Total assets	$12,143	$11,896	$11,871	$10,162
Long-term debt and capital leases (excluding current maturities)	$ 3,121	$ 3,228	$ 3,716	$ 2,833
Stockholders' equity	$ 1,827	$ 1,467	$ 1,913	$ 1,894
Shares of common stock outstanding at year-end	50,816,010	50,453,272	50,063,841	49,699,098
Revenue passengers enplaned (thousands)	88,893	87,399	85,085	77,038
Available seat miles (millions)	130,525	131,780	132,282	123,102
Revenue passenger miles (millions)	86,355	85,206	82,406	72,693
Operating revenue per available seat mile	9.34¢	9.16¢	8.81¢	8.80¢
Passenger mile yield	13.09¢	13.21¢	13.23¢	13.91¢
Operating cost per available seat mile	8.84¢	9.50¢	9.25¢	9.35¢
Passenger load factor	66.16%	64.66%	62.30%	59.05%
Breakeven passenger load factor	62.29%	67.23%	65.58%	62.99%
Available ton miles (millions)	18,150	18,302	18,182	16,625
Revenue ton miles (millions)	10,142	9,911	9,503	8,361
Cost per available ton mile	63.55¢	68.43¢	67.27¢	69.24¢

[1]Summary of operations and other financial and statistical data include $526 million in pretax restructuring charges ($6.59 after-tax per common share).

[2]Summary of operations and other financial and statistical data include $82 million pretax restructuring charge ($1.05 after-tax per common share). Summary of operations excludes $587 million after-tax cumulative effect of changes in accounting standards.

INSURANCE

Insurance companies provide two types of services. One is an identified contract service—mortality protection or loss protection. The second is investment management service.

There are basically four types of insurance organizations:

1. **Stock companies.** A stock company is a corporation organized to earn profits for its stockholders. The comments in this insurance section relate specifically to stock companies. Many of the

comments are also valid for the other types of insurance organizations.

2. **Mutual companies.**   A mutual company is an incorporated entity, without private ownership interest, operating for the benefit of its policyholders and their beneficiaries.

3. **Fraternal benefit societies.**   A fraternal benefit society resembles a mutual insurance company in that, although incorporated, it does not have capital stock, and it operates for the benefit of its members and beneficiaries. Policyholders participate in the earnings of the society and the policies stipulate that the society has the power to assess them in case the legal reserves become impaired.

4. **Assessment companies.** An assessment company is an organized group with similar interests, such as a religious denomination.

The regulation of insurance companies started at the state level. Beginning in 1828, the state of New York required that annual reports be filed with the state controller. Subsequently, other states followed this precedent, and all 50 states have insurance departments that require annual statements of insurance companies. The reports are filed with the state insurance departments in accordance with statutory accounting practices (SAP). The National Association of Insurance Commissioners (NAIC), a voluntary association, has succeeded in achieving near uniformity among the states, so there are no significant differences in SAP among the states.[1]

Statutory accounting emphasizes the balance sheet. In its concern for protecting policyholders, statutory accounting focuses on the financial solvency of the insurance corporation. After the annual reports are filed with the individual state insurance departments, a testing process is conducted by the NAIC. This process is based on ratio calculations concerning the financial position of a company. If a company's ratio is outside the prescribed limit, the NAIC brings that to the attention of the state insurance department.

A.M. Best Company publishes *Best's Insurance Reports*, which are issued separately for life-health companies and property-casualty companies. *Best's Insurance Reports* evaluate the financial condition of more than 3,000 insurance companies. The majority of companies are assigned a Best's Rating, ranging from A+ (Superior) to C- (Fair). The other companies are classified as "Not Assigned." The "Not Assigned" category has ten classifications to identify why a company has not been assigned a Best's Rating.

Some of the items included in Best's data include a balance sheet, summary of operations, operating ratios, profitability ratios, leverage ratios, and liquidity ratios. Most of the ratios are industry-specific. It is not practical to describe and explain them in this text. It should be noted that the financial data, including the ratios, are based on the data submitted to the state insurance departments and are thus based on SAP.

Generally Accepted Accounting Principles (GAAP) for insurance companies developed much later than SAP. The annual reports of insurance companies are based on GAAP. GAAP are primarily governed by SFAS No. 60, "Accounting and Reporting by Insurance Enterprises" and SFAS No. 97, "Accounting and Reporting by Insurance Enterprises for Certain Long Duration Contracts and for Realized Gains & Losses from the Sale of Investments."

The 1934 Securities and Exchange Act established national government regulation, in addition to the state regulation of insurance companies. Stock insurance companies with assets of $1 million and at least 500 stockholders must register with the SEC and file the required forms, such as the annual Form 10-K. Reports filed with the SEC must conform with GAAP.

Exhibit 15-20, pages 661-663, contains the income statement and balance sheet from the 1995 annual report of Aetna Life & Casualty Company. These statements were prepared using GAAP. Review them to observe the unique nature of insurance company financial statements.

Balance Sheet Under GAAP

Assets The balance sheet for an insurance company is not classified by current assets and current liabilities (nonclassified balance sheet). The asset section starts with investments, a classification where most insurance companies maintain the majority of their assets. Many of the investments have a high degree of liquidity, so that prompt payment can be assured in the event of a catastrophic loss. The majority of the investments are typically in bonds, with stock investments being much lower. Real estate investments are usually present for both property-casualty insurance companies and for life insurance companies. Because liabilities are relatively short term for property-casualty companies, the investment in real estate for these companies is usually immaterial. For life insurance companies, the investment in real estate may be much greater than for property-casualty companies because of the generally longer-term nature and predictability of their liabilities.

For debt and equity investments, review the disclosure to determine if there are significant differences between the fair value and the cost or amortized cost. Also review the stockholders' equity section of the balance sheet to determine if there are significant unrealized capital gains (losses).

Assets—Other than Investments   A number of asset accounts other than investments may be on an insurance company's balance sheet. Some of the typical accounts are described in the paragraphs that follow.

Real estate used in operations is reported at cost, less accumulated depreciation. Under SAP, real estate used in operations is expensed.

Deferred policy acquisition costs represent the cost of obtaining policies. Under GAAP, these costs are deferred and charged to expense over the premium-paying period. This is one of the major differences between GAAP reporting and SAP reporting. Under SAP reporting, these costs are charged to expense as they are incurred.

Goodwill is an intangible account resulting from acquiring other companies. The same account can be found on the balance sheet of companies other than insurance companies. Under GAAP, the goodwill account is accounted for as an asset and subsequently amortized to expense. Under SAP, neither the goodwill account nor other intangibles are recognized.

Liabilities   Generally, the largest liability is for loss reserves. Reserving for losses involves estimating the ultimate value, considering the present value of the commitments. The quantification process is subject to a number of subjective estimates, including inflation, interest rates, and judicial interpretations. Mortality estimates are also important for life insurance companies. These reserve accounts should be adequate to pay policy claims under the terms of the insurance policies.

Another liability account found on an insurance company's balance sheet is Policy and Contract Claims. This account represents claims that have accrued as of the balance sheet date. These claims are reported net of any portion that can be recovered.

Many other liability accounts, such as Notes Payable and Income Taxes Payable, are found on an insurance company's balance sheet. These are typically reported in the same manner as other industries report them, except there is no current liability classification.

Stockholders' Equity   The stockholders' equity section usually resembles the stockholders' equity section for companies in other industries. The account—Net Unrealized Gains (Losses) on Securities— can be particularly large for insurance companies because of the

EXHIBIT 15-20 **AETNA LIFE & CASUALTY**
Consolidated Statement of Income and Balance Sheets
1995 Annual Report

(Millions, except share and per-share data) For the years ended December 31,	1995	1994	1993
Revenue:			
Premiums	$ 7,431.4	$ 6,901.3	$ 5,921.7
Net investment income	3,575.1	3,631.4	3,966.6
Fees and other income	1,924.3	1,741.5	1,512.6
Net realized capital gains (losses)	47.2	(55.2)	(61.2)
Total revenue	$ 12,978.0	$ 12,219.0	$ 11,339.7
Benefits and Expenses:			
Current and future benefits	$ 9,027.2	$ 8,652.0	$ 8,189.2
Operating expenses	3,087.5	2,805.9	2,632.8
Amortization of deferred policy acquisition costs	137.1	133.6	101.7
Loss on discontinuance of products	—	—	1,270.0
Severance and facilities charge	—	—	160.7
Total benefits and expenses	$ 12,251.8	$ 11,591.5	$ 12,354.4
Income (loss) from continuing operations before income taxes, extraordinary item, and cumulative effect adjustments	$ 726.2	$ 627.5	$ (1,014.7)
Income taxes (benefits)	252.3	218.1	(412.4)
Income (loss) from continuing operations before extraordinary item and cumulative effect adjustments	473.9	409.4	(602.3)
Income (loss) from discontinued operations, net of tax	(222.2)	58.1	290.3
Income (loss) before extraordinary item and cumulative effect adjustments	251.7	467.5	(312.0)
Extraordinary loss on debenture redemption, net of tax	—	—	(4.7)
Cumulative effect adjustments, net of tax	—	—	(49.2)
Net income (loss)	$ 251.7	$ 467.5	$ (365.9)
Results per Common Share:			
Income (loss) from continuing operations before extraordinary item and cumulative effect adjustments	$ 4.16	$ 3.63	$ (5.42)
Income (loss) from discontinued operations, net of tax	(1.95)	.51	2.61
Income (loss) before extraordinary item and cumulative effect adjustments	2.21	4.14	(2.81)
Extraordinary loss on debenture redemption, net of tax	—	—	(.04)
Cumulative effect adjustments, net of tax	—	—	(.44)
Net income (loss)	$ 2.21	$ 4.14	$ (3.29)
Weighted average common shares outstanding	113,897,633	112,848,653	111,062,954

(continued)

EXHIBIT 15-20   (continued)

Consolidated Balance Sheets
(Millions, except share and per-share data)

As of December 31,	1995	1994
Assets:		
Investments:		
Debt securities:		
Available for sale, at fair value (amortized cost $29,962.5 and $27,208.3)	$31,860.3	$25,938.1
Held for investment, at amortized cost (fair value $1,584.1)	—	1,587.3
Equity securities, at fair value (cost $597.8 and $594.0)	659.7	614.6
Short-term investments	607.8	344.4
Mortgage loans	8,327.2	10,389.9
Real estate	1,277.3	1,283.7
Policy loans	629.4	533.8
Other	688.6	838.0
Total investments	$44,050.3	$41,529.8
Cash and cash equivalents	$ 1,712.7	$ 2,277.2
Reinsurance recoverables and receivables	109.4	129.4
Accrued investment income	618.3	596.8
Premiums due and other receivables	971.5	593.7
Deferred federal and foreign income taxes	271.5	404.2
Deferred policy acquisition costs	1,953.1	1,691.0
Other assets	1,004.4	974.7
Separate accounts assets	29,699.7	24,122.6
Net assets of discontinued operations	3,932.8	3,167.3
Total assets	$84,323.7	$75,486.7

EXHIBIT 15-20   (concluded)

Consolidated Balance Sheets

(Millions, except share and per-share data)

As of December 31,	1995	1994
Liabilities:		
Future policy benefits	$18,372.9	$17,971.5
Unpaid claims and claim expenses	1,563.1	1,389.4
Unearned premiums	142.4	179.4
Policyholders' funds left with the company	22,898.7	23,176.4
Total insurance liabilities	42,977.1	42,716.7
Dividends payable to shareholders	79.2	77.7
Short-term debt	389.6	14.8
Long-term debt	989.1	1,079.2
Current federal and foreign income taxes	154.0	4.2
Other liabilities	2,344.2	1,642.0
Participating policyholders' interests	204.8	170.5
Separate accounts liabilities	29,637.9	24,003.6
Total liabilities	$76,775.9	$69,708.7
Minority interest in preferred securities of subsidiary	$275.0	$275.0
Commitments and Contingent Liabilities (Notes 2, 16, and 17)		
Shareholders' Equity:		
Class A Voting Preferred Stock (no par value; 10,000,000 shares authorized; no shares issued or outstanding)	—	—
Class B Voting Preferred Stock (no par value; 15,000,000 shares authorized; no shares issued or outstanding)	—	—
Class C Non-Voting Preferred Stock (no par value; 15,000,000 shares authorized; no shares issued or outstanding)	—	—
Common Capital Stock (no par value; 250,000,000 shares authorized; 115,013,675 and 114,939,275 issued, and 114,727,093 and 112,657,758 outstanding)	1,448.2	1,419.2
Net unrealized capital gains (losses)	641.1	(1,071.5)
Retained earnings	5,195.6	5,259.6
Treasury stock, at cost (286,582 and 2,281,517 shares)	(12.1)	(104.3)
Total shareholders' equity	$ 7,272.8	$ 5,503.0
Total liabilities, minority interest, and shareholders' equity	$84,323.7	$75,486.7
Shareholders' equity per common share	$63.39	$48.85

expanded use of this account as a result of standards for insurance companies and the material amount of investments that an insurance company may have. Pay close attention to changes in this account, since these unrealized gains or losses have not been recognized on the income statement.

Income Statement Under GAAP

The manner of recognizing revenue on insurance contracts is unique for the insurance industry. In general, the duration of the contract governs the revenue recognition.

For contracts of short duration, revenue is ordinarily recognized over the period of the contract in proportion to the amount of insurance protection provided. When the risk differs significantly from the contract period, revenue is recognized over the period of risk in proportion to the amount of insurance protection.[2]

Policies relating to loss protection typically fall under the short-duration contract. An example would be casualty insurance in which the insurance company retains the right to cancel the contract at the end of the policy term.

For long-duration contracts, revenue is recognized when the premium is due from the policyholder. Examples would be whole-life contracts and single-premium life contracts.[3] Likewise, acquisition costs are capitalized and expensed in proportion to premium revenue.

Long-duration contracts that do not subject the insurance enterprise to significant risks arising from policyholder mortality or morbidity are referred to as *investment contracts*. Amounts received on these contracts are not to be reported as revenues but rather as liabilities and accounted for in the same way as interest-bearing instruments.[4] The contracts are regarded as investment contracts since they do not incorporate significant insurance risk. Interestingly, many of the life insurance policies currently being written are of this type.

With the investment contracts, premium payments are credited to the policyholder balance. The insurance company assesses charges against this balance for contract services and credits the balance for income earned. The insurer can adjust the schedule for contract services and the rate at which income is credited.

Investment contracts generally include an assessment against the policyholder on inception of the contract and an assessment when the contract is terminated. The inception fees are booked as recoveries of capitalized acquisition costs, and the termination fees are booked as revenue at the time of termination.

In addition to their insurance activities, insurance companies are substantially involved with investments. Realized gains and losses from investments are reported in operations in the period incurred.

Ratios

As previously indicated, many of the ratios relating to insurance companies are industry-specific. An explanation of industry-specific ratios is beyond the scope of this book. The industry-specific ratios are frequently based on SAP financial reporting to the states, rather than the GAAP financial reporting that is used for the annual report and SEC requirements.

Ratios computed from the GAAP-based financial statements are often profitability- and investor-related. Examples of such ratios are return on common equity, price/earnings ratio, dividend payout, and dividend yield. These ratios are explained in other sections of this book.

Insurance companies tend to have a stock market price at a discount to the average market price (price/earnings ratio). This discount is typically 10% to 20%, but at times it is much more. There are likely many reasons for this relatively low market value. Insurance is a highly regulated industry that some perceive as having low growth prospects. It is also an industry with substantial competition. The regulation and the competition put pressure on the premiums that can be charged. The accounting environment likely also contributes to the relatively low market price for insurance company stocks. The existence of two sets of accounting principles, SAP and GAAP, contributes to the lack of understanding of insurance companies' financial statements. Also, many of the accounting standards are complex and industry-specific.

The nature of the insurance industry leads to standards that allow much subjectivity and possible manipulation of reported profit. For example, insurance companies are perceived to underreserve during tough years and overreserve during good years.

REAL ESTATE COMPANIES

Real estate companies typically construct and operate income-producing real properties. Examples of such properties are shopping centers, hotels, and office buildings. A typical project would involve selecting a site, arranging financing, arranging for long-term leases, construction, and subsequently operating and maintaining the property.

Real estate companies contend that conventional accounting —recognizing depreciation but not the underlying value of the property—misleads investors. In some cases, these companies have taken the drastic step of selling major parts or all of the companies' assets to realize greater benefits for stockholders. Some real estate companies have attempted to reflect value by disclosing current value in addition to the conventional accounting. Such a company is The Rouse Company. The Rouse Company arrives at current value using future income potential, assuming that the property is held for the long-term development and sales programs. This is an attempt to indicate annual progress and reflect how investors perceive real estate values.

Exhibit 15-21, pages 667-669, contains the balance sheet and a partial footnote from the 1995 annual report of The Rouse Company. Notice at the end of 1995 that the conventional balance sheet had a total shareholders' equity of $42,584,000, while the current value disclosure had a total shareholders' equity of $1,539,155,000. The Rouse Company statement of income and statement of cash flows follow the conventional format. Real estate companies emphasize earnings before depreciation and deferred taxes from operations. The Rouse Company annual report contains extensive discussion of the current value disclosure.

Observe that the balance sheet of The Rouse Company is a non-classified balance sheet, and it does not emphasize liquidity. The first listing under assets is property, while the first listing under liabilities is debt. The most liquid assets are listed last.

SUMMARY

Financial statements vary among industries, and they are especially different for banks, utilities, transportation companies, and insurance companies. In each case, the accounting for these firms is subject to a uniform accounting system. Changes in analysis are necessitated by the differences in accounting presentation.

Oil and gas companies' financial statements are affected significantly by the method that they choose to account for costs associated with exploration and production. Another important aspect of the financial statements of oil and gas companies is the footnote requirement that relates to supplementary information on oil and gas exploration, development, and production activities. Cash flow is also particularly significant to oil and gas companies.

Real estate companies emphasize the underlying value of the property and earnings before depreciation and deferred taxes from operations.

EXHIBIT 15-21   THE ROUSE COMPANY AND SUBSIDIARIES
Balance Sheet and Partial Footnote
1995 Annual Report

THE ROUSE COMPANY AND SUBSIDIARIES
Consolidated Cost Basis and
Current Value Basis Balance Sheets
December 31, 1995 and 1994 (In thousands)

	1995		1994	
	---	---	---	---
	Current Value Basis (Note 1)	Cost Basis	Current Value Basis (Note 1)	Cost Basis
Assets				
Property (Notes 4, 5, 6, 7, 11, and 18):				
Operating properties:				
Property and deferred costs of projects	$ 4,323,010	$ 3,006,356	$ 4,232,913	$ 2,937,565
Less: Accumulated depreciation and amortization	—	519,319	—	490,158
	4,323,010	2,487,037	4,232,913	2,447,407
Properties in development	62,030	56,151	70,866	65,348
Properties held for sale	22,602	22,602	8,809	8,809
Land held for development and sale	149,324	134,168	153,637	132,293
Total property	4,556,966	2,699,958	4,466,225	2,653,857
Prepaid expenses, deferred charges, and other assets	160,854	151,068	159,956	151,223
Accounts and notes receivable (Note 8)	36,751	36,751	31,233	31,233
Investments in marketable securities	2,910	2,910	30,149	30,149
Cash and cash equivalents	94,922	94,922	49,398	49,398
Total	$ 4,852,403	$ 2,985,609	$ 4,736,961	$ 2,915,860

(continued)

EXHIBIT 15-21   (continued)

	1995		1994	
	Current Value Basis (Note 1)	Cost Basis	Current Value Basis (Note 1)	Cost Basis
Liabilities				
Debt (Note 11):				
Property debt not carrying a Parent Company guarantee of repayment	$ 1,990,041	$ 1,990,041	$ 1,998,445	$ 1,998,445
Parent Company debt and debt carrying a Parent Company guarantee of repayment:				
Property debt	138,488	138,488	223,731	223,731
Convertible subordinated debentures	126,750	130,000	105,950	130,000
Other debt	231,884	221,000	116,500	120,700
	497,122	489,488	446,181	474,431
Total debt	2,487,163	2,479,529	2,444,626	2,472,876
Obligations under capital leases (Note 18)	58,786	58,786	60,044	60,044
Accounts payable, accrued expenses, and other liabilities	185,561	185,561	205,317	205,317
Deferred income taxes (Note 14)	445,613	81,649	412,729	82,597
Company-obligated mandatorily redeemable preferred securities of a trust holding solely Parent Company subordinated debt securities (Note 12)	136,125	137,500	—	—
Shareholders' equity (Notes 16 and 17)				
Series A Convertible Preferred stock with a liquidation preference of $225,250 in 1995 and $225,252 in 1994	45	45	45	45
Common stock of 1¢ par value per share; 250,000,000 shares authorized; issued 47,922,749 shares in 1995 and 47,571,046 shares in 1994	479	479	476	476
Additional paid-in capital	309,943	309,943	306,674	306,674
Accumulated deficit	(267,883)	(267,883)	(212,169)	(212,169)
Revaluation equity	1,496,571	—	1,519,219	—
Total shareholders' equity	1,539,155	42,584	1,614,245	95,026
Commitments and contingencies (Notes 18, 19, and 20)				
Total	$ 4,852,403	$ 2,985,609	$ 4,736,961	$ 2,915,860

EXHIBIT 15-21   **(concluded)**

**Current value basis
financial statements**

(a) Current value reporting

The Company's interests in operating properties, land held for development and sale, and certain other assets have appreciated in value and, accordingly, their aggregate current value substantially exceeds their aggregate cost basis net book value determined in conformity with generally accepted accounting principles. The current value basis financial statements present information about the current values to the Company of its assets and liabilities and the changes in such values. The current value basis financial statements are not intended to present the current liquidation values of assets or liabilities of the Company or its net assets taken as a whole.

Management believes that the current value basis financial statements more realistically reflect the underlying financial strength of the Company. The current values of the Company's interests in operating properties, including interests in unconsolidated real estate ventures, represent management's estimates of the value of these assets primarily as investments. These values will generally be realized through future cash flows generated by the operation of these properties over their economic lives. The current values of land held for development and sale represent management's estimates of the value of these assets under long-term development and sales programs.

Shareholders' equity on a current value basis was $1,539,155,000 or $26.30 per share of common stock at December 31, 1995, and $1,614,245,000 or $27.75 per share of common stock at December 31, 1994. The per-share calculations assume the conversion of the Preferred stock.

The process for estimating the current values of the Company's assets and liabilities requires significant estimates and judgments by management. These estimates and judgments are made based on information and assumptions considered by management to be adequate and appropriate in the circumstances; however, they are not subject to precise quantification or verification and may change from time to time as economic and market factors, and management's evaluation of them, change.

The current value basis financial statements are an integral part of the Company's annual report to shareholders, but they are not presented as part of the Company's quarterly reports to shareholders. The extensive market research, financial analysis, and testing of results required to produce reliable current value information make it impractical to report this information on an interim basis.

(b) Bases of valuation (Detail of bases of valuation presented)

Special industry ratios were reviewed in this chapter. The following ratios are helpful when analyzing a bank:

$$\text{Earning Assets to Total Assets} = \frac{\text{Average Earning Assets}}{\text{Average Total Assets}}$$

$$\text{Return on Earning Assets} = \frac{\text{Net Income}}{\text{Average Earning Assets}}$$

$$\text{Interest Margin to Average Earning Assets} = \frac{\text{Interest Margin}}{\text{Average Earning Assets}}$$

$$\text{Loan Loss Coverage Ratio} = \frac{\text{Pretax Income (Before Security Transactions)} + \text{Provision for Loan Losses}}{\text{Net Charge-Offs}}$$

$$\text{Equity Capital to Total Assets} = \frac{\text{Average Equity}}{\text{Average Total Assets}}$$

$$\text{Deposits Times Capital} = \frac{\text{Average Deposits}}{\text{Average Stockholders' Equity}}$$

$$\text{Loans to Deposits} = \frac{\text{Average Total Loans}}{\text{Average Deposits}}$$

The following ratios are helpful in analyzing utility performance:

$$\text{Operating Ratio} = \frac{\text{Operating Expense}}{\text{Operating Revenue}}$$

$$\text{Funded Debt to Operating Property} = \frac{\text{Funded Debt (Long-Term)}}{\text{Operating Property}}$$

$$\text{Percent Earned on Operating Property} = \frac{\text{Net Income}}{\text{Operating Property}}$$

$$\text{Operating Revenue to Operating Property} = \frac{\text{Operating Revenue}}{\text{Operating Property}}$$

The ratios that follow are especially suited to transportation. Additional insight can be gained by looking at revenues and expenses on a per unit of usage basis.

$$\text{Operating Ratio} = \frac{\text{Operating Expense}}{\text{Operating Revenue}}$$

$$\text{Long-Term Debt to Operating Property} = \frac{\text{Long-Term Debt}}{\text{Operating Property}}$$

$$\text{Operating Revenue to Operating Property} = \frac{\text{Operating Revenue}}{\text{Operating Property}}$$

QUESTIONS

Q 15-1.   What are the main sources of revenue for banks?

Q 15-2.   Why are loans, which are usually liabilities, treated as assets for banks?

Q 15-3.   Why are savings accounts liabilities for banks?

Q 15-4.   Why are banks concerned with their loans/deposits ratios?

Q 15-5.   To what agencies and other users of financial statements must banks report?

Q 15-6.   Why must the user be cautious in analyzing bank holding companies?

Q 15-7.   What is usually the biggest expense item for a bank?

Q 15-8.   What does the ratio total deposits times capital measure?

Q 15-9.   What ratios are used to indicate profitability for banks?

Q 15-10.   Why are banks concerned about the percentage of earning assets to total assets?

Q 15-11.   What does the loan loss coverage ratio measure?

Q 15-12.   What type of ratio is deposits times capital?

Q 15-13.   Give an example of why a review of bank assets may indicate risk or opportunity you were not aware of.

Q 15-14.   Why review the disclosure of the market value of investments versus the book amount of investments for banks?

Q 15-15.   Why review the disclosure of foreign loans for banks?

Q 15-16.   Why review the disclosure of allowance for loan losses for a bank?

Q 15-17.   Why review the disclosure of nonperforming assets for banks?

Q 15-18.   Why could a review of savings deposit balances be important when reviewing a bank's financial statements?

Q 15-19.   Why review the footnote that describes commitments and contingent liabilities for a bank?

Q 15-20.   Utilities are very highly leveraged. How is it that they are able to carry such high levels of debt?

Q 15-21.   How does demand for utilities differ from demand for other products or services?

Q 15-22.   Why are plant and equipment listed first for utilities?

Q 15-23.   Are inventory ratios meaningful for utilities? Why?

Q 15-24.   What does the funded debt to operating property ratio measure for a utility?

Q 15-25.   Is times interest earned meaningful for utilities? Why or why not?

Q 15-26.   Are current liabilities presented first in utility reporting?

Q 15-27.   For a utility, why review the account, Construction Work in Progress?

Q 15-28.   For a utility, describe the income statement accounts, Allowance for Equity Funds Used During Construction, and Allowance for Borrowed Funds Used During Construction.

Q 15-29.   Differentiate between successful-efforts and full-costing accounting as applied to the oil and gas industry.

Q 15-30.   Some industries described in this chapter are controlled by federal regulatory agencies. How does this affect their accounting systems?

Q 15-31.   When reviewing the financial statements of oil and gas companies, why is it important to note the method of costing (expensing) exploration and production costs?

Q 15-32.   Oil and gas companies must disclose quantity estimates for proved oil and gas reserves and the major factors causing changes in these resource estimates. Briefly indicate why this disclosure can be significant.

Q 15-33.   For oil and gas companies, there is the potential for a significant difference between the reported income and cash flows from operations. Comment.

Q 15-34.   Is it more desirable to have the operating ratios increasing or decreasing for utilities and transportation companies?

Q 15-35.   What type of ratio is operating revenue to operating property? Will it exceed 1:1 for a utility?

Q 15-36.   What is the most important category of assets for transportation firms?

Q 15-37.   Briefly describe the revenue section of the income statement for a transportation firm.

Q 15-38.   In a transportation firm, what types of things will change operating revenues? Operating expenses?

Q 15-39.   If a transportation firm shows a rise in revenue per passenger mile, what does this rise imply?

Q 15-40.   How is the passenger load factor of a bus company related to profitability?

Q 15-41. Explain how the publication *Financial Analysis of the Motor Carrier Industry* could be used to determine the percentage of total revenue a firm has in relation to similar trucking firms.

Q 15-42. Annual reports filed with state insurance departments are in accordance with what accounting standards?

Q 15-43. Annual reports that insurance companies issue to the public are in accordance with what accounting standards?

Q 15-44. Why could an insurance company with substantial investments in real estate represent a risk?

Q 15-45. For an insurance company, describe the difference between GAAP reporting and SAP reporting of deferred policy acquisition costs.

Q 15-46. Briefly describe the difference between accounting for intangibles for an insurance company under GAAP and under SAP.

Q 15-47. Briefly describe the unique aspects of revenue recognition for an insurance company.

Q 15-48. Insurance industry-specific financial ratios are usually prepared from financial statements prepared under what standards?

Q 15-49. Insurance companies tend to have a stock market price at a discount to the average market price (price/earnings ratio). Indicate some perceived reasons for this relatively low price/earnings ratio.

Q 15-50. Real estate companies contend that conventional accounting does not recognize the underlying value of the property and that this misleads investors. Discuss.

PROBLEMS

P 15-1. The following are statistics from the annual report of McEttrick National Bank:

	1995	1994
Average loans	$16,000,000	$13,200,000
Average total assets	26,000,000	22,000,000
Average total deposits	24,000,000	20,000,000
Average total capital	1,850,000	1,600,000
Interest expenses	1,615,000	1,512,250
Interest income	1,750,000	1,650,000

Required

a. Calculate the total deposits times capital for each year.
b. Calculate the loans to total deposits for each year.
c. Calculate the capital funds to total assets for each year.
d. Calculate the interest margin to average total assets for each year.
e. Comment on any trends found in the calculations of (a) through (d).

P 15-2.   The following are statistics from the annual report of Dover Bank:

	1995	1994	1993
Average earning assets	$50,000,000	$45,000,000	$43,000,000
Average total assets	58,823,529	54,216,867	52,000,000
Income before securities			
transactions	530,000	453,000	420,000
Interest margin	2,550,000	2,200,000	2,020,000
Pretax income before securities			
transactions	562,000	480,500	440,000
Provision for loan losses	190,000	160,000	142,000
Net charge-offs	180,000	162,000	160,000
Average equity	4,117,600	3,524,000	3,120,000
Average net loans	32,500,000	26,000,000	22,500,000
Average deposits	52,500,000	42,500,000	37,857,000

Required   a. Calculate the following for 1995, 1994, and 1993:
1. Earning assets to total assets
2. Return on earning assets
3. Interest margin to average earning assets
4. Loan loss coverage ratio
5. Equity to total assets
6. Deposits times capital
7. Loans to deposits

b. Comment on trends found in the ratios computed in (a).

P 15-3.   Super Power Company reported the following statistics in its statements of income:

	1995	1994
Electric revenues:		
Residential	$11,800,000	$10,000,000
Commercial and industrial	10,430,000	10,000,000
Other	600,000	500,000
	22,830,000	20,500,000
Operating expenses and taxes*	20,340,000	18,125,000
Operating income	2,490,000	2,375,000
Other income	200,000	195,000
Income before interest deductions	2,690,000	2,570,000
Interest deductions	1,200,000	1,000,000
Net income	$ 1,490,000	$ 1,570,000

*Includes taxes of $3,200,000 in 1995 and $3,000,000 in 1994.

Required   a.   Calculate the operating ratio and comment on the results.
b.   Calculate the times interest earned and comment on the results.
c.   Perform a vertical common-size analysis of revenues, using total revenue as the base, and comment on the relative size of the component parts.

P 15-4.   The following statistics relate to Michgate, an electric utility:

	1995	1994	1993
	(In thousands of dollars, except per share)		
Operating expenses	$ 850,600	$ 820,200	$ 780,000
Operating revenues	1,080,500	1,037,200	974,000
Earnings per share	3.00	2.90	2.60
Cash flow per share	3.40	3.25	2.30
Operating property	3,900,000	3,750,000	3,600,000
Funded debt (long-term)	1,500,000	1,480,000	1,470,000
Net income	280,000	260,000	230,000

Required   a.   Calculate the following for 1995, 1994, and 1993:
1.   Operating ratio
2.   Funded debt to operating property
3.   Percent earned on operating property
4.   Operating revenue to operating property
b.   Comment on trends found in the ratios computed in (a).
c.   Comment on the trend between earnings per share and cash flow per share.

P 15-5.   Local Airways had the following results in the last two years:

	1995	1994
Operating revenues	$ 624,000	$ 618,000
Operating expenses	625,000	617,000
Operating property	365,000	360,000
Long-term debt	280,000	270,000
Estimated passenger miles	7,340,000	7,600,000

Required   Calculate the following for 1995 and 1994:
a.   Calculate the operating ratio and comment on the trend.
b.   Calculate the long-term debt to operating property ratio. What does this tell about debt use?
c.   Calculate the operating revenue to operating property and comment on the trend.
d.   Calculate the revenue per passenger mile. What has caused this trend?

P 15-6.   Chihi Airways had the following results for the last three years:

	1995	1994	1993
	(In thousands of dollars)		
Operating expenses	$1,550,000	$1,520,000	$1,480,000
Operating revenues	1,840,000	1,670,400	1,620,700
Long-term debt	910,000	900,500	895,000
Operating property	995,000	990,000	985,000
Passenger load factor	66.5%	59.0%	57.8%

Required   a. Calculate the following for 1995, 1994, and 1993:
                    1. Operating ratio
                    2. Long-term debt to operating property
                    3. Operating revenue to operating property

                b. Comment on trends found in the ratios computed in (a).
                c. Comment on the passenger load factor.

P 15-7.

Required   Answer the following multiple-choice questions related to insurance finan-
                cial reporting.

                a. Which of the following does not represent a basic type of insurance
                    organization?
                    1. Stock companies
                    2. Bond companies
                    3. Mutual companies
                    4. Fraternal benefit societies
                    5. Assessment companies

                b. Which of these statements is not correct?
                    1. The balance sheet is a classified balance sheet.
                    2. The asset section starts with investments.
                    3. The majority of the investments are typically in bonds.
                    4. For life insurance companies, the investment in real estate may be
                        much greater than that for property-casualty companies.
                    5. Real estate investments are reported at cost less accumulated
                        depreciation and an allowance for impairment in value.

                c. Generally, the largest liability is for loss reserves. The quantification
                    process is subject to a number of estimates. Which of the following
                    would not be one of the estimates?
                    1. Investment gains/losses
                    2. Inflation rate
                    3. Interest rates
                    4. Judicial interpretations
                    5. Mortality estimates

d. The manner of recognizing revenue on insurance contracts is unique for the insurance industry. Which of the following statements is not true?
1. In general, the duration of the contract governs the revenue recognition.
2. When the risk differs significantly from the contract period, revenue is recognized over the period of risk in proportion to the amount of insurance protection.
3. For long-duration contracts, revenue is recognized when the premium is due from policyholders.
4. Realized gains and losses from investments are reported in operations in the period incurred.
5. For investment contracts, termination fees are booked as revenue over the period of the contract.

e. Which of the following statements is not true?
1. Statutory accounting has emphasized the balance sheet in its concern for protecting the policyholders by focusing on the financial solvency of the insurance corporation.
2. All 50 states have insurance departments that require annual statements of insurance companies. These annual reports are filed with the state insurance departments in accordance with Statutory Accounting Practices (SAP).
3. After the annual reports are filed with the individual state insurance departments, a testing process is conducted by the NAIC. If a company's ratio is outside the prescribed limit, the NAIC brings that to the attention of the company.
4. A.M. Best Company publishes *Best's Insurance Reports*, which are published separately for life-health companies and property-casualty companies. The financial data, including the ratios, are based on the data submitted to the state insurance departments and are thus based on SAP.
5. Many stock insurance companies must register with the Securities and Exchange Commission and file the required forms, such as the annual Form 10-K. Reports filed with the SEC must conform with GAAP.

Cases

CASE 15-1 Allowance for Funds

The following financial information is from the New England Electric System and Subsidiaries 1994 annual report:

NEW ENGLAND ELECTRIC SYSTEM AND SUBSIDIARIES
Consolidated Statement of Income
Year Ended December 31

	1994	1993	1992
	(Dollars in thousands, except per-share amounts)		
Operating Revenue	$2,243,029	$2,233,978	$2,181,676
Operating Expenses:			
Fuel for generation	220,956	227,182	237,161
Purchased electric energy	514,143	527,307	525,655
Other operation	494,741	492,079	423,330
Maintenance	161,473	146,219	162,974
Depreciation and amortization	301,123	296,631	302,217
Taxes, other than income taxes	125,840	120,493	114,027
Income taxes	128,257	121,124	110,761
Total Operating Expenses	1,946,533	1,931,035	1,876,125
Operating Income	296,496	302,943	305,551
Other Income:			
Allowance for equity funds used during construction	10,169	3,795	2,732
Equity in income of generating companies	9,758	11,016	13,052
Other income (expense) net	(3,856)	(1,154)	936
Operating and other income	312,567	316,600	322,271
Interest:			
Interest on long-term debt	93,500	100,777	114,182
Other interest	11,298	9,809	5,420
Allowance for borrowing funds used during construction	(7,793)	(2,816)	(2,204)
Total Interest	97,005	107,770	117,398
Income after interest	215,562	208,830	204,873
Preferred dividends of subsidiaries	8,697	10,585	10,572
Minority interests	7,439	8,022	9,264
Net Income	$ 199,426	$ 190,223	$ 185,037

	1994	1993	1992
Common shares outstanding	64,969,652	64,969,652	64,969,652
Per-share data:			
Net income	$ 3.07	$ 2.93	$ 2.85
Dividends declared	$ 2.285	$ 2.22	$ 2.14

NEW ENGLAND ELECTRIC SYSTEM AND SUBSIDIARIES
Consolidated Balance Sheet

Year Ended December 31	1994	1993
	(Dollars in thousands)	
Assets		
Utility plant, at original cost	$4,914,807	$4,661,612
Less: Accumulated provisions for depreciation and amortization	1,610,378	1,511,271
	3,304,429	3,150,341
Net investment in Seabrook 1 under rate settlement (Note C)	38,283	103,344
Construction work in progress	374,009	228,816
Net utility plant	3,716,721	3,482,501
Oil and gas properties, at cost (Note A)	1,248,343	1,220,110
Less: Accumulated provision for amortization	964,069	884,837
Net oil and gas properties	284,274	335,273
Investments:		
Nuclear power companies, at equity (Note D)	46,349	46,342
Other subsidiaries, at equity	42,195	44,676
Other investments	50,895	28,836
Total investments	139,439	119,854
Current assets:		
Cash	3,047	2,876
Accounts receivable, less reserves of $15,095 and $14,551	295,627	275,020
Unbilled revenues (Note A)	55,900	43,400
Fuel, materials, and supplies, at average cost	94,431	74,314
Prepaid and other current assets	76,718	69,004
Total current assets	525,723	464,614
Accrued Yankee Atomic cost (Note D)	122,452	103,501
Deferred charges and other assets (Note A)	296,232	290,135
	$5,084,841	$4,795,878

(continued)

Consolidated Balance Sheet

	December 31	
	1994	**1993**
Capitalization and Liabilities		
Capitalization (see accompanying statements):		
Common share equity	$1,580,838	$1,529,868
Minority interests in consolidated subsidiaries	55,066	55,855
Cumulative preferred stock of subsidiaries	147,016	147,528
Long-term debt	1,520,488	1,511,589
Total capitalization	3,303,408	3,244,840
Current liabilities:		
Long-term debt due within one year	65,920	12,920
Short-term debt	233,970	71,775
Accounts payable	168,937	128,342
Accrued taxes	11,002	10,332
Accrued interest	25,193	23,278
Dividends payable	37,154	36,950
Other current liabilities (Note A)	93,251	153,812
Total current liabilities	635,427	437,409
Deferred federal and state income taxes	751,855	705,026
Unamortized investment tax credits	94,930	99,355
Accrued Yankee Atomic cost (Note D)	122,452	103,501
Other reserves and deferred credits	176,769	205,747
Commitments and contingencies (Note E)		
	$5,084,841	$4,795,878

Selected note to consolidated financial statements

3. Allowance for funds used during construction (AFDC)

The utility subsidiaries capitalized AFDC as part of construction costs. AFDC represents the composite interest and equity costs of capital funds used to finance that portion of construction cost not eligible for inclusion in the rate base. In 1994, an average of $30 million of construction work in progress was included in the rate base, all of which was attributable to the Manchester Street Station repowering project. AFDC is capitalized in "Utility plant," with off-setting noncash credits to "Other income" and "Interest." This method is in accordance with an established rate-making practice, under which a utility is permitted a return on, and the recovery of, prudently incurred capital costs through their ultimate inclusion in the rate base and in the provision for depreciation. The composite AFDC rates were 7.6 percent, 7.4 percent, and 8.6 percent, in 1994, 1993, and 1992, respectively.

Required
a. Describe the allowance for equity funds used during construction.
b. Describe the allowance for borrowing funds used during construction.
c. How does capitalizing interest on borrowed funds affect income in the year of capitalization versus not capitalizing this interest? Explain.
d. Would net income tend to be higher than cash flow if there is substantial capitalization of interest on the borrowed funds during the current period? Explain.
e. How does capitalizing the allowance for equity funds used during construction affect income in the year of capitalization versus not capitalizing these charges?
f. Would net income tend to be higher than cash flow if there is substantial capitalization of the allowance for equity funds used during construction for the current year?
g. Describe how a utility that has substantial construction work in progress could have a material cash flow problem in relation to the reported income.
h. Compute the following for 1994 and 1993. Comment on each.
   1. Operating ratio
   2. Funded debt to operating property
   3. Percent earned on operating property
   4. Operating revenue to operating property
   5. Times interest earned
i. Using the balances at December 31, 1994, compute the percentage relationship between construction work in progress and net utility plant. Comment.

CASE 15-2 In Progress

The following financial information is from the Southern Indiana Gas and Electric Company 1994 annual report:

SOUTHERN INDIANA GAS AND ELECTRIC COMPANY
Consolidated Statement of Income
Year Ended December 31

	1994	1993	1992
	(Dollars in thousands, except per-share amounts)		
Operating Revenues:			
Electric	$ 260,936	$ 258,405	$ 243,077
Gas	69,099	71,084	63,828
Total operating revenues	330,035	329,489	306,905

(continued)

Consolidated Statements of Income (concluded)

	1994	1993	1992
Operating Revenues (bro't. fwd.)	$ 330,035	$ 329,489	$ 306,905
Operating Expenses:			
Operation:			
Fuel for electric generation	83,382	81,080	81,239
Purchased electric energy	5,489	9,348	2,914
Cost of gas sold	42,319	51,269	46,653
Other	48,911	40,718	36,103
Total operation	180,101	182,415	166,909
Maintenance	30,355	26,775	22,146
Depreciation and amortization	37,705	36,960	36,233
Federal and state income taxes	19,302	18,306	16,490
Property and other taxes	10,205	13,468	14,232
Total operating expenses	277,668	277,924	256,010
Operating Income	52,367	51,565	50,895
Other Income:			
Allowance for other funds used			
during construction	3,972	3,092	988
Interest	988	930	1,015
Other, net	2,685	2,533	2,101
	7,645	6,555	4,104
Income Before Interest Charges	60,012	58,120	54,999
Interest Charges:			
Interest on long-term debt	18,604	18,437	17,768
Amortization of premium, discount,			
and expense on debt	852	773	446
Other interest	1,589	747	461
Allowance for borrowing funds			
used during construction	(2,058)	(1,425)	(434)
	18,987	18,532	18,241
Net Income	41,025	39,588	36,758
Preferred Stock Dividends	1,105	1,105	1,267
Net Income Applicable to			
Common Stock	$ 39,920	$ 38,483	$ 35,491
Average Common Shares Outstanding	15,755	15,755	15,755
Earnings per Share of Common Stock	$2.53	$2.44	$2.25

The accompanying Notes to Consolidated Financial Statements are an integral part of these statements.

SOUTHERN INDIANA GAS AND ELECTRIC COMPANY
Consolidated Balance Sheet

	December 31	
	1994	1993
	(In thousands of dollars)	
Assets		
Utility plant, at original cost:		
Electric	$ 907,591	$879,476
Gas	114,951	107,864
	1,022,542	987,340
Less: Accumulated provision for depreciation	456,922	424,086
	565,620	563,254
Construction work in progress	112,316	72,615
Net utility plant	677,936	635,869
Other Investments and Property:		
Investment in leveraged leases	34,746	34,924
Investments in partnerships	23,411	25,023
Environmental improvement funds held by Trustee	10,526	22,613
Nonutility property and other	12,783	9,861
	81,466	92,421
Current Assets:		
Cash and cash equivalent	6,042	5,983
Restricted cash	22,018	8,749
Temporary investments, at market	5,444	4,676
Receivable, less allowance of $231 and $166, respectively	25,582	28,541
Inventories	46,441	38,190
Coal contract settlement	7,685	5,610
Other current assets	2,355	3,048
	115,567	94,797
Deferred Charges:		
Coal contract settlement	—	7,685
Unamortized premium on reacquired debt	6,621	7,100
Postretirement benefits other than pensions	8,011	4,125
Demand side management program	11,530	7,411
Other deferred charges	16,109	11,433
	42,271	37,754
	$ 917,240	$860,841

The accompanying Notes to Consolidated Financial Statements are an integral part of these statements.

(continued)

Consolidated Balance Sheet   (concluded)

	December 31	
	1994	**1993**
	(In thousands of dollars)	
Shareholders' Equity and Liabilities		
Common Stock	$ 102,798	$ 102,798
Retained Earnings	218,424	204,449
Less: Unrealized loss on debt and equity securities	106	—
	321,116	307,247
Less: Treasury Stock, at cost	24,540	24,540
Common shareholders' equity	296,576	282,707
Cumulative Nonredeemable Preferred Stock	11,090	11,090
Cumulative Redeemable Preferred Stock	7,500	7,500
Cumulative Special Preferred Stock	1,015	1,015
Long-Term Debt, net of current maturities	264,110	261,100
Long-Term Partnership Obligations, net of current maturities	9,507	12,881
Total capitalization, excluding bonds subject to tender (see Consolidated Statements of Capitalization)	589,798	576,293
Current Liabilities:		
Current portion of adjustable rate bonds subject to tender	31,500	41,475
Current maturities of long-term debt, interim financing, and long-term partnership obligations:		
Maturing long-term debt	7,803	763
Notes payable	22,060	11,040
Partnership obligations	3,374	3,849
Total current maturities of long-term debt, interim financing, and long-term partnership obligations	33,237	15,652
Other current liabilities:		
Accounts payable	35,183	33,939
Dividends payable	125	135
Accrued taxes	6,849	7,941
Accrued interest	4,599	4,517
Refunds to customers	14,844	3,398
Accrued coal liabilities	22,018	8,749
Other accrued liabilities	16,339	10,125
Total other current liabilities	99,957	68,804
Total current liabilities	164,694	125,931
Deferred Credits and Other:		
Accumulated deferred income taxes	120,576	117,267
Accumulated deferred investment tax credits, being amortized over lives of property	24,702	26,549
Regulatory income tax liability	4,052	7,197
Postretirement benefits other than pensions	8,384	4,125
Other	5,034	3,479
	162,748	158,617
	$ 917,240	$ 860,841

Selected note to consolidated financial statements
(d) Utility plant

Utility plant is stated at historical original cost of construction. Such cost includes payroll-related costs, such as taxes, pensions, and other fringe benefits, general and administrative costs, and an allowance for the cost of funds capitalized as a cost of construction. While capitalized AFUDC does not represent a current source of cash, it does represent a basis for future cash revenue through depreciation and return allowance. The weighted average AFUDC rate (before income taxes) used by the Company was 9.5% in 1994, 10.5% in 1993, and 11.5% in 1992.

Required

a. Describe the allowance for other funds used during construction.
b. How does capitalizing interest on borrowed funds affect income in the year of capitalization versus not capitalizing this interest? Explain.
c. Would net income tend to be higher than cash flow if there is substantial capitalization of the allowance for equity funds used during construction for the current year?
d. Compute the following for 1994 and 1993. Comment on each.
   1. Operating ratio
   2. Funded debt to operating property
   3. Percent earned on operating property
   4. Operating revenue to operating property
   5. Times interest earned
e. Using the balance at December 31, 1994, compute the percentage relationship between construction work in progress and net utility plant.
f. Comment on trends, considering only net income, earnings per share of common stock, allowance for other funds used during construction, and allowance for borrowing funds used during construction.

CASE 15-3 Loans and Provision for Loans

Sylvania Savings Bank included the following footnote in its 1984 annual report:

Loans

Net loans at December 31, 1984, were $175,617,000, an increase of 23% over $142,264,000 at December 31, 1983. During the year, commercial loans increased by 25%, real estate loans increased by 3%, and consumer loans increased by 74%. Net loans represented 68% of total earning assets at December 31, 1984, compared to 64% at December 31, 1983. The average yield on the loan portfolio for 1984 was 13.2% compared to 12.7% for 1983. Non-earning loans at December 31, 1984 were $2,469,000, as compared to $4,528,000 at December 31, 1983. During 1984, net loan charge-offs amounted to $1,239,000, compared to $1,414,000 in 1983. To offset these charge-offs, the 1984 provision for possible loan losses was $1,430,000, compared to $1,425,000 in 1983. As a result of these provisions, the Reserve for Possible Loan Losses totaled $1,786,000 at December 31, 1984, and $1,595,000 at December 31, 1983. As a percent of loans less unearned discount, the reserve was 1.01% in 1984 and 1.11% in 1983.

Required   Give your opinion as to significant information in this footnote.

CASE 15-4 You Can Bank on It

The financial data included in this case are from selected parts of the 1995 annual report of Mid Am, Inc.

MID AM, INC.
CONSOLIDATED STATEMENT OF CONDITION

December 31 (Dollars in thousands)	1995	1994
Assets		
Cash and due from banks	$ 102,600	$ 85,332
Interest-bearing deposits in other banks	3,372	2,232
Federal funds sold	72,558	8,160
Securities available for sale	461,997	212,437
Investment securities	—	71,700
Mortgage-backed investment securities	—	180,309
Loans held for sale	12,642	12,963
	653,169	573,133
Loans, net of unearned fees and income of $829 and $1,648	1,475,651	1,433,289
Allowance for credit losses	(14,859)	(14,722)
Net loans	1,460,792	1,418,567
Bank premises and equipment	49,489	50,171
Interest receivable and other assets	41,301	36,918
TOTAL ASSETS	$ 2,204,751	$ 2,078,789

CONSOLIDATED STATEMENT OF CONDITION (concluded)

	1995	1994
Liabilities		
Demand deposits (non-interest-bearing)	$ 223,945	$ 190,423
Savings deposits	593,807	586,140
Other time deposits	1,042,390	959,929
Total deposits	1,860,142	1,736,492
Federal funds purchased and securities sold under agreements to repurchase	87,548	80,136
Capitalized lease obligations and debt	48,405	65,434
Interest payable and other liabilities	13,818	11,475
	2,009,913	1,893,537
Shareholders' Equity		
Preferred stock—no par value		
Authorized—2,000,000 shares		
Issued and outstanding—1,422,744 and 1,608,000 shares in 1995 and 1994, respectively	35,569	40,200
Common stock—stated value of $3.33 per share		
Authorized—35,000,000 shares		
Issued—19,492,726 and 17,359,629 shares in 1995 and 1994, respectively	64,975	57,865
Surplus	91,723	75,624
Retained earnings	9,529	17,769
Treasury stock—522,361 and 1,400 common shares in 1995 and 1994, respectively	(8,424)	(20)
Unrealized gains (losses) on securities available for sale	1,466	(6,186)
Commitments and contingencies (Notes 13 and 14)		
TOTAL LIABILITIES AND SHAREHOLDERS' EQUITY	$ 2,204,751	$ 2,078,789

CONSOLIDATED STATEMENT OF EARNINGS

Years Ended December 31, (Dollars in thousands, except per-share data)	1995	1994	1993
Interest Income			
Interest and fees on loans	$130,300	$110,917	$107,688
Interest on deposits in other banks	218	146	218
Interest on federal funds sold	3,610	1,206	1,606
Interest on taxable investments	25,209	24,750	26,683
Interest on tax exempt investments	3,206	3,552	3,192
	162,543	140,571	139,387
Interest Expense			
Interest on deposits	72,527	54,689	57,907
Interest on borrowed funds	7,789	4,875	3,150
	80,316	59,564	61,057
Net interest income	82,227	81,007	78,330
Provision for credit losses	3,002	1,224	3,991
Net interest income after provision for credit losses	79,225	79,783	74,339
Non-interest Income			
Trust department	1,337	1,195	910
Service charges on deposit accounts	6,200	6,036	5,819
Mortgage banking	8,522	6,694	12,317
Brokerage commissions	9,540	7,137	5,158
Collection agency fees	3,399	3,928	2,390
Net gains on sales of securities	350	1,231	2,719
Other income	6,607	6,333	4,689
	35,955	32,554	34,002
Non-interest Expense			
Salaries and employee benefits	41,282	40,183	35,441
Net occupancy expense	5,113	5,269	5,070
Equipment expense	7,385	7,589	6,740
Other expenses	24,636	25,538	25,711
	78,416	78,579	72,962
Income before income taxes	36,764	33,758	35,379
Applicable Income Taxes			
Currently payable	9,587	9,732	9,392
Deferred	2,210	773	1,306
	11,797	10,505	10,698
Net income	$ 24,967	$ 23,253	$ 24,681
Net income available to common shareholders	$ 22,216	$ 20,336	$ 21,763
Earnings Per Common Share			
Primary	$1.16	$1.07	$1.16
Fully diluted	$1.11	$1.03	$1.11

Note 4. Loans and Allowance for Credit Losses

Loans outstanding are as follows:

December 31, (Dollars in thousands)	1995	1994
Real estate loans:		
Construction	$ 63,086	$ 69,942
Mortgage	885,714	871,704
Commercial, financial, and agricultural loans	357,290	327,871
Installment and credit card loans	164,055	155,380
Other loans	6,335	10,040
Total	1,476,480	1,434,937
Less:		
Unearned income	(22)	(38)
Unamortized loan fees	(807)	(1,610)
Allowance for credit losses	(14,859)	(14,722)
Total net	$ 1,460,792	$ 1,418,567

Most of the Company's business activity is with customers located within the respective local business area of its banks which encompasses Western Ohio and Southeastern Michigan. The portfolio is well diversified, consisting of commercial, residential, agri-business, consumer, and small business loans. There are no significant concentrations in any one industry, and the amounts related to highly leveraged transactions are not significant.

The Company evaluates each customer's creditworthiness on a case-by-case basis. The amount of collateral obtained is based on management's evaluation of the customer. Collateral held relating to commercial, financial, agricultural, and commercial mortgages varies but may include accounts receivable, inventory, property, plant and equipment, and income-producing commercial properties.

Changes in the allowance for credit losses are as follows:

Years Ended December 31 (Dollars in thousands)	1995	1994	1993
Balance at beginning of period	$ 14,722	$ 15,157	$ 15,718
Additions (reductions):			
Provision for credit losses	3,002	1,224	3,991
Charge-offs	(4,379)	(3,406)	(7,175)
Recoveries on loans charged off	1,478	1,747	2,119

Transfer of other real estate
    owned allowance relating to
    in-substance foreclosure loans
	36	—	—

Effect of conforming year-ends of pooled entities	—	—	504
Balance at end of period	$ 14,859	$ 14,722	$ 15,157

At December 31, 1995, the recorded investment in impaired loans amounted to $9,245,000, of which $7,868,000 of impaired loans have a specific allowance of $2,307,000 and the remaining $1,377,000 of impaired loans have no specific allowance as the fair value of the collateral securing the loans exceeded the investment in the loan. The average recorded investment in impaired loans for the year ended December 31, 1995, was $9,939,000. Interest income recognized on the cash basis in 1995 related to impaired loans was $686,000.

At December 31, 1994, the outstanding principal balance of loans placed on non-accrual status amounted to $6,017,000.

Other non-performing assets at December 31, 1995 and 1994 include other real estate owned of $763,000 and $1,102,000, respectively, which have been recorded at estimated fair values less estimated selling costs.

In the normal course of business, the Company has made loans to certain directors, executive officers, and their associates under terms consistent with the Company's general lending policies. Loan activity relating to these individuals for the three years ended December 31, 1995 is as follows:

(Dollars in thousands)	Balances at Beginning of Period	New Originations/ Advances	Loan Repayments	Other	Balances at End of Period
Year ended December 31, 1995	$ 21,787	$11,558	$ 9,736	$(4,234)	$19,375
Year ended December 31, 1994	$ 20,406	$14,120	$10,774	$(1,965)	$21,787
Year ended December 31, 1993	$ 19,466	$ 9,369	$ 7,135	$(1,294)	$20,406

Required

a. Compute the following for 1995 and 1994 (use ending balance sheet accounts):
1. Earning assets to total assets
2. Return on earning assets
3. Interest margin to average earning assets (use year-end total earning assets)
4. Loan loss coverage ratio
5. Equity capital to total assets
6. Deposits times capital
7. Loans to deposits

b. Comment on the trends indicated by the ratios computed in (a).

CASE 15-5 Proved Reserves

Amerada Hess Corporation included the information in this case as part of the Supplementary Oil and Gas Data with its 1995 annual report.

The Corporation's net oil and gas reserves have been estimated by DeGolyer and MacNaughton, independent consultants. The Corporation is offering for sale its Canadian operations and approximately 15% of its December 31, 1995, United States reserves on a barrel of oil equivalent basis. Reserves in Abu Dhabi, which the Corporation anticipates selling in the first half of 1996, represent approximately 60% of crude oil reserves in other areas. The reserves in the tabulation below include proved undeveloped crude oil and natural gas reserves that will require substantial future development expenditures. The estimates of the Corporation's proved reserves of crude oil and natural gas (after deducting royalties and operating interests owned by others) follow:

Oil and Gas Reserves	Total	United States	Canada	Europe	Other Areas
Net Proved Developed and Undeveloped Reserves:					
Crude Oil, Including Condensate and Natural Gas Liquids (Millions of Barrels)					
At January 1, 1993	652	203	40	371	38
Revisions of previous estimates	66	16	—	43	7
Extensions, discoveries, and other additions	28	5	3	20	—
Purchases of minerals in-place	3	—	1	2	—
Production	(79)	(26)	(5)	(41)	(7)
At December 31, 1993	670	198	39	395	38
Revisions of previous estimates	49	13	(2)	35	3
Extensions, discoveries, and other additions	12	8	2	2	—
Purchases of minerals in-place	8	4	—	—	4
Sales of minerals in-place	(3)	—	—	(3)	—
Production	(92)	(25)	(5)	(56)	(6)
At December 31, 1994	644	198	34	373	39
Revisions of previous estimates	68	11	—	44	13
Extensions, discoveries, and other additions	95	30	3	61	1
Sales of minerals in-place	(17)	(11)	(2)	(4)	—
Production	(95)	(23)	(4)	(62)	(6)
At December 31, 1995	695	205	31	412	47

(continued)

Natural Gas (Millions of Mcf)

At January 1, 1993	2,640	1,009	597	1,034	—
Revisions of previous estimates	127	30	(5)	102	—
Extensions, discoveries, and other additions	189	82	65	42	—
Purchases of minerals in-place	20	11	4	5	—
Production	(323)	(183)	(61)	(79)	—
At December 31, 1993	2,653	949*	600	1,104	—
Revisions of previous estimates	142	105	(1)	38	—
Extensions, discoveries, and other additions	167	101	50	16	—
Purchases of minerals in-place	4	3	—	1	—
Sales of minerals in-place	(76)	—	—	(76)	—
Production	(309)	(156)	(68)	(85)	—
At December 31, 1994	2,581	1,002	581	998	—
Revisions of previous estimates	53	6	(10)	57	—
Extensions, discoveries, and other additions	270	200	10	7	53
Sales of minerals in-place	(100)	(23)	(39)	(38)	—
Production	(323)	(147)	(79)	(97)	—
At December 31, 1995	2,481	1,038*	463	927	53

Net Proved Developed Reserves:
Crude Oil, Including Condensate
and Natural Gas Liquids
(Millions of Barrels)

At January 1, 1993	436	173	40	191	32
At December 31, 1993	514	169	38	271	36
At December 31, 1994	505	171	33	263	38
At December 31, 1995	540	157	31	310	42

Natural Gas (Millions of Mcf)

At January 1, 1993	2,002	851	576	575	—
At December 31, 1993	2,260	794	579	887	—
At December 31, 1994	2,210	838	558	814	—
At December 31, 1995	2,036	755	458	823	—

*Excludes 527 million Mcf of carbon dioxide gas for sale or use in company operations.

Required   a. Prepare a vertical common-size analysis of Net Proved Developed and Undeveloped Reserves Crude Oil, Including Condensate and Natural Gas Liquids (millions of barrels). Only use balances at December 31. Use December 31, 1993, as the base. Do a similar common-size analysis for natural gas (millions of Mcf).

b. Prepare a vertical common-size analysis of Net Proved Developed Reserves Crude Oil, Including Condensate and Natural Gas Liquids (millions of barrels). Only use balances at December 31. Use December 31, 1993, as the base. Do a similar common-size analysis for natural gas (millions Mcf).

c. Comment on the common-size analysis in (a) and (b).

CASE 15-6 Heavenly Flying

Exhibit 15-15 includes consolidated statements of income for Delta Air Lines, Inc.

Required a. Prepare a vertical common-size analysis of this statement, through operating income for 1995, 1994, and 1993. Use total operating revenues as the base.

b. Comment on trends found in (a).

CASE 15-7 Insight

Exhibit 15-21 includes the Consolidated Cost Basis and Current Value Basis Balance Sheets from the 1995 annual report of The Rouse Company and Subsidiaries. These balance sheets contain substantial differences between operating properties on a current value basis versus cost basis and between deferred income taxes on a current value basis versus cost basis. The current value basis statements also have a significant revaluation equity account.

Required a. Comment on the following accounts, describing why there is a difference between the current value and the cost basis:
1. Operating properties
2. Deferred income taxes
3. Revaluation equity

b. Comment on the subjectivity in arriving at the current values.

Endnotes

1   Arthur Anderson & Co., *Insurance* (Essex, England: Saffren Press Ltd., 1983), p. 87.
2   *Statement of Financial Accounting Standards No. 60,* "Accounting and Reporting by Insurance Enterprises" (Stamford, CT: Financial Accounting Standards Board, 1982), paragraph 13.
3   *Statement of Financial Accounting Standards No. 60,* paragraph 15.
4   *Statement of Financial Accounting Standards No. 97,* "Accounting and Reporting by Insurance Enterprises for Certain Long-Duration Contracts and for Realized Gains and Losses from the Sale of Investments" (Stamford, CT: Financial Accounting Standards Board, 1987), paragraph 15.

16 Personal Financial Statements and Accounting for Governments and Not-for-Profit Organizations

THIS CHAPTER BRIEFLY COVERS THREE TYPES of financial reporting that have not been discussed in previous chapters: (1) personal financial statements, (2) governments, and (3) not-for-profit organizations other than governments.

PERSONAL FINANCIAL STATEMENTS

Personal financial statements of individuals, husband and wife, or a larger family group are prepared for obtaining credit, income tax planning, retirement planning, and estate planning. *Statement of Position 82-1* (SOP 82-1) covers guidelines for the preparation of personal financial statements.[1] SOP 82-1 concludes that:

> The primary users of personal financial statements normally consider estimated current value information to be more relevant for their decisions than historical cost information. Lenders require estimated current value information to assess collateral, and most personal loan applications require estimated current value information. Estimated current values are required for estate, gift, and income tax planning, and estimated current value information about assets is often required in federal and state filings of candidates for public office.[2]

SOP 82-1 concludes that personal financial statements should present assets at their estimated current values and liabilities at their estimated current amounts at the date of the financial statements. This contrasts with commercial financial statements, which predominantly use historical cost information. SOP 82-1 provides guidelines for determining the estimated current value of an asset and the estimated current amount of a liability. Exhibit 16-1 presents these guidelines.[3]

Form of the Statements

The basic statement prepared for personal financial statements, a **statement of financial condition**, resembles a balance sheet. It states assets at estimated current values and liabilities at estimated current amounts. A tax liability is estimated on the difference between the stated amounts of the assets and liabilities and the tax basis of these assets and liabilities. For example, land may cost $10,000, which would be the tax basis, but may have an estimated current value of $25,000. The estimated tax liability on the difference between the $10,000 and the $25,000 would be estimated.

The difference between the total assets and total liabilities, designated **net worth**, is equivalent to the equity section in a commercial balance sheet. The statement of financial condition is prepared on the accrual basis. Assets and liabilities are presented in order of liquidity and maturity.

The optional statement of changes in net worth presents the major changes (sources of increases and decreases) in net worth. Examples of changes in net worth would be income, increases in the estimated current value of assets, and decreases in estimated income taxes. The **statement of changes in net worth** presents changes in terms of realized increases (decreases) and unrealized increases (decreases). Examples of realized increases (decreases) are salary, dividends, income taxes, and personal expenditures. Examples of unrealized increases (decreases) are an increase in the value of securities, an increase in the value of a residence, a decrease in the value of a boat, and estimated income taxes on the differences between the estimated current values of assets and the estimated current amounts of liabilities and their tax bases. Comparative financial statements may be more informative than statements of only one period.

For personal financial statements, the statement of changes in net worth replaces the income statement. SOP 82-1 includes guidelines on disclosure (Exhibit 16-1). These guidelines are not all-inclusive. Examples of disclosure include the methods used in determining current values of major assets, descriptions of intangible assets, and assumptions used to compute the estimated income taxes.

Most individuals do not maintain a complete set of records, so the necessary data must be gathered from various sources. These sources include brokers' statements, income tax returns, safe deposit boxes, insurance policies, real estate tax returns, checkbooks, and bank statements.

EXHIBIT 16-1   Guidelines for Determining the Estimated Current Values of Assets and the Estimated Current Amounts of Liabilities

General

12.   Personal financial statements should present assets at their estimated current values and liabilities at their estimated current amounts. The estimated current value of an asset in personal financial statements is the amount at which the item could be exchanged between a buyer and seller, each of whom is well informed and willing, and neither of whom is compelled to buy or sell. Costs of disposal, such as commissions, if material, should be considered in determining estimated current values.[A] The division recognizes that the estimated current values of some assets may be difficult to determine and the cost of obtaining estimated current values of some assets directly may exceed the benefits of doing so; therefore, the division recommends that judgment be exercised in determining estimated current values.

13.   Recent transactions involving similar assets and liabilities in similar circumstances ordinarily provide a satisfactory basis for determining the estimated current value of an asset and the estimated current amount of a liability. If recent sales information is unavailable, other methods that may be used include the capitalization of past or prospective earnings, the use of liquidation values, the adjustment of historical cost based on changes in a specific price index, the use of appraisals, or the use of the discounted amounts of projected cash receipts and payments.

14.   In determining the estimated current values of some assets (for example, works of art, jewelry, restricted securities, investments in closely held businesses, and real estate), the person may need to consult a specialist.

15.   The methods used to determine the estimated current values of assets and the estimated current amounts of liabilities should be followed consistently from period to period unless the facts and circumstances dictate a change to different methods.

Receivables

16.   Personal financial statements should present receivables at the discounted amounts of cash the person estimates will be collected, using appropriate interest rates at the date of the financial statements.

Marketable Securities

17.   Marketable securities include both debt and equity securities for which market quotations are available. The estimated current values of such securities are their quoted market prices. The estimated current values of securities traded on securities exchanges are the closing prices of the securities on the date of the financial statements (valuation date) if the securities were traded on that date. If the securities were not traded on that date but published bid and asked prices are available, the estimated current values of the securities should be within the range of those prices.

18.   For securities traded in the over-the-counter market, quotations of bid and asked prices are available from several sources, including the financial press, various

(continued)

EXHIBIT 16-1   (continued)

quotation publications and financial reporting services, and individual broker-dealers. For those securities, the mean of the bid prices, of the bid and asked prices, or of the prices of a representative selection of broker-dealers quoting the securities may be used as the estimated current values.

19.   An investor may hold a large block of the equity securities of a company. A large block of stock might not be salable at the price at which a small number of shares were recently sold or quoted. Further, a large minority interest may be difficult to sell despite isolated sales of a small number of shares. However, a controlling interest may be proportionately more valuable than minority interests that were sold. Consideration of those factors may require adjustments to the price at which the security recently sold. Moreover, restrictions on the transfer of a security may also suggest the need to adjust the recent market price in determining the estimated current value.[B]

Options

20.   If published prices of options are unavailable, their estimated current values should be determined on the basis of the values of the assets subject to option, considering such factors as the exercise prices and length of the option periods.

Investment in Life Insurance

21.   The estimated current value of an investment in life insurance is the cash value of the policy less the amount of any loans against it. The face amount of life insurance the individuals own should be disclosed.

Investments in Closely Held Businesses

22.   The division recognizes that the estimated current values of investments in closely held businesses usually are difficult to determine. The problems relate to investments in closely held businesses in any form, including sole proprietorships, general and limited partnerships, and corporations. As previously stated, only the net investment in a business enterprise (not its assets and liabilities) should be presented in the statement of financial condition. The net investment should be presented at its estimated current value at the date of the financial statement. Since there is usually no established ready market for such an investment, judgment should be exercised in determining the estimated current value of the investment.

23.   There is no one generally accepted procedure for determining the estimated current value of an investment in a closely held business. Several procedures or combinations of procedures may be used to determine the estimated current value of a closely held business, including a multiple of earnings, liquidation value, reproduction value, appraisals, discounted amounts of projected cash receipts and payments, or adjustments of book value or cost of the person's share of the equity of the business.[C] The owner of an interest in a closely held business may have entered into a buy-sell agreement that specifies the amount (or the basis of determining the amount) to be received in the event of withdrawal, retirement, or sale. If such an agreement exists, it should be considered, but it does not necessarily determine estimated current value.

EXHIBIT 16-1 (continued)

Whatever procedure is used, the objective should be to approximate the amount at which the investment could be exchanged between a buyer and a seller, each of whom is well informed and willing, and neither of whom is compelled to buy or sell.

Real Estate (Including Leaseholds)

24. Investments in real estate (including leaseholds) should be presented in personal financial statements at their estimated current values. Information that may be used in determining their estimated current values includes:
   a. Sales of similar property in similar circumstances.
   b. The discounted amounts of projected cash receipts and payments relating to the property or the net realizable value of the property, based on planned courses of action, including leaseholds whose current rental value exceeds the rent in the lease.
   c. Appraisals based on estimates of selling prices and selling costs obtained from independent real estate agents or brokers familiar with similar properties in similar locations.
   d. Appraisals used to obtain financing.
   e. Assessed value for property taxes, including consideration of the basis for such assessments and their relationship to market values in the area.

Intangible Assets

25. Intangible assets should be presented at the discounted amounts of projected cash receipts and payments arising from the planned use or sale of the assets if both the amounts and timing can be reasonably estimated. For example, a record of receipts under a royalty agreement may provide sufficient information to determine its estimated current value. The cost of a purchased intangible should be used if no other information is available.

Future Interests and Similar Assets

26. Nonforfeitable rights to receive future sums that have all the following characteristics should be presented as assets at their discounted amounts:
   • The rights are for fixed or determinable amounts.
   • The rights are not contingent on the holder's life expectancy or the occurrence of a particular event, such as disability or death.
   • The rights do not require future performance or service by the holder.
Nonforfeitable rights that may have those characteristics include:
   • Guaranteed minimum portions of pensions.
   • Vested interest in pensions or profit-sharing plans.
   • Deferred compensation contracts.
   • Beneficial interests in trusts.
   • Remainder interests in property subject to life estates.
   • Annuities.
   • Fixed amounts of alimony for a definite future period.

(continued)

EXHIBIT 16-1   (continued)

Payables and Other Liabilities

27.   Personal financial statements should present payables and other liabilities at the discounted amounts of cash to be paid. The discount rate should be the rate implicit in the transaction in which the debt was incurred. If, however, the debtor is able to discharge the debt currently at a lower amount, the debt should be presented at the lower amount.[D]

Noncancellable Commitments

28.   Noncancellable commitments to pay future sums that have all the following characteristics should be presented as liabilities at their discounted amounts:
*   The commitments are for fixed or determinable amounts.
*   The commitments are not contingent on others' life expectancies or the occurrence of a particular event, such as disability or death.
*   The commitments do not require future performance or service by others.
Noncancellable commitments that may have those characteristics include fixed amounts of alimony for a definite future period and charitable pledges.

Income Taxes Payable

29.   The liability for income taxes payable should include unpaid income taxes for completed tax years and an estimated amount for income taxes accrued for the elapsed portion of the current tax year to the date of the financial statements. That estimate should be based on the relationship of taxable income earned to date to total estimated taxable income for the year, net of taxes withheld or paid with estimated income tax returns.

Estimated Income Taxes on the Differences Between the Estimated Current Values of Assets and the Estimated Current Amounts of Liabilities and Their Tax Bases

30.   A provision should be made for estimated income taxes on the differences between the estimated current values of assets and the estimated current amounts of liabilities and their tax bases, including consideration of negative tax bases of tax shelters, if any. The provision should be computed as if the estimated current values of all assets had been realized and the estimated current amounts of all liabilities had been liquidated on the statement date, using applicable income tax laws and regulations, considering recapture provisions and available carryovers. The estimated income taxes should be presented between liabilities and net worth in the statement of financial condition. The methods and assumptions used to compute the estimated income taxes should be fully disclosed. Appendix B to this statement of position illustrates how to compute the provision.

EXHIBIT 16-1   (concluded)

[A] Paragraph 27 defines the estimated current amount of a liability.

[B] For further discussion on valuing marketable securities, see the AICPA Industry Audit Guide, *Audits of Investment Companies* (New York: AICPA, 1973), pp. 15-17.

[C] The book value or costs of a person's share of the equity of a business adjusted for appraisals of specific assets, such as real estate or equipment, are sometimes used as the estimated current value.

[D] For a further discussion of the setting of a discount rate for payables and other liabilities, see APB Opinion 21, "Interest on Receivables and Payables," paragraph 13.

Suggestions for Reviewing the Statement of Financial Condition

1. Usually the most important figure, the net worth amount, indicates the level of wealth.

2. Determine the amount of the assets that you consider to be very liquid (cash, savings accounts, marketable securities, and so on). These assets are readily available.

3. Observe the due date of the liabilities. In general, we would prefer the liabilities to be relatively long term. Long-term liabilities do not represent an immediate pressing problem.

4. When possible, compare specific assets with their related liabilities. This will indicate the net investment in the asset. For example, a residence with a current value of $90,000 and a $40,000 mortgage represents a net investment of $50,000.

Suggestions for Reviewing the Statement of Changes in Net Worth

1. Review realized increases in net worth. Determine the principal sources of realized net worth.

2. Review realized decreases in net worth. Determine the principal items in realized decreases in net worth.

3. Observe whether the net realized amount increased or decreased and by how much.

4. Review unrealized increases in net worth. Determine the principal sources of the increases.

5. Review unrealized decreases in net worth. Determine the principal sources of the decreases.

6. Observe whether the net unrealized amount increased or decreased and the amount.

7. Observe whether the net change increased or decreased and the amount.

8. Observe the net worth at the end of the year.

Illustration of Preparation of the Statement of Financial Condition

For Bill and Mary, assume assets and liabilities, effective income tax rates, and the amount of estimated income taxes are as follows at December 31, 1997:

Account	Tax Bases	Estimated Current Value	Excess of Estimated Current Values over Tax Bases	Effective Income Tax Rates	Amount of Estimated Income Taxes
Cash	$ 8,000	$ 8,000	—	—	—
Savings accounts	20,000	20,000	—	—	—
Marketable securities	50,000	60,000	$10,000	28%	$ 2,800
Options	-0-	20,000	20,000	28%	5,600
Royalties	-0-	10,000	10,000	28%	2,800
Auto	15,000	10,000	(5,000)	—	—
Boat	12,000	8,000	(4,000)	—	—
Residence	110,000	130,000	20,000	28%	5,600
Furnishings	30,000	25,000	(5,000)	—	—
Mortgage payable	(60,000)	(60,000)	—	—	—
Auto loan	(5,000)	(5,000)	—	—	—
Credit cards	(5,000)	(4,000)	—	—	—
Total estimated income tax					$16,800

Bill and Mary
Statement of Financial Condition
December 31, 1997

Assets:	
Cash	$ 8,000
Savings accounts	20,000
Marketable securities	60,000
Options	20,000
Royalties	10,000
Auto	10,000
Boat	8,000
Residence	130,000
Furnishings	25,000
Total assets	$ 291,000
Liabilities:	
Credit cards	$ 4,000
Auto loan	5,000
Mortgage payable	60,000
Total liabilities	69,000
Estimated income taxes on the difference between the estimated current values of assets and the estimated current amounts of liabilities and their tax bases	16,800
Net worth	205,200
Total liabilities and net worth	$ 291,000

Comments

1. Many would consider the net worth, $205,200, a relatively high amount.

2. Liquid assets total $88,000 (cash, $8,000; savings accounts, $20,000; and marketable securities, $60,000).

3. Most of the liabilities appear to be long term (mortgage payable, $60,000).

4. Compare specific assets with related liabilities:

Auto:		Residence:	
Current value	$10,000	Current value	$130,000
Auto loan	5,000	Mortgage payable	60,000
Net investment	$ 5,000	Net investment	$ 70,000

Illustration of Preparation of the Statement of Changes in Net Worth

For Bill and Mary, the changes in net worth for the year ended December 31, 1997, follow:

Realized increases in net worth:	
Salary	$ 70,000
Dividend income	5,000
Interest income	6,000
Gain on sale of marketable securities	2,000
Realized decreases in net worth:	
Income taxes	20,000
Real estate taxes	2,000
Personal expenditures	28,000
Unrealized increases in net worth:	
Marketable securities	11,000
Residence	3,000
Unrealized decreases in net worth:	
Boat	2,000
Furnishings	4,000
Estimated income taxes on the differences between the estimated current values of assets and current amounts of liabilities and their tax bases	12,000
Net worth at the beginning of year	176,200

Bill and Mary
Statement of Changes in Net Worth
For the Year Ended December 31, 1997

Realized increases in net worth:	
Salary	$ 70,000
Dividend income	5,000
Interest income	6,000
Gain on sale of marketable securities	2,000
	83,000
Realized decreases in net worth:	
Income taxes	20,000
Real estate taxes	2,000
Personal expenditures	28,000
	50,000
Net realized increase in net worth	33,000

Net realized increase in net worth (bro't. fwd.)	<u>$ 33,000</u>
Unrealized increases in net worth:	
Marketable securities	11,000
Residence	<u>3,000</u>
	14,000
Unrealized decreases in net worth:	
Boat	2,000
Furnishings	4,000
Estimated income taxes on the differences	
between the estimated current values of	
assets and the estimated current amounts of	
liabilities and their tax base	<u>12,000</u>
	18,000
Net unrealized decreases in net worth	<u>4,000</u>
Net increase in net worth	29,000
Net worth at the beginning of year	176,200
Net worth at the end of the year	<u>$ 205,200</u>

Comments

1. Most of the realized increases in net worth is salary ($70,000).
2. The major decreases in realized net worth are income taxes ($20,000) and personal expenditures ($28,000).
3. The net realized increase in net worth totaled $33,000.
4. The principal unrealized increase in net worth is marketable securities ($11,000).
5. The principal unrealized decreases in net worth are estimated income taxes on the differences between the estimated current value of assets and the estimated current amounts of liabilities and their tax bases ($12,000).
6. The net unrealized decreases in net worth totaled $4,000.
7. The net increase in net worth totaled $29,000.
8. The net worth at the end of the year totaled $205,200.

ACCOUNTING FOR GOVERNMENTS

The accounting terminology utilized by governments differs greatly from that used by profit-oriented enterprises. Governments use such terms as *appropriations* and *general fund.* Definitions of some of the terms that will be encountered follow:

—   **Appropriations.**   Provision for necessary resources and the authority for their disbursement.

—   **Debt service.**   Cash receipts and disbursements related to the payment of interest and principal on long-term debt.

—   **Capital projects.**   Cash receipts and disbursements related to the acquisition of long-lived assets.

—   **Special assessments.**   Cash receipts and disbursements related to improvements or services for which special property assessments have been levied.

—   **Enterprises.**   Operations that are similar to private businesses in which service users are charged fees.

—   **Internal services.**   Service centers that supply goods or services to other governmental units on a cost reimbursement basis.

—   **General fund.**   All cash receipts and disbursements not required to be accounted for in another fund.

—   **Proprietary funds.**   Funds whose purpose is to maintain the assets through cost reimbursement by users or partial cost recovery from users and periodic infusion of additional assets.

—   **Fiduciary funds (nonexpendable funds).**   Funds whose principal must remain intact (revenues earned may be distributed).

—   **Encumbrances.**   Future commitments for expenditures.

Thousands of state and local governments in the United States account for a large segment of the gross national product. State and local governments have a major impact on the citizens. No organization has had a clear responsibility for providing accounting principles for state and local governments. The American Institute of Certified Public Accountants (AICPA), the National Council on Governmental Accounting, and the Municipal Finance Officers Association have provided significant leadership in establishing accounting principles for state and local governments.

During the early 1980s, many thought that governmental accounting could benefit from the establishment of a board similar to the Financial Accounting Standards Board (FASB). A group of government accountants and CPAs organized a committee known as the Governmental Accounting Standards Board Organizing Committee. The Committee recommended the establishment of a separate standard-setting body for governmental accounting.

In April 1984, the Financial Accounting Foundation amended its articles of incorporation to accommodate a Governmental Accounting Standards Board (GASB). Thus, GASB became a branch of the Financial Accounting Foundation.

Governmental Accounting Standards Board Statement No. 1, Appendix B, addresses the jurisdictional hierarchy of the GASB and the FASB. Appendix B of *Governmental Accounting Standards Board Statement No. 1* establishes the following priorities for governmental units:

1. Pronouncements of the Governmental Accounting Standards Board.

2. Pronouncements of the Financial Accounting Standards Board.

3. Pronouncements of bodies composed of expert accountants that follow a due process procedure, including broad distribution of proposed accounting principles for public comment, for the intended purpose of establishing accounting principles or describing existing practices that are generally accepted.

4. Practices or pronouncements that are widely recognized as being generally accepted because they represent prevalent practice in a particular industry or the knowledgeable application to specific circumstances of pronouncements that are generally accepted.

5. Other accounting literature.[4]

Governmental Accounting Standards Board Statement No. 1 also adopts the National Council on Governmental Accounting pronouncements and the American Institute of Certified Public Accountants audit guide entitled *Audits of State and Local Governmental Units* as the basis for currently existing GAAP for state and local governmental units.

State and local governments serve as stewards over public funds. This stewardship responsibility dominates state and local government accounting.

State and local government accounting revolves around fund accounting. A **fund** is defined as an:

Independent fiscal and accounting entity with a self-balancing set of accounts recording cash and/or other resources together with all related liabilities, obligations, reserves, and equities which are segregated for the purpose of carrying on specific activities or attaining certain objectives in accordance with special regulations, restrictions, or limitations.[5]

Government transactions are recorded in one or more funds designed to emphasize control and budgetary limitations. Examples of funds, established for a specific purpose, are highway maintenance, parks, debt repayment, endowment, and welfare. The number of funds utilized depends on the responsibilities of the particular state or local government and the grouping of these responsibilities. For example, highway maintenance and bridge maintenance may be grouped together.

Some governments do their accounting using a method that resembles a cash basis, others use a modified accrual basis, and some use an accrual basis. A single government unit may use more than one basis, depending on the fund. For example, the City of Toledo, Ohio, uses a modified accrual basis for the governmental and expendable trust funds and uses an accrual basis of accounting for the proprietary and nonexpendable trust funds. The trend is away from the cash basis and toward the modified accrual basis. Some states have passed a law requiring governments to use a modified accrual basis.

The manner of handling depreciation can be much different than it is for a commercial business. Review the notes to the financial statements to determine how the state or local government unit handles depreciation. The City of Toledo, Ohio, describes its handling of depreciation in a footnote to its 1995 annual report, as follows: "Depreciation expense relating to Proprietary Fund Fixed assets is charged to operations. Accumulated depreciation on general fixed assets of the City is recorded on a memorandum basis in the General Fixed Assets Account Group."

The 1995 annual report of Lucas County, Ohio, describes the handling of depreciation as follows: "Depreciation is not provided for the General Fixed Assets Account Group. Depreciation for the Proprietary Funds is determined by allocating the cost of fixed assets over their estimated useful lives on a straight-line basis."

State and local governments prepare a **budget**, a detailed plan of operations for each period. This includes an item-by-item estimate of expenditures. When the representatives of the citizens (city council, town meeting, and so on) approve the budget, then the individual expenditures become limits. An increase in an approved expenditure will require approval by the same representatives who set up a *legal* control over expenditures. This differs from the budget for a commercial business, which is merely a plan of future revenues and expenses.

A great variance exists in the quality of disclosure in the financial reporting of state and local governments. Some poorly reported items have been pension liabilities, marketable securities, inventories, fixed assets, and lease obligations.

The Government Finance Officers Association of the United States and Canada presents a Certificate of Achievement for Excellence in Financial Reporting to governmental units and public employee retirement systems whose comprehensive annual financial reports are judged to conform substantially to program standards. These standards are considered to be very rigorous. The municipal bond rating of the governmental unit should also be determined. Standard & Poor's and Moody's evaluate and grade the quality of a bond relative to the probability of default. One rating is assigned to all general obligation bonds (backed by the full faith and credit of the government unit). Bonds not backed by the full faith and credit of the government unit, such as industrial revenue bonds, are rated individually. These ratings do not represent the probability of default by the governmental unit.

When reviewing the financial reporting of governmental units, visualize the reporting in a pyramid fashion. The funds are typically grouped into major categories, which are supported by individual funds that serve to account for each of the separate government activities. Exhibit 16-2 illustrates the pyramid concept of financial reporting for a governmental unit.

When reviewing a governmental unit, the following suggestions are helpful:

1. Determine if a Certificate of Achievement has been received.
2. Determine the municipal bond rating of the governmental unit.
3. Review the combined balance sheet.
4. Review the combined statement of revenues, expenditures, and changes in fund balances.
5. Review the disclosure of debt.
6. Review footnotes and other disclosures.
7. In addition to reviewing the absolute numbers, prepare selected common-size analyses.

EXHIBIT 16-2   **The Financial Reporting "Pyramid"**

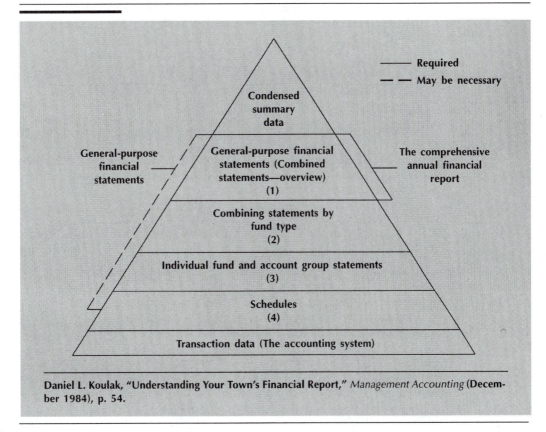

Daniel L. Koulak, "Understanding Your Town's Financial Report," *Management Accounting* (December 1984), p. 54.

The City of Toledo, Ohio, presents detailed financial statements and in recent years has been awarded Certificates of Achievement for Excellence in Financial Reporting. The total financial report consists of more than 100 pages. Selected parts follow:

1. Combined Balance Sheet—All Fund Types and Account Groups (Exhibit 16-3, pages 712-715).
2. Combined Statement of Revenues, Expenditures, and Changes in Fund Balances—All Government Fund Types and Expendable Trust Funds (Exhibit 16-4, pages 716-717). (Notice that proceeds from debt are recorded on this statement as revenue. Principal retirement, interest, and fiscal charges are recorded as expenditures.)
3. Partial Footnote 1—Organization and Summary of Significant Accounting Policies (Exhibit 16-5, page 717). (Notice that a modified accrual basis of accounting is utilized by the Governmental and Expendable Trust Funds, whereas an accrual basis of accounting is utilized by the Proprietary and Nonexpendable Trust Funds. Agency Fund assets and liabilities are recognized on the modified accrual basis of accounting.)
4. Income Tax Revenues (Exhibit 16-6, page 718).
5. Ratio of Net General Bonded Debt to Assessed Value and Net Bonded Debt per Capita—Last Ten Years (Exhibit 16-7, page 718).

ACCOUNTING FOR NOT-FOR-PROFIT ORGANIZATIONS OTHER THAN GOVERNMENTS

Not-for-profit organizations account for a substantial portion of economic activity in the United States. There are over 20,000 not-for-profit organizations in the United States.[6] Examples of not-for-profit organizations include hospitals, religious institutions, professional organizations, universities, and museums.

Not-for-profit accounting principles were derived from numerous not-for-profit industry accounting manuals and audit guides. Examples were AICPA audit guides for Colleges and Universities, Audits of Voluntary Health and Welfare Organizations, and audits of providers of Health Care Services.

The FASB was concerned about the lack of uniformity in the accounting for not-for-profit organizations and the lack of overall quality of not-for-profit organizations' financial reporting. To address this concern, four accounting standards relating to not-for-profits were issued by the FASB. These standards are: (1) SFAS No. 93, "Recognition of Depreciation by Not-for-Profit Organizations," (2) SFAS No. 116, "Accounting for Contributions Received and Contributions Made," (3) SFAS No. 117, "Financial Statements of Not-for-Profit Organizations," and (4) SFAS No. 124, "Accounting for Certain Investments Held by Not-for-Profit Organizations." A brief description of these accounting standards and how they impact financial reports follows:

1. SFAS No. 93, "Recognition of Depreciation by Not-for-Profit Organizations" (August 1987)[7]

Prior to SFAS No. 93, most not-for-profit organizations did not recognize depreciation. SFAS No. 93 requires not-for-profit organizations to recognize depreciation on long-lived tangible assets. SFAS No. 93 includes these requirements relating to depreciation:

1. Disclose the amount of depreciation expense for each period.
2. Disclose depreciable assets by major classes as of the balance sheet date.
3. Disclose accumulated depreciation for each asset class or in total as of the balance sheet date.
4. Disclose the methods used to calculate depreciation.

SFAS No. 93 exempts individual works of art or historical treasures from the depreciation requirements. For this exemption, two requirements must be met:

1. The asset must have "cultural, aesthetic, or historical value that is worth preserving perpetually."
2. The organization that owns the artwork or historical treasure must be able to preserve the asset so that its potentially unlimited service potential will remain intact.

2. SFAS No. 116, "Accounting for Contributions Received and Contributions Made" (June 1993)[8]

SFAS No. 116, applies to *all not-for-profit organizations as well as to any entity that receives or makes contributions.* Some key aspects of SFAS No. 116 will be summarized.

Contributions Received   Contributions received are to be recognized as revenues or gains in the period received. In addition, these contributions are to be recognized as assets, decreases in liabilities, or as expenses in the same period. Contributions received are to be measured at their fair values and reported as restricted support or unrestricted support.

Contributed services received are to be recognized if one of the following conditions holds:

1. The service creates or enhances nonfinancial assets; or
2. These services involve specialized skills that would most likely be paid for if they were not donated (i.e., electrical services, plumbing services, accounting services, etc.).

(discussion continues on p. 719)

EXHIBIT 16-3   CITY OF TOLEDO, OHIO
Combined Balance Sheet
All Fund Types and Account Groups
December 31, 1995
(Amounts in thousands)

| | | GOVERNMENTAL FUND TYPES | | |
	GENERAL	**SPECIAL REVENUE**	**DEBT SERVICE**	**CAPITAL PROJECTS**
ASSETS AND OTHER DEBITS				
Equity in Pooled Cash	$ —	$ 2,159	$ 107	$ 2,250
Other Cash	24	1	—	—
Investments at Cost	—	2,591	—	—
Funds on Deposit—Employees				
Deferred Compensation Program	—	—	—	—
Receivables (Net of Allowance				
for Uncollectible Accounts):				
Taxes	28,907	—	—	—
Accounts	1,550	2,530	—	598
Special Assessments	—	43,764	3,133	1,120
Notes	—	784	—	—
Due from Other Funds	—	—	—	11,061
Due from Other Governments	—	—	—	—
Prepaid Expenditures and Expenses	308	277	—	—
Inventory of Supplies	985	1,624	—	1,031
Restricted Assets:				
Equity in Pooled Cash	—	—	—	—
Other Cash	—	6	65	—
Investments at Cost	4,558	1,791	522	38,207
Accounts Receivable	—	—	—	—
Due from Other Funds	—	—	—	—
Due from Other Governments	—	—	—	—
Property, Plant, and Equipment				
(Net of Accumulated Depreciation)	—	—	—	—
Deferred Debt Issuance Cost	—	—	—	—
Amount Available in Debt				
Service Funds	—	—	—	—
Amount to Be Provided for:				
Retirement of General Long-Term				
Obligations	—	—	—	—
Compensated Absences	—	—	—	—
Total Assets and Other Debits	$36,332	$55,527	$ 3,827	$54,267

EXHIBIT 16-3   (continued)

	PROPRIETARY FUND TYPES		FIDUCIARY FUND TYPES	ACCOUNT GROUPS		
ENTERPRISE	INTERNAL SERVICE		TRUST AND AGENCY	GENERAL FIXED ASSETS	GENERAL LONG-TERM OBLIGATIONS	TOTAL (MEMORANDUM ONLY)
$ 706	$23,427		$21,905	$ —	$ —	$ 50,554
281	—		—	—	—	306
50,780	—		1,552	—	—	54,923
—	—		34,876	—	—	34,876
—	—		—	—	—	28,907
8,141	5		5	—	—	12,829
—	—		—	—	—	48,017
2,841	—		465	—	—	4,090
818	1,120		—	—	—	12,999
308	—		—	—	—	308
180	—		—	—	—	765
2,415	511		—	—	—	6,566
—	—		—	—	—	—
826	—		—	—	—	897
21,400	1,151		—	—	—	67,629
782	—		—	—	—	782
47,228	—		—	—	—	47,228
125	—		—	—	—	125
307,440	8,995		—	88,930	—	405,365
993	—		—	—	—	993
—	—		—	—	658	658
—	—		—	—	144,777	144,777
—	—		—	—	29,136	29,136
$ 445,264	$35,209		$58,803	$88,930	$ 174,571	$ 952,730

(continued)

EXHIBIT 16-3   (continued)

| | GOVERNMENTAL FUND TYPES | | | |
	GENERAL	SPECIAL REVENUE	DEBT SERVICE	CAPITAL PROJECTS
LIABILITIES				
Accounts Payable	$ 2,501	$ 1,089	$ 31	$ 1,395
Escrow	—	23	—	278
Retainages	19	—	—	755
Due to Other Funds	3,904	6,799	5	353
Due to Other Governments	—	1	—	56
Deferred Revenue	14,502	43,764	3,133	5,058
Other Current Liabilities	3,172	502	—	55
Accrued Compensated Absences	—	—	—	—
Payable from Restricted Assets:				
Accounts Payable	—	—	—	—
Escrow	31	—	—	—
Retainages	—	—	—	—
Due to Other Governments	—	—	—	—
Other Current Liabilities	—	—	—	—
Debt:				
Notes Payable	209	31,000	—	9,110
General Obligation Bonds Payable	—	—	—	—
Police and Fire Pension General Obligation Bonds	—	—	—	—
Special Assessment Bonds Payable with Governmental Commitment	—	—	—	—
Revenue Bonds Payable	—	—	—	—
Capital Lease Obligation	—	—	—	—
Other Long-Term Debt	—	—	—	—
Deferred Compensation	—	—	—	—
Landfill Closure and Post-Closure Care	—	—	—	—
Total Liabilities	24,338	83,178	3,169	17,060
FUND EQUITY				
Contributed Capital	—	—	—	—
Investment in General Fixed Assets	—	—	—	—
Retained Earnings (Deficit):				
Reserved for Debt Service	—	—	—	—
Reserved for Replacement	—	—	—	—
Reserved for Improvement	—	—	—	—
Unreserved	—	—	—	—
Fund Balances (Deficit):				
Reserved for Encumbrances	738	9,916	—	14,276
Reserved for Inventory of Supplies	985	1,624	—	1,031
Reserved for Capital Improvements	4,558	—	—	19,384
Reserved for Long-Term Notes Receivable	—	783	—	—
Reserved for Debt Service	—	—	658	—
Reserved for Prepaid Expenditures/Expenses	—	277	—	—
Reserved for Subsequent Years Expenditure	436	471	—	—
Reserved for Budget Stabilization	4,308	—	—	—
Unreserved	969	(40,722)	—	2,516
Total Fund Equity (Deficit)	11,994	(27,651)	658	37,207
Total Liabilities and Fund Equity (Deficit) and Other Credits	$ 36,332	$ 55,527	$ 3,827	$ 54,267

EXHIBIT 16-3   (concluded)

	PROPRIETARY FUND TYPES		FIDUCIARY FUND TYPES	ACCOUNT GROUPS		
	ENTERPRISE	INTERNAL SERVICE	TRUST AND AGENCY	GENERAL FIXED ASSETS	GENERAL LONG-TERM OBLIGATIONS	TOTAL (MEMORANDUM ONLY)
	$ 1,723	$ 359	$ 47	$ —	$ —	$ 7,145
	64	—	831	—	—	1,196
	12	—	—	—	—	786
	48,046	1,120	—	—	—	60,227
	—	—	7,993	—	—	8,050
	—	—	—	—	—	66,457
	116	16,011	5,513	—	—	25,369
	—	—	6,840	—	29,136	35,976
	1,331	—	—	—	—	1,331
	1,182	—	—	—	—	1,213
	95	—	—	—	—	95
	—	—	—	—	—	—
	841	—	—	—	—	841
	17,300	1,500	—	—	621	59,740
	18,707	14	—	—	91,079	109,800
	—	—	—	—	18,425	18,425
	—	—	—	—	2,067	2,067
	52,717	—	—	—	—	52,717
	—	—	—	—	23,200	23,200
	—	—	—	—	3,834	3,834
	—	—	34,876	—	—	34,876
	—	—	—	—	6,209	6,209
	142,134	19,004	56,100	—	174,571	519,554
	23,926	57,663	—	—	—	81,589
	—	—	—	88,930	—	88,930
	8,975	—	—	—	—	8,975
	46,518	—	—	—	—	46,518
	14,345	—	—	—	—	14,345
	209,366	(41,458)	—	—	—	167,908
	—	—	—	—	—	24,930
	—	—	—	—	—	3,640
	—	—	—	—	—	23,942
	—	—	465	—	—	1,248
	—	—	—	—	—	658
	—	—	—	—	—	277
	—	—	—	—	—	907
	—	—	—	—	—	4,308
	—	—	2,238	—	—	(34,999)
	303,130	16,205	2,703	88,930	—	433,176
	$ 445,264	$ 35,209	$ 58,803	$ 88,930	$ 174,571	$ 952,730

EXHIBIT 16-4   CITY OF TOLEDO, OHIO
Combined Statement of Revenues, Expenditures, and Changes in
Fund Balances—All Governmental Fund Types and Expendable Trust Funds
For the Year Ended December 31, 1995 (Amounts in thousands)

	GENERAL	SPECIAL REVENUE	DEBT SERVICE	CAPITAL PROJECTS	FIDUCIARY FUND TYPES EXPENDABLE TRUSTS	TOTAL (MEMO-RANDUM ONLY)
			GOVERNMENTAL FUND TYPES			
REVENUES:						
Income Taxes	$ 129,789	$ —	$ —	$ —	$ —	$ 129,789
Property Taxes	14,496	—	—	—	—	14,496
Special Assessments	3	17,414	796	141	—	18,354
Licenses and Permits	2,984	20	—	—	—	3,004
Intergovernmental Services	20,010	27,947	782	2,164	—	50,903
Charges for Service	9,948	934	—	118	124	11,124
Investment Earnings	4,042	808	34	1,717	185	6,786
Fines and Forfeitures	3,831	561	—	—	—	4,392
All Other Revenue	1,043	104	—	1,092	448	2,687
Total Revenues	186,146	47,788	1,612	5,232	757	241,535
EXPENDITURES:						
Current:						
General Government	18,493	151	—	—	428	19,072
Public Service	1,616	23,485	—	—	—	25,101
Public Safety	109,306	1,231	—	—	618	111,155
Public Utilities	—	2,826	—	—	—	2,826
Community Environment	5,722	9,995	—	—	3,050	18,767
Health	14,255	3,528	—	—	—	17,783
Parks and Recreation	5,119	238	—	—	122	5,479
Capital Outlay	3,143	1,036	—	24,514	—	28,693
Debt Service:						
Principal Retirement	1,317	100	8,075	676	—	10,168
Interest and Fiscal Charges	2,499	2,025	5,857	1,320	—	11,701
Total Expenditures	161,470	44,615	13,932	26,510	4,218	250,745
Excess (Deficiency) of Revenues over Expenditures	24,676	3,173	(12,320)	(21,278)	(3,461)	(9,210)
Other Financing Sources (Uses):						
Operating Transfers (In)	—	849	12,546	28,731	3,844	45,970
Operating Transfers (Out)	(28,931)	(5,147)	(52)	(11,462)	(650)	(46,242)
Bond Proceeds	6,070	432	112	16,835	—	23,449
Note Proceeds	—	—	—	171	—	171
Other Financing Sources (Uses)	11	157	—	—	—	168
Total Other Financing Sources and (Uses)	(22,850)	(3,709)	12,606	34,275	3,194	23,516
Excess (Deficiency) of Revenues and Other Financing Sources, over Expenditures and Other Financing Uses	$ 1,826	$ (536)	$ 286	$ 12,997	$ (267)	$ 14,306

EXHIBIT 16-4 (concluded)

	GOVERNMENTAL FUND TYPES				FIDUCIARY FUND TYPES EXPENDABLE TRUSTS	TOTAL (MEMO-RANDUM ONLY)
	GENERAL	SPECIAL REVENUE	DEBT SERVICE	CAPITAL PROJECTS		
Excess (Deficiency) of Revenues and Other Financing Sources, over Expenditures and Other Financing Uses (bro't. fwd.)	$ 1,826	$ (536)	$ 286	$ 12,997	$ (267)	$ 14,306
Fund Balances (Deficit) at Beginning of Year	10,317	(26,776)	372	24,796	2,341	11,050
Residual Equity Transfers	(44)	(26)	—	(586)	—	(656)
Increase in Reserve for Inventory	(105)	(313)	—	—	—	(418)
Fund Balance (Deficit) at Year-End	$ 11,994	$ (27,651)	$ 658	$ 37,207	$ 2,074	$ 24,282

EXHIBIT 16-5 CITY OF TOLEDO, OHIO
Partial Footnote 1—Organization and Summary of Significant Accounting Policies

C. Basis of Accounting

The modified accrual basis of accounting is utilized by the Governmental and Expendable Trust Funds. Under this method of accounting, the City recognizes revenue when it becomes both measurable and available to finance current City operations. Revenues accrued at the end of the year include: individual income taxes during the fourth quarter that are received within 60 days after year-end; property taxes for the budget year to which they apply, where taxpayer liability has been established and such taxes are received during the year or within 60 days after year-end; and intergovernmental revenues for the year, which are received within 60 days after year-end or based on expenditures recognized where agreements stipulate funds must be expended for a specific purpose or project before any reimbursements will be made to the City. Expenditures are recorded when the related fund liability is incurred. Principal and interest on general long-term debt are recorded as fund liabilities when due or when amounts have been accumulated in the debt service fund for payments to be made early in the following year.

The accrual basis of accounting is utilized by the Proprietary and Nonexpendable Trust Funds. Revenues are recognized when earned, and expenses are recognized when incurred. Unbilled Water and Sewer Funds' utility service receivables are recorded at year-end.

Agency Fund assets and liabilities are recognized on the modified accrual basis of accounting, since these Funds are custodial in nature and do not involve measurement of results of operations.

EXHIBIT 16-6 CITY OF TOLEDO, OHIO
Income Tax Revenues
Last Ten Years (Amounts in thousands)

Fiscal Year	Tax Revenues	Tax Rate
1986	$ 95,651	2 1/4%
1987	102,267	2 1/4
1988	109,542	2 1/4
1989	106,702	2 1/4
1990	107,980	2 1/4
1991	104,870	2 1/4
1992	110,423	2 1/4
1993	115,755	2 1/4
1994	124,975	2 1/4
1995	129,789	2 1/4

Source: City of Toledo Income Tax Department

EXHIBIT 16-7 CITY OF TOLEDO, OHIO
Ratio of Net General Bonded Debt to Assessed Value and
Net Bonded Debt per Capita—Last Ten Years

Fiscal Year	Population (1)	Assessed Value (2)	Gross General Bonded Debt (2)	Less Balance in Debt Service Fund (2) & (3)	Net General Bonded Debt (2)	Ratio of Net Bonded Debt to Assessed Value	Net Bonded Debt per Capita
1986	354,635	$2,773,893	$61,550	$ 31	$61,519	2.2%	$173.47
1987	354,635	2,796,482	66,395	70	66,325	2.4	187.02
1988	354,635	3,091,093	68,820	26	68,794	2.2	193.99
1989	354,635	3,111,062	52,640 (4)	113	52,527	1.7	148.12
1990	332,943	3,106,052	63,260	180	63,080	2.0	189.46
1991	332,943	3,227,440	57,110	208	56,902	1.8	170.91
1992	332,943	3,196,025	68,995	251	68,744	2.2	206.75
1993	332,943	3,162,416	62,550	312	62,238	2.0	186.93
1994	332,943	3,277,973	74,450	373	74,077	2.3	222.50
1995	332,943	3,257,493	91,079	658	90,421	2.8	271.58

(1) *Source:* U.S. Bureau of the Census.
(2) Amounts shown in thousands of dollars. *Source:* Lucas County Auditor.
(3) The City has paid its general bonded debt service for the tax years shown from current income tax revenues. The amount required is transferred to the debt service funds from the capital improvement fund.
(4) Gross general bonded debt was adjusted downward in 1989 to reflect reductions for bonded debt supported by special revenue sources.

Contributed services recognized should be disclosed by nature and amount for the period. Service contributions are to be valued at the fair value of the services or the resulting increase in assets.

Under SFAS No. 116, donated works of art, historical treasures, or similar assets can be excluded if the following conditions are met:

1. Contributed items are held for public service purposes rather than for financial gain.

2. Contributed items must be protected, kept unencumbered, cared for, and preserved.

3. The organization must have a policy of using funds from the sales of collected items to purchase additional collection pieces.

Contributions received are to be segregated into permanent restrictions, temporary restrictions, and unrestricted support imposed by donors. Restricted contributions shall be reported as an increase in either permanently restricted net assets or temporarily restricted net assets. Unrestricted contributions received are to be reported as unrestricted support and increases in unrestricted net assets. Contributions received are to be measured at fair value.

Conditional promises are to be recognized in the financial statements when the condition(s) has been substantially met. If the nature of the conditional promise is ambiguous, it should be interpreted as conditional.

Contributions Made   Contributions made are to be recognized as expenses in the period in which they are made. These contributions are to be reported as decreases in assets or increases in liabilities. Contributions made are to be measured at the fair value of the asset contributed or the liability discharged. Conditional promises to give are recognized when the conditions are substantially met.

3. SFAS No. 117, "Financial Statements of Not-for-Profit Organizations" (June 1993)[9]

Prior to SFAS No. 117, there were significant differences in the financial reports of not-for-profit organizations. The intent of SFAS No. 117 is to provide consistency in the financial statements of not-for-profit organizations. SFAS No. 117 addresses financial statements, the content of financial statements, and the classification of financial statement information.

Not-for-profit organizations are to present three aggregated financial statements. These include a statement of financial position, a statement of activities, and a statement of cash flows. SFAS No. 117 specifies the content of each of these required financial statements.

Concerning the statement of financial position, SFAS No. 117 directs that it is to include aggregated information about the assets, liabilities, and net assets. SFAS No. 117 requires the statement of activity to provide information concerning the effects of transactions on the amount and nature of net assets, the interrelationships between those transactions and other events, and how resources are used by the organization to provide services. The statement of activity is also to disclose the changes in the amounts of permanently restricted net assets, temporarily restricted net assets, and unrestricted net assets.

In regards to the content of the statement of cash flows, SFAS No. 117 requires that not-for-profit organizations comply with SFAS No. 95, "Statement of Cash Flows." In addition, SFAS No. 117 amends SFAS No. 95 concerning its description of financing activities. Financing activities now include receipts of donations restricted for acquiring, constructing, or improving long-lived assets or establishing or increasing permanent or term endowments.

For the statement of financial position, SFAS No. 117 requires that assets and liabilities should be reported in relatively homogenous groups. They should also be classified to provide information about their interrelationships, liquidity, and financial flexibility. New assets are to be classified as either permanently restricted, temporarily restricted, or unrestricted. Revenues, expenses, gains, and losses are to be separated into reasonably homogeneous groups for the statement of activities. They also are to be classified as affecting permanently restricted, temporarily restricted, or unrestricted net assets.

4. SFAS No. 124, "Accounting for Certain Investments Held by Not-for-Profit Organizations" (November 1995)[10]

This statement applies to investments in equity securities that have a readily determinable fair value and to all investments in debt securities. These investments are to be shown at their fair values in the statement of financial position. This statement does not apply to investments in equity securities that are accounted for under the equity method or to investments in consolidated subsidiaries. Disclosure requirements in the statement of financial position include the aggregate carrying value of investments by major categories and the basis for determining the carrying values of equity securities without readily determinable fair market values. Any shortfall in the fair value of donor-restricted endowment funds below the amount required by donor stipulations or by law must also be disclosed.

For the statement of activities, any realized or unrealized gains and losses are to be shown. Some of the disclosure requirements for the statement of activities include the composition of the investment return, which consists of investment income, realized gains and losses on investments not reported at fair value, and net gains and losses on investments that are reported at fair value.

Applicability of GAAP to Not-for-Profit Organizations

Some individuals were of the opinion that the applicability of GAAP to not-for-profit organizations was unclear. SOP 94-2 was issued to address the applicability of GAAP to not-for-profit organizations.[11]

SOP 94-2 concludes that not-for-profit organizations should follow the guidance in effective provisions of ARBs, APB Opinions, and FASB Statements and Interpretations unless the specific pronouncement explicitly exempts not-for-profit organizations or their subject matter precludes such applicability (SOP 94-2, paragraph .09).

Exhibit 16-8, pages 722-724, contains major portions of the 1995 and 1994 financial statements of the Institute of Management Accountants. These statements are for the years ended June 30, 1995 and 1994. These statements do not reflect SFAS No. 124. SFAS No. 124 is effective for annual financial statements issued for fiscal years beginning after December 15, 1995.

Budgeting by Objectives and/or Measures of Productivity

Accounting for nonprofit institutions differs greatly from accounting for a profit-oriented enterprise. The accounting for a profit-oriented business centers on the entity concept and the efficiency of the entity. The accounting for a nonprofit institution does not include an entity concept or efficiency. The accounting for a profit-oriented business has a bottom-line net income. The accounting for a nonprofit institution does not have a bottom line.

Some nonprofit institutions have added budgeting by objectives and/or measures of productivity to their financial reporting to incorporate measures of efficiency. The article, "Budgeting by Objectives: Charlotte's Experience," reported several objectives incorporated in the budget of Charlotte, North Carolina. Four primary objectives guided the budget: (1) the property tax rate should not increase, (2) continued emphasis should be placed on making the best use of city employees and the present computer capability, (3) any budget increase should be held to a minimum, and (4) a balanced program of services should be presented.[12]

This article also reports measures of productivity that Charlotte has used. These measures of productivity include: (1) customers served per $1,000 of sanitation expense, (2) number of tons of refuse per $1,000 expense, and (3) street miles flushed per $1,000 expense.[13]

Budgeting by objectives and/or measures of productivity could be added to the financial reporting of any nonprofit institution. The objectives and measures of productivity should be applicable to the particular nonprofit institution.

EXHIBIT 16-8 The IMA 1995 Financial Report (in Part)

INSTITUTE OF MANAGEMENT ACCOUNTANTS, INC. AND AFFILIATES
Combined Statement of Financial Position
Years Ended June 30, 1995 and 1994
(Dollars in thousands)

	1995	1994
ASSETS		
Cash and cash equivalents	$ 1,091	$ 865
Marketable securities	10,777	10,676
Receivables, net allowance for doubtful accounts	644	707
Property, equipment, and software, net	4,764	4,846
Other assets	1,003	1,115
Total assets	$18,279	$18,209
LIABILITIES, DEFERRED REVENUES, AND NET ASSETS		
Accounts payable and accrued expenses	$ 1,958	$ 2,041
Bonds payable, net of discount	4,072	4,214
Total liabilities	6,030	6,255
Deferred revenues		
Membership dues	3,796	3,840
Other	1,011	998
Total deferred revenues	4,807	4,838
Net assets		
Unrestricted		
IMA		
Current Operating Fund	176	298
Reserve Fund	4,932	5,064
ICMA	1,173	717
IMAMEF		
Board Designated	100	100
Undesignated	940	937
IMAFAR	121	—
Total net assets	7,442	7,116
Total liabilities, deferred revenues, and net assets	$18,279	$18,209

SUMMARY

This chapter reviewed financial reporting for personal financial statements and accounting for governments and other not-for-profit organizations. Accounting for these areas differs greatly from accounting for profit-oriented businesses. This difference has been narrowed substantially for not-for-profit organizations other than governments.

EXHIBIT 16-8 (continued)

INSTITUTE OF MANAGEMENT ACCOUNTANTS, INC. AND AFFILIATES
Combined Statement of Activities and Changes in Net Assets
Years Ended June 30, 1995 and 1994
(Dollars in thousands)

	1995	1994
REVENUES AND SUPPORT		
Membership dues and fees	$ 8,051	$ 8,179
Bequest—unrestricted	—	17
Education programs	2,248	2,247
Annual conference	531	570
Advertising and sales of publications	1,720	1,627
CMA exam fees	1,413	1,270
Interest and dividends	527	468
Gains on sales of securities	728	354
Other	942	555
Total revenues and support	16,160	15,287
EXPENSES		
Payments to chapters	1,099	1,114
Chapter and member services	2,329	2,170
Education programs	2,467	2,259
Annual conference	464	566
Publications and library	1,954	1,843
CMA program	780	728
Research expenditures	289	296
Administration and occupancy costs	5,665	5,825
Other	787	543
Total expenses	15,834	15,344
Changes in net assets	326	(57)
Net assets, beginning of year	7,116	7,173
Net assets, end of year	$ 7,442	$ 7,116

(continued)

Statement of Position 82-1 presents guidelines for the preparation of personal financial statements. SOP 82-1 concludes that personal financial statements should present assets at their estimated current values and liabilities at their estimated current amounts at the date of the financial statements. This differs from commercial financial statements that predominantly use historical information.

The accounting for governments (state and local governments) revolves around fund accounting. Government transactions are recorded in one or more funds designed to emphasize control and budgetary limitations. Some governments do their accounting using a method that resembles a cash basis, others use a modified accrual basis, and some use an accrual basis.

EXHIBIT 16-8   (concluded)

INSTITUTE OF MANAGEMENT ACCOUNTANTS, INC. AND AFFILIATES
Combined Statement of Cash Flows
Years Ended June 30, 1995 and 1994
(Dollars in thousands)

	1995	1994
CASH FLOWS FROM OPERATING ACTIVITIES		
Changes in net assets	$ 326	$ (57)
Adjustments to reconcile changes in net assets to		
net cash provided by (used for) operating activities		
Depreciation, amortization, and		
valuation allowances	503	489
(Gains) on sales of securities	(728)	(354)
Changes in assets and liabilities		
Decrease in receivables	60	3
Decrease (increase) in other assets	112	(246)
Decrease in accounts payable and accrued expenses	(83)	(282)
Decrease (increase) in deferred revenues	(31)	105
Cash provided by (used for) operating activities	159	(342)
CASH FLOWS FROM INVESTING ACTIVITIES		
Capital expenditures	(415)	(599)
Purchases of investments	(2,371)	(6,180)
Proceeds from sales of investments	2,998	5,016
Cash provided by (used for) investing activities	212	(1,763)
CASH FLOWS FROM FINANCING ACTIVITIES		
Repayment of current portion of long-term debt	(145)	(135)
Cash (used for) financing activities	(145)	(135)
Increase (decrease) in cash and cash equivalents	226	(2,240)
Cash and cash equivalents		
Beginning of year	865	3,105
End of year	$ 1,091	$ 865

See notes to combined financial statements (notes not included).

Not-for-profit accounting for organizations, other than governments, has changed substantially. It now resembles accounting for profit organizations. A major difference is that not-for-profit organizations issue a statement of activities instead of an income statement.

Some nonprofit institutions have added budgeting by objectives and/ or measures of productivity to their financial reporting to incorporate measures of efficiency.

QUESTIONS

Q 16-1.   May personal financial statements be prepared only for an individual? Comment.

Q 16-2.   What is the basic personal financial statement?

Q 16-3.   Is a statement of changes in net worth required when presenting personal financial statements?

Q 16-4.   Are comparative financial statements required when presenting personal financial statements?

Q 16-5.   When preparing a personal statement of financial condition, should assets and liabilities be presented on the basis of historical cost or estimated current value?

Q 16-6.   In a personal statement of financial condition, what is the equity section called?

Q 16-7.   What personal financial statement should be prepared when an explanation of changes in net worth is desired?

Q 16-8.   Is the presentation of a personal income statement appropriate?

Q 16-9.   GAAP as they apply to personal financial statements use the cash basis. Comment.

Q 16-10.   Is the concept of working capital used with personal financial statements? Comment.

Q 16-11.   List some sources of information that may be available when preparing personal financial statements.

Q 16-12.   Give examples of disclosure in footnotes with personal financial statements.

Q 16-13.   If quoted market prices are not available, a personal financial statement cannot be prepared. Comment.

Q 16-14.   List some objectives that could be incorporated into the financial reporting of a professional accounting organization.

Q 16-15.   Do not-for-profit organizations, other than governments, use fund accounting? Comment.

Q 16-16.   The accounting for governments is centered on the entity concept and the efficiency of the entity. Comment.

Q 16-17.   For governmental accounting, define the following types of funds:
1.   General fund
2.   Proprietary fund
3.   Fiduciary fund

Q 16-18.   How many funds will be used by a state or local government?

Q 16-19.   The budget for a state or local government is not as binding as a budget for a commercial business. Comment.

Q 16-20.   Which organization provides a service whereby it issues a certificate of conformance to governmental units with financial reports that meet its standards?

Q 16-21.   The rating on an industrial revenue bond is representative of the probability of default of bonds issued with the full faith and credit of a governmental unit. Comment.

Q 16-22.   The accounting for not-for-profit institutions does not typically include the concept of efficiency. Indicate how the concept of efficiency can be incorporated in the financial reporting of a not-for-profit institution.

Q 16-23.   Could a profit-oriented enterprise use fund accounting practices? Comment.

PROBLEMS

P 16-1.   For each of these situations, indicate the amount to be placed on a statement of financial condition at December 31, 1997.

    a. Bill and Pat Konner purchased their home at 2829 Willow Road in Stow, Ohio, in August 1980 for $80,000. The unpaid mortgage is $20,000. Immediately after purchasing the home, Bill and Pat added several improvements totaling $10,000. Real estate prices in Stow have increased 40% since the time of purchase.

        From the facts given, determine the estimated current value of the home.

    b. Joe Best drives a Toyota, for which he paid $10,000 when it was new. Joe believes that since he maintains the car in good condition, he could sell it for $12,000. The average selling price for this model of Toyota is $9,000.

        From the facts given, determine the estimated current value of Joe's car.

    c. Sue Bell is 40 years old and has an IRA with a balance of $20,000. The IRS penalty for early withdrawal is 10%. The marginal tax rate for Sue Bell is 30% (tax on gross amount).

        What is the estimated current value of the IRA and the estimated income taxes on the difference between the estimated current values of assets and the estimated current amounts of liabilities and their tax bases?

    d. Bill Kell guaranteed a loan of $8,000 for his girlfriend to buy a car. She is behind in payments on the car.

        What liability should be shown on Bill Kell's statement of financial condition?

    e. Dick Better bought a home in 1976 for $70,000. Currently the mortgage on the home is $45,000. Because of the current high interest rates, the bank has offered to retire the mortgage for $40,000.

        What is the estimated current value of this liability?

P 16-2.   For each of these situations, indicate the amount to be placed on a statement of financial condition at December 31, 1997.

    a. Raj Reel owns the following securities:

        1,000 shares of Ree's
        2,000 shares of Bell's

Ree's is traded on the New York Stock Exchange. The prices from the most recent trade day follow:

    Open   19
    High $20\frac{1}{2}$
    Low   19
    Close   20

Bell's is a local company whose stock is sold by brokers on a workout basis (the broker tries to find a buyer). The most recent selling price was $8.

        What is the estimated current value of these securities? (Assume that the commission on Ree's would be $148 and the commission on Bell's would be $170.)

b. Charlie has a certificate of deposit with a $10,000 balance. Accrued interest is $500. The penalty for early withdrawal would be $300.

What is the estimated current value of the certificate of deposit?

c. Jones has an option to buy 500 shares of ABC Construction at a price of $20 per share. The option expires in one year. ABC Construction shares are presently selling for $25.

What is the estimated current value of these options?

d. Carl Jones has a whole-life insurance policy with the face amount of $100,000, cash value of $50,000, and a loan outstanding against the policy of $20,000. Susan Jones is the beneficiary.

What is the estimated current value of the insurance policy?

e. Larry Solomon paid $60,000 for a home ten years ago. The unpaid mortgage on the home is $30,000. Larry estimates the current value of the home to be $90,000. This estimate is partially based on the selling price of homes recently sold in the neighborhood. Larry's home is assessed for tax purposes at $50,000. Assessments in the area average one-half of market value. The house has not been inspected for assessment during the past two years. Larry would sell through a broker, who would charge 5% of the selling price.

What is the estimated current value of the home?

P 16-3. For Bob and Carl, the assets and liabilities and the effective income tax rates at December 31, 1997 follow:

Accounts	Tax Bases	Estimated Current Value	Excess of Estimated Current Values over Tax Bases	Effective Income Tax Rates	Amount of Estimated Income Taxes
Cash	$ 20,000	$ 20,000	—	—	_____
Marketable securities	45,000	50,000	5,000	28%	_____
Life insurance	50,000	50,000	—	—	_____
Residence	100,000	125,000	25,000	28%	_____
Furnishings	40,000	25,000	(15,000)	—	_____
Jewelry	20,000	20,000	—	—	_____
Autos	20,000	12,000	(8,000)	—	_____
Mortgage payable	(90,000)	(90,000)	—	—	_____
Note payable	(30,000)	(30,000)	—	—	_____
Credit cards	(10,000)	(10,000)	—	—	_____

Required a. Compute the estimated tax liability on the differences between the estimated current value of the assets and liabilities and their tax bases.

b. Present a statement of financial condition for Bob and Carl at December 31, 1997.

c. Comment on the statement of financial condition.

P 16-4. For Mary Lou and Ernie, the assets and liabilities and the effective income tax rates at December 31, 1997 follow:

Accounts	Tax Bases	Estimated Current Value	Excess of Estimated Current Values over Tax Bases	Effective Income Tax Rates	Amount of Estimated Income Taxes
Cash	$ 20,000	$ 20,000	—	—	_____
Marketable securities	80,000	100,000	20,000	28%	_____
Options	-0-	30,000	30,000	28%	_____
Residence	100,000	150,000	50,000	28%	_____
Royalties	-0-	20,000	20,000	28%	_____
Furnishings	40,000	20,000	(20,000)	—	_____
Auto	20,000	15,000	(5,000)	—	_____
Mortgage	(70,000)	(70,000)	—	—	_____
Auto loan	(10,000)	(10,000)	—	—	_____

Required

a. Compute the estimated tax liability on the differences between the estimated current value of the assets and liabilities and their tax bases.

b. Present a statement of financial condition for Mary Lou and Ernie at December 31, 1997.

c. Comment on the statement of financial condition.

P 16-5. For Bob and Sue, the changes in net worth for the year ended December 31, 1997 follow:

Realized increases in net worth:	
Salary	$ 60,000
Dividend income	2,500
Interest income	2,000
Gain on sale of marketable securities	500
Realized decreases in net worth:	
Income taxes	20,000
Interest expense	6,000
Personal expenditures	29,000
Unrealized increases in net worth:	
Stock options	3,000
Land	7,000
Residence	5,000
Unrealized decreases in net worth:	
Boat	3,000
Jewelry	1,000
Furnishings	4,000
Estimated income taxes on the differences between the estimated current values of assets and the estimated current amounts of liabilities and their tax bases	15,000
Net worth at the beginning of year	150,000

Required a. Prepare a statement of changes in net worth for the year ended December 31, 1997.

b. Comment on the statement of changes in net worth.

P 16-6. For Jim and Carl, the changes in net worth for the year ended December 31, 1997 follow:

Realized increases in net worth:	
Salary	$ 50,000
Interest income	6,000
Realized decreases in net worth:	
Income taxes	15,000
Interest expense	3,000
Personal property taxes	1,000
Real estate taxes	1,500
Personal expenditures	25,000
Unrealized increases in net worth:	
Marketable securities	2,000
Land	5,000
Residence	3,000
Stock options	4,000
Unrealized decreases in net worth:	
Furnishings	3,000
Estimated income taxes on the differences	
between the estimated current values of	
assets and the estimated current amounts	
of liabilities and their tax bases	12,000
Net worth at the beginning of year	130,000

Required a. Prepare a statement of changes in net worth for the year ended December 31, 1997.

b. Comment on the statement of changes in net worth.

P 16-7. Use Exhibit 16-4, City of Toledo, Ohio, Combined Statement of Revenues, Expenditures, and Changes in Fund Balances.

Required a. Prepare a vertical common-size statement for Exhibit 16-4, using only total revenues and expenditures (memorandum only). Use total expenditures as the base.

b. Comment on significant items in the vertical common-size analysis.

P 16-8. Use Exhibit 16-6, City of Toledo, Ohio, Income Tax Revenues.

Required a. Prepare a horizontal common-size analysis of taxes collected. Use 1986 as the base.

b. Comment on significant trends indicated in the horizontal common-size analysis prepared for (a).

(continued)

P 16-9.   Use Exhibit 16-7, City of Toledo, Ohio, Ratio of Net General Bonded Debt to Assessed Value and Net Bonded Debt per Capita.

Required   a.   How much has assessed value increased from 1986 to 1995?
                b.   How much has net general bonded debt increased from 1986 to 1995?
                c.   Give your opinion of the significance of the change in debt between 1986 and 1995.

P 16-10.   Use Exhibit 16-8, Institute of Management Accountants financial statements.

Required   a.   How much was the combined change in net assets between 1994 and 1995?
                b.   Prepare a horizontal common-size analysis for total revenue and expenses for 1994 and 1995. (Use 1994 as the base.)
                c.   Prepare a vertical common-size analysis for the combined revenues and expenses for 1994 and 1995. (Use total revenues as the base.)
                d.   Comment on significant items in the horizontal and vertical common-size analyses.

Cases

CASE 16-1 Governor Lucas—This Is Your County

The 1995 Lucas County, Ohio, financial report contains approximately 200 pages and has consistently received the Certificate of Achievement for Excellence in Financial Reporting. This case includes selected parts.

Required

a. Prepare a vertical common-size analysis of the combined balance sheet. Use only the total assets and other debits side of the balance sheet. Use the 1995 totals (memorandum only) and the 1994 totals (memorandum only).

b.
1. Of the governmental fund types, which fund has the most total assets?
2. What is the total for pooled cash and cash equivalents for 1995?
3. What is the total for accrued wages and benefits for 1995?

c. Describe the following:
1. General fund
2. Special revenue funds
3. Capital projects funds

d. Briefly describe the basis of accounting.

e. From Table 3:
1. Total Nominal Expenditures: Prepare a horizontal common-size analysis. Use 1986 as the base.
2. Total Real Expenditures: Prepare a horizontal common-size analysis. Use 1986 as the base.
3. Compare the trend in (2) with the trend in (1).
4. Total Real Expenditures, 1995, is stated in terms of what year? Show the computation for the 1995 Total Real Expenditures ($109,960,000).

f. From Table 4:
1. Using horizontal common-size analysis, determine the tax revenue by source that increased the most between 1986 and 1995.
2. Convert Table 4 to a vertical common-size analysis. Use total revenue as the base.
3. Comment on major trends found in (2).

LUCAS COUNTY, OHIO
COMBINED BALANCE SHEET
ALL FUND TYPES AND ACCOUNT GROUPS
DECEMBER 31, 1995
(AMOUNTS IN 000s)

	GOVERNMENTAL FUND TYPES			
	General Fund	Special Revenue	Debt Service	Capital Projects
Assets and other debits:				
Pooled cash and cash				
equivalents (Note C)	$ 2,362	$ 13,862	$ 147	$ 1,503
Investments (Note C)	8,452	49,589	526	5,378
Segregated cash accounts (Note C)	—	2,314	—	—
Receivables (net of allowances				
for uncollectibles)				
Taxes (Note J)	21,337	55,089	—	6,019
Accounts	150	664	—	2
Special assessments	3	—	14,502	—
Accrued interest	1,521	31	—	—
Loans	—	719	—	—
Due from other funds (Note D)	20	95	—	—
Due from other governments	1,986	5,803	90	553
Prepaid items	—	—	—	—
Inventory: Materials and supplies	—	1,472	—	—
Property, plant, and equipment (Note E)				
Land	—	—	—	—
Land improvements	—	—	—	—
Buildings, structures, and improvements	—	—	—	—
Furniture, fixtures, and equipment	—	—	—	—
Less: Accumulated depreciation	—	—	—	—
Construction-in-progress (Note E)	—	—	—	—
Amount available in debt service fund	—	—	—	—
Amount to be provided for retirement of				
general long-term obligations	—	—	—	—
Total assets and other debits	$35,831	$129,638	$15,265	$13,455

LUCAS COUNTY, OHIO
COMBINED BALANCE SHEET (continued)
ALL FUND TYPES AND ACCOUNT GROUPS
DECEMBER 31, 1995
(AMOUNTS IN 000s)

| | PROPRIETARY FUND TYPES | | FIDUCIARY FUND TYPES | ACCOUNT GROUPS | | | |
	Enterprise	Internal Service	Trust and Agency	General Fixed Assets	General Long-Term Obligations	1995 Totals (Memorandum Only)	1994 Totals (Memorandum Only)
$ 936	$ 3,748	$17,430	$ —	$ —	$ 39,988	$ 25,902
3,352	13,413	3,260	—	—	83,970	88,301
—	—	29,944	—	—	32,258	25,289
—	—	—	—	—	82,445	14,779
2,747	98	107	—	—	3,768	3,771
—	—	—	—	—	14,505	15,245
—	—	—	—	—	1,552	822
—	—	—	—	—	719	565
100	356	—	—	—	571	656
1,631	—	—	—	—	10,063	13,215
—	—	—	—	—	—	320
17	90	—	—	—	1,579	639
412	89	—	15,427	—	15,928	16,054
71,970	—	—	—	—	71,970	67,694
4,783	30	—	117,782	—	122,595	111,510
12,353	1,094	—	24,306	—	37,753	35,833
(38,789)	(730)	—	—	—	(39,519)	(37,413)
15,773	—	—	4,525	—	20,298	21,986
—	—	—	—	810	810	914
—	—	—	—	101,750	101,750	98,820
$ 75,285	$18,188	$50,741	$162,040	$102,560	$603,003	$504,902

(continued)

LUCAS COUNTY, OHIO
COMBINED BALANCE SHEET (continued)
ALL FUND TYPES AND ACCOUNT GROUPS
DECEMBER 31, 1995
(AMOUNTS IN 000s)

	GOVERNMENTAL FUND TYPES			
	General Fund	Special Revenue	Debt Service	Capital Projects
Liabilities:				
Accounts payable	$ 1,594	$ 5,682	$ —	$ 1,280
Accrued wages and benefits	2,065	3,414	—	—
Due to other funds (Note D)	73	99	—	—
Due to other governments	1,071	1,057	—	—
Claims payable—current	—	—	—	—
Deferred revenue (Note J)	11,750	53,945	14,444	5,874
Matured bonds payable	—	—	3	—
Matured interest payable	—	—	8	—
Accrued interest payable	—	—	—	—
Unapportioned monies	—	—	—	—
Deposits	—	—	—	—
Payroll withholdings	—	—	—	—
Deferred compensation payable—employees	—	—	—	6,000
Notes payable (Note F)	—	—	—	—
Bonds payable (Note G)	—	—	—	—
OWDA loans payable (Note G)	—	—	—	—
OWPC loans payable (Note G)	—	—	—	—
Claims payable—noncurrent	—	—	—	—
Landfill obligation—noncurrent (Note Q)	—	—	—	—
Obligations under capital leases (Note G)	—	—	—	—
Total liabilities	16,553	64,197	14,455	13,154
Equity and other credits:				
Contributed capital (Note M)	—	—	—	—
Investment in general fixed assets	—	—	—	—
Retained earnings: Unreserved	—	—	—	—
Fund balances (deficit)				
Reserved—				
Reserved for encumbrances	2,835	12,551	—	2,922
Reserved for inventory	—	1,472	—	—
Reserved for loans receivable	—	719	—	—
Unreserved—				
Designated for debt service	—	—	810	—
Designated for charity	—	31	—	—
Undesignated	16,443	50,668	—	(2,621)
Total equity and other credits	19,278	65,441	810	301
Total liabilities, equity, and other credits	$35,831	$129,638	$15,265	$13,455

LUCAS COUNTY, OHIO
COMBINED BALANCE SHEET (concluded)
ALL FUND TYPES AND ACCOUNT GROUPS
DECEMBER 31, 1995
(AMOUNTS IN 000s)

	PROPRIETARY FUND TYPES		FIDUCIARY FUND TYPES	ACCOUNT GROUPS			
	Enterprise	Internal Service	Trust and Agency	General Fixed Assets	General Long-Term Obligations	1995 Totals (Memorandum Only)	1994 Totals (Memorandum Only)
$ 335	$ 67	$ 142	$ —	$ —	$ 9,100	$ 7,733	
515	135	1	—	11,894	18,024	16,690	
102	297	—	—	—	571	656	
49	—	—	—	—	2,177	2,271	
—	1,701	—	—	—	1,701	2,432	
—	—	—	—	—	86,013	19,623	
—	—	—	—	—	3	3	
9	—	—	—	—	17	14	
4	—	—	—	—	4	5	
—	—	14,338	—	—	14,338	14,858	
—	—	5,184	—	—	5,184	5,176	
—	—	2,076	—	—	2,076	906	
—	—	24,865	—	—	24,865	20,197	
—	—	—	—	—	6,000	9,780	
740	—	—	—	58,289	59,029	57,392	
23,251	—	—	—	3,767	27,018	27,022	
912	—	—	—	1,316	2,228	1,398	
—	9,911	—	—	—	9,911	8,900	
—	—	—	—	12,500	12,500	12,600	
98	—	—	—	14,794	14,892	15,845	
26,015	12,111	46,606	—	102,560	295,651	223,501	
43,151	—	—	—	—	43,151	40,433	
—	—	—	162,040	—	162,040	156,627	
6,119	6,077	—	—	—	12,196	10,587	
—	—	—	—	—	18,308	13,623	
—	—	—	—	—	1,472	565	
—	—	—	—	—	719	565	
—	—	—	—	—	810	914	
—	—	—	—	—	31	87	
—	—	4,135	—	—	68,625	58,000	
49,270	6,077	4,135	162,040	—	307,352	281,401	
$ 75,285	$18,188	$50,741	$162,040	$102,560	$603,003	$504,902	

LUCAS COUNTY, OHIO
NOTES TO THE FINANCIAL STATEMENTS
DECEMBER 31, 1995
Note A—Description of Lucas County and Basis of Presentation

The County: Lucas County is a political subdivision of the State of Ohio. The County was formed by an act of the Ohio General Assembly in 1835. The three-member **Board of County Commissioners** is the legislative and executive body of the County. The **County Auditor** is the chief fiscal officer. In addition, there are seven other elected administrative officials, each of whom are independent as set forth by Ohio law. These officials are: **Clerk of Courts, Coroner, Engineer, Prosecutor, Recorder, Sheriff,** and **Treasurer**. There are also ten **Common Pleas Court Judges**, two **Domestic Relations Court Judges**, two **Juvenile Court Judges**, one **Probate Court Judge**, and five **Court of Appeals Judges** elected on a County-wide basis to oversee the County's justice system.

As defined by generally accepted accounting principles established by the Government Accounting Standards Board (GASB), the financial reporting entity consists of the primary government, as well as its component units, which are legally separate organizations to which the elected officials of the primary government are financially accountable. Financial accountability is defined as appointment of a voting majority of the component unit's board, and either (a) the ability to impose will by the primary government, or (b) the possibility that the component unit will provide a financial benefit to or impose a financial burden on the primary government.

The accompanying financial statements present the County (Primary Government) and its component units. The financial data of the component units are included in the County's reporting entity because of the significance of their operational or financial relationships with the County.

A blended component unit is a legally separate entity from the County, but is so intertwined with the County that it is, in substance, the same as the County. It is reported as part of the County and blended into the appropriate funds.

A discretely presented component unit is an entity that is legally separate from the County but for which the County is financially accountable, or its relationship with the County is such that exclusion would cause the County's financial statements to be misleading or incomplete. The County has no component units to discretely present.

In determining its reporting entity and component units, the County considered all potential component units, including the Lucas County Board of Health, Metropolitan Park District, Lucas County Soil and Water Conservation District, Lucas County Port Authority, Lucas County Recreation Inc., Lucas County Improvement Corporation, Toledo Zoological Society, Toledo Area Sanitary District, Lucas County Board of Education, and Toledo-Lucas County Convention and Visitors Bureau and concluded that such were neither component units nor related organizations of the County and that it would not be misleading to exclude their activities from the County's reporting entity.

Basis of Presentation: The accounts of the County are organized on the basis of funds or account groups, each of which are considered separate accounting entities. The accounting of the operations of each fund is maintained by a set of self-balancing accounts that comprise the assets, liabilities, fund equity, revenues, expenditures/expenses, and statement of cash flows as appropriate. The various funds are summarized by type in the general purpose financial statements.

Total columns on the Combined Statements are captioned "Memorandum Only" to indicate they are presented only to facilitate financial analysis. Data in these columns do not present financial position, results of operations, or cash

LUCAS COUNTY, OHIO
NOTES TO THE FINANCIAL STATEMENTS (continued)
DECEMBER 31, 1995
Note A—Description of Lucas County and Basis of Presentation

flows in conformity with generally accepted accounting principles, nor are such data comparable to a consolidation.

The County uses the following fund types and account groups:

Governmental Fund Types:

- **General Fund:** This fund accounts for the general operating revenues and expenditures of the County not recorded elsewhere. The primary revenue sources are sales and use taxes, property taxes, state and local government fund receipts, investment earnings, and charges for services.
- **Special Revenue Funds:** These funds are used to account for specific governmental revenues (other than major capital projects) requiring separate accounting because of legal or regulatory provisions or administrative action. These funds include: Public Assistance, the Board of Mental Retardation, and the Motor Vehicle and Gas Tax funds, which are major funds of the County.
- **Debt Service Fund:** The Debt Service Fund is used to account for revenues received and used to pay principal and interest on debt reported in the County's general long-term obligations account group.
- **Capital Projects Funds:** These funds are used to account for the acquisition or construction of capital assets. Revenues and financing sources are derived from the issuance of debt or receipts from the General Fund and Special Revenue funds.

Proprietary Fund Types:

- **Enterprise Funds:** These funds are used to account for operations that provide services which are financed primarily by user charges, or activities where periodic measurement of income is appropriate for capital maintenance, public policy, management control, or other purposes.
- **Internal Service Funds:** These funds are used to account for the goods or services provided by certain County departments to other County funds, departments, and other governmental units, on a cost reimbursement basis.

Fiduciary Fund Types:

- **Trust and Agency Funds:** These funds are used to account for and maintain assets held by the County in a trustee capacity or as an agent for individuals, private organizations, other governmental units, and other funds. These assets include: property and other taxes, as well as other intergovernmental resources which have been collected and which will be distributed to other taxing districts located in Lucas County.

Account Groups:

- **General Fixed Assets Account Group:** This account group is used to present the general fixed assets of the County utilized in its general operations, exclusive of those used in Enterprise and Internal Service funds. General fixed assets of Lucas County include land, buildings, structures and improvements, furniture, fixtures and equipment, assets acquired by capital leases, and construction in progress.
- **General Long-Term Obligations Account Group:** This account group is used to account for all long-term obligations of the County.

(continued)

LUCAS COUNTY, OHIO
NOTES TO THE FINANCIAL STATEMENTS (continued)
DECEMBER 31, 1995
Note B—Summary of Significant Accounting Policies

The accompanying financial statements of the County are prepared in conformity with generally accepted accounting principles (GAAP) for local government units as prescribed in statements and interpretations issued by the GASB another recognized authoritative sources. The County has elected not to apply FASB Statements and interpretations issued after November 30, 1989, to its proprietary activities.

Measurement Focus: Governmental and Expendable Trust Funds are accounted for on a spending, or "financial flow," measurement focus. Governmental and Expendable Trust Fund operating statements represent increases and decreases in net current assets. Their reported fund balance is considered a measure of available spendable resources.

Proprietary Fund Types are used to account for the County's ongoing organizations and activities which are similar to the private sector. Proprietary Fund Types are accounted for on a cost of services, or "capital maintenance," measurement focus. Proprietary Fund Type income statements represent increases and decreases in net total assets.

Basis of Accounting: All financial transactions for Governmental and Fiduciary Funds are reported on the modified accrual basis of accounting. Under this accounting method, revenues are recognized when measurable and available to finance county operations. Revenues accrued at the end of the year consist of reimbursements from other governments for grant expenditures, amounts receivable from charges for services, licenses and permits, fines, special assessments, and property taxes. Governmental Fund expenditures are accrued when the related fund liability is incurred, except interest on long-term debt, which is recorded when due. Proprietary Fund financial transactions are recorded on the accrual basis of accounting: revenues are recognized when earned and measurable; expenses are recognized as incurred.

Budgetary Accounting and Control: Under Ohio law, the Board of County Commissioners must adopt an appropriations budget by January 1st of a given year, or adopt a temporary appropriation measure with final passage of a permanent budget by April 1st, for all funds except Fiduciary Fund Types. Budgets are legally required for each organizational unit by object (personal services, material and supplies, charges for services, and capital outlays and equipment).

Each county department prepares a budget which is approved by the Board of County Commissioners. Modifications to the original budget within expenditure objects can be made by the budget manager in the Auditor's Office. The County maintains budgetary control within an organizational unit and fund by not permitting expenditures and encumbrances to exceed appropriations at the object level (the legal level of control). Unencumbered and unexpended appropriations lapse at year-end. Encumbered and unpaid appropriations (reserved for encumbrances) are carried forward to the next year as authority for expenditures.

TABLE 3
LUCAS COUNTY, OHIO
GENERAL GOVERNMENTAL EXPENDITURES AND REVENUES
ADJUSTED FOR INFLATION[1]
LAST TEN FISCAL YEARS
(Amounts in 000s)

Fiscal Year	Total Nominal Expenditures	Total Nominal Revenues	Average[2] CPI-U	Total Real Expenditures	Total Real Revenues
1986	$ 158,787	$ 152,876	328.4	$ 87,757	$ 84,491
1987	167,470	169,090	340.4	89,294	90,158
1988	187,964	185,417	361.5	94,371	93,093
1989	203,026	200,414	370.7	99,404	98,126
1990	215,693	210,308	391.4	100,022	97,524
1991	231,925	226,828	408.0	103,206	100,938
1992	226,783	234,525	420.3	97,970	101,315
1993	240,914	249,025	432.9	101,007	104,408
1994	269,100	278,478	444.0	110,004	113,837
1995	276,567	286,270	456.5	109,960	113,818

[1] Between 1986 and 1995, real expenditures increased by 25.3% or $22.2 million, while real revenues increased by 34.7% or $29.3 million over the same period.
[2] Average Consumer Price Index for all Urban Consumers. 1977 is the base year when the Average CPI-U was 181.5.

TABLE 4
LUCAS COUNTY, OHIO
TAX REVENUES BY SOURCE
LAST TEN FISCAL YEARS
(Amounts in 000s)

Fiscal Year	General Property Tax	Tangible[1] Personal Tax	Property Transfer Tax	County[2] Sales Tax	Total
1986	$ 26,022	$ 9,059	$ 771	$ 28,431	$ 64,283
1987	35,025	10,399	755	31,229	77,408
1988	36,763	10,300	773	34,662	82,498
1989	41,227	10,549	734	35,351	87,861
1990	44,077	10,820	647	33,942	89,486
1991	44,894	10,310	1,411	34,485	91,100
1992	47,729	10,115	1,930	46,250	106,024
1993	52,926	9,915	2,272	45,137	110,250
1994	53,491	10,308	2,341	60,546	126,686
1995	54,563	10,523	2,562	56,161	123,809

[1] Tangible Personal Tax includes: personal property tax, mobile home tax, and grain tax.
[2] Includes county sales tax and hotel lodging tax. 1994 sales tax increase includes sales tax accrual attributed to implementation of GASB #22.

Endnotes

1   *Statement of Position 82-1*, "Accounting and Financial Reporting for Personal Financial Statements" (New York, NY: American Institute of Certified Public Accountants, October 1982).

2   *Statement of Position 82-1*, p. 6.

3   A good article on this subject is: "Personal Financial Statements: Valuation Challenges and Solutions," by Michael D. Kinsman and Bruce Samuelson, *Journal of Accountancy* (September 1987), p. 138.

4   *Government Accounting Standards Board Statement No. 1* (July 1984), Appendix B, paragraph 4.

5   *Governmental Accounting, Auditing, and Financial Reporting* (Chicago, IL: Municipal Finance Officers Association of the United States and Canada, 1968), p. 6.

6   Walter Robbins and Paul Polinski, "Financial Reporting by Nonprofits," *National Public Accountant* (October 1995), p. 29.

7   *Statement of Financial Accounting Standards No. 93*, "Recognition of Depreciation by Not-for-Profit Organizations" (Stamford, CT: Financial Accounting Standards Board, 1987).

8   *Statement of Financial Accounting Standards No. 116*, "Accounting for Contributions Received and Contributions Made" (Norwalk, CT: Financial Accounting Standards Board, 1993).

9   *Statement of Financial Accounting Standards No. 117*, "Financial Statements of Not-for-Profit Organizations" (Norwalk, CT: Financial Accounting Standards Board, 1993).

10   *Statement of Financial Accounting Standards No. 124*, "Accounting for Certain Investments Held by Not-for-Profit Organizations" (Norwalk, CT: Financial Accounting Standards Board, 1995).

11   *Statement of Position 94-2*, "The Application of the Requirements of Accounting Research Bulletins, Opinions of the Accounting Principles Board and Statements of Interpretations of the Financial Accounting Standards Board to Not-for-Profit Organizations" (New York, NY: American Institute of Certified Public Accountants), September 1994.

12   Charles H. Gibson, "Budgeting by Objectives: Charlotte's Experience," *Management Accounting* (January 1978), p. 39.

13   Gibson, p. 39, 48.

Comprehensive Case—
Worthington Industries

Worthington Industries began in 1955, when John H. McConnell started a steel brokerage business in his basement. The company began as a processor of flat rolled steel. In the early years, the company only "slit" or changed the width of steel. Today Worthington performs a wide variety of processes. Portions of its 1996 annual report follow.

Note: Printed with permission of Worthington Industries, Inc.

Consolidated Statements of Earnings
Worthington Industries, Inc. and Subsidiaries

Dollars in thousands, except per share	Year ended May 31	1996	1995	1994
Net sales		$ 1,477,838	$ 1,483,569	$ 1,285,134
Cost of goods sold		1,256,574	1,244,633	1,093,350
	Gross Margin	221,264	238,936	191,784
Selling, general, and administrative expense		95,123	85,102	72,372
	Operating Income	126,141	153,834	119,412
Other income (expense):				
Miscellaneous income		950	573	389
Interest expense		(8,350)	(6,036)	(3,017)
Equity in net income of unconsolidated affiliates —Joint Ventures		7,333	6,216	(555)
Equity in net income of unconsolidated affiliate —Rouge		21,729	32,111	19,406
	Earnings Before Income Taxes	147,803	186,698	135,635
Income taxes		56,461	70,012	50,782
	Net Earnings	$ 91,342	$ 116,686	$ 84,853
	Average Common Shares Outstanding	90,812	90,730	90,378
	Earnings Per Share	$ 1.01	$ 1.29	$ .94

See notes to consolidated financial statements.

Consolidated Statements of Shareholders' Equity
Worthington Industries, Inc. and Subsidiaries

Dollars in thousands, except per share	1996	1995	1994
COMMON SHARES			
Balance at beginning of year	$ 908	$ 906	$ 601
Sale of common shares under stock option plan			
(116,051 in 1996; 198,144 in 1995; 375,155 in 1994)	1	2	4
Par value of shares issued in connection with share split	—	—	301
Purchase and retirement of common shares			
(216,500 in 1996; 1,436 in 1994)	(1)	—	—
Balance at May 31	$ 908	$ 908	$ 906
ADDITIONAL PAID-IN CAPITAL			
Balance at beginning of year	**$102,733**	$ 96,427	$ 81,250
Sale of common shares under stock option plan			
(116,051 in 1996; 198,144 in 1995; 375,155 in 1994)	**1,549**	2,569	3,875
Sale of shares under dividend reinvestment plan			
(90,561 in 1996; 81,102 in 1995; 74,101 in 1994)	**1,820**	1,664	1,471
Par value of shares issued in connection with share split	—	—	(301)
Transactions of unconsolidated affiliate	10	2,073	10,134
Purchase and retirement of common shares			
(216,500 in 1996; 1,436 in 1994)	(243)	—	(2)
Balance at May 31	**$105,869**	$102,733	$ 96,427
MINIMUM PENSION LIABILITY			
Balance at beginning of year	**$ (871)**	$ (1,674)	$ (230)
Transactions of unconsolidated affiliate	**682**	803	(1,444)
Balance at May 31	**$ (189)**	$ (871)	$ (1,674)
TRANSLATION ADJUSTMENT			
Balance at beginning of year	**$ (146)**	$ —	$ —
Foreign currency translation adjustment	**(1,102)**	(146)	—
Balance at May 31	**$ (1,248)**	$ (146)	$ —
RETAINED EARNINGS			
Balance at beginning of year	**$487,708**	$408,234	$356,567
Net earnings	**91,342**	116,686	84,853
Cash dividends declared			
(per share: $.450 in 1996; $.410 in 1995; $.367 in 1994)	**(40,872)**	(37,212)	(33,161)
Purchase and retirement of common shares			
(216,500 in 1996; 1,436 in 1994)	**(3,978)**	—	(25)
Balance at May 31	**$534,200**	$487,708	$408,234

See notes to consolidated financial statements.

Consolidated Balance Sheets
Worthington Industries, Inc. and Subsidiaries

Dollars in thousands	May 31	1996	1995
ASSETS			
Current Assets			
Cash and cash equivalents		$ 19,029	$ 2,003
Accounts receivable, less allowances of			
$2,778 and $2,397 at May 31, 1996 and 1995		224,956	216,443
Inventories			
Raw materials		128,884	142,738
Work in process and finished products		79,141	58,140
		208,025	200,878
Prepaid expenses and other current assets		24,031	32,578
	Total Current Assets	476,041	451,902
Investment in Unconsolidated Affiliates		138,212	104,764
Intangible Assets		65,256	—
Other Assets		28,280	25,381
Property, Plant, and Equipment			
Land		20,658	11,383
Buildings		154,774	122,073
Machinery and equipment		528,965	427,927
Construction in progress		88,877	27,903
		793,274	589,286
Less accumulated depreciation		280,938	254,369
		512,336	334,917
	Total Assets	$ 1,220,125	$916,964

(continued)

Consolidated Balance Sheets   (concluded)

Dollars in thousands May 31	1996	1995
LIABILITIES		
Current Liabilities		
Accounts payable	$ 82,178	$ 87,329
Notes payable	—	38,200
Accrued compensation, contributions to		
employee benefit plans, and related taxes	33,234	31,741
Dividends payable	10,901	9,992
Other accrued items	17,652	8,597
Income taxes	5,829	2,709
Current maturities of long-term debt	1,475	660
Total Current Liabilities	151,269	179,228
Other Liabilities	17,912	18,055
Long-Term Debt	298,742	53,476
Deferred Income Taxes	112,662	75,873
Contingent Liabilities—Note G		
EQUITY		
Shareholders' Equity		
Preferred shares, $1.00 par value, authorized—		
1,000,000 shares, issued and outstanding—none	—	—
Common shares, $.01 par value, authorized—		
150,000,000 shares, issued and outstanding—		
1996—90,830,440 shares; 1995—90,840,328 shares	908	908
Additional paid-in capital	105,869	102,733
Minimum pension liability of unconsolidated affiliate	(189)	(871)
Foreign currency translation adjustment	(1,248)	(146)
Retained earnings	534,200	487,708
	639,540	590,332
Total Liabilities and Shareholders' Equity	$ 1,220,125	$916,964

See notes to consolidated financial statements.

Consolidated Statements of Cash Flows
Worthington Industries, Inc. and Subsidiaries

In thousands Year Ended May 31	1996	1995	1994
OPERATING ACTIVITIES			
Net earnings	$ 91,342	$116,686	$ 84,853
Adjustments to reconcile net earnings to net cash provided by operating activities:			
Depreciation	39,222	34,129	32,385
Gain on sale of short-term investments	—	—	(911)
Provision for deferred income taxes	10,355	15,541	7,911
Equity in undistributed net income of unconsolidated affiliates	(25,153)	(37,847)	(19,345)
Changes in assets and liabilities:			
Accounts receivable	13,456	(26,702)	(20,886)
Inventories	35,175	(15,996)	(25,895)
Prepaid expenses and other current assets	2,443	(7,418)	(6,460)
Other assets	(1,951)	554	(6,576)
Accounts payable and accrued expenses	(25,990)	(11,156)	4,001
Other liabilities	(457)	(1,390)	11,777
Net Cash Provided by Operating Activities	138,442	66,401	60,854
INVESTING ACTIVITIES			
Investment in property, plant, and equipment, net	(108,996)	(61,485)	(46,554)
Acquisition of Dietrich Industries, net of cash acquired	(169,391)	—	—
Investments in unconsolidated affiliates	(8,315)	(10,857)	—
Other, net	—	—	1,287
Net Cash Used by Investing Activities	(286,702)	(72,342)	(45,267)
FINANCING ACTIVITIES			
Proceeds from (payments on) short-term borrowings	(38,200)	28,200	10,000
Proceeds from long-term debt	424,774	27,000	—
Principal payments on long-term debt	(180,473)	(28,490)	(1,165)
Proceeds from issuance of common shares	3,370	4,235	5,350
Repurchase of common shares	(4,222)	—	(27)
Dividends paid	(39,963)	(36,276)	(33,161)
Net Cash Provided (Used) by Financing Activities	165,286	(5,331)	(19,003)
Increase (decrease) in cash and cash equivalents	17,026	(11,272)	(3,416)
Cash and cash equivalents at beginning of year	2,003	13,275	16,691
Cash and Cash Equivalents at End of Year	$ 19,029	$ 2,003	$ 13,275

See notes to consolidated financial statements.

Industry Segment Data
Worthington Industries, Inc. and Subsidiaries

In thousands May 31	1996	1995	1994	1993	1992
SALES					
Net Sales					
Processed steel products	$1,013,099	$1,028,326	$ 920,199	$ 767,682	$668,578
Custom products	321,013	302,096	249,459	241,916	217,731
Cast products	143,726	153,147	115,476	103,644	85,037
	$1,477,838	$1,483,569	$1,285,134	$1,113,242	$971,346
EARNINGS					
Operating Income					
Processed steel products	$ 93,379	$ 112,390	$ 98,062	$ 79,187	$ 70,317
Custom products	18,200	19,754	15,334	20,360	13,948
Cast products	14,562	21,690	6,016	6,544	4,092
	126,141	153,834	119,412	106,091	88,357
Miscellaneous income	950	573	389	598	1,289
Interest expense	(8,350)	(6,036)	(3,017)	(3,421)	(3,986)
Equity in net income of unconsolidated affiliates	29,062	38,327	18,851	4,587	5,440
	$ 147,803	$ 186,698	$ 135,635	$ 107,855	$ 91,100
ASSETS					
Identifiable Assets					
Processed steel products	$ 758,836	$ 507,073	$ 471,458	$ 428,891	$410,051
Custom products	178,679	165,619	138,015	117,856	105,483
Cast products	71,225	78,099	75,733	69,843	62,350
Corporate	73,173	61,409	61,406	59,674	41,273
	1,081,913	812,200	746,612	676,264	619,157
Investment in unconsolidated affiliates	138,212	104,764	51,961	17,945	8,803
	$1,220,125	$ 916,964	$ 798,573	$ 694,209	$627,960
DEPRECIATION					
Depreciation Expense					
Processed steel products	$ 22,054	$ 19,041	$ 19,075	$ 17,745	$ 15,927
Custom products	10,330	8,710	7,047	5,598	5,233
Cast products	4,647	4,362	4,095	3,900	3,879
Corporate	2,191	2,016	2,168	1,961	1,848
	$ 39,222	$ 34,129	$ 32,385	$ 29,204	$ 26,887
EXPENDITURES					
Capital Expenditures					
Processed steel products	$ 79,551	$ 31,869	$ 14,693	$ 9,876	$ 28,081
Custom products	17,423	22,254	19,086	12,640	9,345
Cast products	5,427	4,041	6,787	5,283	1,631
Corporate	6,595	3,321	5,988	1,341	6,063
	$ 108,996	$ 61,485	$ 46,554	$ 29,140	$ 45,120

( ) *Indicates deduction*

Corporate expenses are allocated on a consistent basis among industry segments over the five-year period. Earnings are before income taxes and cumulative effect of accounting changes. "Capital expenditures" are net of normal disposals and exclude amounts in connection with acquisitions and divestitures.

See notes to consolidated financial statements.

Notes to Consolidated Financial Statements
Worthington Industries, Inc. and Subsidiaries

NOTE A—Summary of Significant Accounting Policies

Consolidation: The consolidated financial statements include the accounts of Worthington Industries, Inc. and Subsidiaries (the "Company"). Investments in unconsolidated affiliates are accounted for using the equity method. Significant intercompany accounts and transactions are eliminated. Certain reclassifications were made to prior years' amounts to conform with the 1996 presentation.

Use of Estimates: The preparation of financial statements in conformity with generally accepted accounting principles requires management to make estimates and assumptions that affect the amounts reported in the financial statements and accompanying notes. Actual results could differ from those estimates.

Cash and Cash Equivalents: The Company considers all highly liquid investments purchased with a maturity of three months or less to be cash equivalents.

Inventories: Inventories are valued at the lower of cost or market. Cost is determined using the specific identification method for steel processing and the first-in, first-out method for all other businesses.

Property and Depreciation: Property, plant, and equipment are carried at cost and depreciated using the straight-line method over the estimated useful lives of the assets. Accelerated depreciation methods are used for income tax purposes.

Capitalized Interest: Interest is capitalized in connection with construction of qualified assets. Under this policy, interest of $2,085,000 was capitalized in 1996 and $529,000 in 1995.

Postretirement Benefits Other than Pensions: The Company adopted Financial Accounting Standards Board (FASB) Statement No. 106, "Employer's Accounting for Postretirement Benefits Other than Pensions," effective June 1, 1993. The adoption of this Statement did not have a material impact on the Company's operating results or financial position. As permitted by Statement 106, the Company elected not to restate the financial statements of prior years.

Stock-Based Compensation: During 1995, the FASB issued Statement No. 123, "Accounting for Stock-Based Compensation," effective June 1, 1996. This Statement sets forth standards for accounting for stock-based compensation or allows companies to continue using Accounting Principles Board Opinion (APB) No. 25 with additional disclosures in the notes to consolidated financial statements. It is the Company's intention to continue using APB No. 25 with additional disclosures in the notes beginning in 1997.

Statements of Cash Flows: With respect to noncash activities, the Company recorded its increased equity from the Rouge Steel Company's initial public offering as an increase in investments in unconsolidated affiliates of $3,215,000 in 1995 and $15,451,000 in 1994 and additional paid-in capital (net of deferred taxes) of $2,073,000 in 1995 and $10,134,000 in 1994.

Supplemental cash flow information for the years ended May 31 is as follows:

In thousands	1996	1995	1994
Interest paid	$10,936	$ 6,688	$ 2,973
Income taxes paid	46,131	60,520	39,957

Notes to Consolidated Financial Statements
Worthington Industries, Inc. and Subsidiaries

Fair Value of Financial Instruments: The following methods and assumptions were used by the Company in estimating the fair value of its financial instruments:

Cash and cash equivalents, other assets, and long-term debt—The carrying amounts reported in the balance sheets approximate fair value.

The concentration of credit risks from financial instruments, related to the markets discussed in Business Profile on page 3, is not expected to have a material effect on the Company's consolidated financial position, cash flow, or future results of operations.

In thousands	1996	1995
Short-term notes payable to bank—unsecured	$ —	$38,200
Industrial development revenue bonds and notes	13,476	14,136
Notes payable to banks—unsecured	—	13,000
Revolver—unsecured	85,000	27,000
Senior notes due 2006—unsecured	200,000	—
Other	1,741	—
	300,217	92,336
Less current maturities	1,475	38,860
	$298,742	$53,476

NOTE B—Shareholders' Equity

On September 16, 1993, the Company's Board of Directors authorized a three-for-two split of the common shares, with distribution of the additional shares on October 22, 1993, to holders of record on October 1, 1993. Also on September 16, 1993, the shareholders adopted an amendment to the Certificate of Incorporation of the Company to increase the authorized number of common shares from 100,000,000 shares to 150,000,000 shares. References in this annual report to per-share amounts and to the number of common shares have been adjusted, where appropriate, to give retroactive effect to the share split.

The Board of Directors is empowered to determine the issue prices, dividend rates, amounts payable upon liquidation, voting rights, and other terms of the preferred shares when issued.

NOTE C—Debt

Debt at May 31 is summarized as follows:

The industrial development revenue bonds and notes (IRBs) represent loans to purchase facilities and equipment costing $24,601,000. The IRBs mature serially through 2011 and may be retired in whole or in part at any time. At May 31, 1996, the IRBs have fixed interest rates: $9,945,000 at 5.9% and the remainder at 8.0%.

The Company maintains a $150,000,000 revolving credit agreement with five banks, of which $65,000,000 was available on May 31, 1996. The credit agreement is committed through 2001 and has one annual extension option. The rate of interest is determined at the time of borrowing, based upon a choice of options as specified in the agreement, and was 5.6% at May 31, 1996.

During the year ended May 31, 1996, the Company filed a shelf registration for the issuance of up to $450,000,000 of debt securities and issued $200,000,000 of 7.125% Notes due 2006. The majority of the proceeds were used to repay a bridge loan credit facility that was used to finance the acquisition of Dietrich Industries (see Note K).

Notes to Consolidated Financial Statements
Worthington Industries, Inc. and Subsidiaries

The Company enters into interest rate hedge agreements to manage interest costs and exposure to changing interest rates. At May 31, 1996, agreements were in place that effectively converted $150,000,000 of fixed rate debt to floating. The counterparties to these agreements are major financial institutions.

Various debt agreements place restrictions on financial conditions and require maintenance of certain ratios. One of these restrictions limits cash dividends and certain other payments to $3,000,000 plus 75% of net earnings, as defined, subsequent to May 31, 1976. Retained earnings of $347,333,000 were unrestricted at May 31, 1996.

Principal payments on long-term debt, including lease purchase obligations, in the next five fiscal years are as follows: 1997— $1,475,000; 1998—$5,057,000; 1999—$720,000; 2000—$660,000; 2001—$660,000; and thereafter—$291,645,000.

The Company is guarantor on bank loans for four separate joint ventures. The guarantees totaled $30,700,000 at May 31, 1996, and relate to debt with varying maturities. The Company believes the guarantees will not significantly affect the consolidated financial position or future results of operations.

NOTE D—Income Taxes

Income taxes for the years ended May 31 were as follows:

In thousands		1996	1995	1994
Current:	Federal	$38,704	$45,559	$36,907
	State & local	7,403	8,912	5,964
Deferred:	Federal	10,386	14,382	7,627
	State	(32)	1,159	284
		$56,461	$70,012	$50,782

Under Statement of Financial Accounting Standards Board Number 109, "Accounting for Income Taxes," the liability method is used in accounting for income taxes. Under this method, deferred tax assets and liabilities are determined based on differences between financial reporting and tax bases of assets and liabilities, and are measured using enacted tax rates and laws that will be in effect when the differences are expected to reverse.

Deferred income taxes reflect the net tax effects of temporary differences between the carrying amounts of assets and liabilities for financial reporting and the amounts used for income tax purposes. The components of the Company's deferred tax liabilities and assets as of May 31 are as follows:

In thousands	1996	1995
Deferred tax assets:		
Allowance for doubtful accounts	$ 1,176	$ 1,284
Inventory	(5,352)	1,375
Accrued expenses	4,317	3,888
Income taxes	2,916	2,460
Other	553	388
	3,610	9,395
Deferred tax liabilities:		
Property, plant, and equipment	73,751	45,426
Undistributed earnings of unconsolidated affiliates	38,911	30,447
	112,662	75,873
Net deferred tax liability	$109,052	$66,478

The reasons for the difference between the effective income tax rate and the statutory federal income tax rate were as follows:

	1996	1995	1994
Federal statutory rate	35.0%	35.0%	35.0%
State and local income taxes, net of federal tax benefit	3.4	3.6	3.0
Other	(.2)	(1.1)	(.6)
	38.2%	37.5%	37.4%

Notes to Consolidated Financial Statements
Worthington Industries, Inc. and Subsidiaries

NOTE E—Employee Benefit Plans

Nonunion employees of the Company participate in a current cash profit sharing plan and a deferred profit sharing plan. Contributions to and costs of these plans are determined as a percentage of the Company's pretax income before profit sharing.

Certain operations have noncontributory defined benefit pension plans covering a majority of their employees qualified by age and service. Company contributions to these plans comply with ERISA's minimum funding requirements.

A summary of the components of net periodic pension cost for the defined benefit plans in 1996, 1995, and 1994, and the contributions charged to pension expense for the defined contribution plans follow:

In thousands	1996	1995	1994
Defined benefit plans:			
Service cost (benefits earned during the period)	$1,171	$1,078	$1,089
Interest cost on projected benefit obligation	3,330	3,091	2,875
Actual return on plan assets	(9,480)	(3,884)	(1,222)
Net amortization and deferral	5,582	283	(2,544)
Net pension cost on defined benefit plans	603	568	198
Defined contribution plans	4,307	4,985	3,935
Total pension expense	$4,910	$5,553	$4,133

Pension expense was calculated assuming a weighted average discount rate and an expected long-term rate of return on plan assets of 8%. Plan assets consist principally of listed equity securities and fixed income instruments. The following table sets forth the funded status and amounts recognized in the Company's consolidated balance sheet for defined benefit pension plans at May 31:

In thousands	Plans Whose Assets Exceed Accumulated Benefits		Plans Whose Accumulated Benefits Exceed Assets	
	1996	1995	1996	1995
Actuarial present value of benefit obligations:				
Vested	$37,849	$35,546	$6,399	$6,361
Accumulated	$38,200	$35,945	$6,809	$6,590
Projected benefit obligation	$38,200	$35,945	$6,809	$6,590
Plan assets at fair value	52,199	43,922	6,020	5,022
Projected benefit obligation less than (in excess of) plan assets	$13,999	$7,977	$(789)	$(1,568)
Comprised of:				
Accrued pension cost	$ —	$ —	$ (557)	$(1,361)
Prepaid pension cost	3,244	2,030	(23)	—
Unrecognized:				
Net gain	15,541	10,905	829	60
Prior service cost	(6,505)	(6,950)	(1,292)	(1,393)
Unrecorded net asset (obligation) at transition, net of amortization	1,718	1,992	(48)	(45)
Adjustment to recognize minimum liability	—	—	302	1,171
	$13,999	$7,977	$(789)	$(1,568)

NOTE F—Stock Options

Under its employee stock option plans, the Company may grant employees incentive stock options to purchase shares at not less than 100% of market value at date of grant or nonqualified stock options at a price determined by the Stock Option Committee. Generally, options are exercisable at the rate of 20% a year beginning one year from date of grant and expire ten years thereafter.

Notes to Consolidated Financial Statements
Worthington Industries, Inc. and Subsidiaries

The following table summarizes the option plans:

In thousands, except per share	Price Range Per Share	Number of Options		
		1996	1995	1994
Exercised	$4.68-$19.25	116	198	375
At May 31,				
Granted	$19.25-$21.375	501	882	—
Outstanding	$7.11-$21.375	2,174	1,821	1,164
Exercisable		996	1,115	933
Available for grants		3,117	3,618	4,500

The options outstanding at May 31, 1996 were held by 688 persons, had an average exercise price of $15.57 per share, and have expiration dates ranging from May 1997 to March 2006.

NOTE G—Contingent Liabilities

The Company is a defendant in certain legal actions. In the opinion of management, the outcome of these actions, which is not clearly determinable at the present time, would not significantly affect the Company's consolidated financial position or future results of operations.

NOTE H—Industry Segment Data

Industry segment descriptions on page 3, Company locations on page 34, and segment data on page 24 of the annual report are an integral part of these financial statements.

Sales for processed steel products and custom products include $209,826,000 in 1996, $204,338,000 in 1995, and $161,602,000 in 1994 to a major automobile manufacturer purchasing through decentralized divisions and subsidiaries in different geographical areas.

NOTE I—Related Party Transactions

The Company purchases from and sells to affiliated companies certain raw materials and services at prevailing market prices. Sales for fiscal 1996, 1995, and 1994 totaled $51 million, $61 million, and $62 million, respectively. Accounts receivable related to these transactions were $10 million and $12 million at May 31, 1996 and 1995, respectively. Purchases for fiscal 1996, 1995, and 1994 totaled $167 million, $194 million, and $168 million, respectively. Accounts payable related to these transactions included $18 million and $27 million at May 31, 1996 and 1995, respectively.

NOTE J—Investment in Unconsolidated Affiliates

The Company's investments in affiliated companies which are not majority owned or controlled are accounted for using the equity method. Investments carried at equity and the percentage interest owned consist of Worthington Specialty Processing, partnership (50%), London Industries, Inc. (60%), Worthington Armstrong Venture, partnership (50%), TWB Company, partnership (50%), Acerex, S.A. de C.V. (50%), and Rouge Steel Company (28%).

The market value of the Company's investment in the class A and class B common stock of Rouge at May 31, 1996 ($22.25 per share) was approximately $134 million. At May 31, 1996, the Company's share of the underlying net assets of Rouge exceeded the carrying amount included in investment in unconsolidated affiliates of $101,134,000 by $9,106,000. The excess is being amortized into income by increasing equity in net income of unconsolidated affiliates using the straight-line method over the remaining 12 years.

Financial information for affiliated companies accounted for by the equity method is as follows:

In thousands	1996	1995	1994
Current assets	$ 553,023	$ 569,447	$ —
Noncurrent assets	287,247	227,315	—
Current liabilities	233,441	240,044	—
Noncurrent liabilities	176,618	167,915	—
Minority interests	6,404	21,404	—
Net sales	1,383,343	1,386,824	1,189,470
Gross margin	122,500	170,234	106,309
Net income	88,644	122,116	64,152

The Company's share of undistributed earnings of unconsolidated affiliates included in consolidated retained earnings was $67,935,000 at May 31, 1996.

NOTE K—Acquisition

On February 5, 1996, the Company acquired all of the outstanding capital stock of Dietrich Industries, Inc. for approximately $146 million in cash and $23 million in assumed liabilities, net of cash acquired. Dietrich, based in Pittsburgh, Pennsylvania, is involved primarily in the manufacture and sale of metal framing products for the commercial and residential construction markets. The acquisition was accounted for using purchase accounting with results for Dietrich included since the purchase date. The purchase price exceeded the fair value of the net assets acquired by approximately $66 million which is being amortized over 40 years.

The following pro forma data summarizes the results of operations of the Company for the 12 months ended May 31, 1996 and May 31, 1995, assuming Dietrich was acquired at the beginning of each period presented. In preparing the pro forma data, adjustments have been made to conform Dietrich's accounting policies to those of the Company and to reflect purchase accounting adjustments and interest expense:

In thousands, except per share (unaudited)	Twelve Months Ended	
	May 31, 1996	May 31, 1995
Net sales	$1,660,815	$1,768,931
Net earnings	$92,503	$120,459
Earnings per common share	$1.02	$1.33

NOTE L—Quarterly Results of Operations (Unaudited)

The following is a summary of the unaudited quarterly results of operations for the years ended May 31, 1996 and 1995.

In thousands, except per share	Three Months Ended			
	Aug.	Nov.	Feb.	May
1996				
Net sales	$325,736	$354,544	$360,224	$437,334
Gross margin	47,005	53,011	54,289	66,958
Net earnings	21,508	26,188	20,896	22,750
Earnings per share	$.24	$.29	$.23	$.25
1995				
Net sales	$346,257	$363,276	$370,117	$403,919
Gross margin	52,132	58,008	60,392	68,404
Net earnings	25,448	28,264	28,651	34,323
Earnings per share	$.28	$.31	$.32	$.38

Report of Management

The management of Worthington Industries is responsible for the preparation of the accompanying consolidated financial statements in conformity with generally accepted accounting principles appropriate in the circumstances. Management is also responsible for the determination of estimates and judgments used in the financial statements, and the preparation of other financial information included in this annual report to shareholders. The financial statements have been audited by Ernst & Young LLP, independent auditors.

The management of the Company has established and maintains an accounting system and related internal controls that it believes are sufficient to provide reasonable assurance that assets are safeguarded against unauthorized acquisition, use, or disposition, that transactions are executed and recorded in accordance with management's authorization, and that the financial records are reliable for preparing financial statements. The concept of reasonable assurance is based on the recognition that the cost of a system of internal control must be related to the benefits derived and that the balancing of the factors requires estimates and judgments. Management considers the recommendations of the internal auditors and independent certified public accountants concerning the Company's system of internal control and takes appropriate actions which are cost effective in the circumstances.

The Board of Directors has an audit Committee of Directors who are not members of management. The Audit Committee meets periodically with the Company's management, internal auditors, and independent certified public accountants to review matters relating to financial reporting, auditing and internal control. To ensure auditor independence, both the internal auditors and independent certified public accountants have full and free access to the Audit Committee.

John H. McConnell
John H. McConnell, Chairman & Founder

John P. McConnell
John P. McConnell, Vice Chairman & CEO

Donald G. Barger
Donald G. Barger Jr., Vice President-CFO

Michael R. Sayre
Michael R. Sayre, Controller

Report of Independent Auditors

Shareholders and Board of Directors
Worthington Industries, Inc.

We have audited the accompanying consolidated balance sheets of Worthington Industries, Inc. and Subsidiaries as of May 31, 1996 and 1995, and the related consolidated statements of earnings, shareholders' equity, and cash flows for each of the three years in the period ended May 31, 1996. These financial statements are the responsibility of the Company's management. Our responsibility is to express an opinion on these financial statements based on our audits.

We conducted our audits in accordance with generally accepted auditing standards. Those standards require that we plan and perform the audit to obtain reasonable assurance about whether the financial statements are free of material misstatement. An audit includes examining, on a test basis, evidence supporting the amounts and disclosures in the financial statements. An audit also includes assessing the accounting principles used and significant estimates made by management, as well as evaluating the overall financial statement presentation. We believe that our audits provide a reasonable basis for our opinion.

In our opinion, the financial statements referred to above present fairly, in all material respects, the consolidated financial position of Worthington Industries, Inc. and Subsidiaries at May 31, 1996 and 1995, and the consolidated results of their operations and their cash flows for each of the three years in the period ended May 31, 1996, in conformity with generally accepted accounting principles.

Ernst & Young LLP

Columbus, Ohio
June 14, 1996

Required   a. Prepare the following ratio analyses for Worthington Industries for 1996 and 1995. Make general comments about liquidity, long-term debt-paying ability, profitability, and investor analysis.

Liquidity
1. Days' sales in receivables
2. Accounts receivable turnover (net receivables 1994—$189,741,000; allowance 1994—$2,535,000)
3. Accounts receivable turnover in days
4. Days' sales in inventory
5. Merchandise inventory turnover (1994 inventory—$184,882,000)
6. Inventory turnover in days
7. Operating cycle
8. Working capital
9. Current ratio
10. Acid-test ratio
11. Cash ratio
12. Operating cash flow/current maturities of long-term debt and current notes payable

Long-Term Debt-Paying Ability
13. Times interest earned
14. Debt ratio
15. Debt/equity ratio
16. Debt to tangible net worth
17. Operating cash flow/total debt

Profitability
18. Net profit margin
19. Total asset turnover (total assets 1994—$798,573,000)
20. Return on assets
21. Operating income margin
22. Operating asset turnover (total operating assets 1994—$720,677,000)
23. Return on operating assets
24. Sales to fixed assets (net fixed assets 1994—$307,561,000; construction in progress 1994—$21,375,000)
25. Return on investment (long-term debt + equity 1994—$618,054,000)
26. Return on total equity (total equity 1994—$503,893,000)
27. Gross profit margin

Investor Analysis
28. Percentage of earnings retained
29. Earnings per common share

(continued)

30. Degree of financial leverage
31. Price/earnings ratio (market price 1996, $20.13; 1995, $20.88)
32. Dividend payout
33. Dividend yield
34. Book value per share

b. Prepare a vertical common-size analysis of the statement of income for 1996, 1995, and 1994. Use net sales as the base. Comment on the findings. (Round to one decimal place.)

c. Prepare a horizontal common-size analysis for the statement of income for 1994-1996. Use 1994 as the base year. Comment on the findings. (Round to one decimal place.)

d. Prepare a vertical common-size analysis of the balance sheet for 1996 and 1995. Use total assets as the base. Comment on the findings. (Round to one decimal place.)

e. Prepare a horizontal common-size analysis of the balance sheet for 1996 and 1995. Use 1995 as the base year. Comment on the findings. (Round to one decimal place.)

f. Industry segment data

1. Using common size

   (a) For the period 1992-1996, compare net sales by industry segment.

       (1) For horizontal, use 1992 as the base. (Comment on the findings.)

       (2) For vertical, use total net sales as the base. (Comment on the findings.)

   (b) For the period 1992-1996, compare operating income by industry segment (only use processed steel products, custom products, and cast products).

       (1) For horizontal, use 1992 as the base. (Comment on the findings.)

       (2) For vertical, use total operating income for processed steel products, custom products, and cast products as the base (only use these segments). (Comment on the findings.)

   (c) For the period 1992-1996, compare capital expenditures by industry segment. (Only use processed steel products, custom products, and cast products.)

       (1) For horizontal, use 1992 as the base. (Comment on the findings.)

       (2) For vertical, use total capital expenditures. (Exclude corporate.) (Comment on the findings.)

2. Computing ratios
    (a) For the period 1992-1996, compare operating income with identifiable assets (processed steel products, custom products, and cast products). (Comment on the findings.)
    (b) For the period 1992-1996, compare capital expenditures with identifiable assets (processed steel products, custom products, and cast products). (Comment on the findings.)

Advanced Topics

a. Review the accounting policies of Worthington Industries, Inc. Considering inventories and property, plant, and equipment, would you describe its policies as conservative or liberal (conservative in terms of the lowest possible income and liberal in terms of the highest possible income)?

b. How material is pension expense in relation to net sales? Consider the period 1994-1996.

c. Give your opinion of the materiality of outstanding options at the end of 1996 and 1995.

d. Explain capitalized interest. How significant was capitalized interest during 1996, 1995, and 1994?

e. The company is the guarantor on bank loans for two separate joint ventures. The guarantees totaled $30,700,000 at May 31, 1996. How do accountants describe this guarantee of debt?

f. The company is the defendant in certain legal actions. How is this potential liability accounted for?

g. For fiscal 1996, the market price of the common stock ranged from $16.63 to $22.50. The par value of the common stock was $.01. Why the significant difference between the market value and the par value?

h. Comment on apparent seasonal influences to net sales and revenues and net earnings.

i. Identify noncash activities that relate to the statements of cash flows.

j. Retained Earnings
    1. Identify the retained earnings balance at May 31, 1996.
    2. What amount of retained earnings was unrestricted at May 31, 1996?
    3. In your opinion, do the retained earnings restrictions have a practical significance as of May 31, 1996?

k. Deferred Taxes
    1. How did Worthington Industries describe (define) deferred income taxes?

      2. Identify the deferred tax items.

      3. Which two deferred tax items had significant influences on the increase in deferred taxes for 1996?

l.   1. Compute the net profit margin excluding "equity in net income of unconsolidated affiliates."

      2. Comment on the potential distortion in the net profit margin because of the significant "equity in net income of unconsolidated affiliates."

m. Sales to Fixed Assets

      1. Compute this ratio including construction in progress in property, plant, and equipment.

      2. Compute this ratio excluding construction in progress from property, plant, and equipment.

      3. Which computation is better? Why?

Glossary

Most of the terms in this glossary are explained in the text. Some terms not explained in the text are included because they represent terms frequently found in annual reports.

Accelerated Cost Recovery System (ACRS): Depreciation method introduced for tax purposes in 1981 and subsequently modified. See Modified Accelerated Cost Recovery System (MACRS).

Accelerated depreciation: Any depreciation method in which the charges in earlier periods exceed those in later periods.

Account: A record used to classify and summarize transactions.

Account form of balance sheet: A balance sheet that presents assets on the left-hand side and liabilities and owners' equity on the right-hand side.

Accounting changes: A term used to describe the use of a different accounting principle, estimate, or reporting entity than used in a prior year.

Accounting cycle: A series of steps used for analyzing, recording, classifying, and summarizing transactions.

Accounting errors: Mistakes resulting from mathematical errors, improper application of accounting principles, or omissions of material facts.

Accounting period: The time to which accounting reports are related.

Accounting policies: The accounting principles and practices adopted by a company to report its financial results.

Accounting Principles Board (APB): A board established by the AICPA that issued opinions establishing accounting standards during the period 1959-1973.

Accounting Research Bulletins (ARBs): Publications of the Committee on Accounting Procedure of the AICPA, that established accounting standards during the years 1939-1959.

Accounting system: The procedures and methods used to collect and report accounting data.

Accounts receivable: Monies due on accounts from customers arising from sales or services rendered.

Accrual basis: The accrual basis of accounting dictates: revenue is recognized when realized (realization concept) and expenses are recognized when incurred (matching concept).

Accrued expenses: Expenses incurred, but not recognized in the accounts.

Accrued revenues: Revenues for services performed or for goods delivered that have not been recorded.

Accumulated benefit obligation (ABO): The present value of pension benefits earned to date based on employee service and compensations to that date.

Accumulated depreciation: Depreciation allocates the cost of buildings and machinery over the periods of benefits. The depreciation expense taken each period accumulates in the account, Accumulated Depreciation.

Accumulated postretirement benefit obligation (APBO): The present value of postretirement benefits earned to date based on employee's service to that date.

Acquisitions: Companies that have been acquired.

Additional paid-in capital: The investment by stockholders in excess of the stock's par or stated value as well as invested capital from other sources, such as donations of property or sale of treasury stock.

Adjusting entries: Entries made at the end of each accounting period to update the accounts.

Administrative expense: Results from the general administration of the company's operation.

Adverse opinion: An audit opinion issued whenever financial statements contain departures from GAAP that are too material to warrant only a qualification. This opinion states that the financial statements do not present fairly the financial position, results of operations, or cash flows of the entity in conformity with GAAP.

Aging of accounts receivables: A method of reviewing for uncollectible trade receivables by which an estimate of the bad debts expense is determined. The receivable balances are classified into age categories and then an estimate of noncollection is applied.

Allowance for funds used during construction (AFUDC): The recording of AFUDC is a utility accounting practice prescribed by the state utility commission. It represents the estimated debt and equity costs of financing construction work in progress. AFUDC does not represent a current source of cash, but under regulatory rate practices, a return on and recovery of AFUDC is permitted in determining rates charged for utility services. Some utilities report the estimated debt and equity costs of financing construction work-in-progress in separate accounts.

Allowance for uncollectible accounts: A contra accounts receivable account showing an estimate of the accounts receivable that will not be collected.

American Accounting Association (AAA): An organization of accounting professors and practicing accountants.

American Institute of Certified Public Accountants (AICPA): A professional organization for CPAs.

Amortization: The periodic allocation of the cost of an intangible asset over its useful life.

Annual report: A formal presentation containing financial statements and other important information prepared by the management of a corporation once a year.

Annuity: A series of equal payments (receipts) over a specified number of equal time periods.

Antidilution of earnings: Assumed conversion of convertible securities or exercise of stock options that results in an increase in earnings per share or a decrease in loss per share.

Antidilutive securities: Securities whose assumed conversion or exercise results in an increase in earnings per share or a decrease in loss per share.

Appropriated retained earnings: A restriction of retained earnings that indicates that a portion of a company's assets are to be used for purposes other than paying dividends.

Assets: Probable future economic benefits obtained or controlled by a particular entity as a result of past transactions or events.

Assignment of receivables: The borrowing of money with receivables pledged as security.

Attestation: Any service performed by a CPA resulting in a written communication that expresses a conclusion about the reliability of a written assertion.

Audit committee: A committee of the board of directors comprised mainly of outside directors having no management ties to the organization.

Audit report: The mechanism for communicating the results of an audit.

Auditing: A systematic process of objectively obtaining and evaluating evidence regarding assertions and communicating the results to interested users.

Auditor: A person who conducts an audit.

Authorized stock: The maximum number of shares a corporation may issue without changing its charter with the state.

Average cost method (inventory): A method that lumps the costs of inventory to determine an average.

Balance sheet: The financial statement which shows the financial position of an accounting entity as of a specific date. The balance sheet lists assets, the resources of the firm; liabilities, the debts of the firm; and stockholders' equity, the owners' interest in the firm.

Balance sheet (classified): A form that segregates the assets and liabilities between current and noncurrent.

Balance sheet (financial position form): A form that deducts current liabilities from current assets to show working capital. The form adds remaining assets and deducts the remaining liabilities to derive the residual stockholders' equity.

Balance sheet (unclassified): A form that does not segregate the assets and liabilities between current and noncurrent.

Bargain purchase option: Provision granting the lessee the right, but not the obligation, to purchase leased property at a price that, at the inception date, is sufficiently below the expected fair value of the property at exercise date to provide reasonable assurance of exercise.

Bargain renewal option: Provision granting the lessee the right, but not the obligation, to renew the lease at a rental that, at inception, is sufficiently below the expected fair rental at exercise date to provide reasonable assurance of renewal.

Bond: A security, usually long-term, representing money borrowed by a corporation. Normally issued with $1,000 face value.

Bond discount: The difference between the face value and the sales price when bonds are sold below their face value.

Bond premium: The difference between the face value and the sales price when bonds are sold above their face value.

Bond sinking fund: A fund established by the segregation of assets over the life of the bond issue to pay the bondholders at maturity.

Bonds (serial): A bond issue which matures in installments.

Book value of an asset: The original cost of an asset less any accumulated depreciation (depletion or amortization) taken to date.

Book value per share: The dollar amount of the net assets of a company per share of common stock.

Buildings: A structure used in a business operation.

Business combination: One or more businesses that are merged together as one accounting entity.

Business entity: The viewpoint that the business (or entity) for which the financial statements are prepared is separate and distinct from the owners of the entity.

Callable bonds: Bonds that a corporation has the option of buying back and retiring at a given price before maturity.

Callable obligation: A debt instrument payable on demand of the company.

Callable preferred stock: Preferred stock that may be redeemed and retired by the corporation at its option.

Capital: Owners' equity in an unincorporated firm.

Capital expenditures: Costs that increase the future economic benefits of an asset above those originally expected.

Capital lease: Long-term lease in which the risk of ownership lies with the lessee and whose terms resemble a purchase or sale; recorded as an asset with a corresponding liability at the present value of the lease payments.

Capital stock: The portion of the contribution by stockholders assignable to the shares of stock as par or stated value.

Capitalization: The process of assigning value to a balance sheet account (asset or liability).

Capitalized interest: Interest added to the cost of a fixed asset instead of being expensed.

Cash: The most liquid asset that includes negotiable checks, unrestricted balances in checking accounts, and cash on hand.

Cash basis: A system of accounting which records revenues when received and expenses when paid.

Cash dividend: The payment (receipt) of a dividend in cash.

Cash equivalents: A company's highly liquid short-term investments considered to be cash equivalents and usually classified with cash on the balance sheet.

Cash flows from financing activities: Cash flows relating to liability and owners' equity accounts.

Cash flows from investing activities: Cash flows relating to lending money and to acquiring and selling investments and productive long-term assets.

Cash flows from operating activities: Generally the cash effects of transactions and other events that determine net income.

Cash surrender value: The investment portion of a life insurance policy, payable to the policyholder if the policyholder cancels the policy.

Change in an accounting estimate: A change in the estimation of the effects of future events.

Change in an accounting principle: Adoption of a generally accepted accounting principle different from the one used previously for reporting purposes.

Change in reporting entity: An accounting change that reflects financial statements for a different unit of accountability.

Chart of accounts: A listing of all accounts used by a company.

Chief accountant of the SEC: An appointed official of the Securities and Exchange Commission.

Classified balance sheet: A balance sheet that segregates the assets and liabilities as current and noncurrent.

Collateral: Security for loans or other forms of indebtedness.

Common-size analysis (horizontal): Common-size analysis expresses comparisons in percentages. Horizontal analysis indicates the proportionate change over a period of time.

Common-size analysis (vertical): Common-size analysis expresses comparisons in percentages. Vertical analysis indicates the proportional expression of each item in a given period to a base figure selected from that same period.

Common stock (capital stock): The stock representing the most basic rights to ownership of a corporation.

Common stock equivalent shares: A security that is not in the form of a common stock, but that contains provisions that enable its holder to acquire common stock.

Comparative statements: Financial statements for two or more periods.

Compensated absences: Payments to employees for vacation, holiday, illness, or other personal activities.

Compensating balance requirements: Provisions in loan agreements requiring the borrower to maintain minimum cash balances with the lending institution.

Compensatory option plans: Stock option plans offered to a select group of employees.

Compilation: A professional service in which the CPA presents information that is the representation of management without undertaking to express any assurance on the statements.

Completed-contract method: A method that recognizes revenues and expenses on long-term construction contracts when the contract is completed.

Composite depreciation: A depreciation method which aggregates dissimilar assets and computes depreciation for the aggregation based on a weighted average life expectancy.

Conservatism: The concept which directs that the measurement with the least favorable effect on net income and financial position in the current period be selected.

Conservative analysis: This perspective represents a relatively strict interpretation of the value of assets and what constitutes debt.

Consigned goods: Inventory physically located at a dealer but another company retains title until the consignee sells the inventory.

Consistency: The concept requiring the entity to give the same treatment to comparable transactions from period to period.

Consolidated financial statements: The combined financial statements of a parent company and its subsidiary.

Constant dollar accounting (price-level accounting): The method of reporting financial statement elements in dollars having similar purchasing power. Constant dollar accounting measures general changes in prices of goods and services.

Construction-in-process: Fixed asset account where construction costs are recorded until construction is completed.

Contingent asset: An asset that may arise in the future if certain events occur.

Contingent liabilities: Liabilities whose payment is dependent on a particular occurrence such as settlement of litigation or a ruling of tax court.

Contra account: An account used to offset a primary account in order to show a net valuation, e.g., accounts receivable (primary account) less allowance for doubtful accounts (contra account).

Contributed capital: The sum of the capital stock accounts and the capital in excess of par (or stated) value accounts.

Convertible bonds: Bonds that may be exchanged for other securities of the corporation, usually common stock.

Convertible preferred stock: Preferred stock that can be converted into common stock.

Convertible securities: Securities whose terms permit the holder to convert the investment into common stock of the issuing companies.

Copyright: An exclusive right granted by the federal government to publish and sell literary, musical, and other artistic materials.

Corporation: A separate legal entity having its own rights, privileges, and liabilities distinct from those of its owners.

Cost/benefit: The process of determining that the benefit of an act or series of acts exceeds the cost of performing the act(s).

Cost of goods manufactured: The total cost of goods completed in the manufacturing process during an accounting period.

Cost of goods sold or cost of sales: The cost of goods sold during an accounting period.

Cost principle: The accounting principle that records historical cost as the appropriate basis of initial accounting recognition of all acquisitions, liabilities, and owners' equity.

Cost recovery: A revenue recognition method which requires recovery of the total cost prior to the recognition of revenue.

Credit: An entry on the right side of a T-account.

Cumulative effect of change in accounting principle: The effect that a new accounting principle would have had on net income of prior periods if it had been used instead of the old principle.

Cumulative preferred stock: Preferred stock on which unpaid dividends accumulate over time and must be satisfied in any given year before a dividend may be paid to common stockholders.

Currency swap: An exchange of two currencies as part of an agreement to reverse the exchange on a specific future date.

Current assets: Current assets are assets (1) in the form of cash, (2) that will normally be realized in cash, or (3) that conserve the use of cash during the operating cycle of a firm or for one year, whichever is longer.

Current cost: The current replacement cost of the same asset owned, adjusted for the value of any operating advantages or disadvantages.

Current liabilities: Obligations whose liquidation is reasonably expected to require the use of existing resources properly classifiable as current assets or the creation of other current liabilities.

Current maturity of long-term debt: The portion of a long-term debt payable within the next operating cycle or one year, whichever is longer.

Current replacement cost: The estimated cost of acquiring the best asset available to undertake the function of the asset owned.

Debenture bonds: Bonds issued on the general credit of a company.

Debit: An entry on the left side of a T-account.

Decision usefulness: The overriding quality or characteristic of accounting information.

Declining balance depreciation: The declining balance method applies double the straight-line depreciation rate times the declining book value (cost minus accumulated depreciation) to achieve a declining depreciation charge over the estimated life of the asset.

Default risk: The probability that a company will be unable to meet its obligations.

Defeasance: A method of early retirement of debt in which risk-free securities are purchased and then placed in a trust account to be used to retire the outstanding debt at its maturity.

Deferral: The postponement of the recognition of an expense already paid or of a revenue already received.

Deferred charge: A long-term expense prepayment amortized to expense.

Deferred financing costs, net: An asset account usually classified under other assets; costs associated with the issuance of long-term bonds that have not been amortized.

Deferred taxes: A balance sheet account; classified as an asset or liability depending on the nature of the timing differences. The differences are the result of any situation that recognizes revenue or expense in a different time period for tax purposes than for the financial statements.

Deficit: A negative (debit) balance in retained earnings.

Defined benefit pension plan: A pension plan that defines the benefits that employees will receive at retirement.

Defined contribution pension plan: A pension plan that specifies the employer's contributions and bases benefits solely on the amount contributed.

Depletion: Recognition of the wearing away or using up of a natural resource.

Depreciation expense: The process of allocating the cost of buildings, machinery, and equipment over the periods benefited.

Devaluation: A downward adjustment of the exchange rate between two currencies.

Direct financing type lease: A capital lease in which the lessor receives income only from financing the "purchase" of the leased asset.

Direct write-off method: A method of recognizing specific accounts receivable determined to be uncollectible.

Disclaimer of opinion: Inability to render an audit opinion because of lack of sufficient evidence or lack of independence.

Discontinued operations: The disposal of a major segment of a business.

Discount rate: The interest rate used to compute the present value.

Divestitures: Companies that have been disposed of.

Dividends (cash): Cash payment from current or past income to the owners of a corporation.

Dividends in arrears: The accumulated unpaid dividends from prior years on cumulative preferred stock.

Dividends payable: A current liability on the balance sheet resulting from the declaration of dividends by the board of directors.

Dividends (stock): A percentage of outstanding stock issued as new shares to existing shareholders.

Donated capital: Assets donated to the company by stockholders, creditors, or other parties.

Double-declining-balance depreciation: A method of calculating depreciation by which a percentage equal to twice the straight-line percentage is multiplied by the declining book value to determine the depreciation expense for the period (salvage value is ignored when calculating).

Double-entry accounting: A system of recording transactions in a way that maintains the equality of the equation: Assets = Liabilities + Stockholders' Equity.

Dry holes: Wells drilled which do not find commercial quantities of oil or gas.

Early extinguishment of debt: The retirement of debt prior to the maturity date.

Earnings per share: Net income (after preferred dividends) per share of common stock computed using the weighted average of shares of common stock outstanding during the year.

Economic substance: The "real" nature of a transaction, as opposed to its legal form.

Effective rate of interest: The yield or true rate of interest.

Efficient market hypothesis: A theory to explain the functioning of capital markets in which share prices reflect all publicly available information.

Emerging Issues Task Force (EITF): A task force of representatives from the accounting profession created by the FASB to deal with emerging issues of financial reporting.

Employee Retirement Income Security Act (ERISA): A legislative act passed by Congress in 1974 that made significant changes in requirements for employer pension plans. This act has been amended several times since 1974.

Employee stock ownership plan (ESOP): A qualified stock-bonus, or combination stock-bonus and money purchase, pension plan designed to invest in primarily the employer's securities.

Equipment: Assets used in the production of goods or in providing services.

Equity: Synonymous with the expression shareholders' equity.

Equity in earnings of nonconsolidated subsidiaries: When a firm has investments in stocks, uses the equity method of accounting, and the investment is not consolidated, then the investor firm reports equity earnings (the proportionate share of the earnings of the investee).

Equity method: A method to value intercorporate equity investments by adjusting the investor's cost basis for the percentage ownership in the investee's earnings (or losses) and for any dividends paid by the investee.

Equity-oriented deferred compensation: The amount of compensation cost deferred and amortized to future periods as the services are provided.

Estimated economic life of leased property: The useful life of leased property estimated at inception under conditions of normal maintenance and repairs.

Estimated liability: An obligation of the entity whose exact amount cannot be determined until a later date.

Estimated residual value of leased property: The expected fair or market value of leased property at the end of the lease term.

Ethics: A set of principles referring to ideals of character and conduct.

Exchange rate: The rate at which one unit of currency may be purchased by another unit of currency.

Executory costs: Insurance, maintenance, and local and property taxes on leased property.

Expectations gap: The disparity between users' and CPAs' perceptions of professional services, especially audit services.

Expenses: Outflows or uses of assets or incurrences of liabilities (or a combination of both) during the process of an entity's revenue generating operations.

Extraordinary items: Material events and transactions distinguished by their unusual nature and infrequent occurrence.

Face amount, maturity value: The amount that will be paid on a bond (note) at the maturity date.

Feedback value: An ingredient of relevant accounting information.

Financial accounting: Recording and communication of financial information under GAAP.

Financial Accounting Standards Board (FASB): A body that has responsibility for developing and issuing rules on accounting practice.

Financial leverage: The amount of debt financing in relation to equity financing.

Financial statement (report) analysis: The process of reviewing, analyzing, and interpreting the basic financial reports.

Financial statements: Generally considered to be the balance sheet, income statement, and statement of cash flows.

Finished goods: Inventory ready for sale.

First-in, first-out (FIFO) (inventory): The flow pattern assumes that the first unit purchased is the first sold.

Fiscal year: Any twelve-month accounting period used by an economic entity. (It does not necessarily correspond to the calendar year.)

Footnotes: Present additional information on items included in the financial statements and additional financial information.

Form 8-K: A special SEC filing required when a material event or transaction occurs between Form 10-Q filing dates.

Form 10-K: An SEC form required to be filed within 90 days of a company's fiscal year-end. It is like an annual report but with more detail.

Form 10-Q: An SEC form required to be filed within 45 days of the end of a company's 1st, 2nd, and 3rd fiscal year quarters. It contains interim information on a company's operations and financial position.

Form 20-F: The annual financial report filing with the SEC required of all foreign companies whose debt or equity capital is available for purchase/sale on a U.S. exchange.

Form versus substance: Form refers to the legal nature of a transaction or event; substance refers to the economic aspects of the transaction or event.

Forward contract: Agreement to purchase or sell commodities, securities, or currencies on a specified future date at a specified price.

Forward exchange rate: A rate quoted currently for the exchange of currency at some future specified date.

Franchise: A contractual privilege granted by one person to another permitting the sale of a product, use of trade name, or provision of a service within a specified territory and/or in a specified manner.

Fraud: Intent to deceive.

Full cost accounting: The method of accounting that capitalizes all costs of exploring for and developing oil and gas reserves within a defined area, subject only to the limitation that costs attributable to developed reserves should not exceed their estimated present value.

Full disclosure: Accounting reports must disclose all facts that may influence the judgment of an informed reader.

Fully diluted earnings per share: Net income applicable to common stock divided by the sum of the weighted average common stock and common stock equivalents.

Functional currency: The currency of the primary business environment (i.e., country) of a company's operations.

Fund accounting: Accounting procedures in which a self-balancing group of accounts is provided for each accounting entity established by legal, contractual, or voluntary action.

Future contract: Exchange-traded contract for future acceptance or delivery of a standardized quantity of a commodity or financial instrument on a specified future date at a specified price.

General journal: A journal used to record transactions not maintained in special journals.

General ledger: A record of all accounts used by a company.

Generally accepted accounting principles (GAAP): Accounting principles that have substantial authoritative support.

Generally accepted auditing standards (GAAS): Those auditing standards which have been established in a particular jurisdiction by formal recognition by a standard-setting body, or by authoritative support.

Going concern or continuity: Assumes that the entity being accounted for will remain in business for an indefinite period of time.

Goodwill (cost in excess of net assets of companies acquired): Arises from the acquisition of a business for a sum greater than the physical asset fair value, usually because the business has unusual earning power.

Governmental funds: General, special revenue, project, debt service, and special assessment funds; each designed for a specific purpose and used by a state or local government to account for its normal operations.

Gross profit margin: Gross profit margin equals the difference between net sales revenue and the cost of goods sold.

Group depreciation: A depreciation method which groups like assets together and computes depreciation for the group rather than for individual assets.

Guarantee of employee stock ownership plan (ESOP): An employee stock bonus plan used as a financing vehicle for an employer which borrows money to purchase its own stock. The stock is security for the loan, and the ESOP repays the loan from employer contributions.

Harmonization of accounting principles: The attempt by various organizations (e.g., the FASB, IASC) to establish a common set of international accounting and reporting standards.

Hedge: A process of buying or selling commodities, forward contracts, or options for the explicit purpose of reducing or eliminating foreign exchange risk.

Historical cost: The cash equivalent price of goods or services at the date of acquisition.

Human resource accounting: Attempts to account for the services of employees.

Impairment: A temporary or permanent reduction in asset value.

Imputed interest rate: A rate of interest applied to a note when the effective rate was either not evident or determinable by other factors involved in the exchange.

In-substance defeasance of debt: The debtor irrevocably places cash or other assets in a trust to be used solely for satisfying the payments of both interest and principal on a specific debt obligation.

Income smoothing: An accounting practice that attempts to present a stable measure of income (usually an increasing amount).

Income statement: A summary of the revenues and expenses and gains and losses that result in net income or net loss for a period.

Income taxes: Taxes levied by federal, state, and local governments on reported accounting profit. Income tax expense includes both tax paid and deferred.

Inconsistency: A change in accounting principle from one period to the next, requiring an explanatory paragraph following the opinion paragraph of the auditor's report.

Incorporation by reference: Direction of the reader's attention to information included in the annual report to shareholders, rather than reporting such information in Form 10-K.

Industry practices: Practices leading to accounting reports that do not conform to the general theory that underlies accounting.

Inflation: An increase in the general price level of goods and services.

Initial public offering (IPO): The first or initial sale of voting stock to the general market by a previously privately held concern.

Insolvent: A condition in which a company is unable to pay its debts.

Installment sales: A type of sale which requires periodic payments over an extended length of time.

Institute of Management Accountants (IMA): An organization of management accountants concerned with the internal use of accounting data.

Intangibles: Nonphysical assets, such as legal rights, recorded at historical cost, then reduced by systematic amortization.

Intercompany profit: The profit resulting when one related company sells to another related company.

Interest: The cost for the use of money. It is a cost to the borrower and revenue to the lender.

Interest rate swaps: An agreement to exchange variable rate interest payments based on a specific index for a fixed rate or a variable rate stream of payments based on another index.

Interim reports: Financial reports that cover fiscal periods of less than one year.

Internal control: The process effected by an entity to provide reasonable assurance regarding the achievement of objectives. It consists of three parts: operations controls, financial reporting controls, and compliance controls.

International accounting standards (IAS): The accounting standards adopted by the IASC.

International Accounting Standards Committee (IASC): An organization established in 1973 by the leading professional groups of the major industrial countries.

International Federation of Accountants (IFAC): An association of professional accounting organizations founded in 1977.

Interperiod tax allocation: The process of allocating the taxes paid by a company over the periods in which the taxes are recognized for accounting purposes.

Introductory paragraph: The first paragraph of the standard audit report, which identifies the financial statements covered by the audit report and clearly differentiates management's responsibility for preparing the financial statements from the auditor's responsibility for expressing an opinion on them.

Inventories: The balance of goods on hand.

Inventory-lower-of-cost-or-market (LCM) rule: An inventory pricing method which prices the inventory at an amount below cost if the replacement (market) value is less than cost.

Investments: Usually stocks and bonds of other companies held for the purpose of maintaining a business relationship or exercising control. To be classified as long term, it must be the intent of management to hold these assets as such. Long-term investments are differentiated from marketable securities, where the intent is to hold the assets for short-term profits and to achieve liquidity.

Issued stock: The shares of stock sold or otherwise transferred to stockholders.

Joint venture: An association of two or more businesses established for a special purpose; some in the form of partnerships and unincorporated joint ventures; others in the form of corporations jointly owned by two or more other firms.

Journals: Initial recordings of a company's transactions.

Kiting: A type of misrepresentation fraud used to conceal bank overdrafts or cash misappropriations.

Land: Realty used for business purposes. It is shown at acquisition cost and not depreciated. Land containing resources that will be used up, however, such as mineral deposits and timberlands, is subject to depletion.

Land improvements: Expenditures incurred in the process of putting land into a usable condition, e.g., clearing, grading, paving, etc.

Lapping: A form of concealment that involves crediting current customer remittances to the accounts of customers who have remitted previously.

Last-in, first-out (LIFO) (inventory): The flow pattern assumes that those units purchased last are sold first.

Lease: An agreement conveying the right to use property, plant, or equipment (land and/or depreciable assets) for a stated period of time.

Lease improvement: An improvement to leased property that becomes the property of the lessor at the end of the lease.

Leasehold: A payment made to secure the right to a lease.

Ledger: Summarizes the effects of transactions upon individual accounts.

Lessee: The party to a lease who acquires the right to use the property, plant, and equipment.

Lessor: The party to a lease giving up the right to use the property, plant, and equipment.

Leverage: The extent to which a company's capital structure includes debt financing.

Leveraged buy-out (LBO): A purchase of a company where a substantial amount of the purchase price is debt financed.

Liabilities: Future sacrifices of economic benefits arising from present obligations to other entities.

LIFO liquidation: The reduction of inventory levels below previous levels. This has the effect of increasing income by the amount by which current prices exceed the historical cost of the inventory under LIFO.

LIFO reserves (LIFO valuation adjustment): The amount that would need to be added back to the LIFO inventory in order for the inventory account to approximate current cost.

Limited liability: The concept that stockholders in a corporation are not held personally liable.

Line of credit: An agreement with a financial institution by which an organization obtains authorization for borrowings up to a specified amount.

Liquid assets: Current assets that either are in cash or can be readily converted to cash.

Liquidating dividend: A dividend that exceeds the balance in retained earnings.

Liquidation: The process of selling off the assets of a business, paying any outstanding debts, and distributing any remaining cash to the owners.

Liquidity: The ability of an entity to maintain its short-term debt-paying ability.

Listed company: A company whose shares or bonds have been accepted for trading on a securities exchange.

Loan defaults: Violations of loan agreements that could result in loan principal and interest becoming immediately due.

Loan restructuring: Revision of loan terms in a manner mutually acceptable to the lender and borrower.

Long-term liabilities: Liabilities due in a period exceeding one year or one operating cycle, whichever is longer.

Lower of cost or market: A method to value inventories and marketable securities.

Machinery: An asset listed at historical cost, including delivery and installation, plus any material improvements that extend its life or increase the quantity or quality of service; depreciated over its estimated useful life.

Management discussion and analysis: Part of the annual report package required by the Securities and Exchange Commission.

Management report: Management statements to shareholders which acknowledge management's responsibility for the preparation and integrity of financial statements.

Market value (stock): The price investors are willing to pay for a share of stock.

Marketable securities: Ownership and debt instruments of the government and other companies that can be readily converted into cash.

Matching: The concept that determines the revenue and then matches the appropriate cost incurred in generating this revenue.

Materiality: The concept that exempts immaterial items from the concepts and principles that bind the accountant, and allows these items to be handled in the most economical and expedient manner possible.

Merger: A combination of one or more companies into a single corporate entity.

Minority interest (balance sheet account): The ownership of minority shareholders in the equity of consolidated subsidiaries that are less than wholly owned.

Minority share of earnings: The portion of income that belongs to the minority owners of a firm that has been consolidated.

Misappropriation: The fraudulent transfer of assets from the firm to one or more employees.

Modified Accelerated Cost Recovery System (MACRS): The accelerated cost recovery system as revised by The Tax Reform Act of 1986.

Monetary assets: Cash and other assets that represent the right to receive a specific amount of cash.

Monetary liabilities: Accounts payable and other liabilities that represent the obligation to pay a specific amount of cash.

Monetary unit: The unit used to measure financial transactions.

Mortgage payable: A liability secured by real property.

Multiple-step income statement: Form of the income statement that arrives at net income in steps.

Natural business year: A 12-month period ending on a date that coincides with the end of an operating cycle.

Natural resources: Assets produced by nature such as petroleum, minerals, and timber.

Net assets: Total assets less total liabilities (equivalent to shareowners' equity).

Net operating loss carryback: When tax-deductible expenses exceed taxable revenues, a company may carry the net operating loss back three years and receive refunds for income taxes paid in those years.

Net operating loss carryforward: When tax-deductible expenses exceed taxable revenues, a company may carry an operating loss forward and offset future taxable income.

Net realizable value: The nondiscounted amount of cash, or its equivalent, into which an asset is expected to be converted less direct costs necessary to make that conversion.

Neutrality: A qualitative characteristic of accounting information that involves the faithful reporting of business activity without bias to one or another view.

Noncurrent or long-term assets: Assets that do not qualify as current assets. In general they take longer than a year to be converted to cash or to conserve cash in the long run.

Note payable: A payable in the form of a written promissory note.

Off-balance sheet financing: Refers to a company taking advantage of debt-like resources without these obligations appearing as debt on the face of the balance sheet.

Operating cycle: The period of time elapsing between the acquisition of goods and the final cash realization resulting from sales and subsequent collections.

Operating expenses: Consist of two types: selling and administrative. Selling expenses result from the company's effort to create sales. Administrative expenses relate to the general administration of the company's operation.

Operating lease (lessee): Periodic payment for the right to use an asset, recorded in a manner similar to the recording of rent expense payments.

Option: A financial instrument that conveys to its owner the right, but not the obligation, to buy or sell a security, commodity, or currency at a specific price over a specified time period or at a specific date.

Organization costs: The costs of forming a corporation.

Organizational costs: The legal costs incurred when organizing a business; carried as an asset and usually written off over a period of five years or longer.

Other income and expenses: Income and expenses from secondary activities of the firm not directly related to the operations.

Outstanding shares: The number of authorized shares of capital stock sold to stockholders that is currently in the possession of stockholders (issued shares less treasury shares).

Owners' equity (stockholders' equity): The residual ownership interest in the assets of an entity that remains after deducting its liabilities.

Paid-in capital in excess of par value (or stated value): The proceeds from the sale of capital stock in excess of the par value (or stated value) of the capital stock.

Par value: An amount set by the firm's board of directors and approved by the state. (The par value does not relate to the market value.)

Parent company: A company that owns a controlling interest in another company.

Partnership: An unincorporated business owned by two or more individuals.

Patent: Exclusive legal rights granted to an inventor for a period of 17 years.

Payables: Short-term obligations created by the acquisition of goods and services.

Pension fund: A fund established through contributions from an employer and sometimes from employees that pays pension benefits to employees after retirement.

Percentage-of-completion method: A revenue recognition method which recognizes profit each period during the life of the contract in proportion to the amount of the contract completed during the period.

Periodic inventory method: A method of accounting for inventory which determines inventory at the end of the period.

Permanent accounts: All balance sheet accounts.

Perpetual inventory method: A method of accounting for inventory which records continuously the sales and purchases of individual items of inventory.

Personal financial statements: Financial statements of individuals, husband and wife, or a larger family group.

Pledging: Using assets as collateral for a bank loan.

Pooling of interest: A method of accounting for a business combination that combines all asset, liability, and stockholders' equity accounts.

Postretirement benefits other than pensions: Benefits other than pensions that accrue to employees upon retirement, such as medical insurance and life insurance contracts.

Predictive value: A qualitative characteristic of accounting information based on its relevance and usefulness to a decision maker in forecasting a future event or condition.

Preferred stock: Stock that has some preference over common stock.

Premium: An amount paid in excess of the face value of a security (stock or bond).

Prepaid: An expenditure made in advance of the use of the service or goods.

Present value consideration: The characteristic that money to be received or paid out in the future is not worth as much as money available today. Accountants consider the time value of money when preparing the financial statements for such areas as long-term leases, pensions, and other long-term situations where the future payments or receipts are not indicative of the present value of the asset or the obligation.

Primary earnings per share: Net income applicable to common stock divided by the sum of the weighted-average common stock and common stock equivalents.

Prior period adjustments: Reported as restatements of retained earnings. They include corrections of errors of prior periods, a change in accounting entity, certain changes in accounting principles, and adjustments that result from the realization of income tax benefits of preacquisition operating loss carryforwards of purchased subsidiaries.

Prior service cost: When a defined pension plan is adopted or amended, credit is often given to employees for years of service provided before the date of adoption or amendment. The cost of taking on this added commitment is called the prior service cost.

Privatization: The sale of all or part of a previously government controlled entity to the general public.

Productive-output depreciation: A depreciation method in which the depreciable cost is divided by the total estimated output to determine the depreciation rate per unit of output.

Profitability: The relative success of a company's operations.

Projected benefit obligation (PBO): The present value of pension benefits earned to date based on past service and an estimate of future compensation levels for pay-related plans.

Property dividend: A dividend in a form of asset other than cash.

Property, plant, and equipment: Tangible assets of a long-term nature used in the continuing operation of the business.

Proportionate consolidation: A method of consolidating the financial results of a parent company and its subsidiary in which only the proportion of net assets owned by the parent are consolidated.

Proprietorship: A business owned by one person.

Prospectus: A document describing the nature of a business and its recent financial history.

Proxy: A legal document granting another party the right to vote for a shareholder on matters involving a shareholder vote.

Proxy statement: Information provided in a formal written form to shareholders prior to a company's regular annual meeting.

Public company: A company whose voting shares are listed for trading on a recognized securities exchange or are otherwise available for purchase by public investors.

Purchase accounting: The assets and liabilities of an acquired company accounted for on the books of the acquiring company at their relative fair market values to the acquiring company at the date of acquisition.

Qualified opinion: An audit opinion rendered under circumstances of one or more material scope restrictions or departures from GAAP.

Qualitative characteristics: Standards for judging the information accountants provide to decision makers; the primary criteria are relevance and reliability.

Quarterly statements: Interim financial statements on a quarterly basis.

Quasi-reorganization: An accounting procedure equivalent to an accounting fresh start. A company with a deficit balance in retained earnings "starts over" with a zero balance rather than a deficit. A quasi-reorganization may also include a restatement of the carrying values of assets and liabilities to reflect current values.

Ratio analysis: A comparison of relationships among account balances.

Raw materials: Goods purchased for direct use in manufacturing that become part of the product.

Realization (revenue recognition): A concept that generally recognizes revenue when:

1. The earning process is virtually complete, and

2. The exchange value can be objectively determined.

Receivables: Claims arising from the selling of merchandise or services on account to customers are referred to as trade receivables. Other claims may be from sources such as loans to employees or a federal tax refund.

Redeemable preferred stock: Preferred stock subject to mandatory redemption requirements, or with a redemption feature that is outside the control of the issuer.

Registrar: An independent agent that maintains a record of the number of a company's shares of capital stock that have been issued and to whom.

Relevance: Qualitative characteristic requiring that accounting information bear directly on the economic decision for which it is to be used; one of the primary qualitative characteristics of accounting information.

Reliability: Qualitative characteristic requiring that accounting information be faithful to the original data and that it be neutral and verifiable; one of the primary qualitative characteristics of accounting information.

Replacement cost: The cost to reproduce or replace an asset.

Report form of balance sheet: A balance sheet presentation which presents assets, liabilities, and stockholders' equity in a vertical format.

Reporting currency: The currency used to measure and report.

Representational faithfulness: The agreement of information with what it is supposed to represent.

Research and development (R&D): Funds spent to improve existing products and develop new ones.

Reserves: Accounts classified under liabilities resulting from an expense to the income statement and an equal increase in the reserve account on the balance sheet. These reserve accounts do not represent definite commitments to pay out funds in the future, but they do represent an estimate of funds that will be paid out in the future.

Residual value (salvage value): The estimated net scrap or trade-in value of a tangible asset at the date of disposal.

Retail inventory method: An inventory method that converts the retail value of inventory to an estimated cost.

Retained earnings: The undistributed earnings of a corporation consisting of the net income for all past periods minus the dividends that have been declared.

Retained earnings appropriated: The amount of retained earnings that has been restricted for specific purposes.

Royalties: Payment for a right over some natural resource, or payment to an author or composer.

Sale and leaseback: Sale of an asset with the purchaser concurrently leasing the asset to the seller.

Sales or revenues: Income from the sale of goods or services and lease or royalty payments.

Sales-type lease: A capital lease that generates two income streams. One from the sale of the asset and a second from the financing of the asset.

Scope paragraph: That paragraph of the audit report that tells what the auditor did. Specifically, it states whether or not the audit was conducted in accordance with GAAS.

Securities Act of 1933: A federal statute governing the registration of new securities issues traded in interstate commerce.

Securities Act of 1934: A federal statute establishing recurring reporting requirements for public companies once their securities have been registered with the SEC.

Securities and Exchange Commission (SEC): An agency of the federal government that has the legal power to set and enforce accounting practices.

Segment reporting (product segment information): When operations are diversified, the firm may report results on a segmented basis.

Selling expenses: Result from the company's effort to create sales.

Serial bonds: A bond issue with several different maturity dates.

Simple interest: Interest computed on the principal amount only.

Single-step income statement: Form of the income statement that arrives at net income in a single step.

Sinking fund: An accumulation of cash or securities in a special fund dedicated to paying, or redeeming, an issue of bonds or preferred stock.

Social accounting: Attempts to account for the benefits to the social environment within which the firm operates.

Specific identification (inventory): Identifies the items in inventory as coming from specific purchases.

Standard audit report: The form of audit report recommended by the Auditing Standards Board of the AICPA. This report is rendered at the conclusion of an audit in which the auditor encountered no material scope limitations, and the financial statements conform to GAAP in all material respects.

Stated (contract) rate: The rate of interest used to compute the cash interest payments on bonds or notes.

Stated value: A value assigned by the board of directors to no-par stock.

Statement of cash flows: Provides detailed information on cash flows resulting from operating, investing, and financing activities.

Statement of owners' equity: An accounting statement describing transactions affecting the owners' equity.

Statement of retained earnings: A summary of the changes to retained earnings for an accounting period.

Statements of Financial Accounting Concepts (SFAC): Issued by the Financial Accounting Standards Board and provide the Board with a common foundation and basic reasons for considering the merits of various alternative accounting principles.

Statements of Financial Accounting Standards (SFAS): These statements establish generally accepted accounting principles (GAAP) for specific accounting issues.

Stock appreciation rights: Give the holder the right to receive compensation at some future date based on the market price of the stock at the date of exercise over a pre-established price.

Stock certificate: A document issued to a stockholder indicating the number of shares of stock owned.

Stock dividend: A dividend in the form of additional shares of a company's stock.

Stock options: Allow the holder to purchase a company's stock at favorable terms.

Stock split: Increase in the number of shares of a class of capital stock, with no change in the total dollar amount of the class, but with a converse reduction in the par or stated value of the shares.

Straight-line amortization of bonds: Writes off an equal amount of bond premium or discount each period.

Straight-line depreciation: A method of depreciation that allocates the cost of a tangible asset in a constant over the life of the asset.

Subordinated debt: A form of long-term debt which is "junior," or in a secondary position in relation to the claim on a company's assets for the payment of its other debt obligations.

Subsequent events: Events that occur after the balance sheet date, but before the statements are issued.

Subsidiary: A company whose stock is more than 50 percent owned by another company.

Successful efforts accounting: The method of accounting which capitalizes only the costs which result in the discovery of oil and gas reserves.

Sum-of-the-years'-digits depreciation: This method takes a fraction each year times the cost less salvage value. The numerator of the fraction is the remaining number of years of life. The denominator remains constant, and is the sum of the digits of the years of life.

Summary annual report: A simplified annual report in which data required by the SEC is supplied in the proxy statement and the Form 10-K.

Summary of significant accounting policies: A description of all significant accounting policies of the company. An integral part of the financial statements, this information is typically presented as the first footnote.

Supplies: Items used indirectly in the production of goods or services.

Take-or-pay contract: An executory contract by which one party agrees to pay for the product regardless of whether the product is physically received or not.

Tangible assets: The physical facilities used in the operation of the business.

Taxable income: Income determined in accordance with income tax regulation.

Temporal method of translation: A method of translating foreign financial statements in which cash, receivables, and payables are translated at the exchange rate in effect at the balance sheet date. Other assets and liabilities are translated at historical rates, while revenues and expenses are translated at the weighted-average rate for the period.

Temporary accounts: Accounts closed at the end of an accounting period. They include all income statement accounts and the dividends account.

Temporary differences: Revenue and expense recognized in one period for financial reporting but recognized in an earlier or later period for income tax purposes.

Term bonds: The entire bond issue matures at the same time.

Time period: Assumes that the entity can be accounted for with reasonable accuracy for a particular period of time.

Timeliness: The qualitative characteristic indicating that accounting information should reach the user in time to help in making a decision.

Trademarks: Rights to use distinctive names or symbols granted to the holder for 28 years with option for renewal.

Transaction approach: The recording of events that affect the financial position of the entity and that can be reasonably determined in monetary terms.

Translation adjustments (foreign currency translation adjustments): An account classified under stockholders' equity that represents foreign currency translation gains and losses that have not been charged to the income statement.

Translation gains and losses: Gains and losses due to fluctuations in exchange rates.

Treasury stock: Capital stock of a company, either common or preferred, that has been issued and reacquired by the issuing company but has not been reissued or retired. It reduces stockholders' equity.

Trend analysis: Analysis over more than one accounting period to identify the trend of a company's results.

Troubled debt restructuring: A concession by creditors to allow debtors to eliminate or modify debt obligations.

Unappropriated retained earnings: The unrestricted retained earnings.

Unconsolidated subsidiaries: Subsidiaries whose financial statements are not combined with the parent company.

Understandability: A user-specific quality directing that accounting information be understandable to users who have a reasonable knowledge of business and economic activities and who are willing to study the information with reasonable diligence.

Unearned income: A liability, either current or long-term, for income received prior to the delivery of goods or the rendering of services (also described as deferred income).

Unexpended industrial revenue bond proceeds: An asset account, classified under other assets, representing funds that have not yet been used for the purpose indicated when the bonds were issued.

Unit-of-production depreciation: Relates depreciation to the output capacity of the asset, estimated for the life of the asset.

Unqualified opinion: An audit opinion not qualified for any material scope restrictions or departures from GAAP.

Unrealized decline in market value of noncurrent equity investments: A stockholders' equity account that results from adjusting long-term equity securities to the lower of cost or market value.

Unrealized (gain) loss: A (gain) loss recognized in the financial statements but not associated with an asset sale.

Unusual or infrequent item: Certain income statement items that are unusual or occur infrequently, but not both.

Verifiability: The qualitative characteristic indicating that accounting information can be confirmed or duplicated by independent parties using the same measurement technique.

Vested benefit obligation (VBO): The portion of the pension benefit obligation that does not depend on future employee service.

Vesting: The accrual to an employee of pension rights, arising from employer contributions, not contingent upon the employee's continuing service with the employer.

Warranty obligations: Estimated obligations arising out of product warranties.

Work in process: Goods started, but not ready for sale.

Working capital: The excess of current assets over current liabilities.

Zero coupon bond: A bond that does not pay periodic interest, but is a promise to pay a fixed amount at the maturity date.

Bibliography

1. FUNDAMENTAL CONCEPTS AND INTRODUCTION TO FINANCIAL REPORTING

Benston, G. J. "An Analysis of the Role of Accounting Standards for Enhancing Corporate Governance and Social Responsibility." *Journal of Accounting and Public Policy*, Fall 1982, 5-17.

Beresford, D. R. "The Balancing Act in Setting Accounting Standards." *Accounting Horizons*, March 1988, 1-7.

Bierman, Harold. "Extending the Usefulness of Accrual Accounting." *Accounting Horizons*, September 1988, 10-14.

Christenson, Charles. "The Methodology of Positive Accounting." *The Accounting Review*, January 1983, 1-22.

Cooper, K., and G. D. Keim. "The Economic Rationale for the Nature and Extent of Corporate Financial Disclosure Regulation: A Critical Assessment." *Journal of Accounting and Public Policy*, Fall 1983.

Gerboth, Dale L. "The Conceptual Framework: Not Definitions, But Professional Values." *Accounting Horizons*, September 1987, 1-8.

Koeppen, David R. "Using the FASB's Conceptual Framework: Fitting the Pieces Together." *Accounting Horizons*, June 1988, 18-26.

Rimerman, Thomas W. "The Changing Significance of Financial Statements." *Journal of Accountancy*, April 1990, 79-83.

Solomons, D. "The FASB's Conceptual Framework: An Evaluation." *Journal of Accountancy*, June 1986, 114-124.

Stamp, Edward. "Why Can Accounting Not Become a Science Like Physics?" *Abacus*, Spring 1981, 13-27.

Wyatt, Arthur. "Accounting Standards: Conceptual or Political?" *Accounting Horizons*, September 1990, 83-88.

2. INTRODUCTION TO FINANCIAL STATEMENTS AND OTHER FINANCIAL REPORTING TOPICS

Adhikari, Ajay, and Shawn Z. Wang. "Accounting for China." *Management Accounting*, April 1995, 27-32.

Beresford, Dennis. "What's the FASB Doing About International Accounting Standards?" *Financial Executive*, May/June 1990, 17-24.

Bernard, Victor L., and Thomas Stober. "The Nature and Amount of Information in Cash Flows and Accruals." *The Accounting Review*, October 1989, 624-652.

Bishop, Ashton, and Rasoul H. Tondkar. "Development of a Professional Code of Ethics." *Journal of Accountancy*, May 1987, 97-100.

Bruns, William J., and Kenneth A. Merchant. "The Dangerous Morality of Managing Earnings." *Management Accounting*, August 1990, 22-25.

Carbridge, Curtis, Walter W. Austin, and David J. Lemak. "Germany's Accrual Accounting Practices." *Management Accounting*, August 1993, 45-47.

Cheney, Glenn A. "Soviet-American Financial Coexistence." *Journal of Accountancy*, January 1990, 68-72.

Choi, Frederick D. "A Cluster Approach to Accounting Harmonization." *Management Accounting*, August 1981, 27-31.

Choi, Frederick D., and Richard M. Levich. "Behavioral Effects of International Accounting Diversity." *Accounting Horizons*, June 1991, 1-13.

Collins, Stephen. "The Move to Globalization." *Journal of Accountancy*, March 1989, 82-85.

Cook, J. Michael, and Michael H. Sutton. "Summary Annual Reporting: A Cure for Information Overload." *Financial Executive*, January/February 1995, 12-15.

Davidson, Ronald A., Alexander M. G. Gelardi, and Fangyve Li. "Analysis of the Conceptual Framework of China's New Accounting System." *Journal of Accountancy*, March 1996, 58-74.

Epstein, Marc J., and Moses L. Pava. "Profile of an Annual Report." *Financial Executive*, January/February 1994, 41-43.

Lee, Charles, and Dale Morse. "Summary Annual Reports." *Accounting Horizons*, March 1990, 39-50.

Lowe, Herman J. "Ethics in Our 100-Year History." *Journal of Accountancy*, May 1987, 78-87.

Milan, Edgar. "Ethical Compliance at Tenneco Inc." *Management Accounting*, August 1995, 59.

Nair, R. D., and Larry E. Rittenberg. "Summary Annual Reports: Background and Implications for Financial Reporting and Auditing." *Accounting Horizons*, March 1990, 25-38.

Perera, M. H. "Towards a Framework to Analyzing the Impact of Culture on Accounting." *International Journal of Accounting*, 1989, 42-56.

Rich, Anne J. "Understanding Global Standards." *Management Accounting*, April 1995, 51-54.

Schroeder, Nicholas W., and Charles H. Gibson. "Are Summary Annual Reports Successful?" *Accounting Horizons*, June 1992, 28-37.

Schroeder, Nicholas W., and Charles H. Gibson. "Improving Annual Reports by Improving the Readability of Footnotes." *The Woman CPA*, April 1988, 13-16.

Wallace, R. S. Olusegun. "Survival Strategies of a Global Organization: The Case of the International Accounting Standards Committee." *Accounting Horizons*, June 1990, 1-22.

Wallace, Wanda A., and John Walsh. "Apples-to-Apples Profits Abroad." *Financial Executives*, May/June 1995, 28-31.

Wyatt, Arthur R., and Joseph F. Yospe. "Wake-Up Call to U.S. Business: International Accounting Standards Are on the Way." *Journal of Accountancy*, July 1993, 80-85.

3.   BALANCE SHEET

Davis, M. L. "Differential Market Reaction to Pooling and Purchase Methods." *The Accounting Review*, July 1990, 696-709.

Flamholtz, Eric G., D. Gerald Searfoss, and Russell Coff. "Developing Human Resource Accounting as a Human Resource Decision Support System." *Accounting Horizons*, September 1988, 1-9.

Gibson, Charles H. "Quasi-Reorganizations in Practice." *Accounting Horizons*, September 1988, 83-89.

Heian, J. B., and J. B. Thies. "Consolidation of Finance Subsidiaries: $230 Billion in Off-Balance-Sheet Financing Comes Home to Roost." *Accounting Horizons*, March 1989, 1-9.

Kim, M., and G. Moore. "Economics vs. Accounting Depreciation." *Journal of Accounting and Economics*, April 1988, 111-125.

Samuelson, Richard A. "Accounting for Liabilities to Perform Services." *Accounting Horizons*, September 1993, 32-45.

Sanders, George, Paul Munter, and Tommy Moures. "Software—The Unrecorded Asset." *Management Accounting*, August 1994, 57-61.

Schuetze, Walter P. "What Is an Asset?" *Accounting Horizons*, September 1993, 66-70.

4.   INCOME STATEMENT

Asquith, Paul, Paul Healy, and Krishna Palepu. "Earnings and Stock Splits." *The Accounting Review*, July 1989, 387-403.

Elliott, J. A., and D. R. Philbrick. "Accounting Changes and Earnings Predict-ability." *The Accounting Review*, January 1990, 157-174.

Lilien, Steven, Martin Mellman, and Victor Pastena. "Accounting Changes: Successful Versus Unsuccessful Firms." *The Accounting Review*, October 1988, 642-656.

May, Gordon S., and Douglas K. Schneider. "Reporting Accounting Changes: Are Stricter Guidelines Needed?" *Accounting Horizons*, September 1988, 68-74.

McGough, Eugene. "Anatomy of a Stock Split." *Management Accounting*, September 1993, 58-61.

Pincus, Morton, and Charles Wasley. "The Incidence of Accounting Changes and Characteristics of Firms Making Accounting Changes." *Journal of Accountancy*, June 1994, 1-24.

Ricks, W. E., and J. S. Hughes. "Market Reactions to a Non-Discretionary Accounting Change: The Case of Long-Term Investments." *The Accounting Review*, January 1985, 33-52.

5.   BASICS OF ANALYSIS

Chang, L. S., K. S. Most, and C. W. Brain. "The Utility of Annual Reports: An International Study." *Journal of International Business Studies*, Spring/Summer 1983, 63-84.

Gibson, C. H., and P. A. Boyer. "Need for Disclosure of Uniform Financial Ratios." *Journal of Accountancy*, May 1980, 78.

Ingberman, M., and G. H. Sorter. "The Role of Financial Statements in an Efficient Market." *Journal of Accounting, Auditing, and Finance*, Fall 1978, 58-62.

Wittington, G. "Some Basic Properties of Accounting Ratios." *Journal of Business Finance and Accounting*, Summer 1980, 219-232.

7.   LIQUIDITY OF SHORT-TERM ASSETS; RELATED DEBT-PAYING ABILITY

Davis, H. Z., N. Kahn, and E. Rosen. "LIFO Inventory Liquidations: An Empirical Study." *Journal of Accounting Research*, Autumn 1984, 480-496.

Dopuch, N., and M. Pincus. "Evidence on the Choice of Inventory Accounting Methods: LIFO Versus FIFO." *Journal of Accounting Research*, Spring 1988, 28-59.

Heath, L. C. "Is Working Capital Really Working?" *Journal of Accountancy*, August 1980, 55-62.

Hunt, H. G. III. "Potential Determinants of Corporate Inventory Accounting Decisions." *Journal of Accounting Research*, Autumn 1985, 448-467.

Johnson, W. B., and D. S. Dhaliwal. "LIFO Abandonment." *Journal of Accounting Research*, Autumn 1988, 236-272.

Tse, Senyo. "LIFO Liquidations." *Journal of Accounting Research*, Spring 1990, 229-238.

8.   LONG-TERM DEBT-PAYING ABILITY

Deakin, Edward B. "Accounting for Contingencies: The Pennzoil-Texaco Case." Accounting Horizons, March 1989, 21-28.

Dietrich, J., and R. S. Kaplan. "Empirical Analysis of the Commercial Loan Classification Decision." *Accounting Review*, January 1982, 18-38.

Heian, James B., and James B. Thies. "Consolidation of Finance Subsidiaries: $230 Billion in Off-Balance-Sheet Financing Comes Home to Roost." *Accounting Horizons*, March 1989, 1-9.

Strait, C. M., and J. J. Zautra. "Debt-Service Capacity Revisited." *Journal of Commercial Bank Lending*, September 1980, 26-36.

Thomas, J. K. "Why Do Firms Terminate Their Overfunded Pension Plans?" *Journal of Accounting and Economics*, November 1989, 361-398.

Williams, Georgina, and Thomas J. Phillips. "Cleaning Up Our Act: Accounting for Environmental Liabilities." *Management Accounting*, February 1994, 30-33.

9.   ANALYSIS OF PROFITABILITY

Lev, B. "On the Usefulness of Earnings and Earnings Research: Lessons and Directions from Two Decades of Empirical Research." *Journal of Accounting Research*, Supplement 1989, 153-192.

Lipe, R. C. "The Information Contained in the Components of Earnings." *Journal of Accounting Research*, Supplement 1986, 37-64.

Moses, D. "Income Smoothing and Incentives: Empirical Tests Using Accounting Changes." *The Accounting Review*, April 1987, 358-377.

Rapacciola, Donna, and Allen Schiff. "Reporting Segment Sales Under APB Opinion No. 30." *Accounting Horizons*, December 1991, 53-59.

Worthy, F. S. "Manipulating Profits: How It's Done." *Fortune*, June 15, 1984, 50-54.

10.   ANALYSIS FOR THE INVESTOR

Arnold, J., and P. Maizer. "A Survey of the Methods Used by UK Investment Analysts to Appraise Investments in Ordinary Shares." *Accounting and Business Research*, Summer 1984, 195-207.

Ball, Ray. "The Earnings-Price Anomaly." *Journal of Accounting and Economics*, June/September 1992, 319-346.

Beaver, W., and D. Morse. "What Determines Price-Earnings Ratios?" *Financial Analysts Journal*, July-August 1978, 65-76.

Block, Frank E. "A Study of the Price to Book Relationship." *Financial Analysts Journal,* January/February 1995, 63-73.

Bowen, R. M., L. A. Daley, and C. C. Huber. "Evidence on the Existence and Determinants of Inter-Industry Differences in Leverage." *Financial Management*, Winter 1982, 10-20.

Butler, Kirt C., and Larry H. P. Lang. "The Forecast Accuracy of Individual Analysts: Evidence of Systematic Optimism and Pessimism." *Journal of Accounting Research*, Spring 1991, 150-156.

Chambers, A. E., and S. H. Penman. "Timeliness of Reporting and the Stock Price Reaction to Earnings Announcements." *Journal of Accounting Research*, Spring 1984, 21-47.

Clemente, Holly A. "What Wall Street Sees When It Looks at Your P/E Ratio." *Financial Executive*, May/June 1990, 40-44.

Coggin, T. D., and J. E. Hunter. "Analysts EPS Forecasts Nearer Actual Than Statistical Models." *The Journal of Business Forecasting*, Winter 1982-1983, 20-23.

Cole, Kevin, Jean Helwege, and David Laster. "Stock Market Valuation Indicators: Is this Time Different?" *Financial Analysts Journal*, May/June 1996, 56-64.

Holthausen, Robert W., and D. F. Larcker. "The Prediction of Stock Returns Using Financial Statement Information." *Journal of Accounting and Economics*, June/September 1992, 373-411.

Kross, W., and D. A. Schroder. "An Empirical Investigation of the Effect of Quarterly Earnings Announcement Timing on Stock Returns." *Journal of Accounting Research*, Spring 1984, 153-176.

Livingston, D. T., and J. B. Henry. "Effect of Employee Stock Ownership Plans on Corporate Profits." *Journal of Risk and Insurance*, September 1980, 491-505.

Molodovsky, Nicholas. "A Theory of Price-Earnings Ratios." *Financial Analysts Journal*, January/February 1995, 29-43.

Ou, Jane A., and Stephen H. Penman. "Financial Statement Analysis and the Prediction of Stock Returns." *Journal of Accounting and Economics*, November 1989, 295-329.

Zarowin, P. "What Determines Earnings-Price Ratios Revisited." *Journal of Accounting, Auditing, and Finance*, Summer 1990, 439-454.

11. STATEMENT OF CASH FLOWS

Casey, C. J., and N. J. Bartczak. "Cash Flow—It's Not the Bottom Line." *Harvard Business Review*, July-August 1984, 61-66.

Kronquist, Stacey L., and Nancy Newman-Limata. "Reporting Corporate Cash Flows." *Management Accounting*, July 1990, 31-36.

Largay, J. A. III, and C. P. Stickney. "Cash Flows, Ratio Analysis, and the W.T. Grant Company Bankruptcy." *Financial Analysts Journal*, July-August 1980, 51-54.

Livnat, Joshua, and Paul Zarowin. "The Incremental Informational Content of Cash-Flow Components." *Journal of Accounting and Economics*, May 1990, 25-46.

Nurnberg, Hugo. "Inconsistencies and Ambiguities in Cash Flow Statements Under FASB Statement No. 95." *Accounting Horizons*, June 1993, 60-75.

Rayburn, J. "The Association of Operating Cash Flow and Accruals with Security Returns." *Journal of Accounting Research*, Supplement 1986, 121-133.

Sondhi, A. C., G. H. Sorter, and G. I. White. "Cash Flow Redefined: FAS 95 and Security Analysis." *Financial Analysts Journal*, November/December 1988, 19-20.

12. STATEMENT ANALYSIS: PART II— COOPER TIRE & RUBBER COMPANY

Hooks, Karen L., and James E. Moon. "A Classification Scheme to Examine Management Discussion and Analysis Compliance." *Accounting Horizons*, June 1993, 41-59.

13. EXPANDED UTILITY OF FINANCIAL RATIOS

Altman, E. I. "Financial Ratios, Discriminant Analysis, and the Prediction of Corporate Bankruptcy." *Journal of Finance*, September 1968, 589-609.

Altman, E. I., and M. Brenner. "Information Effects and Stock Market Response to Signs of Firm Deterioration." *Journal of Financial and Quantitative Analysis*, March 1981, 35-51.

Altman, E. I. *Corporate Financial Distress.* New York: John Wiley & Sons, 1993.

Bird, R. G., and A. J. McHugh. "Financial Ratios—An Empirical Study." *Journal of Business Finance and Accounting*, Spring 1977, 29-45.

Bonocure, J. J. "A New Era of Financial Reporting." *Financial Executive*, December 1981, 30-34.

Casey, C. J., Jr. "Variation in Accounting Information Load: The Effect on Loan Officers' Prediction of Bankruptcy." *Accounting Review*, January 1980, 36-49.

Casey, C. J., and N. J. Bartczak. "Using Operating Cash Flow Data to Predict Financial Distress: Some Extensions." *Journal of Accounting Research*, Spring 1985, 384-401.

Dambolena, I. G., and S. J. Khorvry. "Ratio Stability and Corporate Failure." *Journal of Finance*, September 1980, 1017-1026.

Gombola, M. J., and J. E. Ketz. "Financial Ratio Patterns in Retail and Manufacturing Organizations." *Financial Management*, Summer 1983, 45-56.

Imhoff, E. A., Jr. "Analytical Review of Income Elements." *Journal of Accounting, Auditing, and Finance*, Summer 1981, 333-351.

Jaggi, B. "Which Is Better, D & B or Zeta in Forecasting Credit Risk?" *Journal of Business Forecasting*, Summer 1984, 13-16, 22.

Lincoln, M. "An Empirical Study of the Usefulness of Accounting Ratios to Describe Levels of Insolvency Risk." *Journal of Banking and Finance*, June 1984, 321-340.

Makeever, D. A. "Predicting Business Failures." *The Journal of Commercial Bank Lending*, January 1984, 14-18.

McDonald, B., and M. H. Morris. "The Statistical Validity of the Ratio Method in Financial Analysis: An Empirical Examination." *Journal of Business Finance and Accounting*, Spring 1984, 89-97.

Patell, J. M., and M. A. Wolfson. "The Intraday Speed of Adjustment of Stock Prices to Earnings and Dividend Announcements." *Journal of Financial Economics*, June 1984, 223-252.

Patrone, F. L., and D. duBois. "Financial Ratio Analysis in the Small Business." *Journal of Small Business Management*, January 1981, 35-40.

Rege, V. P. "Accounting Ratios to Locate Take-Over Targets." *Journal of Business Finance and Accounting*, Autumn 1984, 301- 311.

Steinbart, Paul John. "The Auditor's Responsibility for the Accuracy of Graphs in Annual Reports: Some Evidence of the Need for Additional Guidance." *Accounting Horizons*, September 1989, 60-70.

Stober, T. L. "The Incremental Information Content of Financial Statement Disclosures: The Case of LIFO Liquidations." *Journal of Accounting Research*, Supplement 1986, 138-160.

Tse, S. "LIFO Liquidations." *Journal of Accounting Research*, Spring 1990, 229-238.

Williamson, R. W. "Evidence on the Selective Reporting of Financial Ratios." *The Accounting Review*, April 1984, 296-299.

14. IMPACT OF CHANGING PRICES ON FINANCIAL STATEMENTS

Bates, H. L., and M. J. Reckens. "Does Replacement Cost Data Make a Difference?" *Journal of Accountancy*, June 1979, 42.

Boatsman, James, and Elba Baskin. "Asset Valuation with Incomplete Markets." *The Accounting Review*, January 1981, 38-53.

Connor, J. E. "Inflation Accounting: An Altestor's View." *Journal of Accountancy*, July 1980, 76-77.

Most, K. S. "Depreciation Expense and the Effect of Inflation." *Journal of Accounting Research*, August 1984, 782-788.

Nichols, Donald. "Operating Income and Distributable Income Under Replacement Cost Accounting: The Long-Life Asset Replacement Problem." *Financial Analysts Journal*, January-February 1982, 68-73.

Rosenfeld, P. "A History of Inflation Accounting." *Journal of Accountancy*, September 1981, 95-126.

Seed, A. H. "Measuring Financial Performance in an Inflationary Environment." *Financial Executive*, January 1982, 40-50.

Short, D. G. "Impact of Price-Level Adjustments on the Meaning of Accounting Ratios." *Journal of Business Finance and Accounting*, Autumn 1980, 377-391.

15. STATEMENT ANALYSIS FOR SPECIAL INDUSTRIES: BANKS, UTILITIES, OIL AND GAS, TRANSPORTATION, INSURANCE, REAL ESTATE COMPANIES

Agnich, J. F. "How Utilities Account to the Regulators." *Management Accounting*, February 1981, 17-22.

Barniv, Ran. "Accounting Procedures, Market Data, Cash-Flow Figures, and Insolvency Classification: The Case of the Insurance Industry." *The Accounting Review*, July 1990, 578-604.

Ho, T., and A. Saunders. "A Catastrophe Model of Bank Failure." *The Journal of Finance*, December 1980, 1189-1207.

Lilien, S., and V. Pastena. "Intramethod Comparability: The Case of the Oil and Gas Industry." *Accounting Review*, July 1981, 690-703.

Palmon, Dan, and Lee J. Zeidler. "Current Value Reporting of Real Estate Companies and a Possible Example of Market Inefficiency." *The Accounting Review*, July 1978, 776-790.

Rose, P. L., and W. L. Scott. "Return-on-Equity Analysis of Eleven Largest U.S. Bank Failures." *Review of Business and Economic Research*, Winter 1980-81, 1-11.

Shick, R. A., and L. F. Sherman. "Bank Stock Prices as an Early Warning System for Changes in Condition." *Journal of Bank Research*, Autumn 1980, 136-146.

16. PERSONAL FINANCIAL STATEMENTS AND ACCOUNTING FOR GOVERNMENTS AND NOT-FOR-PROFIT ORGANIZATIONS

Brown, Victor H., and Susan E. Weiss. "Toward Better Not-For-Profit Accounting and Reporting." *Management Accounting*, July 1993, 48-52.

Charnes, A., and W. Cooper. "Auditing and Accounting for Program Efficiency and Management Effectiveness in Not-for-Profit Entities." *Accounting Organizations and Society 5*, 1980, 87-108.

Chase, Bruce. "New Reporting Standards for Not-For-Profits." *Management Accounting*, October 1995, 34-37.

Downs, G. W., and D. M. Rocke. "Municipal Budget Forecasting with Multivariate ARMA Models." *Journal of Forecasting*, October-December 1983, 377-387.

Hay, E., and James F. Antonio. "What Users Want in Government Financial Reports." *Journal of Accountancy*, August 1990, 91-98.

Ives, Martin. "Accountability and Governmental Financial Reporting." *Journal of Accountancy*, October 1987, 130-134.

Kinsman, Michael D., and Bruce Samuelson. "Personal Financial Statements: Valuation Challenges and Solutions." *Journal of Accountancy*, September 1987, 138-148.

Meeting, David T., Randall W. Luecke, and Edward J. Giniat. "Understanding and Implementing FASB 124." *Journal of Accountancy*, March 1996, 62-66.

Shoulders, Craig D., and Robert J. Freeman. "Which GAAP Should NOPs Apply?" *Journal of Accountancy*, November 1995, 77-78, 80, 82, 84.

Statement of Position of the Accounting Standards Division 82-1, "Accounting and Financial Reporting for Personal Financial Statements." New York: American Institute of Certified Public Accountants, 1982.

Index

A

Accountants, certified public, use of financial ratios, 558-559

Accounting cycle, basic steps in, 52-55

Accounting equation, defined, 53

Accounting for business combinations, 94; methods defined, 94

Accounting for governments, 705-710, 712-718

Accounting for not-for-profit organizations, 710-711, 719-724

Accounting loss, defined, 353

Accounting model, traditional assumptions of, 11-23

Accounting principles, cumulative effect of change in, on the income statement, 169-170; illustrated, 171

Accounting Principles Board (APB), function of, 2; see also American Institute of Certified Public Accountants

Accounting qualities, illustrated, 7

Accounting Research Division, function of, 2

Accounting resources, on the Internet, 222

Accounting standards, domestic, 69

Accounting standards, international, harmonization of, 68-71:
  items included in, 68

Accounting standards, overload, 33

Accounting Standards Division, publications of, 10

Accounting Standards Division Executive Committee (AcSEC), function of, 10

Accounts receivable:
  collectibility of, 257
  as a current asset, 99, 256-265
  days' sales in, 260
  defined, 99
  and electric utilities, 642
  liquidity of, methods of measurement, 260-265
  and personal financial statements, 697

turnover, 263
turnover, in days, 264
turnover, per year, 264
uncollectibility of, 257
see also Receivables

Accrual basis:
  adjusting entries for, 54
  basics of, 22, 23
  compared with cash basis, 23
  defined, 22

Accrued liabilities of Cooper Tire & Rubber Company, 237

Accumulated benefit obligation, in pension plans, 340

Accumulated depreciation, 104; see also Depreciation

Acid-test ratio, 282-284:
  conservative, 282
  formula for, 282
  trends in, illustrated, 284

Adjusting entries, 54

Administrative expenses, defined, 159

Adverse opinion, in an auditor's report, 56

AICPA, see American Institute of Certified Public Accountants

Air carriers, see Transportation companies

Allowance for Doubtful Accounts, 257-258

The Almanac of Business and Industry Financial Ratios, 204

Alternative cash flow, 490

America's Corporate Families: The Billion Dollar Directory, 218

American Institute of Certified Public Accountants (AICPA):
  Accounting Principles Board, 2
  Accounting Research Division, 2
  Accounting Standards Division, publications of, 10
  Committee on Accounting Procedures, 2
  Committee on Accounting Terminology, 2

Profitability (continued)

$$\text{Return on Investment} = \frac{\text{Net Income before Minority Share of Earnings and Nonrecurring Items} + [(\text{Interest Expense}) \times (1 - \text{Tax Rate})]}{\text{Average (Long-Term Liabilities + Equity)}}$$

$$\text{Return on Total Equity} = \frac{\text{Net Income before Nonrecurring Items} - \text{Dividends on Redeemable Preferred Stock}}{\text{Average Total Equity}}$$

$$\text{Return on Common Equity} = \frac{\text{Net Income before Nonrecurring Items} - \text{Preferred Dividends}}{\text{Average Common Equity}}$$

$$\text{Gross Profit Margin} = \frac{\text{Gross Profit}}{\text{Net Sales}}$$

$$\text{Operating Cash Flow Per Share} = \frac{\text{Operating Cash Flow} - \text{Preferred Dividends}}{\text{Common Shares Outstanding}}$$

Investor Analysis

$$\text{Degree of Financial Leverage} = \frac{\text{Earnings before Interest, Tax, Minority Share of Earnings, Equity Income, and Nonrecurring Items}}{\text{Earnings before Tax, Minority Share of Earnings, Equity Income, and Nonrecurring Items}}$$

Earnings Per Common Share:

$$\text{Simple} = \frac{\text{Net Income} - \text{Preferred Dividends}}{\text{Weighted Average Number of Common Shares Outstanding}}$$

$$\text{Price/Earnings Ratio} = \frac{\text{Market Price per Share}}{\text{Fully Diluted Earnings per Share}}$$

$$\text{Percentage of Earnings Retained} = \frac{\text{Net Income} - \text{All Dividends}}{\text{Net Income}}$$

$$\text{Dividend Payout} = \frac{\text{Dividends Per Common Share}}{\text{Diluted Earnings Per Share}}$$

$$\text{Dividend Yield} = \frac{\text{Dividends Per Common Share}}{\text{Market Price Per Common Share}}$$

$$\text{Book Value Per Share} = \frac{\text{Total Stockholders' Equity} - \text{Preferred Stock Equity}}{\text{Number of Common Shares Outstanding}}$$

$$\text{Materiality of Options} = \frac{\text{Stock Options Outstanding}}{\text{Number of Shares of Common Stock Outstanding}}$$

$$\text{Operating Cash Flow/Cash Dividends} = \frac{\text{Operating Cash Flow}}{\text{Cash Dividends}}$$